COMPARATIVE POLITICS

THIRD EDITION

Now in its third edition, this unique textbook remains a favorite for introductory undergraduate courses in comparative politics. It features twelve theoretically and historically grounded country studies that show how the three major concepts of comparative analysis – interests, identities, and institutions – shape the politics of nations and regions. Written in a style free of heavy-handed jargon and organized to address the concerns of contemporary comparativists, this textbook provides students with the conceptual tools and historical background they need to understand the politics of our complex world. This third edition introduces completely new chapters on Nigeria, the European Union, and France.

Jeffrey Kopstein is author of *The Politics of Economic Decline in East Germany 1945–1989* (1997) and more than 40 articles in scholarly journals and books. He is currently Director of the Centre for European, Russian, and Eurasian Studies at the University of Toronto.

Mark Lichbach is Professor and Chair of Government and Politics at the University of Maryland, College Park. He is the author or editor of many books, including the award-winning *The Rebel's Dilemma*, and of numerous articles in scholarly journals.

COMPARATIVE POLITICS

INTERESTS, IDENTITIES, AND INSTITUTIONS IN A CHANGING GLOBAL ORDER

THIRD EDITION

Edited by

JEFFREY KOPSTEIN
University of Toronto

MARK LICHBACH
University of Maryland, College Park

CAMBRIDGE
UNIVERSITY PRESS

CAMBRIDGE UNIVERSITY PRESS
Cambridge, New York, Melbourne, Madrid, Cape Town, Singapore, São Paulo, Delhi

Cambridge University Press
32 Avenue of the Americas, New York, NY 10013-2473, USA

www.cambridge.org
Information on this title: www.cambridge.org/9780521708401

First edition published 2000
Second edition published 2005
Third edition published 2009
Reprinted 2009

Printed in the United States of America

A catalog record for this publication is available from the British Library.

Library of Congress Cataloging in Publication Data

Comparative politics / edited by Jeffrey Kopstein, Mark Lichbach. – 3rd ed.
  p.   cm.
Includes bibliographical references and index.
ISBN 978-0-521-70840-1 (pbk.)
1. Comparative government.   I. Kopstein, Jeffrey.   II. Lichbach, Mark Irving, 1951–
III. Title.
JF51.C6235 2008
320.3–dc22   2007041032

ISBN 978-0-521-70840-1 paperback

To Max and Isaac Kopstein and to Sammi Jo and Yossi Lichbach

May they someday help repair our world.

Brief Table of Contents

Contents

PART THREE. LATE DEVELOPERS

Maps

Preface to the Third Edition

This book originated during many hours of pleasant conversation about teaching comparative politics at the University of Colorado at Boulder. Out of these conversations emerged the idea of an introductory textbook that would convey to students the main currents in contemporary comparative politics. These currents are summed up here under three rubrics: interests, identities, and institutions. We decided to illustrate this framework through a series of country studies cast in world-historical perspective. At the same time, we wanted to avoid weighing down the country studies with a heavy-handed or outdated theoretical apparatus that inevitably discourages even the hardiest of students. The result, we hope, has struck an acceptable balance between conceptual rigor and flexibility.

To the extent that we have accomplished this, most of the credit is due to our contributors, who have cheerfully taken on our framework without losing what is interesting and distinctive about their country's experience. In response to student and instructor demand, we have added new chapters in this third edition on the European Union and Nigeria. We remain grateful to the staff of Cambridge University Press and especially Ed Parsons for his professionalism, enthusiasm, and common sense.

As in the first and second editions, editing this book has been a collaborative act. It represents the tangible result of a long friendship. Although both of us have moved on to different universities, this book has allowed us to continue the conversation that started over coffee and ice cream seventeen years ago.

Contributors

Michael Bratton, Michigan State University
Anthony Gill, University of Washington
Andrew C. Gould, University of Notre Dame
Stephen E. Hanson, University of Washington
Okechukwu Iheduru, Arizona State University
Jeffrey Kopstein, University of Toronto
Paulette Kurzer, University of Arizona
Mark Lichbach, University of Maryland
Laurence McFalls, University of Montreal
Vali Nasr, Tufts University
Peter Rutland, Wesleyan University
Miranda A. Schreurs, University of Maryland
Rudra Sil, University of Pennsylvania
Yu-Shan Wu, Academia Sinica

CHAPTER ONE

What Is Comparative Politics?

Jeffrey Kopstein and Mark Lichbach

Introduction

Imagine that you could design the political order (for example, democracy in the United States, Communist Party dominance in China) for a country of your choosing. Where would you start? Who would get to rule? What rules for political life would you choose? Could you make rules that would be fair to everyone? If not, whom would these rules favor and whom would they disadvantage? Would they be rules that even those at the bottom of the social order, the poorest and least powerful people, would agree to? What would be the rules for changing the rules? These are difficult questions because to answer them in a meaningful way requires an understanding of why and how different countries of the world are governed differently. With so many choices to make, it is easy to see why the job of designing a constitution would be such a difficult one.

It could, however, be made easier. One might start by evaluating the existing possibilities as exemplified by the various forms of government in the states of the world. The state is an organization that possesses sovereignty over a territory and its people. Yet, within our world of states, no two are ruled in exactly the same way. Why should this be the case? Why are societies run, and political orders designed, in so many different ways? What consequences do these differences hold for a people's well-being?

Comparativists (that is, political scientists who study and compare the politics of different countries) believe that it is possible to provide answers to these questions, and in this book students will begin to understand the craft of comparative politics. Even if it is not possible to design a country as one sees fit, it is possible to understand why countries develop the way they do and why they are ruled as they are. By comparing the range of possible political responses to global opportunities and constraints, we can begin to offer explanations for why countries develop as they do and evaluations about the trade-offs involved under different political orders. Understanding and explaining the differences among the politics of countries are really the core concerns of comparative politics.

COMPARATIVE POLITICS AND POLITICAL SCIENCE

Within political science, comparative politics is considered one of the major "subfields." How is it situated in relation to the other subfields? Let us consider two that are among the most closely related: political theory and international relations.

In some ways, the first comparativists were political theorists. Two thousand years ago, the ancient Greek political theorists Plato and Aristotle identified different kinds of political orders – such as aristocracy (literally "the rule of the best"), oligarchy ("the rule of the few"), democracy ("the rule of the people"), and tyranny ("the rule of the tyrant") – and wrote carefully argued treatises on which form of government is the best. Although they offered basic explanations for why one type of government changed into another, they were more interested in justifying what is the right kind of government than in telling us systematically why we get the kind of government that we do. Contemporary political theorists within political science continue this venerable tradition. They continue to write about different kinds of political orders and analyze the structure of ideas about those orders primarily to make judgments about them.

Comparativists, by contrast, tend to suspend their normative evaluation of the world in favor of describing the political world and explaining why it is the way it is. It is important to remember that comparativists do this not because they lack preferences or are unwilling to make normative judgments but rather because as social scientists they are committed first to offering systematic explanations for the world as it is. A comparativist may not like fascism or communism (or even democracy!) but usually considers it challenging enough to answer the question of why some countries become fascist, communist, or democratic in the first place. Comparativists may disagree about whether the acquired knowledge may help make the world a better place or help us make better moral judgments about politics, but they usually agree that the job of describing and explaining is big enough, and perhaps some of the deeper philosophical meanings of our findings can be left to the political theorists. So, for example, rather than evaluating whether democracy is good or not, comparativists spend a great deal of time trying to understand and identify the general conditions – social, economic, ideological, institutional, and international – under which democracies initially appear, become unstable, collapse into dictatorship, and sometimes reemerge as democracies.

What is the relationship between comparative politics and international relations? Like comparativists, most students of international relations consider themselves to be social scientists. Additionally, like comparative politics, the subfield of international relations can also trace its roots to ancient Greek political theory. In this case, the person of interest is Thucydides, who attempted to understand the origins and consequences of the Peloponnesian Wars between the Greek city-states. War, as we all know, is unfortunately an important part of the human condition. Modern scholars of international relations understandably devote a great deal of time and energy to explaining why states go to war with each other. Of course, peoples of different states do not only fight with each other. They also trade goods and services with each other. It is not surprising then that scholars of international relations also study trade between countries.

Comparativists, although acknowledging the importance of war and international trade, concentrate on the politics within countries rather than the politics that occurs between them. This intellectual division of labor between comparativists, who study "domestic politics," and international-relations specialists, who study the "foreign politics" of states, has long characterized political science. With so much to learn, it seemed to be a sensible way of dividing up the discipline.

In the last quarter of the twentieth century, this began to change. For one thing, most scholars of international relations now recognize that what happens within a country may determine whether it wages war or makes peace. Would there have been a Second World War without the election of Hitler's Nazi Party in Germany in 1932? It is difficult to say for certain, but it is much less likely that the politics *between* the European states during the 1930s would have developed the way they did if the politics *within* one of them, Germany, had been different.

Comparativists also understand the huge impact that international relations has upon the politics of almost every country in the world. War and preparing for war have always influenced domestic politics. So has international trade. Today, the ease with which goods and services, people and the ideas they espouse, and, perhaps most importantly, weaponry move around the world have made our planet a much smaller place. Clearly, what transpires between countries influences what happens within them.

Rather than sustain an artificial division between comparative politics and international relations, in this book we explicitly take account of the global context in which the politics of a country takes shape. The international environment often provides a political challenge to which countries have no choice but to respond. In responding as they do, however, they may introduce a new kind of domestic institutional order that other countries find appealing or threatening and to which they in turn also feel compelled to respond. There is an intimate connection between international and domestic politics, and in the next chapter we offer a framework for thinking about this connection.

How Comparativists Practice Their Craft: Concepts and Methods

REGIME TYPES

Although comparativists think about a broad range of questions, they are most frequently interested in the origins and impact of different kinds of government, or what they refer to as "regime type." That is, if we accept that there are different kinds of political orders in the world, what are the main characteristics of those orders, and why do they appear where and when they do? For example, all of the country chapters in this book consider why democracy took root or did not take root in the country in question.

Before inquiring into the origins of democracy, however, one must have a fairly clear concept of what democracy is and what it is not. The classification of countries into regime types is tricky. Most comparativists do not simply accept the word of the rulers of a country that its political institutions are democratic. Instead, they operate with a definition of democracy that contains certain traits: competitive, multiparty elections, freedom of speech and assembly, and the rule of law are the minimum that most comparativists require for a country to be classified as a democracy.

Similarly, when comparativists classify a country as communist, they usually mean that it is ruled by a communist party that seeks to transform the society it rules according to the tenets of Marxist-Leninist ideology. Real countries, of course, never practice perfectly all of the traits of any regime type. They are never perfectly democratic, communist, fascist, or Islamist. Democracies sometimes violate their own laws or conduct elections that are not perfectly free and fair. Beyond a certain point, however, it makes little sense to categorize a country as democratic if it prohibits free speech or falsifies election results. Or, to take an example from this book, if a communist country, such as China today, allows markets to determine economic life, at what point do we cease categorizing it as communist? Comparativists do not agree on the answer to this question, but clearly it is an important one because before we can understand why certain regime types exist in one place and not in another, we have to agree on what that regime type looks like.

TOOLS OF ANALYSIS: INTERESTS, IDENTITIES, AND INSTITUTIONS

Even when they agree on the important differences between democratic, communist, fascist, and Islamic states, comparativists frequently disagree on how best to evaluate the conditions that produce the political regime types in question. This is also a very tricky question. Let us say that you were parachuted into a country and had to figure out quickly what the most important facts about that country were for determining its politics. On what would you choose to concentrate? Comparativists do not always agree on this either. A first group of comparativists maintains that what matters most is material interests. People are rational calculators. They organize politically when it serves their interests and support political regime types that maximize their life chances. They are rational in the sense that they minimize their losses and maximize their gains. If you accept this assumption, then, to get a handle on the politics of a given country, what you should be studying is the structure of material interests in its society and how those interests organize themselves to gain power.

The major interests seen in democratic states are usually organized into interest groups, trade unions, social movements, and political parties. In non-democratic states, it may be illegal for individuals to come together in interest groups or competing political parties, but even in communist and fascist states, political scientists have identified many ways in which people pursue their interests to get the kinds of public policies that benefit them the most.

A second group of comparativists maintains that there is no such thing as "objective" interests outside of some set of values or ideas that defines your interests. Who you think you are – your identity – determines what you really want. Yes, all people require food and shelter, but beyond this minimum what people value most in this world may have very little to do with maximizing their material lot. In fact, it is all too easy to find people who are willing to die for what they believe in (that is, to act against the most important material interest of all – physical survival). Instead, what people demand out of their rulers and what rulers do is to pursue the ideals that they most cherish and enact policies that are consistent with their identities. So, rather than focusing on material interests, to understand politics you are much better off concentrating on the dominant identity of a given society.

Religion and ethnicity are two of the most common forms that identity takes. In democracies, political scientists have consistently shown that religion and ethnicity are very good (although not perfect) predictors of how people vote and what kinds of policies they favor. In the United States, for example, most Jews vote for the Democratic Party and most Southern Baptists vote Republican because these respective parties are considered by both religious groups as having ideas similar to their own on important issues. In India, a state that consists of a multitude of nationalities and religions, parties based primarily on particular ethnic and religious groups have successfully competed against parties that run on a nonethnic platform. And it is not only minority groups that engage in identity politics. The success of anti-immigrant parties throughout Europe and Hindu nationalist parties in India shows that majorities engage in identity politics, too.

Modern societies constantly generate new identities based not only on religion and ethnic belonging but also on gender, sexual orientation, and care for the environment. Democratic societies now have strong and important women's rights, gay rights, and environmental movements. And, of course, identity politics matters not only in democratic settings but also in nondemocratic ones. Communist revolutionaries hoped that if they built a better society, people would begin to define themselves in new ways and that a new "socialist man" would appear who would subordinate his selfish desires to the greater needs of society as a whole. Part of what makes the study of politics so interesting is the constant proliferation of new identities and the myriad ways in which these new identities are either accommodated or rejected by the political order or can undermine the existing order.

A third set of comparativists maintains that both material interests and identities do not really determine on their own how a country's politics works. What matters most are institutions, the long-term, authoritative rules and procedures that structure how power flows. People may deeply desire a certain kind of policy (a new health care system, for example) and have an identity that would support this (say, a widely spread ethic of care that reflects the simple maxim "I am my brother's keeper"), but the rules of the political game may be structured in such a way that numerical minorities can easily block all attempts to change the policy. So, if you want to get a quick analysis of a country's politics, what you should concentrate on are the authoritative rules of the game – the institutions.

Political life is teeming with institutions. Democracies have institutions for electing their leaders, for channeling the flow of legislation, and for determining whether the laws are just or "constitutional." Some of these institutions are so important, such as regularly held free and fair elections, that they are part of what we mean by democracy. Other institutions, such as the rules for electing leaders, have a great impact on the politics of a country, but no single set of electoral rules can be held to be more "democratic" than another. In Great Britain, parliamentary leaders are elected much as in the United States, in a single-member district, "first-past-the-post" election. In Germany, members of the Parliament – the Bundestag – are elected primarily in a multi-member district, "proportional representation" contest in which parties are represented in the legislature according to their share of the popular vote. Both systems have strengths and weaknesses but are equally democratic.

Of course, nondemocratic countries have institutions, too. The most important institution in a communist state is the Communist Party, which has small party cells at all political levels spread throughout the society. Communist states also have elaborate institutions for economic planning and administration. And, of course, there is the institution of the secret police. Iran, as an Islamic republic, not only has an elected parliament but standing over this parliament is an unelected Supreme Revolutionary Council of religious leaders that possesses the right to declare invalid legislation that contradicts its interpretation of Islamic law. As in democratic countries, the institutions of nondemocratic countries shape the political arena and influence what kinds of policies are enacted.

These three ways of studying the determinants of politics – interests, identities, and institutions – represent the dominant concepts in comparative politics, and some admixture of them is present in just about every study, including the chapters in this book. They give us a powerful set of tools for grappling with some of the most important questions that comparativists think about.

Consider again the question of why some countries (or "cases," as comparativists often refer to them) are democratic and others are not. Scholars who stress the importance of interests point to the size of a country's middle class on the assumption that poorer countries have smaller middle classes and diminished chances for sustaining democracy. Comparativists who study identities and values explain the presence or absence of democracy by the strength of a population's commitment to representative government and democratic participation. Institutionalists, by contrast, focus on which kinds of political arrangements (U.S.-style presidentialism or British-style parliamentary government, for example) best ensure that elections, freedom of speech, and the rule of law will continue to be practiced.

Comparativists apply the tools of interests, identities, and institutions not only to the determinants of regime type, that is, why countries are democratic or nondemocratic. They also use these concepts to understand why countries have the kinds of public policies that they do. Even among democracies, one finds important differences. For example, some have large and extensive welfare states – systems to equalize people's material conditions. Others have much smaller ones. Consider the issue of publicly financed health insurance. It is generally acknowledged that most industrialized democratic countries have universal systems of government-funded health insurance and tightly controlled regulations for the provision of medical services. The big exception to this rule is the United States, where health insurance and service provision remain mostly private. Why is this the case? What accounts for this American exceptionalism? An analysis based on interests might point to the influence of powerful groups, such as insurance companies and doctors, who oppose government interference in the market for health care. An analysis based on identities would stress the value most Americans place on individual responsibility and the suspicion that they generally harbor toward governmental intervention in the market. An institutional analysis of this question would point to the structure of political institutions in the United States in order to show how health care legislation can be blocked relatively easily by a determined minority of legislators at several points along its way to passage. Which of these different approaches to the question yields the most powerful insights is, of course, a matter of debate. What comparativists believe is that the answer to the question of U.S. exceptionalism can only be found by comparing U.S. interests, identities, and institutions with those of other countries.

In fact, the concepts of interests, identities, and institutions can be used to assess a broad range of themes that comparativists study. Why do some democratic countries have only two parties, whereas others have three, four, or more? Why do minority ethnic groups mobilize politically in some countries and during some eras but not in others? Why do some people enter politics using parties and elections, whereas others turn to street demonstrations, protest, or even terrorism?

A question that many comparativists have studied using interests, identities, and institutions is that of when revolutions occur. This is an especially fascinating question for students of comparative politics because political change does not always occur slowly and peacefully. Some of the truly momentous changes in political life in countries throughout the world occur quickly and entail a great deal of violence. Notice, for example, that most of the countries in this book have experienced political revolutions at some time in their history. Their political orders, especially in those countries that became democratic early in their history, were born as much through violent revolutionary conflict as through peaceful compromise. Comparativists frequently deploy the concepts of interests, identities, and institutions in order to identify the conditions under which revolutions occur.

Using these tools and the cases they study, comparativists often establish explanations for general families of events such as revolutions, elections, and the onset of democracy itself. When the explanation works well (that is, when it can account for the same phenomenon across a sufficiently large range of cases) and the family of events is general enough, comparativists will use the term "theory" to describe what they are talking about. Theories are important because they help us discover new facts about new cases, and cases are important because they help us build new and more powerful theories.

Comparative Politics and Developmental Paths

A CHANGING FIELD

Comparative politics developed as a subdiscipline in the United States after World War II. At that time, Americans suddenly found themselves in a position of leadership, with a need for deep knowledge about a huge number of countries. The Cold War between the United States and the Soviet Union raised the question of whether countries around the world would become increasingly democratic and capitalist or whether some version of communism would be more appealing. Comparativists initially provided an answer to this question by maintaining that over time most countries would look more and more alike; they would "converge" with each other. Especially as they became wealthier, industrialized, educated, and less bound by unquestioned tradition, states throughout the world would become more democratic. As society changed, "political development" would occur. This approach to comparative politics was called modernization theory.

Even though it yielded important insights and inspired a great deal of research throughout the world, by the late 1960s modernization theory confronted withering criticism on a number of fronts. First, it universalized the particular experience of the West into a model that all countries, independent of time or place, would also follow. Political scientists doing field research in other areas of the world maintained that this was simply not happening. In poorer countries, in particular, democracies often collapsed into dictatorships. Second, and more important, political scientists working in poorer regions of the world argued that even if the history of Europe and North America (the "West") did represent a shift from traditional to modern society, the fact of the West's existence changed the context in which poorer countries had to develop. Some political scientists maintained that the poorer nations of the world lived in a condition of "dependence" on the West. Large Western corporations, so the argument of the dependency theorists ran, supported by their governments at home and by the regimes they controlled in the poorer countries of the world, economically exploited these countries. As long as this relationship existed, the people of these poorer countries (called the "developing world") would remain poor and would live in undemocratic conditions. Even those who did not share this view came to believe that the notion of a unilinear path to the modern world was not supported by the facts and that the West's existence at a minimum changed the context in which the poorer countries of the world had to live. In the face of these trenchant criticisms, most comparativists backed away from thinking in such broad terms and began to concentrate on "smaller" and more tractable questions such as those we have outlined here.

During the 1970s, however, a new wave of democratization began and dozens of countries that had been dictatorships for decades or that had never known democracy at all became democratic. Rather than return to modernization theory, with its sweeping generalizations about the intimate tie between industrial and capitalist society on the one hand and democracy on the other, comparativists have attempted to develop theories that are more sensitive to historical and geographic contexts. That is the point of departure in our book. Although we share the long-term interest of comparativists in the conditions that produce and sustain democracy, our approach acknowledges the uniqueness of the experience of the West and the huge impact that this experience has had and continues to exercise on the political development of the rest of the world.

Our approach is thus "developmental" in that we place the analysis of each country within the context not only of its own history but also within a broader global history of political development. The initial breakthrough of the West into industrial capitalism and political democracy set out a challenge for the rest of the world. The responses to this challenge sometimes took a democratic form, as in the case of France's response to Great Britain's power in the nineteenth century, but sometimes they did not, as in the cases of communism and fascism. In fact, all of the nondemocratic regime types that we examine in this book were responses to the challenge posed by the most powerful capitalist and democratic countries. The international context provides the impetus through which domestic interests and identities create new institutions.

Not every comparativist will agree with our approach. Some maintain that the perspective emphasizing the Western developmental challenge to the rest of the world is too focused on the "West" and ignores indigenous developments that have little to do with the West. Others contend that it is best to leave these larger questions aside altogether because they are basically unanswerable and that the purpose of comparative politics is to approach matters of the "middle range" (that is, questions that are amenable to neat generalizations). Although we acknowledge the hazards of starting with the West and proceeding to the frequently poorer and less democratic areas of the world – the "East" and "South" – the West's impact is too important to ignore. Equally, although we understand that theorizing about such large questions as why countries have the political orders they do is asking a great deal, comparative politics has never shied away from asking big questions about the origins of regime types and their impact on world history. Furthermore, as the country chapters make clear, there is no reason why smaller and more tractable questions cannot be pursued within our framework of interests, identities, and institutions.

PATHS OF DEVELOPMENT

We divide our country chapters into four groups. Each group represents a distinct developmental path. The first group we term "early developers," and we use the examples of Great Britain and France to illustrate what is distinctive about this group. We could also have chosen other Northern and Western European cases such as the Netherlands, Sweden, and Switzerland, as well as the United States and Canada. Great Britain and France, however, offer important features that make them worth studying. In both cases, long-term economic changes created urban middle classes who used their new social power to demand a greater say in the affairs of government. In the case of Great Britain, the economic growth that produced the new middle classes was so rapid and decisive that it has been termed by economic historians an "industrial revolution" and caused Britain to become the most powerful country in the world and remain so for over a century. France, too, became very powerful and created an overseas empire that competed with Great Britain's. In both cases, however, democracy became firmly rooted. In Great Britain, it was never questioned. In France, where the struggle for democracy was much more intense, the proponents of democratic government time and again gained the upper hand.

A second group of countries took a different developmental path. We term them "middle developers." We include in this group Germany and Japan, although we could also have included Italy, Spain, Austria, and several other countries of Central Europe. The key feature of this pattern of development is that these countries all got a "late start" in economic development and had to catch up with the early developers if they were to compete militarily and satisfy the material desires of their people. In all cases, the state played a much larger role in fostering economic development, the traditional agrarian nobility did not really leave the political scene until well into the twentieth century, the military wielded a great deal of influence, and the middle classes were socially far weaker and politically more timid than in the early developers. This combination of external pressure to develop, the dominance of traditional social classes in the modern political world, and the relative weakness of the middle classes laid the groundwork for uncertain democratic politics and authoritarian rule. In the twentieth century, both Germany and Japan developed indigenous responses to the early developers that political scientists have termed "fascist." Fascism offered an alternative way of looking at the world compared with the liberal democracy of the early developers. It stressed ethnic and racial hierarchy over equality, dictatorship over democracy, and military conquest over international trade. Although the fascist response to the challenge of the West was largely defeated in World War II, and both Germany and Japan subsequently entered the family of democratic states, fascist rulers remained in power for much longer in Spain, and fascist ideology continues to attract support in parts of Europe and Asia (for example, postcommunist Hungary and Slovakia and India).

Our third group of countries we term "late developers." We include here Russia and China, although we could also have included other countries in Eastern Europe and Southeast Asia. In both Russia and China, economic development occurred so late after its initial breakthrough in the West that the state was forced to play the dominant role. As both societies entered the twentieth century, the middle class was tiny and weak. The industrial working class was also small, deeply disaffected, and lived in horrible conditions. The majority of both societies consisted of illiterate and landless peasants. The response in both cases was a communist revolution based on an intellectual elite leading the mass peasantry in the name of a yet to be created industrial working class. Communism promised a world based on material equality and a nonmarket planned economy under the leadership of a communist party that supposedly understood the scientific "laws" of historical development. At the beginning of the twenty-first century, the late developers cast off their communist economies and China (but, initially at any rate, not Russia) experienced rapid economic growth. Both, however, remained less than democratic – China was still formally ruled by a communist one-party dictatorship and Russia had significantly backslid on earlier democratic reforms – and both were still attempting to close the economic gap between their own country and the more advanced West.

The countries in our fourth developmental path we term "experimental developers." We have chosen as our cases Mexico, India, Iran, South Africa, Nigeria, and the European Union. These cases are faced with unique developmental problems. Mexico's grand experiment is independence. Is it possible for a country to be autonomous when its northern neighbor happens to be the most powerful country in the world? Until the mid-1990s, Mexico's postrevolutionary political development was characterized by a one-party state and an autarkic economy. These features of Mexico's political development have changed dramatically since the mid-1990s. India's grand experiment is non-revolutionary democracy. Is it possible for a large postcolonial country to be a democracy when it has had a major independence movement but not a social revolution? It is interesting to note that India's one-party dominance and autarkic development have also been strongly challenged by both domestic and international pressures for change. Iran's grand experiment is Islam. Is it possible for a country to be economically and politically powerful and thrive in the modern world after an Islamic revolution? Is there an Islamic path into the modern world? Iran seeks a distinctive path of development that combines political participation and markets in ways that accommodate local religious traditions. One finds here a struggle between pro-Western and anti-Western forces. South Africa's grand experiment is multiracial democracy. Is it possible for ethnoconstitutional democracy in which power is shared along ethnic lines to survive in a country that made a relatively peaceful transition from colonialism and apartheid? Nigeria in some ways combines the developmental challenges of Mexico, India, Iran, and South Africa. It is poor, multi-ethnic, religiously and linguistically diverse, dependent on revenues from oil exports, and only sporadically democratic. The results have sometimes been heartening but mostly they have been sobering and even depressing. Is there a way forward for a country confronting all of the challenges of development at once? Although much wealthier than Nigeria, the European Union's experiment is perhaps the most ambitious of all, for it is essentially an attempt by multiple states in Europe to ensure peace and prosperity over the long term by yielding the most precious resources that states have – their independence and their sovereignty.

These six grand experiments remind us that political development is open-ended. It is by no means inevitable that countries will become democracies. Because new challenges to development exist in today's small world, undiscovered paths may still emerge. It is true that during the 1990s the end of the Cold War and the demise of communism diminished the pride in being part of the "developing world" and hence encouraged the search for alternative paths to development. Many countries that were formerly considered part of the developing world began to redefine their interests, identities, and institutions to compete globally via democracy and markets. This redefinition was not always easy or genuine, and some countries did not stay democratic for long or were democratic on paper only. Still, there is no doubt that, during the 1990s, the global hegemony of democracy and capitalism seemed unchallengeable.

The terrorist attacks of September 11, 2001, and their aftermath brought much of this into doubt. The intention of Osama bin Laden's Al Qaeda network was to launch a global holy war against the world's democracies in the hope of creating Islamic states throughout the Muslim world. Whether this latest challenger to the global rise of democracy and markets will be able to translate its ideas into policies that appeal to significant numbers of people and whether it will be able to translate its dogma into a concrete institutional framework in any state of the Middle East remains an open question. What is clear, at least, is that challengers to liberal democracy have not disappeared.

WHY STUDY COMPARATIVE POLITICS?

Even once we have agreed on the main questions that we care about and the main concepts used in our analysis, we still have the question of how exactly we should go about studying politics. It will not surprise you to read that comparativists are deeply committed to *comparing* and believe that a great deal can be learned by comparisons of just about anything. Not only can we compare but we *must* compare in order to get an accurate picture of political life. Just think about why we take pictures of giant redwood trees with people or automobiles next to them. We do this because it is impossible to understand just how large a redwood is in the absence of something of known size against which we can compare it. So, too, for political life. We compare political orders in order to understand what we are looking at in each one.

All governments grapple with complex global issues: the need to accommodate diverse ethnic and religious identities, the struggle to improve economic security and growth, the quest to provide a strong basis for national citizenship, and the effort to cope with demands for democracy and participation. The world is a laboratory in which countries engage in grand experiments in development. There are a variety of such experiments: many different forms of culture, civil society (informal networks of citizens), economic markets, political democracy, state bureaucracies, and public policies. The comparativist compares and contrasts how two or more countries conduct these experiments. Much of this book involves describing and explaining the similarities and differences among countries.

Why, for example, are political parties different in Britain, France, and Germany? Perhaps they are different because of institutions: The British electoral rules, as in the United States, provide a "first-past-the-post" system that normally leads to two dominant parties. The German electoral system, by contrast, is based on proportional representation, which encourages the formation of multiple parties. On the other hand, perhaps the differences in parties can be attributed to differences in identities. France's tradition is one of radical revolution and Great Britain's one of slow and evolutionary change. To take another example, why did Britain and Germany react differently to the oil shocks and budget crises of the 1970s and then the highly competitive international economy of the 1990s and the beginning of the twenty-first century? Perhaps they reacted differently because of the configuration of interests. Interest groups work more closely with government in Germany than in Britain. On the other hand, perhaps the differences can be attributed to identities. German workers value more highly the protections offered by the state against the ups and downs of the market and were therefore less willing to accept cuts in their benefits (employment security, duration and size of payment from the state in case of unemployment, health and disability insurance) than were their British counterparts. We try, in other words, to construct plausible explanations for the variations we observe. Comparison thus allows us to test our ideas about comparative politics. When done well, this sort of comparison provides us with a powerful set of explanations and theories that can help us understand not only the countries from which we developed them but also new countries that we have yet to consider.

The purpose of this book is therefore not to cram your head with information about politics in faraway places and times long ago. Comparing cases and explanations helps us to study politics because it forces us to think in a rigorous way. It forces us to think theoretically. It also forces us to confront in a particularly acute way the problem of applying theories to reality. Recall our example of the absence of universal public health insurance in the United States. It is quite common to read that it does not exist because of powerful interest groups who oppose it. But did not powerful interest groups oppose its introduction in other countries? It will not surprise you to learn that Canadian doctors and insurance companies were just as opposed to universal public health insurance as their U.S. counterparts. Yet Canada enacted universal publicly funded health insurance as far back as 1963. By helping us to eliminate wrong answers, this small comparison of two cases illustrates how powerful a tool comparison is for helping us zero in on the correct answer to an important question.

You are not likely to become a social scientist, however. As policymakers and advisers, or simply as citizens wishing to participate in politics, we have two reasons for comparing countries. First, comparison encourages us to broaden our knowledge of political alternatives and possibilities. It also allows us to recognize diversity. Such knowledge permits us to make informed judgments about our leaders and political life. Second, the laboratory of political experiences may be transferable. Nations can learn from one another. They can locate ideas for solving their own problems. They can borrow foreign models or adapt their acquired knowledge to perfect their own institutions. In short, comparison allows us to draw positive lessons from successful experiments and negative lessons from failed experiments.

Comparison, in sum, allows social scientists to describe and explain and allows policymakers to understand and choose. There are, however, many obstacles to comparing countries that differ in language, size, culture, and organization. The end result of our comparisons might be to recognize the differences rather than the similarities of experiences and experiments. Comparing the problems of two or more countries might lead us to conclude that each country is unique. The dimensions of this uniqueness, however – the precise way in which each country is unique – can only be discovered through comparison.

Americans, for example, might conclude that they are very different from the rest of the world. As we have seen, American exceptionalism is a major theme of comparative politics. Americans need to recognize, however, how big, important, rich, and powerful the United States is compared with the rest of the world. In order to understand the United States itself – to describe, explain, and evaluate U.S. politics – Americans must consider circumstances different from their own. When they do so, they gain perspective on their own society.

Comparison, therefore, has always been used by scholars, students, and citizens to produce a better-informed and more critical understanding of the political world in which we live.

CHAPTER TWO

The Framework of Analysis

Jeffrey Kopstein and Mark Lichbach

Introduction

The core idea of this book is simple: three important aspects of domestic politics – interests, identities, and institutions – are explored in a set of country studies cast in world-historical and developmental perspective. We teach, in short, the following framework.

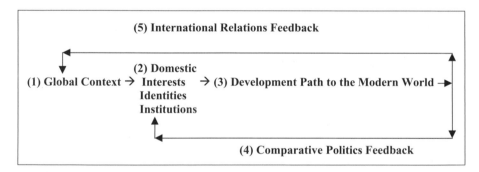

To put it in words: (1) The global context influences (2) domestic interests, identities, and institutions, which produce (3) developmental paths to the modern world, which, in turn, generate (4) comparative-politics feedback effects on domestic interests, identities, and institutions and (5) international-relations feedback effects on the global context. Our approach allows us to raise important empirical questions about comparing governments and significant normative concerns about evaluating good and bad governments. Let us turn to each of the five parts of our framework.

Global Context

Today's world is small. Our book therefore has a "globalist" slant. The global context for comparative politics involves tensions between nations and states, contradictions between global homogenization and local diversity, and conflict among states at particular points in history.

NATIONS AND STATES

The first thing to understand about the world is that it is divided into nations and states and that nations and states are often in tension with one another. What are these two sets of things that dominate the globe, and why are they in tension?

When we speak of modern states, we mean first that states have external independence. Political scientists call this external independence sovereignty. Governments have armies, navies, and air forces to maintain their external security. They send and receive ambassadors to other states and belong to the global club of states, the United Nations. Sovereignty also has a second, internal dimension. The international community of states generally recognizes and accepts the right and power of the government to make laws and monopolize force within its boundaries. This means that states have internal control over their populations. They maintain internal order, collect taxes, regulate economic life, confine people in prisons, and conscript or recruit citizens into the armed forces. States vary, however, in how much external independence and internal control they in fact exert. Some states, such as the United States and Great Britain, possess independence that is widely accepted externally, and they also exercise significant control over their populations. Other states, such as Afghanistan or Sudan, enjoy much less external independence and exercise so little control over their populations that political scientists argue about whether they actually have a state.

States are populated by "peoples." Peoples are often called nations. The origins of nations and their defining characteristic may be linguistic, religious, racial, or the perception of a common history or shared fate. Nationhood is largely a subjective category. If a people considers itself to be a nation, then we must at least begin to think of it as a nation.

Global society is thus divided into states that are defined organizationally and nations that are defined culturally. Because a state is a set of governing institutions and a nation a community of people, some – especially nationalists – argue that the two should coincide in a nation-state. Nationalists maintain that the only proper form of government is one in which the boundaries of the state correspond with the boundaries of the nation. They claim that only in a nation-state, where people identify with the state because the rulers of the state are also members of the nation, will people accept the government as the legitimate representative of their community that is entitled to make laws on their behalf.

Although nationalists believe that national identity should coincide with state boundaries, when we look at a map of the world we quickly discover that the relationship between state and nation is highly imperfect. In fact, they rarely coincide. Very few states are composed of a single national group. Some states, such as Russia and India, are composed of several or even many nations. Some nations, such as the Kurds, are spread out over many states and have never governed themselves. Finally, there are some nations, such as the Jews and the Armenians, that are spread out over many states and that have one central governing state more or less serving as a focal point for their nationalist aspirations.

State and nation often do not coincide because of history. "State-building" (the formation of a state) frequently does not coincide with "nation-building" (the formation of a sense of national unity). It may surprise you to learn, for example, that late into the nineteenth century, many people in large parts of France did not even speak French as their first language. These people had to be "made" into French men and women. It may also surprise you to learn that more than two centuries ago, when the United States gained its independence, there were fewer than 20 governments in the world that we would designate today as states. Most political entities were principalities, city-states, empires, and tribal areas without fixed and legally recognized boundaries. Today, the entire surface of the globe is divided into independent states that make claims to control national territories and their populations.

GLOBALIZATION AND HETEROGENEITIES

The second thing to understand about the world is that it is a whole and that the whole and the parts are also often in conflict with one another. Consider, first of all, the world as a whole. Regional and global forces respond to and shape a set of common and converging global interests, identities, and institutions. Markets, cultures, and institutions operate not only within countries but among them as well.

Interests, identities, and institutions have all become global. Trade, finance, and production are now global activities. Global markets exist not only for land and capital but also, increasingly, for labor. Economic problems are consequently global problems. Growth and prosperity are global problems. Inequality and poverty are global problems. The gap in political and social equality and economic prosperity between those living in the Northern and Southern hemispheres is a global problem. Diseases and epidemics are global problems. Environmental problems are also now global. And, of course, so is terrorism. In sum, it is not possible for a country to isolate itself from global economic trends, cycles, and shocks.

Examples abound of the ways in which Western values dominate and define social and cultural identities throughout the world. For instance, English is the international language used in business, politics, the arts, and the sciences. Innumerable technical standards derived from the West define the global business culture. The notion of universal human rights derives from Western ideas of justice. At a more mundane level, consumer culture itself has become global. People throughout the world increasingly wear the same kinds of clothing, eat many of the same kinds of food, listen to the same music, and watch the same television programs. The global masses who consume Coca-Cola soft drinks and McDonald's hamburgers, wear Nike sneakers and Levi's blue jeans, and watch Steven Spielberg films attempt to move up the material and status hierarchy and enter the world of Armani apparel, Chanel perfume, Dom Perignon champagne, and Perrier mineral water. Much of the upwardly mobile global middle class, in turn, strives to acquire the lifestyle of Lear Jets, Porsche cars, and the transnational managerial elites' Rolex watches. These aspirations, at each level, are the same around the world.

Not only have interests and identities become global but institutions have also. Examples of regional or continent-wide institutions include the European Union and the North American Free Trade Agreement (the comprehensive regional trade agreement signed by the United States, Canada, and Mexico in 1994). Global actors such as the United Nations, the World Bank, the International Monetary Fund, and the World Trade Organization issue extensive supranational regulations and exert an extraordinary amount of influence. International nongovernmental organizations such as the Roman Catholic Church, the International Red Cross, Greenpeace, and Amnesty International affect the lives of ordinary people in large and small ways.

Global markets, Western values, and international institutions exercise an important common, one might even say homogenizing, influence across borders. In some ways, huge sections of the world have converged, and the result is diminished diversity of political and economic institutions. And the more states and societies begin to resemble each other, the more pressure there is on nonconforming states to change their ways to fit in.

LOCAL HETEROGENEITIES

The worldwide movement toward variations on a common theme of democracy and markets, a theme originally developed in the West, has generated its own antithesis. Notwithstanding global trends, there persist important and interesting differences among states. States attempt to develop distinctive national policies to deal with the global economy and evolve institutional variations of democracies and markets. In some market economies such as those in Great Britain and the United States, the state plays a primarily regulatory role, setting out the rules of the game in which people and companies compete. In Germany and Japan, in contrast, the state has a much stronger hand in guiding the market, frequently involving itself in such areas as finance and wage negotiations. Despite some global convergence, the idea of different paths to the modern world – for example, variations on democracy, authoritarianism, and communism – is still relevant. Since the 1980s, political scientists have debated whether global economic competition will force all advanced industrial economies to adopt similar social policies and levels of taxation.

There is little evidence at the dawn of the twenty-first century that this is actually occurring, and in fact the pressures of economic competition have intensified the search within different countries for ways to adapt that preserve their national identities, unique structures of domestic interests, and distinctive institutional orders. Similarly, although the states of the democratic West exerted a great deal of pressure on the states of the Middle East to democratize, especially after September 11, 2001, this pressure has been strenuously resisted and the search by the people of this region for a distinctive Islamic path to the modern world has intensified.

Comparativists often ask whether the principle of sovereignty will remain globally dominant in the twenty-first century. It is too early to answer this question definitively, but there are several challenges to sovereignty from society itself that are turning up in many countries at the same time:

- Various kinds of subnationalism involving territorially based minorities have attempted to separate nations from states. Whether it be Scots in Great Britain, Quebecois in Canada, the Baltic peoples of the Soviet Union, or the Sikhs in India, ethnic and cultural groups have sought with varying degrees of success to crown their own sense of separateness with a state of their own.
- Religious fundamentalism in Judaism, Christianity, and Islam challenges the individualism, materialism, and secularism of the Western state.
- The rise of gender and sexuality in politics – the struggle for political representation of women, gays, lesbians, and the transgendered – also challenges the nation-state from below by questioning dominant definitions of political membership.
- The authority of the state is also challenged from below by libertarians – who want deregulation of markets, privatization of state services, severe cutbacks in welfare-state expenditures and public-sector taxes – and by environmentalists, who seek to control the effects of economic growth.

Comparativists often study these challenges to the state under the rubric of social movements and revolutions. Student revolts, terrorism, and fascist and Marxist revolutions have come in waves that affect many countries at the same time. Why? Herein lies another paradox of globalization – the increasing interdependence of the world – and heterogeneity: The source of globalization, the West, is also frequently the source of the challenges to it, and thus of heterogeneity, or diversity. Democracy, fascism, and communism, for example, were all conceived in the West.

In your reading you will find contradictory global and local forces that characterize the current community of nations and states. Although since the 1800s there has been a consolidation of the world into nation-states, there has also been a set of challenges to the state: those from below, which challenge the state through the growing independence of civil society; and those from above, which challenge the state through the growth of regional and supranational forces that put into question these global trends in global ways.

WORLD-HISTORICAL TIME AND CONFLICTS AMONG STATES

Modern sovereign states developed in response to the experiences and challenges of other states. Our historical point of departure in this book is the profound and irreversible changes that occurred in the northwest part of Europe, and especially Great Britain, approximately 250 years ago. This most important critical juncture in modern history is often subsumed under the rubric of the Industrial Revolution, which ran its course roughly from 1780 to 1850. In a very short period, new technologies of mass production, the creation of large urban areas containing a growing proportion of the population, the commercialization of agriculture, the increasing ability to manipulate nature due to rapid advances in scientific knowledge, and new methods of organizing people in administrative bureaucracies combined in Great Britain and a few other countries to generate a new society of unprecedented power that succeeded during the nineteenth century in conquering much of the rest of the planet.

The rest of the world had to respond to the British challenge. Comparativists have spent much time documenting and explaining these responses. To take just one example, once Great Britain became *the* major power in the world, Germany felt pressure to catch up. In responding, however, Germany could not simply repeat the British experience because that would have taken, many Germans believed, far too long. Instead, Germany developed its own set of political and economic institutions that exercised an important impact on its subsequent political and economic history. In fact, as we will see later, Germany still lives with the institutional legacies of its initial response to the British "challenge."

Any global order thus involves competition in world-historical space and time that affects the evolution of states. Here are the questions comparativists ask: What was the competitive international situation in which a state found itself when it attempted to modernize and industrialize? Who were its principal rivals and competitors among sovereign states? In other words, who developed first, had a head start, and could serve as a benchmark? And who developed later, had to play catch-up in order not to be left behind, and hence looked for negative and positive role models?

The developmental logic of countries thus differs partly because the countries began their development during different world-historical eras. Great Britain, for example, embarked on the path to development before any of the other states and thus laid down the political, economic, and military challenge to which other states responded. In Europe, France, Germany, and Russia responded to the British challenge out of fear of being considered backward as a country and fear of political humiliation, but they did so in their own ways, and hence their developmental histories differ from Britain's and from each other's. Outside of Europe, Japan, China, Mexico, India, Iran, Nigeria, and South Africa, the other countries studied in this book, attempted to find their own ways into the modern world of competitive sovereign states. Each used the resources – human, institutional, and economic – available at the time it responded to the challenges that came from the outside world.

To understand the way states are today, it is crucial to look at the strategic and defensive modernization that these states undertook to preserve their national interests, identities, and institutions. Global political competition affects all countries of the world. Late development brought challenges in the form of malevolent Western colonialism and imperialism. It also brought opportunities in the form of benevolent liberal democratic hegemons and positive and negative models of development that permitted the late and experimental developers to learn from the positive experiences and avoid the negative experiences of countries that preceded them historically.

In sum, we stress that domestic politics must be understood in world-historical perspective; that our descriptions and explanations must take into account particular historical situations; and that domestic economies, cultures, and politics are invariably affected by the competitive international environment of states.

Domestic Interests, Identities, and Institutions

What aspects of domestic politics are affected by the global context of development? We advance three concepts that are relatively simple but very powerful. First, people are rational beings who pursue their interests. Second, people are meaning-seeking beings who are defined by their identities. Third, people's interests and identities are shaped by and pursued within institutions. Interests, identities, and institutions are all, in turn, shaped, as shown in our country chapters, by the global context of development. The global context of development, therefore, matters to comparativists because it produces certain patterns of interests, identities, and institutions that persist over time and shape the countries in which we live.

INTERESTS

Politics is partly about the pursuit of interests. One reason that people become involved in politics is to get the things they want from the government and to ensure that the state enacts laws and policies that advance their interests. Of course, what people want varies greatly. Still, there is no denying that a large part of politics in any society revolves around the question of who gets what. I may want a higher economic standard of living and you may want a cleaner environment. How these differences in interests are resolved tells us much about a country's politics.

We therefore assume that individuals have preferences, goals, and objectives. They also face temporally fixed constraints, limitations, and resources. People are problem solvers who try to optimize their gains and minimize their losses. They therefore make choices among available alternatives in order to reach their goals. In politics, what this means is that material interests determine policy preferences. People react to the incentives they face and devise strategies and tactics to pick the alternative that best enables them to satisfy their material self-interest.

Material interests are often pursued not only by individuals but also collectively. People who share an interest attempt to act as if they were a single individual. It is not easy to do this because of what political scientists call the collective-action problem: People who want to act as a unified group often find that individuals are narrowly focused on their own personal situation and refuse to contribute their time or resources to collective causes. Yet, people do band together in pursuit of their common concerns and join political parties, interest groups, and social movements that become important bodies. Professional associations, trade unions, health lobbies, and environmental organizations are but a few of the many kinds of interest groups that people join in order to pursue their interests.

Comparativists frequently focus on a particular category of collective interest that they term "class." For example, when they write of the "working class," they are referring to the large group of people who make their living by selling their labor. Of course, with such a large group it is unlikely that they will speak with a single voice or act as if they all had the same interest. The concept of class therefore can be a very tricky one to use.

Comparativists also note that interest groups are more powerful in some countries than in others. More than a century ago, Alexis de Tocqueville observed the propensity among the inhabitants of the United States to join groups and participate in associational life. Since then, other comparativists have painted a more complex picture. In some countries, such as Germany and Japan, large numbers of people join trade unions. In others, such as the United States and Canada, this number is much smaller. In dictatorial countries such as Russia under Joseph Stalin or China under Mao Zedong, it may be very difficult for interest groups to form because the leaders have the power and will to prevent them from coming into existence. One measure of whether a country is becoming more democratic then is whether the people have the right to form interest groups and through these groups to influence political decisions. The kinds of interest groups and their strength determine much about the politics of a country.

So many interest groups are often at work in a country that its politics become gridlocked. All too often such is the case in the United States. In countries such as India and South Africa, ethnic interest groups frequently alter the legislative agendas of ruling coalitions and presidents. Another focus for comparativists therefore is how conflict and cooperation among interest groups get worked out in different societies. In Great Britain, as in the United States, politics revolves around the intense competition among interest groups that comparativists call "pluralism." In Japan and Germany, on the other hand, social groups often seek to cooperate and avoid conflict, even of the peaceful kind, through institutionalized bargaining arrangements called "corporatism."

Comparativists doing interest-based analyses typically ask: What is the distribution of resources in society? What are the major interest groups in a society? What are their political preferences? What are the obstacles to collective action, and which groups have managed to overcome the obstacles to acting collectively? Are there coalitions between well-endowed or poorly endowed groups that can tilt the balance in the case of conflict? Who are the winners and losers of conflicts?

In sum, the pursuit of material interests through interest-group politics is affected by the global context and, in turn, interest groups battle over alternative paths of development. The pursuit of material interests thereby affects the distribution of economic rewards in society and consequently represents one important way of approaching comparative politics.

IDENTITIES

Politics is also about identity. Although evidence shows that people all over the world often pursue common goals, and thus can be said to share certain interests, people also frequently define what is in their interest differently. Based on particular sets of beliefs and values that we often refer to as culture, they will even define their material interests differently. What people are willing to give their life for, how much hardship they will bear during war, or how many hours on weekends they are willing to work varies across societies. Likewise, the kinds of ideas, political language, and even physical demeanor that people expect from their politicians also vary greatly across nations and states.

Think, for example, how religion and ethnicity influence politics. If people define their identity in religious terms – that is, if they say to themselves, "We are primarily Jewish, Christian, or Muslim, and not German, French, or Iranian" – they will define their interests differently from people who do not tend to define their identity on the basis of religion. In turn, they will support different kinds of governmental policies toward religion, schooling, and popular culture. Ethnicity and national sentiments have a similar kind of influence on how people define themselves. If someone defines herself primarily in ethnic terms, she will tend to care most about how many people of her own ethnic group or nation are in politics. She will tend to define her interests in ethnic terms. It is common, for example, for people of an ethnic group to want a state that will defend its rights to schooling in their language and cultural traditions and to want politics and administration to be controlled by people of their ethnic group.

Just as people with different economic or material interests can clash over their differences, people with different identities also frequently disagree on politics. Although the Soviet Union was a single country, it consisted of many different ethnic groups that never managed to transcend their own particular identities. One contributing factor to the breakup of the Soviet Union was the failure of the Communist Party to create a unifying "Soviet" identity among the many ethnic groups in the country. Often, however, the results of identity politics can be tragic. During the Yugoslav civil wars of the 1990s, people who speak basically the same language began to define their identities so differently (often in terms of religious and ethnic differences) that they were willing to kill one another in order to live in areas that were ethnically "pure." In the aftermath of the Iraq war, many Sunni and Shiite Muslims who had lived side by side for several centuries no longer felt they could live together in the same neighborhood, or even the same country.

Of course, people may possess not simply one identity but several competing identities, and it is not obvious which one will dominate or how people will ultimately act based on their identities. Someone might be, for example, a woman and black and feel equally strongly about both of these identities. Political leaders often play an important role in mobilizing some identities and neutralizing others. In France, for example, right-wing politicians have tried since the 1990s to convince the French that their traditional notions of who is French – someone born on French soil – should be changed and that the true French are those who have been born into the French culture. The idea here is to exclude as many immigrants from citizenship and public life as possible. On the other hand, at the same time, German politicians have been working to alter the notion of who is a German, an idea that to this day remains based on blood ties to other Germans, in order to make German identity more inclusive. Similarly, successive Indian governments have worked very hard at catering to the various subnational identities within the country while simultaneously carving out a distinctive Indian national identity that will be more important to people than all of their other identities.

Religion and ethnicity are only two of the more important kinds of identities. One can easily point to a politics of gender, environmental, and regional identities. Each of these identities informs what people want out of politics, what they are willing to do, and how they define their interests.

The subject can be made even broader, however. Comparativists frequently study attitudes in society toward such issues as the role of government, the kinds of institutions that people want, and the degree of their commitment to democracy. Such studies may take the form of quantitative public-opinion surveys about attitudes and opinions or may be microlevel ethnographic studies of civic associations, such as Greenpeace, the National Rifle Association, or the Parent-Teacher Association.

Material interests frequently trump social identities. In 1992, for example, Bill Clinton won the U.S. presidential election with the slogan "It's the economy, stupid." But it is easy to be cynical and think that people care only about money. In fact, many types of social identities can trump material interests, allowing identity politics to prevail. For example, in Iran, Ayatollah Khomeini thought that "economics is for donkeys." The world has seen a revival of traditional communities, religious fundamentalism, ethnic and racial identities, and gender identifications that have not been washed away by (and have actually been strengthened as a reaction against) Western materialism.

In fact, social identities can even influence what people think their material interests are. The great German social scientist Max Weber showed how the early Protestants' concern about the fate of their immortal souls caused them to work as efficiently as they could and consume as little as possible in the hope that their worldly success would be a sign that they were members of the "elect" and not the "damned." This work ethic, the Protestant ethic, as Weber termed it, created a huge increase in productivity and savings and laid the foundation for modern capitalism. The impact of identities on material life, however, extends well beyond the West. Because identity can discipline a labor force for economic development, authoritarian states often try to impose ideas on societies in order to promote economic growth. Stalin in the Soviet Union and Mao in China were ideologically committed to socialism. They sought to create a dedicated population of true believers who would suspend their own material desires in the present in order to build utopian, egalitarian societies in the future. In Iran at the beginning of the twentieth century, secular nationalism replaced Islam in part to encourage economic development. Now that secular nationalism has been replaced by Islam, many hope that it, too, will encourage economic development.

Comparativists doing identity-based analyses of politics will ask: What are the dominant ideas of a society? What do people value most? How do these values shape political behavior? What ideals do people expect their leaders to share? Why do some identity groups conflict and others live in relative harmony? How do leaders use identities to mobilize their populations for projects they deem important?

INSTITUTIONS

We now turn from interests and identities to institutions. Institutions provide an important arena in which politics takes place. When comparativists speak of institutions, they usually mean the authoritative rules and organizations that structure political life. We first explore how the global context influences domestic institutions and how these institutions, in turn, affect developmental paths by influencing identities and interests. We then explain why many comparativists consider the study of politics to be synonymous with the study of institutions.

INSTITUTIONS AS CONSEQUENCES (OF THE GLOBAL CONTEXT) AND AS CAUSES (OF INTERESTS AND IDENTITIES)

Comparativists often start their analysis by examining the state. The state is an organization that maintains control over a particular territorial jurisdiction. It is important to note, however, that this control may be stronger or weaker depending upon a great number of circumstances. An important factor affecting how societal interests and identities influence politics and public policy is whether the state is strong or weak. But what do we mean by a "strong" or "weak" state? Comparativists usually think of state strength as being determined by two factors: autonomy and capacity.

Consider autonomy. The state may be autonomous from the interests and identities of civil society. This means that it cannot be easily influenced by specific groups in society – business associations, working-class unions, or religious identity groups, for example – that try to penetrate and capture the state to use it to pursue their narrow concerns rather than to pursue the broader public good. The state's political and administrative leaders in a strong state are capable of formulating and defining their own preferences for what they would like to see the state do. Hence, the state could be autonomous in the sense of making its own decisions.

Now consider capacity. The state might also have great power and capacity in relation to the interests and identities of society. That is, a strong state will have the resources and the ability to use those resources effectively to implement its decisions and strategies in order to address the problems, challenges, and crises of development, in spite of what class interests and religious identities might prefer.

Many late developers believe that a strong – autonomous and capable – state is good for economic development. A strong state can pursue the general good of all society. It does not have to follow the narrow interests or identities of a single subnational group that has selfish reasons for not contributing to the public welfare.

Of course, strong states need not always be democratic ones. In fact, there is a certain amount of tension between strong states and democracy. A strong state does not have to accept the notion that the public good is the sum of the interests and identities that emerge from voting and lobbying. Rather, a strong state can pursue the "true" public good of the entire nation. In other words, some argue that a strong state can rectify the selfishness found in society. The Japanese state, for example, embodied in the persons of its bureaucrats and civil servants, has often operated autonomously of business and labor interests and has had the capacity to implement its choices over the opposition of both groups.

Such common variations of democratic institutions as divided government, checks and balances, federalism, and weak political parties were therefore avoided by states that followed the early developers because they were thought to decrease state power and promote political fragmentation, instability, and gridlock. Many late developers have come to believe, however, on the basis of recent experience, that a strong state *hinders* economic development because it burdens society with high taxes and other policies that are designed to feather the beds of the bureaucrats that constitute the strong state rather than foster economic growth for the population as a whole. At the same time, those states that fail to provide for the minimum of public safety and services, such as Iraq and Afghanistan, are usually considered to be failed states.

Ironically, former totalitarian states such as the Soviet Union proved weaker than the supposedly weak democracies, such as the United States. Democracies, especially those with a powerful president or prime minister, can be strong because the state power they wield is considered legitimate by most people. Under these circumstances, democratic states may even reinforce national unity and provide the key to resolving political conflicts over interests and identities.

INTERESTS AND IDENTITIES, AND THE STRUGGLE OVER INSTITUTIONS

We have maintained that competition between states generates the demand for economic development that, in turn, generates individuals and groups with material interests and social identities. Interest groups and identity groups with different preferences about development then come into conflict with each other.

We have also argued that political institutions empower some groups and constrain others, thereby transforming interests and identities into public policies. Bureaucratic and democratic institutions thus influence the formation of interests and identities, restrict and promote their expression, and finally mold them into policies associated with paths of development.

Interest groups and identity groups realize that institutions influence the outcome of their policy struggles over a path of development and therefore seek to retain or change institutions in order to gain the political power needed to satisfy their own interests and identities. An important part of politics thus involves generally unequal groups fighting over the making and remaking of political institutions. As we will see in the chapter on Russia, for example, the struggle over the rules of the game after the collapse of communism was especially intense. But this is, in fact, an age-old part of politics. In Britain during the eighteenth and nineteenth centuries, middle-class interests fought against monarchs and aristocrats. They sought a parliament to limit the king and enhance their own status and power. In Germany during the nine-teenth and early twentieth centuries, urban industrial and rural landowning elites fought against lower-class workers' and peasants' interests. They sought a strong state that would preserve their influence. In both cases, democratic and bureaucratic institutions were the outcomes of interest- and identity-driven political struggles. Hard bargains were struck. In some cases, elections were introduced, but the right to vote was extended to the lower classes only gradually. In other cases, landowning and urban elites enjoyed disproportional representation in Parliament. Although some believed that the bargains made everyone in the country better off by permitting economic development, oth-ers believed that the bargains bestowed much greater advantages on some than others.

Because institutions are so central to politics, they stand at a pivotal point in our framework. Although the global context influences domestic interests, identities, and institutions, the institutions, which are often contested, shape and filter interests and identities into developmental paths.

Developmental Paths to the Modern World

Global competition forces countries to adopt a developmental path. States and societies choose domestic and foreign policies in politics and economics to compete in the global order. What do such policies, paths, and regime types entail?

With respect to domestic policy, states do many things. Governments pur-sue extractive policies. They take goods and services from their citizens in the form of money (taxes) and time (military service). Governments also pursue distributive policies in which they return goods and services to their citizens; for example, roads and social security payments. Governments organize and pay for systems of public education. Governments also pursue regulatory policies in which they set the rules for property rights, human rights, and occupational safety. Finally, governments sometimes attempt to shape the equality of opportunity and/or the equality of results.

Governments also pursue foreign policies. Some states expend a great deal of energy on preserving the global status quo. Others are "revolutionary" and attempt to change the global order. Some states pursue war as a tool of statecraft. Others remain relatively peaceful, except under the most extreme circumstances.

The domestic and foreign policy choices often combine into what is called a *development strategy* or *grand strategy*, as shown in Table 2.1. Different world-historical circumstances favor certain grand strategies over others. Take, for example, economic policy. During the Cold War, Japan developed its export-oriented consumer goods industries and India chose to develop its

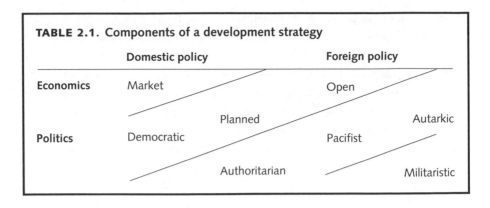

TABLE 2.1. Components of a development strategy

	Domestic policy		Foreign policy	
Economics	Market		Open	
		Planned		Autarkic
Politics	Democratic		Pacifist	
		Authoritarian		Militaristic

nascent industries by protecting them from foreign competition. The global trading system may influence whether nations adopt import-substitution industrialization, as in India's case during the Cold War, or export-led industrialization, as in Japan's attempt to compete in the world automobile market. World markets might influence whether states are free traders or protectionist, whether they institute a laissez-faire market economy or a state-directed one, and whether they pursue peaceful or aggressive foreign policies.

A major theme of this book is therefore democratic capitalism and its alternatives. *There is no single developmental path to the modern world.* States can and do make their own developmental choices and often evolve local institutional variations of globally or regionally dominant political economies. Theories suggesting that all states move through common stages and converge in the end, such as some versions of modernization theory, are wrong. Looked at historically, there have been multiple paths to the modern world. There has been no inevitable triumph of democracy, markets, and peace. Domestic interests, identities, and institutions have combined in the past and continue to combine today with the global context to support undemocratic, anticapitalist, closed, and militaristic paths. And a key source of local variation in institutions today is the existence of alternatives to and variations on democracy, markets, and peace.

We therefore need to develop a comparative and historical understanding of the alternative paths to the modern world adopted in different international environments. We offer four sets of country studies that have been chosen to exemplify the different developmental logics of countries that began their journey into the modern world during different world-historical eras.

- Early Developers: Britain and France
- Middle Developers: Germany and Japan
- Late Developers: Russia and China
- Experimental Developers: Mexico, India, Iran, South Africa, the European Union, and Nigeria

These cases should remind us that development is open-ended. Because new challenges to development exist in today's small world, undiscovered paths may still emerge.

You should note three things about our choice of cases. First, our global and developmental perspective allows us to choose states on theoretical and substantive grounds and thus to set contemporary issues of policy and performance in a larger setting. Second, we have chosen cases that are today's engines of development for the Western, Middle Eastern, Asian, African, and Latin American regions of the world. Third, all of our cases have had revolutions of one type or another rooted in world-historical problems of development, which, in turn, influence country-specific patterns of development.

You should also note two features of developmental paths. First, paths are competing political alternatives. People always debate the choice of a developmental path, and these debates inevitably involve a power struggle among competing interests and identities. In early twentieth-century China, for example, the urban intelligentsia advocated a liberal path based on urban middle-class interests, Western liberal values, and democratic institutions. The nationalists pushed an authoritarian path rooted in conservative, rural elite interests, a strong nationalist ideology, and statist institutions. The communists advocated a communist path based on peasant interests, Marxist ideology, and totalitarian institutions controlling civil society. Similar debates among liberals, conservatives, and socialists can be located in every Western country during the 1930s. Fascist, communist, and liberal movements that vied for political power also can be found in Russia during the late nineteenth and early twenty-first centuries.

Second, the debate among proponents of various paths leads to governing or developmental coalitions, combining state and societal actors, that form behind grand strategies of development, and these coalitions attempt to implement their development strategies using institutions designed for that purpose. Under fascism, rural and urban elites used the state to repress workers, peasants, and groups defined as ethnically "alien." Under post–World War II corporatist systems in Europe, business, labor, and government worked together. During the 1990s, and in many parts of the world at the beginning of the twenty-first century, market-oriented (or what are sometimes called neoliberal) development coalitions became dominant in many countries. Such policy coalitions, however, face formidable problems. They are vulnerable to shifts in global context and can be quite unstable. Some members leave voluntarily and others are purged. Many, for example, have traced the failure of democracy in Weimar Germany to cabinet instability, and others have traced cabinet instability to the failure of the democrats to put together a viable developmental coalition. Hitler and the Nazi Party then seized power and proposed a new grand strategy of conquest and genocide for Germany and Europe. This example teaches us that although state–society coalitions are difficult to construct, their success defines development – for better or worse.

In sum, comparativists believe that the world-historical time in which countries modernized or industrialized has influenced their development strategy. This book therefore chooses its cases based on the international situation within which states found themselves when they first attempted to develop.

Comparative-Politics Feedback

A particular developmental policy backed by a specific regime coalition may or may not be successful. Based on the rule of thumb "If it ain't broke, don't fix it," one would expect that when development is working well for everyone in the country, regimes would want to consolidate their developmental path.

Often, a developmental path performs poorly everywhere and for nearly everyone except a very small group of beneficiaries. A path such as the creation of a predatory, nondevelopmental state could produce little economic growth, wasteful and inefficient allocation of resources, crime and violence, corruption, worker absenteeism, and alcoholism. Moreover, developmental strategies can produce misdevelopment, uneven development, or exploitative development. For example, the British approach to colonial development in India involved a divide-and-rule strategy that produced distorted development: interests, identities, and institutions were constructed to favor Britain and not India. And, more generally, developmental experiments can fail and result in either stagnant or collapsed states. Although some regimes are by definition interim, transitional, and provisional, there are dead-end developmental paths that did not look so dead-end at the time they were adopted. The dustbin of history is littered with colonial administrations, occupation governments, world empires, principalities, city-states, tribal areas without fixed territorial boundaries, bureaucratic authoritarianism, feudalism, slave states, apartheid systems, and fascist and communist regimes.

Poor economic performance in failed and misshapen development experiments leads to uncertainty, poverty, and social tensions: civil disorder and political anarchy, leadership succession crises, illegitimacy, and alienation. Developmental models are thus constantly being rethought. For example, until 1990, countries throughout the world sought to emulate the Japanese economic "miracle"; when Japan sank into a prolonged recession, it was no longer considered a "model." The result of such new thinking can be evolutionary or revolutionary change of domestic interests, identities, and institutions in order to pursue new developmental paths.

Failed developmental paths also can be altered by revolutionary changes of interests, identities, and institutions from above. National elites can coalesce into a new regime whose purpose is to resist the global order. For example,

German and Japanese "revolutions from above" during the nineteenth century and first half of the twentieth century remade social classes, solidified national identities, and created militant and strong states that sought to reshape the global order rather than adapt to it.

Of equal importance, failed developmental paths are sometimes changed by revolution from below, often after failed attempts at revolution from above. For example, economic and political liberalization under Soviet President Mikhail Gorbachev created new interests, identities, and institutions that brought about the collapse of the Soviet Union. It appears that certain developmental paths and the coalitions behind them run their course wherever and whenever they are tried and therefore contain the seeds of their own revolutionary demise. Not long ago, for example, many academics and policymakers believed that late-developing countries needed strong states to mobilize resources for industrialization, assure territorial integrity, collect taxes, and staff bureaucracies. As resistance movements began to think otherwise and toppled many such states, global thought shifted. It is now widely argued that strong populist authoritarian regimes, military/bureaucratic absolutisms, patrimonial states that concentrate power in rulers and their families, and corporatist and state-led industrialization generate problems, such as bloated public sectors, mismanagement, corruption, waste, and inefficiency, that result in such economic imbalances as inflation, currency overvaluation, and balance-of-payments crises. Neoliberal regimes based on expanded free markets that have been created in turn have also generated severe problems. At the same time, however, some comparativists now believe that "shock-therapy" policies of rapid marketization, advocated for many states by the international financial institutions, can also produce instability and the possibility of revolution. If strong states provide too much control, weak states provide no framework at all for capitalist development. Different developmental regimes, in short, contain different flaws that eventually lead to the appearance of resistance movements in a set of similarly situated countries.

International-Relations Feedback

National development also influences the global context within which a regime finds itself. Consider some examples. British power helped define the eighteenth- and nineteenth-century worlds. In the aftermath of World War II, the United States imposed its own vision on the global economic order. The decision by the U.S. Federal Reserve Bank to raise interest rates from 1979 to 1982 contributed to the world debt crisis by increasing the amount that debtor states in poorer regions of the world had to pay for borrowed money. German authoritarianism and fascism plunged the world into global war. Japanese authoritarianism had the same result. The Soviet Union's and China's internal patterns of development led them to try to export communist regimes to the rest of the world. During the Cold War, Mexico and India legitimized and encouraged a third way of development for a large number of states. Iran's decision, along with the rest of the major oil-producing states, to raise oil prices in the 1970s shook the developed world. Its Islamic Revolution shook regimes throughout the Arab and Muslim worlds. And, finally, South Africa's bold experiment in multiracial democracy has important implications for other deeply divided states.

In sum, developmental paths may contribute to global peace and prosperity. They also contribute to global war and poverty. A nation's development can thus have an impact far beyond a single nation's borders.

The two feedback loops of our framework – comparative-politics feedback and international-relations feedback – yield a path-dependent view of history. Once a state starts down a developmental path, where it goes next is affected by where it has been. Choices made at critical junctures in a state's history not only set a state down a certain path but also preclude alternative paths. A state's contemporary problems thus originate in the historical crises and challenges it has faced. The developmental choices a country makes today are partly a result of the choices that were put in place when it began to develop in a particular world-historical context.

For example, interests, identities, and institutions can persist even through revolutions. First, economic markets and the interests they define show continuity. Today's close connection between interest groups and government in Germany, for example, can be traced to the developmental choices of Germany's nineteenth-century rulers. Second, cultural identities and the values and beliefs that people cherish are resilient. Religion and ethnicity often reemerge after a revolution and affect developmental priorities and choices. Fundamentalist Islam in today's Iran, for example, survived the Shah's regime and was shaped by his industrialization policies. Finally, institutions that define and resolve conflicts among different interests and identities in a country can also survive revolution. Contemporary Russia's interests, identities, and institutions are part of the historical legacy of communism.

The two feedback loops also offer a "punctuated-equilibrium" view of how the present is shaped by the past. What comparativists mean by this is that countries have developmental regimes, supported by developmental coalitions, that are separated by identifiable political crises or critical junctures that produce breakpoints and turning points in a country's history. In other words, a country's global context, its domestic interests, identities, and institutions, and, most significantly, its developmental path to the modern world can change and lead to a new developmental regime. Germany, for example, made the transition from empire, to the democratic Weimar Republic, to two states divided by capitalism and communism, and finally to a new united and democratic Germany. Regime changes are often closely identified with leadership changes. Thus, the change of leadership from Gorbachev to that of Boris Yeltsin in Moscow involved a redefinition of Russian state institutions and national identity. Our country chapters are chronologically organized to take account of the historical changes in regimes associated with changing global contexts; domestic interests, identities, and institutions; and developmental paths.

Our Approach to Comparison

Comparison is essential to comparative politics, and we have made it central to this book. Our approach to comparison involves, first, a common set of tools with which we fashion country studies that reveal distinctive paths of development, and second, explicit comparisons among two or more cases designed to establish the causes and consequences of the significant differences among countries.

First, we have provided a set of tools to study substantive problems rather than a blueprint to develop a theory of comparative politics. Because politics in Britain is interestingly different from politics in France, which is interestingly different from politics in Germany, we have not forced the chapters into a common, encyclopedia-like framework. That is, for each country we have not devoted three pages to interests, four to identity, and five to institutions. Rather, we have allowed our authors to use our common tools to bring out what is unique and significant about each country. This approach gives students a better sense of British politics, French politics, and South African politics than would be possible if every country's politics were forced through a homogenizing boilerplate framework that drains the countries of their uniqueness. Our framework permits the authors to tell the story of their own country in their own way and hence makes for more interesting reading.

Second, after each part of the book – divided into early developers, middle developers, late developers, and experimental developers – we include a section called "stop and compare." These sections should really be called "stop and think" because we ask students to use the comparative method to draw empirical and moral lessons from the country studies by establishing the similarities and differences within and between each of our four sets of cases.

Here are the sorts of questions we ask: How are Britain and France variations of early development, and how are they different from the United States? How are Germany and Japan variations of middle development, which are different from the early developers? How do our two late developers, Russia and China, differ from one another, and how are they different from the early and middle developers? Finally, what are the similarities and differences among contemporary experimental developers – Mexico, India, Iran, South Africa, Nigeria, and the European Union – and what sorts of contrasts do they make with the early, middle, and late developers we have studied?

By alternating country studies with explicit sections on comparison, we demonstrate how comparativists think. Comparativists mix the specific and the general. They begin with cases, turn to theory, and then return to the cases in a never-ending sequence of induction and deduction.

Conclusion

This book guides the beginning political science student through the master concepts, dominant theories, and substantive problems of comparative politics. The country chapters that you are about to read take you on a journey through space and time. Why would you, a college student, be interested in joining this tour through the countries of today's small world?

Our global framework implies that what happens in other countries is important to you, no matter where you live. Take the United States, for example. Although the United States is large, important, and rich, and spans a continent separated from the rest of the world by oceans, Americans are dependent on the economics and the politics of countries around the world. Our political and economic security, our material welfare, and the well-being of our environment are wrapped up with political change and development in the rest of the world. The transportation and communication revolutions that have contracted time and space have created global interdependence. The process is accelerating: It is only since the 1960s that we have had pictures of the globe as a "whole" world, and it is only since the 1990s that the Internet has provided instant multimedia communication to people around the world. In short, a state – even a powerful one such as the United States – that seeks to be isolated, autonomous, and sheltered from global forces is doomed to fail. A state that accepts the inevitability of contacts between different societies, and hence attempts to integrate itself into today's small and interdependent world, can potentially succeed. Americans thus need to know and understand what is going on elsewhere. Citizens in the United States and in other countries must be aware of the world in which they live. They need to be cognizant of the potential dangers and challenges, as well as the possible opportunities, that will confront them in the decades ahead. The same would apply to any student reading this book in any country of the world.

Our approach allows you to be exposed to the theoretically and substantively important currents in contemporary comparative politics. Moreover, we do not expect you to be interested in names and dates for their own sake but because understanding the contemporary world is made easier by knowing some of the more important ones.

At critical points along our journey, we will stop and make comparisons in order to explain and evaluate what we see. Let us repeat our framework: (1) The global context influences (2) domestic interests, identities, and institutions that produce (3) developmental paths to the modern world, that in turn generate (4) comparative-politics feedback effects on domestic interests, identities, and institutions, and (5) international-relations feedback effects on the global context. Let us begin.

PART ONE

EARLY
DEVELOPERS

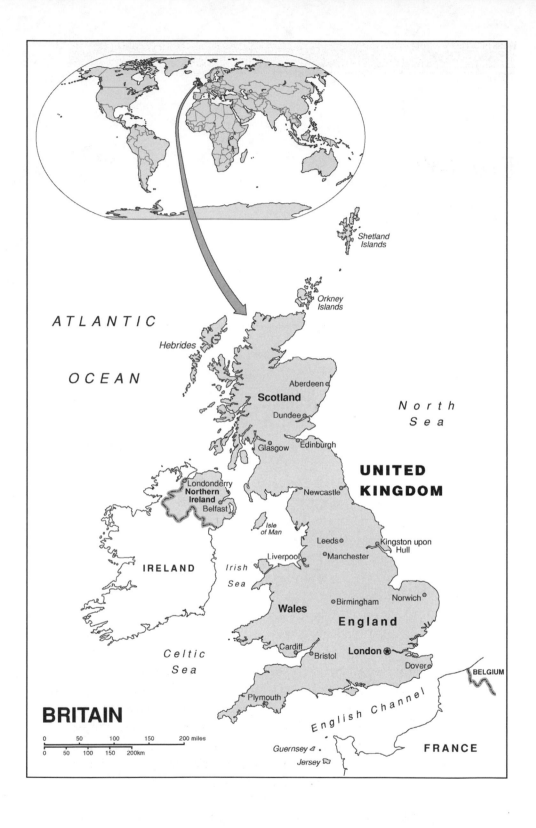

ATLANTIC

OCEAN

Shetland Islands

Orkney Islands

Hebrides

Aberdeen

Scotland

North Sea

Dundee

Glasgow Edinburgh

Londonderry
Northern Ireland

Belfast

UNITED

KINGDOM

Newcastle

Isle of Man

IRELAND

Irish Sea

Liverpool

Leeds Kingston upon Hull

Manchester

Birmingham Norwich

Wales **England**

Celtic Sea

Cardiff

Bristol

London ✹

Dover

Plymouth

English Channel

BELGIUM

BRITAIN

| 0 | 50 | 100 | 150 | 200 miles |

| 0 | 50 | 100 | 150 | 200km |

Guernsey

Jersey

FRANCE

CHAPTER THREE

Britain

Peter Rutland

Introduction

Britain is the usual starting point for comparative politics textbooks because its political system has some similarities with the U.S. system, but also some important differences. Furthermore, most people see the British political system as very successful, having endured for centuries, and thus worthy of study and emulation. Britain has strong and stable political institutions, a firmly established national identity, and a society in which individual freedoms are well protected and social interests vigorously defended.

Britain does indeed enjoy highly stable political institutions that have been in place for centuries. But this very stability has inhibited much-needed structural reform. Britain is headed into the twenty-first century with nineteenth-century political institutions. Important constitutional reforms introduced in the 1990s include the reform of the House of Lords (the upper house of Parliament), and the introduction of parliaments for Scotland and Wales for the first time in 300 years. Britain has also come under increasing pressure to integrate British institutions with those of the **European Union (EU)**, which it joined in 1973.

But these reforms are inadequate to address the deep contradictions within the British model that have provoked a sense of profound political malaise. The system of prime ministerial government produces strong leadership, but vests excessive power in the hands of the prime minister. The sense of crisis goes beyond tinkering with political institutions. The July 2005 bombings on public transport in London were a shocking reminder that some members of Britain's Muslim community are deeply alienated from the British way of life. It is not only immigrants who are uncertain about what it means to be British. For older generations, British national identity is still overshadowed by the legacy of empire and the victory over Germany in World War II ("Britain's finest hour"). This has made it psychologically difficult for Britain to become an active and committed member of the European Union. There is a deep division between Europhiles, those who support Britain's membership in the EU, and Euroskeptics, who oppose further integration with Britain's neighbors. Also in the 1990s Britain introduced radical constitutional reforms in a bid to satisfy the demands of nationalists in Scotland, Wales, and Northern Ireland. Hence, British identity is still very much a work in progress.

Moving from identity to interests, Britain's entrenched social hierarchy led to a period of class warfare between capital, the state, and organized labor that lasted from the early 1800s to the 1990s. This struggle polarized the political system, paralyzed public policy making, and hampered Britain's ability to adapt to a changing global economy. Only since Prime Minister Tony Blair's Labour Party gave up its struggle to transform market capitalism in the mid-1990s has the country managed to shake off this legacy of social confrontation. In contrast with most of continental Europe, Britain has now embraced U.S.-style capitalism, with a lower level of social protection from the state. But prosperity remains elusive for a large and growing underclass.

THE BRITISH MODEL

Britain pioneered the system of liberal democracy that has now spread in some form or other to most of the world's countries. Its political institutions – especially its legal tradition – had a very strong influence on the political system that was created in the United States.

The United States sees itself as the most pristine model of democracy because it introduced the first written constitution in 1787 and has lived under that same constitution for more than 200 years. Britain in contrast lacks a formal written constitution, so it is hard to put a date on the introduction of liberal democracy to that country. The story usually begins with the **Magna Carta** of 1215, when powerful regional lords forced King John to sign a charter respecting their feudal rights in return for the taxes and troops they provided the king. Parliament emerged as the institution through which the lords, and later common citizens, could negotiate their rights with the king. Under the leadership of Oliver Cromwell, from 1642 to 1648 the Parliament fought a civil war with the king in defense of these rights, culminating in the execution of King Charles I. But the monarchy was subsequently restored. In the **Glorious Revolution** of 1688, the Protestant William of Orange deposed the Catholic king James II, and took office as a constitutional monarch who accepted that ultimate sovereignty rested with the Parliament. Since then, there have been no violent political upheavals in Britain.

One of the main virtues of the British model is its capacity to adapt gradually over time. The British model is based on an evolving set of social conventions, and not on a set of ideas captured in a single document. Many of these practices, such as the system of common law (a legal system based on judicial decision rather than legislation), jury trials, freedom of speech, a bill of rights, and the notion of popular sovereignty – were already established by the seventeenth century and formed the bedrock upon which the U.S. Constitution itself was based. But many of the features of the contemporary British model cannot be found in the United States, such as **parliamentary sovereignty** (the idea that ultimate political authority rests with the Parliament); constitutional monarchy (a monarch who is the formal head of state, but with very limited political powers); and an ideologically polarized party system.

The British political system is a product of that country's unique history. There is an old story about the Oxford college gardener who, when asked how he kept the lawn so immaculate, replied: "That's easy, you just roll it every day . . . for 300 years." This continuity argument raises the question of whether Britain's democratic experience can ever be successfully "exported" elsewhere, or whether other countries are merely supposed to marvel at the unique virtues of the **"Westminster model"** of parliamentary sovereignty.

The U.S. model of democracy comes more ready for export. Its essence is captured in a short document, based on a fairly simple set of principles: the equality of all men, the rule of law, and the separation of powers – an institutional system of checks and balances. This has enabled the United States to play the leading role in the spread of democracy around the world since the end of World War II. It was U.S. – and not British – advisers who oversaw the writing of new constitutions in postwar Germany and Japan. This also reflects the fact that the United States was a rising power over the course of the twentieth century, while Britain's prominence steadily eroded.

But the British model is no less important than the U.S. model in understanding the global spread of democracy. As the British Empire shrank after 1945, it left a series of democratic political systems modeled along British lines in its former colonies. The white-settler colonies of Australia, New Zealand, and Canada were granted their independence between 1867 and 1907. Then came decolonization in India (1947), Africa (the 1950s), and the Caribbean islands (the 1960s). Cross-national analysis shows that countries that were formerly British colonies are more likely to be stable democracies than are countries that were the colonies of, say, France or Spain. In part, this is because they follow the Westminster model of parliamentary democracy, which seems generally more stable than presidential systems in developing countries. India, the jewel in Britain's imperial crown (being by far the largest of its possessions), has remained a democracy for half a century despite a very low level of economic development, which is usually seen as an obstacle to democracy. The British ex-colonies in Africa do not fit this pattern, however. With the exception of Botswana, they have all slipped into periods of military or one-party rule since independence.

The Long Road from Empire to Europe

AN ISLAND NATION

If you ask someone from England the most important date in English history, they will almost certainly say 1066. That was when the invading Norman army of William the Conqueror defeated the Anglo-Saxon forces of King Harold at the Battle of Hastings. The French-speaking Norman aristocracy took over England and started the long and bloody process of welding it into a unified state. Britain has not been invaded since 1066. The Spanish Armada was repulsed in 1588, as were Hitler's forces in 1940. The Britons are proud of having preserved their sovereignty against foreign invasion for more than 900 years. This feeds British patriotism and a feeling that Britain is fundamentally distinct from the rest of Europe.

The fact that Britain is an island meant that it relied on the Royal Navy for its security. Unlike the states of continental Europe, it did not require a large standing army to protect itself from its neighbors. Author George Orwell once suggested that this reliance on the navy is the reason that Britain became a democracy. Unlike the absolutist monarchs of Europe, Britain's rulers did not have a large army that they could also use to put down social unrest. Instead, they had to meet popular discontent with compromise. (The United States, like Britain, also dispensed with a standing army and relied on its navy for defense.) All of the powers in continental Europe introduced compulsory military service during the nineteenth century, but Britain continued to rely on a small, professional, volunteer army, most of which was stationed overseas. Only in the middle of World War I was the military draft introduced, and it was dropped immediately thereafter. It was reintroduced in 1940 and finally abolished in 1960. Most other European countries still had compulsory military service until the 1990s.

THE END OF EMPIRE

By the nineteenth century, Britain's global naval power and advanced manufacturing industry made it the dominant imperial power. Both conquest and trade were constitutive of British national identity. Its pantheon of heroes included pirates who robbed Spanish galleons laden with silver (Francis Drake) and the clerk who rose to be the conqueror of India (Robert Clive). British colonies covered one-quarter of the planet in an empire on which "the sun never set." After World War I, Britain lost its position as global economic leader to the United States. Its empire was challenged by growing independence movements in its colonies. Britain lacked the manpower, and ultimately the political will, to fight these colonial wars. After World War II, Britain agreed to independence for India and Palestine, then Malaya, and then for its possessions in East and West Africa. As U.S. Secretary of State

Dean Acheson observed in 1963, Britain "had lost an empire but not yet found a role." Most former British colonies joined the **British Commonwealth** (now called the Commonwealth of Nations), a loose association of 53 countries, founded in 1931. It now has a largely ceremonial role, organizing sporting and cultural exchanges. Seventeen Commonwealth countries still retain the British House of Lords as their final court of appeal. Britain initially clung to a network of smaller colonial possessions around the globe, but these, too, were slowly jettisoned. In 1968, to save money, Britain decided to close all of its military bases east of the Suez Canal, with the exception of Hong Kong.

Just as memories of empire were fading, in 1982, Argentina's military rulers decided to seize the Falkland Islands, a worthless British territory a few hundred miles off the Argentine coast. Prime Minister Margaret Thatcher sent a naval task force to liberate the islands, which was accomplished at the cost of 5,000 Argentine and 125 British lives. The **Falklands War** boosted Thatcher's waning popularity ratings and helped her win a second term as prime minister in 1983.

The British Empire achieved symbolic closure in July 1997 when Britain returned Hong Kong to the People's Republic of China on the expiration of its 99-year lease on the territory. China promised to preserve a special status for Hong Kong for 50 years and respect its economic and political rights. These rights did not include democratic government: Only in the last few years of its lease had Britain made half-hearted efforts to introduce democratic elections to Hong Kong.

Some older Britons look back at the empire with unembarrassed nostalgia, clinging to the myth that British rule brought civilization to the more primitive corners of the globe – from railways to the rule of law. Visions of empire are sustained in the British imagination by a steady flow of movies and TV dramas. The uglier side of imperial rule was edited out of collective memory. Only in the past decade has there been public debate about Britain's role in the transatlantic slave trade; the brutal suppression of the Kenyan "Mau Mau" revolt in the 1950s; or the 1842 war with China, whose goal was to force China's rulers to allow the import of opium.

Although Britain slipped from its dominant role in the international order, it clung to a place at the table of leading powers. As one of the "big three" allied nations that won World War II, it was given one of the five permanent seats on the United Nations Security Council in 1945. It acquired nuclear weapons in the 1950s. The Labour Party advocated unilateral nuclear disarmament in the 1980s, a policy that won little public support. Despite fierce opposition from within his own Labour Party, Prime Minister Tony Blair decided to commission a new generation of submarine-launched missiles to replace the existent Trident system. The proposal passed the House of Commons in March 2007 thanks to support from the Conservative Party.

Britain owes its prominent role in world affairs since 1945 to its "special relationship" with the United States. This began with Franklin Roosevelt and Winston Churchill during World War II and was carried over into the Cold War. As part of the U.S.-led NATO (North Atlantic Treaty Organization) alliance, Britain kept 50,000 troops in West Germany until the end of the Cold War. Britain sent troops to support U.S.-led military actions in Korea in 1950 and Iraq in 1990 and 2003. There have been some rocky periods in the relationship, however. The United States blocked the Anglo-French seizure of the Suez Canal in 1956, and Britain refused the U.S. request to send troops to Vietnam in 1965.

The close partnership between Britain and the United States continued under Prime Minister Margaret Thatcher and U.S. President Ronald Reagan in the 1980s, when they were united in opposition to the Soviet "evil empire." After the Cold War, British Prime Minister Tony Blair and U.S. President Bill Clinton forged close ties, both seeking an elusive, centrist **"Third Way"** in their domestic reforms (neither socialist nor conservative), while cooperating in humanitarian intervention in the former Yugoslavia.

Britain often put the special relationship with Washington ahead of closer integration with Europe. For example, Britain's decision to use U.S. Polaris submarine missiles to provide its nuclear deterrent in 1962 encouraged France to veto the United Kingdom (UK)'s application to join the European Economic Community (EEC), the forerunner of the European Union (EU). (France had been hoping to jointly develop a European submarine missile system.) In 2003, France and Germany, Britain's European partners, refused to support the U.S.-led war in Iraq, but Tony Blair persuaded Parliament to send 45,000 British troops to take part in the invasion. As the war dragged on, Blair's resolute support of the United States became increasingly unpopular with the British public and within the Labour Party itself. Roughly one-third of the Labour members of Parliament opposed the war from the outset.

THE RELUCTANT EUROPEAN

Although Britain was one of the victors in World War II, it was economically drained by the struggle, and was neither able nor willing to become involved in building a new political structure on the shattered continent. In 1952, it refused to join the European Coal and Steel Community, an early forerunner of the European Union, fearing that plans for a common industrial policy would infringe upon its national sovereignty. The European Economic Community (EEC, a broader European economic regional alliance launched in 1957) emerged as Britain's major trading partner, and its economic growth outpaced that of Britain. Twice during the 1960s, Britain tried to join the EEC but was rejected, mainly because Paris feared that British entry would weaken France's influence.

It was not until 1973 that Britain entered the renamed European Community. Much of the next decade was spent haggling over the terms of Britain's membership. In 1984, the Euroskeptic Margaret Thatcher won a reduction in Britain's high contribution to the common budget, half of which went to support inefficient European farmers through the Common Agricultural Policy, a policy aimed at integrating and regulating agricultural production in member countries. Thatcher warily signed the Single European Act (1986), which promoted the free flow of goods, labor, and capital, but also introduced qualified majority voting in place of the veto that the larger countries formerly enjoyed. Thatcher favored free trade but opposed EU-mandated labor and welfare programs. She wanted a Europe of nation-states rather than a federal Europe ruled by supranational institutions that lacked democratic accountability. Many Conservatives objected to the fact that the European Court of Justice had the power to invalidate British laws that contradict EU law. Thatcher's resistance to European integration caused splits within the Conservative Party and led to her removal as prime minister in 1990.

Britain, together with the Scandinavian EU member countries, declined to enter the economic and monetary union that was agreed to at Maastricht in 1991, when the EC renamed itself the European Union. Britain reluctantly incorporated EU regulations (the *acquis communautaire*) into British law, but refused to adopt the single European currency (the **euro**), which was introduced in stages beginning in 1999. Britain's links to Europe grew closer with the opening of the Eurotunnel for trains under the English Channel in 1995. In the next decade Britain's strong economic growth drew in hundreds of thousands of young job-seekers from Europe. By 2007 London was home to an estimated 500,000 Poles and 300,000 French.

Even as economic ties between Britain and the Continent continued to deepen, Britain was reluctant to pursue political integration with Europe. Britain was a strong supporter of "widening" the EU to include the former communist countries of Eastern Europe, in part because it was thought this might delay a political "deepening" of the union. (Ten more countries joined the EU in May 2004, and Romania and Bulgaria joined in January 2007, raising the number of members to 27.) But closer political union would undermine Britain's ability to run an independent, liberal economic policy and weaken its strategic alliance with the United States. A "federal Europe" would challenge the principle of parliamentary sovereignty, which lies at the very heart of the British political tradition.

Who Are the British? Contested Identities

We all have an image of who the British are: Lady Diana, the Beatles, Austin Powers, Helen Mirren. The British seem to be confident and self-assured, even complacent. But this image of comfortable homogeneity is an illusion. Britain was always riven by deep social-class divisions at home and doubts over the viability and morality of its empire abroad. Britain's political identity as the country enters the twenty-first century is more fragile than outsiders usually suppose.

The political identity of many older Britons is tied to the lost empire that disappeared from the world atlas more than half a century ago. Britain's reluctance to join its neighbors in European integration stems from the fear that such a step would undermine British identity. And the Scots, Irish, and Welsh are still there to remind us that "British" should not be conflated with "English." The Celtic periphery makes up 10 million of Britain's population of 60 million and has won increased political autonomy in the last quarter of the twentieth century. Despite 900 years of continuous self-rule, Britain's ethnic identity remains contested and ill-defined.

FORGING A BRITISH NATION

"Britain" and "Great Britain" are synonyms, referring to the main island that includes England, Scotland, and Wales. The United Kingdom is the political unit that includes Great Britain and Northern Ireland. The 60.6 million inhabitants of the United Kingdom have a complex and shifting hierarchy of identities. They identify themselves as English, Scottish, Welsh, or Irish, and at the same time they are aware of themselves as British subjects. Regional identities within each of the countries are also quite strong, with many counties and cities having distinct dialects and proud traditions.

The contemporary United Kingdom is an ethnically diverse society with strong national communities in Wales, Scotland, and Northern Ireland. While the empire existed, the four peoples of the British Isles were united in a common endeavor of mutual enrichment through global conquest. With the end of the empire, that powerful practical and ideological cohesive force is now lacking. Since the 1990s, an emergent "European" identity has been added to the mix.

The south of England was occupied by Angles and Saxons who crossed from the European continent during the sixth to ninth centuries, while Vikings conquered the North. The French-speaking Normans displaced the Anglo-Saxon rulers in 1066 and set about creating a unified kingdom. By the end of the sixteenth century, a notion of the English people was quite firmly established – as reflected in the patriotic plays of William Shakespeare. Through the stick of conquest and the carrot of commerce, the English absorbed the Celtic peoples of Wales (1535), Ireland (1649), and Scotland (1707). Local parliaments were dissolved, and a unitary state was created and run from London.

The process of absorption was different in each of the three Celtic regions. English lords moved into Wales and took over the land, but the peasantry maintained their distinct Welsh identity. Today, about one-fifth of the three million residents of Wales still speak the distinctive Welsh language at home. In Scotland, the indigenous feudal elite was divided. Most of the lowland lords sided with London and helped subjugate the recalcitrant Highlanders. This culminated in the defeat of the Jacobite rebels at Culloden (1745), the last battle fought on British soil. Most of the rebellious clans were deported to America. The Scottish elite played a leading role in the forging of the British nation and the expansion of its empire. During the eighteenth century, Edinburgh, the Scottish capital, rivaled London as an intellectual center. It was there that Adam Smith developed the conceptual framework of liberal capitalism.

Like the Welsh, the five million Scots still maintain a strong sense of national identity, although the Gaelic language has almost disappeared. Scotland preserved its own legal and educational systems, independent from the English model. The Scottish National Party (SNP) believes that Scotland's identity would be best preserved through the creation of an independent Scottish state. Their cause was boosted during the 1960s by the discovery of oil and gas in the North Sea off eastern Scotland. Even so, Scotland remained a net recipient of subsidies from the British national budget. Also during the 1960s, a nationalist movement, **Plaid Cymru**, arose in Wales. Its main goal was the preservation of Welsh language and culture. The nationalists won concessions from London in language policy: Welsh road signs, a Welsh TV station, and the teaching of the Welsh language in schools. Plaid Cymru routinely wins around 10 percent of the vote in Wales in elections.

Whereas the focus of Welsh nationalism is culture, the Scottish movement is broader, with economic and political goals. As a result, its support fluctuates, depending on the level of voter disaffection with the mainstream parties. The SNP usually wins between 12 and 20 percent of the vote but managed to garner 30 percent in 1974. This led the Labour government to steer more public spending into the Celtic regions. Under the 1974 Barrett formula, Scotland, Wales, and Northern Ireland get 15, 10, and 5 percent of the spending in England – more than their share of the total population in the United Kingdom. The Labour Party also promised to create regional assemblies in each country with the power to pass laws and raise taxes, a reform known as **"devolution."** Scots were split on the idea because the SNP still wanted outright independence. A referendum was held in 1979, and only 12 percent of Welsh and 33 percent of Scots voted in favor of a regional assembly.

The idea of devolution was dropped, but then it was revived during the 1990s by the Labour Party under its new leader, Tony Blair. The new Labour government held referenda on devolution in September 1997. Seventy-four percent of Scots voted in favor of a new Scottish parliament, and 64 percent approved giving the body tax-raising powers in the form of an extra 3 percent income tax (the "tartan tax"). The Welsh were rather lukewarm about self-government. Their referendum backed a Welsh parliament by the slimmest of margins (50.3 percent to 49.7 percent), on voter turnout of only 50 percent. A proposal to create a new elected regional assembly in North-East England was decisively rejected, by 78 percent to 22 percent, in a November 2004 referendum.

Despite a number of scandals since they started work in 1999, the two new regional parliaments have been moderately successful, broadening the range of political participation. The new Welsh executive became the first government anywhere in the world to have a majority of female ministers. Many Britons fear that the creation of the Scottish parliament will lead ineluctably to full independence for Scotland. In the May 2007 elections the SNP for the first time won more votes than Labour, and formed a minority government. It remains committed to Scottish independence.

THE IRISH QUESTION

Catholic Ireland was brought under British control only after brutal military campaigns by Oliver Cromwell (1649) and William of Orange (1689). English lords moved in to take over the land, while Scottish Protestants established a colony in Ulster (present-day Northern Ireland). The English banned the Irish language, which survived only in the more remote regions. Unscrupulous landlords, cheap food imports from the United States, and the failure of the potato crop resulted in famine in the 1840s and a mass exodus from the Irish countryside. A growing movement for Irish independence was met with proposals for autonomy ("home rule") from London. These plans foundered initially over land reform and later because of opposition from the Ulster Protestants.

The year 1916 saw an abortive nationalist uprising in Dublin. In the wake of World War I, as Ireland sank into civil war, the British decided to cut their losses. In 1921, London granted independence to the southern Republic of Ireland while maintaining Northern Ireland as part of the United Kingdom. Northern Ireland was granted its own parliament (Stormont), which was controlled by the 1.6 million strong Protestant majority. The 800,000 Catholics of the province lived in segregated housing estates and went to separate (Catholic) schools. The Protestants controlled the police force and steered jobs and public spending to their own community.

In 1968, a civil rights movement sprang up, demanding equal treatment for the Catholics and borrowing the tactics of the U.S. civil rights movement. Its peaceful protests were brutally dispersed by the Protestant police. The Irish Republican Army (IRA), a long-dormant terrorist group, mobilized to defend the Catholics, their goal being that Northern Ireland leave the United Kingdom and join a united Ireland. In 1969, 16,000 British troops were sent to take over the job of policing the province from the discredited Ulster constabulary. Over the next three decades, Northern Ireland was wracked by a three-way "low-intensity" conflict among the British army, the IRA, and sundry Protestant paramilitaries. Riots, bombings, and assassinations became part of everyday life. The British government fought back with special courts and internment without trial. From time to time, the IRA planted bombs on the British mainland, and they managed to kill several top British officials. All told, the conflict caused more than 3,600 deaths and 40,000 injuries. At least the British army managed to prevent the conflict from escalating into open civil war or Bosnian-style ethnic cleansing. On occasion, human rights went by the board. For example, six Irishmen accused of planting a bomb in Birmingham, England, in 1975 were imprisoned for 16 years before they were declared innocent and released.

The British abolished the Stormont parliament in 1972, but efforts to introduce power sharing between Catholics and Protestants foundered on opposition from hard-line Protestant **Unionists**, who staunchly defended remaining part of the United Kingdom. The Protestants were living in a seventeenth-century time warp, adhering to values of God, queen, and country that had long been forgotten in mainland Britain. More concretely, the Protestants feared exchanging their majority status in Ulster for minority status in a united Ireland – particularly because the Irish Republic's laws were still based on the Catholic faith (banning divorce and abortion, for example).

Britain and Ireland drew closer as they both became further integrated into the European Union, and in 1985 London agreed to grant Dublin a direct role in any future peace settlement for the North. London promised the Unionists that Ulster would only join a united Ireland if a majority in the North voted in favor of it. Peace talks resumed in 1993, and a complex peace deal was agreed in 1998, under the chairmanship of former U.S. Senator George Mitchell. The IRA and Protestant paramilitaries promised to disarm, and in return their convicted comrades would be released from prison. Protestant and Catholic politicians in the North agreed to share power in an assembly elected by proportional representation. The "Good Friday" accord was approved in a referendum, winning 71 percent support in the North. Despite some continuing violence from renegade extremists, hopes for peace were high. The leaders of the main Protestant and Catholic parties, David Trimble and John Hume, were awarded the Nobel Peace Prize in 1998. Prisoner releases began, but the IRA refused to disarm and Protestant leaders balked at sharing power with their Catholic counterparts. In the June 2001 British parliamentary elections, in Northern Ireland extremist parties hostile to the accord won more support than the centrist parties on both the Unionist and Catholic sides.

After the September 11, 2001, terrorist attacks in the United States, the IRA sensed that world opinion was turning against terrorism, and they started to give up (or "decommission") some of their weapons under the supervision of an independent commission headed by a retired Canadian general.

However, low-level sectarian violence continued, and the IRA refused to disband. In October 2002, the London government suspended the Northern Ireland Assembly and Executive for the fourth time since 1998 as relations between the leaders of the two communities broke down. Elections to the Assembly in November 2003 saw further losses for the moderate parties that had championed the peace process (the Ulster Unionists and the mainly Catholic Social Democratic and Labour Party) at the expense of the hard-line Democratic Unionist Party and republican Sinn Fein. In September 2005 the monitoring commission finally certified that the IRA had put all its weapons "beyond use," and in May 2006 the Assembly reconvened to prepare for fresh elections in March 2007. On March 26, 2007, the hard-line leaders of both sides (Ian Paisley for the Democratic Unionists and Gerry Adams for Sinn Fein) agreed to form a united coalition government and sealed the deal with a historic handshake. Paisley became the first minister of the province with Sinn Fein's Martin McGuinness as his deputy.

Ireland was the first – and last – British colony. The Northern Ireland "troubles" are a blot on British democracy and the most painful reminder of the legacy of empire.

A MULTICULTURAL BRITAIN

Another important echo of empire was the appearance in the 1960s of a community of immigrants from Asia and the West Indies. These Asians and blacks broke the image of social and ethnic homogeneity that had prevailed in Britain for decades.

Facing a labor squeeze, as early as 1948 Britain started to recruit workers from Jamaica and Trinidad, former British colonies in the West Indies. These black workers were joined by a flow of migrants from India and Pakistan, a process accelerated by the expulsion of Asians from Kenya and Uganda in 1965. More restrictive immigration laws were introduced, which slowed but did not halt the flow. By 2001, there were 1.2 million blacks (half African, and half from the Caribbean); 1.1 million Indians; 1 million Muslim Pakistanis and Bangladeshis; and 250,000 other Asians, mainly Chinese. This meant that 7.9 percent of the population belonged to nonwhite minorities. (White immigrants accounted for another 4 percent.) Four out of ten immigrants live in London, where they make up one-quarter of the city's population.

Race is not the only issue. The South Asian migrants are Hindus and Muslims, and their arrival posed a challenge to Britain's avowed status as a Christian nation. Few Americans realize that the Church of England is the established state religion, with the queen as its official head. Anglican religious education used to be legally compulsory for all pupils in state schools, with separate (state-funded) schools for Roman Catholics and Jews. In practice, less than 10 percent of the British population are regular churchgoers. With the appearance of Muslim and Hindu pupils in the 1970s, most state schools stopped teaching religion, and new "faith schools" were opened for those religions. The new immigrants forced Britain to acknowledge the fact that it was in reality a secular, urban, individualist culture, and that its old self-images of queen, church, and empire were sorely outdated.

Immigration was also a political challenge. Many older Britons harbored racist attitudes from the days of empire, and some young workers saw the immigrants as a threat to their jobs and state housing. The racist National Front Party arose in the late 1960s, and there were occasional street battles between racist skinheads and immigrant youths from the 1970s to the present. The situation began to change as the first cohort of British-born blacks and Asians passed through the educational system and entered the professions. Whereas their parents had kept a low social and political profile, the second generation was more assertive in demanding a full and equal place in British society. But it took several decades before the new immigrant communities won political representation. In 1987, four minority candidates won seats in Parliament, rising to 10 in 1997 and 15 in 2005 (of which 12 were Labour). Tony Blair appointed the first black minister in 1997, and he named a black woman to head the House of Lords.

London is now a vibrant, multicultural city. Intermarriage rates across racial lines are high (in comparison with the United States): around 50 percent for both blacks and Asians. The media deserve much of the credit for helping to redefine Britain as a multiracial community. However, accusations of racism in the police force were highlighted by the failure to prosecute the skinheads who killed a black youth, Stephen Lawrence, in London in 1997. In May 2001, race riots broke out in several northern cities, highlighting the tension in poor white and immigrant communities competing for scarce jobs and housing. During the 1990s, attention focused on the problems posed by an influx of asylum seekers, mainly from Eastern Europe but also from countries as far flung as Afghanistan and Somalia. More than 500,000 entered the United Kingdom from 1991 to 2001, with 100,000 arriving in 2002 alone. Four out of five applicants were rejected, but housing and processing them caused public outrage. Immigration was a major issue in the 2005 election, with the Conservatives attacking the Labour government for allegedly liberal asylum policies that were encouraging refugees to head for Britain. The government responded by tightening border controls.

After September 11, attention focused on the activities of radical Muslim clerics who were recruiting potential terrorists from young men who attended their mosques in England. These fears turned into horrible reality on July 7, 2005, when four young Muslim men set off bombs on three subway trains and a London bus, killing 52 and injuring 700. This was the first suicide bombing in Europe. There was a second attempted attack on July 21, but the three bombers failed to detonate their charges. Three of the July bombers were born in Britain to families from Pakistan, the fourth had been born in

Jamaica. The fact that the bombers were born and raised in England was a profound shock to the British public. Analysts pondered to what extent this home-grown terrorism was due to cultural and social alienation, or was driven by foreign policy issues such as UK involvement in the war in Iraq. Muslim community leaders mobilized to try to reach out to the disaffected youth, while Prime Minister Blair pledged to "pull up this evil ideology by its roots." The government stepped up state funding to Muslim schools, and tried to liaise with "moderate" Muslims while marginalizing their "extremist" counterparts. In an echo of the veil controversies in France, in October 2006 an English teacher was suspended for wearing a full-face veil. Prime Minister Blair supported the school's decision, arguing that the veil was a "mark of separation."

Unfortunately, the July 2005 bombings could not be treated as an isolated incident. In a November 2006 speech Dame Eliza Manningham-Buller, director of the Security Service (MI5), said there were some 200 groups in Britain, with 1,600 members, intent on committing acts of political violence, while polls suggested that "over 100,000 of our citizens consider that the July 2005 attacks in London were justified." According to a Pew Global Attitudes Project survey released in June 2006, only 7 percent of Muslims in Britain saw themselves as British citizens first, while for 81 percent their primary identity was Muslim. Fifteen percent even believed violence against civilian targets could "sometimes" be justified.

The government pushed through bills increasing police powers to meet the terrorist challenge, which critics claimed amounted to an attack on civil liberties. The strict 2006 Terrorism Act made it a criminal offence to encourage others to commit acts of terrorism, including the glorification of terrorism, the circulation of terrorist publications, or training in terrorist techniques. Suspects can be held without charge for up to 28 days. In November 2005 the Commons rejected the government's proposal to extend the detention for up to 90 days – the first time Blair's government was defeated in the House. Forty-nine Labour MPs voted against the government. Already in June 2005 the government had introduced a bill to introduce compulsory identity cards for all residents, including biometric information. The House of Lords rejected various versions of the bill 12 times before it was finally passed in 2006. The Conservatives promised to cancel the plan, which aims to introduce the cards for all residents by 2010, if they win the next election.

BRITISH POLITICAL INSTITUTIONS

The British political system is characterized by a high level of stability. Its main strength has been the evolution of institutions able to defuse the deep conflicts in British society before they turn violent. The core features of what is known as the Westminster model – parliamentary sovereignty, prime ministerial government, and two parties alternating in power – have remained basically unchanged for more than a hundred years.

THE PATH TO PARLIAMENTARY DEMOCRACY

The U.S. political system is based on a written constitution, a contract among the people to form a new state based on certain agreed principles. In contrast, the linchpin of the British system is the notion of parliamentary sovereignty. The Parliament, representing the people, has the power to enact any law it chooses, unrestrained by a written constitution. Another difference is that the U.S. system strives for a separation of powers among the executive, legislative, and judicial branches. In contrast, the British system of parliamentary sovereignty fuses the executive with the legislature, while the House of Lords also serves as the nation's highest court.

Parliamentary sovereignty rests on the notion of popular sovereignty, where voters get to choose their leaders through frequent direct elections. At first, in the eighteenth century, the number of voters who got to participate was very small, perhaps 2 percent of the population. It took 200 years of social conflict before the franchise spread to the majority of citizens. It is remarkable that an institution originally designed to protect the interests of medieval nobles – the Parliament – also came to be accepted by industrial workers in the twentieth century as a vital instrument for the protection of their interests.

Regional *parlements* emerged in France as a forum for nobles to resolve disputes. (The word *parlement* means "talking place" in French, the language also used by the English nobility at the time.) The institution spread to England in the late thirteenth century, providing a forum for the monarch to bargain with the nobles over taxes. Over time, the monarch grew more powerful and came to be seen as the divinely chosen ruler of the kingdom (whose right to rule was subject to approval by the pope). In 1534, King Henry VIII broke with the Church of Rome and established a separate Church of England, with himself as head. The rhetoric of king and Parliament gradually shifted from divine right to that of serving the interests of the people and nation.

The upper chamber of Parliament (the House of Lords) consisted of **hereditary peers**, lords appointed by the monarch, whose title automatically passes down to their eldest sons. The lower chamber (the House of Commons) consisted of representatives elected by property owners in the public at large. Conflict between king and Parliament over the right to raise taxes erupted into civil war (1642–1648). After a brief period of military-theocratic rule by Oliver Cromwell, in the Glorious Revolution of 1688 the Parliament installed William of Orange as a constitutional monarch with limited powers. In the eighteenth century, the Parliament's role developed into what has come to be known as the Westminster model (named after Westminster, the London district where the Houses of Parliament are located.). One of its most important features is the emergence of two distinct parties – Her

Majesty's Government on one side and **Her Majesty's Opposition** on the other. The idea that one can disagree with the government without being considered a traitor was novel, and is still a rarity in many authoritarian regimes. The two-party system came to be seen as integral to the Westminster model.

In his classic 1971 book *Polyarchy*, Robert Dahl argued that liberal democracy develops along two dimensions: contestation and participation. "Contestation" means that rival groups of leaders compete for the top state positions; "participation" refers to the proportion of the adult population who play an active role in this process through elections. Over the course of the twentieth century, many countries have made an abrupt transition from closed authoritarian regimes to competitive, democratic regimes. In these cases, contestation and participation emerge simultaneously. In the British case, however, the politics of contestation were firmly established long before mass participation appeared on the scene.

THE HOUSE OF COMMONS

The centerpiece of the British political system is the House of Commons. The House of Commons consists of 646 members of Parliament (MPs) elected from single-member constituencies. The winner is the candidate who scores the largest number of votes, the same "first-past-the-post" system as in the United States. Although a handful of members sit as Independents, the vast majority of MPs run for election as members of a political party. The Commons must submit itself for election at least once every five years in what is called a General Election. (If an MP dies or resigns between elections, an individual by-election is held for that seat.) After the election, the leader of the party with a majority of MPs is invited by the queen to form a government. If no single party has an absolute majority, party leaders negotiate and the monarch appoints a coalition government. That has not happened since 1935, because the winner-take-all electoral system typically throws up two strong parties.

The best example of British democracy in action is **Prime Minister's Questions**. For thirty minutes once a week, the prime minister stands before the Commons and answers questions, largely unscripted, from members of Parliament of all parties. The ritual often strikes foreign observers as rather silly. The questions are not really intended to solicit information but to score political points and make the other side look foolish. Members of Parliament from all parties shout, whistle, and laugh to express their encouragement or displeasure. The drama is enhanced by the fact that the two main parties sit on ranked benches facing each other, just yards apart. (Since 1989, question time has been televised.)

The spectacle seems juvenile, more akin to a college debate than a legislative assembly. However, the game has a serious purpose: public accountability. Week after week, the members of the government have to take the stand and defend their policies. It is a kind of collective lie-detector test in which the failings of government policy are ruthlessly exposed to ridicule by the opposition. Problems or scandals are speedily brought to light: A controversial newspaper article will stimulate questions in Parliament within days. And a minister who is caught lying to the Commons must immediately resign.

Prime Minister's Questions illustrates the radical difference between the U.S. and British legislatures. A sitting U.S. president never has to confront his political adversaries face to face. Once a year he goes to Congress to give a State of the Union address, with no questions allowed. (The televised debates once every four years are between presidential *candidates*.) The president's communications with the public are carefully managed through public statements, photo-ops, and the occasional press conference.

FROM CABINET TO PRIME MINISTERIAL GOVERNMENT

The head of the government is known as the prime minister. The prime minister nominates a cabinet of about 20 ministers, who are appointed by the queen to form Her Majesty's Government. There are another 70 to 80 ministers and deputy ministers without cabinet rank. Whereas U.S. cabinet members work for the president, their British counterparts are accountable to Parliament. All ministers are members of Parliament, either from the Commons or the Lords, and they must account for their actions, individual and collective, to that body. On the other hand, the prime minister can pick whom he or she wants to be a minister. Individual ministers are not confirmed by the legislature as in the United States.

The cabinet meets weekly in the prime minister's residence, **No. 10 Downing Street**. The prime minister chairs and directs cabinet meetings, and votes are usually not taken. The most senior ministers are those heading the Foreign Office, the Treasury, and the Home Office (dealing with police, prisons, etc.). The ministers rely on the permanent civil service to run their departments, with only a handful of personal advisers brought in from outside. The total number of outside appointees when a new government takes power is fewer than 100, compared with more than 2,000 political appointees in the United States.

There is no clear separation of powers between the executive and legislative branches under the British system. On the contrary, the two are fused together. The public elects the House of Commons knowing that the majority party will form the executive branch. The prime minister comes from the party with a majority in the Commons, and this majority always votes according to party instructions. This means that the legislative program of the ruling party is almost always implemented. The government rules as long as it can sustain its majority in the Commons. A government will resign after defeat in the Commons on what it deems to be a vote of confidence.

This system gives the prime minister tremendous power, in what Lord Hailsham, a leading Conservative, called "an elective dictatorship." The power of the prime minister is augmented by the fact that he or she chooses when to call an election. The Commons can vote to dissolve itself at any time, leading to a general election just six weeks later. Thanks to having control over the majority party in the Commons, the prime minister can choose when to face the electorate. This gives a tremendous political advantage to the incumbent government. The prime minister carefully monitors opinion polls and economic data, and calls an election when support is at a peak (although an election must be called no later than five years after the previous election).

If the U.S. Congress is a *policy-making* legislature, Westminster is at best a *policy-influencing* legislature. In Britain, the government is responsible for introducing virtually all legislation: It is extremely rare for a bill proposed by an individual MP to make it into law. Members of Parliament are expected to vote in accordance with party instructions (the party "whip"), except when a vote is declared a matter of personal conscience. An MP who defies the whip may be expelled from the party and denied its endorsement at the next election, which will usually prevent her or his reelection. Even so, in about 10 to 20 percent of votes in the Commons, a small number of rebels defy the party whip. The parliaments of 1974–1979 and 1992–1997 saw frequent revolts by dissident MPs from the ruling party, but they had only a marginal effect on the government's capacity to enact its program. In an attempt to bolster the Parliament's powers, 14 new committees giving MPs oversight over ministry activities were introduced in 1979.

During the 1980s, when Margaret Thatcher was prime minister, there were complaints that the prime minister was becoming too powerful, even "presidential," in her ability to dictate policy to the cabinet and ministers. In particular, Thatcher took over direct control of foreign policy, at the expense of the foreign secretary. These complaints returned after Tony Blair became prime minister in 1997. After his reelection in 2001, Blair created special units for European and foreign/defense affairs inside the prime minister's office, further undercutting the role of the foreign office and defense ministry. Under Blair, many key policies were forged in meetings with individual ministers, especially with the powerful Chancellor of the Exchequer (treasury secretary) **Gordon Brown**, and the Cabinet ceased to be the main decision-making forum.

The upper chamber of Parliament, the House of Lords, has only a limited capacity to block or delay government legislation. Any act that is passed in three readings by the Commons and Lords and signed into law by the queen supersedes all preceding laws and precedents and must be implemented by the judiciary. The judicial branch has only a narrow ability to interfere with the government's actions because there is no written constitution to which they can appeal to declare a law invalid. The lack of a bill of rights troubled many liberal observers.

For centuries Britain had a unitary system of government: there was no federal structure that could block the powers of the Westminster Parliament. There were separate ministries for Scotland, Wales, and Northern Ireland, whose main task was spending regional development funds. Local governments have very limited powers, and the national government sets the rules by which they raise and spend money. Eighty percent of the funding for local councils comes from the national government, and there are strict rules over how it can be spent. Margaret Thatcher was so annoyed by the policies of the Labour-controlled Greater London Council that she had Parliament abolish the council in 1986. (It had been created only in 1964.) The New Labour government of Tony Blair set about reversing the centralization of the Thatcher years, creating a new Greater London Authority in 1999 and moving ahead with plans for the introduction of new parliaments in Wales and Scotland.

THE ELECTORAL SYSTEM

Britain operates a first-past-the-post, or winner-take-all, electoral system, similar to that in the United States. This produces clear winners and strong alternating majority parties in the House of Commons. However, it is criticized for offering voters an exceptionally narrow range of alternatives (two) and denying third parties adequate representation.

Each of the 646 Members of Parliament is elected from a single-member constituency in which the candidate with the highest number of votes wins. This first-past-the-post electoral system works to the advantage of the two leading parties, which tend to finish first and second in every race. Britain's third-largest party, the Liberal Democrats, has 15 to 25 percent support in nearly every constituency in the country, but this is not enough to displace a Labour or **Tory** (another name for Conservative) incumbent with 40 to 60 percent support. Hence, the Liberal Democrats win very few parliamentary seats.

Another problem with the first-past-the-post system is that the winner may well have only a plurality and not an absolute majority of the votes cast, because there are usually more than two candidates competing for each seat. This also means that at national level there is no guarantee that the party that wins the most seats will have won a majority of the popular vote. In fact, no government since the coalition that won in 1935 has gained more than 50 percent of the votes cast in a British election – yet this did not prevent those governments from having absolute control of the Commons and pursuing an aggressive legislative program.

The first-past-the-post system is unpredictable in the degree to which voter preferences are translated into parliamentary seats. Table 3.1 shows the results of the 1992 and 1997 elections (excluding Northern Ireland). The

TABLE 3.1. 1992 and 1997 General elections

	1992 election			1997 election		
	Actual: share of vote (%)	No. of MPs	Hypothetical: no. of MPs under PR[a]	Actual: share of vote (%)	No. of MPs	Hypothetical: no. of MPs under PR[a]
Conservatives	42.8	336	273	31.4	165	199
Labour	35.2	271	222	44.4	419	286
Liberal Democrats	18.3	20	114	17.2	46	109
Scots/Welsh nationalists	2.4	7	16	2.5	10	16
Referendum Party[b]	–	–	–	2.7	0	17
Others	1.3	0	0	1.7	0	0

The table shows the actual results (excluding Northern Ireland) in the first two columns, and the hypothetical results if seats were awarded according to proportional representation (PR).
[a] Dividing the total votes by total seats.
[b] The Referendum Party was formed by billionaire industrialist James Goldsmith to push for Britain's exit from the EU.

third column illustrates a hypothetical case: how many seats each party would have won if they had been allocated in strict proportion to the share of total votes cast – a system of proportional representation, or PR. Note how small differences in the votes gained by the rival parties produce huge differences in the number of seats won.

In 1992, both Labour and Tories won more seats than they would have had under a PR system, whereas the Liberal Democrats got only one-fifth of the seats they would have had under PR. In 1997, the Liberal Democrats won twice as many seats as they did in 1992, although they garnered fewer votes than in the previous election. The Conservatives did worse in 1997 than they would have under PR, whereas Labour scooped up two-thirds of the seats with only 44 percent of the national vote.

In June 2001, Labour scored a second consecutive victory in national elections. They won 413 seats (6 fewer than in 1997), while their share of the vote slipped by 2.5 percent to 40.7 percent. The Conservatives polled 31.7 percent of the vote but garnered only 166 seats, and the Liberal Democrats increased their seats by 6 to 52, with 18.5 percent of the vote. (Other parties won 9.3 percent of the total vote and 28 seats.) In May 2005 Tony Blair won an unprecedented third term. Labour only narrowly led the Conservatives, by 35.2 percent to 32.3 percent of the popular vote, but this translated into 355 seats for Labour and only 197 for the Tories.

The Liberal Democrats, with 22.0 percent of the vote, picked up a mere 62 seats.

The unequal relationship between votes and seats is exacerbated by the unequal geographical concentration of voters and the economic divide between the prosperous southeast and the depressed north and west. Labour does well in London and in northern cities but usually wins few seats in the southern suburbs and rural areas. (An exception was the 1997 election, when Labour did well even in the south.) The gap in regional voting patterns actually increased during the 1970s and 1980s. As a result of this pattern, four out of five constituencies are "safe seats" that rarely change hands between parties in an election. Despite this, voter turnout was relatively high, usually 80 percent, although it slipped to 69 percent in 1997 and 57 percent in 2001, recovering to 61 percent in 2005.

Under the first-past-the-post system, minor parties with a regional concentration, such as the Scottish and Welsh nationalists, can win seats on their home turf. The third-largest party in Britain, formerly the Liberals and now called the Liberal Democrats, wins seats mainly in the alienated periphery where their supporters are concentrated: Scotland, Wales, and the southwest of England. Elsewhere, they win few seats.

There have been growing calls for a reform of the British electoral system in order to make the results more representative of voter opinion. The Liberal Democrats have the most to gain from the introduction of European-style proportional representation. Most advocates of PR suggest a compromise system, such as that operating in Germany, where half the seats are reserved for single-member races (to ensure that there is an MP responsible for each district) and half for party lists (to ensure proportional representation at national level). Britain now has some experience with the PR system. Elections to the European Parliament using the PR system took place in Britain in 1999. And the two new parliaments in Scotland and Wales are elected by PR (single-seat constituencies, topped up by additional members from a national party list to ensure proportionality).

Defenders of the existing British system argue that it produces a strong government with the power to implement its legislative program. Proportional representation would spread power among three or more parties, which would require coalition governments of more than one party. This may be undemocratic because in most countries coalition governments are usually formed in backroom deals that take place after the election. Neither Labour nor the Tories are likely to introduce PR because this would undermine their capacity to form single-party governments. The Liberal Democrats hope that if a future Parliament is equally split between Labour and Conservatives, the Labour Party might introduce PR in return for Liberal Democratic support. In its 1997 election manifesto, Labour promised to hold a referendum on electoral reform, but it dropped the idea after the election.

POLITICAL BEHAVIOR

Voter loyalty to political parties is quite high in Britain, although it has fallen since the Second World War. During the 1990s, the fierce partisan loyalties and "tribal" divisions of previous decades gave way to more centrist, middle-class politics. In 1950, 40 percent of those polled "strongly identified" with a single party, but this figure had halved by 1992. In the 1950s, social class and income level were good predictors of voting behavior, although even then one-quarter of industrial workers voted Conservative and not Labour (which was attributed to deferential or patriotic values). The protracted economic crisis of the 1960s and 1970s eroded party loyalties as voters started to shop around for new ideas. Social-class origin could explain 70 percent of voting behavior in the 1950s but only 50 percent by the 1970s. Voting became less a matter of habit and more a matter of choice. Voter behavior became more volatile, harder to predict, and more likely to be swayed by party campaigns. Voter turnout fell, especially among young people.

Given the large number of "safe" seats, the parties pour their efforts into winning the "marginal" seats, those that may change hands at every election. In **marginal seats**, the parties canvas every household and record the voting intentions of each family member. On election day, party volunteers stand outside polling stations to record voters' registration numbers. The data are collated at party headquarters, and supporters who have not voted are reminded to go to the polls.

Tight limits on campaign spending have mostly prevented the spread of U.S.-style money politics in Britain. There are no limits on donations to national parties, however, which has fueled repeated scandals. It is the role of the media, rather than money, that has been the main source of controversy in British politics. (Unlike in the United States, broadcast media advertising is banned.) The British are avid newspaper readers (average daily circulation is 14 million). In contrast with those in the United States, most British papers are not politically neutral but actively campaign for one of the parties. The papers are not controlled by political parties, as in much of Europe, but are owned by quixotic business magnates who enjoy playing politics. In 1997, the *Observer* newspaper concluded that the second most influential man after Prime Minister Tony Blair was **Rupert Murdoch**, the Australian who owns one-third of Britain's newspapers. Two-thirds of the newspapers usually back the Tories, but in 1997 most papers switched to Labour, which helps to explain Labour's dramatic victory that year. Most newspapers are hostile to Europe, which caused problems for Europhile Tony Blair. Unlike the press, the television stations are required to be politically neutral and are generally valued for their objectivity. The BBC is state-financed, whereas the three other broadcast stations are commercially owned and depend on advertising for their financing.

Civil society is deeply rooted in Britain, with a broad range of interest groups. Such groups expanded during the 1970s as voters became disillusioned with the mainstream political parties and turned toward "postmaterialist" values. The environmentalist group **Greenpeace** saw its membership swell tenfold to more than 400,000, in part thanks to media coverage of its spectacular protests. Groups protesting new road construction and defending animal rights continued to be active throughout the 1990s. However, environmental issues did not really transform the agendas of the mainstream political parties.

THE DIGNIFIED CONSTITUTION

Queen Elizabeth II ascended to the throne in 1953. She is the head of state but has only limited influence over the affairs of government. The queen meets the prime minister each week for a private chat over tea. The most important function of the monarch is to select a prime minister to form a government, usually after a general election. If that government wins majority support in the Commons, the monarch's effective role is at an end.

The last time the monarch played a significant role in British politics was in 1910. The House of Lords blocked a high-spending welfare budget passed by the House of Commons. Liberal Prime Minister Herbert Henry Asquith called an election, which he won, and he asked the king to create enough new peers to tip the voting in the upper chamber. The Lords gave in and accepted a new law abolishing its right to delay bills involving public spending. They retained the right to return non-spending bills to the Commons, although if passed a second time by the Commons, such bills became law after a two-year delay (reduced to one year in 1949).

The House of Lords is a bizarre anachronism. In a democracy, it does not make sense to give a legislative role to the descendants of medieval knights. The Lords consisted of 750 hereditary peers and 600 life peers. Hereditary peers are exclusively male, and they pass their title to their first sons. The system of life peers was introduced in 1958. They are mostly retired politicians, men and women, who are nominated by the prime minister and appointed by the queen. Their heirs do not inherit their seat in the House of Lords.

The ultraconservative hereditary peers gave the Tories a guaranteed majority in the upper chamber, so Labour had a strong interest in reforming the House of Lords. However, reform of the Lords proved difficult because the House of Commons did not want to create a new elected second chamber that could rival its power. But a second chamber is useful in scrutinizing laws passed on party lines in the Commons. For example, the Lords introduced substantial amendments to the 2001 Anti-Terrorism Crime and Security Bill and delayed the controversial bill to ban fox hunting. (Rural interests opposed to the ban drew more than 400,000 people to a protest rally in September 2004.) In 1998, the Blair government announced its intention to phase out the hereditary peers, but was unable to come up with an acceptable plan for an elected component to the Lords. Proposals to have an upper chamber composed of elected representatives from the nations and regions of Britain were seen as too much of a threat to the legitimacy of the Commons. The independent Wakeham Commission recommended the creation of an autonomous Appointments Commission to nominate new life peers, whose numbers should reflect the party strengths of the Commons, with an additional 20 percent independents. But having an upper chamber consisting entirely of appointees raised fears of cronyism, with the Lords becoming a superfluous mirror of the Commons.

The idea of reforming the monarchy is not on the agenda. Having a ceremonial, nonpolitical head of state preserves the authority of Parliament, and few people advocate abolishing the monarchy in favor of an elected or appointed president. The main argument is over money. Each year, the Commons votes a budget for the queen and her extended family in recognition of their public duties. During the 1990s, as the royal family fell prey to divorce and scandal, the public began to wonder whether they were getting value for their money. The queen's vast personal wealth is exempt from tax, but in response to public criticism in 1995, she voluntarily started to pay income tax. Defenders of the monarchy often fall back on the argument that royal pageantry is good for the tourism industry.

The life of the royals is a reality TV soap opera that provides endless copy for the tabloid press in Britain and throughout the world. Princess Diana, the wife of Prince Charles, was probably the best-known woman on the planet. Her dramatic divorce and subsequent untimely death in a car accident in August 1997 produced an extraordinary outpouring of emotion in Britain, equivalent to that following the death of President John F. Kennedy in the United States. Diana, whom Blair called the "people's princess," had come to represent the new England, breaking down barriers of class, gender, and race through her charity work.

RIVAL INTERESTS AND THE EVOLUTION OF BRITISH DEMOCRACY

The British political system revolves around strong, well-organized social groups defending their respective economic and political interests. Over the course of history, these rival groups developed a set of political institutions to reflect and broker their competing interests. Social interests and political institutions evolved in a parallel and intertwined process. By the seventeenth century, British thinkers were describing the emergence of a "civil society" consisting of a dense network of independent social actors linked through mutual respect, accepted social norms, and the rule of law.

In class terms, British history was dominated by the powerful landowning aristocracy, which was later joined by a resilient and rapacious commercial bourgeoisie. The rising capitalist class, along with elements of the landed aristocracy, went to war against the king and his aristocratic supporters in the middle of the seventeenth century to decide which institution would rule – the monarch or the elected Parliament. The institutions that emerged as a compromise in the wake of the civil war (parliamentary sovereignty and constitutional monarchy) have persisted to the present day.

Many social groups, such as the peasantry, religious minorities, and women, were shut out from civil society and struggled to find a political voice. But during the nineteenth century, the rising class of industrial workers forged a powerful trade-union movement and later a parliamentary political party to defend its interests. Each of these social classes (lords, peasants, capitalists, and workers) lived a different life, went to different schools, and even spoke different dialects.

Despite this highly stratified social system, Britain emerged as a peaceful, stable democracy. Strong political institutions emerged that were able to express and absorb these competing class interests. Stability is the most widely praised attribute of the British political system. The general level of social unrest and political violence (Northern Ireland excepted) has been quite low. Britain has functioned with the same set of political institutions, without coups or revolutions, since 1689. There are few nations in continental Europe that can make such a claim. Germany has gone through four regimes since its formation in 1871; France is on its fifth republic since 1815.

Britain's institutions emerged gradually over time and were the product of experience rather than design. The operating principle was Anglo-Saxon pragmatism (what works) as opposed to French rationalism (what is best). This stable set of political institutions was embedded in a broad consensus of political values. This consensus was particularly strong among the tightly knit ruling elite, who have shown a high degree of cohesiveness over the years. Prominent among these consensus values was the notion of loyalty to the monarch, church, and empire. The very strength of the divisive social-class system was also, ironically, a source of stability. Everyone was fully aware of the existence of the class system and their family's location within it. They all "knew their place."

THE RIGHTS TRADITION

An important part of Britain's consensus values was the recognition of individual rights and the notion of limited government. Over the centuries, medieval England built up a body of common law: the accumulated decisions of court cases that defined and protected individual rights. Such rights included the right to trial by jury and habeas corpus, meaning protection against arrest without a court hearing (literally, the right to one's own body). Such rights to personal liberty and private property were spelled out in the Magna Carta, a contract that was presented to King John in 1215 by a few dozen leading nobles. That document was designed to protect the privileges of a narrow and oppressive aristocracy, but it set the precedent for the sovereign's power being negotiated and conditional. Over the ensuing centuries, the same rights were slowly extended to broader sections of the population.

The rights to personal liberty and property did not initially extend to religion. Although the 1689 Act of Toleration granted freedom of worship to those outside the Church of England, it was not until the 1820s that bans on Catholics and Jews serving in the military or in public office were lifted. Despite the absence of a bill of rights, the individualist, rights-oriented tradition ran deep in British political life.

In 1951, Britain ratified the European Convention on Human Rights, which created a supranational European Court of Human Rights in Strasbourg, France. Since 1966, British citizens have been able to appeal to that court (and the court has reversed British legal decisions in some fifty cases). In 1998, the Blair government introduced the Human Rights Act, which formally incorporated the European Convention on Human Rights into domestic law. This moved the United Kingdom closer to U.S.-style judicial review. Though the 1998 act gives judges the right to challenge laws, their decision has no power unless parliament chooses to act on it. Thus the Law Lords declared part IV of the 2001 Anti-Terrorism Crime and Security Act, on the detention of terrorism suspects, to be in violation of the European Convention. But the law continued in force until it was replaced by the 2005 Prevention of Terrorism Act.

An important difference from the United States is that the right to bear arms was not part of the British tradition. On the contrary, British monarchs were keen to keep a monopoly of force in their own hands, systematically tearing down nearly all of the lords' castles in the sixteenth century. Restrictions on personal gun ownership are very tight. British police usually patrol unarmed, and guns are used in fewer than 100 murders per year in Britain (compared with some 10,000 in the United States). After the massacre of 16 children by a deranged gunman in Dunblane, Scotland, in 1996, private possession of handguns was completely banned.

THE IMPACT OF INDUSTRIALIZATION

From the seventeenth century on, Britain emerged as the preeminent maritime power, pulling ahead of Holland, Spain, and finally France. This was due to the skill, enterprise, and ruthlessness of its sailors in trade and in war. Napoleon described England as a "nation of merchants" (often mistranslated as "a nation of shopkeepers"). Trade was the main source of England's wealth, and it generated a new capitalist class that gradually merged with the old landed aristocracy.

Britain was the first country to experience the agricultural revolution. Peasants were driven from their subsistence plots to make way for extensive farming methods. With no source of livelihood, many opted for emigration. About one-quarter of the population left the British Isles (some unwillingly, as convicts) for America, Canada, Australia, and other outposts of the empire. This provided an important safety valve, reducing the surplus population and easing social discontent. In a TV interview, singer Mick Jagger was asked why there had never been a revolution in England. He replied that it was because all the people who did not like the place had left. Whereas the United States was formed as a nation of immigrants, Britain was a nation of emigrants.

Britain was also the first country to experience the Industrial Revolution, in the first decades of the nineteenth century. Industry and empire grew together. Britain became "the workshop of the world," selling its manufactured goods throughout its global trading network. However, the governing coalition of old landlords and new bourgeoisie was terrified that the example of the 1789 French Revolution could be replicated in Britain. Growing protests from the expanding working class were met with a mixture of repression and reform. The 1832 Reform Act loosened the property requirements for voting, but even then only 5 percent of the adult population was enfranchised. A two-party system emerged in the House of Commons, with reformist and reactionary elements grouping themselves into the parties of Liberals and Conservatives. Further reform acts in 1867 and 1884 gave the vote to 20 percent and then 40 percent of the population.

It was the arrival of organized labor that forced open the doors of Parliament to the mass electorate. Faced with mounting labor unrest, Britain's ruling class opted for compromise rather than confrontation. By giving most adult men the right to vote, they provided an outlet for workers' political frustrations and turned them away from industrial violence. Trade unions had started to form on a craft basis in the 1840s, and by the 1880s they were expanding to the masses of unskilled workers. Heavily influenced by the Methodist revival, a Protestant movement, British workers were generally deferential to their masters and accepting of the status quo. Their initial focus was on improving wages and conditions rather than gaining political rights. For decades, they had precious little to show for their loyalty, as they were crowded into Dickensian slums and labored long hours in the "dark satanic mills" of the Industrial Revolution.

In 1900, the unions formed the Labour Representation Committee (LRC) to advance their interests in Parliament. They realized that they needed legislative protection after a court case had threatened severe civil penalties for strike action. The LRC renamed itself the Labour Party and won 50 seats in the 1906 parliamentary election in alliance with the Liberal Party.

The Liberal government that ruled from 1906 to 1914 introduced some elements of a **welfare state**, such as rudimentary public health care, school meals, and public pensions. These measures were not merely a response to the rise of labor. They were also prompted by the shocking discovery that one-third of the recruits for the British army in the Boer War between British and Dutch interests in South Africa (1899–1902) were medically unfit to serve. To match the mass armies of Germany and Russia, Britain would have to start looking after its workers. Joseph Chamberlain, the reform-minded cabinet minister who served as colonial secretary during the Boer War, advanced the philosophy of "social imperialism" – welfare spending in return for the workers' political loyalty in imperial ventures. This was clearly an echo of Otto von Bismarck's model of welfare capitalism in Germany. The program did not include equal rights for women. The Liberal government resisted a vigorous protest movement for voting rights for women (the Suffragettes). It would take the shock of World War I to change public opinion on the issue.

The British elite came through the Industrial Revolution with its medieval institutions remarkably intact. The aristocracy went from country house to London club, educating their sons at Oxford and Cambridge and sending them off to fight in the colonies in the family regiment. There were a few innovations during the nineteenth century. The new Harry Potter-style "public" schools (in theory open to anyone who could pay the stiff fees) were designed to forge a new elite of like-minded young men by means of a rigid regimen of sport and Latin. In 1854, officials in government service were organized into a politically neutral career civil service, in which recruitment and promotion were to be based on merit rather than political connections.

LABOUR'S RISE TO POWER

The bloodbath of World War I was a major challenge to the integrity of the British state. Britain would have lost the war had the United States not intervened. The conflict killed one in ten of the adult male population, drained the economy, and sapped the enthusiasm of the British state for foreign ventures. Still, Britain got off lightly: The war caused the complete collapse of the political systems of Germany, Russia, Austria-Hungary, and Turkey.

In recognition of the people's sacrifices for the war effort, in 1918 all adult males were given the vote, irrespective of their property holdings, as were women over the age of 28. (The "flappers" – 18- to 28-year-old women – were enfranchised 10 years later.) Thus, it was not until 1929 that "one person, one vote" became the law in Britain, showing that democracy is a quite recent historical development.

The Labour Party fought the 1918 election as coequal of the Conservatives and Liberals and came out of the 1924 election as the largest single party. Although they did not control a majority of seats in the House of Commons, they formed a minority government. It had taken the trade unions only two decades to ascend from the political wilderness to the pinnacle of power. The euphoria was not to last, however. The 1924 government fell within a year, and economic recession triggered a decade of poverty and industrial conflict.

It was not until World War II that a major shift could be seen in the distribution of power within the British political system. British patriotism blossomed in 1939–1941, when the nation fought alone against Nazi-occupied Europe under a coalition government headed by Conservative Prime Minister Winston Churchill. In return, the people demanded a brighter future once the war was won. In 1942, the government released the Beveridge Report, promising full employment and state-provided health care, insurance, and pensions. This was not enough to satisfy the voters. In 1945, they turned out Churchill and for the first time in history elected a majority Labour government, although Labour won only 48 percent of the vote.

That government introduced a radical socialist program. Health care, jobs, and housing were seen as social rights to which everyone was entitled. The government introduced a comprehensive welfare state: a National Health Service, state pensions, and state-funded higher education. They expanded state-subsidized housing (called council housing because it was provided by local councils). (In 1945, one-third of Britons were still living in houses without bathrooms.) The government also had radical socialist goals that went beyond a welfare state, to challenge the very foundations of capitalism. Laws were passed taking into public ownership ("nationalizing") about one-quarter of private industry, including coal mines, electric and gas utilities, steel mills, docks, railways, and long-distance trucking. The expropriated private owners, who were paid modest compensation, opposed nationalization but were powerless in the face of Labour's parliamentary majority.

The postwar government also granted independence to India and Palestine, recognizing that Britain did not have the will or the resources to fight to retain these possessions. But the Labour government did support the United States in forming NATO to oppose Soviet expansionism and reintroduced the draft to help fight the Cold War. The new commitment to socialism at home and the Cold War abroad provided a double anesthetic to dull the pain caused by the loss of empire.

THE POSTWAR CONSENSUS

During the 1950s, British politics slipped into a familiar pattern that would last until 1979. The Labour and Conservative parties alternated in power, and both accepted the basic institutions of postwar Britain. The Tories acquiesced in the retreat from empire and realized that it would be political suicide to try to dismantle the welfare state. Labour knew that the British public did not want more nationalization, not least because problems soon emerged in the management of state-owned industry. Both parties accepted **Keynesianism**, the economic analysis of John Maynard Keynes, who argued that state intervention with public spending could have prevented the Great Depression of the 1930s.

This consensus left little for the two parties to debate. It is ironic that a political system built around two-party adversarial politics should have produced such a consensus in the 1950s. Anthony Downs offered one explanation for this in his 1957 book, *An Economic Theory of Democracy*. In a two-party system, Downs reasoned, leaders will compete for the "median voter" in the middle of the policy spectrum. Hence, both party programs will tend to converge.

During the 1950s and 1960s, successive governments managed to avoid another depression. However, they were too ambitious in trying to "fine-tune" the economy by adjusting interest rates and the money supply to ensure simultaneous economic growth, low inflation, and full employment. The country fell into a debilitating "political business cycle." Attempts by Conservative governments to lower inflation typically led to a recession and a rise in unemployment, causing a surge of support for Labour. In turn, Labour efforts to boost economic growth would cause inflation, sometimes leading to financial crises when international investors deserted the British pound sterling (in 1967 and 1976).

Despite the introduction of the welfare state, relations between labor and management were tense and confrontational. Unlike in Germany or Scandinavia, after the war there was no attempt to introduce corporatist institutions, such as works councils, to give labor a say in the management of private industry. With unemployment held at 3 to 4 percent, workers were able to threaten strike action to push for better wages and conditions. The economy was plagued by waves of strikes, which came to be known as the **"British disease."** British industry was slow to adopt the latest technology, and Britain was overtaken in industrial output by Germany, France, Japan, and even Italy. London was still a major center of international finance, however. The easy profits from banking, or the prestige of a career in the civil service, tended to draw the "brightest and best" away from careers in industry.

The 1960s were not all gloom and doom. While industry was rusting, London was "swinging." A new youth subculture was invented in Britain and exported to the rest of the world. Music and the arts flourished, putting Britain back on the world map as a cultural superpower. By the end of the 1970s, Britain was earning more from exports of rock music than it was from steel.

The 1964–1970 Labour government tried to address the problem of industrial stagnation by promoting tripartite negotiations among the state, employers, and unions to set prices and incomes. But Labour could not challenge the power of the unions. The unions financed the Labour Party, and their 10 to 12 million members dominated the 250,000 individual party members in elections to choose parliamentary candidates and the party's National Executive Committee. Industrial unrest led to the Labour Party's defeat in 1970, and a prolonged strike by coal miners brought down the Tory government in 1974. The 1974–1979 Labour government was undermined by a wave of strikes by garbage collectors, railway workers, and nurses that culminated in the 1978 "winter of discontent."

Exasperated by the dominant role of unionists and left-wing radicals in their party, a group of centrist Labour leaders broke away to form a new **Social Democratic Party** (**SDP**). Their centrist program appeared to reflect the views of the majority of voters. However, the winner-take-all party system (see Table 3.1) makes it very difficult for third parties to gain a foothold in Parliament. In the 1983 election, the SDP-Liberal alliance won 26 percent of the votes (only 2 percent less than Labour) but won only 23 of the 635 seats in the House of Commons at that time. The SDP eventually merged with the Liberal Party to form the Liberal Democrats.

By the end of the 1970s, the British model seemed to be in irreversible decline. The economy stagnated, while inflation hit double figures. Journalists began to write about the "ungovernability" of Britain and a system "overloaded" with the demands of competing interest groups.

THATCHER TO THE RESCUE?

At this point, change came from an unexpected source – the Conservative Party. In 1975, the Conservatives selected Margaret Thatcher as their new leader. Thatcher was an aggressive intellectual with an iron will and razor-sharp debating skills. Unusual for a Tory leader, she came from humble social origins – her father was a grocer. She earned a degree in organic chemistry at Oxford before switching to a legal career to have more time to raise her children.

Thatcher was influenced by the writings of the libertarian Friedrich Hayek and the monetarist Milton Friedman. Her philosophy of popular capitalism drew heavily upon U.S. ideas of rugged individualism and free-market economics. Thatcher concluded that the British model was not working, and her solution was to try to minimize state interference in the economy and society. "Thatcherism" had a profound impact on the British political system, shattering the postwar consensus on the welfare state and locking Labour out of power for 18 years.

Thatcher's bracing New Right rhetoric caught the attention of the British public and gave the Conservatives a clear victory in the 1979 election. She had ambitious plans to deregulate the economy and to privatize large chunks of state-owned industry, and she pledged to follow a tight monetary policy in order to control inflation, whatever the effect on unemployment. Unlike in the United States, the New Right in Britain did not have a social agenda (abortion had been legal since 1967), although they promised to be tough on crime.

Thatcher's first task was to break the power of the trade unions. She introduced new legislation to make it more difficult to call strikes (by requiring pre-strike ballots and cooling-off periods). She doubled spending on police and equipped them with riot gear so that they could take on rock-throwing strikers. Thatcher used the courts to seize the union's assets during an illegal coal **miners' strike** in **1984**, and she went on to shut down most of the state-owned coal mines. By 1990, the number of coal miners had fallen from 300,000 to 50,000. Thatcher broke the back of organized labor. Worker unrest shrank to historically unprecedented levels and was lower than in almost any other country in Europe.

Economic growth was sluggish during Thatcher's first term, and it was probably only her victory in the 1982 Falklands War that won her reelection in 1983. One of the most successful elements of her "popular capitalism" was allowing tenants to buy public housing with low-cost mortgages. From 1979 to 1989, home ownership leapt from 52 percent to 66 percent of all households. Thatcher also sold off many of the nationalized industries: British Telecom, British Gas, and the electric and water utilities. Privatization generated cash for the budget and profits for the millions of citizens who applied for shares in the new companies. Tax rates were cut: The top personal income tax rate fell from 90 percent to 40 percent. Workers were encouraged to opt out of the state pension system and invest some of their payroll taxes in a private retirement account, a measure that was expected to cut state pension spending to a projected 6 percent of Gross Domestic Product (GDP) by 2030, compared with 14–17 percent in continental Europe. A deregulatory program for the financial markets in 1983–1986, called the "Big Bang," enabled London to reinforce its position as the world's leading international financial center.

By the late 1980s, the economy was growing, living standards were rising, and productivity and profits were booming. However, inequality was rising. Average incomes rose 37 percent during 1979–1993, but the earnings of the top 10 percent of the population leaped by 61 percent while those of the bottom decile fell 18 percent. Unemployment climbed to 10 percent from a level of 5 percent in the 1970s, but fell again to 5 percent by 1989. Still, one-third of the population lived in poverty, and there arose a large underclass of jobless youth, which led to a surge in drug use and crime. Ironically, demographic changes and the rise in unemployment caused state welfare spending to increase during the Thatcher years despite her intention to cut public spending.

In 1988, Thatcher introduced an ambitious "New Steps" program to change the way state services were delivered. This reform provided much of the intellectual inspiration for the "reinventing government" movement in the United States. State agencies had to introduce independent cost accounting for each stage of their operations. State services were contracted out to private companies or voluntary agencies through competitive tendering. Many state offices were turned into independent agencies, which then bid to provide government services, from sewage to prisons. Local governments, the National Health Service, and the education system were forced to adopt these reforms. From 1979 to 1993, the number of civil servants was slashed by 30 percent, and about 150 new semi-independent government agencies were created. (This reform had the unfortunate by-product of creating more than 40,000 new patronage positions for central ministers.) The reforms increased efficiency and cut costs but led to increased corruption. They triggered widespread protests, especially over the unpopular "poll tax," introduced in 1988, which replaced the former local property tax with a flat per capita tax.

THE FALL OF THATCHER

Thatcher secured reelection to an unprecedented third successive term in 1989. However, after 10 years under the "Leaderene," strains were beginning to show in the upper ranks of the Conservative Party. Many traditional Conservatives disliked Thatcher's radical reforms, and her authoritarian style alienated many colleagues. Her vocal opposition to further European integration, such as the introduction of a single currency, lost her the support of the internationalist wing of the party. Between 1979 and 1992, membership in the Conservative Party slumped from 1.5 million to 500,000.

Thatcher's departure came not with a bang but with an uncharacteristic whimper. Her popularity steadily eroded throughout the 1980s, dipping to 29 percent in 1990, and she came to be seen as an electoral liability. At that time, the Conservative leader was selected by an annual ballot of members of Parliament. Usually, no candidates ran against the incumbent, but in 1989 an obscure MP came forward to challenge Thatcher, winning 33 votes. The next year, she faced a serious opponent in the form of ex–defense minister Michael Heseltine. Thatcher beat Heseltine in the first round by 204 votes to 152 (with 16 abstentions). Under party rules, a candidate winning less than two-thirds of the vote has to face a second round. Even though she would probably have won, Thatcher chose to resign, partly in order to clear the way for her chosen successor, **John Major**.

Major, like Thatcher, came from humble origins. His father was a circus trapeze artist turned garden-gnome manufacturer. Major left school at 16 and worked his way up from bank teller to senior executive before entering politics. Major was reasonably popular, but he lacked Thatcher's charisma. Despite a deep recession that began in 1990 in which GDP fell by 3.6 percent, Major won the 1992 election, thanks mainly to the inept Labour campaign.

Major pressed ahead with privatization of British Rail and the nuclear power and coal industries. But the Conservative Party was badly split over Europe, with a hard-core right wing opposing further integration. The British public was skeptical about the Brussels bureaucracy but generally favored

EU membership. (In a 1996 poll, 42 percent approved and 24 percent disapproved.) In 1990, Britain joined the **Exchange Rate Mechanism** (**ERM**), the precursor to the single European currency. But in 1991 Britain opted out of the "social chapter" of the Maastricht treaty on European integration. This would have introduced the EU's generous labor legislation to Britain (longer vacations, shorter working hours) and was opposed by employers.

The key turning point in the Major administration was September 1992, when the British pound came under attack from international speculators. Despite desperate government efforts, the pound was forced to leave the ERM. This was a major humiliation and left the government's financial strategy in ruins. Major's approval rating plummeted from 49 percent to 25 percent after the devaluation crisis, and it never recovered.

Conservative Party credibility was further battered by a series of sex and corruption scandals. Tory MPs were caught taking cash to ask questions in the Commons, and government officials were implicated in illegal arms sales to Iraq and Malaysia. The biggest policy disaster came with the 1996 discovery that **"mad cow" disease** (BSE), an incurable disease that attacks the brain stem, had spread from cattle to humans, killing 14 people. The government initially downplayed the problem and delayed ordering the mass slaughter of cattle. (A government minister even appeared on TV feeding hamburgers to his daughter.) Eventually all of Britain's cattle had to be killed and burned. And to this day British people are not allowed to give blood in the United States.

Dissent over relations with the EU was ravaging the Conservative Party, and John Major found it increasingly difficult to control his MPs. In 1995, Tory rebels defeated a government proposal to introduce an extra tax on heating fuel, a measure that would have hurt the poor. The same year, 89 Tory MPs voted against Major's reappointment as their leader. Clearly, the Tories had been in power for too long. But was Labour in a fit state to replace them?

THE RISE OF NEW LABOUR

After the 1992 election, the Labour Party feared that it would never be able to defeat the Tories and might even be overtaken by the Liberal Democrats as the main opposition party. In 1994, the party selected the young, charismatic Tony Blair as its new leader. Blair set about fashioning a new Labour Party that would recapture the middle-class and working-class voters who had defected to the Tories.

Following their defeat in 1979, the Labour Party was split between parliamentary leaders anxious to improve the party's electoral chances and trade-union bosses keen to retain their control over the party. The party's 1918 constitution had given Labour MPs the right to choose the party leader, but in 1981 an electoral college was introduced, with 40 percent of the votes in the hands of the trade unions. In 1983, **Neil Kinnock** became the Labour leader, and he waged a vigorous campaign to diminish union power and expel left-wing militants from the party.

After their electoral defeat in 1987, the Labour leadership started to expunge leftist policies from the party program, dropping their commitment to reverse Thatcher's privatizations, to strengthen union power, and to give up Britain's nuclear weapons. Intraparty reforms shifted the balance of power away from union bosses toward the parliamentary leadership. The union vote at the annual party conference was cut from 90 percent to 50 percent, while the share of union contributions in the party budget fell from 80 percent to 40 percent thanks in part to an influx of cash from sympathetic business interests. The unions had been weakened by Thatcher's defeat of the miners and by changes in the economy. The share of manufacturing in total employment fell from 38 percent in 1956 to 19 percent in 1990, and the proportion of the workforce in unions fell from a peak of 53 percent in 1978 to 30 percent in 1995.

Kinnock resigned following the humiliating 1992 electoral defeat. After the untimely death of Kinnock's successor, John Smith, in 1994 Tony Blair took over as party leader. Blair, a deeply religious, 41-year-old lawyer from a middle-class background, sought to turn Labour into a modern, European, social-democratic party of the center. He wanted to redefine Labour's identity in order to convince the middle-class voter that Labour no longer favored the redistributive, "tax and spend" policies of the past. Britain had become a society of "two-thirds haves and one-third have-nots," and Labour would never get back into power by appealing to the "have nots" alone.

But what would "New Labour" stand for? It would not be enough simply to steal Thatcher's reform agenda. Blair used focus groups to try out ideas, such as communitarianism and the "stakeholder society," before hitting on the formula of the "Third Way." As Andrew Marr explained (*Observer*, August 9, 1998): "The Third Way can be described, so far, by what it is not. It isn't messianic, high spending old socialism and it isn't ideologically driven, individualist conservatism. What is it? It's mostly an isn't." Many of the planks of Blair's new program were pulled straight from nineteenth-century liberalism. The state should stay out of economic management while providing moral leadership, investing in education and welfare, and devolving power to the regions. The centrist Third Way was encapsulated in the Labour slogan "Tough on crime, tough on the causes of crime." New Labour agreed with Margaret Thatcher that free markets were the best way to create prosperity, and they even accepted her reforms of public-sector management. In 1995, the Labour Party finally removed from its constitution Clause IV (put there in 1918), which called for state ownership of industry. All of this change was anathema to old-style socialists in the party.

Tony Blair described New Labour as a "pro-business, pro-enterprise" party, albeit one with a compassionate face. He stressed the values of community and moral responsibility in contrast with Thatcher's brazen individualism. (Famously, the "Iron Lady" had once said, "There is no such thing as 'society.'") Blair also appealed to British patriotism. He even said in May 1998: "I know it is not very PC [politically correct] to say this, but I am really proud of the British Empire."

New Labour was also more open to women. In 1993, the party decided that half of the new candidates selected by local parties for the next parliamentary election must be chosen from women-only short lists. (In 1996, a court struck down this rule as discriminatory.) As a result of these efforts, in the 1997 election 102 women were elected as Labour MPs. The total number of woman MPs from all parties rose from 60 in 1992 to 120 in 1997, dropping to 118 in 2001 and rising to 128 in 2005 (20 percent of the total).

Tony Blair turned to an expensive and sophisticated U.S.-style media campaign to sell the New Labour image to the public. Along with a New Labour, there was to be a New Britain: sophisticated, multicultural, and hip (from "Rule Britannia" to "Cool Britannia"). Labour's main slogan was the patriotic "Britain Deserves Better." In a bid to reassure the voters that their tax-and-spend policies were behind them, Labour pledged to maintain the Conservative government's spending limits for at least two years after the election. No new welfare initiatives were planned beyond a new scheme to make 250,000 unemployed youths take up government-sponsored jobs as a condition to qualify for welfare benefits.

Labour won a landslide victory in the May 1997 election. The Conservatives lost half their seats, and 10 percent of voters switched from Tory to Labour – the largest swing in the past century. Major went down to defeat despite a strong economic recovery, scotching the widely held notion that British election results are driven by economic performance. In June 1997, he was replaced as party leader by the uncharismatic 36-year-old William Hague.

Voters did not choose Labour because they preferred its program to that of the Tories, as their policies were nearly identical. Rather, the Tories were seen as divided, corrupt, and inept, whereas New Labour was trusted to do a more competent job of governing the country.

The only significant policy difference between the two parties was over Europe. Most Tories were skeptical about European integration. Prime Minister Major pursued a vague "wait and see" line, but two-thirds of Tory candidates spoke out against the EU. As recently as 1983, the Labour Party had called for Britain's withdrawal from the EU, which it saw as a capitalist plot. But Blair was adamantly pro-Europe, although he promised to hold a referendum before taking Britain into the single European currency.

One of the first acts of the new Labour government was the granting of independence to the Bank of England, a striking example of their rejection of the old policies of Keynesian demand management. Since its founding in 1694, the Bank of England had followed government advice in setting interest rates. From now on, like the U.S. Federal Reserve, the independent board of directors could fix rates as they pleased in order to prevent a rise in inflation. The head of the Treasury, Gordon Brown, followed a tight monetary and fiscal policy, although he borrowed heavily to fund higher spending on health, education, and welfare.

BLAIR AT THE HELM

On June 7, 2001, the Labour government won a second consecutive landslide victory, while the Conservative Party scrambled to hold onto second place. People started to wonder whether the Conservatives, once the "natural party of government," would ever manage to win an election again. William Hague resigned as Conservative Party leader in the wake of the electoral defeat. Previously, Tory leaders had been elected by Tory MPs. In 2001, for the first time, the MPs picked the two leading contenders, and the party's 320,000 members selected the final winner. The pro-European Kenneth Clarke lost to former army officer Iain Duncan Smith. The Conservative Party remained deeply divided over European integration, and was split between modernizers and traditionalists.

In September 2003, Labour lost the Brent by-election, the first such loss since Tony Blair became party leader in 1994, but the Conservatives finished third behind the Liberal Democrats. In October 2003, the Conservative Party congress removed the ineffective Duncan Smith as leader and replaced him with the centrist Michael Howard.

Tony Blair proved to be a skillful political leader, asserting strong control over the Labour Party and steering public opinion in what David Goodhart has called a "media driven popular democracy." Blair used this power to pursue an ambitious agenda of domestic and foreign reform, with mixed results.

On the home front, Blair's New Labour has forged ahead with the most ambitious constitutional reforms that Britain has seen in the past one hundred years. First, there was the decentralization of power through the creation of Scottish and Welsh parliaments. Second was the abolition of hereditary peers in the House of Lords. However, Blair was unable to break the deadlock over whether to replace the Lords with an elected or appointed chamber. In March 2007 the House of Commons voted in favor of a fully elected Lords, but some MPs voted for this proposal in a bid to kill reform, since they knew the government opposed a fully elected second chamber.

The third major reform was the introduction of a bill of rights and judicial review through the European Court of Human Rights. In 2003, a new department for constitutional affairs was introduced that will take over the judicial appointment process, although the final decision will still rest with the minister of justice (choosing from a list of nominees). This means the abolition of the post of lord chancellor, who formerly served as head judge, speaker of the House of Lords, and member of the cabinet, fusing all three branches of government in a single individual. There are plans to remove the law lords from the House of Lords and create a separate supreme court.

Some complained that Blair had introduced these reforms in a top-down manner, without extensive public comment. Constitutional expert Vernon Bogdanor explained (in *Prospect*, April 20, 2004): "We are transforming an uncodified constitution into a codified one, but in a piecemeal and pragmatic way."

On the foreign policy front, Blair developed a close partnership with U.S. President Bill Clinton, whose views matched Blair's own, and he had ambitious goals for Britain to shape a new, more just world order at America's side. Blair laid out his vision for Britain's global leadership role in a key speech in Chicago on April 22, 1999, in the midst of the NATO war to force Yugoslav troops out of Kosovo. Blair also enthusiastically pursued humanitarian interventions in Sierra Leone and East Timor.

Blair followed the same strategy when Clinton was replaced as U.S. president by the conservative and initially isolationist George W. Bush. Blair even supported Bush's plan to build a missile-defense system, which led to the United States withdrawing from the 1972 treaty barring such a system's deployment. After the September 11, 2001, terrorist attacks in the United States, Blair expressed unequivocal support for the war on terror, mounting a diplomatic crusade to line up allies for the U.S. campaign. British troops took part in the war in Afghanistan. In return, Blair hoped to persuade Bush to tackle the roots of terror by restarting the peace process between Israelis and Palestinians and launching a war on poverty in Africa. Alas, such hopes were sadly misplaced, as Bush failed to act on any of these suggestions.

Things came to a head with the Iraq war. Blair persuaded the British Parliament that Iraq was in possession of weapons of mass destruction that could be launched at 45 minutes' notice, according to an intelligence report released in September 2002 (later known as the "dodgy dossier"). Blair encouraged Bush to go through the United Nations, first sending UN weapons inspectors into Iraq in August 2002 and then going back to the United Nations for endorsement of military action in February 2003 – when the UN inspectors were still asking for more time. Blair failed to foresee the strong Franco-German resistance, which forced the United States to go ahead with the invasion without UN support. British public opinion was against going to war without UN approval. In February 2003 750,000 people marched through London in opposition to the war, the largest protest gathering in British history. Parliament approved military action on March 18, 2003, although one-third of Labour MPs voted against, and two senior ministers resigned in protest.

Criticism focused on the "45 minutes" chemical weapons claim contained in the "dodgy dossier." Reporter Andrew Gilligan of the BBC said that Blair's advisers had "sexed up" the intelligence claims in the dossier. A defense-ministry weapons expert, David Kelly, admitted that he was Gilligan's source and committed suicide on July 17, 2003. The subsequent **inquiry** by Lord **Hutton**, a senior judge, exonerated the government of any wrongdoing but led to the resignation of the BBC chairman and chief executive. The subsequent insurgency in Iraq, and obviously inadequate planning for postwar reconstruction, added to the criticism heaped on Blair. But he had managed to survive the biggest political crisis of his career.

Left-wing Labour MPs continued to oppose the Iraq war. In summer 2006 Blair was criticized for his reluctance to call on Israel to call a cease-fire in Lebanon in the summer. (At the height of the crisis, at an international meeting President Bush hailed the prime minister with a casual "Yo, Blair . . . ," which many took to symbolize the inferiority of Britain in its "special relationship" with the United States.) In March 2007, 90 Labor MPs voted against the government's plan to develop a new generation of nuclear missile submarines to replace the four aging Trident submarines that make up Britain's nuclear deterrent.

Meanwhile, relations between the United Kingdom and Europe were in the doldrums. In October 2002, France and Germany rejected the British plan to reform the Common Agricultural Policy. Tony Blair welcomed the draft EU constitution in July 2003, having successfully resisted attempts by some EU members to extend majority voting to foreign affairs and taxation, which would have threatened Britain's capacity to pursue independent policies in these areas. The rejection of the new draft constitution by French and Dutch voters in 2005 was something of a relief to Blair, since it meant he did not have to put the measure before the British public. Back in 1997, Blair had promised to hold a referendum to take Britain into the euro zone if five economic conditions were met. Public skepticism about abandoning the pound sterling for the euro caused Blair to postpone the referendum. Blair scored a symbolic victory when, thanks to his vigorous lobbying, the International Olympic Committee awarded the 2012 games to London, and not Paris.

New Labour has had only limited success in delivering the promised improvements in public services through decentralization and increased competition. The public remains very dissatisfied over the quality of the health and education services, not to mention the accident-prone railways. (In October 2001, the privatized Railtrack collapsed and was taken back into public ownership.) British society saw a surge in petty crime, causing Blair to introduce tough measures to crack down on "anti-social behavior." The 2004 Civil Partnership Act legalized civic unions for gay couples, and by the end of 2006, 15,000 couples had registered. In 2003, Blair introduced legislation allowing universities to charge fees of up to £3,000 per year. The economy grew at a steady 2.7 percent between 1997 and 2006, while unemployment was held to 5.5 percent, below the EU average. Pensioner poverty fell by one-third and child poverty by one-sixth, but the Gini coefficient, a measure of overall income inequality, did not budge during Labour's decade in power. Labour ramped up public spending on health and education, causing government spending to rise from 39 percent of GDP in 1997 to 42 percent in 2006. Globalization of the economy meant that the British state, like all states, had less discretion in national economic policy than it did during the 1950s and 1960s. Increasingly, British policy is driven by informal networks of transnational corporate elites, not represented in the institutional structures of the Westminster model.

Blair's government displayed at times an unstable mix of cynical populism and lofty idealism, explains David Goodhard, editor of *Prospect* magazine (June 19, 2003). New Labour moved away from the collective interest politics of previous decades toward identity politics and a focus on the individual citizen and consumer. Blair distanced himself from the traditional ideology and activist base of the Labour Party, and this left him vulnerable when political crises flared up, such as the outbreak of foot and mouth disease in May 2001, or the war in Iraq. Labour Party membership fell from 405,000 in 1997 to 280,000 in 2002, and the trade unions started cutting their financial contributions to the party to protest continuing privatization.

Despite discontent with the war in Iraq and poor public services, Blair was able to win a third term in the election he called in May 2005. But Labour squeaked home with 35 percent support, the lowest share of the vote of any government in British history. Tory leader Michael Howard closed the gap with Labour by campaigning for tougher immigration rules, but the divisions in his party prevented him from attacking Blair's pro-European policies.

The Blair government was dogged by a series of scandals. The most serious was the legal investigation that was launched in 2006 over the possible "sale" of peerages by Blair's top fund-raiser, Lord Levy, in return for loans to the Labour Party. (Individual donations to parties are capped at £5,000, but loans did not have to be reported.) Labor suffered losses in the May 2006 local council elections, due to concerns over the "cash for peerages" and other scandals, the war in Iraq, and shortfalls in hospital funding.

Increasingly, Blair came to be seen as a liability rather than an asset for the Labour Party. In September 2004 Blair stated he would step down at the end of a third term. After the 2005 election, dissatisfaction with Blair's leadership grew. In September 2006 17 Labour MPs signed a letter calling on him to step down, and eight junior members of the government resigned. In September 2006 Blair announced that he would resign within a year. There was already a successor in the wings, in the form of Gordon Brown. It was later revealed that back in 1994 Brown had refrained from running against Blair for the post of party leader in return for a promise that Blair would give him control over some areas of domestic policy. This was known as the "Granita Pact," named after the restaurant in which the alleged deal was struck. Brown supporters also claimed that Blair had promised to step down and allow Brown to become party leader at some point in the future.

Blair followed through on his promise, resigning as Labour Party leader and prime minister in June 2007. In accordance with tradition the Queen invited Brown to be prime minister the same day that Blair tendered his resignation – without the need for a fresh general election. Brown, a Scottish university lecturer and journalist who lost an eye in a school rugby game, had headed the Treasury since 1997, and took much of the credit for Britain's strong economic performance. He is seen as closer to traditional Labour values than Blair. The main policy difference between the two men is Brown's wariness about Britain joining the euro.

By 2007 the Conservative Party also had a new leader. In the wake of the 2005 election, Howard was replaced as leader of the Conservative Party by the 39-year-old **David Cameron**. For the first time, the Conservative leader was chosen by a ballot of the entire party membership. Cameron promised to make people "feel good about being Conservative again." Cameron projects a modern image – he smoked pot as a student, sometimes cycles to work, and took paternity leave when his wife gave birth. He is a self-styled "compassionate conservative" (and not a "neoconservative"), who nevertheless takes a traditionalist stance on many issues, such as opposition to further European integration. He supported the war in Iraq, and promises to reverse the government's ban on foxhunting and the introduction of identity cards. In many respects, he is the Conservative equivalent of Tony Blair, a determined centrist. Opinion polls in 2007 showed the Conservatives with a lead over Labour, for the first time in a decade. Fear of a possible Conservative victory seems to have persuaded Brown to drop the idea of calling a snap general election in September 2007 to consolidate his authority as Britain's new leader.

Conclusion

Britain has a robust and successful political system that seems to have recovered from the economic stagnation and class warfare of the 1970s and 1980s. The Westminster model is no longer the "envy of the world," as was complacently assumed by many Britons during the nineteenth century. But the parliamentary system, with strong parties competing for office, has proved its mettle in producing strong governments capable of exercising leadership to tackle Britain's social and economic problems. The experience of countries in the "third wave" of democratization, during the 1970s and 1980s, seems to confirm that parliamentary systems are more successful than presidential systems in reconciling conflicting interests in society and, hence, promoting less violence and greater stability.

The major challenge facing Britain is the same one that confronts the other European countries: crafting transnational institutions to manage the global economy while maintaining the capacity to tackle social problems that arise at the national and regional levels, and also preserving national and subnational identities. Britain has been a follower rather than a leader in this process of international institution-building (such as the European Union), which is a reflection of its diminished role in the international system since the end of its empire.

BIBLIOGRAPHY

Butler, David, and Denis Kavanagh. *The British General Election of 1997*. New York: St. Martin's Press, 1998.

Dunleavy, Patrick, Richard Heffernan, Philip Cowley, and Colin Hay. *Developments in British Politics*. Volume 8. New York: Palgrave Macmillan, 1997.

Foley, Michael. *The British Presidency: Tony Blair and the Politics of Public Leadership*. New York: Manchester University Press, 2001.

Geddes, Andrew, and Jonathan Tonge, eds. *Labour's Landslide*. New York: Manchester University Press, 1997.

Hutton, Will. *The State We're In*. London: Jonathan Cape, 1995.

Kavanagh, Denis. *Thatcherism and British Politics: The End of Consensus?* New York: Oxford University Press, 1990.

King, Anthony, et al., eds. *Britain at the Polls 1992*. London: Chatham House, 1993.

Marquand, David, and Anthony Seldon. *The Ideas That Shaped Modern Britain*. London: Fontana Press, 1996.

Riddell, Peter. *The Unfulfilled Prime Minister: Tony Blair's Quest for a Legacy*. London: Politicos, 2006.

Robins, Lynton, and Bill Jones, eds. *Half a Century of British Politics*. New York: Manchester University Press, 1997.

Seldon, Anthony. *Major: A Political Life*. London: Trafalgar Square, 1998.

Seldon, Anthony, ed. *The Blair Effect: The Blair Government 1997–2001*. New York: Little, Brown, 2001.

Seldon, Anthony, and Denis Kavanagh, eds. *The Blair Effect: 2001–05*. New York: Cambridge University Press, 2005.

Stephens, Philip. *Tony Blair: The Making of a World Leader*. New York: Viking, 2004.

Stothard, Peter. *Thirty Days: Tony Blair and the Test of History*. New York: Harper Collins, 2003.

Thatcher, Margaret. *The Downing Street Years*. New York: HarperCollins, 1993.

Toynbee, Polly, and David Walker. *Better or Worse? Has Labour Delivered?* London: Bloomsbury, 2005.

Trench, Alan, ed. *Has Devolution Made a Difference? The State of the Nations 2004*. Charlottesville, VA: Imprint Academic, 2005.

TABLE 3.2. Key Phases in Britain's Political Development

Time period	Regime	Global context	Interests/ identities/ institutions	Developmental path
1688–1832	constitutional monarchy, parliamentary sovereignty	imperial expansion	elite consensus on values, interests	capitalism, limited state
1832–1914	parliamentary sovereignty, electoral democracy	global hegemony based on naval power	extension of franchise	industrialization, free trade, gold standard
1918–1945	rise of Labour Party, three-party system, coalition governments	hegemony weakened, struggling to retain empire	intense social conflict	defensive
1945–1970	two-party competition	retreat from Empire, Cold War, U.S. alliance, exclusion from Europe	Keynesianism, welfare-state consensus	slow growth, full employment, some immigration
1970–1979	two-party deadlock	entry into European Union, global recession	severe labor unrest, N. Ireland conflict	crisis
1979–1987	Margaret Thatcher dominant	economic globalization, second Cold War	organized labor crushed	neoliberalism: deregulation, privatization
1987–2007	Tony Blair's New Labour dominant, constitutional reform	economic globalization, European integration, war on terror	economic boom, Scottish devolution, Lords reform, worries over immigration	neoliberalism: reformed welfare state, multiculturalism, citizens' rights

IMPORTANT TERMS

British Commonwealth cultural association linking 53 former colonies of Britain.

"British disease" a high level of strike activity caused by powerful trade unions taking advantage of low unemployment to push for higher wages.

Gordon Brown former Chancellor of the Exchequer (head of the Treasury), who succeeded Tony Blair as leader of the Labour Party and prime minister in June 2007.

David Cameron the leader of the Conservative Party since 2006.

devolution the creation of regional assemblies in Wales and Scotland, debated since the 1970s and introduced in 1999.

euro a currency unit introduced in January 1999 as an accounting currency for Germany and the 10 other members of the European Monetary Union. It fully replaced the participating countries' notes and coin in July 2002.

European Union (EU) now an organization of 27 European countries. It originated as the six-member European Coal and Steel Community in 1951 and became the European Economic Community in 1958, gradually enlarging its membership and becoming known as the European Community (EC). The 1991 Maastricht treaty, which came into effect in 1993, enlarged its authority and changed its name to the EU.

Exchange Rate Mechanism (ERM) the common currency band of European Union currencies, which Britain joined in 1990 and was forced to leave in 1992.

Falklands War the 1982 conflict that resulted after Argentina had seized the British-owned Falkland Islands and a British naval task force was sent to recapture them.

Glorious Revolution the 1688 removal of the Catholic King James II by Protestant William of Orange, who accepted the principle of parliamentary sovereignty.

Greenpeace an environmental action group that saw its membership expand during the 1980s.

hereditary peers members of the House of Lords appointed by the monarch and whose title automatically passes down to their sons.

Her Majesty's Opposition the second-largest party in the House of Commons, which is critical of the government but loyal to the British state as symbolized by the monarch.

Hutton inquiry investigation into the government's actions leading Britain into the 2003 war with Iraq.

Keynesianism a philosophy of state intervention in the economy derived from the work of John Maynard Keynes, who argued that the Great Depression could have been avoided by increasing state spending.

Neil Kinnock the Labour Party leader during the 1980s who introduced reforms to decrease the power of trade unions in the party.

"mad-cow disease" scandal a political scandal in 1996 that followed the Conservative government's delay in taking urgent measures to stop the spread of the BSE disease, which was infecting humans.

Magna Carta the contract guaranteeing the rights of noble families that King John agreed to sign in 1215.

John Major Conservative Party leader who replaced Margaret Thatcher as prime minister in 1990 and resigned after losing the 1997 election.

"marginal" seats those seats in the House of Commons that are closely contested and are likely to change hands between parties in an election (the opposite of "safe" seats).

Rupert Murdoch the Australian-born magnate who owns one-third of Britain's newspapers and has considerable political influence.

1984 miners' strike the coal miners' strike that was defeated by Margaret Thatcher, clearing the way for legislation limiting the power of trade unions.

No. 10 Downing Street the prime minister's residence and the place where the cabinet meets.

parliamentary sovereignty the power of Parliament, representing the people, to enact any law it chooses, unrestrained by a written constitution or the separation of powers.

Plaid Cymru the nationalist party in Wales that advocates more rights for the Welsh people, including use of the Welsh language.

Prime Minister's Questions the thirty-minute period once a week during which the prime minister stands before the House of Commons and answers questions from MPs.

Social Democratic Party (SDP) a group of moderate socialists who broke away from the Labour Party in the early 1980s.

"Third Way" the new, moderate philosophy introduced by Tony Blair after he became Labour Party leader in 1994.

Tory the colloquial name for a member of the Conservative Party.

Unionists the Protestant majority in Northern Ireland, who want to keep the province part of the United Kingdom.

welfare state the program of state-provided social benefits introduced by the Labour Government of 1945–1951, including the National Health Service, state pensions, and state-funded higher education.

Westminster model the British system of parliamentary sovereignty, prime ministerial government, and two parties alternating in power.

STUDY QUESTIONS

1. What were the main features of the bipartisan consensus in British politics that lasted from the 1950s to the late 1970s?

2. Why did some observers argue that Britain was "ungovernable" in the 1970s?

3. Which aspects of British society were the targets of Margaret Thatcher's "revolution"?

4. Why did Margaret Thatcher fall from power in 1990?

5. What does Tony Blair mean by the "Third Way"?

6. What factors have been holding Britain back from greater participation in the European Union?

7. When did most British citizens get the right to vote, and why?

8. Why did Labour defeat the Conservatives so soundly in 1997?

9. How does the power of the prime minister compare with that of the U.S. president?

10. What are the strengths and weaknesses of the first-past-the-post electoral system compared with proportional representation? Is Britain likely to introduce PR in the near future?

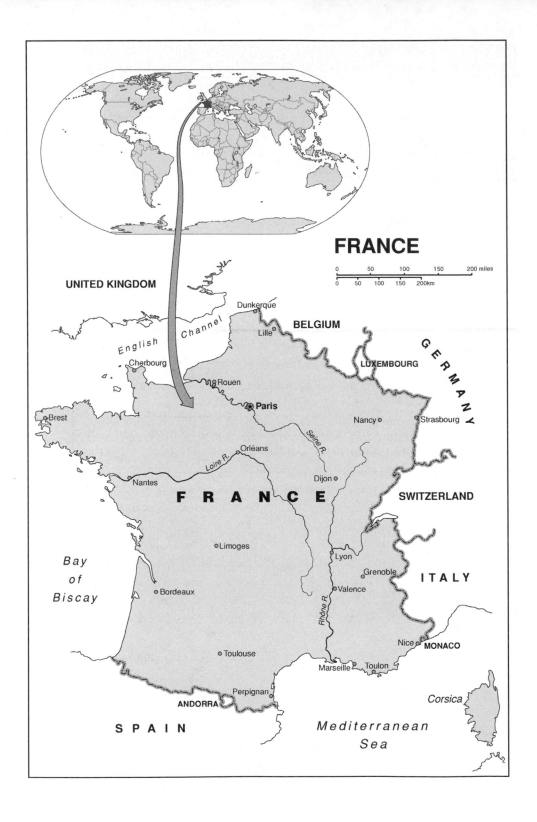

CHAPTER FOUR

France

Laurence McFalls

Introduction

The United States and France have a long-standing love–hate relationship of mutual respect, envy, and suspicion. The French came to the rescue of the American revolutionaries in their War of Independence from Britain, and twice in the twentieth century, American soldiers, proclaiming, "La Fayette, we are here," helped France repel German invaders. Despite – or perhaps because of – their ancient alliance, France and the United States have suspected and accused one another of disloyalty and imperial ambitions. Eager to assert its autonomy after having become a nuclear power, France in 1966, for example, withdrew from the North Atlantic Treaty Organization's U.S.-led integrated command structure. The day after September 11, 2001, France's left-liberal newspaper of reference *Le Monde* headlined, "We are all Americans," but in early 2003, when France failed to back the U.S.-led invasion of Iraq, the United States retaliated not only by renaming some favorite foods "freedom fries" and "freedom toast" but by trying to drive a wedge between the "old" and "new" Europe.

Ambivalence and occasional animosity have been not only diplomatic but cultural and popular as well. In American minds, France represents elegance and sophistication, but also snobbery, frivolity, and cowardice (during the Iraq war, *Google* responded to the search request "French military victories" with "Do you mean 'French military defeats'?"). In French minds, Americans are naïve "big children," whom they nonetheless admire for their dynamism and entrepreneurial spirit. While France in trade talks has fought the United States in favor of *l'exception culturelle* in order to protect French and world culture from "Hollywoodization," the French have lionized lowbrow comedian Jerry Lewis and adored kitsch television series such as *Starsky and Hutch*.

To be sure, the United States occupies a greater space in the French *imaginaire* than France does in the American. With a population of 60 million and a landmass the size of Texas, France is no longer the powerhouse that dominated the European continent from the Middle Ages well into the nineteenth century and that controlled a worldwide empire well into the twentieth. From a contemporary American perspective, France is an intermediate, "has-been" power, whose continuing pretensions to *grandeur* are a misplaced irritant at best. No doubt, the tensions that characterize Franco-American relations owe something to France's relative decline and to the United States' ascendancy to superpower status since World War II, but in fact it is possible, and necessary, to trace them back to fundamental differences in interests, identities, and institutions that have distinguished French and American societies for at least four centuries. No one has offered a finer analysis of these differences than the French nobleman **Alexis de Tocqueville**, who already some 170 years ago expressed France's ambivalent appreciation of the United States in his two-volume study of *Democracy in America*. Americans tend to read Tocqueville's masterpiece, which won him election to the *Académie française*, as a celebration of the vibrancy of their civil society, of the participatory dynamism of their local governments, and of the wisdom of their federalist constitutional order, among other elements of a successful American recipe for reconciling the competing values of personal liberty and social equality. By contrast, American readers like to overlook less endearing, but unfortunately enduring, American traits such as racism, conformism, vulgar materialism, and anti-intellectualism that Tocqueville observed in the United States of the 1830s. As a French patriot, who devoted his life to public service and scholarly analysis, Tocqueville was not interested in the United States for its own sake, but as a comparative foil for France. Indeed, for Tocqueville, the United States constituted a natural experiment, a unique case of a new society founded on the democratic principle of social equality, free from a hereditary nobility with its claims to privileges and leadership. He also feared that America's egalitarianism made it susceptible to tyranny when a mass of socially leveled individuals faced a powerful, increasingly centralized state. Indeed, Tocqueville looked to America as an example of both the dangers and opportunities that France faced after the revolutions of 1789, 1830, and 1848 had destroyed the aristocratic principle and had sent France, as we shall shortly see, down its long, tortuous path to modern democratic stability.

While Tocqueville's ambivalence about American democracy reflected and anticipated long-standing and contemporary tensions in Franco-American relations, the French nobleman was paradoxically an unequivocal admirer of France's ancient Anglo-Saxon nemesis, Great Britain. But Britain, too, was for Tocqueville an exceptional case, a fortuitous land that had avoided the two, interrelated forces of modernity: social equalization and political centralization. In England, as we saw in the last chapter, the landed gentry had, during the Civil War of 1642–1649 and the Glorious Revolution of 1688, succeeded in resisting the centralization of power in the monarchy and had retained its social and political preeminence. For Tocqueville, Britain thus did not stand at the avant-garde of political development. Indeed, its insular position, like that of the United States, allowed Britain, as well as its former colony, to avoid the full onslaught of democratic modernity that hit continental Europe. As Tocqueville wrote in his second masterpiece, *The Old Regime and the Revolution*, France, for better but mostly for worse, represented the ideal-typical, or most "normal," path to political modernity, at least within the western European context.

The Medieval Origins of the French State

One of, if not *the*, classic questions of comparative politics is: Why did the modern bureaucratic state first emerge in Western Europe (and we might add: and why with such a vengeance in France)? Debate still rages, but a crucial explanatory factor lies paradoxically in the fragmented, competitive nature of political authority in the age of **feudalism** that followed the collapse of the Roman Empire in the west in the wake of the "barbarian" invasions of the fifth to tenth centuries. Various Germanic tribal leaders, including the Franks, coveted the title and power of the Roman emperor. Between them, they succeeded in destroying all of the major social, economic, political, and cultural institutions of the late Empire, except for one: the Roman Catholic Church. For over one thousand years, Western Europe was thus characterized by political division and religious unity. The upshot was a constant power struggle not only between political authorities but between them and the church hierarchy under the secular as well as spiritual leadership of the pope in Rome. In the year 800, Charlemagne, the king of the Franks, succeeded in uniting into the Holy Roman Empire most of the territories that would one day become France, Germany, Italy, and the Benelux countries, the founders in 1957 of what would become today's European Union. Divided by his grandsons, Charlemagne's empire had had little chance of survival since even its heroic founder's authority depended on his coronation by the pope. In other words, the division of authority between the spiritual leadership of the pope and the political leadership of the emperor meant that even a successful conqueror of Western Europe would have to come up with sources of legitimacy beyond religious benediction to consolidate his or her power. In any case, the remnants of Charlemagne's empire did not survive the next round of barbarian invasions of the tenth century, including that of the Normans, who settled in the northern part of the Frankish kingdom, whence they successfully invaded England in 1066.

The constant rivalry between feudal leaders on the one hand and between them and the church on the other proved to be the developmental dynamic from which the modern state emerged on the European continent. The consolidation of the French state in fact owed much to the Norman conquest of England. Since no one has repeated William the Conqueror's exploit of 1066, unrivaled Norman rule of the island kingdom allowed it to project power back onto the European mainland, where under the complexities of cross-cutting feudal obligations the English royalty was in some areas the subordinate of Frankish kings and in others their superiors. These confusions came to a head in a succession crisis and series of armed struggles known as the Hundred Years War spanning the fourteenth and fifteenth centuries. Whereas the English succeeded in projecting power across the Channel thanks to the coherence of king and nobility after the conquest and the compromise of the Magna Carta, the French monarchy suffered the typical weakness of feudal devolution of authority, whereby the nobility exercised local authority nominally by grace of the king but where in fact the latter could count on the support of his nobles only by their goodwill. Finally, only in 1431, when, as historical legend would have it, the French king's sister disguised as the peasant girl Jeanne d'Arc heroically rallied the troops, did the French manage to drive the English from the continent. Having learned his lesson, Charles VII convinced his nobility in 1439 to allow him to establish a permanent standing army in exchange, fatally, for the aristocracy's exemption from royal taxes to fund it. This unholy compromise sowed the seeds, as we shall see, for the Revolution that shook France and the world 350 years later, but at the same time it also marked the conception, if not birth, of the European state system.

Even before they began the long struggle to monopolize the control of the means of force on the territories nominally under their control, the monarchs of Western Europe had begun to develop other crucial means of social control. Although they continued their struggle with the church to guide their subjects' spiritual beliefs – the French king even went so far as to hold the pope captive in a palace in Avignon during the fourteenth century, Europe's secular leaders began willy-nilly to develop techniques for more effectively governing their subjects' and their own material affairs. Starting in the twelfth and thirteenth centuries, they granted charters to universities, new institutions that not only competed with monasteries as centers of learning in their faculties of theology but trained experts of applicable knowledge in their faculties of law, arts, and sciences. Deprived of religious authority, Western Europe's monarchies necessarily acquired a comparative advantage in the codification of law and the rationalization of taxes and other fiscal obligations. Since the laws and obligations they rendered more effective were those that maintained the feudal order and the interests of the dominant class, the aristocracy hardly contested this aggrandizement of monarchical power. Yet as with the concession of a permanent royal army, the feudal nobility would learn to regret the convenience of an effective crown.

Whereas in insular England the aristocracy prevented the monarchy from establishing an army and seizing control of the governance of local, daily affairs, on the continent the more constant, immediate threat of war and invasion favored territorial rulers in their bids to raise armies and to monopolize the control of social resources. In fits and starts, this process gave rise to a new political order called **absolutism**, with suzerains, the nominal holders of ultimate authority over a given territory in the feudal order, becoming sovereigns, the effective final arbiters of authority within their lands. The absolutist monarchs of continental Western Europe did not, of course, exercise absolute authority; they lacked the technical means of modern dictatorships, for example. What was absolute – and novel – about their rule was their claim *potentially* to control all aspects of life within their realms. Historians generally tend to describe Ferdinand and Isabella of Spain as the first absolute monarchs, but France usually occupies the rank of the prototypical absolute monarchy, attaining its high point under the long reign of Louis XIV (1642–1710), the *roi soleil*, whose memorable "L'État, c'est moi" embodied the absolutist principle.

Absolutism and the Origins of Contemporary French Institutions, Interests, and Identity

Two centuries, however, separated Charles VII's establishment of a standing royal army from Louis XIV's glorious reign, two centuries that laid the foundations for the institutions, interests, and identities of contemporary France. With the close of the Hundred Years' War, the French monarchy consolidated its rule, notably under Louis XI, whose reign ushered in the French Renaissance, characterized by the construction of the celebrated chateaux along the Loire River and the incorporation into court life of geniuses the likes of Leonardo da Vinci. The French kings did not yet rule unilaterally, though. They still depended, especially in matters of taxation, on the collaboration of the late feudal representative institution of the Estates General, created in 1302. Similar to the two houses of the English Parliament, the Estates separately represented the three orders of feudal society: the nobility, the clergy, and the remaining Third Estate of commoners. In addition, a panoply of local and regional courts and deliberative bodies such as the *Parlements* of Paris and of Languedoc vied with the kings for legislative and judicial authority. In the late sixteenth century, moreover, the monarchy nearly collapsed in the face of the succession crisis and civil war provoked by the death of Henri II, last of the Valois line. Heightened by the conversion of a significant portion of the southern aristocracy to Protestantism, this political and religious struggle within the nobility ceased only when popular uprisings in the late 1580s threatened the aristocratic principle per se. A double compromise saved the kingdom in 1589: the Protestant pretender to the throne, Henri IV, founder of the Bourbon dynasty, converted to Catholicism but in turn introduced official religious tolerance through the Edict of Nantes of 1598.

Beginning under Henri IV's reign, seventeenth-century France witnessed the consolidation and institutionalization of the absolutist monarchy through the successive efforts of four particularly capable royal administrators: Sully, Richelieu, Mazarin, and Colbert. Sully's preoccupation was the securing of an independent financial base for the monarchy. By developing indirect forms of taxation and the sale of state offices, Sully and the monarchy netted the short-term windfalls of privatization of public goods and rendered the Estates General obsolete: the last time they convened before 1789 was in 1614. The long-term effects of Sully's initiative of farming out tax collection and other state functions to private entrepreneurs were: a loss of control over tax receipts, two-thirds of which remained in private hands; growing popular frustration with tax inequities and poor public services; and the emergence of a new class of financiers with a strong identification with the state and an interest in maintaining its structural deficits. Following Sully as de facto ruler of France, Cardinal Richelieu attacked the administrative fragmentation and inconsistencies of what was still largely a feudal monarchy. His method, too, was indirect in that he simply added a new, more rational layer of administration, a reform which initiated the centralized structure of the contemporary French state. Dividing the kingdom into 32 relatively equal *généralités*, he placed them under the supervision of royal *intendants* loyal and responsible to no one but the monarch.

The administrative and fiscal structures of the bourgeoning absolutist state faced a critical test under Richelieu's successor, Cardinal Mazarin, who governed France from 1642 to 1661, during Louis XIV's minority. France's interventions into the Thirty Years' War, which ravaged Central Europe from 1618 to 1648, put such a strain on the tax system that the Parlement of Paris finally refused Mazarin's unilateral tax measures. Thus, at the very moment that the Peace of Westphalia in 1648 consecrated the modern concept of the territorial state, Europe's largest state descended into a five-year civil war. Unlike the contemporaneous English Civil War, the so-called Fronde in France resulted not in the breaking of royal power and absolutist ambition but in a figurative decapitation of the aristocracy. Traumatized by his near loss of power, the young Louis XIV, first with the help of Mazarin, then largely on his own, systematically constructed an absolutist state that became the explicit model emulated by monarchs elsewhere on the continent (and in restoration Britain as well, until the Glorious Revolution of 1688 definitively established parliamentary supremacy). Louis XIV's methods were military, political, social, and economic: He expanded the army by a factor of ten to

300,000 men (out of a total population of under 20 million) and founded a royal police force to maintain order in the growing towns. He did not eliminate the representative bodies inherited from the feudal age but failed to convene them and withdrew their right to criticize royal decrees. His most famous measure, however, was the construction of the enormous palace at Versailles, but not as a megalomaniacal end in itself. From 1682 on, he required that the high nobility take up residence at his court in Versailles. Thereby Louis XIV could not only keep an eye on potential rivals but keep them occupied with court intrigues, drain their purses with frivolous expenses for social prestige, and most importantly distract them from their local interests and power bases. Cut off from the countryside and the peasants who sustained them, the upper nobility became a truly parasitic class serving no economic, judicial, military, or social function. At the same time, however, the absolutist state upheld their feudal rights and privileges, inevitably to the growing frustration of commoners in town and country.

Beyond the clever political manipulation and expansion of existing structures and resources, Louis XIV also sought to create new sources of state power. He charged his minister Colbert with the development of state-owned enterprises not only in such strategic sectors as armaments but also in the production of luxury goods such as the huge wall-hangings produced by the state firm Gobelins. With this pro-active economic policy, Colbert introduced a historically new function and tool for the state: the promotion of economic growth and innovation. Generally called mercantilism, the state-led pursuit of prosperity and trade surpluses in order better to fill the sovereign's coffers is to this day called **colbertisme** in France. A product of seventeenth-century absolutism, *colbertisme* provides a telling example of the interlocking character of institutions, interests, and identities. In France, the state's long-standing institutional capacity to steer economic development through public ownership of key economic sectors and through the training of qualified experts in public service has shaped private interests, notably with higher civil servants and upper management regularly moving back and forth between public and private sectors in industry and finance. French national identity also derives in part from the *colbertiste* tradition, drawing pride in state-inspired accomplishments from Gobelins tapestries to the nationwide high speed rail network of *trains à grande vitesse* (TGV).

Louis XIV's long reign (1642–1710) sowed the seeds of modern-day economic nationalism but also those of absolutism's self-destruction. Having drained the kingdom's capacities with excessive territorial and dynastic ambitions and having outlived his sons and grandsons, the *roi soleil* left France in the hands of five-year-old Louis XV. The occasion was rife for the aristocracy to avenge itself of lost power and prestige. The nobility did not, however, dismantle the absolutist state. Instead, in a process known as the feudal reaction, they transformed it into their private reserve, restricting

access to high offices of army and administration to those who could prove
birth from four aristocratic grandparents. The repressive capacities of the
absolutist state firmly under their control, the aristocracy quite rationally
used them not to develop new commercial or industrial activities, as did the
British aristocracy of the eighteenth century, but rather to reinforce the feudal obligations of the peasantry and other taxable commoners. This strategy
was in fact the only one open to the nobility, for under the absolutist state and
the absentee landlordism of Louis XIV's reign, the peasantry had acquired
de facto control of much of the land, while the commercial, financial, and
bourgeoning industrial resources of the realm were under the control of the
townsmen, or bourgeoisie (from the French *bourg*, fortified town). What is
more, since the French aristocracy drew its material revenues from its legal
control of the land and since the products of French agriculture that lent
themselves to profitable commercialization were the labor-intensive production of wine and wheat, the aristocracy had every interest in seeing peasants
tied to the land by feudal obligation. As Tocqueville observed in *The Old
Regime and the Revolution*, the feudal reaction of the eighteenth century did
not mean that the peasantry and other commoners in France were objectively
worse off than elsewhere in Europe. On the contrary, French absolutism had
given them relative autonomy, which was precisely what made them subjec-
tively more resentful of aristocratic power and privilege than was the case
elsewhere.

The French Revolution

In hindsight, the great revolution of 1789 was a foregone conclusion. To get
there, however, the absolutist state had to lose control of the repressive social
order it had come to sustain. History's great revolutions erupt not from social,
economic, and political injustices alone – these are omnipresent – but from
their convergence with a breakdown of the political and institutional mechanisms for imposing them. To survive, a state must be able to face down any
internal or external challenges to its authority within its territorial boundaries.
In eighteenth-century France, the challenges were great but not insurmount-
able. Indeed, historians still debate whether Louis XVI, with better decisions
or advice, might not have been able to ward off the worst – from his own
point of view, that is – or at least have saved his head in a constitutional
compromise. Fortunately, we need not engage in such counterfactual speculation here since the immediate precipitants of the revolution point to two
obvious causes: budget deficits and under-taxing of the wealthy. To be sure,
the causes of the French Revolution were manifold. Tocqueville, for example,
analyzes not only the legitimate frustrations of the peasantry but also the lack
of communication between the social classes, the complicity of the church in

maintaining inequalities, the utopian idealism of the *philosophes'* critiques of the absolutist state, and the bad timing of Louis XVI's reform efforts, among many others. All of these grievances and mistakes came to a head, though, when the monarchy found itself in a grave fiscal crisis resulting, externally, from war and, internally, from the aristocracy's centuries-old exemption from taxation.

Indeed, since 1774, the monarchy had found itself in a budget crisis that grew even worse when the French crown decided to intervene in favor of the rebellious colonies in the American War of Independence in order to avenge France for its losses in the previous, costly Seven Years' War (experienced as the French and Indian War in America). In a futile attempt to bring order into its affairs, the monarchy in 1788 for the first and last time actually took the trouble to calculate its budget, finding itself to be in a 20 percent budget overrun, with half of the deficit arising from service of the debt. The king's treasury minister, Calonne, proposed a solution that included a new property tax to which the aristocracy would be subjected alongside the commoners. In a bid to secure some form of approval for this radical measure, Calonne revived a supposedly representative institution unused since 1626, a hand-picked Assembly of Notables. But even Calonne's men refused to acquiesce to a principle as repugnant as the taxation of nobles! When in May 1788 the Parlement of Paris refused approval as well, Louis XVI ordered the arrest of its leaders, kicking off the revolution's first phase of aristocratic revolt against the very state that maintained aristocratic privilege. Still, the king needed some sort of legislative approval for his new tax, so he decided to convene the Estates General for the first time since 1614. This institutional mechanism introduced two new dangers: It represented, theoretically at least, the interest of all society, and it mobilized expectations since it entailed the public designation of delegates and the drawing up of lists of grievances. These *cahiers de doléances* have proven to be an invaluable source for historians such as Tocqueville, who could read the state of opinion and the interests of all classes of French society straight from the grievances they addressed to their "good king."

On the eve of the revolution, French society was fragmented into numerous classes and strata whose divergent interests would not only drive the revolution forward to catastrophe but shape French politics, society, and the state for centuries to come. The peasantry, for example, was divided between those who owned or controlled little or no land, equipment, or animals, those who had enough to engage in subsistence agriculture, and those who generated enough surplus to acquire other goods and even more land. These wealthier peasants, although perhaps still nominally subjected to feudal obligations such as the forced labor of the *corvée*, shaded into the bourgeoisie. Originally a political label to describe town dwellers who enjoyed personal exemptions and collective rights within the feudal order, the bourgeoisie, under absolutism, had become an economic class with a panoply of potentially conflicting interests. Including intellectuals, liberal professionals such as doctors and lawyers, artisans and craftsmen, merchants, bankers, rentiers, and – increasingly since the mid-eighteenth century – industrialists, the bourgeoisie had many competing interests, but one common enemy: the aristocracy, whose social prestige and political privileges frustrated bourgeois ambitions. One of these ambitions, perhaps hypocritical, was to accede to the status of noble through the purchase of feudal estates, titles, and royal offices. Indeed, the frontier between *roturiers* (commoners) and nobles had grown confused under absolutism with the rise of the *noblesse de robe*, royal officeholders of nonnoble origin who over time succeeded in acquiring hereditary title. Even the traditional feudal-military *noblesse d'épée* was rife with divisions. Some of the enlightened elites close to the monarchy recognized the necessity of rational reform of the cumbersome feudal-absolutist state whereas their poorer, disempowered cousins in the provinces clung to feudal privileges in a rearguard effort to ward off bourgeois ascension. Finally, on top of the schisms among and between commoners and nobles, social and political conflict under the old regime was further confused by the cross-cutting material, institutional, and ideal interests of the Second Estate, namely the clergy, divided between noble officials and common priests, between monastic orders with huge property holdings and poor parishes, and between regions with differences in religious practices and loyalties.

We cannot here trace out the infinitely complex interplay of interests, institutions, and identities that convulsed France between the convening of the Estates General in 1789 and the final defeat of Napoleon Bonaparte's revolutionary armies in 1815. The history of the French Revolution fills thousands of volumes and debate still rages as to whether it contributed positively to the emergence of the modern democratic state. More radically and universally than the earlier English or American revolutions, the French Revolution established the principles of popular sovereignty and equal rights, but it did so at the cost of ideological terror and massive warfare. In its initial, peaceful phase, the revolution of 1789 looked like an attempt to adjust the rickety institutions of the absolutist state to the interests of a society breaking out of feudal agrarian stagnancy. After aristocratic refusal of the king's tax reforms prompted the convening of the Estates General in May 1789, the Third Estate, with delegates representing over 95 percent of the population, became the focal point for contesting royal authority. Having obtained a number of representatives equal to the sum of those representing the First and Second Estates, the Third Estate, emboldened by pamphleteers such as the Abbé Sieyès (who answered his pamphlet's title "What Is the Third Estate?" resoundingly with "the entire nation"), proclaimed itself constituent National Assembly on June 17. Finding their meeting hall closed by royal order on June 20, the representatives of the Third Estate/National Assembly met on a tennis court and swore in the "Serment du jeu de paume" to continue to assemble until they had drafted a constitution for the kingdom. Louis XVI hesitated to disperse the delegates by force, and a week later all three orders convened together.

Had the revolution ended there, with the proclamation of a constitutional monarchy, it would have remained, like its English and American antecedents, a political affair settled largely between elites with more or less internecine violence. The strategic blunders of the king, however, propelled events toward popular upheaval and profound social revolution. In a context of famine and rapidly rising bread prices in Paris in particular, the king ordered mercenary troops to mobilize around the city and on July 12 fired his popular, reformist finance minister Necker. With rumors circulating about a counterrevolutionary coup against the National Assembly and a plan to starve the city, the Parisian masses, the celebrated *sansculottes*, stormed the royal *Invalides* armory and liberated the prisoners, albeit only seven, of the Bastille fortress in the first great popular *journée* of the revolution, July 14. Over the months and years to come, the *sansculottes* would push the revolution radically forward in a sequence of *grandes journées*, culminating notably on September 21, 1792, in the proclamation of the republic. Still, the revolution would not have had a transformative effect on French society as a whole if the overwhelming mass of the population, the peasantry, had not taken part immediately after the storming of the Bastille. Again, in a context of famine, fear of brigandage, real threats of counterrevolutionary plots, disinformation and disorder, a vast movement known as the Great Fear spread across the French countryside between July 20 and August 6. Fully aware of the legal and political underpinnings of the feudal order that left them beholden to parasitic aristocratic landlords and unfair taxes, the peasants stormed aristocratic manors and castles, carefully identifying and destroying the feudal documents codifying their servitude and obligations. Since the peasants in many cases were already landowners themselves they did not, however, attack property rights. Indeed, throughout the revolution, only nobles who emigrated and fought against the revolution had their land confiscated. Faced with peasant revolt and to recover control of the situation, the National Assembly on the night of August 4, 1789, solemnly proclaimed, with full noble participation, the end of feudalism.

Within a few months and with minimum bloodshed, France had de facto become a constitutional monarchy with a sovereign, popularly representative parliament, equal political and social rights, and an economic order founded on the principle of private property – in short, all the essential ingredients of a liberal representative democracy and a capitalist socioeconomic order. As we know, the revolution did not end there and instead bequeathed France with a political order that lacked stability or legitimacy or both well into the twentieth century. It also left the French hungry for both radical equality and powerful central authority, the complementary but contradictory characteristics typical of modern democratic societies, according to Alexis de Tocqueville. Before exploring the enduring legacy of the revolution for French politics down to the present, however, we must briefly suggest why the revolution could not stop with the dramatic events of 1789. Two factors, which, following Tocqueville, we can link to the institutional dynamics of the absolutist state, drove the revolution on to death and destruction: namely, the treasonous behavior of the crown and the powerful conflicts of interest within French society. It is perhaps understandable, if not forgivable, that Louis XVI, his queen, Marie Antoinette, their courtiers, and aristocratic allies consistently tried to turn back the constitutional and democratic advances of the revolution. After all, centuries of absolutism had trained them to disregard representative bodies and decentralized sources of authority, and the remaining absolutist monarchs on the continent actively plotted with them to restore absolutism. Events such as the king and queen's "flight to Varennes" in June 1791, when they tried to rejoin counterrevolutionary forces near the Belgian border, and the king's subsequent connivance in provoking a proclamation of war against Austria, pushed the revolutionary regime to more and more radical measures as it struggled for survival against external and internal enemies.

The counterrevolutionary forces could indeed count on divisions and conflicts of interest within French society to push the revolution toward collapse or toward ever more authoritarian means. As Tocqueville observed in *The Old Regime and the Revolution*, the absolutist centralization of authority had left Frenchmen equal in their political impotence but isolated from one another in their frustrations. Revolutionary leaders thus inherited a society torn by narrow sectarian interests, and so reverted to the absolutist impulse to centralize power and atomize citizens. These structural tendencies toward divisiveness and authoritarianism of French politics and society were, however, exacerbated by a more immediate, conjunctural legacy of French absolutism: its fiscal crisis, which, as the revolution's immediate cause, still required resolution. In November 1789, the constituent assembly nationalized church property and issued a new currency, the *assignat*, backed by these nationalized goods. What seemed like a good idea at the time not only prompted a hyperinflationary cycle provoking ongoing food shortages and riots but antagonized much of the church hierarchy and the faithful in soon-to-be-counterrevolutionary regions such as the Vendée. A year later, the introduction of the Civil Constitution of the Clergy, requiring that priests swear allegiance to the state as religious functionaries, created an enduring cleavage in French politics: Well into the twentieth century, the single best predictor of a region's left–right voting behavior was its clergymen's refusal (right) or acceptance (left) of the oath.

Through such immediate conflicts, the revolution in the long run forged and solidified political identities that characterize the French polity down to the present. In the short run, however, revolutionary politics intensified social conflict. Perhaps the most important tension of the revolution was that between the popular classes in town and country. The food shortages that preceded the revolution only grew worse in the periods of disruption and of civil and international war that followed 1789. The Parisian *sansculottes* in particular were sensitive to the price of bread and exercised direct pressure on the National Assembly, which responded with the *maximum*, a price ceiling on grains. For the peasantry, the revolutionary regime's price controls and wartime requisitions of foodstuff and livestock became as onerous as their previous feudal obligations. Described by Barrington Moore as "the arbiters of the Revolution," who had pushed through the abolition of feudalism but sanctified the nonegalitarian principle of private property, the peasantry remained the arbiters of French politics right through the nineteenth century. Fearful that the revolutionary republican regime might violate their recently acquired equal right to own property, the better-off peasants in particular provided a conservative ballast to French society, while poorer peasants and landless laborers remained socially, economically, and hence politically dependent on large landowners, including monarchist former nobles, of course. In the western region of the Vendée, peasants turned to active counterrevolutionary insurgency, but everywhere in France they jealously guarded their holdings, however small, ultimately throwing the weight of their numbers in support of **Napoleon Bonaparte**. Military hero of the revolutionary wars turned dictator in 1799, Napoleon offered France price stability with the introduction of a new currency, the franc, legal security (including title to land) through a new civil code, and relative social cohesion through the redirection of conflict toward imperial wars of conquest. In 1804, Napoleon declared himself emperor, pursuing his exportation of both revolutionary ideals and the centralized bureaucratic structure of the French state across Europe, at least until his disastrous decision to invade Russia in 1812 finally undid his empire and spelled defeat of the revolutionary armies and the restoration of the Bourbon monarchy in 1815.

The French Revolution would of course never have come to such a denouement if the political elites who brought about the constitutional revolution of 1789 had maintained some cohesion. Unlike in eighteenth-century Britain, where the commercial interests of the landed and urban elites represented in Parliament fortuitously converged around the growing trade in wool and textiles, in revolutionary France the bourgeoisie in particular were sharply divided in their interests and ideologies. Indeed, most of the political drama of the revolution revolved not around the conflict between the Third Estate, on the one hand, and the clergy and the nobility, on the other, but around rivalries within the Third Estate's bourgeois leadership. Introducing for the first time the spatial, left–right image of the political spectrum, the revolutionary leaders quickly organized themselves into, and sat as, factions in the National Assembly and subsequently in the Convention, France's first representative legislature elected by universal manhood suffrage, which deposed the king and proclaimed the republic. Drawing names from their seating location (the "Montagnards"), their geographical origins (the "Girondins"), or their meeting places (the "Jacobins" and the "Feuillants"), these protoparties engaged in a bloody soap opera – too complex to summarize here – of maneuvering, infighting, and ultimately mutual self-destruction in the Terror and Thermidorian reaction of the mid-1790s. The most famous of these political clubs were the Jacobins, who organized mass membership across the country, came under the infamous leadership of Maximilien Robespierre, and introduced the most radical phase of the revolution, featuring a new calendar and the civic religion of the Cult of the Supreme Being. Paradoxically for such a virulent faction, the Jacobins subscribed to the philosopher Jean-Jacques Rousseau's doctrine that no intermediate associations should come between the citizen and the state, understood as the legitimate embodiment of the general will. To this day the term *Jacobinisme* describes policies and opinions that favour the centralized, unitary character of the French state, a character, as Tocqueville argued, inherited from absolutism and only reinforced through the violence and upheaval of the revolution.

Nineteenth-Century France in Search of Stable Institutions and Identity

In short, France entered the nineteenth century with a modernized, rationalized, highly centralized bureaucratic state, the fruit of an absolutist monarchy, a revolutionary republic, and a militaristic empire. The question that would occupy French politics over the course of the century was what regime form the state would take. With the defeat of Napoleon at Waterloo in 1815, the question was settled from without: the international Congress of Vienna redrew Europe's map to keep France in check and attempted to reintroduce absolutist regimes across the continent and in France. Still, the revolutionary principles of equal rights and constitutionalism once unleashed could be repealed only with difficulty if at all. Thus, in France, the restored Bourbon monarch, Louis XVIII, had to grant a constitutional charter and governed with a bicameral parliament including a hereditary Chamber of Peers and a Chamber of Deputies elected with an extremely restrictive wealth-based suffrage for which only 90,000 Frenchmen qualified. Even such feeble constitutionalism proved too much for Louis' successor, Charles X, who in response to the election of a relatively liberal Chamber of Deputies decreed the dissolution of Parliament and the suspension of civil liberties on July 26, 1830. The bourgeois liberal press protested, but so too did the Parisian masses. In the face of riots, the king, fearing for his head, fled to England, while the hero of the American and French Revolutions and leader of the parliamentary opposition, the aged General La Fayette, embraced Louis-Philippe, duke of Orléans, on the balcony of Paris's city hall and proclaimed him "King of the French."

Cousin once-removed of Louis XVI, Louis-Philippe thus established the "July Monarchy" and introduced an enduring schism in the monarchist camp between the more bourgeois *orléanistes* and the more reactionary, aristocratic *légitimistes*. Embracing the legacy of the constitutionalist first phase of 1789 as well as the tricolor flag of the republic, Louis-Philippe claimed to represent the "juste milieu" (or fine balance) between monarchism and republicanism. Also called the "bourgeois monarchy," Louis-Philippe's 18-year reign did indeed liberalize the monarchy: Education was secularized, civil liberties restored, and suffrage extended to more than twice as many younger, somewhat less plutocratic men. A time of growing wealth, corruption, and rotating-door parliamentary governments, the July monarchy was a golden age of hypocrisy – and of social criticism as articulated in the brilliant novels of Victor Hugo, Gustave Flaubert, and Honoré Balzac. Hugo's *Les Misérables* well describes the revolutionary ferment and popular dissatisfactions of industrializing France in the 1830s and 1840s. Finally, in early 1848 in a context of economic downturn, a protest movement initiated by bourgeois liberal nationalists in a series of political dinner banquets gave way to popular protests in the streets of Paris. Fearing the worst of the *grandes journées* of the revolution, Louis-Philippe, too, abdicated and fled, leaving a provisional revolutionary government including representatives of the new Parisian proletariat to organize France's Second Republic.

Part of a revolutionary current that swept all of Europe in 1848, the Second Republic is one of the most fascinating, if briefest, interludes in France's political development. Like the revolution of 1789, the Second Republic has been seen as prototypical for the difficulties of the emergence of liberal democracy in industrializing societies. A keen, firsthand observer of this dramatic phase of French history, the German exile Karl Marx developed his historical materialist theory of economic and political development on the basis of what he observed there and described in still-insight-rich journalistic texts such as *The Class Struggle in France* and *The Eighteenth Brumaire of Louis Bonaparte*. For Marx, the Parisian working class's uprising of February 1848 was a premature proletarian revolution, as the results of the universal manhood suffrage elections of the republic's constituent assembly proved. These produced a democratic and republican majority, but the peasant and petty bourgeois majority of French society, not to mention the upper classes, feared the egalitarian excesses of the Parisian "mob." When the new government consequently reversed the provisional government's anti-unemployment program, the Parisian workers revolted again in June 1848. This time, however, they were brutally repressed. This unrest played into the hands of the reactionary "party of order," a coalition of conservative bourgeois republicans and monarchists, who won the first regular legislative elections of May 1849. When the petty bourgeois democrats protested the following month, their leaders were arrested, and the following year the party of order abolished universal suffrage and returned education to the hands of the church. Their power uncontested and seemingly uncontestable, the conservative and reactionary upper classes quarreled among themselves in parliament, providing the pretext for the democratically elected president of the republic, Louis Bonaparte, to carry out an anti-parliamentary coup d'état with the support of the army on December 2, 1851. As Marx lucidly analyzed in his *Eighteenth Brumaire* (the title alluding to the date in the revolutionary calendar of Napoleon's coup d'état of 1799), Louis Bonaparte, the nephew of Napoleon, had acceded to the presidency thanks to the massive support of the peasantry, who in the face of their own economic decline with industrialization had harkened back to the myth of their imperial savior Napoleon.

In what Marx called a farcical repetition of the tragic collapse of the First Republic into dictatorship, Louis Bonaparte followed in his uncle's footsteps and proclaimed himself emperor Napoleon III on the first anniversary of his coup. The Second Empire, however, represented a new form of authoritarian regime that anticipated the mass-based, populist dictatorships of the twentieth century. Elected to the presidency before the abolition of universal suffrage, Louis Bonaparte presented himself as an enemy of the traditional elite and defender of the democratic masses. Thus, he had both his coup and his proclamation of the empire approved by popular plebiscite, and during his 18-year reign he preserved at least the formal trappings of representative democratic institutions, even introducing liberal reforms toward the end of his reign, suggesting that he might have allowed a transition to democratic rule, as happened with some late twentieth-century authoritarian regimes. Indeed, his mode of government presaged the developmentalist bureaucratic authoritarian regimes of modern southern Europe and Latin America. **Bonapartism** thus describes not only an ideological current in France favorable to modernizing authoritative, if not authoritarian rulers but, more generally, a developmental strategy whereby a powerful state bureaucracy supplants a divided or weak bourgeoisie to propel capitalist industrial development forward. Along with ambitious public works programs, including the reconstruction of Paris with its famous grand boulevards designed to prevent the erection of revolutionary barricades, Napoleon III provided state subsidies for railroad construction, and organized a concentrated financial

banking sector in order to provide long-term credit for large-scale industrial development. In keeping with the *colbertiste* tradition, Napoleon III's industrial policies reinforced the enduring symbiosis between the state bureaucracy and the private economic sector in France.

Because Napoleon's popular dictatorship rested on his ability to offer something to everyone, like modern authoritarian regimes elsewhere, the Second Empire tried to defuse social conflict with appeals to nationalism and expansionist foreign policies. The latter proved to be Bonaparte's undoing when the authoritarian Prussian chancellor, Otto von Bismarck, outmaneuvered Napoleon into declaring war in 1870. The ensuing Franco-Prussian War allowed Bismarck to unify Germany, to seize Alsace and much of Lorraine from France, and to take Napoleon prisoner at Sedan by the beginning of September of the same year. The revolutionary cycle begun in 1848 thus ended much like that which had started in 1789. Bismarck, however, did not dictate the form that the new French regime would take. Instead, he insisted the French elect a new government with whom he could negotiate a peace treaty, while German troops surrounded Paris. Whereas the Parisian masses had forced the imperial legislature to proclaim a republic and to pursue the war effort, the rest of the war-weary country returned a pacifist monarchist majority in the elections of February 1871. Meeting in Bordeaux, the Chamber elected the *orléaniste* Adolphe Thiers, an elderly protagonist of the 1830 revolution, to preside over the new government. Installed in the suburb of Versailles, the new government ordered the disarming of the National Guard in Paris. The city rebelled and proclaimed itself a revolutionary Commune under a radical democratic and socialist government. This new political experiment did not last long as the Communards and the Versaillais engaged in a bloody civil war while bemused German troops looked on. In the end 20,000 Parisians were dead, including the radical and working-class leadership, shot by firing squad at the famous Père Lachaise cemetery. This bloodbath gave birth surprisingly to France's longest lasting, most stable, and perhaps most successful regime since the ancien régime.

France's Third Republic and Social Stalemate

The child of military defeat, civil war, and antirepublican electoral results, the Third Republic emerged from a long, uncertain gestation period. Republicanism's fortunes began to change with the first postwar by-elections of June 1871. Now that the pursuit of the war was no longer an issue, republican candidates swept 99 of the 114 seats at stake. Sensing a shift of political winds, Thiers anticipated a new ideological current within republicanism, called "opportunisme," when he came out in favor of a republic as the regime which "divides the least." He added that the republic would be a conservative

one or not all. With these remarks, Thiers succinctly evoked the interplay of interests, institutions, and identities at work in the emergence of the Third Republic. To overcome nearly a century of political instability due to conflicting class interests and competing ideas about what constituted the French political community and about what legitimated rule, the founders of the Third Republic had to come up with a compromise: a regime form that minimized social and political divisions by maximizing immobility. As the Franco-American political scientist Stanley Hoffmann wrote of the Third Republic, it was a regime "with plenty of brakes and no motor."

Building such a static political machine, however, required huge efforts on the part of both monarchist and republican politicians. In the case of the monarchists, it would be only a slightly sarcastic exaggeration to say that they had to dig deep into their pockets of political stupidity to snatch defeat from the jaws of victory. In the face of Thiers' opportunistic defection to the republican camp, the *orléanistes* and *légitimistes* in the Chamber of Deputies conspired against him in 1873 to topple his government and to form a new one under the Duke de Broglie with the mandate to restore the Bourbon pretender, the Count of Chambord, to the throne. The count, however, placed *légitimiste* principle ahead of expediency and refused to accept the *orléanistes*' symbolic demand that the monarchy adopt the tricolor flag. The monarchist majority thus found itself with no monarch to embody the political community. Almost despite itself, and by a one-vote majority, the Chamber grudgingly adopted the constitutional laws and the name of the republic in January 1875. In the meantime, however, an electoral college of parliamentarians (the Chamber of Deputies and the Senate convened simultaneously as the National Assembly) had elected the monarchist General Mac-Mahon, "hero" of the bloody repression of the Paris Commune, to the seven-year presidency of the still-indeterminate regime form. In the so-called May 16 crisis of 1877, Mac-Mahon staged the monarchists' last stand against the nascent Third Republic, exercising his constitutional prerogative to dissolve the Chamber. When the republicans won a slim majority in the ensuing elections, fought around the religious and constitutional differences between president and parliament, strong presidentialism and monarchism lost their attraction: The presidents of the Third Republic never again dared to use their power to dissolve the Chamber, preferring instead to play the figurehead role in a resolutely parliamentarian regime.

The republicans' relative electoral success first in the by-elections of 1871 and then in 1877 were not due to the monarchists' strategic blunders alone. Like the conservative republican Thiers, the "opportuniste" republican leaders, notably Léon Gambetta, understood the need to portray the republic as a socially conservative option. They also understood the importance of what would today be called "identity politics" for shaping interests and forging stable institutions. Gambetta in particular realized that the republicans could

win and sustain parliamentary majorities only if the peasantry, still the majority of the French population after a century of slow but steady industrialization, could not only trust the republic but identify with it as well. A powerful orator, Gambetta took the then-radical initiative of going out to campaign in the countryside to convince peasants that the republicans were not the dangerous *partageux* (literally "sharers") who had confiscated their goods during the most radical phases of the revolution. In the longer run, though, the peasants had to be liberated from the conservative clutches of the clergy and large landowners. The Third Republic's strategy for turning "peasants into Frenchmen" (to cite the title of a well-known study of the period), and more importantly Frenchmen loyal to the republican ideal of the nation, was primarily educational. The education minister Jules Ferry, in 1881–1882, thus introduced a trinity that is almost as sacred to French republicanism as the revolutionary motto "Liberté, Égalité, Fraternité," namely "l'enseignement gratuit, laïc et obligatoire" (free, secular, and mandatory education for all). To this day, the principle of **laïcité** (a commitment to secular, humanist education as a source of common political values and identity) remains the major legacy of the Third Republic and a lightning rod for French political debate (as witnessed in recent debates on the banning of "ostentatious" religious symbols such as headscarves in French public schools).

Uniform education across the country along with other nation-building policies such as universal male military conscription, imperialist expansion in Africa, and propaganda to recover the "lost" territories of Alsace and Lorraine succeeded in forging modern French national identity. From Celtic Brittany to Italian Nice, from French Flanders to the French Basque lands, French citizens did not even speak the same language or celebrate the same history until the Third Republic sent its *instituteurs* to every last village to stamp out obscurantism, local languages and dialects, and the power of priests. The republic's mission of *laïcité* of course rekindled the anger and opposition of devout Catholics to anything that smacked of the revolution. What is more, the positive project of *laïcité* often descended into knee-jerk anticlericalism, a church- and priest-bashing that helped conceal the diverging interests and opinions within the republican camp. Although a papal encyclical of 1891 allowed a certain reconciliation of practicing Catholics with the republican regime, the fundamental cleavage between clericalism and anticlericalism defined politics in the Third Republic right up until World War I (and beyond). The **Dreyfus affair** of the late 1890s dramatically illustrated this virulent dividing line within French political culture: Catholics, monarchists, and reactionaries blindly defended the army's false, anti-Semitic accusations of treason leveled against the Jewish officer Alfred Dreyfus while republicans, notably the novelist Émile Zola, fought many years to have Dreyfus's conviction to Devil's Island overturned, a conviction for which the French army only in 1995 offered a full apology!

While anticlericalism may have been the ideological decoy that distracted French republicans from their divergences, protectionism consolidated the regime's social basis. Legislated in 1892, the Méline tariffs provided protection to both industry and agriculture, thereby preserving many small-scale family firms and peasant farming. Thus, on the eve of the First World War, France's economy and population remained 56 percent rural and 40 percent agrarian, at a time when Britain and Germany had become overwhelmingly urban and industrial. This relative underdevelopment had a long-term silver lining for France: the survival well into the late twentieth century of vibrant small-town and country life preserved the local charms (and cheeses!) that make France the world's current number one tourist destination. At the beginning of the twentieth century, however, France's social, economic, and political stagnation generated fatalism and defeatism. Although the Third Republic could muster the resources and popular support to roll back slowly, with last-minute American help, the German invaders of 1914, the regime enjoyed only "obedience without love" in the words of the cynical republican philosopher Alain. While the Republic did produce some remarkable, popular, and democratic leaders such as Gambetta and Ferry, the socialist Jean Jaurès, and the victor of World War I, Georges Clemenceau, the rise and fall of governments at the rate of almost one per year and with little connection to the outcome of elections left the general public largely estranged from politics while significant minorities continued to yearn for the arrival of a Bonapartist strongman on horseback.

While France's "blocked society" (in Stanley Hoffmann's words) may have gotten the government it deserved, it would be a mistake to write off the Third Republic as a dead-end route to political and socioeconomic modernity. After all, the regime established universal manhood suffrage and guaranteed democratic citizenship rights not only before Germany but before Britain as well. For better and for worse, it built a colonial empire, and it survived and won a world war. After the war, it weathered the economic crises of the 1920s and 1930s that destroyed the fragile new democracies of Germany, Italy, Spain, and Eastern Europe, and even in the face of the Great Depression it succeeded in integrating the working classes into the political order.

From the *Front populaire* to the Vichy State

Indeed, since the bloody repression of the Paris Commune of 1871, the industrial working classes had been by and large excluded from political life in the Third Republic. Their political weakness was due not only to their defeat and decapitation in 1871 as in 1848 but to their structural fragmentation in an industrial economy characterized by a few heavy industrial firms (in the coal and steel sector of the northeast) and a plethora of small-scale, specialized, relatively high-skill industries. As elsewhere in continental Europe, various socialist movements and parties embracing revolutionary or electoral strategies sought to organize the working classes with growing success in the 1890s. In France, Karl Marx's son-in-law Jules Guesdes, for example, took a radical stance in opposition to Jean Jaurès's reformist collaboration with bourgeois democrats. In 1905, the socialist Left nonetheless succeeded in uniting within a single party, the SFIO (or the French Section of the Workers' International), forerunner to today's *Parti socialiste* (PS). This unity did not survive the 1920 party congress of Tours, at which the radical Left, loyal to Moscow's new Communist International, broke away to become the French Communist Party (PCF). In addition to this schism between communists and socialists, the working-class movement in France included another major, resolutely anti-electoral, current: anarcho-syndicalism. Inspired by the direct action of the *grandes journées* of the French Revolution, the anarcho-syndicalist movement in France cultivated the myth of the general strike as a heroic tool for bringing about immediate, radical, social change. This idea has taken deep root in the French labor movement. Divided and relatively disorganized outside of the public sector, French unions to this day do not function as collective bargaining agents but put on strikes seemingly at random but with maximum public disturbance in order to generate a "social climate" favorable to their interests.

To the credit of both the French Left and the Third Republic, France in the 1930s did not succumb to the temptation of fascism, at least not immediately. In February 1934, in a context of a political corruption scandal and growing economic hardship, French fascist leagues inspired by the successes of Hitler and Mussolini staged a violent march on the National Assembly building. In a dramatic last minute show of unity, due in part to the Communist International's change of strategy after Hitler's consolidation of power in Germany, the left-wing parties organized a counterdemonstration against the fascist threat and in defense of the republic. With the Left united and the Communists willing to support if not participate in a coalition between the SFIO and the parties of the Center-Left, a *Front populaire* ("Popular Front") government swept into power under the premiership of the socialist millionaire Léon Blum in the elections of 1936. With their first taste of power since 1871 and their aspirations high, the French working classes immediately launched a general strike, which the Blum government defused with the introduction of important, still-celebrated social reforms such as the 40-hour work week and paid vacations. To combat the financial crisis and kick-start the economy, the Popular Front also nationalized the Bank of France and the railroads. As usual under left-wing governments, the resistance of business interests and petty bourgeois anxiety over property rights put a break on reforms as the centrist Radicals withdrew their support for Blum and the far Left denounced his timidity. Meanwhile the Catholic bourgeoisie rallied to the fascist leagues' anti-Semitism, embracing the slogan "Sooner Hitler than Blum." As the centrists vacillated, toppling and rejoining Popular Front governments in response to internal and external crises, the Third Republic lost its will to survive even before the *Blitzkrieg* brought the reputedly world's-strongest army to its knees by June 1940. On July 11, the same Chamber that had brought Blum to power four years earlier abdicated full powers to the increasingly senile hero of World War I, Field Marshal Philippe Pétain. The collaborationist and rabidly anti-Semitic regime, based in the spa town of Vichy, took on the name of the "French State" and abandoned the republican slogan of "Liberté, Égalité, Fraternité" for the authoritarian motto "Famille, Travail, Patrie" (Family, Work, Fatherland).

Blame for France's darkest hour can be spread across the political spectrum. The Right was of course still rife with monarchism, Bonapartism, and authoritarian impulses, always ready to dismantle the republic. On the far Left, the Communists were beholden to Moscow and had withdrawn support for the Popular Front with the Hitler-Stalin pact of 1939 and would become heroes of the Resistance only after Hitler invaded the Soviet Union in 1941. The centrist and center-left defenders of democracy and republicanism were so concerned with preserving the petty bourgeois and peasant basis of the "blocked society" that they feared the social democratic reforms that Britain and even the United States embraced to weather the economic crises of the 1930s. Finally, even members of the resolutely democratic SFIO, such as the future socialist president **François Mitterrand**, were willing at least initially to work under the Vichy regime to preserve some semblance of French national autonomy. In June 1940, only an obscure if visionary general, **Charles de Gaulle**, speaking by radio from London, called on the "Free French" to fight on against the Nazis. After the Second World War, almost everyone in France claimed to have heard de Gaulle's speech and to have supported the Resistance, but the truth is that most went about their business as usual and many went beyond the call of "duty" to the Nazis, denouncing Jewish neighbors and participating in their deportation to death camps. Only in the 1980s and 1990s did the French begin seriously to confront their collaborationist past, the case of Maurice Papon being particularly illustrative of the complexity, complicity, and cover-ups characterizing collaboration and resistance. Officially recognized "resistant," close political ally of de Gaulle, commander in the Legion of Honor, center-right parliamentarian and member of the government, Papon was first accused in 1981 of participating in the deportation of Bordeaux Jews. He came to trial and conviction only in 1997, and even at his death in 2007, Papon caused controversy in the French presidential campaign, when his family and lawyer insisted he be buried with his revoked cross of the Legion of Honor.

From Liberation to the Brink of Civil War

The myths of Resistance and Liberation in 1944 by de Gaulle's Free French forces alongside the Anglo-American Allies of course had foundational qualities for postwar French national identity. France could claim the status of a victorious power and blame initial defeat and the Vichy interlude on the institutional defects of the Third Republic. Thus, when de Gaulle's provisional republican government called elections in October 1945, 96 percent of the voters, who for the first time included all adult women, chose, in a referendum parallel to the parliamentary vote, to make the new assembly constituent. Virtually no one wanted a return to the institutions of the Third Republic, and the centrist republican Radicals, who had carried the former republic and around whom power had always pivoted, were practically eliminated from France's partisan landscape. With 26 percent of the vote, the Communists (PCF), pumped up by their leadership role in the Resistance and by the Red Army's victory over Nazi Germany, were the big winners, but they were closely followed by the SFIO, whose democratic credentials were relatively untarnished by Vichy, and by the new but short-lived center-left Christian democratic *Mouvement républicain populaire* (MRP). Representing three-quarters of the electorate, these parties formed a grand coalition labeled "tripartism" under the nonpartisan leadership of General de Gaulle, as they had already in the provisional government. Almost immediately, however, de Gaulle resigned the premiership, his personal presidentialist, if not neo-Bonapartist ambitions conflicting with the partisan parliamentarians of the tripartist government. The three governing parties were divided among themselves on constitutional questions, with the PCF favoring a unicameral parliamentary regime and the socialists and the MRP preferring various bicameral or presidential checks on parliament precisely in order to prevent the Communists from taking advantage of their power as largest party. The PCF prevailed in the constitutional negotiations, but in the subsequent referendum of May 1946, a narrow majority of voters, more on anticommunist than constitutional grounds, rejected the new republic's proposed foundational laws. Ensuing elections for a new constituent assembly reproduced the tripartist majority, though now with the MRP narrowly as leading party, and constitutional haggling continued. De Gaulle briefly returned from his first of three political "retirements" to plead in favor of a presidential regime and to encourage voters to reject the tripartists' new proposal of a bicameral parliamentary regime in which they promised to establish proportional representation. In the constitutional referendum of October 1946, only 36 percent of voters approved, 31 percent disapproved, and 31 percent abstained. Thus France again ingloriously gave birth to another republic, the Fourth.

Also called "la mal aimée" (the unloved), the Fourth Republic was in many senses a remake of the immobility and instability of the massively (96 percent) rejected Third, only worse. The regime did retain the office of the president of the republic, elected by the members of the National Assembly and the Council of the Republic (the upper chamber of Parliament, itself elected by a complex, partly indirect proportional system), and ultimately the president would put an end to the republic in a semi-constitutional coup d'état. During the Fourth Republic's short existence, however, power resolutely resided in the National Assembly, which made and broke councils of ministers with alarming regularity. One historian has calculated that the Fourth Republic suffered a ministerial crisis that threatened or toppled the government on average once every nine days of its $11\frac{1}{2}$-year existence. It is, however, all too easy and too common to dismiss the Fourth Republic as a failure from birth, as yet another aborted attempt to install a left-leaning if not revolutionary regime in a fundamentally conservative society, or as a proof that a highly democratic, proportionally representative parliamentary regime cannot govern a country as fractious as France.

The Fourth Republic, in fact, succeeded in radically modernizing France, though to be sure within the institutional framework of Jacobinism and *colbertisme* inherited from the past. The two new major institutions associated with the Fourth Republic were actually immediate responses to the postwar crisis of reconstruction, initiated even before the Republic's constitutional foundation. General de Gaulle's tripartist governments established the **École nationale d'administration** (**ENA**) to train civil servants untainted by Vichy before the first postwar elections and shortly thereafter created the *Commissariat general du Plan*, an indicative economic planning agency under the future architect of what would become the European Union, **Jean Monnet**, as first commissioner. The ENA quickly produced a technocratic elite, the so-called *énarques*, who to this day dominate not only public administration in France but the leadership of all political parties from the Center-Left to the Center-Right as well as much of the private business sector. The *énarques* embody the *colbertiste* tradition of coziness between state and economic interests, with the state assumed, in Jacobin fashion, to take the leading role as purveyor of the general will and the common good. Among the modernizing initiatives of the bureaucratic/technocratic Fourth Republic were the mechanization of agriculture, which spelled the beginning of the end of French peasant society; the introduction of a social security system including universal health care; and the massive development of publicly owned nuclear power stations.

Despite the French *dirigiste* (state-interventionist) tradition, it would be a mistake to overemphasize the specificity of state planning of the economy in France. The more liberal British state had introduced it to combat the Depression, and massive state intervention proved necessary everywhere to reconstruct war-ravaged Europe. The United States' introduction of the Marshall Plan in 1947 helped not only to fund European economic recovery, to subsidize American exports, and to combat Soviet/communist influence, but also to encourage economic planning and international cooperation. Paradoxically, the experience of wartime economic integration, albeit under Nazi hegemony, had also strengthened the idea that Europe's economic and political salvation might lie in collaboration rather than competition between nations, especially the dominant powers, France and Germany. Thus in 1950, Jean Monnet convinced French Foreign Minister Robert Schuman to present to German Chancellor Konrad Adenauer a plan, which in 1951 led to the creation of the European Coal and Steel Community, the first formal institutional forerunner of today's European Union. By the end of the Fourth Republic, French politicians, diplomats, and bureaucrats had lain much of the groundwork for the Treaty of Rome, founding the European Economic Community on March 25, 1957.

While France was thus moving toward European integration, its colonial empire was disintegrating. Following military defeat at Diên Biên Phu in 1954, the Fourth Republic abandoned French Indochina and in 1956 granted independence to Tunisia and Morocco, thus laying the groundwork for the dismantling of its remaining African empire in the early 1960s. The political instability of the Fourth Republic, however, prevented it from weathering the most sensitive case of decolonization, namely that of Algeria, considered an integral part of the republic by over a million European settlers since French conquest in 1830. When a National Liberation Front began an armed struggle to assert the sovereignty of the disenfranchised indigenous majority, a civil war erupted and almost engulfed metropolitan France. The ensuing struggle, which in many respects presaged the tragedy of America's contemporary intervention in Iraq, would merit lengthy excursuses on terrorism, counterterrorism, and civilian-military relations, but for the purposes of a synopsis of French political development, it will have to suffice to suggest that a politically divided parliamentary republic confronted by an army whose republican loyalties were hardly guaranteed and by a retired, popular, heroic general who had been campaigning against the republic's constitutional order since its inception had little chance to survive the threat of civil war. When French settlers rioted in Algiers on May 13, 1958, with the connivance of parts of the army and of leading supporters of General de Gaulle, the last government of the Fourth Republic fell. To avoid threatened violence and army-supported insurrection in France proper, the president of the republic asked de Gaulle, who had announced that he was willing to take control without specifying whether he meant constitutionally or not, to form a government. To the credit of de Gaulle's democratic credentials, he scrupulously respected legal procedure and obtained a parliamentary majority for his nonpartisan government on June 1. The following day Parliament honored his request to confer constituent powers to the government, thereby bringing a formal end to France's Fourth Republic. In a referendum held on September 28, 1958, the French electorate approved a new constitution tailored to de Gaulle's principles and ambitions.

France's Fifth Republic: A Stable Democratic Institutional Order?

Half a century later, France's Fifth Republic has today apparently withstood the test of time, but its implantation and consolidation depended on the personal authority and Machiavellian genius of its founder. Once elected to the presidency by a college of parliamentarians and local officials, de Gaulle had to quell the crisis that had brought him to power in the first place: the Algerian war and army insurrection. Again to de Gaulle's credit as a democrat and a republican, he recognized the untenability of French Algeria and did not hesitate to betray those in the army and the die-hard French Algerians who had precipitated his return to power. De Gaulle's "betrayal" provoked terrorist attacks and his attempted assassination, but ultimately he had read French opinion right. With 400,000 French troops unable to secure order in Algeria, de Gaulle negotiated the Évian agreements of 1962, which granted Algeria independence after more than 90 percent of French voters approved them in a referendum. Exercising a form of authority reminiscent of the plebiscitarian Bonapartist Second Empire, de Gaulle understood that his ability to exercise power in the Fifth Republic depended on his demonstration of popular approval. Thus, in a second 1962 referendum, which he called unilaterally, provoking constitutional protest, he asked the French electorate to approve the direct, universal-suffrage election of the president for the traditional seven-year term. The socialist leader François Mitterrand denounced de Gaulle's populist, Bonapartist practices as a "permanent coup d'état," but his opposition to the emergent constitutional order did not keep Mitterrand from running for the presidency in the first direct election of 1965. Paradoxically, Mitterrand's strong showing – he forced de Gaulle into a second, run-off round – helped to consolidate the regime's democratic character: As the winner of a closely contested election, de Gaulle was brought down from the mythical level of charismatic hero to the mundane level of the ordinary politician.

With the popular election of the president, the Fifth Republic became a hybrid presidential–parliamentary regime form, unique in French history and among other western democracies. As in the American presidential system, the president of the Fifth Republic is head of state and assumes effective responsibility for the executive branch of government, but he also designates a head of government, the prime minister and, upon the latter's recommendation, appoints the remaining cabinet ministers. The president chairs the council of ministers and exercises considerable influence over its agenda. Unlike in the American system, but as in the British parliamentary regime, the government, that is, the prime minister and council, are subject to the confidence of the lower chamber of the legislative branch, the National Assembly. The president must therefore appoint a prime minister and a government from the party or, given the fragmentation of the French party system, the coalition of parties that holds the majority of the 577 seats in the National Assembly. Until 1986, the president was always able to appoint a government drawn from the same family of parties that had brought him to power, but when the left-wing alliance that had finally brought François Mitterrand to the presidency in 1981 lost its majority in the legislative elections of 1986, Mitterrand had to appoint the Gaullist leader Jacques Chirac to the premiership, introducing what the French call **cohabitation**. Contrary to expectations of constitutional gridlock and crisis, the first experience of cohabitation proved the institutional resilience of the Fifth Republic. Mitterrand refused to become a figurehead, preserved his prerogatives and initiative in the "high politics" areas of defence and foreign policy, and exercised a certain moderating influence on the right-wing government without blocking its policy orientations. Since then, both left- and right-wing presidents have well survived cohabitations, and the French electorate seems to have acquired a taste for the centrist consensus that the unusual constitutional arrangement favors.

The relative weakness of parliament vis-à-vis both the president and the government might explain the success of cohabitation. The president can dissolve the National Assembly, but usually does so only immediately after entering office in order to obtain a favorable majority. In addition to enjoying considerable latitude to govern by issuing rules and regulations by executive order, the prime minister and the government can force legislation through Parliament by declaring it an issue of confidence that can be overturned only if the opposition can cobble together a majority to censure and topple the government. Designed to combat the governmental instability of the Fourth Republic, the powers of the Assembly are restricted to approval of the budget and the elaboration of legislative texts, of which fewer than 20 percent emanate from private members (as opposed to the government). Divided into only six, unwieldy permanent committees, the 577 deputies of the National Assembly can exercise little oversight or investigative power over the government. As for the upper chamber, the 321-seat Senate, a third of whose members are renewed every three years by an electoral college of deputies and local elected officials, it "enjoys" the same powers as the Assembly, except that of censuring the government. Given its more conservative composition and being out of synch with other electoral cycles, the Senate theoretically can have a moderating influence on legislation, but being elected to the Senate is more of a sinecure than a legislative responsibility. Since 1974, however, members of parliament, and of the opposition in particular, have at least acquired the ability to contest the constitutionality of legislation: 60 senators or 60 deputies, as well as the president of the republic and of each chamber, can demand a judicial review of legislation, decrees, and treaties by the nine-member Constitutional Council. Also responsible for settling contested election results, the Constitutional Council, on the basis of one of its own decisions in 1971, has become the self-proclaimed guardian of fundamental civil rights and republican principles.

A certain consolation for the relative powerlessness of the members of parliament is the fact that virtually all of them occupy other political positions at the local and regional levels. Most famously, Jacques Chirac, for example, when he was not prime minister or president, was simultaneously deputy for a rural part of central France and mayor of Paris! Known – and denounced – as the *cumul des mandats* (the accumulation of offices), this practice allows politicians, particularly those in the opposition, to develop a powerbase, to gain administrative experience, and to forge a public profile. Since decentralization legislation in 1982 introduced a new level of regional government that organizes metropolitan France's 36,000 *communes* (municipalities) and 96 *départements* into 22 regions, most with prerevolutionary historical roots, the presidency of a regional council has become a new political springboard. For example, Ségolène Royal, the socialist candidate for the presidency of the republic in 2007, could campaign on, among other things, her experience in education, economic development, and transport as president of the Poitou-Charentes region. Since decentralization has largely freed the *départements* from the powerful tutelage of the central government's prefects (the postrevolutionary successors to the absolutist *intendants*), the presidencies of departmental general councils, like the position of mayor in a larger city, also provide meaningful outlets for ambitious parliamentarians. Finally, the proof that municipal offices offer tangible power and other benefits (as well as encouraging ground-level political recruitment) lies in the fact that France's countless *communes* jealously guard their autonomy, refusing attempts at consolidation into more rational administrative units: Villages and hamlets with a few dozen residents may have long lost their primary school but still insist on electing a mayor and council and on maintaining a community hall.

This plethora of local public office holders has a no-doubt unintentional institutional feedback effect on France's presidency and party system: Since a candidate need gather only 500 signatures from among these numerous and often cantankerous or nonpartisan office holders in order to appear on the national ballot for the first round of the presidential election, French electors have found themselves with a choice of up to 16 candidates in the first round of presidential voting, with candidates representing the interests of everyone from hunting and fishing sportsmen to the most radical spokespersons of the Marxist-Leninist fringe. This embarrassment of choice contributed, as we shall shortly see, to the electoral fiasco of 2002, but more generally it has reinforced both the fragmentation and the polarization of the French political party system within a constitutional order where, as in the United States, the primacy of the presidency has a structuring effect on all other electoral contests. No presidential candidate, not even the Fifth Republic's founder de Gaulle, has been able to win a majority of votes in the first round of elections, and only a handful of deputies well entrenched in their districts ever enter the National Assembly after only one round (with the exception of the 1986 elections held with proportional representation). After the free-for-all of the first round, only the top two contenders face one another in the second, decisive ballot one month later. This sequence allows a multiplicity of parties to test their luck or to act as spoilers but then forces an alignment or coalescence around two candidates, usually but not always one from the left and one from the right of the ideological spectrum.

The particular case of the Fifth Republic fuels the general debate among institutionalist analysts of party systems as to whether electoral rules cause or, alternatively, reflect the relative fragmentation of party systems. As under the Third Republic, the two-round majoritarian electoral system has, under the Fifth Republic, tended to produce a relatively stable left–right cleavage in electoral politics while fostering recurrent divisions and fusions within the partisan camps of the Left and the Right. In light of France's fractious political and social history, it is not clear, however, whether this polarized fragmentation results from the strategic logic of partisan competition or from deep-seated sociological cleavages in interests and political identities. On the Right, political parties under the Fifth Republic have continued to be either loose electoral coalitions around powerful personalities or ideological nuances such as those that caused *orléanistes* and *légitimistes* as well as monarchists and conservative republicans to converge or diverge in the nineteenth century or, in the case of the different organizational manifestations of the Gaullist movement, to be mass-based fronts uniting the disparate interests of bourgeois nationalists, peasants, and populist petty bourgeois and working-class elements as under Bonapartism. On the Left, the parties have tended to be sociologically and organizationally anchored in the interests of civil servants, schoolteachers, and unionized workers but continue to be ideologically fractured. Perhaps the most significant political development under the Fifth Republic, however, has been the decline if not disappearance of the PCF, with a drop in Communist support from a solid 20 percent in the 1960s to well below 10 percent today. This erosion of the PCF has followed not only from the relative socioeconomic decline of the industrial sector and the ensuing further disorganization of the working class (union membership has dropped to less than 10 percent of the French labor force) and from the discredit and collapse of Soviet communism but also from the effective strategic maneuvering of the *Parti socialiste* (PS). Founded under the leadership of François Mitterrand in 1971, after the divisions between the old SFIO and other leftist and center-left parties of different ideological persuasion had allowed two right-wing candidates to face each other in the second round of the 1969 presidential election, the PS succeeded in luring the PCF first into a common platform and electoral alliance and then, from 1981 to 1984, into government, thus sapping the PCF of its revolutionary raison d'être.

The electoral success of the united Left in 1981 marked, as we shall shortly see, the most important political, social, and economic challenge that the Fifth Republic has faced to date. Designed by and for a right-wing leader, the Fifth Republic, like the Third up until the Popular Front election of 1936, had largely rested on the exclusion of the working classes and the Left. Unlike the conservative caretakers of the "blocked society" of the Third Republic, however, de Gaulle was a modernizer who did not hesitate to use the statist levers inherited from the Fourth Republic and the *colbertiste* tradition vigorously to pursue economic development, notably around "national champion" firms, both private and public. Indeed, during the "trente glorieuses," that is, the 30 glorious years following the Liberation, France enjoyed the highest economic growth rates in Western Europe at over 5 percent per year. Relative undervaluation of the French franc, high investment rates thanks to state participation in the industrial and financial sectors, inflationary policies to diminish debts and deficits, and low wages due to the feeble organization of labor all contributed to French competitiveness and high growth rates, but economic inequality also increased with growth. De Gaulle was of course not indifferent to working-class interests: His government initiated the construction of low-cost high-rise housing estates in France's suburbs, a policy that has come to haunt France in recent years. Substituting national pride for social solidarity, de Gaulle's foreign policies defended "une certaine idée de la France" from what he railed against as Anglo-American hegemony. In addition to withdrawing from NATO's American-led command structure and denouncing U.S. domination of the international financial system (the Bretton Woods fixed exchange rate system that allowed the United States to accumulate deficits at no expense), de Gaulle twice vetoed Britain's entry into the European common market. Although he pushed European integration as a means to France's historic reconciliation with Germany, de Gaulle jealously guarded French sovereignty within the European Economic Community and steered its policies in France's favor, notably the Common Agricultural Policy, which to this day disproportionately subsidizes French farmers.

De Gaulle's heavy-handed policies antagonized intellectuals as well as workers. In 1968, traditional May Day demonstrations sparked an anti-authoritarian and what has come to be called "postmaterialist" student protest movement in Paris, which in turn encouraged spontaneous strikes in firms around the country. At the height of the unrest, in a climate echoing past revolutions, army trucks had to transport essential goods, and President de Gaulle mysteriously disappeared for several hours (he had flown to Germany by helicopter to consult a general to assure himself of army backing). De Gaulle knew, however, that he could count on the conservatism of the provinces once again to quell the revolutionary élan concentrated in the capital. He dissolved the National Assembly and organized counterdemonstrations, while the Prime Minister, Georges Pompidou, charged a young secretary of state, Jacques Chirac, to negotiate generous concessions to the labor unions: a 35 percent increase in the minimum wage and a 10 percent raise for the rest, albeit gains that were quickly wiped out by inflation. The Gaullists won a clear majority in the ensuing June elections, but feeling the need to renew his own mandate, de Gaulle called a referendum on decentralization in April 1969. When his proposal narrowly failed to pass, de Gaulle, as promised, resigned, and died the following year. The proof that May 1968 and its aftermath had not really constituted a serious left-wing challenge to the Gaullist Fifth Republic, however, came with the election of de Gaulle's successor: His prime minister, Pompidou, rode easily into office over a divided Left and another lackluster conservative candidate in the second round.

France without de Gaulle: Democratic Consolidation or Lack of Leadership?

With President Pompidou's death in April 1974, the Fifth Republic faced new challenges as the Left was now united behind François Mitterrand, the Right was divided with no clear Gaullist successor, and the theretofore booming economy suddenly faced the stagnation and inflation ("stagflation") of the first oil crisis. Pompidou's easy election in 1969 had postponed the Right's reckoning with a future without de Gaulle. The minister of finance and economy under both de Gaulle and Pompidou, Valéry Giscard d'Estaing, nonetheless succeeded in profiling himself as a critic and a more centrist, liberal alternative to Gaullist nationalism and dirigisme. He owed his narrow victory over Mitterrand in the second round of the 1974 presidential election, however, to the backing of Jacques Chirac, who had positioned himself as heir to the Gaullist nationalist and populist mantle. Giscard appointed Chirac to the premiership, but their alliance was uneasy as Chirac, in 1976, reshaped the Gaullist movement into a powerful electoral machine for himself, the

Rassemblement pour la République (RPR). Giscard in turn created a federation of independent center-right parties in 1978, the *Union pour la démocratie française* (UDF), to back his aspirations for reelection. Given this re-creation of the Right's traditional divisions and the fact that the economy was mired in **la crise** (the somewhat oxymoronic term the French have come, over the past three decades, to use to describe the enduring situation of relative decline that followed the exceptional boom of the "trente glorieuses"), the only surprise of the 1981 presidential election should have been that Giscard even came close to holding onto power.

In conservative France, however, François Mitterrand's victory in May 1981 and the united Left's convincing victory in the following month's National Assembly elections came as a political earthquake. In polemical exaggeration of the PCF's minor ministerial role in the government of Pierre Mauroy, the right-wing press railed against the "socialo-communist" regime while rumors circulated that the army would not tolerate a left-wing government. Meanwhile, on the Left, utopian expectations of a revolutionary transformation of daily life were rife for disappointment. Although the new government did nationalize the "commanding heights" of the economy, notably the banking sector, where the state had been heavily involved since 1945, Mitterrand and Mauroy's strategy for pulling France out of *la crise* was classic Keynesian re-inflation of the economy through increased consumer spending and state investment by way of wage increases and budget deficits. Described later as "Keynesianism in one country" (in allusion to Stalin's strategy of "socialism in one country"), the Socialist-led government's economic policy exposed France's integration into the European and global economies. Indeed, France's reflationary policies ran counter to the neoliberal monetarist policies adopted at the time not only in Thatcher's Britain and Reagan's America but also, albeit less dogmatically, in France's largest trade partner, traditionally inflation-shy Germany. As prices and budget and trade deficits rose, the value of the franc collapsed, forcing three major devaluations in two years. As early as March 1983, the Mauroy government had to reverse policies, tying the franc to the deflationary strong deutsche mark policies of the German Bundesbank. Mitterrand appointed a new government under Laurent Fabius in 1984 with PCF support but no ministerial participation. Although the economy stabilized and the government changed the electoral law to a system of proportional representation to save as many seats in the National Assembly as possible, the 1986 elections gave the Right a solid majority, leaving the socialist president no choice but to appoint the Gaullist leader Jacques Chirac to the premiership of a government that not only continued monetarist policies but reversed the strategic nationalizations of 1981.

Despite the disappointments and reversals of Mitterrand's first *septennat* (seven-year term), his presidency proved the resilience of the institutions of the Fifth Republic and their adaptability to the conflicting interests and identities of the French Left and Right. Initially critical of the "permanent coup d'état" of the presidential republic, Mitterrand must be credited for his careful, strategic defense of institutional continuity in a context first of radical policy initiatives in 1981–1983 and then of policy reversals. He demonstrated that *alternance* was possible under the Fifth Republic, that is, not only that the Left of revolutionary tradition could come to power without changing the regime form but also that the Right could overturn the Left by peaceful means, and that the Left and Right could cohabit within the two-headed executive. In short, competitive democracy had finally become banal in France two centuries after the French Revolution! Thanks to his mastery and defense of the democratic institutions of the republic, Mitterrand did not become a lame duck after his party's defeat in 1986. Instead, he devoted himself to the cause of European integration, committing France to the Single European Act of 1987 and then negotiating economic and monetary union in what would become the **Maastricht treaty** of 1992, establishing the European Union and initiating the move to a single European currency, the euro. Both dignified and avuncular (his nickname in the popular press was "Tonton," the familiar diminutive for uncle), Mitterrand profited from the Right's habitual clash of personalities and from its propensity for questionable business dealings, and presented himself as the centrist, unifying embodiment of the nation to handily win the 1988 presidential election over "his" prime minister, Jacques Chirac. Consistent with their reendorsement of Mitterrand, who had promptly dissolved the National Assembly, French voters returned a Socialist majority under the premiership of Mitterrand's intrapartisan rival Michel Rocard.

The end of the first cohabitation did not, however, mark a return to the status quo ante of Fifth Republic politics, for the presidential election of 1988 also brought the electoral breakthrough of Jean-Marie Le Pen, leader of the extreme right *Front national* (FN). Thanks to the proportional representation of the 1986 National Assembly elections, Le Pen and 34 other FN members had acceded to Parliament, gaining more visibility for their xenophobic, anti-immigration, and anti-European platform. Le Pen had actually won a seat with the right-wing populist Poujadist movement exactly 30 years earlier as the youngest deputy of the Fourth Republic. He quit his seat, however, to fight as a volunteer in French Algeria, later admitting to have tortured "terrorists." In 1974, his presidential bid as leader of the recently founded FN garnered only 0.75 percent of the vote, and in 1981 he failed to secure the 500 signatures necessary to appear on the ballot. But in the context of *la crise*, growing political disenchantment, and the collapse of the PCF as an outlet for antisystem protest during the early 1980s, the *Front national* became a lightning rod for dissatisfaction, gaining seats and publicity in municipal elections in 1983 and then tying the PCF with 6 percent of the vote in the 1986 National Assembly vote. Two years later, the full measure of racist, reactionary, populist and/or simply enraged opinion among French electors – ironically often in rural areas with little or no experience with immigration – became clear when Le Pen received over 14 percent of the vote in the first round of the presidential election. Despite (or perhaps because of?) countless court convictions for hateful inflammatory speech, Holocaust denial, and defamation, Le Pen has remained a fixture and an embarrassment on the French political landscape, his consistent support among a significant minority of voters always calling into question the strength of France's liberal democratic and republican values.

Le Pen and the FN owe a good part of their success, of course, to the failings of the democratic Left and Right, in particular to their inability, within a context of European integration and global competition, to defend numerous interests within French society and to articulate a convincing image of France's identity and place in the world. *La crise* has prevented France from growing its way out of problems of inequality and social exclusion. Instead, a *fracture sociale* widened as those, often but not exclusively in the civil service and public sector, with protected, well-paid jobs and generous social security benefits resisted – rightly or wrongly – any reforms aimed at greater flexibility and efficiency as neoliberal ploys of Anglo-Saxon inspiration; others, typically the young, women, and immigrants, had to make do with low-wage, low-benefit, short-term contract jobs or join the ranks of the unemployed (about 10 percent of the working population for the past 20 years). France's relative economic and political decline pushed Mitterrand and his successors to pursue European integration as a means for disciplining and redressing the economy as well as for giving France a stronger voice within a larger political community, but this strategy also left the French with a keen sense of lost sovereignty and diminished national pride as France found itself increasingly a smaller fish in the bigger pond of an expanding European Union.

Thus, Mitterrand's second term and both terms of his successor Jacques Chirac came under the shadow of decadence. Although the government of Prime Minister Michel Rocard, between 1988 and 1991, succeeded with the help of four UDF ministers in forging a centrist consensus on social welfare reform and in making a dent in unemployment, Rocard's personal animosity toward Mitterrand finally ended with his forced resignation. Mitterrand appointed France's first female prime minister, Édith Cresson, but her scandal-plagued administration lasted less than a year, as did that of her successor, Pierre Bérégovoy. Indeed, at the time, it seemed that Mitterrand was more concerned with the completion of monuments to his "reign" such as the new National Library that bears his name. In a referendum held on

September 1992, Mitterrand did still manage to convince French voters to approve the Maastricht treaty on European union and, by extension, in de Gaulle's tradition, to renew their support for the president – but only by the narrowest of margins. A few months later, the legislative elections of 1993 disavowed the socialist government, giving a landslide majority of 472 out of 577 seats to the RPR and the UDF. Since Jacques Chirac refused to assume the premiership again in cohabitation with Mitterrand, his former finance minister, Edouard Balladur, took on the job and, to Chirac's chagrin, became highly popular and a leading contender for the 1995 presidential election. Ever the clever campaigner, however, Chirac positioned himself as an "outsider" and to the left of Balladur, promising to heal the *fracture sociale*. (The "Balladurians" were subsequently marginalized in Chirac's first administration, a fact which explained some of the animosity between Chirac and his party's candidate to succeed him in 2007, Nicolas Sarkozy.)

In principle, Chirac should have enjoyed smooth sailing at the start of his term. His prime minister, Alain Juppé, had a huge majority in Parliament, and he himself a fresh mandate to take on *la crise*. But France was also committed to meeting the financial and budgetary criteria set by the European Union for the introduction of the single currency, so when Juppé introduced budget-tightening measures in the autumn of 1995, a wave of strikes and demonstrations reminiscent of May 1968 brought France to a standstill by mid-December. Despite the disruption, the strikes enjoyed widespread popular support and sowed the seeds for a renaissance of the French Left in the libertarian, anarcho-syndicalist tradition. The strikes generated a new form of social and political activism outside the partisan arena, with local action being tied to a critical discourse on globalization and the neoliberal orientation of the world economy. Among the "children" of 1995 is the group ATTAC, founded in France with chapters around the world pursuing an alternative globalization or "altermondialisation." The best-known activist from this movement is José Bové, peasant leader, scourge of McDonald's and Monsanto, and 2007 presidential candidate. Although at opposite ends of the ideological spectrum, Bové and Jean-Marie Le Pen are both prototypically French in their violent, romantic contesting of order even if the former's historical roots are agrarian and anarchist and the latter's are monarchist and populist-authoritarian. For better or for worse, Bové and Le Pen are a reminder that France's Fifth Republic still exists against the backdrop of a dialectic of revolution and reaction.

With his government's reform efforts stalled in the face of popular opposition, President Chirac took the risk of dissolving the National Assembly with a huge center-right majority a year before its term expired. His move backfired horribly and from 1997 to 2002 he was forced to cohabit with a socialist prime minister, Lionel Jospin, leading a comfortable left-wing majority of the

PS, the PCF, and, represented for the first time in France, the Green Party. Thanks to a favorable international economic climate, Jospin's government presided over a reduction in unemployment from 12.2 percent to 8.6 percent, but his concrete economic policies – the reduction of the work week to 35 hours, a new youth employment contract scheme, and his (partial) privatization of national standard-bearers such as France Telecom and Air France – raised controversy among his political allies as well as opponents. His introduction of civil unions for homosexual partners and the discovery of his Trotskyist activism in his youth, however, incensed conservative opinion. In September 2000, he convinced President Chirac to back a constitutional referendum to reduce the presidential term of office to five years in sync with the legislative period: Both men shared an interest in preventing future cohabitations – and in making their presidential candidacies more palatable to voters who might not be able to stomach the prospect of seven more years of either Chirac or Jospin. Almost 84 percent of voters approved the change, but barely 30 percent of electors bothered to vote, thereby signaling their lack of support to either the president or the prime minister. Nineteen months later, the fiasco of the 2002 presidential election proved the unpopularity of both men and, more importantly, called into question the entire political order of the Fifth Republic.

On April 21, 2002, the incumbent president faced the humiliation of receiving only 19.9 percent of votes in the first round of the election. Even worse, Jospin, who with 23.3 percent had outpolled Chirac in the first round of the 1995 election, won only 16.2 percent while, ironically, the Trotskyist fringe candidate Arlette Laguiller scored an astonishing fifth-place finish of 5.7 percent. Meanwhile, on the far Right, Jean-Marie Le Pen had improved his support from 15 percent in 1995 to almost 16.9 percent and beyond all expectations found himself in the second round, to be held two weeks later. The result sent shock waves through France as tens of thousands of left-wing voters took to the streets to "defend the Republic," but also in act of contrition. Explanations and excuses for the disaster abounded: A record number of voters (28.4 percent) had stayed away from the polls in the first round, many expecting a repeat of the Chirac–Jospin confrontation of 1995. For the same reason, numerous critical PS members and supporters had voted for "Arlette," the sympathetic self-educated bank clerk who had been on every presidential ballot since 1974. On the Right, the decision to make security a central campaign issue with veiled undertones of anti-immigrant, anti-Muslim racism had played to the advantage of the aging, contested FN leader, Le Pen, who after all represented the real thing. Virtually the entire political spectrum from the respectable Right to the far Left rallied around Chirac, who handily trounced Le Pen with 82.2 percent of the vote.

Chirac's victory was hardly one for liberal democracy, but he took it as an occasion to do that at which he excelled: constructing a new electoral machine. For the June legislative elections, his backers created the *Union pour la majorité présidentielle* (UMP), unifying the RPR with smaller center-right formations and most of the UDF (the rump organization remaining under François Bayrou, who was to make a remarkable comeback in the first round of the 2007 presidential election). Subsequently renamed *Union pour un mouvement populaire*, the UMP easily carried the National Assembly vote as the PS fought without a leader: Jospin had immediately resigned from office following the April 21 debacle. After five years of cohabitation, Chirac again enjoyed a majority tailored to his person, but his second term proved as fruitless as his first. He appointed a fairly obscure provincial politician, Jean-Pierre Raffarin, to be his entirely subordinate prime minister, and the latter initially enjoyed popularity due to his distance from the corrupt Parisian political elite. Indeed, Chirac's previous prime minister, the president of the UMP, and the Gaullist leader's heir apparent, Alain Juppé, had been under investigation for nepotistic abuse of office while working as Chirac's right-hand man while the latter was mayor of Paris. Convicted in 2004 and disqualified from public office until 2006, Juppé was symptomatic of the sleaze surrounding the Gaullist machine as investigators circled like vultures waiting for Chirac's presidential immunity from potential prosecution to end. In such a climate, Raffarin's timid reform efforts, including tax cuts for the rich, could hardly remain popular, especially as European Union convergence criteria required France, now fully integrated into the single-currency eurozone, to squeeze its budget deficit to under 3 percent of GDP.

With European integration and globalization taking the blame for France's laggard economic and budgetary performance in the discourses not only of the far Left and of the far Right but also of the president of the republic, Chirac and Raffarin seemed to be headed for political suicide. Then the president announced on the national holiday, July 14, 2004, that he would submit approval of the new European Union Constitution (drafted under the leadership of former president Giscard d'Estaing) to a referendum to be held the following May 29. A classic Gaullist/Bonapartist tactic to plebiscite his personal authority and to divide the opposition, Chirac's referendum initiative achieved the latter but royally failed to accomplish the former. Socialist voters were split down the middle, torn between their loyalties to the European ideals and their distrust of a complex constitutional text that seemed to place economic liberalism ahead of social solidarity. In the end, fear of competition from Eastern Europe and perhaps, a few years down the road, from Turkey pushed economically precarious middle- and working-class voters to bring the referendum to a 54.7 percent rejection. Unlike his hero de Gaulle, who had resigned 35 years earlier when his referendum failed, Chirac stayed in office and sacked his prime minister. Henceforth, however, he was a lame duck president, apparently primarily interested in frustrating the efforts of the interior minister and president of the UMP, Nicolas Sarkozy, to succeed him in 2007. He thus appointed to the premiership the foreign minister, Dominique de Villepin, who had acquired presidential stature with a remarkable speech at the United Nations in opposition to the Iraq war in early 2003. De Villepin's bubble quickly burst, though, when police brutality sparked rioting in the Parisian suburb of Clichy-sous-Bois on October 27, 2005. Over the next 18 days, violence spread to the depressed, low-cost housing estates that have become the ghettos for unemployed immigrants and minorities around all of France's major cities. De Villepin allegedly delayed declaring a state of emergency and stemming the violence in order to make Sarkozy, his rival, but also his interior minister, look bad. In fact the prolongation of the crisis merely played into the heavy-handed law-and-order discourse of Sarkozy, who, himself the son of a Hungarian immigrant, described the rioting children of immigrants as "rabble." Any remaining hope that de Villepin could displace Sarkozy as the Right's pretender to the presidency quickly disappeared a few months later when he tried to force a flexible hire-and-fire scheme for first-time employees through Parliament. After hundreds of thousands of students and trade unionists took to the streets and closed schools and universities for several weeks in a movement again reminiscent of May 1968, Chirac disavowed the controversial legislation and, in the process, his prime minister. His presidency was washed out.

Conclusion: French Interests, Institutions, and Identity in the Face of European Integration and Globalization

The French use an expression that they rarely need to complete. It starts, "*Plus ça change* [the more things change]," and everyone knows without saying that it ends, "*plus c'est la meme chose* [the more they stay the same]." It applies particularly well to French politics. The Fifth Republic has indeed demonstrated remarkable continuity over the course of its five-decade history and also with respect to a millennium of French history. These continuities are not just rhetorical or symbolic but sociologically profound as well. The Fifth Republic has, for example, had a tiresomely unchanging cast of characters: France's longest-serving president, François Mitterrand, began political service under Vichy, while Fourth-Republic *énarque* Jacques Chirac was minister, premier, president, or mayor of Paris for over forty years; and Jean-Marie Le Pen has been the star of the extreme Right for over fifty years. During the 2007 presidential election campaign, the leading candidates had to practice the highly personalized politics initiated by de Gaulle and slipped into character roles of the past: Sarkozy, the Mac-Mahon of the 2005 suburban riots, inherited Chirac's talent for machine politics and for co-opting electoral themes from the Left and the far Right, whereas Ségolène Royal, the PS candidate, was something of a female François Mitterrand, simultaneously defending leftist republican ideals and more conservative national pride. These recurrent character roles do not, however, simply reflect a lack of political imagination or the institutional difficulties of acquiring and maintaining power in the hybrid presidential-parliamentary regime and the fragmented, polarized party system reinforced by the two-round electoral system. They are also the product of deep-rooted conflicting interests in French society and of challenges to French identity in the context of a changing global order.

Ever since the prerevolutionary age of monarchical absolutism, material interests in France have been divided between economic actors dependent on the state (at the time: aristocrats, financiers, monopoly holders), those in new private commerce and industry (the burgeoning bourgeoisie), and those in local, subsistence activities (peasants, artisans). For reasons we have seen in this chapter, the monarchist, republican, or Bonapartist state in France has intervened to accelerate, to slow down, to direct, or to redistribute economic development in order to maintain internal social order or to face external competition. From an Anglo-American perspective, this prominent economic role of the French state is a developmental aberration, a brake on liberalism, on capitalism, and purportedly on democracy. While France has certainly suffered authoritarian interludes over the centuries since the 1789 revolution, their causes have had little to do with state constraints on economic competition and much to do with the virulence of political competition. Despite postwar planning and the strength of the PCF in the two decades following the Liberation, France has had a capitalist market economy ever since the revolution established the principles of private property and formal individual equality. But it is a variety of capitalism peculiar to France, just as Britain, the United States, Germany, Italy, and – today – China, among other societies, have their own historically grounded models of capitalism.

Political debate in and about France today centers largely on the virtues and vices of the "French model" of contemporary capitalism, though mostly on its purported vices. France has indeed been mired in *la crise* since the mid-1970s, and virtually every leader since then has dashed the electorate's hopes of recovery. France has of course previously experienced long periods of relative decline, the entire Third Republic, for example, and other countries have as well – once stellar Japan since 1990 and Britain throughout France's "trente glorieuses," for example. But it would be a mistake to overstate France's economic difficulties. French (and Franco-European multinational) firms, from Airbus to Alstom, from Dassault to Danone (Dannon), from Renault to Ricard, remain world leaders in their sectors; the country remains an export leader and ran a foreign trade surplus throughout the crisis years of the 1990s; and although British per capita gross domestic product (GDP) has nominally surpassed France in recent years, any visitor to the two countries will recognize that France's standard of living and infrastructure (transport, housing, health, commerce) remains superior. Still, France has some serious problems, particularly in the effectiveness of its large public sector. As historian Timothy Smith has neatly summarized, France has succeeded in matching Scandinavian levels of social spending while maintaining (not quite) American levels of socioeconomic inequality. France offers generous social services in health, education, and child care, yet clearly not enough to keep young people, immigrants, and women from merely scraping by. As even the best-intentioned politicians of the Fifth Republic have learned, they cannot provide more without straining French capital and competitiveness, nor provide less without provoking revolt among civil servants, students, and the underprivileged. Beyond the traditional quantitative interest in redistributable growth, France, too, has seen the rise of a new qualitative, or "postmaterialist," interest in sustainable, ecologically viable activity. This movement has, however, taken on a distinctively French form; for example, José Bové's anarcho-agrarian environmentalist activism in favor of small-scale, specialized organic farming (and not just in the traditional luxury, export sectors of wine and cheese) resonates well in a country that still had a significant peasant farm economy a generation ago.

Whether the relatively new generation of leaders to emerge from the 2007 elections can turn the stalemated institutional structure of the Fifth Republic into a tool for renewing the French model of capitalism to the satisfaction of competing socioeconomic and environmental interests remains to be seen. Their ability to do so will, however, largely depend on their ability to rearticulate and rally their compatriots around a coherent vision of France's place in the world. The notion that "la France éternelle" has long had a powerful, unified sense of identity is a myth, of course. In medieval times, the heroism of Jeanne d'Arc, appropriated as patron saint by the *Front national*, was more a symptom of divisions between the aristocracy and the crown than of a budding national consensus. The Third Estate, as we saw, proclaimed itself to embody the nation during the French Revolution, but nineteenth-century vacillations between popular empire, monarchisms, and republicanisms proved that France's universalist values and "mission civilisatrice" were a fig leaf for a fractured political community. The Third Republic educated peasants into Frenchmen and propounded the doctrine of France's "natural" hexagonal borders, the better to recover lost territories on the Rhine, while de Gaulle's defense of "une certaine idée de la France" from the Liberation through the founding years of the Fifth Republic was decidedly vague in its certitude. The point, of course, is that any society requires a foundational or aspirational myth to maintain a minimum of coherence. Since de Gaulle's departure and the end of the postwar boom, the Fifth Republic has been at the quest of such a myth. Presidents Giscard, Mitterrand, and Chirac all embraced the noble project of European integration as a myth of salvation, but the near miss of the 1992 Maastricht treaty referendum and the crash and burn of the European constitutional referendum of 2005 have proved that the European ideal has opened division, wounds, and fears as well as hopes that France might find its role within a larger, more powerful political community.

Indeed, the European strategy of opening borders contradicts the logic of identity construction that usually builds on distinction from the "other." The French republican tradition, however, has concealed this dynamic of exclusion that accompanies the inclusive definition of the political community. The principles of individual equality and universal human rights inherited from the revolution have enabled France, much like the republican United States, to integrate millions of immigrants, notably Italians and Poles beginning in the nineteenth century and Spaniards and Portuguese in the twentieth. But republican "political correctness," such as census taking that refuses to record the ethnic origins of citizens born in France, has also kept the French from confronting growingly obvious problems of integration and discrimination, notably for citizens and immigrants originating from former colonies in North and sub-Saharan Africa. The suburban ghetto riots of November 2005 testify to the failure of France's integration policies but also – paradoxically – to a certain strength of the republican tradition. Unlike in Britain, where significant parts of the immigrant community have gravitated toward Islamist extremism, the young rioters, predominantly of North African descent, wanted into the French community's jobs, elite schools, and political representation. Immigration, like European integration, has become figuratively and literally a political football in France, where a few months after the riots the entire political class (except for Jean-Marie Le Pen) both sincerely and cynically celebrated the nation's multiracial "Black-Blanc-Beur" World Cup soccer team ("beur" being the slang self-label of the descendants of North African immigrants) and its captain of Algerian heritage, Zinedine Zidane.

Perhaps trivial, President Chirac's invitation of the 2006 World Cup team to the Elysée Palace, after its narrow defeat in the final and Zidane's controversial head-butt and expulsion from the match, was emblematic of France's current predicaments. A show of republican unity designed to paper over the country's ethnic and socioeconomic tensions, Chirac's ceremony also sought to express, and politically to profit from, the nation's outpouring of sympathy for the team captain's wounded pride. Zidane at that moment embodied contemporary France: a has-been superstar with an uncertain future but a rich past to fall back on. In the United States, someone like Zidane would consider running for president. In France, *plus ça change* . . .

Things do change in France, of course. Political commentators, for example, heralded the 2007 presidential election as a breakthrough. The second round not only almost brought a woman to power for the first time but opposed two candidates who were toddlers at the founding of the Fifth Republic and who had made it to the top not by being party hacks but by the force of their personalities. The victor, with 53 percent of the record 84 percent turnout vote, Chirac's interior minister Nicolas Sarkozy, apparently owed success to his casting himself as an outsider who would break with Chirac and with France's past and who would liberalize France's economy within a hundred days of assuming office. The defeated Socialist candidate, Ségolène Royal, announced that she too would seek to modernize and renew the French Left by bringing it more into line with the market orientations of the British Labour Party or the German Social Democrats. This apparent liberalizing shift of the French party system seemed to signal an end to French exceptionalism. Indeed, already in the first round of voting, support for the PCF had sunk to an insignificant 2 percent while the aging Jean-Marie Le Pen's drop to only 10 percent suggested the beginning of the end of France's flirt with the far Right. Despite these changes, Sarkozy's victory also recalled recurrent patterns of French political life. The new president's outsider status, his Machiavellian raw ambition, and his authoritarian and populist outbursts have won him the label of a latter-day Bonaparte, while his evocations of the values of work, family, and country resonate with the traditional reactionary Right. Sarkozy's election rekindled rioting in the suburban immigrant ghettos, and when he left France the day after his election to holiday on a billionaire friend's yacht, he stirred outrage on the Left while recalling the age-old coziness between the business interests and right-wing regimes in France. A third consecutive presidential victory for the Right, Sarkozy's election also underscored the historical weakness of the Left in France. Despite dramatic breakthroughs in 1791, 1848, 1871, 1936, and 1981, left-wing politics have been more a revolutionary myth than a reality. France remains a profoundly conservative country, especially as the instinct of centrist forces within the left–right spectrum is to veer to the right in a crunch, as often happened in the Third and Fourth Republics. This tendency repeated itself in 2007 when centrist politics made a comeback in the form of UDF leader François Bayrou's 18 percent showing in the presidential election's first round. Although Bayrou adopted stances close to Royal's and made it clear that he did not support Sarkozy in the second round, the vast majority of UDF politicians and voters, when push came to shove, rallied around the UMP candidate. During his first months in office, Sarkozy certainly introduced a new style of presidentialist politics as he hyperactively intervened in the daily affairs of his government, relegating his prime minister to an entirely subordinate, administrative role and reinforcing his neo-Bonapartist image. Time alone will tell, however, whether Sarkozy's promised "rupture" with the politics of the past has truly marked a new beginning for French politics. For now, once again, *plus ça change. . . .*

BIBLIOGRAPHY

Agulhon, Maurice. *The French Republic, 1879–1992*. Oxford: Blackwell, 1995.

Anderson, Perry. *Lineages of the Absolutist State*. London: Verso, 1974.

Bell, David S. *François Mitterrand: A Political Biography*. Cambridge: Polity Press, 2005.

Bloch, Marc. *Strange Defeat*. New York: W. W. Norton, 1999.

Debray, Régis. *Charles De Gaulle: Futurist of the Nation*. Translated by John Howe. London: Verso, 1994.

Hoffmann, Stanley, et al. *In Search of France: The Economy, Society and Political System in the Twentieth Century*. New York: Harper Torchbooks, 1963.

Larkin, Maurice. *France since the Popular Front: Government and People, 1936–1996*. New York: Oxford University Press, 1997.

Lefebvre, Georges. *The Coming of the French Revolution*. Princeton, NJ: Princeton University Press, 1989.

Marx, Karl. *The Eighteenth Brumaire of Louis Bonaparte*. New York: International Publishers, 1963.

Mendras, Henri. *La seconde révolution française (1965–1984)*. Paris: Gallimard, 1994.

Moore, Barrington. *Social Origins of Dictatorship and Democracy*. Boston: Beacon Press, 1966

Paxton, Robert O. *Vichy France, 1940–1944*. New York: Columbia University Press, 2001.

Rousso, Henry. *The Vichy Syndrome: History and Memory in France since 1944*. Translated by Arthur Goldhammer. Cambridge, MA: Harvard University Press, 2006.

Skocpol, Theda. *States and Social Revolutions*. Cambridge: Cambridge University Press, 1979.

Smith, Timothy B. *France in Crisis: Welfare, Inequality and Globalization since 1980*. Cambridge: Cambridge University Press, 2004.

Strayer, Joseph R. *On the Medieval Origins of the Modern State*. Princeton, NJ: Princeton University Press, 1970.

Tocqueville, Alexis de. *The Old Regime and the French Revolution*. Tranlsated by Stuart Gilbert. New York: Anchor Books, 1983.

Todd, Emmanuel. *La nouvelle France*. Paris: Seuil, 1990.

Weber, Eugen. *Peasants into Frenchmen: The Modernization of Rural France, 1870–1914*. Stanford, CA: Stanford University Press, 1976.

TABLE 4.1. Key Phases in France's Political Development

Time period	Regime	Global context	Interests/ identities/ institutions	Developmental path
800–1589	feudal monarchy	competing claims to political and religious authority	Three Estates: nobility, clergy, commoners (peasants, townsmen)	territorial consolidation
1589–1715	absolutism	emergent international state system	bureaucratization, disempowerment of landed nobility	centralization of political authority, mercantilism
1715–1789	feudal reaction	growing international competition, emergent capitalism	polarization between landed aristocracy and commoners (Third Estate)	labor-repressive agricultural, authoritarian-ism
1789–1804	Revolution	war, intervention	heightened conflict, terror, ideology	preconditions for capitalism, liberal democracy
1804–1875	post-revolu-tionary instability	birth of contemporary state system, global capitalism	unresolved conflicts among classes, ideologies	liberalism, Bonapartism
1870–1940	Third Republic	imperialism, World Wars	repression and rebirth of working-class movements	conservative modernization
1940–1944	Vichy	occupation	collaboration, resistance, liberation	reactionary authoritarian-ism
1946–1958	Fourth Republic	economic cooperation/ integration	rise of technocratic elites	technocratic modernization
1958–1981	Fifth Republic (Gaullist)	Cold War, struggle for autonomy	prosperity vs. rise of "postmaterialist" interests	from neo-Bonapartism to neoliberalism
1981–2007	Fifth Republic (post-Gaullist)	deepening and widening of European integration	dualist split between protected and marginalized social strata	ongoing crisis of the French model of capitalism

IMPORTANT TERMS

absolutism historically linked to the emergence of the sovereign state, absolutism describes a form of rule in which a monarch claims, and more or less effectively exercises, a monopoly of political authority on a delimited territory. Absolutism centralizes political functions (justice, defense, taxation) previously fragmented and devolved to the aristocracy under feudalism but maintains the nobility's social and economic privileges.

alternance literally "alternation," this term describes a change of government between the right and left ends of the political spectrum. Under the Fifth Republic, the predominance of right-wing parties until 1981 made the question of *alternance* a test of the regime's democratic character and vialibility. Successive *alternances* and experiences of *cohabitation* since 1981 have proved the Gaullist constitution's success.

Napoleon Bonaparte born on the island of Corsica in 1769, Napoleon Bonaparte died in British captivity on the island of St. Helena in 1821. At the age of 26 he was already a general and hero of revolutionary army campaigns in Italy and Egypt. He took power in France through a coup d'état in 1799 before proclaiming himself emperor of the French in 1804. His expansionary foreign policy rallied the nation but ended in disaster in 1815.

Bonapartism derived from the periods of imperial rule of Napoleon I and his nephew Louis Bonaparte (Napoleon III), this term describes both an ideological current in French politics that favors the authoritative, even authoritarian, leadership of a charismatic politician and a socioeconomic development strategy whereby the state, under a powerful leader, assumes responsibility for modernization and industrialization.

cohabitation originally seen as a possible defect in the Fifth Republic's constitutional order, cohabitation describes the situation where the president must nominate a prime minister who does not hold the same partisan allegiances because the president does not command a majority in the lower house of parliament, the National Assembly. Since 1984, France has experienced three periods of cohabitation.

colbertisme initiated by and retrospectively named for Louis XIV's minister Jean-Baptiste Colbert (1619–1683), this economic doctrine was the French version of mercantilism. The label still applies generally to the prominent role of the French state in directing economic development.

la crise following three "glorious" decades of record economic growth since 1945 ("les trente glorieuses"), France has been bogged down in three decades of relative stagnation commonly called "la crise." Shorthand for a complex of phenomena ranging from high unemployment to poor integration of immigrants, the expression describes more a national mood of self-doubt than a concrete economic crisis, as France remains a world leader in many sectors.

Charles de Gaulle born in 1890, de Gaulle was wounded and taken German prisoner as an officer in World War I. He rose to the rank of general at the beginning of World War II, subsequently refusing to accept the Vichy government's capitulation and calling for resistance by radio from London. He led the provisional government upon Liberation in 1944 but opposed the parliamentary constitutional order of the nascent Fourth Republic. In 1958 he founded and became the first president of the Fifth Republic, resigning office in 1969, the year before his death.

Dreyfus affair the false accusation and condemnation for espionage of the Jewish officer Alfred Dreyfus in 1894 became a political crisis revealing the cleavages of the Third Republic and lasting until 1906 when the novelist Émile Zola publicly denounced the scandal in his celebrated newspaper article "J'accuse" in 1898.

École nationale d'administration one of France's elite "grandes écoles," the ENA was founded in 1945 to train administrators for government and business in the wake of collaboration and the Vichy government. Known as "énarques," its graduates are often denounced as a coterie of technocrats with undue power and influence. They practice "pantouflage," literally "house-slippering," that is, an all-too-comfortable moving back and forth between government and business.

feudalism this social order predominated in Europe for over a millennium from the fall of the Roman Empire until the French Revolution. Feudal society was divided into three orders: the nobility, the clergy, and the rest – or respectively those who fought, those who prayed, and those who worked. The third order, or estate, of commoners consisted overwhelmingly of peasants tied to the land and under obligation to their lords but also included townspeople (the "bourgeoisie") collectively exempt from many feudal obligations.

Jacobinisme derived from the radical revolutionary faction known as the Jacobins, this term describes the tendency toward the centralization of political authority and the ideological valorization of the state as the embodiment and articulator of the general will and collective well-being of society.

laïcité roughly translatable as secularism, this term in French political discourse describes the republican principle not only of separation of church and state but also of relegation of religion to the private sphere. The principle of *laïcité* has recently and controversially been invoked to justify the prohibition of "ostentatious" religious symbols (such as the Muslim headscarf) from public places such as schools.

Maastricht treaty signed in February 1992 in the Dutch city of Maastricht, this treaty founded the European Union and initiated the movement toward the single European currency, the euro. Submitted for approval by referendum in France in September 1992, the treaty sharply divided opinion, passing by a narrow margin of 51 percent.

François Mitterrand France's longest-serving president (1981–1995), Mitterrand won election only at his third candidacy and after having had a long political career under Vichy, the Fourth Republic, and the Fifth Republic. He succeeded in bringing the Left to power by refounding the Socialist Party in 1971 and making an electoral alliance with the Communist Party, ultimately undermining its postwar stranglehold on 20 percent of the electorate. Born in 1916, Mitterrand concealed and battled cancer, outliving his second term by one year until 1996.

Jean Monnet born in 1888, Monnet was one of the architects of the Allied victory in World War II, having convinced U.S. president Roosevelt to begin rearmament before the American entry into the war. His wartime planning skills qualified him to organize France's postwar reconstruction as planning commissioner. Recognizing the benefits of closer cooperation and integration for economic and political reconstruction, Monnet became the instigator of the European Economic Community and today's European Union. He died in 1979.

Alexis de Tocqueville born in 1805, this French nobleman became one of the most astute observers of *Democracy in America* and a brilliant historian of *The Old Regime and the Revolution* in France. A statesman as well as a literary giant, Tocqueville died in 1859 in self-imposed internal exile under the Second Empire before he could finish his history of the revolutionary period and aftermath.

STUDY QUESTIONS

1. How did international competition on the European continent shape France's early political development during feudalism and absolutism as distinct from that of England?

2. How did absolutism shape social classes and interests and how, in turn, did those interests exacerbate the tensions inherent in absolutist rule?

3. How did competing interests during the revolutionary period prevent the consolidation of stable political institutions?

4. What interests and institutions favored the emergence of representative democracy in nineteenth-century France? Which ones militated against it?

5. What were the competing conceptions of the French political community and identity in the postrevolutionary period?

6. To what degree and how did the Third Republic succeed in reconciling competing interests, identities, and institutional models?

7. Would the Third Republic have survived if Nazi Germany had not invaded in 1940?

8. Is it fair to describe the Fourth Republic as a failure?

9. Why did François Mitterrand denounce the institutions of the Fifth Republic as a "permanent coup d'état"?

10. Did the *alternance* of 1981 normalize French democracy?

11. What are the current challenges to the French political system? Which ones are new and which ones can be traced back through the millennial history of the country?

STOP AND COMPARE

EARLY DEVELOPERS: BRITAIN AND FRANCE

An important part of democracy is the role of parliaments. Much of Great Britain's history has been a constant refinement of the principle of representative parliamentary government. Through a long series of struggles and reforms, British parliamentary government emerged triumphant over the rule of kings and queens. In the course of these changes, the monarchy remained a symbol of national integration and historical continuity, but the real political power came to reside in the prime minister and his or her cabinet of ministers. Of course, even in Britain, parliamentary and cabinet government did not necessarily mean the same thing as democracy: The right to vote – the franchise – was only gradually extended to the lower classes and women, and the final reforms came about during the twentieth century.

Despite the important upheavals in British history, political scientists continue to view the British experience as one of successful gradualism, of a gradual extension of the freedoms of liberal democracy to ever-larger groups of people. In the creation of liberal democracy, the British were undoubtedly aided by the simultaneous and successful rise of a commercial and capitalist economy during the eighteenth and nineteenth centuries. This was the age of the Industrial Revolution. Although the transition to a new kind of economy was not easy, for the first time in history an economy generated large amounts of goods that could be consumed by a large number of people. To be sure, at first these goods were enjoyed only by the new "middle" classes, but over time the new lifestyle spread to the working class as well. Accompanying these changes in material living standards came changes in the way people thought about their place in the world. One's position and life chances were no longer set in stone from birth. Upward mobility was now a possibility for people who never would have thought such a world possible a mere century earlier. It was in this context that common people could begin to demand a political voice commensurate with their contribution to the public good. The argument was a powerful one, and gradually the old feudal/aristocratic oligarchy gave way to wider sections of society in search of political representation.

Of course, a further important feature of the British experience was the creation of a global empire between the seventeenth and the nineteenth centuries. Industrialization both contributed to and was assisted by the military, economic, and political conquest of large parts of Africa and Asia. The empire provided raw materials for manufacture, markets for export, a "playground" for military elites, and a source of national pride that made it easier for the British to try to universalize their particular experience. As other countries in Europe began to compete economically and militarily, however, and as locally subjected peoples from Ghana to India recognized the incongruity of British ideals of parliamentary democracy and law with continued imperial domination, the costs of empire began to rise. By the beginning of the twentieth century, Britain had clearly fallen from the imperial heights it had once occupied, and domestic discussion began to focus on issues of economic decline and how to extricate the country from costly imperial commitments. With Britain divested of its empire, its economy continued to decline throughout the twentieth century relative to other European countries, and much of contemporary British politics has concerned ways to reverse this decline. In Britain's (mostly) two-party system, both parties have proposed cures for what ails the economy, but neither has been able to offer recipes for regaining the national confidence (indeed, some say arrogance) that was once taken for granted.

Notwithstanding such troubles, the British experience continues to be the benchmark against which comparativists think about the developmental experience of other countries. The British (or what is sometimes called the Westminster) model of government became the standard against which other countries measure their own progress.

Britain's experience could not be duplicated, however. Even France, the country whose experience we pair with Britain's, initially developed in Britain's shadow and bridged early and late developmental paths. The logic of pairing France and Britain is, nevertheless, compelling. Like Britain, France's history is largely one of the people emerging victorious over kings. The difference is that, in France, the monarchy and the old feudal oligarchy were displaced not through a long series of conflicts and compromises but largely through a major revolution in 1789 in which the monarch was executed and the aristocracy hounded out of political life. Over the course of the next century, French political history was tumultuous, the political pendulum swinging back and forth between democratic development and periods of authoritarian or populist regimes. Despite these changes, what remained a constant in French political life was the notion that power ultimately resided with the people. Even such populist demagogues as Napoleon and, later, his nephew Louis Bonaparte (Louis-Napoleon) never managed to depart fully from the notion of popular sovereignty. Indeed, they could not, if only because postrevolutionary France depended on its people to serve in its armies and mobilize for war.

If the British political experience is one of subjugating monarchical power to representative institutions, the French democratic experience is one of regulating a strong centralized state through plebiscitary mandate. War was a staple of political life on the European continent and preparing for it an important part of what states did. The French state was no exception; in fact, it became a model for others to emulate (and eventually surpass). Even before the French Revolution, French monarchs and their states played an important part in encouraging economic development and collecting taxes for the purposes of military preparation. The revolution did little to change this and in many ways intensified the power of the French state. In fact, one way of thinking about the revolution is in terms of a rebellion against the taxing power of the French monarchy and its resurrection in the form of more or less democratically elected heads of state who, because of their popular mandate, had more power to draw on private resources for public goals than ever before. Given its pattern of development, it is perhaps not surprising for us to learn that after much experimentation with various forms of representative government in the latter part of the nineteenth century and first part of the twentieth, France has settled on a strong, popularly elected presidency with a five-year term of office.

This contrast between parliamentary rule in Britain and presidential rule in France has become a model one for political scientists. Such differences in democratic institutions have important long-term effects on politics and policies. Given the importance and centralized nature of the French state, it is natural that the state became highly involved in economic development during the twentieth century. French economic planning, a subtle and highly developed system of state guidelines and state-induced market incentives, has often been contrasted with the heavy-handed Soviet communist model, not merely in the differences in style but also because for a very long time the French model seemed to work so well. More recently, however, the impacts of European integration and increased global trade have brought the feasibility of the model under question and led to a debate in France on the future of French-style economic planning and whether it will have to adapt to the competing model of Anglo-American capitalism. Britain has also experienced a debate between Euroskeptics and Europhiles.

Finally, globalization has also meant that both Britain and France are now home to large numbers of people born in other countries. Right-wing sentiment against "foreigners" has emerged, and politicians have raised questions about national identity. Questions of identity are nothing new to Britain and France. British identity has always been contested – the Celtic periphery of Scots, Irish, and Welsh have frequently challenged the hegemony of the

STOP AND COMPARE

English. French identity has long been split between a Catholic and conservative France rooted in the rural peasantry and a secular and progressive
France rooted in the urban classes. Yet, for both Britain and France, the
presence of so many "non-Europeans" in their midst is something quite new.
How democracies, especially two of the oldest and most stable ones, manage
the tensions among multiculturalism, national unity, and democratic politics
is a topic that will capture the interest of comparativists for years to come.

PART TWO

MIDDLE
DEVELOPERS

GERMANY

0   50   100 miles
0   50   100km

DENMARK

North Sea

Baltic Sea

Kiel

Rostock

Lübeck

Hamburg

Emden   Bremerhaven

Bremen   Elbe R.

POLAND

Hannover

⊛ Berlin

Magdeburg

NETHERLANDS

Duisburg   Essen

Düsseldorf   Kassel   Leipzig

Cologne   Dresden

Bonn

GERMANY

BELGIUM

Wiesbaden   Frankfurt am Main

LUXEMBOURG

CZECH
REPUBLIC

Rhine R.   Mannheim

FRANCE

Stuttgart   Danube R.

Munich

SWITZERLAND   LIECHTENSTEIN   A U S T R I A

CHAPTER FIVE

Germany

Andrew C. Gould

Introduction

In October 1990, the East German state (the **German Democratic Republic – GDR**) collapsed and its territory and people were absorbed by the West German state (the **Federal Republic of Germany – FRG**), even though just over a year earlier almost no one had expected this to happen. Yet, the strange fate of East Germany makes sense as part of Germany's path through the modern world, which has been influenced strongly by external political and economic challenges. A precarious military-strategic position in Europe made it difficult for one German polity to rule over everyone who is in one way or another conceivably German; German political organizations frequently competed with one another for people and territory. Only rarely did one kingdom, empire, or state succeed in dominating all other German polities. Even today, millions of German-speaking people and considerable territories that were formerly governed by various German rulers remain outside of the unified German state.

The challenges that Germans faced and their responses were characteristic of what happens when a major power takes a middle path through political and economic development. Germany was at a disadvantage with respect to the early developers. In politics, German rulers could not match France in establishing strong central authority over a vast territory. In economics, German industrial development lagged behind Britain's. Along with these strategic and economic disadvantages, however, the rapid diffusion of new ideas into Germany offered certain opportunities. Germany's newer bureaucracies skipped over traditional practices and instead adopted only the latest organizational techniques. German industries, unimpeded by false starts, implemented advanced technology on a massive scale. In the struggle with the early developers, Germany developed powerful political institutions (a professional army and an authoritarian monarchy), mobilizing identities (ethnic conceptions of nation), and significant economic interests (heavy industry and labor-repressive agriculture), all of which imperiled liberalism and democracy.

The German experience demonstrates that backwardness compared with early developers has powerful and wide-ranging effects. When Germany was attempting to catch up, its industries modernized, its state engineered massive social and economic changes, and its leading political ideologies emphasized power, obedience, and material well-being rather than political freedom. But the culmination of this approach, the fascist regime of Adolf Hitler's Nazi Party, ultimately failed to deliver social order, prosperity, and global leadership atop a new world order. In the wake of World War II, when two new superpowers emerged in virtually unassailable positions, German elites no longer sought to remake their country into the world's greatest power. Postwar Germany was divided into two and one of the new German states, the FRG, became a medium-sized power almost entirely dependent upon the United States for its security, with no offensive military capability of its own. During the Cold War, Germany's economy grew to become one of the world's most successful, and democracy, freedom, and the rule of law began to flourish in the heart of the European continent.

Contemporary interests, identities, and institutions in Germany stem from Germany's path through the modern world. With regard to interests, the reliance of major German industrialists on the state and big banks for funding during the nineteenth and twentieth centuries, and the struggles of many small- and medium-sized firms to stay afloat, stemmed from Germany's economic position and attempts to catch up with France and Britain. In the early twenty-first century, the German government is seeking to transform the state's intricate involvement in the market, especially in the labor market, a difficult reform process that does not win strong support even from leading firms, much less from labor unions and those who have protected employment. The almost bewildering variety of contemporary German identities – from right-wing nationalism, to ecological activism, to recent immigrants seeking a new status – also flows from previous episodes of identity formation and reformulation. Some key institutional features of the contemporary German state, including the post-unification relocation of the capital from **Bonn** back to **Berlin**, show the pull of past practice. Other political institutions, notably the **Basic Law** (**Grundgesetz**) of 1949, are explicitly crafted to prevent any reemergence of authoritarianism. In this chapter, we explore how Germany's particular developmental sequence created domestic and international legacies that strongly influence the country today.

Origins of a Middle Developer, 100 B.C.–A.D. 1800

If you place key moments in German history, even familiar ones, in the analytic framework of this text, then you can see just how much influence the global context has on the development of a given country. To start the analysis, and in contrast with nationalist myths of a pure beginning, the origins of modern Germany did not lie uniquely within German lands but instead in the contact between two societies. Early German and Roman cultures blended and grew together during the expansions and contractions of the Roman Empire across Europe. Roman influence, starting in the first century B.C., brought a common culture of Christianity, a common elite language of Latin, and a common experience of the Roman legal code. As the Roman Empire declined during the fifth century, Germanic warriors reinvigorated their practice of honor-based pacts of loyalty that provided a political foundation for new feudal kingdoms.

Germany at this time resembled the rest of Europe. As in the rest of Europe from the eighth through the twelfth centuries, aspiring German kings were usually at war with one another. As in other parts of Europe, strong cities emerged during the thirteenth through sixteenth centuries, especially along the Rhine River and the Baltic Sea. In contrast to the personalistic and custom-bound rule in feudal kingdoms, cities governed themselves through written laws and representative institutions. Also during the sixteenth century, a wave of religious revival swept across Germany and Europe; the Protestant Reformation and Catholic Counter-Reformation left German territories religiously divided.

Germany became a middle developer during the seventeenth and eighteenth centuries because this is when German rulers could not match the successes of monarchs in France and England. Whereas each of the early developers became unified under absolutist or would-be absolutist rulers, Germany remained politically divided. For instance, starting in 1618, the Thirty Years' War devastated the population and economy of many German states; it ended with the 1648 Peace of Westphalia, which signaled the ascendancy of France under Louis XIV as a European power and which highlighted the inability of Germany's nominal imperial ruler (Ferdinand III, Holy Roman Emperor) to stem the growing sovereignty of the many different and competing German states and principalities. The weakness of pan-German political institutions and the persistence of political divisions accentuated other differences within the German lands, such as the cleavage between Protestants and Catholics and the contrast between economically advanced regions in western and southern Germany and the backward agricultural economies and social structures east of the Elbe River.

Competing Modern States, 1800–1871

German polities were middle developers in building a modern state, that is, in building a political organization that could successfully claim to be the only organization with the right to use violence over the German territory and its people. The two most powerful political units were the **Austrian Empire** in the southeast and **Prussia** in the northeast. They competed with each other and with dozens of other would-be states in what is now modern Germany. The winnowing down of German states accelerated under the renewed military conquests of an early developer. In 1806, the French emperor Napoleon Bonaparte invaded, consolidated many German states into larger units, and imposed a common legal code. German leaders sought both to imitate and resist Napoleon by rationalizing their own bureaucracies and building stronger armies. It is characteristic of these changes that Francis II dissolved his virtually moribund Holy Roman Empire, which ineffectively claimed to organize political rulers throughout German lands, and instead focused on ruling with his hereditary name and title as Francis I, Emperor of Austria. When the armies of Francis I (Austria), Frederick William III (Prussia), George III (Great Britain), Alexander I (Russia), and the other allies finally defeated Napoleon in 1815, Austria and Prussia emerged even stronger than before compared to the other German states. As an eastern power, Prussian military might was centered on its capital in Berlin, but the peace treaty agreed to at the **Congress of Vienna** awarded Prussia control over many economically advanced territories in the west along the Rhine River.

Two main social and political groups contended for influence in Germany during the nineteenth century. The first group included many people energized by the broader European liberal movements for nationalism and constitutionalism. They were liberals in the nineteenth-century meaning of the term: They favored large and free markets, the separation of church and state, and constitutional representative government. German liberals sought to build a German nation that encompassed all of the people then divided into various polities; they wanted a national market unhindered by internal boundaries; and they wanted to limit monarchical power by building new political institutions, such as a national electoral system, a parliament, and a written constitution. Leading intellectuals, professors, government officials, industrialists, professionals, and various members of the middle classes played key roles in the liberal movement.

The second group contending for influence was the landed elite (**Junkers**) of eastern Prussia. These owners of large tracts of land employed agricultural labor in conditions of near servitude to produce grain for world markets. They were deeply conservative politically and sought to forestall any political change that threatened their control over land and people, including any changes in the system of German states, in the ways the various states were governed internally, and in the harsh conditions of life for their agricultural workers. Their estates produced grain for the world market at very competitive prices, but their approval of market economics did not extend to the conditions of production for their workers. In fact, their economic success rested on political power and economic exploitation.

German monarchs successfully resisted most of the political demands of the liberal group and allied themselves with the landed elite. For example, in 1830, liberal revolutions took place in France, Belgium, and Switzerland. Liberalism was strong in the Rhineland as well, but the Prussian king in Berlin avoided changes by taking advantage of his government's physical separation from most of the revolutionary action and his additional military resources based in the east. Even less change occurred in Austria than in Prussia.

Next, in 1848, important political reforms again engulfed many countries of Europe. In Germany, widespread revolutionary activity in the Rhineland, Berlin, and Vienna led to a call for the election of a national assembly of delegates. Elections were held in all of the German states, from Prussia to Austria and the many other states. The delegates met in Frankfurt to draw up a new constitution for a unified German state, but the Prussian and Austrian monarchs used force to preserve their rule, and the **Frankfurt Parliament** proved unable to reform, overthrow, or even unify the conservative states; the parliament disbanded without achieving any of its intended aims.

The rejection of liberalism had the unintended consequence of setting in motion future revolutionary movements. In the spring of 1841, **Karl Marx** was a 23-year-old student whose dissertation was accepted by the University of Jena. Marx had planned for a career as an academic philosopher, but the Prussian government's imposition of strict controls on university appointments meant that he had to write for a different audience. His new job as the editor of a newspaper financed by liberals and run by radicals, the *Rheinische Zeitung*, ended abruptly when the Prussian censor closed the paper for being too critical. Unable to find work in Germany, Marx left for France in 1843, where he met his lifelong collaborator, Friedrich Engels. In 1848, he and Engels wrote the *Communist Manifesto*, closing with the statement: "The proletarians have nothing to lose but their chains. They have a world to win. Working men of all countries, unite!" Marx returned to Germany during the revolutionary movements of 1848 and advocated an alliance with liberal reformers, but the failure of this revolution finally convinced him and many other activists and supporters that real reform was impossible without more fundamental changes in the economy and society.

In the battle for supremacy among the German powers, the Prussian monarchy adopted the economic dimension of the liberal program but used its military strength both to dominate the smaller German states and to reject the political dimensions of liberalism. Prussia sponsored a growing free-trade zone among the German states, and the size of its own market made it costly for other states to avoid joining. Prussia defeated Austria in war in 1866, paving the way for the formation of the North German Confederation under Prussian leadership in 1867. The final steps in Germany's first modern unification required that France be forced to accept the change in the German situation. The Franco-Prussian War of 1870 matched two nondemocratic rulers – France's emperor Louis-Napoleon (Napoleon Bonaparte's nephew) against the king of Prussia, Wilhelm I. The war had widely divergent consequences. Louis-Napoleon lost the war and was replaced by a democratic regime, the Third Republic (1870–1940); Prussia won the war and used its victory to consolidate a larger German state under authoritarian rule.

The Prussian king – advised by his chancellor, Otto von Bismarck – had himself crowned the emperor of Germany while at the French palace of Versailles in 1871. The title of emperor was chosen to evoke memories of the Holy Roman Empire that had been disbanded in 1806; the new regime became known as the Second Empire. The new borders were fixed by military victory. Unified Germany encompassed Prussia (including its eastern territories along the Baltic in what is now Poland and Russia) and virtually all of the non-Austrian German states. It also included territory taken from France, the economically advanced provinces of Alsace and Lorraine. Austria and Switzerland remained outside of the new German empire as independent countries.

Unification under Authoritarian Leadership, 1871–1919

Germany's late unification gave its newly constructed state institutions a great deal of influence over society. The state's initiative played a crucial role in changing Germany, even if the state was not always successful in its efforts. In other words, the developmental path of relatively late state-building in Germany gave the German state, compared with early state-building in Britain and France, an opportunity to attempt to reshape society, the economy, and politics.

The leaders of the German state reshaped society in unintended ways when they set about recasting institutions and reformulating identities. First, the mainly Protestant leaders attacked Catholicism. In the early 1870s, the state leaders pursued a **cultural struggle** (**Kulturkampf**) with laws and regulations to make it difficult for Catholic priests to carry out their work. Political activists responded by founding a political party, the **Center Party** (**Zentrumspartei**). The party's top decision makers were Catholic lay leaders, and Center Party candidates received the implicit and explicit aid of the church. The long-term effects of the Kulturkampf, however, were neither what the German political elite wanted nor what the Catholic Church expected. Instead of a retreat from politics, the struggle against Catholicism induced Catholics to mobilize in their own political party. Instead of increasing the power of the Catholic Church in politics and society, as the Catholic hierarchy would have preferred, the Kulturkampf brought about the emergence of professional party leaders who were not priests, even though they were Catholic. The state reconciled with the church during the 1870s, but the Center Party remained to represent German Catholics, and it went on to become one of Germany's largest political parties.

As the regime made its peace with a recast Catholic community, the leaders next turned their attention to the emerging political movements among the working classes. The Socialist Worker's Party was formed in 1875 from various radical groups, and it won only 9 percent of the vote in 1877. Bismarck, however, blamed the party for Germany's economic situation: "As long as we fail to stamp on this communist ant-hill with domestic legislation," he said, "we shall not see any revival in the economy." In 1878, Bismarck won majority support in the Reichstag (parliament) for severe antisocialist legislation. The government closed Socialist Party offices and publications, prohibited its meetings, and generally harassed its organizers. Many left-wing activists fled from Germany, especially to Switzerland, and sought to keep their efforts alive in exile.

Despite the repression, many workers and other supporters continued to identify themselves as working class and to support the Socialist Party. Most of the antisocialist laws lapsed in 1890, and the party reemerged under a new name as the **Social Democratic Party** (Sozialdemokratische Partei Deutschlands, SPD). The Socialists climbed at the polls in 1898 with 27 percent of the vote. In the final elections under the empire in 1912, the Social Democratic Party won even more – 35 percent of the vote. The typical Socialist voter was a young, urban worker who was Protestant but did not go to church, and who was German rather than a member of the Polish or another minority group. The party attracted little support from Catholics or people living in rural areas. Still, the Social Democrats had almost a million members in 1912, a substantial accomplishment, as its members were expected to pay regular dues as in many other European parties. Like other mass parties in Europe, the Social Democrats reached beyond the purely political realm to organize funeral societies, buying cooperatives, book-lending libraries, gymnastic societies, choral clubs, bicycling clubs, soccer teams, Sunday schools, and dance courses.

The new German state had to foster economic development in difficult circumstances. Most importantly, from 1873 to 1896 there was a Europe-wide depression. Agricultural prices fell with the introduction of inexpensive Russian and midwestern American grain on world markets; industrial prices also fell, employment figures were unstable, production rose, and profits decreased. One response to these difficult conditions lay beyond state control: Many Germans emigrated from Europe to North and South America.

German firms enjoyed some "advantages of backwardness." They could adopt advanced machinery and industrial organization from British examples without having to devise these things themselves. But there were also disadvantages of backwardness. In order to acquire expensive technology and survive early competition with established businesses, many German firms relied on large banks and the state for the necessary capital funds. From 1875 to 1890, both the eastern German grain growers (the Junkers) and the big industrialists sought and won state protection from imports in the form of high tariffs; Germany's relatively large working class would have preferred free trade and cheaper food.

One can argue that the institutions of the Second Empire were on their way to becoming more democratic during the early twentieth century. The Social Democratic Party and the Center Party were gaining in strength, and liberal industrialists were gaining in influence over the old Junker elite. As the success of industrialization began to materialize in the 1890s, for example, many leading industrialists saw that they could compete on the world market and broke with the Junkers to seek lower tariff barriers. Industrialists, like workers, now favored low tariffs and the resulting lower prices on food. Several shifts in cabinet formation resulted, followed by a victory for low-tariff delegates in the Reichstag election of 1912.

For all of the democratic gains at the ballot box under the empire, however, Germany's position within the global context made a transition to democracy problematic. German leaders ruled over a middle developer and felt threatened by the early developers. Frustrated in their ambitions to challenge Britain and France as leading imperial powers, the German elite responded to a crisis in southeastern Europe and opted for war in 1914. Their basic hope was for a quick victory to expand Germany's base from which to challenge the established powers. But the quick German victory did not materialize. Instead, the forces of Germany and its ally in this war, Austria-Hungary, bogged down in trench warfare against those of the Triple Entente (Britain, France, and Russia). The German high command's next gamble to win the war quickly – by introducing submarine warfare in the Atlantic – did not weaken Britain and France sufficiently before the feared and ultimately decisive intervention of American troops and resources.

As in other countries affected by the Great War, as World War I was called, massive mobilization had political consequences for Germany. Eleven million men, amounting to 18 percent of the population, were in uniform. Workers and families scrambled to support the war effort. Massive propaganda campaigns encouraged a strong national feeling and the sense that every German person was a valuable member of the nation. Similar campaigns in the other great powers boosted the feelings of national belonging in every state and increased the pressure for political reform to give every member of the nation an equal set of citizenship rights.

Although there was a gradual democratization of political life under the Second Empire, the transition to a full democracy came abruptly. As it became clear that Germany was losing the war, several navy and army units mutinied. This was followed by uprisings in Berlin and William II's abdication as emperor of Germany in 1918. As in France at the end of Emperor Louis-Napoleon's rule, loss in war combined with military defections and domestic uprising sparked the transition from authoritarianism to democracy.

Democracy and Competitive Capitalism, 1919–1933

With the fall of the Second Empire, a democratic, constitutional regime took command of the German state. Under the **Weimar Republic**, all adult men and women had the right to vote in elections to the Reichstag. Elections were also held to select a president. In turn, the president usually requested the leader of the strongest parliamentary party to serve as the chancellor, form a cabinet, and lead the government. If the chancellor's party could not form a majority on its own, the chancellor had to put together a coalition of parties in the Reichstag in order to govern. Given the absence of a single party that could command a majority, most governments were coalition governments composed of several parties. Not all coalition governments are weak, but in the case of Weimar Germany many were.

Adherents of the empire retained considerable influence even under the new regime. The new democratic leaders never purged reactionary officers from the army or police. Instead, the democrats relied on the old authoritarians. For example, the Social Democratic leaders of the new German government called on the army to suppress demonstrations in a bid to restore order to rioting cities, quell the threat of a communist revolution, and prevent a German example of the recently successful 1917 revolution in Russia. In addition, most of the judges had received their legal training under the empire and continued to interpret the law in an antidemocratic fashion. Many of the highly trained and well-placed civil servants were holdovers from the previous era. Whereas the first president was a leading Socialist, **Friedrich Ebert**, the second and only other president, **Otto von Hindenburg**, was a Junker and former army officer. It was Hindenburg who appointed Hitler as chancellor in 1933.

If the usual distribution of vote shares had been sustained as the country moved into the early 1930s, the Weimar Republic might well have survived. The leading parties in the regime during the 1920s were the Social Democratic Party, which usually received about 25 percent of the vote, and the Center Party, which usually received about 15 percent of the vote. Farther to the left, the Communist Party also polled steadily in the 15 percent range. On the center-right, various bourgeois, liberal, and traditional-nationalist parties accounted for most of the remaining 45 percent of the vote. The governments worked reasonably well, as long as parties in the center of the political spectrum remained strong.

Important aspects of the Weimar Republic's demise were the increasing strength of extreme left-wing and right-wing parties committed to the destruction of the republic and the failure of the center-right parties to retain their constituencies. Beginning with the election of 1930, the new **National Socialist German Workers' Party** (**Nazi Party**) started to capture a substantial share of the vote, mostly from the old center-right, bourgeois, and liberal parties. In 1933, in the last democratic election, for example, the Socialists received almost their typical amount at 20 percent, and the Center Party won its usual 15 percent. The Communists received a somewhat higher than normal 17 percent. It was the collapsing center-right and right-wing parties that provided the Nazis with a plurality of 33 percent of the vote, paving the way for Hitler to be named chancellor.

Our perspective on global contexts and paths to development illuminates important causes of the democratic collapse and fascist takeover that stand up to comparative analysis. First, Germany's size and middle-developer status interacted in ways dangerous for democracy. Germany was a big country, and many of its people had seemingly reasonable expectations that Germany would become the next great power. Yet, years of competition with the early developers, especially Britain and its ex-colony, the United States, and now added competition with a late developer, the Soviet Union, seemed to leave Germany lagging behind. For many people in Germany and in other populous middle developers (such as Japan and Italy), one temptation was to change the nature of the competition and embark on a military strategy to remake the world order with their nation on top. The temptation had already faded in the countries that had suffered serious defeats in attempts to use force and authoritarianism to improve their global position (Sweden in 1648; France in 1815 and 1870); the temptation was also weak in smaller countries with no realistic hope of a military path to greatness. Thus, one can see World War I, World War II, and the authoritarian regimes that pushed them forward as part of a common tendency among large middle developers to seek to improve their global position by military means. It is interesting to note that this tendency remains even today in several other large countries with frustrated developmental ambitions.

Second, Germany's middle-developer status allowed an antidemocratic class at the top of its social structure to exercise considerable influence. Although Germany's rapid industrial development helped to produce a substantial middle class and working class, both of which are frequently in favor of democratic regimes in other states, there also remained a small but powerful class of landed elites who used labor-repressive modes of agriculture on their estates. These Junkers were also highly placed in the German state and could use their position to maintain their social and economic status. As we have noted, it was Hindenburg, a Junker president of the Weimar Republic, who appointed Hitler as chancellor. Although most Junkers certainly preferred more traditional conservatives to the Nazis, the Nazis had a better hold on mass support and were seen as useful tools in the larger struggle against communism. Other landed elites using labor-repressive modes of agriculture (such as plantation owners in the southern United States) had fought against full democracy; in these and similar cases, it seemed to require a major military defeat to force these small but powerful groups to relinquish key aspects of their authority.

Third, Germany's path to development set up political institutions that made it more difficult to reach agreements among social and political forces. Other middle-developing democratic regimes (in Sweden, Norway, Denmark, and Czechoslovakia) survived the interwar years without succumbing to domestic fascist movements. These liberal democracies survived at least in part because their democratic regimes were supported by strong coalitions between socialist and agrarian parties. Such a democratic urban-rural coalition did not form in Germany, nor did one form in the two other Western European countries that succumbed to fascist movements (Italy and Spain). Thus, it may be that the inability of predominantly urban socialists and predominantly rural agrarian parties to reach agreement fatally weakened the German, Italian, and Spanish democracies during the interwar years. Taken together, all three reasons imply that Germany's global position and domestic institutions tended to undermine attempts at democracy and competitive capitalism.

Nazism in Power, 1933–1945

Germany's Nazi regime was similar to other fascist regimes in several key organizational aspects. Hitler used his legal appointment as chancellor of the Weimar Republic to consolidate his command of the Nazi Party and put his party in control of the state. Within weeks, Hitler took advantage of communist resistance as a pretext to prohibit and suppress the Communist Party. During the rest of 1933, other parties were strongly encouraged to dissolve and allow their members to join the Nazi Party; for the remainder of the regime's rule, the Nazi Party was the only legal party in Germany. In principle, Nazis sought to enroll all Germans from every social class in various party-affiliated organizations. With these steps toward constructing a one-party, mobilizing, authoritarian regime, German Nazism can be seen as similar to the fascism in Italy under Benito Mussolini and, to a lesser degree, Spain under Francisco Franco.

What separates Nazi Germany from other cases of fascism, however, is the world war it initiated and the genocide it committed. Widespread support for militarism and expansionism, especially to the east, were part of Hitler's initial program and appeal. Hitler prepared for war from the start and successfully annexed Austria in 1938 and the Sudetenland in Czechoslovakia in 1939 without provoking a military response. There is evidence that Hitler hoped to avoid having to fight until the middle 1940s, and many Germans believed that war, when it did come, would be short. Nevertheless, the German invasion of Poland in September 1939 led the British and French to declare war. When German forces entered Paris in 1940, many Germans hoped for both victory and peace, but as the fighting dragged on over Britain and deep in Soviet Russia, this combined outcome became unlikely. From 1939 until the Nazi regime's fall in 1945, Germany, Europe, and the rest of the world's major powers were at war.

The Nazi regime undertook a brutal and virtually unique policy, the mass murder of civilians based on beliefs about their racial background, that both demands and evades explanation. The **Holocaust**, as the Nazi destruction of European Jewry is called, could not have gone forward without a combination of (1) racist beliefs, (2) the organizational capabilities of a modern state, (3) a fascist political regime, and (4) a leader who favored killing not just as a means to another end but also as a major policy objective in its own right. Of the three major fascist regimes of the period, only the Nazi regime carried out a campaign to exterminate all European Jews and people belonging to many other groups (Sinti and Roma, homosexuals, psychiatric patients, and the handicapped). In Italy, for example, the early fascist leadership openly included some people of Jewish descent, and Mussolini did not seek a campaign against Jews. Prior to the Holocaust, traditional forms of anti-Semitism were influential in Germany (but also throughout much of predominantly Christian Europe), as were modern, scientific forms of racism and population theories (these, too, were present elsewhere in Europe and in the United States). Other demagogues sought power in all of the major Western countries, but these potential leaders were less successful than Hitler. Taken alone or in various partial combinations, racist ideas, modern states, nondemocratic regimes, and murderous leaders have contributed to terrible outcomes throughout history and around the world, but the full combination of all four has so far come together only under Hitler's regime.

The choices made in the 1930s and early 1940s carried unintended consequences. Whereas many Junkers welcomed Hitler, although at arm's length, in a bid to bring order to their rapidly changing society, the result of Nazism and its failure was the Junkers' elimination from a role in German politics. Germany lost its eastern territories, and the landed elite lost their grip on military and political power. World War II weakened all of the European powers, including Germany, and left two other powers at the top of the global military system: the Soviet Union and the United States. The global context of a bipolar, Cold War world was thus ushered into being by the developmental path and choices taken by Germany's political leaders.

Occupation (1945–1949), Division (1949–1990), and Unification (1990–)

Germany today is strongly democratic, capitalist, and internationally cooperative with other democratic, capitalist states. The radical transformation from its past took place in three basic steps. The victorious Allied powers occupied and administered Germany in four zones with virtually no central state apparatus from 1945 to 1949. Two new German states then emerged from the occupation: the Federal Republic of Germany (FRG), based on the American, British, and French zones in western Germany, and the German Democratic Republic (GDR), based on the Soviet zone in the east. The two-Germanys situation seemed destined to last for generations, yet a third period began with the fall of Soviet communism in Central Europe in 1989, the rapid collapse of the GDR, and the unification of the German states in 1990.

Germany's place in the global arena changed decisively. During the Cold War, each of the German states was tied to one of the major powers. The FRG became one of the world's leading economic developers, albeit without its own offensive military capabilities. The economy of the GDR languished and remained tied to the less successful command economies of the Soviet bloc. The collapse of the Soviet Union sparked the final decay of the GDR. Reunited Germany now occupies a leading position among the nations of the world and within Europe. Like all other major powers in the early twenty-first century, however, Germany lags far behind the United States in military power, especially in the ability to conduct large-scale military operations outside of its home territory. As we shall see, these changes in the global context influence the makeup of Germany's current interests, identities, and institutions, as well as its overall development path.

Interests in Contemporary Germany

Germany's economy ranks at the very top of the world's large, industrialized economies. According to the World Bank, Germany had the world's third-largest economy overall in 2005, as measured by its Gross National Income (GNI) of $2.8 trillion (only the United States and Japan had larger economies – China was fourth; the United Kingdom had Europe's second largest with $2.3 trillion). The economy yielded a per capita GNI of $35,000, roughly the same as in France and the United Kingdom. This average income per person is impressive, especially considering Germany's population of 83 million people. Only two countries in the world have both a higher per capita GNI and a larger population, the United States ($44,000 per person, 300 million people) and Japan ($39,000 per person, 128 million people).

Germany today benefits greatly from competing economically within the current system rather than attempting to subvert it through military force as it had attempted to do earlier. Germany is the world's leading exporter of goods and services. German exports in 2004 were valued at $912 billion (the United States had $819 billion and Japan had $566 billion). Whereas, prior to World War II, Germany had achieved impressive economic growth but still lacked the imperial success of Great Britain, now German economic and political ambitions seem well served by the current distribution of power. Germany is a member of the Organization for Economic Cooperation and Development (OECD) and a leader in the Group of Eight (G8), which is composed of the leaders from the world's eight largest economies. Several constraints on German sovereignty have been lifted since 1990 as a result of unification. The German-Polish border was finally settled at the **Oder-Neisse line**; the old Allies from World War II no longer occupy Berlin. Although Germany is a member of the United Nations, it still lacks a seat on the powerful Security Council, which includes, by contrast, Great Britain and France.

Within Europe, Germany is, along with France, one of the key states that pushed for greater economic and political cooperation in the European Union. In contrast with its own past, Germany adopted a radically new stance toward other European states. In order to avoid future military conflicts and to guide growing intra-European trade, West German leaders supported the drive for closer economic and political cooperation among European countries. The FRG was one of the six founding members of the European Coal and Steel Community in 1951, and it was a major supporter of the Rome Treaties of 1957 that built the European Economic Community and related institutions of cooperation. During the 1970s and 1980s, the United States and Japanese economies put severe pressure on European industries. In response, West Germany took the lead, along with France, in pushing for a stronger European cooperation, notably in the Single European Act, which went into effect in 1987 and significantly reduced barriers to trade and institutional obstacles to Europe-wide political cooperation. Unified Germany in the 1990s supported the Treaty on European Union of 1992, which strengthened the EEC and other institutions, transforming them into the European Union. Germany also pushed for European Monetary Union (EMU) in 1999 and EU expansion in 2004, so that the EU now includes 27 member countries, including most of the former communist countries in Central Europe.

As a whole, Germany's material interests lie in maintaining and working within the current world economic system. But that does not mean that all Germans have exactly the same interests. What are the various interests in Germany? Which interests emerged as dominant, and how do they seek to position Germany in the world economy?

One way to see the different interests in a society is to look at the major factors of production in the economy: labor, capital, and land. As you might expect, these factors have distinct interests. Owners of labor – that is, workers – favor low food prices and high wages. Owners of capital – factory owners – favor low food prices, low wages, and high prices for their own products. Owners of land favor low costs for labor and industrial products – the inputs for agricultural production – and high prices for agricultural products.

Since the end of World War II, the impact of the generally expanding world trade on these different interests has helped to sustain democratic and capitalist institutions in Germany. Productive labor and capital are both relatively abundant in Germany. The German workforce is highly skilled and productive. Germany imported more workers as immigrants, especially during the 1960s, and the German workforce remains one of the world's most technically adept. One problem is relatively high unemployment; it reached 10 percent in 1997, remained at 8 or 9 percent through 2003, and hit 11 percent in 2005 – a major challenge for German governments. With regard to capital, Germany possesses a massive industrial base, some of which survived from before World War II but much of which was built after the war along highly efficient lines. To take one measure of Germany's capital abundance, in 1953 West Germany was the seventh most industrialized country in the world, measured by industrialization per capita, and by 1980 it was the third most industrialized country (behind only the United States and Sweden). German industry relies on being able to sell its goods in European and other foreign markets.

Germany, however, has a relatively scarce supply of agriculturally productive land; there are too many people and too small a territory. In West Germany, there were fully 414 people per square kilometer of arable land. By contrast, for example, in the land-abundant United States, there are only about 41 people per square kilometer of arable land. Agriculture adds just 1 percent to German GDP (whereas it adds 2 percent to the U.S. GDP and 3 percent to that of France); agriculture produces just 1 percent of Germany's merchandise exports (compared with 2 percent of U.S. merchandise exports). Thus, unlike industry and labor, most of German agriculture was not in a position to produce on a global scale at competitive prices; Germany could not meet its demand for agricultural products from domestic sources.

One can see the practical political effects of these economic interests in at least two ways. First, industry and labor have won the fight with agriculture to put Germany in the free-trade camp. German industry and labor now have strong interests in an open international trading system in which they use their strength to compete on a world market and avoid flooding their own market with too many goods. Given the size of these two sectors in Germany, their joint interests overrode those of the opposing agriculturalists, who would have preferred trade restrictions and higher food prices. As a result, the main political parties agree on the basic outlines of economic policy. The center-left Social Democratic Party, with a stronghold in the working class, favors free-trade industrialization. The center-right **Christian Democrats** (composed of the allied parties of the Christian Democratic Union and the Christian Social Union), with strong support from industrialists, also favor free-trade industrialization. Both have pushed for the reduction of trade barriers on a global scale and within Europe.

The second political impact of interests is that the main parties advocate even greater economic free trade and are willing to compensate the losers under this policy. Even during the late 1990s, when world financial crises unsettled global markets, the major political parties remained strongly in favor of the continued economic integration of Europe, including monetary union with other European countries. A major concession that the government regularly has to make in order to deepen European integration is to its farmers. As compensation to landowners and farmers for the losses caused by economic integration and free trade, to this day the European Union spends the bulk of its budget on support for farmers. Both of Germany's two main political parties have supported the relatively generous welfare provisions of the German state that cushion the blows of international economic competition and allow the employed workforce to maintain its high level of technical skills, albeit at the cost of relatively high unemployment rates and pension costs.

The social classes that make up German society come out of a tradition of stark class distinctions. However, the experiences of fascism, the post–World War II economic success, and now the transition to a service-oriented economy have dulled long-standing divisions. One can take the occupational composition of the workforce as a measure of changes in Germany's class structure. In 1950, 28 percent of workers were in agriculture or self-employed, 51 percent were manual workers (mostly in industry), and 21 percent were salaried, nonmanual workers (so-called white-collar and service workers). By 1994, only 10 percent were in agriculture or self-employed and only 38 percent were manual workers, whereas fully 52 percent were salaried, nonmanual workers. Thus, as in the rest of the industrialized world, Germany has developed a combined industrial and postindustrial social structure.

Identities in Contemporary Germany

Gradually, after World War II, antidemocratic values weakened. The failure to win world domination shook many people's faith in the fascist alternative to democracy. After the war, many Germans avoided overt politics and turned inward – toward family, work, and the pursuit of personal well-being – and abandoned a belief in grander political ends. The relative economic success of the West German economy during the 1950s and 1960s reinforced the value placed on the pursuit of prosperity.

Support for democracy has grown. In a 1950 survey, German respondents were asked about political competition. Fully 25 percent said that it is better for a country to have only one political party, and another 22 percent were undecided about this question or gave no response. A bare majority, just 53 percent, said that it is better for a country to have several parties. It would be hard to say that a political culture is democratic if such a slight majority of people believe that political competition among parties is a good idea. Things have changed, however. In a 1990 survey, just 3 percent of respondents said that it is better to have only one party, and only 8 percent were undecided or gave no response. The overwhelming preponderance of respondents, 89 percent, stated that it is better for a country to have several political parties.

A strong faith in democracy developed at the elite and mass levels. The German political philosopher Jürgen Habermas has described "constitutional patriotism" as the ultimate political value. Support for democracy is also reflected in public-opinion polls. In a survey carried out in the 1990s, 50 percent of respondents in Germany stated that they were "very satisfied" or "fairly satisfied" with the way democracy worked in Germany; 37 percent stated they were "not very satisfied"; and only 11 percent were "not at all satisfied." Although this measure of support for democracy was not as high as in the United Kingdom – where 61 percent reported that they were "very" or "fairly satisfied" – the distribution of responses to this question in Germany was about average among EU countries. There were important differences between the former East Germany and West Germany: only 30 percent of respondents in the former East stated that they were "very" or "fairly satisfied," compared with 55 percent in the former West. The indicators of public opinion suggest that there is widespread support for human rights as a basic value and broad support for the current version of democratic institutions in Germany.

Still, the 83 million people living in Germany do not share a single identity. One dimension on which Germans differ is how they situate themselves with respect to the rest of Europe and the possibility of a European identification that transcends national identifications. In a survey conducted in the late 1990s, 49 percent of respondents said that they consider themselves to be "German only." Another 35 percent of respondents said that they considered themselves to be "German and European." Seven percent said that they considered themselves "European and German," and 5 percent chose "European only." The distribution of national versus European identity in Germany was about average for the EU countries. Among the bigger countries, German national identity is located halfway between the weak national identity in France (where just 31 percent chose "French only") and the strong national identity in the United Kingdom (where 60 percent chose "British only").

Many Germans are relatively new residents of the German state, and this also leads to varied identities. In the post–World War II period from 1949 to

1989, while Germany was divided, approximately 13 million refugees whom the FRG identified as German (by ethnic background) arrived from Poland, the Soviet Union, and the GDR. The territory of the GDR in 1948 was home to about 19 million people. The GDR's population shrank during the decades of division, mostly because of legal and illegal migration to the FRG. In 1989 alone, some 344,000 people from the GDR left for the FRG, along with 376,000 ethnic-background Germans from the Soviet Union and elsewhere in Eastern Europe. As mentioned earlier, what was left of the GDR's population, 16 million people, came under FRG control in 1990. The nearly automatic right of ethnic-background Germans to immigrate and acquire German citizenship was curbed partially in the 1990s and early 2000s with requirements to prove German language abilities and cultural assimilation.

Many people who live in Germany are considered by the German state to be foreigners; indeed, there are more foreigners in Germany than in any other European country. In the mid-2000s, over 10 million people living in Germany were born elsewhere (12.5 percent of Germany's total population, comparable to the 12.3 percent figure for the United States and above the median 9 percent for other European countries, according to OECD data). About 7.3 million people were citizens of other countries (8.9 percent of the population, the largest percentage for any big OECD country and above the OECD median of 5 percent). Many people from Turkey and southern Europe (the former Yugoslavia, Greece, and Italy) arrived during the 1960s under the government's policy of encouraging the temporary migration of foreigners to work in German industries that needed more labor. Almost a million people left Germany during the 1970s when the government provided incentives for foreign workers and their families to leave Germany, yet most of the immigrants did not leave. The single largest group of foreign citizens in Germany is from Turkey; other large groups of foreign nationals are from Italy, Greece, and Poland.

Although there are signs of change toward a more permanent official status, the conventional term for foreign workers in the 1950s and 1960s, "**guest workers**" (*Gastarbeiter*), underscored the state's attempt to emphasize the temporary nature of their stay in Germany, despite their growing and deep involvement in the German economy and society. Many of the hardships faced by these immigrant groups are common to the experience of immigrant laborers in other industrialized countries: low wages, dangerous employment, few opportunities for advancement, racism, victimization by crime, discrimination in housing and employment, and the near-constant threat of legal deportation. The difficult situation of many immigrants considered non-ethnic Germans is exacerbated by their exclusion from political rights. It was virtually impossible for foreign workers, or even their children, to earn the right to vote, become a citizen, or run for public office. The *jus sanguinus* legal tradition of defining citizenship by descent, rather than by place of birth, remains strong. A child born in Germany to two non-German parents does not automatically have German citizenship. A 1999 reform allows a child of non-German parents to apply for and acquire German citizenship if at least one parent has held a permanent resident permit for three years and has actually resided in Germany for eight years.

Religious identities among the Christian and formerly Christian population are roughly evenly divided among Protestants, Catholics, and those who declare themselves unaffiliated, with about 26 million people in each group (in addition there are 900,000 Orthodox Christians, mainly immigrants from Greece and Serbia). Protestants are predominant in the old East (where Protestantism had long prevailed); the nonreligious are more prevalent there as well (in the aftermath of a secularizing, Communist regime).

There are growing groups of Jews and Muslims. A 1925 census recorded almost 565,000 Jews in the Weimar Republic. Just several thousand German Jews survived the Holocaust, and only about 30,000 Jewish people lived in Germany in the 1980s, predominantly in Berlin. With the collapse of Communism in the east, many Jews from the Baltic countries and the former Soviet Union moved to Germany and the Jewish population has grown to just over 100,000 people by the mid-2000s (according to German government statistics).

Muslims constitute an exceptionally heterogeneous and diverse group. There were fewer than 7,000 Muslims in the FRG in 1961; estimates for the number of Muslims in Germany in the first decade of the 21st century are between 3 and 4 million people and about 4% of the population. Most of the approximately 2.4 million Turkish-origin residents of Germany, including several hundred thousand Kurds, are Muslim. There are approximately 600,000 Muslims from Bosnia-Herzegovina and Albania, North Africa, and the Arab Middle East. Around 100,000 are Iranian, stemming from the flight of more secular Muslims from Iran beginning in the 1980s. Around 2% of Muslims are German converts to Islam. A majority of Muslims in Germany are Sunni, around 65%, and there are also Alevites, Imamites, and some Turkish Shiites. Germany's Muslims hold diverse views and values. In a 2006 Pew Global Attitudes survey, the greatest concern of Germany's Muslims was unemployment – 56% said they were very worried about this; other religious and cultural matters ranked much lower – only 23% of Muslim respondents were very worried about extremism and only 18% were very worried about the decline of religion. Half of the respondents said that there was a struggle between extremist and moderate Muslims in Germany; among those who saw a struggle, just 14% said they identified with the extremists.

The identities of men and women with respect to gender roles are changing, too. Germany emerged from World War II with gender identities rooted in the past. In the FRG, the law still reflected greater rights for men than for women, especially in regard to marriage and property. In the GDR, strict legal equality was undermined by pervasive informal occupational segregation by gender. Nearly 90 percent of women in the communist East had worked outside of the home, whereas not even half of women did in the West. Pay and working conditions were better in the West, but the advancement of women into the higher ranks of important professions remained slow. A movement for women's rights developed during the 1970s in the FRG, as in virtually all Western democracies. By force of example, this movement has changed how men and women think of themselves. Institutional changes have reinforced these new conditions, although not as dramatically as in some other countries. Abortion laws were almost liberalized in the 1970s but were turned back by a conservative majority on the Constitutional Court, which cited right-to-life provisions in the Basic Law. After unification, the differences in abortion laws between West and East proved to be a difficult political issue and negotiators agreed to allow temporarily different laws in the former East and West. The liberal abortion law for the East finally expired in 1992, and a moderately pro-choice, all-German law was declared unconstitutional in 1993, again by a more conservative Constitutional Court. The parliament crafted a new compromise law in 1995 that fits the court's ruling; most abortions are technically illegal, but no one can be prosecuted, and public funds may be used if the woman falls below an income threshold. There is substantial variation in the practical availability of abortion services from state to state. Many women seeking abortions travel within Germany or to neighboring countries such as the Netherlands.

Institutions in Contemporary Germany

The founding document of the Federal Republic of Germany is the 1949 Basic Law (*Grundgesetz*), which officially became the Constitution of the United German People in October 1990. Between 1949 and 1990, although political actors used it much like a constitution, the Basic Law was usually not called a constitution, given the prominent role that the occupying Western powers had in its formulation and given the reluctance to recognize as permanent the division of Germany into two parts. Under the Western occupation, political life began to reemerge mainly at the regional rather than the national level. In September 1948, the Allied military governors and provincial leaders convened a constituent assembly of 65 delegates to draft a provisional constitution. The aims of the framers were to avoid the perceived weaknesses of the Weimar system, to prevent a renewed fascist movement, and to lock western Germany into the Western alliance. The resulting document strengthened the chancellor and the legislature over the bureaucracy and army, and it decentralized power to the various regional governments. The framers placed the rule of law and basic liberal institutions at the very heart of the system. Their proposed Basic Law was ratified by regional parliaments in May 1949. It has been amended several times, and its provisional character has faded; it was not replaced during unification, but rather its terms were used to incorporate the former East Germany into the FRG.

The two largest political parties in post–World War II West Germany grew out of the Christian Democratic and Socialist camps from the Weimar era in radically new ways. The Christian Democratic Union (Christlich-Demokratische Union, CDU) and the Christian Social Union (Christlich-Soziale Union, CSU) comprise the Christian Democratic camp. Although officially two parties, most political scientists consider them to function as one party for they do not nominate candidates to compete in the same district; the CSU contests elections in predominantly Catholic Bavaria, whereas the CDU contests them in the rest of the FRG. The two parties are often referred to collectively as the CDU/CSU. A major transformation is that the CDU explicitly sought support from Protestants as well as Catholics. Various Christian Democratic parties won local elections in the occupied zones after World War II, and many of them came together once CDU leader Konrad Adenauer became chancellor with the support of the CSU. The CDU/CSU supporters were not just former Center Party voters but also those who had supported liberal and socialist parties in the past. A second major transformation was that the party, especially Economics Minister Ludwig Erhard, who later became chancellor himself, strongly championed free-market economics. The CDU/CSU has been a center-right party, advocating capitalism with strong social protections, close ties to the United States and other Western powers, and strong anticommunism. It formed every government, in coalition with smaller parties, from 1949 to 1966 and from 1982 to 1998.

The Social Democratic Party (Sozialdemokratische Partei Deutschlands, SPD) was transformed by the unexpected successes of the CDU/CSU and the SPD's long years in opposition until 1966. The party emerged from under the Nazi-era ban on its activities as the best-organized party in occupied Germany. Yet its failure to win elections during the 1950s convinced its leading figures, such as future chancellors Willy Brandt and Helmut Schmidt, of the need to break from its overdependence on orthodox Marxist rhetoric and almost exclusively working-class support. With major reforms at the 1959 Bad Godesberg party conference, the SPD officially stated its policy of reaching out to religious believers and to middle-class voters, changes that gradually began to have their effect on voters, who gave them increasing support in the early 1960s. The successful participation of the SPD in the Grand Coalition government with the CDU from 1966 to 1969 demonstrated the ability of its leading figures to manage the economy and politics in pro-democratic and pro-capitalist ways and paved the way for its electoral success in 1969 and the formation of its own governing coalition with the Free Democratic Party through 1982. It returned to power in coalition with the Green party from 1998 to 2005.

Two medium-sized parties have played pivotal roles in modern German politics as well. The Free Democratic Party (Freie Demokratische Partei,

FDP) stands for individualism and free economic competition. In the immediate post–World War II years, the party was formed by Weimar-era liberals, although the anticlerical emphasis of German liberalism was pared away to leave the focus on free-market economics. Although the FDP has never polled more than 13 percent of the vote in national elections, it has frequently been able to give one of the two larger parties the necessary support to form a government. With roots in the environmentalist and antinuclear social movements in the 1970s, another party, the Greens, first won parliamentary representation in the 1983 elections. For much of the 1980s, the party was divided into a more fundamentalist faction that advocated far-reaching reforms to reject capitalist development and to protect the environment, and a more realist faction advocating less drastic reform while working within the system. After reunification in 1990, the Greens joined with Bundnis90, former East German counterparts who had been leading dissidents under the GDR, but the alliance between the wealthier and poorer partners has not been smooth. The Greens served in government as a junior coalition partner with the SPD following the 1998 and 2002 elections.

Some other parties have won seats in the **Bundestag** (the lower house of parliament), although not participation in the formation of a government. The Party of Democratic Socialism (PDS) attained 36 seats in 1998; it had been formed by leading figures from the former Communist Party of the GDR such as Gregor Gysi, and won in districts of the former East Germany, mainly with support from older voters dissatisfied with the rapid pace of postunification change. The PDS performed poorly in the 2002 elections, winning just 2 seats, and merged with other left groups in the former West Germany to form the new Left Party, which went on to win 54 seats in 2005.

In part because of the Basic Law's well-crafted institutional design, Germany has sustained its political democracy since 1949. At the most basic level, Germany qualifies as a political democracy because all of the major actors in German society expect that elections for the highest offices in the state will be held on a regular basis into the foreseeable future. This situation contrasts with the Weimar Republic, where many leading political actors either sought to end the practice of elections or at least reasonably expected that elections would be suspended at some point. According to the Basic Law of 1949, elections to the national legislature are held every four years. (The Basic Law's exceptions to this rule occur when the legislature is deadlocked. If this happens, it provides for the **federal president [Bundesprasident]** to call early elections. So far, this has happened only twice, in 1972 and 1982.) The intervals between German national elections are not quite as regularly spaced as election intervals in presidential systems, such as the United States, but they are more regular than in other parliamentary systems, such as that of the United Kingdom.

For the most part, the powers of the president are severely restricted compared with the relatively powerful role for the president under the Weimar system. Although the president is the official head of state, the president's powers are mainly restricted to the calling of elections and ceremonial functions, and one person can serve for no more than two terms as president. The president can pardon criminals and receives and visits other heads of state. The president promulgates all federal laws with a signature (the authority to refuse to sign is disputed, and presidents have signed all but perhaps five laws). The president is not popularly elected. According to the Basic Law, every five years a special federal convention convenes for the sole purpose of selecting the president; it is composed of the delegates to the legislature, an equal number of representatives from the state assemblies, and several other prominent persons. The selection by the federal convention has so far led to presidents with moderate views, at the end of distinguished careers, and well respected by the political elite. Johannes Rau began serving his presidential term in July 1999 at the age of 68; he had previously served as the deputy national chairman of the Socialist Party and as prime minister of Germany's largest state, North-Rhine-Westphalia. His 2004 successor, 61-year-old Horst Kohler, was chosen by the majority in the federal convention held by parties in opposition to the SPD-Green government – the CDU/CSU and the FDP. Trained as an economist and political scientist, Kohler served in the economics and finance ministries of CDU governments, rising to deputy minister of finance from 1990 to 1993, during which time he helped to negotiate the Maastricht treaty on European Economic and Monetary Union and undertook major responsibilities for the process of German unification. Some presidents have been able to influence national debates by means of skillful speech making, as when Richard von Weizsacker (president 1984–1994; CDU) gave a 1985 speech commemorating the fortieth anniversary of the end of World War II that cautioned Germans not to forget the nation's past and to guard against a revival of nationalist sentiment.

The **federal chancellor (Bundeskanzler)** is the real executive power in the German system. Although the chancellor is responsible to the legislature, as in other parliamentary systems, he or she may appoint and dismiss other cabinet ministers at will, rather like U.S. presidents. The relatively regular interval between elections gives the chancellor a somewhat firm idea about the political struggles that lie ahead and enhances the authority of the legislature and the chancellor over that of the president. Another source of the chancellor's authority is Article 67 of the Basic Law, the so-called **constructive vote of no confidence**, which states that the legislature may dismiss the chancellor only when a majority of the members simultaneously elects a successor. This brake on the authority of the legislature helps prevent weak chancellors from emerging. For example, the only time that a constructive vote of no confidence succeeded was in 1982, when the Free Democratic

TABLE 5.1. German Chancellors since World War II

1949–1963	Konrad Adenauer (CDU)
1963–1966	Ludwig Erhard (CDU)
1966–1969	Kurt Georg Kiesinger (CDU)
1969–1974	Willy Brandt (SPD)
1974–1982	Helmut Schmidt (SPD)
1982–1998	Helmut Kohl (CDU)
1998–2005	Gerhard Schroder (SPD)
2005–	Angela Merkel (CDU)

Party (FDP) withdrew from the ruling coalition and went along with a vote of no confidence regarding Social Democratic Party (SPD) Chancellor Helmut Schmidt. A new FDP and CDU/CSU coalition in the legislature selected Helmut Kohl as chancellor. With a majority behind him from the beginning and with several election victories thereafter, Kohl served as chancellor from 1982 until 1998. In other parliamentary governments, legislatures can agree to dismiss a sitting government but then may fail to agree on a strong successor, agreeing instead only to select weak figures unable to take real initiatives on their own.

The lower house (Bundestag) of the bicameral legislature produces the executive. The lower house is directly elected, whereas the upper house (**Bundesrat**) is composed of delegates chosen by the 16 federal states (*Länder*). The leader of the largest party in the lower house usually puts together a two-party coalition (neither of the two largest parties controls a majority of seats alone); the coalition in turn supports the party leader as chancellor. The chancellor must maintain a legislative majority in order to stay in power. With majority support, however, the chancellor has a relatively free hand in appointing and dismissing members of the cabinet. For example, the Social Democratic Party won the single largest block of seats in the 1998 and 2002 elections; after each election, its leader, Gerhard Schroder, formed a coalition with the Green Party to control a majority of seats. His cabinets were dominated by SPD politicians, but some key posts were given to Green Party politicians, notably the post of foreign minister to Joschka Fischer. After the 2005 elections, neither of the two big parties could form a majority alone or in coalition with one of the smaller parties; the government was formed by a new grand coalition of the SPD and the CDU/CSU with Angela Merkel (CDU) as chancellor.

The rules for translating votes into seats comprise a crucial institution in any democracy. Germany employs a mixed-member proportional formula (a subtype of proportional representation). Each voter makes **two ballot choices** in a national German election for representatives in the lower house. One choice is for a candidate to represent the voter's district. The winning candidates in each district take half the seats in the lower house. A voter's second choice is for a national party overall in the lower house. The other half of the seats are awarded such that the proportion of seats per party matches the votes per party on the second ballot choice. The two types of representatives give the system its mixed-member label; once in place, however, the two types of members behave the same and have identical powers in the legislature.

Germany's mixed-member proportional system preserves the influence of medium-sized and large parties and minimizes the impact of small parties with widely dispersed supporters. Germany's medium-sized parties gain national representation via the second ballot choice more easily than under a plurality electoral system, in which the voter makes only one choice for a given office and the top vote-getter in a district wins the office (as is the case in the United States and United Kingdom). Most notably, two German parties have won seats in the legislature by securing a national vote of more than 5 percent on the second ballot choice, even though their candidates did not win any districts on the first ballot choice. The Free Democrats have been a crucial player in legislative politics since 1949, while typically winning about 10 percent of the popular vote. Similarly, the Greens have become almost as influential since the 1980s although securing only around 5 percent to 10 percent of the popular vote. Grand-coalition governments of the SPD and the CDU/CSU ruled from 1966 to 1969 and after the 2005 elections, but all of the other coalition governments have involved one of the big parties with one of the medium-sized parties.

The big winners in the electoral system are the two largest parties. Germany's electoral system includes three special rules, two of which aid the largest parties. One is the "5 percent rule": A party must win at least 5 percent of the national vote on the second ballot choice in order to get a matching share of seats. Thus, small parties with support distributed across many districts are eliminated from gaining representation (for instance, the extreme right-wing Republican Party won 3 percent of the national second-choice vote but no seats in 1994; similar results emerged in 1998 and 2002). Even the medium-sized Free Democrats and the Greens are perennially concerned about falling below the 5 percent threshold; their coalition partners in government have periodically advocated strategic voting in order to ensure that the medium-sized parties do not fall below that mark. During the SPD-FDP coalition of 1969–1982, SPD supporters offered crucial support to the FDP on their second ballot choice; in 1998, the FDP relied upon second ballot choices of CDU supporters, while the Greens relied upon second ballot choices of SPD supporters. The 5 percent threshold thus increases the reliance of the medium-sized parties on their larger partners. A second important rule is the "three-district waiver" exception to the 5 percent rule: If a party wins a seat in at least three districts, then the national 5 percent rule is waived, and the party is also awarded seats according to its share of the total vote on the second ballot choice. This second modification permitted the former East German Communist Party, campaigning as the Party of Democratic Socialism, to win national representation after unification in the elections of the 1990s based on its victories in the former East Berlin, despite its very small national vote share. This second modification is the only one that aids very small parties, and it comes into play only if the small party's supporters are concentrated in a few districts. In 2002, however, the PDS won only two districts and thus did not qualify for additional seats by the three-district waiver. Finally, the "excess mandate provision" holds that if a party wins more district mandates than the proportion of the popular vote on the second choice would otherwise award the party, then the party gets to retain any extra seats, and the size of the legislature is increased accordingly. Although of relatively little consequence for most of the Federal Republic's electoral history, the excess mandate provision during the 1990s began to help the big parties that can win seats in many districts; it gave the CDU 6 extra seats in 1990, and then in 1994 gave the CDU 12 extra seats and the SPD 4. In 2005, the CDU received 9 and the SPD received 7 of these so-called overhang seats.

All of these rules, combined with the way voters actually cast their ballots, produce governments. To take a specific example, the 2002 elections gave five parties seats in the lower house: Social Democratic Party (SPD), 251 seats; Christian Democratic Union (CDU)/Christian Social Union (CSU), 248 seats; Bundnis90/Greens, 55 seats; Free Democratic Party (FDP), 47 seats; Party of Democratic Socialism (PDS) – socialist, former communist – 2 seats. Over a dozen other parties were on ballots in one or more states but did not qualify for national representation. As in previous elections, the extreme right-wing parties were fragmented and ineffectual at the national level. These seat totals for the five parties in the legislature produced an 11-seat majority for the SPD-Green alliance, so SPD Chancellor Schroder remained in power, although he shuffled some individual cabinet posts. As we have seen, Germany's bicameral system can provide other opportunities for the opposition and their supporters despite a government's majority in the lower house. The opposition was able to play a strong role in influencing Schroder's sweeping economic reform plans in 2003 after elections in the states of Hesse and Lower Saxony in February of that year gave victories to the CDU; with the CDU in power in those states, their delegates to the Bundesrat gave a majority to opposition parties. The final legislation agreed to in December 2003 required the government to compromise from its original proposals.

Germany's federal structure gives the republic's constituent units a great deal of power. Sixteen states make up the republic. The combination of federalism in the state and bicameralism in the legislature gives Germany a substantial amount of institutional overlap that differs both from unitary systems (such as in the United Kingdom and France) and from other federal systems that have sharper federal–state distinctions (such as in the United States). Compared with regional governments in Europe, the states possess a good deal of power in relation to the central government. Each state has a premier and a legislature. The state legislatures send delegates to the assembly that elects the president and also send delegates to the national legislature's upper house (the Bundesrat). The Basic Law reserves certain powers for the states, including education, police and internal security, administration of justice, and the regulation of mass media. The states are also responsible for administering federal laws and collecting most taxes. Changes since the Basic Law of 1949 have been designed to enhance or at least preserve the states' powers. They now have at least a joint role in higher education, regional economic development, and agricultural reform. Reforms in 1994 were designed to give the various states a voice in policy making at the European level; until then, the federal government had a larger role to play.

The Basic Law recognizes freedom of religion, but Article 140 grants important public authority to religious institutions that had exercised such authority under the Weimar Republic. Most notably, Lutheran and Catholic churches are granted "public corporation" status that includes, among its key features, a provision that the government directs a percentage of the tax payments from persons who identify with these religions to their respective churches (the amounts are substantial – about 8–10 percent of what individuals owe in taxes). Individual states make decisions on granting public corporation status to other religions, and they have done so for several Christian sects and Jews. In contrast, no Muslim organization has been awarded public corporation status.

There are hundreds of Muslim organizations in Germany, many with strongly competing goals and values, and several high-profile efforts to form single, umbrella organizations for Muslims have failed to incorporate key groups and/or have splintered soon after their formation. In the 1970s and 1980s, the federal government relied mainly upon organizations associated with the Turkish state to manage the affairs of Muslims in Germany, notably the Turkish State Directorate for Religious Affairs. The main organizational network of political Islam in Germany was the Islamic Community Milli Görüs, organized by Turkish Muslims who opposed the secularizing character of the official organization. Beginning in the 1990s, however, German governments have sought to co-opt and to incorporate both types of organizations into German-centered institutions. Several states have established special councils for state–Islam relations and the federal government – especially through the Ministry of the Interior, the courts, and the Federal Office for the Protection of the Constitution (Bundesamt für Verfassungsschutz) – has attempted to nationalize the political and religious organization of Muslims in Germany. Recently, for instance, in November 2006, the Interior Ministry launched the German Conference on Islam (DIK), which is intended to be a two- to three-year process of negotiation and communication between the federal government and representatives of Muslims living in Germany.

The economy itself can be seen as an institution, especially because its key actors are linked in stable relationships that go beyond mere monetary exchange. Many terms have been used to describe the economy of the Federal Republic of Germany: neocorporatism, social democracy, and coordinated market economy, to name three important ones. These terms seek to capture Germany's blend of social and market institutions in a single economy. In fact, a term that Germans commonly use to describe their economic order is a "**social market economy**." A social market economy rests not only on market principles of supply and demand but also on extensive involvement by the state and societal institutions. Germany has institutions that are designed to ensure the smooth functioning of free economic exchange. Prior to the European Monetary Union, Germany's central bank, for example, was for a long time one of the most independent and powerful central banks in the world. In fact, Germany's central bank was the main model for the European Central Bank. Germany's bank sought to keep interest rates and inflation low and the currency stable. There is no purer example of a firm commitment to market principles than a central bank free of political influence. On the social side of the equation, the German state guarantees a free university education for all who qualify academically, and basic health care and adequate income for all its citizens. In addition, the state supports organized representation in the workplace and vocational training for workers, rather than letting these matters be handled by firms or unions alone.

At the heart of Germany's social market economy is the "social partnership" of business and labor. According to the political scientist Lowell Turner, social partnership is defined as "the nexus – and central political and economic importance – of bargaining relationships between strongly organized employers (in employer associations) and employees (in unions and works councils) that range from comprehensive collective bargaining and plant-level co-determination to vocational training and federal, state and local economic policy discussions." In addition to labor and business, there are also important "framing and negotiating roles" for two other actors, large banks and the government. In this kind of system, negotiated agreements between the social partners of business and labor shape politics and economics at all levels: national, regional, and local. As an example of national peak agreements, one could point to the Concerted Action of 1967 or the Solidarity Pact in 1993. There are also industry-wide or simply firm-level agreements regarding, for example, vocational training and industrial policy.

The Solidarity Pact of 1993 nicely illustrates a peak bargain under social partnership. The federal government agreed not to let old industries in the former East Germany simply wither away. Instead, it sought an active role for itself in industrial restructuring. Eastern industries benefited from temporary assistance, as did labor, because employment was protected. Western industrialists were also given opportunities for developing infrastructure (such as roads, railroads, and government offices), while they promised to invest in the old eastern industrial core rather than simply dismantling it and confining their production to the already developed western regions. Unions, in return, promised to hold back wage demands in both the East and West and promised to support the program of adjustment in the East rather than adopt a posture of militant opposition. Although this bargain worked to the benefit of all sides, it was the product of institutionalized negotiation, not simple economic logic.

Scholars and policymakers do not agree on the future of German social partnership. In the view of many, the Solidarity Pact of 1993 was just an isolated episode in a period more noted for conflicting interests. The early 1990s witnessed a new phase of economic globalization: Would the institutions of social partnership survive the neoliberal economic policy atmosphere? Would they hold up against rapid financial movements across international borders? Could they be maintained in the face of widening international economic competition as the costs of communication and transportation continued to fall? During the early 1990s, it was plausible that Germany's more moderate social partnership would succumb to the new conditions. Unemployment rose to over 10 percent in late 1995 and grew to over 12 percent in early 1997. Because unions typically find it difficult to maintain their bargaining position in the face of persistent joblessness among workers, German unions will likely find it hard to sustain their influential role. Furthermore, the increasing integration of European economies weakens the position of national-level actors, especially labor unions. Finally, the prospect of extending the European Union to the east introduces the possibility that employers will use low-cost labor in less-developed member countries rather than continue to invest in the developed core.

Others are more optimistic that German social partnership may be resilient after all. Although recognizing the difficulties facing partnership, especially the challenges facing organized labor, one can point to more positive signs. In the first place, the eastern decay has not spread to the West; instead Western institutions have spread to the former East Germany. Employer associations, industrial unions, comprehensive collective-bargaining arrangements, elected works councils, and legally mandated codetermination have all taken root in the old East. The economic integration of the East, although not complete and not as painless as Chancellor Helmut Kohl argued it would be in 1990, certainly has not led to an economic collapse. According to these optimists, few companies actually relocated to low-wage countries during the 1980s. They further maintain that there will likely be little relocation to the East during the next few decades. Investment in the East, moreover, may serve to stimulate demand for exports from Germany and may also open up even more markets for German goods. In addition to these favorable trends, the international financial crises of the late 1990s – first in Asia, then in Russia, and then in Latin America – dampened enthusiasm for unregulated free markets, even among global investors. In times of uncertainty, many international financial decision makers sought the greater security provided by more institutionalized forms of industrial organization. European Union institutions leave a great deal of leeway to national-level institutions, by the principle of "subsidiarity" (the notion that decisions should be made at the most local level possible), and because each individual government, especially governments of big countries such as Germany, has a major say in what happens at the European level. Finally, Germany's major firms have actually sought to preserve key elements of its social market economy, such as their successful efforts to maintain policies of generously supported early retirement for workers.

Persistent unemployment (reaching levels above 11 percent) and poor economic performance were cited by the Schroder government as the reasons for major cuts in social spending and labor-market reforms in 2003. Although key reforms did pass, making it easier for firms to hire workers without providing them protections against firing, for example, two key features of the German labor market did not change: sectorwide wage agreements and workers' codetermination. Both of these institutions involve businesses, labor unions, workers' elected representatives, and the state in managing change on the shop floors of Germany's leading industries. Thus, even as Germany's Social Democratic and Green coalition governing parties attempted to put forward major changes in the state and the economy, the core features of social partnership continued to play key roles. After the 2005 elections, under a CDU/CSU and SPD coalition government, the prospects for major transformations of state–economy relations and social partnership are not strong.

The new German judiciary and the legal philosophy of the state is the product of a deliberate attempt by post-Nazi era political actors to transform radically an institution that had not protected basic civil and human rights. On the side of institutional redesign, the Basic Law created a Federal Constitutional Court with the power of judicial review. The practice of judges reviewing state actions for conformity with a higher law – in this case, the Basic Law – was completely foreign to the German legal tradition before 1949. The change was strongly championed by the U.S. occupiers, who had at their disposal the model of the U.S. Supreme Court and who were clearly thinking of the old German judiciary that did not strike down any of the Nazi government's decrees.

A distinctive and controversial aspect of German law and legal institutions, however, concerns what Americans would call freedom of speech. Unlike in the United States, "hate speech" is unconstitutional in Germany, and the organizations that promote it are banned after being investigated by the Federal Office for the Protection of the Constitution. It is illegal, for example, to organize a Nazi party, to deny publicly the historical fact of the Holocaust, or to sell or distribute Nazi propaganda. How does the German state justify actions and policies that Americans would consider unacceptable, and even unconstitutional, departures from liberal democratic practices? Germans view their democracy as a "militant democracy" that is unwilling to permit antidemocratic forces to use the protections of the liberal state to help undermine it. These ideas and the institutions that are in place to back them up are one obvious reaction to Germany's authoritarian past.

The German judiciary nevertheless also shows some continuity in its institutional practices. On the side of persistence, German judges are closely integrated with the state bureaucracy, and their posts are like those of high bureaucrats. They are rarely former politicians, prosecutors, or other types of attorneys, as is often the case in the United States. Instead, aspiring jurists begin their careers as apprentices to sitting judges; they then rise through the hierarchy and, if they are successful, never leave the judicial branch. The dominant institutional philosophy of judging puts the judge in the role of actively applying the law to individual cases in a deliberate pursuit of the truth, unlike U.S. judges, who more commonly see themselves as impartial arbiters between two conflicting parties. German judges do not set precedents as do their Anglo-American counterparts; the job of German judges is simply to apply the law correctly, not interpret it or adapt it to circumstances unforeseen by the framers of a statute. Despite the otherwise federal structure of the judiciary, the German legal code is uniform across all of the various state governments.

Germany's Post–World War II Developmental Path

Whereas Germany had relied upon state-led development for most of its unified history, the post–World War II German state acted as a cooperative partner in social and economic development. The FRG itself led much of the world's post–World War II economic growth, partly financed internationally by the U.S. Marshall Plan for European recovery. Germany's economic development was grounded domestically in its close cooperation among top businesses, organized labor unions, and the state. The state still influences Germany's society and economy through institutions similar to those found in many other European countries. The economic slowdown and persistent unemployment in the early twenty-first century present challenges for its governments that are seeking to streamline the state and energize economic growth, yet Germany today is still a model for those seeking to strike a new balance between the strengths of the free market and the support of significant social protections. In its foreign economic policy, Germany promotes deep economic integration with world markets and especially within an expanded European Union. In foreign security policy, Cold War Germany was the forward base of U.S. power in Europe. Germany remains a key U.S. ally in the early twenty-first century, although it advocates greater multilateralism when confronting terrorists and rogue states around the world.

Germany's path of political development was profoundly shaped by its long period as a middle developer (see Table 5.2 at the end of the chapter). Germany began much like the rest of Europe. Yet, compared with England and France, Germany's lateness in developing a single territorial state and a strong industrial base, and then new challenges from even later developers, such as Russia, put Germany in a difficult position. Germany was also a relatively large middle developer, like Japan, and thus it acquired domestic interests, identities, and institutions different from smaller middle developers, such as Sweden and Denmark. The temptation to use a massive state apparatus for military conquest in a bid to improve its global position did not disappear in Germany until after World War II. Germany's persistent reliance on the state to address many important tasks fostered a distinctive set of interests, identities, and institutions that made it hard to develop or sustain democratic political institutions. As a result, for much of its history, Germany's economic development was state-led, and its political order was authoritarian.

Germany's global context predisposed it to adopt the state-led path to development. The Second Empire was the prize Prussia won by defeating its military rivals, notably France. With a heavy reliance on its army and bureaucracy, the state aided the growth of heavy industry in a bid to catch up with leading industries in Britain. In politics, the state strongly discouraged dissent and refused to permit elections to the highest public offices. The Second Empire never became a democracy. The Weimar Republic departed from the imperial pattern to adopt competitive capitalism and democratic, constitutional government. In stark contrast with the preceding regime, the two political parties at the core of most of Weimar's coalition governments were the Socialist Party and the Catholic Center Party. The global context, however, remained unfavorable for capitalist democracy in Germany. In addition to the burden of reparations payments to France and Britain after World War I, Germany still faced stiff industrial competition from the Western economies. After the establishment of communist rule in Russia during the 1920s, Germany felt threatened and discriminated against, now from both the West and the East. The economic crisis brought on by the Great Depression was the final blow to the Weimar Republic. In the end, the Nazi Party offered Germans a chance to take a new version of antiliberal, state-led development. Thus, the durability of the Second Empire, the difficult experiment with democracy under Weimar, and the reversion to state-led development under Nazi rule all point to the importance of the state for much of Germany's existence.

The path of state-led development was difficult to change because of the feedback effect through domestic institutions. The legacies of the Second Empire, including strong authoritarian enclaves in the army, bureaucracy, and presidency, made the survival of the Weimar Republic precarious. The

Second Empire's support for Protestant nationalism against Catholicism and class-based sentiments left contradictory legacies. On the one hand, Catholic and working-class identities and institutions developed in opposition to the regime and then went on to be bulwarks of the Weimar Republic. On the other hand, the legacy of strong nationalism and the experience of stigmatizing various groups as unpatriotic and non-German fed into support for the Nazi Party and the overthrow of the democratic system.

Germany's state-led development also fed back into the international system itself. German militarism provoked Soviet defensive action and the fortress mentality of communist regimes, and it also provoked the established Western powers to use force in defense of the liberal international order. The defeat of Nazi Germany in World War II laid the groundwork for a new global rivalry between the United States and the Soviet Union. These two main powers occupied and divided Germany. The U.S. and international support for West Germany's reindustrialization and reintegration into the world economic and political systems helped to set Germany down a new path.

Germany's new global position as one of the world's leading economic powers supports a revised set of interests, identities, and institutions and a kind of democratic capitalism that can be described as embedded liberalism. Germany stands for strongly liberal economic policies, and its industries are fiercely competitive in the international marketplace. Its institutions sustain a firmly democratic regime with a constitutional framework. The market is combined with the social partnership of strong labor unions, business leaders, and key administrative agencies. Germany's political parties, labor unions, and federal institutions all consistently support the basic practices of constitutional, parliamentary democracy. As for political values, most political scientists agree that Germany is as solidly democratic today as any country in Europe.

The continuing globalization of the economy presents a new set of challenges and opportunities for Germany. With the collapse of the Soviet Union, a unified Germany is exercising even greater influence in European and world politics, especially through its leading role in the strengthened European Union. The German social welfare system so far remains more or less intact, despite some cuts in recent years. Germany also maintains a high level of wage equality and keeps government budgets largely in balance, but at the cost of relatively high unemployment. Germany has attracted labor immigrants and political refugees, many of whom are Muslim, but there are few political or religious institutions that successfully facilitate integration into German society; moreover, current efforts at improved integration are frequently confounded by internal diversity among Muslims, by competition between Muslim organizations, and by debates among Germans about whether and how to recognize their society's new ethnic and religious heterogeneity. The question of how Germany's distinctive set of interests, identities, and institutions will respond to new global challenges remains an exciting issue to follow in the coming years.

BIBLIOGRAPHY

Bairoch, Paul. "International Industrialization Levels from 1750 to 1980." *Journal of Economic History* 11, no. 2 (Fall 1982): 269–333.

Dahrendorf, Ralf. *Society and Democracy in Germany*. New York: Norton, 1967.

Ertman, Thomas. *Birth of the Leviathan: Building States and Regimes in Medieval and Early Modern Europe*. Cambridge: Cambridge University Press, 1997.

Eurobarometer Surveys of public opinion. Accessed at http://ec.europa.eu/public_opinion/index_en.htm.

Federal Statistical Office, Germany. Official statistics and reports accessed at http://www.destatis.de/e_home.htm.

Gerschenkron, Alexander. *Economic Backwardness in Historical Perspective: A Book of Essays*. Cambridge, MA: Harvard University Press, 1962.

Gould, Andrew C. *Origins of Liberal Dominance: State, Church, and Party in Nineteenth Century Europe*. Ann Arbor: University of Michigan Press, 1999.

Janos, Andrew C. "The Politics of Backwardness in Continental Europe, 1780–1945." *World Politics* 41, no. 3 (April 1989): 325–358.

Klausen, Jytte. *The Islamic Challenge: Politics and Religion in Western Europe*. Oxford: Oxford University Press, 2005.

Laurence, Jonathan. "Managing Transnational Islam: Muslims and the State in Western Europe." In Craig Parsons and Timothy Smeeding, eds. *Immigration and the Transformation of Europe*. New York: Cambridge University Press, 2006.

Luebbert, Gregory M. *Liberalism, Fascism, or Social Democracy: Social Classes and the Political Origins of Regimes in Interwar Europe*. New York: Oxford University Press, 1991.

Moore, Barrington. *The Social Origins of Dictatorship and Democracy: Lord and Peasant in the Making of the Modern World*. Boston: Beacon, 1966.

Organization for Economic Cooperation and Development (OECD). Statistics can be accessed at http://www.oecd.org/statsportal/.

Rogowski, Ronald. *Commerce and Coalitions: How Trade Affects Domestic Political Alignments*. Princeton, NJ: Princeton University Press, 1989.

Suval, Stanley. *Electoral Politics in Wilhelmine Germany*. Chapel Hill: University of North Carolina Press, 1985.

Turner, Lowell, ed. *Negotiating the New Germany: Can Social Partnership Survive?* Ithaca, NY: Cornell University Press, 1997.

Wehler, Hans-Ulrich. *The German Empire, 1871–1918*. Leamington Spa: Berg Publishers, 1985.

World Bank. World Development Indicators 2006. Accessed at http://devdata.worldbank.org/wdi2006/contents/index2.htm.

TABLE 5.2. Key Phases in Germany's Political Development

Time period	Regime	Global context	Interests/identities/institutions	Developmental path
1800–1870	competing monarchies (authoritarian)	industrial and political revolutions	strong landed elite Protestant nationalism and Catholic resistance authoritarian institutions evade reform	state-building
1871–1918	Second Empire (authoritarian)	European imperialism	industry and landed elite strong nationalism and working-class and Catholic subcultures authoritarian with elections	state-building
1919–1933	Weimar Republic (democratic)	rise of U.S. economic power; communist revolution in Russia	strong industry socialism, Catholicism, nationalism, weak democratic values, and fear of communism democracy with powerful reserved domains for authoritarian office-holders in army and bureaucracy	competitive capitalism
1933–1945	Third Empire (authoritarian)	great power rivalry and global depression	strong industry fascism and anti-Semitism authoritarian	totalitarian overthrow of world order
1945–1949	foreign occupation (military)	U.S. and Soviet military dominance	reindustrialization, fascism discredited parties, unions, and local governments rebuild	international aid
1949–1990	Federal Republic of Germany (democratic)	Cold War and economic growth in capitalist countries	automobiles and high-technology industry democratic values grow, new immigrants, feminism, and environmentalism parties, unions, federal state	embedded liberalism Leninism
	German Democratic Republic (authoritarian)		heavy industry, communist indoctrination but increasing disaffection one-party state	
1990–	Federal Republic of Germany (democratic)	U.S. as sole superpower and global-ization	advanced industry and services, strong democratic values, cultural nationalism, feminism, environmentalism parties, unions, federal state, EU	embedded liberalism

IMPORTANT TERMS

Austrian Empire the south-east German polity governed from Vienna by the Habsburg dynasty and the main rival to Prussia for control over German territory. It was officially founded in 1804 by the Habsburgs in response to Napoleon; it was succeeded by the Austro-Hungarian Empire in 1867, which was then dissolved in 1918. Formerly Habsburg lands became the states of Austria, Hungary, Czechoslovakia, and portions of Poland, Rumania, Italy, and Balkan states.

Basic Law (Grundgesetz) founding 1949 document of the Federal Republic of Germany that serves as its constitution. Originally designed to be replaced by "a constitution adopted by a free decision of the German people," it has never been replaced but has been amended several times, including to incorporate the new states from the East in 1990.

Berlin city in northeastern Germany, capital of reunified Germany since 1990. It was earlier the capital of the kingdom of Prussia, the Second Empire, the Weimar Republic, and the Third Reich. It was occupied and divided after World War II. The support of the United States during the Berlin airlift (1948–1949) kept Soviet forces from taking the western sector. The Berlin wall (1961–1989) kept easterners from leaving for the West. Berlin's eastern half was the capital of the German Democratic Republic.

Bonn city on the Rhine River in western Germany, from 1949 to 1990 the provisional capital of West Germany. After 1990, it continued to house many federal offices during the move back to Berlin. It was occupied by French revolutionary forces in 1794 and was awarded to Prussia in 1815.

Bundesrat (Federal Council) the second, or upper, house of the Parliament in which each state (*Land*) receives at least three votes and larger states receive up to three additional votes based on population; there are 69 votes total. A state's delegation must cast all of its votes together as the state government instructs, and no split votes can be registered, even from states governed by coalitions of parties. The Bundesrat's approval is required in about two-thirds of legislation, where the states' powers are involved. Secondary in power to the Bundestag but important when different parties control the two houses.

Bundestag (Federal Diet) the primary, or lower, house of the Parliament. Its delegates are chosen by popular vote, with all seats up for election normally every four years. The exact number of seats can vary slightly from one election to another because of the "excess mandate provision" and the "three-district waiver" electoral rules (603 delegates were seated after the 2002 election; 614 after the 2005 election).The Bundestag's approval is required for all legislation, as in most parliamentary systems, and it exercises more oversight of cabinets than do most parliaments. Its majority party or a coalition selects the chancellor.

Center Party (Zentrumspartei) the political party that emerged in defense of Catholic interests in the 1870s under the Second Empire. It was the second-largest party for much of the Weimar Republic (with 15 percent to 20 percent of the vote), and it frequently was in the governing coalition. Its predominantly Catholic supporters for the most part did not defect to the Nazi Party during the early 1930s, but its deputies voted for the Enabling Act that gave Hitler dictatorial powers in 1933.

Christian Democrats the Christian Democratic Union (CDU) and the Christian Social Union (CSU), allied parties on the center-right. The CDU campaigns in all states except Bavaria, where it is allied with the more conservative CSU. The CDU's founding in the post–World War II era broke from the tradition of the Catholic Center Party by including Protestants as well as Catholics. Since 1949, one of Germany's two main political party groupings.

Congress of Vienna the 1815 great-powers conference after the defeat of French Emperor Napoleon Bonaparte. The powers agreed to give Prussia control over most of the Rhine territories in order to keep France in check, greatly expanding Prussia's role in Germany overall.

constructive vote of no confidence requirement in the Basic Law that the Bundestag, in order to dismiss the chancellor, must simultaneously agree on a new chancellor. It was designed to limit the power of the parliament and strengthen the chancellor. Attempted twice but successful only once, it has generally had the intended effect.

Friedrich Ebert leader of the moderate wing of the Social Democratic Party and first president of the Weimar Republic.

federal chancellor (Bundeskanzler) head of the government, usually the head of the leading political party. Once the chancellor is selected by the Bundestag, he or she can count on majority support most of the time. The chancellor has more authority than prime ministers in most parliamentary systems.

federal president (Bundesprasident) head of state with largely ceremonial authority. The president is selected by a federal convention of all Bundestag deputies and an equal number of delegates selected by the state legislatures. The position has a five-year term and is usually filled by senior politicians; activist presidents can use the office to influence public opinion.

Federal Republic of Germany (FRG) Bundesrepublikdeutschland (BRD), the current German state. Founded in 1949 and based on the U.S., British, and French zones of occupation, it was often known as West Germany until 1990. It acquired the German Democratic Republic (GDR) in the unification of 1990.

Frankfurt Parliament (1848–1849) the all-German Parliament elected in 1848 that met in the city of Frankfurt and attempted to unify and reform the many German states along more liberal or democratic principles. Its inability to do so began a long period of authoritarian predominance in German states.

German Democratic Republic (GDR) Deutsche Demokratische Republik (DDR), the German state based on the Soviet zone of occupation from 1949 until 1990, often known as East Germany.

guest workers (*Gastarbeiter*) frequently used term for immigrant workers in the 1950s and 1960s that underscored their temporary status in Germany.

Otto von Hindenburg the Junker former army officer who became the second president of the Weimar Republic and appointed Hitler as chancellor in 1933.

Holocaust the Nazi attempt to kill all European Jews during World War II. 5.7 million Jewish people were killed. Other so-called undesirable people – including Roma, homosexuals, psychiatric patients, the handicapped, and political opponents, especially Communists – were also targeted for destruction. A total of between six and seven million people lost their lives. Auschwitz and Treblinka were two major death camps.

Junkers the landed nobility of eastern Prussia. Their vast estates east of the Elbe River produced grain for Germany and the world market but only by keeping agricultural laborers in near slavery. They formed the core of the Prussian state administration and the Second Empire's administration, and never fully accepted the legitimacy of the Weimar Republic.

Kulturkampf (cultural struggle) the attempt by the Second Empire to break the authority of the Catholic Church in unified Germany by means of legislation, regulation, and the harassment of priests, mainly between 1871 and 1878. It reduced the church's authority in some areas but generally sparked a revival of political Catholicism and popular religiosity.

Karl Marx founding thinker of modern socialism and communism. Born in 1818 in Trier, in the Rhine province of Prussia, he became involved in various German and French radical movements during the 1830s and 1840s. He wrote *The Communist Manifesto* (in 1848, with Friedrich Engels) and many other polemical and analytical works. The guiding personality in the Socialist International movement in the 1860s, he died in London in 1883.

National Socialist German Workers' Party (Nazi Party) the fascist party taken over by Adolph Hitler in 1920–1921. It became the largest political party in the Weimar Republic in the early 1930s, winning 38 percent of the vote in July 1932 and 33 percent in November. Hitler's appointment as chancellor in 1933 was followed by the end of the republic and the beginning of one-party Nazi rule until 1945.

Oder-Neisse line the contemporary eastern border of Germany with Poland along these two rivers.

Prussia the North German state governed from Berlin by the Hohenzollern dynasty beginning in 1701 that grew in military strength and gained control of most of what is now Germany and western Poland during the eighteenth and nineteenth centuries. It formed the core of the Second Empire in 1871. Subsequently a state within Germany, it was disbanded during the Allied occupation in 1947.

Social Democratic Party Germany's oldest political party, generally on the center-left. It emerged in the 1870s as a working-class protest party, and its main wing helped to found and frequently govern the Weimar Republic. Since 1949, one of Germany's two main political parties.

social market economy a term for tempering the free market with concern for social consequences. It is based on a "social partnership" of business and labor, along with the state and banks, to shape politics and economics at the national, regional, and local levels in order to cushion and guide economic change.

two-vote ballot procedure the voting method to select delegates in the Bundestag that is a form of proportional representation. The first vote is for a candidate to represent the voter's district. Half of the seats are awarded as a result. The second vote is for a party overall. The remaining seats are distributed so that the overall share of seats for each party matches the second ballot choices.

Weimar Republic the German state and democratic regime that was formed after the fall of the Second Empire in 1919 and lasted until 1933. It was named for the city where its constitution was written. Bitter and polarized partisan competition from the communist Left and the extreme nationalist right wing made it difficult for the moderate and mostly Social Democratic and Center Party governments to operate.

STUDY QUESTIONS

1. Consider Germany in 1815. In what ways was it like the rest of Europe? How was it different?

2. Why were Germany's political institutions under the Second Empire authoritarian rather than democratic?

3. Why did the Weimar Republic fail to survive as a democracy?

4. What were the main features and policies of the Nazi regime?

5. How did the Allies reshape interests, identities, and institutions in occupied Germany from 1945 through 1949?

6. What were the major differences between the FRG and the GDR between 1949 and 1989?

7. How did Germany's interests, identities, and institutions change as a result of reunification in 1990?

8. What are the major political parties in the FRG?

9. What impact has the FRG had on Europe and the world since World War II?

10. How is the global context after 1990 affecting Germany's developmental path?

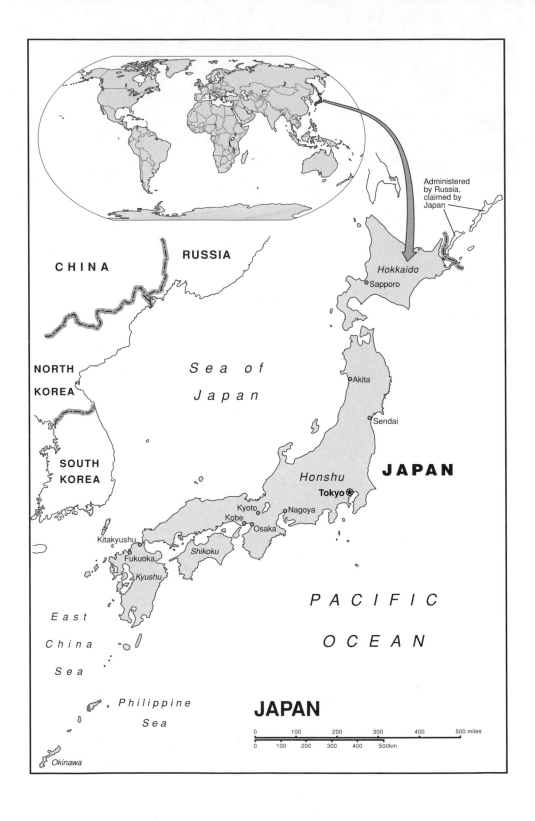

CHINA

RUSSIA

*Sea of
Japan*

NORTH
KOREA

SOUTH
KOREA

Administered
by Russia,
claimed by
Japan

Hokkaido
Sapporo

Akita

Sendai

JAPAN

Honshu

Tokyo

Kyoto
Kobe
Nagoya
Osaka

Kitakyushu

Fukuoka

Shikoku

Kyushu

*East
China
Sea*

*Philippine
Sea*

JAPAN

Okinawa

**PACIFIC

OCEAN**

| 0 | 100 | 200 | 300 | 400 | 500 miles |
| 0 | 100 | 200 | 300 | 400 | 500km |

CHAPTER SIX

Japan

Miranda A. Schreurs

Introduction

Japan is a fascinating country for political scientists to study. Within the space of a century, Japan went from being an almost completely isolated feudal society to the world's second richest country and a stable democracy.

Japan's interests, identities, and institutions have both been shaped by and played a significant role in shaping the global order. Under the threat of Western imperialism, Japan fought for its economic and political autonomy. As a result, Japan was the only imperial power in Asia, itself becoming a colonizer rather than a colonized state. Like Germany, Japan experimented with democracy in the 1920s before succumbing to militarist powers in the 1930s. Japan launched the Pacific War with the bombing of Pearl Harbor on December 7, 1941, and had conquered much of East and Southeast Asia before Japan's eventual defeat with the U.S. atomic bombings of Hiroshima and Nagasaki, respectively on August 6 and 9, 1945. Japan was occupied by the U.S.-led allied forces from its defeat in war until it regained sovereignty in April 1952. The subsequent democratic transition of postwar Japan can be considered among one of the most successful cases of democratization that occurred during what Samuel Huntington has referred to as the Second Wave of countries to democratize.

The Japanese Constitution, which was drafted with great U.S. influence, includes an article (**Article 9**) that renounces war as a sovereign right of the nation. Although this article is the subject of much debate and there have been calls for constitutional revision, Japan is arguably one of the most pacifist countries in the world today. Japan's security is guaranteed by the U.S.-Japan Security Treaty and Japan is the most important U.S. ally in Asia. Because Japan does not function as a "normal" state in the *realpolitik* sense of the word (that is, as a state that wields power through military strength), Japan has had to rely on economic and "soft" power in its foreign relations.

Despite much Western influence over Japanese institutions and interests, Japan retained and developed many unique institutions as well. Other countries have shown great interest in the institutional and cultural factors that were behind Japan's remarkable postwar economic growth. These include the close working relationship between government and industry, the special role played by Japan's highly educated bureaucracy in economic decision making, and the importance of long-term personal relationships. Japan developed a liberal form of economics that included a far greater degree of government-intervention and planning than existed in the United States.

Japan is also of interest because of the unique form of parliamentary democracy that has taken root in the post-occupation period. Japan has been ruled by the **Liberal Democratic Party** (**LDP**) ever since the party's founding in 1955, except for a brief interlude in the 1990s. Although a recession plagued the country for most of the decade after the bursting of Japan's economic bubble in 1989, the LDP survived as the dominant party. Electoral reform in 1994 was aimed at leading the state toward a two-party dominant system. This has yet to happen. An important development in this direction, however, was the electoral victory of the **Democratic Party of Japan** (**DPJ**) in the July 2007 House of Councillors election.

As we will see, many of the interests, identities, and institutions that shaped Japan in the second half of the twentieth century as the country struggled to catch up with the West have been under pressure. Ever since Japan caught up with North America and Europe economically – arguably starting in the 1970s, it has struggled to adapt its political, social, and economic institutions to a changing global context. Many of the structures that worked so well for Japan in its phase of catch-up economic development have proved less well adapted to a world in which Japan is among the world's richest and strongest economies. Today, Japan is trying to redefine itself as not just a major economic might, but also an important political power.

The Geography of Japan

Japan is a vast archipelago made up of over 3,000 islands extending 1,300 miles from the Sea of Japan to the Pacific Ocean, the distance from New York City to Miami, Florida. There are five large islands where the majority of the population live: Honshu, the main island, where both the ancient capital of Kyoto and the modern capital of Tokyo are found; Hokkaido, the northernmost island, which today is increasingly closely tied to Russia in its trade; Okinawa, which was returned to Japan only in 1972 and is home to the largest U.S. military base in the Pacific; Kyushu; and Shikoku.

Japan's 127 million inhabitants make it the world's tenth most populated country and also one of its most densely populated. The population density is made more intense by Japan's mountainous terrain. Eighty percent of the country is mountainous, meaning that a population that is only somewhat less than half that of the United States lives in a territory about the size of California, but only 20 percent of which is arable. In fact, it has been estimated that 50 percent of the Japanese population lives on just 2 percent of its land! Japan lacks much in the way of natural resources and must import virtually all of its oil and natural gas.

Japan is a largely homogenous nation; 99.4 percent of the population is Japanese and only 0.6 percent other ethnicities, primarily Korean and some Chinese. It has among the highest life expectancies of any country (over 80 years for both men and women) and among the lowest infant mortality rates. Although one of the richest nations in the world, the high cost of living means that per capita income on a purchasing power parity comparison was only roughly $33,100 compared to $43,800 for the United States in 2006.

The Historical Roots of Institutions, Identities, and Interests

To understand why Japan was able to modernize so quickly and to develop a stable democracy in the post–World War II period, it is important to examine briefly the impact of the global historical context on the development of Japanese institutions, identities, and interests.

TOKUGAWA JAPAN, 1603–1867

In 1600 Ieyasu Tokugawa succeeded in military battle to unify a country that had essentially been divided into 260 feudal fiefdoms, each headed by a **daimyo**, a feudal lord. Although still technically ruled by the imperial family, Japan's emperors had become too weak to keep real power. For the next two-and-a-half centuries (1603 to 1867) the Tokugawa shogunate ruled Japan from Edo (Tokyo) while the emperor maintained his residence in Kyoto. During this time, the daimyo were required to spend every other year in Edo working on behalf of the **shogun** and to leave their families in Edo when they traveled back to their feudal lands, an extremely expensive proposition that effectively prevented rival powers from emerging. This system of alternate residency known as *sankin kōtai* not only helped solidify the Tokugawa clan's power, it was an important element behind the development of a relatively strong economy. The fact that the daimyo and their retainers had to travel from across the vast archipelago to Edo every other year meant that an elaborate road system developed. This road system helped to support local economies and the process of urbanization. By 1720 Edo had a population of well over one million, making it the world's largest city. Urbanization helped stimulate demand from rural areas and the development of commodity and financial markets. The Edo period is known as a time of peace when various cultural arts such as kabuki and ukiyo-e flourished. Confucianism places a high value on learning and a large number of schools were created for the samurai (warriors in service to the daimyo) as well as for commoners. By the beginning of the Meiji period, Japan had obtained a fairly high literacy rate. These factors were all important for Japan's later rapid economic, political, and cultural transformation.

Japan was a Confucian, class-based society, with samurai at the top of the hierarchy, followed by peasants, artisans, and merchants. The only group that was considered lower than the merchants were the *eta*, the outcasts, whose professions, which included leather-work, were considered impure. Although Christian (primarily Jesuit and Franciscan) missionaries attempted to spread their religion in Japan, by the late sixteenth century they had become the targets of persecution and by the turn of the seventeenth century, Christianity was banned. Japan remained a nation of Buddhists and Shintoists.

Japan was remarkably isolated from the world during the Edo period. In the 1630s, Japan closed its ports to foreigners, except the Dutch and Chinese, who were granted permission to trade out of the port of Nagasaki in Kyushu. Foreign books were also banned until 1720. Given Japan's isolation, it must have been a real shock when in the summer of 1853 **Commodore Matthew Perry** steamed into Edo Bay with four armed ships carrying a letter to the Japanese emperor from U.S. President Millard Fillmore requesting (and in essence demanding) that Japan open its ports to American ships for trade and supplies. Recognizing the superior military power of the Americans, the shogunate acquiesced and a peace and friendship treaty that allowed for limited trade was signed. Perry's voyage was to mark the beginning of similar demands by other countries and Japan's forced acceptance of what are known as "unequal treaties." These were trade agreements that gave Westerners extraterritorial rights in Japan so that if, for example, they committed a crime on Japanese soil, they would not be subject to Japanese law, but only their own country's courts.

Perry's visit also marked the beginning of a century of rapid and at times turbulent changes in Japanese politics, economics, and society as Japan sought first to prevent domination by the West, as it saw what had happened in neighboring China and throughout much of Southeast Asia, and then to "catch up" with the Europe and North America. Japan's late entry onto the world stage had fateful consequences not only for Japan's development, but also for relations between Asia and the West.

THE MEIJI ERA, 1868–1912

The shogun's acquiescence to American demands was viewed by some as a betrayal of the Japanese nation and led to national uprisings under the slogan *sonno joi*, "revere the emperor, expel the barbarians." In 1868 the period of shogun rule was brought to an end in a process known as the **Meiji**

Restoration. Young Prince Mutsuhito became Japan's 122nd emperor. He took the name Meiji ("enlightened government"). The Meiji Era was an immensely important period of institutional and cultural transformation. The emperor moved the imperial capital to Tokyo ("eastern capital") and a centralized government was created. A circle of oligarchs (**genro**), many of whom were from the nobility that supported the "restoration" of the emperor, advised the emperor and were the true wielders of power. They effectively used the name of the emperor to legitimize the revolutionary changes they imposed upon the country. State Shintoism was made the ideology of the country; it reified the emperor as the divine ancestor of the Sun Goddess Amaterasu. Militarists were later to politicize state Shintoism and use it to support their expansionist quest. There was to be no bourgeois middle-class revolution from below in Japan.

During the Meiji Era, profound changes were made to virtually all sectors of society. With the goal of achieving *fukoku kyohei* ("rich country, strong military") Japan's leaders set out to modernize the country. They brought in Western advisors and teachers and sent hundreds of Japanese students abroad to study everything Western, including science and technology, the political systems and constitutions of Europe and the United States, the concept of universities, hospitals, and even Western dress and social customs. By the end of the Meiji Era, Japan's reformists had succeeded in containing popular revolts from below while creating a modern state and world power, a new economy, and a rebuilt society, all truly remarkable feats given the short period of time in which they occurred.

The Meiji leaders eventually adopted a constitution in 1889 based on the Prussian parliamentary model. (The U.S. constitutional model was rejected as being too liberal.) The Meiji Constitution created an authoritarian parliamentary system. It provided for the establishment of an imperial **Diet** (a parliament), with a popularly elected House of Representatives. In addition, a House of Peers, composed largely of nobility (the former daimyo and court nobility) who received their title by birthright, was formed. The power of the elected House of Representatives, however, was strongly limited. Sovereignty rested with the emperor. The emperor appointed his cabinet ministers, had legislative superiority over the Diet, could make emergency decrees, and enter into treaties. Only the emperor could amend the constitution, and the military was directly responsible to him and not to the Diet. The special powers of the emperor, including emergency powers, were in reality wielded not so much directly by the emperor as by his ministers and a special Privy Council that advised the emperor. In addition, the genro, who had masterminded the Meiji Constitution, held much influence into the beginning of the twentieth century. Suffrage, moreover, was limited to males who held substantial property, in other words, only 1 percent of the population, most of whom were landlords.

During the Meiji period many of Japan's most famous universities were established, including Tokyo, Kyoto, Keio and Waseda. Powerful financial and industrial conglomerates known as **zaibatsu** also solidified their positions. They were usually tied to rich families that had begun to do business in the Edo Era; many of their names remain familiar today, such as Mitsubishi (shipping), Mitsui (banking), and Sumitomo (mining). The *zaibatsu* worked closely with the government and, in later periods, the military.

A BRIEF INTERLUDE WITH DEMOCRACY: THE TAISHO DEMOCRACY, 1918–1932

By the Taisho Era (the period of rule of the Taisho emperor, which began in 1912) the power of the oligarchs had waned and that of the political parties – of which there were many – in the House of Representatives had grown. It appeared that Japan might develop a more representative form of democracy. Indeed, during this period of **Taisho democracy**, the first commoner became prime minister, a competitive party system took root, and suffrage was extended to all males (in 1925). There was, however, considerable discontent with the government for its failure to deal with inflation and labor unrest and sharp ideological differences had emerged in society.

Left-wing movements and activism grew in the early part of the 1920s influenced by developments in Russia. An illegal Communist Party formed in 1922, and socialist parties, which had existed since the early 1920s despite government suppression, became more vocal. The growing appeal of the Left at a time when suffrage had been greatly expanded was viewed by conservatives as a threat to the imperial family and the essence of the Japanese nation. In 1925, just after universal male suffrage was granted, conservatives pushed through a Peace Preservation Law, which made illegal organizations and movements that had as their goal changing the political system. A 1928 amendment by emergency imperial decree strengthened the law and made left-wing activism essentially punishable by death. A 1941 amendment went one step further and allowed for preventive arrest. The Peace Preservation Law marked the beginning of the empowerment of ultrarightists and the elimination of open political debate.

Japan as a Military Power and a Colonial Force

Japan's rapid industrialization during the Meiji Era was considered critical to the strengthening of the military. Japan tested its military strength in the Sino-Japanese War of 1894–1895. Japan's victory over China attested to the success of the Meiji Restoration and was a humiliating blow to a greatly weakened China. As a result of this war, Korea was made a protectorate of

Japan, and Taiwan, the Liadong Peninsula, and the Pescadores were ceded to Japan. Concerned about competition from Japan in China, however, Russia, France, and Germany forced Japan to return the Liadong Peninsula to China. This was but one of many events that were to leave the Japanese feeling that they were not respected as equals by Western powers, which in turn nourished a resentful nationalism.

Japan achieved another military victory that surprised the world when it defeated Russia in the 1904–1905 Russo-Japanese War. In defeat, Russia recognized Japanese paramount political, military, and economic interests in Korea as well as Japanese control of the railways of Inner Manchuria and Port Arthur (Lüshun). Russia also ceded to Japan the southern portion of Sakhalin and the adjacent islands. (These islands are now commonly referred to as the Northern Territories or Kurile islands.) Russia seized these islands in the closing days of World War II, but Japan has disputed Russian claims. Because of this territorial dispute, Russia and Japan have yet to sign a treaty officially ending the Second World War! Japan formally colonized Korea in 1910, joining Western countries as the only Asian nation to be a colonizer.

During World War I, Japan joined the Allied powers, declaring war on Germany in 1914 and seizing German-leased territories in China. At the end of the war Japan was recognized as one of the "Big Five" and obtained a permanent seat in the League of Nations. Japan had become a major foreign power.

Still, Japan's late development relative to Western powers and its status as an Asian, rather than a Western, power meant that it was not perceived or treated as an equal by the West. Japan failed to convince Western powers to include a racial equality clause in the Treaty of Versailles. Many in Japan felt wounded by this unequal treatment. By the 1930s, ultrarightists and militarists had gained the upper hand and the hopes for a democratic Japan faded. Japan strengthened its grip on Manchuria, formally detaching it from China in 1931. In 1937, Japan attacked China, beginning the Pacific War. Japan allied itself with Germany and Italy in World War II. Seeking to curb Japanese imperialism, the United States slapped economic sanctions on Japan. Japan responded by attacking Pearl Harbor and extending its sphere of influence into Southeast Asia in a quest to secure oil and to become the dominant power in Asia. Japan declared war on the United States in 1941 and capitulated on August 14, 1945.

Japan's colonization of Korea, China, Taiwan, and its military advance into large parts of Southeast Asia was done in the name of expelling Western imperialists from Asia and creating a Greater East Asia Co-Prosperity Sphere. The often brutal colonization and military rule of Japan left bitter memories in much of Asia.

Occupation of Japan

The U.S. occupation of Japan has received renewed attention as a result of the U.S.-led war in Iraq. The George W. Bush administration compared the occupation of Iraq with the postwar occupations of Japan and Germany. Pulitzer Prize–winning author John Dower, a leading authority on the occupation of Japan, has argued, however, that the differences with the situation in Iraq are great. Although young Japanese soldiers were trained in the war for suicide missions as kamikaze pilots, once the occupation of Japan began there were no serious cases of violence against the occupying forces, a major difference with Iraq.

The demilitarization and democratization of the country was rapid. **General Douglas MacArthur** was appointed by President Harry S. Truman to be the Supreme Commander of the Allied Powers (SCAP) and head of the Allied occupation of Japan. Although the officials who were considered the masterminds of the war were purged, imprisoned, and in a small number of cases tried by the Tokyo War Crimes Tribunal, the government was left intact; SCAP worked with and through the Japanese bureaucracy and Diet.

Two months after the occupation began, MacArthur called for the "liberalization of the constitution" and democratization in five key areas – the emancipation of women, permitting the unionization of labor, liberalizing education, establishing an effective judicial system that would protect human rights, and dismantling of the *zaibatsu* to create a more liberal and democratic economic system. The democratization process happened remarkably quickly.

In February 1946, six months into the occupation, the Japanese government presented a draft constitution to SCAP headquarters. Unhappy with the Japanese draft, MacArthur had his staff prepare a more liberal model, which was then debated in the Diet. The new constitution went into effect in May 1947.

The occupation of Japan was so successful in large part because it was considered legitimate by the Japanese, who were weary of war. When the occupation began, Japan was a demoralized, exhausted, malnourished, and ravaged country. Japan's cities had been heavily bombed and much of its heavy industry destroyed. Soldiers and colonists were repatriated to a country that was too poor to provide them with work. In this context, it proved relatively easy to blame the military for Japan's ill-fated imperialism. Moreover, when the war ended, it was the emperor, considered divine by his people, who ordered that the military disarm. Rather than trying Emperor Hirohito as a war criminal as some wanted, MacArthur argued that because of his divine status in the eyes of the people and because his advisors and the military were the ones to really decide to invade China and launch the war, he should remain as emperor. The emperor's endorsement of the occupation and its reforms helped to legitimize SCAP's activities.

It can also be argued that it was important that Japan was led by a man generally supportive of SCAP policies during most of the occupation. **Shigeru Yoshida** served as prime minister from May 1946 to May 1947 and again from October 1948 to October 1954. During his time as prime minister, he chose to align Japan with the United States politically and economically, focus Japan's political attentions on economic development, and allow the United States to take on the role of protecting Japan. His policies, commonly referred to as the Yoshida Doctrine, became the basic guiding ideologies of the conservative Liberal Democratic Party (LDP) when it formed in 1955 out of the merger of the Liberal Party and the Democratic Party.

Other reforms included the passage of an antimonopoly law and the breakup of the *zaibatsu*, which SCAP believed had played a major role in Japan's militarization. The 1946 Land Reform led to the redistribution of land from absentee landlords and large landowners to tenants at fixed 1945 prices. The land reform reduced rural unrest and contributed to a relatively high degree of equalization of wealth in society.

The Japanese Constitution and the Establishment of a New Political Order

The 1946 Constitution remains in force in Japan today and has never been amended. It differs from the Meiji Constitution in several key aspects. First, sovereignty was placed with the people rather than with the emperor as had been the case in the past. The emperor's status was changed from head of state to symbol of state, and his functions were limited to ceremonial ones. The House of Representatives (also known as the Lower House) was greatly empowered. The House of Peers was abolished and in its place an elected House of Councillors was created. The bicameral Diet was made the highest organ of state and given sole law-making authority. The constitution stipulated that the prime minister and the majority of ministers should be members of the Diet and that the prime minister should be elected by the parliament, a major difference with the Meiji cabinet, which was a transcendental cabinet, that is, one that was to be "above" the parliament. The new political structure was based largely on the British parliamentary model.

Second, the new constitution emphasized respect for fundamental human rights and individual freedoms. Freedom of the press was assured. Political parties that had been banned were given the right to form, paving the way for the reestablishment of the **Japan Socialist Party** and the Japan Communist Party (JCP). Citizens were given the right to seek redress against unjust actions by government under a revised judicial system. The age of suffrage was reduced from 25 to 20. The constitution also established equality of the sexes before the law (a right which is not written into the U.S. Constitution). Despite there having been a women's movement in Japan in the prewar period, women did not gain the right to vote until the occupation granted it to them, and this was then enshrined in the new constitution. Interestingly, in the first postwar election, in April 1946, women won 7.8 percent of the seats in the Lower House of the Diet, a percentage they were not to repeat until more than a half a century later. In the House of Representatives election in September 2005, women won 45 seats or 9.4 percent of the 480-member chamber. They held 17.4 percent of the seats in the House of Councillors after the July 2007 election.

Third, the constitution is pacifist. The preamble of the constitution begins:

> We, the Japanese people, acting through our elected representatives in the National Diet, determined that we should secure for ourselves and our posterity the fruits of peaceful cooperation with all nations and the blessings of liberty all over this land, and resolved that never again shall we be visited with the horrors of war through the action of government, do proclaim that sovereign power resides with the people.

In addition, Article 9 explicitly denounces the right to war:

> Aspiring sincerely to an international peace based on justice and order, the Japanese people forever renounce war as a sovereign right of the nation and the threat or use of force as a means of settling international disputes. In order to accomplish [this] aim, land, sea, and air forces, as well as other war potential, will never be maintained. The right of aggression of the state will not be recognized.

These pacifist elements of the Japanese constitution have been central to defining Japan's approach to foreign policy. It remains a matter of historical debate with considerable implications for nationalism as to whether Article 9 was MacArthur's idea or if it was proposed by Kijūrō Shidehara, who served briefly as prime minister until the first postwar election was held in 1946. The interpretation of these elements of the constitution and what they mean for Japan's ability to contribute to international peacekeeping efforts and to new security threats have been hotly debated for years.

The "Reverse Course" and Japan's Emergence as a Key U.S. Ally

The initial goals of the U.S. occupation were to demilitarize and democratize Japan and help it regain basic economic functions in order to be self-sufficient. Beyond that Japan was of little interest to the United States. The onset of the Cold War altered U.S. thinking about Japan, which suddenly took on a new strategic significance, and a **"reverse course"** was initiated in 1947.

The reverse course slowed and on occasion reversed the democratic reforms introduced by the United States in the early phase of the occupation. Initially, for example, SCAP had encouraged labor unions as a critical element of democratic politics. Concerned about growing labor unrest and labor's ties to the Japan Communist Party, SCAP intervened, banning a planned nationwide strike in 1947. Behind the reverse course were concerns about the spread of communism. Global politics once again conspired to intervene in Japanese politics.

The victory of Mao Zedong's communist forces over the Kuomintang (the Nationalists) in 1949, the outbreak of the Korean War in 1950, and the Soviet Union's grip on Central and Eastern Europe created concern in Washington that communism could spread to a weak Japan. The JCP, the only party to speak out against Japan's military aggression, reemerged after the war as a legal party, but suffered renewed repression by SCAP, which launched its own "Red Purge" in 1950. Although the JCP was greatly weakened, it survived as a party. Many labor leaders were also removed as part of the Red Purge. The politics of this period created a deep-seated ideological divide between conservatives, who supported the United States in most of its policy initiatives, and the parties of the Left and, especially, the Japan Socialist Party and the JCP, which opposed Japan's strong alignment with the United States.

The Cold War was instrumental in the U.S. decision to have Japan establish a National Police Reserve for the maintenance of domestic order. In 1954, the Police Reserve was turned into the Japanese Self-Defense Forces (SDF) for the protection of the country. Although the SDF are now one of the largest military forces in the world, because of Article 9 they are restricted to national self-defense. In the 1990s, however, a new interpretation of Article 9 has led to Japan's participation in noncombat roles in UN peacekeeping operations.

In 1951, the United States and Japan concluded the San Francisco Peace Treaty, formally ending the U.S. occupation of Japan, and the U.S.-Japan Security Treaty. The occupation formally ended on April 28, 1952, one month after the U.S. Senate had ratified the agreement. The security treaty engendered considerable opposition both within Japan from left-leaning parties and internationally, as it gave the United States the right to maintain troops in Japan and as a base for U.S. activity in East Asia even after the occupation ended. This is interesting to ponder in light of the U.S.-led occupation of Iraq and questions concerning the stationing of troops there after the country technically regained its sovereignty. In Japan's case, the U.S. military operates independently of, but in close cooperation with, the SDF.

The U.S.-Japan Security Treaty was renewed in 1960, permitting the continued stationing of U.S. troops in Japan, but this was done over the strong objections of parties of the Left, the radical *Zengakuren* student movement, and labor unions. In fact, the treaty was rammed through the Diet under highly questionable circumstances; the Socialist Party members of Parliament and their male secretaries were dragged out of the Diet by the police that Prime Minister Nobusuke Kishi had called in so that the Liberal Democrats could vote to renew the treaty. Fearing that democracy itself was at stake, there were massive demonstrations in front of the Japanese Diet that resulted in one of Japan's most serious political crises of the postwar period and led to the cancellation of President Dwight D. Eisenhower's planned visit to Japan to celebrate the treaty's renewal and to the resignation of Prime Minister Kishi. The treaty, however, was passed and in subsequent years was generally accepted by society. The United States currently maintains approximately 53,000 troops in Japan, about half of whom are based in Okinawa. The question of whether or not U.S. troops should remain in Japan continues to be an important and divisive political question for Japan, and has been especially hotly debated in Okinawa. The United States somewhat reduced its troop size in Okinawa following widespread demonstrations in the mid-1990s after the public erupted in anger when three U.S. servicemen raped a young Japanese girl. Since then, the situation has calmed somewhat, although the Iraq war engendered renewed debate about Japan's close military alliance with the United States and its implications for Japan's own security.

Understanding Japan's "Economic Miracle"

Few would ever have predicted that Japan would emerge from its war-ravaged state in 1945 to become one of the world's richest nations by the end of the 1960s. The Japanese "economic miracle" is one of the most studied aspects of Japanese politics and economics. Numerous factors contributed to Japan's economic recovery, many of which were external to Japan and can be considered circumstantial.

When World War II ended, for example, Japan received financial and technical assistance from the United States. The American banker John Foster Dulles was sent to Japan in 1948 as an economic advisor and introduced austerity measures, including wage and price controls, balanced budgets, and currency-exchange controls, among others. The yen–dollar exchange rate was fixed at 360 yen to the dollar; this rate remained in place until the collapse of the Bretton Woods system in 1973. It can be argued that the favorable exchange rate aided Japan's export expansion. Japan's economic recovery received a major stimulus from the demand for military and other supplies for UN troops fighting in the Korean War. The dollar purchases gave Japan a means to pay for its imports and reequip its industries. Steel and other heavy industries did especially well. Finally, it has been argued that Japan benefited enormously from being able to concentrate on economic development while leaving its defense largely to the United States. Japan's budgetary expenditures on the SDF remained at less than 1 percent of the national budget until well into the 1980s.

Beyond these external conditions, however, there were important domestic factors at work as well. First was the stabilization of the party system. There was a consolidation of political parties in 1955 when the conservative Liberal Democratic Party formed out of a merger of the Liberal Party and the Democratic Party. In reaction to the formation of the LDP, the socialist Left also merged to form the Japan Socialist Party (JSP). The socialists, however, had historically been ideologically divided between those supportive of a radical, Marxist socialism and those supporting a more moderate socialism that worked within the system. The JSP split in 1959 when the more moderate wing of the party, in connection with the JSP's opposition to the security treaty, broke off to create the Democratic Socialist Party (DSP). In addition, the Communist Party represented a share of the left-leaning vote. As a result of the division of the left-leaning opposition, the LDP was able to maintain a majority in the Lower House of the Diet – even if at times a bare majority. The dominance of the LDP in postwar Japanese politics provided for a high degree of policy stability.

In 1960, Prime Minister Hayato Ikeda announced a goal for Japan to double the national income in a decade. Over the course of the decade, Japan expanded its range of export goods from textiles and low-end goods ("made in Japan" in the 1950s was a symbol often associated with cheap toys and plastic goods) to heavy industry – including steel, chemicals, ship building, and automobiles – and electronic goods, such as radios, televisions, cameras, calculators, and computers. By 1967, Japan's Gross National Product (GNP) had surpassed that of Great Britain, France, and West Germany. So successful was Japan at importing technologies, improving upon them, and then reexporting new designs that Japan began to develop trade surpluses with the United States, and trade frictions between the two countries began to grow. For much of the 1970s and 1980s, the United States worked to open Japan's economy to U.S. goods, which were often barred by protectionist policies.

Japan's economic wealth was more evenly distributed than in many developing countries, and with a growing economic pie there was relatively limited unrest in Japan, although labor engaged in annual wage offensives. Most Japanese considered themselves to be part of the middle class even though by American or European standards the average Japanese lived in a rather small home – largely an issue of space rather than wealth. In the 1970s, Prime Minister Kakuei Tanaka, one of the more colorful and controversial prime ministers of Japan, who in his later years was accused of massive corruption, decided that it was important to keep rural areas connected to the increasingly economically dominant cities of the Kantō (the area surrounding Tokyo and Yokohama) and Kansai (the areas surrounding Osaka, Kyoto, and Kobe) regions. He initiated a program called Reconstruction of the Japanese

Archipelago. It was this program that led to the building of Japan's famous bullet trains, the *shinkansen*, which permit travel between Tokyo and Kyoto in as little as three hours.

One of the most intriguing informal institutional systems at play in postwar Japan is known as administrative guidance, or **gyōsei shidō** in Japanese. One of the consequences of SCAP's purging of politicians who were associated with Japan's militarism was that the bureaucracy became very influential. Many of Japan's postwar parliamentarians and prime ministers were bureaucrats who turned into politicians because of the sudden opening of electoral positions as a result of the purges. This helped create links between parliamentarians (and especially the LDP) and the bureaucracy.

Bureaucrats were highly involved in the formulation of legislation. In fact, most bills originated in the bureaucracy rather than in the House of Representatives even though important committees in the Diet, such as the Policy Affairs Research Committee, did influence the shape of bills and the Diet had ultimate authority to vote on legislation. More recently, politicians have begun to initiate more legislation, but the bureaucracy still remains powerful and heavily involved in policy formulation.

The influence of the Japanese bureaucracy had prewar origins, as the ministries were powerful under the old system as well, and considerable continuity between the prewar and postwar bureaucracy meant that competencies were maintained. Bureaucrats, moreover, had moral authority in a society that respects educational attainment. Entering the bureaucracy was considered a prestige track for male graduates of Japan's elite universities, although this is somewhat less true today than in the past. Japan has a career civil service, and entrance to the bureaucracy requires passing extremely difficult exams and interviews. Until the Equal Employment Opportunity Law was passed in 1986, women were permitted to take the exams, but were often screened out during the interview process. In the meantime, the doors of the bureaucracy have been opened to more women and women are beginning to assume more powerful posts, including as bureaucratic ministers.

The **Ministry of Economy, Trade, and Industry** (**METI**) (known as the Ministry of International Trade and Industry [MITI] prior to the government restructuring of 2001) and the Ministry of Finance were particularly important to Japan's economic development. They used administrative guidance or what Richard Samuels called a process of negotiation or "reciprocal consent" between ministries and industries to push the economy in particular directions. The ministries had various tools in their hands to do this, including preferential tax treatment and the provision of low-interest loans.

Administrative guidance was aided by the close connections that existed between bureaucrats and, especially, the large corporations, where lifetime employment was quite common. Japan is a network society. Personal relationships such as those established during high school and in universities are immensely important. These networks helped to link bureaucrats with industries. In addition, because Japan's bureaucracy is a career civil service, as one ascends the ladder of hierarchy, the number of available positions diminishes. Bureaucrats who know they have hit the glass ceiling within their ministries typically retire from the ministry and take up positions either in industry or government-created institutions. This process is so well known that is has a special name: *amakudari* or literally "descent from heaven." The idea behind *amakudari* was that it would provide direct communication links between bureaucrats and industry officials.

The role that women played in this system should not be underestimated either. There are fairly strong gender role divisions in Japan. Throughout most of the postwar period, women could work, but they were expected to retire upon marriage or at the latest with childbirth, not to reenter the workforce until their role as mothers and primary child-care giver was complete. When they did reenter the workforce, it was usually as part-timers. Women therefore provided Japanese companies with highly educated, but cheap employees. Lifetime employment, moreover, was not a privilege conferred upon women. Employers could more easily let women go, providing companies with flexibility during economic downturns. Salaries reflected this gender divided system as well. A male employee's wages increased upon marriage and with the birth of children and men earned more than women. Since the 1986 Equal Employment Law went into effect, such gender discrimination is now illegal, and as a result the position of women has improved somewhat. Still, during the recession that began in the early1990s, women, who now make up the majority of university graduates, had a much harder time than their male counterparts in finding employment.

Opposition to the Conservative Agenda

Japan's economic success made it the envy of many countries. Yet, there were also controversial elements to Japan's rapid economic growth and the conservative party's approach to politics. We have already discussed the Japan Socialist Party's opposition to the Security Treaty and its view that the SDF were unconstitutional. In comparison with the German Socialist Party, which distanced itself from Marxism at its 1959 Bad Godesburg summit, the JSP maintained its Marxist orientation and opposition to Japan's close security relationship to the United States. Interestingly, the downfall and near total collapse of the JSP, which throughout most of the postwar period had managed to garner about one-third of the electorate's support, came when it compromised on its positions, accepted the U.S.-Japan Security alliance and the SDF, and agreed to go into a coalition government with the LDP in 1994 in exchange for the position of prime minister. The JSP paid a heavy price for its dramatic policy shift. In 1996, the party was all but wiped out by disenchanted supporters.

Japan's conservative politics engendered criticism from various quarters for other reasons as well. In the 1960s and 1970s, there were widespread consumer movements and environmental movements. Consumer movements protested policies that favored industrial expansion at the expense of consumers, who had to pay high prices for imported goods and were paying more for televisions manufactured in Japan than Americans were paying for those same televisions. Environmental movements arose because of the severe, health-threatening pollution that resulted from the failure to enact any pollution controls. So bad was pollution in Tokyo in the 1970s that vendors sold oxygen on street corners. In the fishing community of Minamata, which had the misfortune of being selected as a site for a petro-chemical complex in the 1950s, mercury poisoning resulted in severe birth defects and fatalities.

The dominance of the LDP had led to Japan being identified as a system dominated by one party. The LDP's majority was always relatively slim, however, and this gave the parties of the Left some opportunity to influence policy developments. During the early 1970s, the LDP was threatened with a loss of electoral support. Communists and socialists had won mayoral and gubernatorial positions in Japan's major cities and the LDP feared a similar loss at the national level. To prevent this from occurring, the LDP adopted policies that were being called for by the social movements and leftist mayors and governors. Thus, during the 1970s, the LDP expanded social programs and introduced advanced pollution controls.

Another problem with the close ties that formed among the LDP, the bureaucracy, and industry was the potential for corruption of both politicians and bureaucrats and the political apathy this generates within the public. The LDP was in power for so long that it is perhaps not so surprising that corruption scandals began to plague the party, and the influence of the bureaucracy meant that it was a target as well. One of the most riveting examples of corruption led to the arrest of Shin Kanemaru, a godfather-type politician who was the effective head of the largest faction of the LDP and mentor to Kakuei Tanaka, who also fell into disgrace. Kanemaru was arrested for accepting bribes from Sagawa Kyūbin, a delivery company, and asking the company to put him in touch with the *yakuza*, the Japanese mafia, so that they might take care of his detractors. When the police raided his homes and offices they found over 3 billion yen in bond certificates, tens of millions in bank notes, and over 200 pounds of gold bars! The police discovered that many of the contributions came from construction companies. Tanaka also was implicated in the scandal but died before ever serving any time. The failure to apply harsh punishments commensurate with the size of the crimes committed disillusioned many of the public.

Other scandals made the public even more distrustful of the government. These included the government's inept handling of rescue efforts after the devastating 1995 Hanshin earthquake, in which at least 6,000 in the Kobe area died; a case in which the Ministry of Health and Welfare permitted hemophiliacs to be given untreated blood and as a result thousands are HIV-positive; numerous nuclear accidents, including one at the Tokaimura uranium reprocessing plant in which poorly trained employees caused a criticality accident and died of nuclear radiation; and Naoto Kan, head of the opposition Democratic Party of Japan (newly formed in 1998), resigned after admitting to having failed to pay into the mandatory national pension scheme. Jun'ichiro Koizumi, who was prime minister from 2001 to 2006, subsequently also admitted to having failed to make all payments, but managed to avoid calls for his resignation in part by deflecting national attention by making a historic visit to North Korea. The pension scandals angered the public, which under planned pension reforms was being asked by politicians to pay more into the pension scheme.

The Politics of Reform

ECONOMIC REFORM

In 1989, the Japanese economy was soaring. Japan's remarkable economic growth had some predicting that Japan would surpass the United States economically. Land prices had reached astronomical levels. The real estate value of land adjacent to the Imperial Palace grounds in downtown Tokyo was so high that it led to estimates that the palace grounds themselves – an area similar in size to Central Park in New York – were worth more than the entire real estate value of California! Japan's wealth was staggering and the Japanese model became an object of study. Universities across the United States were teaching the Japanese business model and Japanese became one of the most studied foreign languages in the country. Japanese individuals, companies, and banks invested their money in real estate and development projects at home and abroad. In Japan a rural construction boom ensued as golf courses and leisure facilities were built and the government instituted a policy to promote "leisure" in response to international complaints that the Japanese worked too hard.

But then the economic bubble burst. Real estate prices began to tumble, and banks found themselves sitting upon huge sums of nonperforming loans. The huge speculation boom, which went far beyond what would have occurred had banks been using more stringent accounting practices, led to many companies and banks going bankrupt. In addition, excessive public spending produced a huge government deficit, measured at 130 percent of Gross Domestic Product (GDP) in 2001, the highest of any industrialized country. Concerns about Japan's aging society and the long-term viability of the public pension system also weighed upon policy makers.

As a result of the lackluster performance of Japan's economy, various economists both inside and outside of Japan have pushed the government to adopt structural reform measures, pushing Japan toward a more American-style liberal economic system. Japan's previously touted economic model involved extensive government involvement in the economy, but clearly this involvement had produced its own unique set of pathologies. Prime Minister Koizumi initiated efforts to decrease the size of government, reducing the number of ministries and agencies from 22 to 13. He also created a new Council on Economic and Fiscal Policy to advise the prime minister and appointed Harvard-trained Heizo Takenaka as the first minister of financial services, economic and fiscal policy to address reform of the banking system. The International Monetary Fund pressured the government to survey the extent of the bank loan problem. Given that Japan finances a huge percentage of the U.S. government deficit through the purchase of government bonds, the health of the Japanese economy is immensely important to the United States as well as the global economy.

The government was urged to pursue deregulation of its 77 state-backed corporations, many of which were involved in construction and public works, such as the Highway Public Corporation, and transportation. The biggest initiative in this regard, and one which Prime Minister Koizumi staked his political career on, was the privatization of Japan Post. Unlike most postal services, Japan Post not only provided postal and package delivery services, it offered banking and life insurance services. It was widely considered to be the largest holder of personal savings in the world and provided much of the financial capital necessary to support the LDP's many public works projects, such as the building of highways, dams, and airports. Koizumi's administration's argument behind privatization was that it would allow for more flexible and efficient use of the massive funds held by the corporation. A bill calling for the splitting of Japan Post into four separate companies narrowly passed the Lower House of the Diet in 2005, but many of Koizumi's own party failed to back him in the vote. The bill subsequently failed to pass in the Upper House when many LDP politicians defected to the opposition. Rather than accepting defeat, Koizumi played a risky and controversial move. He dissolved the Lower House of the Diet, called for new elections, and refused to support the candidacy of any incumbent who did not give clear support to the bill. In the September 2005 election, Koizumi beat the odds and won a super-majority in the Lower House, making it possible to pass bills without support from the Upper House. The Democratic Party of Japan suffered a devastating defeat, dropping from 175 to 113 seats.

Large companies have been pressured to move away from their lifetime employment structure and to streamline their operations. Institutional structures that functioned well in Japan's phase as a developmental state when it was trying to catch up with the West proved a drag on the economy in a more globalized economic system in which Japan was one of the most mature economies. The growing feeling among many of Japan's political leaders was that Japan had to develop a more flexible economic system if it was to remain competitive in the twenty-first century.

Given that Japan does not have a very well-developed social welfare net or unemployment system and that job mobility is more limited than in the United States, however, there was considerable resistance to some of the reforms. Japan's society is rapidly aging and many were concerned about what the closing of Japan Post would mean for the elderly in rural areas, who used Japan Post for their postal, banking, and insurance needs. The development of a welfare net to catch those who lose out in the structural reform process has not received much attention from the government although programs are being established to help small and medium enterprises and encourage entrepreneurs. Prime Minister Koizumi's immediate successor lacked his charisma. Shinzo Abe's administration, moreover, was plagued by financial scandals (four bureaucratic ministers were forced to resign and Agriculture Minister Toshikatsu Matsuoka committed suicide just before he was to face questions before the Diet related to money scandals). Most devastating, however, was when his administration had to admit that the government has lost track of 64 million pension claims. Abe tendered his own recognition just one year into his job. Yasuo Fukuda became prime minister in September 2007.

POLITICAL REFORM

The scandals that plagued the ruling party in the late 1980s and 1990s and power struggles within the heavily factionalized LDP led to a splintering of the party in 1992. In that year, Morihiro Hosokawa left the LDP with a small group of followers to form a new party, which was named the Japan New Party, promising to pursue economic, political, and social reforms. Ichiro Ozawa, another reformist politician, also abandoned the LDP and formed his own new party, the Shinseitō. In the next election in 1993, the LDP received the largest number of votes, but not a majority, and this opened the door for the first non-LDP government to form since 1948. An unwieldy eight-party coalition was formed, including all of the old opposition parties except the Japan Communist Party, plus the two newly formed parties, and Hosokawa became prime minister. Although the coalition government did not survive for long, it marked the beginning of a new era in postwar Japanese politics of coalition governments and the beginning of the unraveling of what is commonly known as the 1955 system – a system where the LDP was in power and the Japan Socialist Party, the Democratic Socialist Party, the Japan Communist Party, and the Clean Government Party (Kōmeitō, a party formed in

1964 with the backing of a Buddhist group, Soka Gakkai) were in perpetual opposition.

One of the real achievements of Hosokawa's government was electoral reform. Japan's electoral system had been based on a complicated medium-sized, multi-member district system in which each electoral district elected, in most cases, between three and five representatives. As each voter had a single nontransferable vote, this meant that the top vote getters, sometimes getting as little as ten percent of the vote, took office. This system pitted members of the same party against each other as well as against other parties and was immensely expensive. The coalition government argued that the system bred corruption, was unfair (as electoral redistricting had not kept pace with Japan's rapid urbanization and as a result the weight of a rural individual's vote was much greater than that of an urban dweller's vote), worked to the advantage of the LDP as a party because of its strong rural support base, and worked against the development of party ideologies. There was interest in creating a new electoral system that might eventually lead to a two-party system similar to the British system, where control of government moves between the Labour Party and the Conservative Party, and that of the United States, where it moves between the Democratic Party and the Republican Party.

In complicated negotiations, a new electoral system was agreed upon for the House of Representatives, the more powerful of Japan's two houses. The new system adopted a combination proportional-representation system and a single-member district system. The system was modified again by changes to the Electoral Law, most recently in 2000. Under the new system, 300 seats are elected in single seat races and another 180 votes are determined by proportional representation. Each voter gets two votes, one for a candidate and one for a party.

In the 1994 election, the LDP again failed to obtain a majority. The LDP was able to prevent another opposition coalition government from forming, however, by creating a grand coalition with the largest of the opposition parties, the Social Democratic Party of Japan (SDPJ, formerly the JSP). As noted previously, as a condition of joining the coalition, the SDPJ was given the right to choose one of their own to be prime minister. While Tomoiichi Murayama was able to enjoy a year as prime minister, in the next election he saw his party decimated at the polls in part because the compromises it had made to enter the grand coalition with the LDP – eliminating its rejection of the SDF and the U.S.-Japan Security Treaty – alienated many of its left-wing supporters.

In subsequent elections, the LDP was able to stay in power by forming coalitions with one or more of many smaller parties, most prominently New Kōmeitō. The largest opposition party in Japan is now the Democratic Party of Japan. The Japan Communist Party continues to win a small number of seats in the Diet as well. After the 2005 House of Representatives election, the LDP had 296 seats, the DPJ had 113 seats, New Kōmeitō 31, the JCP 9, the Social Democratic Party 7, and other parties 24.

Japan's party landscape has gone through a bewildering set of changes in the past two decades. Dozens of small political parties formed, merged with other parties, changed their names, and then disappeared. New Party Sakigake, formed in 1993, for example, changed its name to the Sakigake Party in 1998, and then to Midori no Kaigi (Environmental Green Political Assembly) in 2002, before closing its doors in 2004 when it failed to garner sufficient support to send any representatives to the Diet. Other parties to come and go include the New Conservative Party, the Liberal Party, the Sun Party, the New Fraternity Party, the New Peace Party, Japan New Party, Japan Renewal Party, New Frontier Party, and the Democratic Socialist Party.

In 2005, a handful of disgruntled LDP politicians broke off from the LDP and formed People's New Party, New Party Nippon, and New Party Daiichi. People's New Party had four seats in the Lower House after the 2005 election, and the other two parties one each.

In a changing domestic and global context, the LDP has tried to redefine itself as a party. It is interesting to reflect on why Prime Minister Koizumi backed the kind of radical economic and fiscal reforms described, and why he was willing to pit himself so strongly against members of his own party in pushing forward reforms – such as the privatization of Japan Post – that threatened the electability of some LDP politicians in rural areas. The LDP had survived as a ruling party in large part because of the backing the party received from rural voters. Rural voters who had benefited from the party's agricultural policies and public works projects were loyal supporters of the LDP. The urbanization of Japan, however, meant that the rural population was rapidly aging and declining. Koizumi recognized the need for the party to court more urban and neoliberal voters if it were to maintain its dominance in Japanese politics.

Another important aspect of political change in Japan since the 1990s has been the empowerment of civil society. There were many restrictions that hampered the formation of a vibrant civil society in Japan. The devastating 1995 Hanshin earthquake and the important role played by voluntary groups in rescuing victims helped to make more favorable government attitudes about civil society. There has also been pressure on Japan to open the way for a greater role for civil society in decision making as a result of international conferences, such as the United Nations Conference on Environment and Development or the United Nations Conference on Women, where nongovernmental organization participation is expected. In the past decade, there have been important changes to laws governing the establishment of nonprofit organizations and the creation of Freedom of Information laws. Thus, along with the changes in Japan's party structure, there has been a pluralization of decision-making institutions in the past decade as new interests and identities gained a greater foothold.

Carving out a New International Role and Vision for Japan in a Changing Global Order

The LDP also had to deal with the international consequences of its economic success. The 1970s and 1980s were years of Japan bashing when the United States and Europe began to feel Japan's growing economic muscle and experience large trade imbalances with Japan. Although Japan was in fact a net importer in large part because of its need to import most of its energy and raw materials, it was a net exporter to the United States, many European countries, and East and Southeast Asia. The United States in particular pushed Japan to remove formal and informal trade barriers affecting automobiles, steel, computers, machine tools, among other products. This was not always easy for the LDP to do. The protectionist policies clearly benefited Japanese industry, which was a financial backer of the party in Japan's expensive electoral system. They also benefited Japan's small but influential agricultural sector, an important voting block for the LDP.

As in other countries, Japan's interests and identities were tied to its institutions, and the Japanese resented the outside world's effort to delink them. In the 1980s, Japan was lobbied to open its doors to citrus fruit and beef exports, which it eventually did. Efforts to push open the rice market, however, were less successful. While the government argued that rice had a special cultural significance and was a necessary element of Japan's food security and therefore must be protected, there were clearly electoral reasons why the LDP was reluctant to remove tariffs on rice. Negotiations also addressed informal trade barriers, which made it difficult for foreign companies to set up operations in Japan. An example of an informal trade barrier is the long-term relationships among corporations which lead firms to favor familiarity and loyalty over price. The close links between firms and suppliers that are found in Japan's **keiretsu**, the postwar version of the *zaibatsu*, have made it difficult for foreign companies to break into the market. Other examples are the close networks between Japanese companies and the bureaucracy that emerge from practices such as *amakudari*, discussed earlier. Such informal institutional factors, however, are difficult to change. It can also be argued that for many years U.S. companies ignored the Japanese market, dismissing it as too difficult to enter for linguistic and cultural reasons.

Japan has opened most of its markets under pressure from the United States and Europe and because of its accession to the World Trade Organization (WTO). Japan, moreover, is now itself concerned about other countries using protectionist barriers to block its exports – as was the case when the United States slapped import duties on steel. Thus, Japan is a strong supporter of the WTO and its free trade policies. In the 1980s, Japanese firms also began to move more of their manufacturing overseas closer to markets and where cheaper labor is available. Thus, many Japanese automobile manufacturers produce automobiles for the U.S. market in the United States and many electronic firms do parts assembly in China. This too has raised issues for Japan, as there are growing concerns about industrial flight from Japan.

As a result of its economic strength, Japan also found itself pressured to do more for international society, given its status as the world's second-largest economy. Conservative elements of the LDP used this international pressure as an opportunity to push for revisions to Japan's security policies. Prime Minister Yasuhiro Nakasone, who was prime minister from 1982 to 1987 and had a close relationship with both Ronald Reagan and Margaret Thatcher, pushed for an expansion of Japan's budget for the Self-Defense Forces, exceeding the de facto 1 percent limit that Prime Minister Takeo Miki established in 1976. Japan began to pay for more of the costs of maintaining U.S. bases in Japan and agreed to defend the seas between its islands and its major sea lanes. During the 1990s, these changes to Japan's security program were pushed even further as a result of the first Persian Gulf War. Under considerable international pressure and despite strong domestic concerns, the Japanese Diet agreed to permit the use of Japanese SDF personnel in noncombat roles in UN peacekeeping operations. The Japanese population could be persuaded of this in part because of the extensive international criticism Japan received for not contributing more to the first Persian Gulf War even though Japan paid $13 billion to support the war efforts. Thus, in a major reinterpretation of Article 9, Japan has participated in UN peacekeeping operations in support roles in Angola, Cambodia, Mozambique, El Salvador, the Golan Heights, Kenya and Zaire (to aid refugees of the genocide in Rwanda), and East Timor. The International Peace Cooperation Law, which went into effect in 1992, restricted Japanese SDF involvement to cases where a cease-fire is in operation and all parties consent to Japan's involvement. Weapons can only be used for self-defense. Since 2001, the Japanese Diet passed two special measures permitting the deployment of the SDF to provide logistical support to U.S. military operations against terrorism in Afghanistan and Iraq. The LDP and the DPJ, however, disagree on the form that future Japanese peacekeeping operations should take.

Another foreign policy area where Japan began to exert more influence was in assistance to developing countries. This has been done through both Japan's role as one of the largest contributing nations to multilateral development banks, including the Asian Development Bank, the International Monetary Fund, and the World Bank, and the work of the United Nations. It has also been done through official development assistance (ODA). Japan emerged in the 1990s as one of the world's largest providers of ODA although Japan's aid figures in percentage terms of GDP are well below many other countries. Japanese aid has been used to develop infrastructure, including roads, schools, hospitals, dams, and energy facilities, overseas. A large percentage of Japanese aid, primarily in the form of low interest loans, went to Southeast Asia and China, regions where Japan has tried to strengthen its economic and political ties and overcome the negative images of the wartime past. In response to criticisms that Japanese assistance was often contributing to projects that were environmentally destructive, threatening the way of life of indigenous peoples, or lining the pockets of corrupt officials in developing countries, Japanese ODA practices have been substantially revised. Environmental protection, sustainable development, and human health are now among the primary areas for which Japan provides ODA; this includes loans for sewage construction, fresh water projects, health care, reforestation, and the like. In the 1990s and early 2000s, the largest share of Japanese ODA went to China, much of it in the form of environmental assistance. This aid is to end in 2008, however. This is because of a growing sentiment in Japan that China, with its large military and newly launched international space program, no longer needs Japanese development assistance.

Since the mid-1990s, Japan has attempted to create a foreign policy more independent of the United States. This has been greeted with mixed success in Asia. Asia has not forgiven Japan for the war in the Pacific, nor has Japan been very good about apologizing to Asia for the atrocities it committed during the war. Japanese politicians have continued to upset China, Korea, and other Asian states by invoking wartime memories with, for example, official visits to Yasukuni Shrine, a Shinto shrine that memorializes and enshrines Japan's war dead, including some of the Pacific War's most notorious war criminals. Prime Minister Koizumi made several visits to the shrine, causing protests and riots elsewhere in Asia. The Ministry of Education's approval of a history textbook that gave scant attention to Japan's wartime atrocities led to wide-scale riots against Japanese in China in 2005. Nevertheless, although Japan has never openly apologized to Asia for the offenses of World War II, the government has taken some measures to improve ties and to put the war into the past. In 1992 in a highly symbolic visit, Emperor Akihito (who ascended to the throne upon his father's death in 1989, ending the **Shōwa period** and beginning the Heisei "Peace" Era) traveled to China and expressed regret about the past. The Japanese government also agreed to make modest compensation payments to Korean "comfort" women who were victims of institutionalized rape by the military during the war.

Prime Minister Yasuo Fukuda, elected in September 2007, has made improving relations with Asian neighbors a major foreign policy goal. He is pursuing the development of stronger bilateral economic, political, and cultural ties with Asian neighbors. Japan is intensely aware of China's growing economic strength and its already powerful military and thus, improving ties to China is deemed highly important.

Relations with North Korea, however, remain tense. Japan has been a member of the six-party talks addressing North Korea's nuclear weapons program. Although Prime Minister Koizumi made two widely publicized visits to North

Korea, relations between the two nations have remained strained. This is due to a combination of factors, but central to them is the utterly bizarre case of 13 Japanese kidnap victims and their North Korean families. In late 2002 North Korea admitted to having kidnapped 13 Japanese in the 1970s to train North Koreans spies in Japanese language and culture. Intense public interest in the case – a story that could have come straight out of a James Bond movie – placed great pressure on the Japanese government not only to get the five surviving kidnap victims back to Japan, but also their children and spouses, and the remains of those who are believed dead. Prime Minister Fukuda expressed strong reservations to U.S. President George W. Bush regarding his plans to take North Korea off the list of terrorist-sponsoring nations as a reward for the North's agreement in 2007 to disable its nuclear facilities.

Conclusion

Japan is struggling to determine what its role should be in a post–Cold War world in which alliance structures and the economic situation of states are changing. Many in Japan are questioning whether Japan can continue to operate as a state with such strong restrictions on the deployment of its military. Many others in Japan are arguing that Japan should remain pacifist and make nonmilitary contributions to the global system. The rapid growth of China is of great interest and concern to Japan and as a result Japan has been working to improve its relations with China and other countries in Asia.

Long considered a follower of U.S. foreign policy, since the mid-1990s Japan has begun to show somewhat more policy independence from the United States although it still closely monitors U.S. reactions to its policy positions. Japan has become an international leader in the provision of official development assistance and has become a more powerful international player in Asia. Still, there is a lot of questioning in Japan about what the future holds.

This sense of uncertainty also pervades the political and economic systems. Efforts to create a two-party electoral system in Japan have failed to date and there is growing public apathy about politics. On the economic front, years of reform efforts may slowly be beginning to pay off, but many uncertainties remain.

Japan has an extremely well-educated population, low crime rates, high life expectancy, and a relatively high GNP per capita. Thus, on many of the most important indicators of a nation's well-being, Japan ranks well compared with other "rich" countries, including the United States. Maintaining this performance as society ages and its economy enters an era of slower growth will be one of the most important challenges for the Japanese government.

BIBLIOGRAPHY

Allinson, Gary D., and Yasunori Sone. *Political Dynamics in Contemporary Japan*. Ithaca, NY: Cornell University Press, 1993.

Beasley, W. G. *The Rise of Modern Japan: Political, Economic, and Social Change since 1850*. New York: St. Martin's Press, 2000.

Dower, John W. *Embracing Defeat: Japan in the Wake of World War II*. New York: Norton, 1999.

Duus, Peter. *The Rise of Modern Japan*. Boston: Houghton-Mifflin, 1976.

Gluck, Carol. *Japan's Modern Myths: Ideology in the Late Meiji Period*. Princeton, NJ: Princeton University Press, 1985.

Hayes, Louis D. *Introduction to Japanese Politics*. Fourth ed. Armonk, NY: M.E. Sharpe, 2004.

Hook, Glenn D., Julie Gilson, Christopher W. Hughes, and Hugo Dobson. *Japan's International Relations: Politics, Economics, and Security*. Second ed. New York: Routledge, 2005.

Johnson, Chalmers. *MITI and the Japanese Miracle: The Growth of Industrial Policy, 1925–1975*. Stanford, CA: Stanford University Press, 1982.

Kingston, Jeff. *Japan's Quiet Transformation: Social Change and Civil Society in the Twenty-first Century*. New York: Routledge Curzon, 2004.

Pekkanen, Robert. *Japan's Dual Civil Society: Members without Advocates*. Stanford, CA: Stanford University Press, 2006.

Pempel, T. J. *Regime Shift: Comparative Dynamics of the Japanese Political Economy*. Ithaca, NY: Cornell University Press, 1998.

Richardson, Bradley. *Japanese Democracy*. New Haven, CT, and London: Yale University Press, 1997.

Samuels, Richard J. *The Business of the Japanese State: Energy Markets in Comparative and Historial Perspective*. Ithaca, NY: Cornell University Press, 1987.

Schreurs, Miranda A. *Environmental Politics in Japan, Germany, and the United States*. Cambridge: Cambridge University Press, 2002.

Schlesinger, Jacob M. *Shadow Shoguns: The Rise and Fall of Japan's Postwar Political Machine*. Stanford, CA: Stanford University Press, 1999.

Schwarz, Frank, and Susan J. Pharr, eds. *The State of Civil Society in Japan*. Cambridge: Cambridge University Press, 2003.

Stockwin, J. A. A. *Governing Japan*. Third ed. Oxford: Blackwell Publishers, 1999.

Tsai, Kelly, and Saadia Pekkanen, eds. *Japan and China in the World Economy*. New York: Routledge, 2005.

Scheiner, Ethan. *Democracy without Competition in Japan: Opposition Failure in a One-Party Dominant State*. Cambridge: Cambridge University Press, 2005.

Schoppa, Leonard. *Race for the Exits: The Unraveling of Japan's System of Social Protection*. Ithaca, NY: Cornell University Press, 2006.

Vogel, Steven. *Japan Remodeled: How Government and Industry are Reforming Japanese Capitalism*. Ithaca, NY: Cornell University Press, 2006.

TABLE 6.1. Key Phases in Japan's Political Development

Time period	Regime	Global context	Interests/identities/ institutions	Developmental path
1603– 1867	Tokugawa shogunate (military authoritarian/ imperialism)	growing foreign trade pressures, European domination of China/U.S.– forced opening of Japan	powerful shogunate/ competition among feudal daimyo/ shogun-led unification of country	unification of state through dominance of feudal domains by shogunate
1868– 1912	Meiji Period (oligarchy/ authoritarian/ imperialism)	European imperialism/ Asian power struggles	political and industrial elite/political and industrial reform/ authoritarian with elections	adoption of Western political institutions and capitalism
1912– 1926	Taisho democracy (democratic/ imperialism)	World War I and Treaty of Versailles, failure of West to accept Japan as an equal	political and industrial elite/democracy, socialism, communism, imperialism/democracy with powerful bureaucrats and oligarchs	capitalism and imperialism
1926– 1945	militarism (authoritarian/ imperialism)	global depression, rise of fascism and communism, World War II	military elite/fascism, imperialism/authoritarian	capitalism, imperialism, and militarism
1945– 1952	foreign occupation (military/ democratic)	Start of U.S.-Soviet Cold War, Communist victory in China, Korean War	economic development/militarism discredited/rebuilding of industry and democratic institutions	international assistance and occupation
1955– 1993	one-party dominance (democratic)	Cold War, economic growth	big business/democratic values grow, pacifism, consumerism, environmentalism/ one-party dominant democratic system	capitalism and liberalism
1994– present	coalition government (democratic)	end of Cold War, improved Asian regional relations	economic stagnation/ globalization, expanded overseas role for SDF/ pluralization, strengthening of civil society	capitalism, liberalism, and globalization

IMPORTANT TERMS

amakudari literally, "descent from heaven," this phrase refers to the common practice whereby retiring civil servants take up positions in Japanese corporations and public interest bodies.

Article 9 of the Japanese constitution states "the Japanese people forever renounce war as a sovereign right of the nation and the threat or use of force as a means of settling international disputes." It has been the basis for the maintenance of a pacifist foreign policy although over the years it has been reinterpreted to allow for the creation of Self Defense Forces and participation in U.N. Peace-keeping Operations.

daimyo were the lords of the 260 feudal fiefdoms of Japan. The victory in war of the Tokugawa clan in 1600 led to a system in which the daimyo were required to pay tribute to the Tokugawa government.

Democratic Party of Japan (DPJ) is the second largest party in Japan. Founded in 1998 by the merger of several smaller parties, it has the best chance of any party to beat the LDP in elections. In the July 2007 House of Councillors election, the DPJ won a majority of seats. This was the first time ever that the LDP lost control of the upper house.

Diet a German word for parliament. Japan's Diet was created in 1890 based on the Prussian model. The Diet was weak in the pre–World War II era, but the 1946 Constitution greatly strengthened its powers.

fukoku kyohei literally "rich nation, strong army," this phrase symbolized Meiji Japan's desire to catch up economically and militarily with the West.

genro the oligarchs who advised the emperor and effectively ran Japan during the Meiji Era.

gyōsei shido translated as "administrative guidance," this term symbolizes the power of the Japanese bureaucracy and its influence in helping to steer the Japanese economy during its growth years.

Japan Socialist Party (JSP) the largest opposition party in postwar Japan from its formation in 1955 to its disastrous electoral performance in the 1995 House of Representatives elections. The party changed its name in English to the Social Democratic Party of Japan (SPDJ) in 1991.

keiretsu the term for the economic conglomerates that are prevalent in postwar Japan and are the successors to the prewar *zaibatsu*.

Liberal Democratic Party (LDP) the conservative governing party of Japan from its formation in 1955 to its electoral defeat in 1993. From 1994 on the LDP has again governed in coalition with other small parties.

General Douglas MacArthur was appointed Supreme Commander of the Allied Powers (SCAP) by President Harry S. Truman and was in charge of the occupation of Japan. He was a very powerful figure and had a hand in the writing of the Japanese constitution.

Meiji Restoration refers to the 1868 revolt that led to the downfall of the Tokugawa clan, the revival of the position of the emperor, and the implementation of a crash course of modernization for Japan.

Ministry of Economy, Trade, and Industry (METI), formally known as the Ministry of Trade and Industry (MITI), played an important role in the economic development of Japan. Many of Japan's smartest university graduates worked for METI.

Commodore Matthew Perry sailed four "black ships" into Edo Bay in 1853 demanding the opening of Japanese ports to foreign trade. Perry's voyages to Japan were behind the great political reforms of the Meiji Restoration.

reverse course refers to a shift in the emphasis of U.S. occupation policies in Japan after the onset of the Cold War. The focus of policies shifted from the demilitarization and democratization of Japan to the limited rearming of Japan and its economic recovery.

Shigeru Yoshida Japanese prime minister from 1946 to 1947 and again from 1949 to 1954 who chose to focus on economic development and allow the United States to guarantee Japan's security. His policies are referred to as the Yoshida Doctrine and became the guiding ideology of the LDP.

shogun the military leaders and the Tokugawa clan which ruled Japan from 1603–1868.

Shōwa period the name of the reign of Emperor Hirohito (1926–1989), a tumultuous period in Japanese history.

Taisho democracy the brief interlude during the period from 1918 to 1932 when parties gained political influence and a more pluralist democracy began to function.

zaibatsu the family-owned financial conglomerates of the prewar era.

STUDY QUESTIONS

1. Why was Japan able to avoid the fate of many other Asian countries that became colonies of the West? How did Japan go from being an isolated state under the Tokugawa Shogunate to becoming a world power during the Meiji Era?

2. Was the Meiji Constitution democratic? Why, or why not?

3. What explains Japan's imperialism and the rise of militarists in the 1930s?

4. What lessons can we take from the Allied occupation of Japan? Why was the occupation of Japan so successful?

5. Japan's "economic miracle" stunned the world. How can Japan's rise from postwar destitution to economic powerhouse be explained?

6. How would you characterize postwar Japanese democracy? How does the postwar constitution differ from the Meiji Constitution?

7. Why was the Yoshida Doctrine so important to Japan's defense posture and economic development in the postwar period?

8. Why might one consider the 1990s as the beginning of a period of economic and political reform in Japan? What are the driving factors behind these reforms?

9. Do you think that Japan should maintain a strict interpretation of Article 9? Why, or why not?

10. What characteristics of Japanese politics would you consider to be uniquely Japanese?

STOP AND COMPARE

EARLY DEVELOPERS AND MIDDLE DEVELOPERS

Once Great Britain and France developed, all other countries were forced to respond. Germany and Japan were among the first to do so. By the middle of the nineteenth century, Germany was not yet unified and Japan faced Western imperialism. German and Japanese variations on the grand strategies of development found in the early developers are the direct result of international competition – military, economic, and cultural – between early and middle developers.

If Great Britain's and France's historical experiences are models of development and revolution from below, Germany and Japan represent instances of development and revolution from above. Compared with their predecessors, the middle and lower classes in Germany and Japan were weaker and the upper classes stronger. The state, in alliance with the upper classes, helped initiate economic development. Above all, what drove the entire process was military competition with more advanced states.

This developmental path had fateful consequences for liberal democracy and ultimately world peace. After abortive attempts at representative democracy, both Germany and Japan thus went through a period of fascism before they could participate in the world economy on an equal basis with the developed West.

MIDDLE DEVELOPERS: GERMANY AND JAPAN

French power on the European continent guaranteed throughout the first 70 years of the nineteenth century that Germany remained a fragmented group of kingdoms and principalities. Among these separate states, however, some were more powerful than others. The most militarily capable was Prussia, which, under the leadership of Chancellor Bismarck, succeeded in defeating the French in the Franco-Prussian War of 1870 and unifying the German states under Prussian leadership in 1871. From the outset, German economic and political development reflected the fact that it came in response to French and British advancement. The fact that the need for military power came in anticipation of, rather than in response to, economic development meant that the path taken by Britain and France, which was largely a story of rising middle classes gradually securing power over monarchs and nobilities, would not be a historical possibility for Germany. Unable to rely on an economically ingenious and politically assertive rising middle class, Germany industrialized by allowing capital to concentrate in relatively few large banks, permitting industrialists to reduce risk through the creation of cartels, and creating a modern military officer corps and state apparatus on the basis of premodern agrarian elites. The coalition on which power rested consisted of an alliance of "iron and rye" that had little interest in genuine parliamentary rule. The parliament, known as the Reichstag, was neither fairly elected nor did it have sovereignty over the kaiser, whose governmental ministers continued to be appointed from the ranks of the noble elite.

Although this pattern of development forestalled democracy, it succeeded quite spectacularly in military competition and economic development. By the beginning of the twentieth century, Germany could field land armies superior to those of the French and could float ships on a par with those of the British. German chemical, machine-building, and metal industries were as advanced as those of its competitors. Such rapid development, occurring really in fewer than 40 years, had a price. German craftsmen and especially industrial workers, who were often first-generation city dwellers, lived mostly in very difficult circumstances. Radical working-class parties, such as the Social Democrats, could easily recruit the disaffected and the poor into mass politics. The ruling elite responded in two ways: first by banning the Social Democrats, and when that could not be sustained, by relying on a kind of militaristic German nationalist appeal for solidarity among classes against other nations. Unfortunately, this latter strategy worked. Perceiving the balance of forces to be temporarily on their side, and by tradition inclined toward military solutions to social and diplomatic problems, the kaiser and his advisers exploited a crisis in European security relations in 1914 to launch a continent-wide war, which ultimately became known as World War I.

Defeat in this war forced the kaiser to abdicate and led to a fundamental democratization of German politics. This first try at parliamentary democracy, known as the Weimar Republic (1920–1933), suffered from innumerable handicaps. The old elites had not been decisively replaced either in the economy or in the state bureaucracy; the victory of democracy was associated in many people's minds with a humiliating loss in war (in a country that lived by the cult of war) and an equally humiliating peace treaty signed at Versailles; the country was saddled with heavy reparations payments to the victors; and the political institutions led to a fragmented party system and the temptation to rule by emergency presidential decree. This last factor became the fateful one when Adolf Hitler's Nazi Party managed to gain a plurality of seats in the Reichstag in the 1932 elections. Hitler had revived much of the older militaristic thinking of the pre-Weimar era, but he now laced the new ideology with large doses of revenge and racism. After spending the middle of the 1930s preparing for war, in 1939 Germany initiated, for the second time in the twentieth century, a Europe-wide conflict that cost the lives of millions.

Because war emanated from Germany twice during the twentieth century, the Allied victors decided that this would not happen again. The ultimate price that Germany paid for defeat was, in some sense, to return to the situation from which it had started: national division. The Soviet zone of occupation became communist East Germany, or what was called the German Democratic Republic, and the three Western zones of occupation (those of Britain, the United States, and France) became West Germany, or the Federal Republic of Germany.

Apart from division, the Western allies and democratically minded Germans were also determined to remake Germany from the inside in order to ensure that democracy would genuinely take root there. To that end, Germany developed a set of policies, as well as constitutional and institutional innovations, designed to foster democratic stability and prevent extremist politics from ever returning. For example, although Germany continues to have a multiparty system, there are constitutional features to guarantee that it does not become too fragmented, unstable, or gridlocked in indecision. Another such arrangement is corporatism. Most Germans are organized into trade unions or employer associations. The German government through its public offices attempts to ensure that these two groups hammer out agreements that ensure just wages, low unemployment, and high growth rates. In turn, the government attempts to soften many of the rougher edges of capitalist economics through a comprehensive welfare state. The net impact of these policies is designed to ensure that economic downturns do not occur often and, when they do occur, that they do not turn public opinion against democracy. Perhaps more crucially, corporatist policies are supposed to prevent the most rancorous debates over wages, prices, and welfare and move them off the parliamentary floor and out of politics in general.

Such policies helped secure for the Federal Republic quite remarkable growth rates throughout the postwar era and also created a society that, for the first time in Germany's history, genuinely seems to value liberal democracy for its own sake. However, the challenges of reunification, European unity, and global capitalist competition have induced slower growth rates, much higher unemployment, and a new domestic debate on whether the German model can be sustained into the future. In the first years of the twenty-first century, the German government brought the entire German social market model into question by tinkering with such bedrocks of the

German model as health care, unemployment insurance, and state employment. Such questioning of the German model and initial moves to alter it are indeed troubling to most Germans precisely because it was this model that brought the country affluence and, after 1989, national unity – two things that had eluded Germany for the previous century.

Although Japan lies thousands of miles away from the European continent, grouping it together with Germany makes a great deal of sense to comparativists. For one thing, like Germany, Japan confronted external challenges to its sovereignty that forced it into rapid economic development in order to compete militarily. For another, the responses to these challenges were remarkably similar. Finally, the long-term path on which these responses set Japan led it to a similar form of militarism that also could only be overcome by fundamental restructuring after World War II.

Japan entered the early modern period a fragmented country dominated by alliances of local feudal lords (called daimyo), several of whom tried for over a century to gain control over the country. Under the leadership of the Tokugawa family (1603–1868), however, Japan at the start of the seventeenth century overcame its feudal fragmentation. Through concentration of power in the hands of the shogun, the institution of a rigid class system in which the warrior samurai nobility were given the lion's share of privileges, and the isolation of the island through a prohibition on foreign travel and a ban on the practice of Christianity, successive Tokugawa rulers succeeded in crafting out a distinctive Japanese identity and a unified Japanese state.

As effective as this system was in solving the problems of political unification – and the fact that it lasted for 250 years suggests that it was effective – the arrival of U.S. Commodore Perry's "black ships" in 1853, with the purpose of forcing Japan to open its borders to trade and foreign influence, posed challenges that the Tokugawa order was not equipped to confront. In the mid-1860s, a series of rebellions among low-level samurai, who incorporated nonprofessional soldiers and even peasants into their army under a nationalist banner of expelling the foreign "barbarians," succeeded in overthrowing the last Tokugawa shogun from office and replaced him in 1868 with an emperor whom they considered to be the true emperor of Japan, the 15-year-old Meiji.

The Meiji Restoration, as historians have subsequently dubbed it, set Japan down a course of economic and military modernization with the purpose of securing the country from foreign control. The slogan of the time, "rich country, strong military," captured the essence of what the Meiji Restoration was about. As in Germany, our other middle developer, industrial modernization occurred primarily in the form of a "revolution from above." A modern army and navy were created, feudal-style control over localities was replaced with a modern local government, and class privileges were formally abolished, thus reducing the power of the old samurai class, in theory, to that of the commoners. As in Germany, industrialization was accomplished at break-neck speed under the guidance of a national bureaucracy and with capital controlled by large, family-owned industrial conglomerates called *zaibatsu*. Also as in Germany, the Japanese Meiji elite sought a political model that could accommodate the kinds of changes that were taking place. The constitutional model they settled on, not surprisingly, was that of imperial Germany, with its parliamentary electoral rules that favored the landed elite and a government that remained dominated by military institutions and values.

Fundamental democratization occurred in Japan for the first time only in 1925 with a series of electoral reforms. Unfortunately, the old Meiji ruling elites who remained on the political scene, especially within the officer corps, never fully supported democracy. When the political and economic crises of the 1930s hit, consistent pressure from right-wing extremists and the military high command constrained the actions of civilian government. The ideas of the far Right and the military about what Japan needed were somewhat diffuse, but they can be summarized relatively easily: solve Japan's economic and domestic problems through the colonization and economic domination of continental Asia. To achieve these goals, starting in 1936 Japan engaged in a series of wars in China that yielded even more power to the military. The military viewed the United States as the main obstacle to Japan's plans for Asia, and it finally pushed Japan to attack Pearl Harbor in 1941 as a preemptive strike against U.S. might.

The devastating end of the war was the U.S. decision to drop the atomic bomb twice on Japan, after which the U.S. occupation inaugurated a series of political and economic reforms that changed life in Japan. A new constitution that forbade foreign military involvement, the complete removal of the emperor from political life, and a series of new institutions and political rules designed to bring constitutional democracy all brought about fundamental change. Japan lives with the result to this day.

Despite these changes, the nature of the Japanese political and economic model shows considerable continuities, or at least influences, from the past that remain a constant source of fascination for comparativists. Government and business continue to work closely together (although Japan's government is the "smallest" in the industrialized world), and capital remains far more concentrated than in the Anglo-American model. Furthermore, Japan continues to use a combination of hierarchy in political and social culture and a remarkable degree of equality in salaries and living standards. Japanese workers are highly unionized but almost never go on strike. Japan's trade tariffs are among the lowest in the world, but it continues to be a country that foreign businesses have trouble penetrating. Finally, Japan's parliament, although democratically elected, continues in many ways to "pass" laws drafted in ministries rather than craft the laws itself. The latest round of globalization, however, has brought about considerable rethinking among the Japanese, who have started to question seriously whether these long-term characteristics of the Japanese model will be able to continue on into the future. As in Germany, where the fundamental democratization of the postwar period was accompanied by a selective retention of important aspects of the earlier model that seemed to work, the need to rethink the postwar political-economic model has led to considerable unease within Japan.

PART THREE

LATE
DEVELOPERS

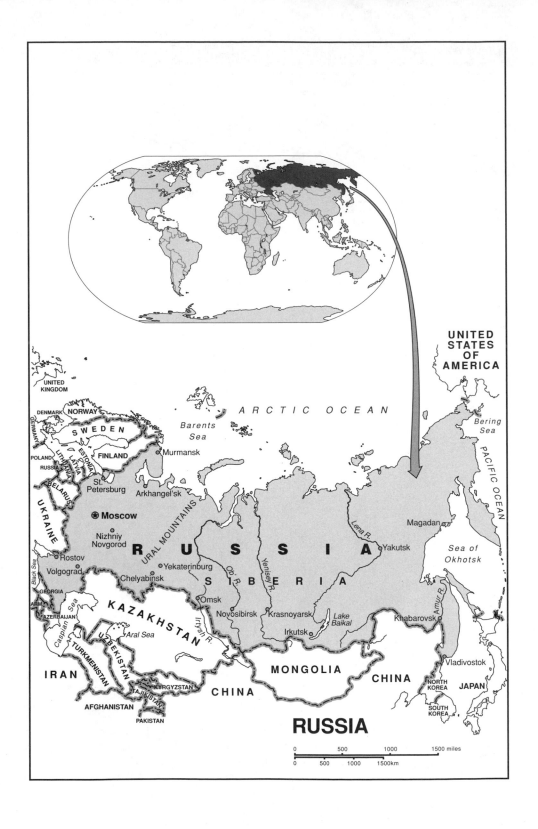

RUSSIA

CHAPTER SEVEN

Russia

Stephen E. Hanson

Introduction

Russia has long puzzled and surprised observers of international politics. For seven decades, Russia was at the center of a communist regime – the Union of Soviet Socialist Republics, or USSR – that competed with the United States for global supremacy (see Table 7.1 at the end of the chapter). After the collapse of the USSR in 1991, Russia suffered a prolonged period of political, military, and economic decay. During the two terms of President **Vladimir Putin**, the Russian economy rebounded strongly, but this growth was accompanied by a return to political authoritarianism. There is no consensus among specialists about how this one-time superpower became so weak so quickly; nor do scholars agree in their evaluations of Putin's efforts to revive the country. Indeed, it seems that Russia simply does not fit conventional analytic categories.

Geographically, Russia is the biggest country in the world, spanning 11 time zones. Most of its population is in Europe; most of its territory is in Asia. Although about four-fifths of its population are ethnically Russian, the Russian Federation contains hundreds of other ethnic groups, some of which have engaged in serious struggles for greater autonomy or – in the case of **Chechnya** – full independence. Should we call Russia a European, an Asian, or a "Eurasian" state? Is Russia a nation or an empire? Might Russia eventually break up into smaller regional units? Or is it emerging again as a revitalized great power in world politics?

Economically, Russia is largely industrialized and urbanized, with less than one-fifth of its population living in rural areas. Its population is highly educated. Yet many of its factories are inefficient, technologically backward, and environmentally unsafe; its villages still often lack paved roads, sewage systems, and basic services; and its economy remains heavily dependent on exports of oil, natural gas, and minerals. Should we call Russia an advanced, a developing, or an underdeveloped state? Or does Russia's economy deserve some new theoretical category of its own?

Culturally, Russia has played a key role in European intellectual and artistic history, producing such well-known writers and composers as Lev Tolstoy, Fyodor Dostoevsky, and Pyotr Tchaikovsky. Yet for centuries – and even today – prominent Russian thinkers have claimed that their country can never be truly "Westernized" because of what they claim is the essential mysticism, communalism, and idealism of the Russian "soul." Should we call Russia's culture Western, non-Western, or something else entirely?

Neither Western analysts nor Russians themselves have come up with consistent answers to these questions. Indeed, since the collapse of the communist empire in 1991, life in Russia has become even more unpredictable and confusing. As the twenty-first century dawns, Russians are engaged in a seemingly endless debate about their country's identity. Early hopes for a rapid transition to Western-style democracy and capitalism have been dashed, and although the public mood has improved with the stabilization of the economy under Putin, there remains a pervasive anxiety about Russia's future.

Faced with the paradoxical nature of Russia's geography, economy, politics, and culture, many political scientists have been tempted to agree with Winston Churchill that Russia is "a riddle wrapped in a mystery inside an enigma." Detailed descriptions of Russian institutions seem to become outdated almost as soon as they are written. However, the comparative and theoretical approach to political analysis presented in this book can help us explain Russia's troubled history.

This chapter argues that contemporary Russian interest groups have been decisively shaped by the ideological identity and distinctive institutions imposed on the country by **Vladimir Lenin** and his followers from 1917 to 1991 in an effort to catch up with and overtake the West. In short, the USSR was a failed ideological experiment to design an alternative anticapitalist model of industrial society. Ironically, the collapse of Soviet institutions left Russia once again on the periphery of the global capitalist system, facing challenges of economic backwardness, ethnic conflict, and international insecurity similar to those confronting the country in the early twentieth century. This time, however, there is no consensual or coherent ideology to organize Russia's response to these challenges. Thus, an analysis of the rise and fall of the Soviet Union is crucial for understanding Russian politics today.

The Rise and Fall of the USSR

FROM MARX TO LENIN

What did "communism" mean to the founders of the Soviet regime and their heirs? To answer this question, we must begin with an examination of the

Western European theorist who originally invented the idea of communism – **Karl Marx**. To be clear, Marx himself did not provide a blueprint for the Soviet system. Indeed, he died 34 years before the Russian Revolution of 1917. Those who wish to blame Marx for Soviet tyranny forget how little control philosophers and theorists have over the ways in which their ideas are interpreted decades or centuries later. Still, the Soviet leaders all considered themselves Marx's faithful disciples. We therefore need to understand Marx's ideas in order to make sense of the rise and fall of the Soviet Empire.

Karl Marx was born in 1818 in what is now Germany. When Marx was growing up, the vast majority of German-speakers, like the vast majority of human beings elsewhere, lived in small peasant villages ruled by various local lords and princes. The Industrial Revolution that had already transformed England and the United States had yet to reach Germany, where merchant activity was largely confined to the larger cities and towns. Thus, Marx wrote about capitalism as it was first being developed on the European continent.

When Marx was just 29 years old, he and his best friend, Friedrich Engels, composed the most influential revolutionary essay ever written: the *Communist Manifesto*. The starting point for the analysis contained in the *Manifesto* – and indeed for all of Marx's later works – is a theoretical approach that later became known as historical materialism, which asserts that economic forces have ultimately determined the course of human social history. Politicians and philosophers may think that they are battling over principles, but in Marx's view they are really always fighting over the question of which groups get which shares of a society's overall wealth. The ruling ideas in each historical period, according to Marx, are always the ideas of a particular society's ruling class.

Marx argued that every stage of history has been marked by class struggle. Society has always been divided into two main classes: those who own property, and those who are forced to work to survive. The ruling class, Marx claimed, takes all the wealth that is left over once people's basic survival needs are met – what Marx called surplus value. However, the oppressed class always struggles to regain this surplus, which, after all, the workers themselves have produced. Eventually, class struggle ignites a full-scale social revolution against the old order, leading to the emergence of a new and more advanced form of economic organization.

According to Marx, three main types of class society have shaped human history to date: slavery, feudalism, and capitalism. Slavery was the dominant "mode of production" in the earliest human civilizations, such as those of ancient Greece, Egypt, and Rome. After the fall of the Roman Empire, slavery in Europe gave way to feudalism, in which the main class struggle was between the ruling aristocracy and the oppressed peasantry. After 1500 or so, this mode of production also began to weaken and finally disintegrate.

The third and final type of class society, capitalism, emerged in its full-fledged form in England and the United States during the 1700s. In the *Communist Manifesto*, Marx and Engels predicted – correctly, as we now know – that it would eventually encompass the entire globe. Capitalists themselves naturally argue that this new mode of production promotes individual freedom and wealth. In reality, Marx insisted, capitalism is simply another form of class exploitation with its own distinct type of class struggle. The ruling class under capitalism, the bourgeoisie, consists of those who hire workers for wages and/or own the factories, banks, and housing upon which workers are dependent. The oppressed class, the proletariat, consists of all those who own nothing more than their own labor power and are therefore forced to compete for a job in order to survive – that is, the vast majority of people. Surplus value, in the form of capitalist profits, goes straight into the pockets of the ruling class, whereas the proletariat must continually struggle to raise their wages above a very low level.

Marx was convinced that the capitalist system, like slavery and feudalism before it, would eventually be destroyed in a social revolution – this time eliminating class divisions among human beings altogether and ushering in communism, an era of global harmony and abundance. Marx argued that the experience of working together under the dehumanizing conditions of capitalism would serve to strip the proletariat of all forms of identity that had previously divided it. Subjected to the same forms of underpaid, repetitive, mechanized labor, workers would stop caring about one another's race, ethnicity, religion, or nationality and recognize their common humanity. The proletarian revolution, then, would be a revolution of the vast majority of human beings, united as one, to take control over the global economic system. Freed from the tyranny of wage slavery and the terror of unemployment, workers would henceforth work together in conditions of free, creative cooperation. The *Communist Manifesto* concludes: "The proletarians have nothing to lose but their chains! They have a world to win! Working men of all countries, unite!"

Yet there was a central paradox in Marx's thinking. On the one hand, Marx called for workers to unite and struggle for better conditions and wages in order to build proletarian solidarity and learn to exploit the vulnerabilities of the bourgeois system. On the other hand, Marx expected that workers under capitalism would become increasingly miserable over time, making revolution inevitable. What should communists do, then, if every successful workers' struggle against the bosses made workers less miserable and more satisfied with capitalism? Should communists support change within the existing system? Or should they continue to promote global revolution regardless of how capitalism reformed itself? Marx himself never quite resolved this strategic paradox.

In fact, no Marxist revolution has ever taken place in a developed capitalist country. Instead, communist revolution occurred first in 1917 in Russia – a country that had then only barely entered the capitalist age, with over 80 percent of its population consisting of peasants and only around 8 percent industrial workers. Why? Ironically, precisely because of Russia's underdevelopment, Marx's ideas were relatively more consistent with the interests of Russian workers and intellectuals. Although reforms had moderated the worst abuses of Western European capitalism, Russia during the early twentieth century was still suffering through the early period of industrialization, with its characteristic disregard for worker health and safety and its total lack of legal channels for worker representation. The Russian proletariat, small as it was, was thus much more revolutionary than were the better-off workers of the West. Meanwhile, many Russian intellectuals saw in Marxism a way to escape their country's economic and military backwardness without having to adopt the Western capitalist system. By achieving "socialism" – the first stage of communist society – it seemed that Russia could miraculously leap ahead of countries such as England and France in historical development. Finally, Marx's inspiring vision of communism proved especially powerful in a tsarist empire that had become embarrassingly weak, poor, and corrupt. Such factors help to explain the rapid spread of Marxist ideas in a feudal country – and the political evolution of the man who eventually founded a Marxist regime there, Vladimir Il'ich Lenin.

Vladimir Ulyanov – Lenin's real name – was born in the provincial town of Simbirsk, Russia, in 1870. When Lenin was 17 years old, his older brother Alexander was arrested for participating in a plot to assassinate the tsar and was later executed. This event placed the entire Ulyanov family under a cloud of suspicion. Lenin was allowed to attend law school in the capital city of St. Petersburg, but shortly after he began his legal studies, he was expelled for participating in student demonstrations against the regime. He began to read radical literature and soon became a convinced Marxist. By 1900, he had become prominent enough within Russian revolutionary circles to be invited to join the leading Russian Marxists in exile in Switzerland, where they lived and worked in order to avoid harassment and arrest by the tsarist police.

In 1902, Lenin published his most famous essay, entitled *What Is to Be Done?* Lenin's ideas on party organization in this work ultimately inspired revolutionaries in China, Vietnam, Cuba, and elsewhere to create one-party regimes modeled on the Leninist example. Lenin's essay contained three main arguments, all of which became quite controversial among Marxists. First, Lenin bluntly insisted that the working class by itself could never make a successful anticapitalist revolution. More than 50 years after the publication of the *Communist Manifesto*, it had become clear that workers would always be satisfied with gains in local wages, benefits, and representation; in this sense,

Lenin argued, workers had a kind of "trade-union consciousness" instead of the revolutionary consciousness needed for the successful overthrow of global capitalism. Second, Lenin argued that the movement must be led instead by Marxist intellectuals devoted at all times to revolutionary activity. A special organization of these intellectuals – a "party of professional revolutionaries" – was needed to guide the proletariat toward its eventual and inevitable victory over the bourgeoisie. Finally, Lenin insisted that the party of professional revolutionaries itself be organized as a strictly hierarchical, disciplined, and unified body. Attempts to introduce "bourgeois" forms of voting or legal procedure into the communist camp would only turn it into an ineffective debating society. Instead, the party should practice what Lenin would later term **"democratic centralism"** – meaning that debate within the party should end the moment the party's Central Committee had made a decision on any given issue.

It would be a long time, however, before Lenin and his followers built a party that in reality looked anything like his original institutional proposal. Indeed, Lenin's insistence on his model of organization at a congress of Russian Marxists in 1903 led to a split between two different factions: the Bolsheviks, or majority – so named because of Lenin's success in getting a bare majority of delegates present to vote to prohibit part-time party membership – and the Mensheviks, or minority, who argued for a more decentralized and inclusive organization of Marxists and workers. By 1904, even many of those Russian Marxists who had originally supported Lenin joined the Mensheviks to protest what they saw as his increasingly dictatorial behavior – ironically leaving the Bolsheviks very much a minority among Russian Marxists until 1917.

Indeed, had it not been for dramatic changes in Russia's global environment, Lenin's party might have faded into historical insignificance. However, the outbreak of World War I in 1914 revived the Bolsheviks' fortunes. The tsarist regime found itself hopelessly outgunned by the Germans and began to disintegrate quickly. In addition, the war's unprecedented bloodshed discredited the capitalist system, making Bolshevik ideology appear relatively more attractive. Finally, the war divided the Western European Marxist parties, each of which initially voted to support its own capitalist government in a war against their fellow proletarians – leaving Lenin as one of the few Marxists who could claim to have opposed World War I consistently from the start.

Lenin was outraged by what he saw as the spinelessness of German, French, and other Western socialists. He argued in his essay *Imperialism* that European Marxists had become hopelessly corrupted by payoffs from capitalist imperial expansion. The proletarian revolution, he concluded, was therefore more likely to begin in Russia, in the periphery of the global capitalist system, than in the developed countries of the West. Lenin made it clear, too, that his own

Bolshevik Party was ready to lead the Russian proletariat in its revolutionary struggle. Once Russia proved to the workers of the world that socialist revolution was possible, Lenin argued, communism would spread like wildfire throughout the West and beyond.

The opportunity to act on this theory soon arose when the tsar, Nicholas II, suddenly abdicated in March 1917 in response to mounting losses on the battlefield, peasant uprisings in the countryside, and bread riots in the cities. This "February Revolution" – so named because the old Russian calendar was then about two weeks behind the modern Western calendar – left Russia in a state of near anarchy. A **provisional government** made up of former members of the tsarist Parliament tried, with the support of the United States, Britain, and France, to revive the Russian economy and to continue the war against Germany. But this government had very little real authority, and in the cities, actual power devolved to what were called **soviets**, or councils, of workers and soldiers. Meanwhile, in the countryside, peasant revolts spread; many of the old nobility were killed or forced to flee.

Lenin did not, in any way, cause the collapse of tsarism; he had been in Switzerland for most of the war. He returned to the capital city of Petrograd (formerly St. Petersburg) in April 1917, advocating the overthrow of the provisional government, the establishment of a socialist republic based upon the soviets, and the immediate cessation of the war. Although the radicalism of these proposals at first stunned many of his own closest supporters, by the summer, mounting war casualties and the disintegrating economy rapidly turned the tide of public opinion among workers and soldiers in the Bolsheviks' favor.

On November 7 – the so-called October Revolution – Lenin and his supporters successfully seized power in Petrograd. Within a year, they had wiped out all other organized political forces within the territory they controlled. Not only were tsarist and capitalist parties banned, but socialists who opposed the Bolsheviks were also suppressed. A new secret police force, the Cheka – later to become the KGB – was set up to hunt down "enemies of the revolution." Even the soviets, the spontaneous organizations of the workers themselves, were soon reduced to little more than rubber stamps for the party's central decrees. Party cells were set up in every factory, every school, and every public organization to help "guide" the proletariat to communism.

Lenin's theoretical expectation that Bolshevik victory would spark communist revolutions throughout the capitalist world turned out to be unfounded, however. From 1918 to 1920, Lenin and Leon Trotsky, head of the newly formed Red Army, fought an enormously destructive and bloody civil war against various supporters of tsarism, liberalism, anarchism, and anti-Bolshevik socialism. But after having reconquered most of the territory of the former Russian empire, Lenin began to realize that the final global victory of the proletariat might be delayed indefinitely. Global capitalism, apparently, had stabilized.

To survive in power, then, the Bolsheviks had to revive the ruined Russian economy. In March 1921, Lenin introduced the **New Economic Policy**, which freed grain markets and allowed small-scale capitalism in the cities. Trade and agriculture began to recover soon afterward. Simultaneously, however, Lenin further strengthened one-party rule by implementing a "ban on factions" within the party's ranks. In 1922, he promoted a young disciple by the name of **Joseph Stalin** to the new position of general secretary of the Communist Party, entrusting him with the task of ensuring party discipline through control over personnel decisions.

Another vexing problem was that the new Soviet state occupied a territory containing hundreds of different religions and ethnic groups. According to Marx, of course, such identities were supposed to disappear entirely with the victory of communism over capitalism. In reality, such groups as the Ukrainians, the Georgians, and the Muslim peoples of Central Asia tended to perceive the new regime in Moscow as a continuation of the former Russian empire. Lenin appointed Stalin to be the new commissar for nationalities, expecting him to find a reasonable balance between the need for the party's central control and the concerns of non-Russians – after all, Stalin himself was an ethnic Georgian. To Lenin's dismay, Stalin immediately tried to eliminate all forms of national autonomy, even using physical violence to intimidate ethnic leaders who resisted his will. Ultimately, the new "Soviet Union" formed in 1923 did include several "national republics" for the largest and most powerful nationalities of the regime. Real political power, however, was concentrated in the Kremlin in Moscow (to which the Soviet capital had been relocated from Petrograd in 1918).

Shortly after promoting Stalin to these important positions, Lenin suffered a series of strokes that ultimately left him incapacitated. As Lenin lay on his deathbed in 1923, a fierce struggle for power broke out. In the last letter he was able to dictate, Lenin warned that such internecine battles could fatally weaken the party. In particular, his protégé Stalin had concentrated "immense power in his hands" and was "too rude" to occupy the post of general secretary. Lenin's warnings were ignored. Lenin died in January 1924. Within five years, Stalin emerged as the sole leader of the Soviet regime.

FROM LENIN TO STALIN

How did Iosef Djugashvili, the son of a poor cobbler in the small, mountainous country of Georgia, eventually become Joseph Stalin, one of the most powerful and brutal tyrants in history? This question is of immense historical importance because Stalin, even more than Lenin, shaped the playing field upon which Russian and other post-Soviet politicians now struggle for power. Moreover, by forging a communist bloc extending from Asia to Europe, Stalin also helped to create the basic contours of international politics in the second half of the twentieth century.

From the comparative point of view, however, the two main arguments that have been advanced to explain Stalin and Stalinism are rather unsatisfying. Some analysts argue that Stalin defeated his rivals for power and then established a tyranny simply because he was the most power hungry, the most brutal, and the most opportunistic of any of Lenin's heirs. Although Stalin obviously wanted power and was willing to use violent means to get it, it makes little sense to accuse Stalin of simple opportunism. In order to rise within Lenin's Bolshevik Party in the first place, Stalin had to fight for 14 years for an illegal organization that until 1917 had few resources, only a few thousand loyal supporters, and a leader who lived in exile in Western Europe. During this period, the tsarist police arrested him a half-dozen times. If this was a strategy to attain future political power, it was one we can only recognize as such in retrospect. Certainly no ordinary rational politician would have chosen Stalin's early career path!

The second argument often made to explain Stalin's behavior is a psychological one: in short, that Stalin was a paranoid schizophrenic who thought that hidden enemies were always plotting against him. Again, this analysis may be clinically accurate. But this hardly explains how Stalin rose to the leadership of the world's largest state. Somehow, Stalin's personal psychology did not prevent him from convincing many intelligent men and women that he was a socialist genius and not a lunatic. How he did so must be explained in terms of the larger political, social, and global environment in which Stalin's personality was situated.

An alternative point of view, which will be defended here, is that Stalin rose to power and remained in control of the USSR until his death because he, like Lenin, was an institutional innovator within the Marxist ideological tradition. In short, Stalin was a convinced communist, as well as a staunch supporter of Lenin's ideas about party organization. Stalin was in a position to gain unprecedented political power at the head of the Leninist party only because he had identified enough with it early in life to have faith in its eventual triumph. This is why Lenin gave Stalin the crucial post of party general secretary: Stalin had proven his loyalty in times of trial, so Lenin thought he could be counted on to defend the party's interests.

Certainly, Stalin did his best to enforce Leninist norms of strict party discipline and control over a potentially hostile society, using his position to attack and purge any party member who dared disagree with the "general line" of the party leadership – within which, of course, he himself was a key figure. In this respect, however – despite Lenin's complaints about Stalin's "rude" behavior – he was only following Lenin's own principles of "democratic centralism." Shortly after Lenin's death, Stalin promoted thousands of young workers to party membership in a mass campaign called the "Lenin levy," creating an even larger base of personal supporters within the Communist Party. None of Stalin's opponents possessed either the institutional levers or the organizational skills of the future dictator – a factor that cannot be ignored in accounting for his rise to power.

Stalin's victory was not only institutional, however; it was also ideological. Stalin, in fact, proposed a very distinct set of answers to the most troubling issue confronting Marxists in the Soviet Union in the wake of their revolutionary victory: namely, how to build socialism in a largely peasant country without the support of proletarian revolutions in more advanced capitalist countries. The policies that flowed from Stalin's analysis ultimately annihilated millions of people and left a burdensome economic legacy for post-Soviet Russia. Yet Stalinism was arguably the most consistent ideological response to the question of what was to be done after Lenin's death.

In order to see this, we must briefly examine the views of Stalin's primary opponents. There were three main positions in the debate: the Left, the Right, and the Center. The Left was led by the famous revolutionary Leon Trotsky, who had played a crucial role in the Bolshevik takeover, almost single-handedly building up the new Red Army and leading it to victory during the civil war. But after Lenin was incapacitated, Trotsky became disillusioned with what he saw as the gradual bureaucratization of the party and the loss of the Soviet Union's revolutionary momentum. Trotsky exhorted Soviet workers to redouble their efforts to build a strong industrial infrastructure as rapidly as possible and argued that the Bolsheviks should strive to foment revolutions throughout Western Europe. Unfortunately for Trotsky, after three years of world war, a year of revolution, and three years of civil war, most party members and ordinary workers were tired of revolutionary appeals. Some thought Trotsky might be harboring designs to take power for himself through a military coup. In the fall of 1923, the Left Opposition was overwhelmingly outvoted in the party's Central Committee, and by 1924 Trotsky's power and influence began to decline rapidly.

The Right Opposition in the 1920s was led by Nikolai Bukharin, a well-known Marxist theorist who edited the party's newspaper, *Pravda* (meaning "truth"). After an early alliance with Trotsky, Bukharin became convinced that the Left's proposals for continuous revolutionary advance were not feasible. Instead, Bukharin advocated a slow, evolutionary path to socialism in the USSR. Specifically, he argued that Lenin's New Economic Policy allowing small-scale capitalism should be continued "seriously and for a long time." The peasantry should be encouraged to get rich. Within factories, efficient management should be promoted – even if that meant keeping in place the same capitalist bosses as before the revolution. Eventually, Bukharin claimed, this policy would allow the Soviet people gradually to "grow into socialism." Such a policy was certainly more realistic than Trotsky's romantic leftism. Yet it failed to appeal to those who genuinely believed in the ideals of 1917.

Many party members, workers, and intellectuals asked why they had fought for communism if the end result was simply to establish a "New Economic Policy" that looked more like a "New Exploitation of the Proletariat."

The Center Leninist position during the 1920s was advocated by Grigorii Zinoviev, who had been one of Lenin's most loyal supporters during the pre-1917 period. Zinoviev led the Bolshevik Party in the newly renamed city of Leningrad (formerly St. Petersburg and then Petrograd). He also directed the Comintern, a global organization of communist parties loyal to Moscow, which Lenin had founded in 1919. Zinoviev argued that both the Left and the Right had gone too far: The Left called for revolution without rational analysis or professionalism, whereas the Right called for rational economic policies without any revolutionary vision. Surely, true Leninism – as he now began to refer to the regime's ideology – required both revolution and professionalism simultaneously! Unfortunately, Zinoviev himself had little idea of how to bring about a "Leninist" synthesis of these two concepts. His most original idea – enthusiastically supported by Stalin – was to place Lenin's mummified body on display in Moscow's Red Square so that generations of grateful proletarians could line up to see the founder of Soviet communism.

Neither Trotsky, nor Bukharin, nor Zinoviev proposed any practical policies for dealing with Russia's severe economic backwardness in a way that seemed consistent with the Soviet regime's socialist identity. Stalin did. In December 1924, Stalin proposed an alternative vision that appeared far more realistic in the context of the international isolation of the Soviet regime: "**socialism in one country**." The basic idea behind "socialism in one country" was simple: It was time to stop waiting for revolutions in other capitalist countries and start building socialism at home. This theoretical position contradicted Trotsky's calls for continuous revolutionary advance in Western Europe, as well as Zinoviev's hopes to inspire the world communist movement from Moscow without actually risking revolutionary changes within the USSR itself. Bukharin, assuming that Stalin's idea of "socialism in one country" was identical to his own evolutionary socialism, threw his support behind Stalin in the power struggle against Trotsky and Zinoviev. By 1928, however, having defeated his latter two opponents, Stalin began to attack Bukharin as well, accusing him of being an opportunist who had sold out to the "bourgeois" rich peasants and industrialists. Stalin lined up large majorities to vote against the Right opposition in the Central Committee, and in 1929 he expelled Bukharin and his supporters from the party leadership.

Now the unchallenged leader of the regime, Stalin revealed that his vision of "socialism in one country" required a new revolutionary assault on Soviet society. Like Lenin, Stalin proposed to translate Marxist identity into concrete institutions that would structure the interests and incentives of millions of ordinary people – this time, in the economic and not just the political realm.

Marx himself had said very little about how economic institutions should be organized in the postrevolutionary period; certainly, he had provided no guidance concerning how a single socialist state surrounded by capitalist ones could transform a largely peasant economy into an industrial power. However, Marx had indicated that he expected the "dictatorship of the proletariat" to organize state control over both the industrial and agricultural sectors of the economy, to eliminate private property wherever possible, and to organize production according to a common plan. Stalin now expanded on these principles to propose the revolutionary restructuring of the entire Soviet economy on the basis of **five-year plans** drawn up by the state and enforced by the Communist Party. Stalin insisted that although the Soviet economy was a century behind the West in developmental terms, that distance had to be made up in a decade – or the capitalists would "crush us."

The Stalinist planning system contained three key elements: **collectivization** of agriculture, a novel form of "planned heroism" in industry, and the creation of a huge system of prison labor camps known as **gulags**. The first of these, collectivization of agriculture, represented Stalin's "solution" to the dilemma of how to deal with the huge peasant population in forging a socialist Soviet Union: Basically, he decided to enslave or kill the entire peasantry. Again, Stalin put his argument in clear Marxist terms. The peasantry as a class, Marx had argued, was a leftover from feudalism. Capitalism was destined to destroy the peasantry and the aristocracy alike; there would be no place for peasant villages in the socialist future. Those who benefited from private property in agricultural production, Stalin reasoned, formed a sort of peasant bourgeoisie – kulaks, meaning "the tight-fisted ones" – while the poor peasants who worked for them were essentially part of the proletariat. Proletarian revolution in the countryside required class struggle against the kulaks and eventually, as Stalin put it, "the liquidation of the kulaks as a class." In place of the old system of private peasant farming, Stalin proposed the creation of new "collective farms" (*kolkhozy*) and "state farms" (*sovkhozy*), where peasants would work for the greater good of the proletariat – under strict party supervision.

In reality, the drive to create collective and state farms amounted to an all-out assault on the countryside by Stalin's party supporters, by the army, and by various thugs and brigands who took advantage of the chaos to loot, steal, and rape. All over the Soviet Union, peasants battled to preserve their autonomy, even killing their own livestock rather than letting their pigs, cows, and chickens fall under party control. By 1932, the collectivization drive had generated a famine throughout the agricultural regions of the USSR during which millions of people starved to death. Even so, Stalin's goal of gaining party control over the production of food was realized. Indeed, even at the height of the famine, Stalin continued to export grain to the West in order to earn hard currency for the regime. By the mid-1930s, most of the land in the country had been collectivized, excluding only tiny private plots where peasants were allowed to work for themselves and their families.

The second key element of Stalin's socioeconomic system was the imposition of centrally planned production targets for every manager and worker within the Soviet Union. The State Committee on Planning, or Gosplan, had been formed in the mid-1920s to provide general projections for future economic development in the USSR; in this respect, the organization acted in ways similar to planning bureaucracies in Western capitalist countries, such as France. But, in 1929, Stalin gave Gosplan officials the unprecedented task of supervising the rapid industrialization of an enormous country. The specific institutional mechanisms used to ensure this result were designed to elicit a sort of "professional revolutionary" economic activity comparable to that expected of good Leninist party members. Specifically, monthly and yearly production targets, calculated in terms of gross output, were issued for workers and state managers of every factory and collective farm in the USSR. However, the party did not promote workers or managers who simply attained these targets – in fact, just "fulfilling" the plan was held to be a "bourgeois," unrevolutionary sort of behavior. Those who consistently overfulfilled their plan targets, thus supposedly demonstrating their superior revolutionary enthusiasm and dedication – the so-called shock workers and heroic managers – were given monetary bonuses, special housing, better food, and even trips to Moscow to visit the dictator himself.

This system of incentives encouraged an atmosphere of constant, chaotic activity, as workers and managers struggled to produce higher and higher volumes of cement, coal, and steel, urged on by the state planners and party leadership. However, Soviet citizens soon learned that overfulfillment of plans by too great an amount could also sometimes get them into trouble. According to a principle known as "planning from the achieved level," Gosplan was instructed to raise plan targets to the point attained in the previous planning period. Thus, if a worker somehow produced double his or her required amount of coal in one year, he or she might be required to attain the same absurd amount of production the next – and failure to do so, again, could lead to arrest and imprisonment. Thus, Stalinist institutions encouraged individuals to overfulfill their plans, but not by too much. Managers and workers were given incentives to be "revolutionary," but in a manner that was simultaneously "disciplined and professional."

During the First Five-Year Plan, an industrial infrastructure was built in the Soviet Union in an incredibly short period of time; this result looked all the more impressive against the backdrop of the Great Depression then enveloping the capitalist West. Over time, however, the constant demands to "fulfill and overfulfill the plan" during the 1930s alienated even those groups who most benefited from Stalin's policies – the proletariat and party officials. A "final-exam economy," in which constant "cramming" to complete plan assignments before the final deadline was followed by the imposition of even greater work demands, could not but produce exhausted and exasperated managers and workers.

Thus, the third key component of Stalin's economic system, the creation of the gulag system, was vital to its overall functioning. The gulags – short for "chief directorate of labor camps" in Russian – were originally set up during the civil war to incarcerate those who opposed Lenin's plans for Communist Party rule. Under Stalin, however, their scope expanded rapidly; tens of millions of people were arrested as "class enemies" of the "proletarian dictatorship." Gulag inmates were put to work building canals, paving roads, digging coal, and constructing monuments to Lenin and Stalin, often under the most brutal conditions imaginable. The contribution of the gulag system to overall Soviet production under Stalin is hard to estimate, but it clearly played a crucial role in the attainment of the ambitious industrialization targets of the 1930s. Moreover, the constant threat of the gulag undoubtedly did much to inspire ordinary people's continued efforts to overfulfill the plan.

However, the types of economic activity encouraged by Stalin's incentive structure were not conducive to the long-run performance of the system. Already during the 1930s, all sorts of dysfunctional behaviors emerged within Soviet enterprises. First, because plan targets were formulated simply in terms of gross quantities of output, the quality of Soviet production often suffered greatly; as a result, the basic infrastructure of Soviet industry began to crumble and decay almost as soon as it was built. The problem of quality control was even more severe in such sectors of economic production as consumer goods and services, which were given low priority by Stalin. Second, the system was poorly equipped to handle technological change. Shutting down assembly lines in order to introduce new, up-to-date machinery meant failing to meet one's monthly and annual production targets, so Soviet managers tended to rely on their existing equipment. Third, Stalinist industrialization was an environmental disaster; to fulfill and overfulfill plans mattered more than long-term concerns with people's health or the preservation of nature. Today, former Soviet factory towns are some of the most polluted places on Earth. Fourth, collectivized agriculture was enormously inefficient and wasteful. Indeed, by the late Soviet era, approximately 65 percent of all vegetables and 90 percent of all fresh fruit were produced on the mere 2 to 3 percent of the land given to peasants' private plots!

Finally, the Stalinist system was prone to rampant institutional corruption. The official banning of most forms of private property and markets meant that all kinds of buying, selling, and stealing of state resources went on in black markets and within personal networks. Managers often colluded with local party officials to lower plan targets, falsify production reports, or otherwise protect enterprises from the demands of central planners. Given the absence of both unemployment and bankruptcy procedures, the only way to curtail such behavior was to arrest the perpetrators – but because almost everyone was involved in some form of informal evasion of their official responsibilities, rooting out corruption completely was impossible.

Stalin knew full well that his vision of socioeconomic socialism was, despite its external successes, falling victim to such forms of corrosion from within. But having sacrificed decades of his life – and millions of other people's lives – to establish this system, he was not about to rethink his policies. Instead, he tried to explain the corruption of the planning system as the work of "hidden class enemies" within the USSR and "survivals of capitalist psychology" within people's minds. In 1936, Stalin began a massive blood purge of everyone he thought was conspiring with the global bourgeoisie against socialism. In Stalin's mind, this supposed conspiracy included the Right, Left, and Center oppositions of the 1920s, economists and plant managers, independent artists and intellectuals, and the entire general staff of the Red Army. Between 1936 and 1938 – the period known as the Great Terror – Stalin killed about 75 percent of the Communist Party's Central Committee, including Zinoviev and Bukharin, who were tortured and forced to testify that they were agents of capitalist intelligence services, and then executed. In 1940, one of Stalin's agents assassinated Trotsky, then living in exile in Mexico City. Meanwhile, millions more Soviet citizens were imprisoned or killed.

How did such a coercive system maintain itself? Every institutional order, no matter how oppressive, requires the allegiance of some social group whose interests it advances, and the Stalinist system is no exception. In fact, one small group did quite well within the framework of Stalinist industrialization, namely, blue-collar workers in their twenties and early thirties who had joined the party during Stalin's rise to power. Many of these men (and women, although this group was predominantly male) found themselves promoted extremely rapidly during the period of the First Five-Year Plan to positions of management and within the party hierarchy. They rose even further when their immediate supervisors were killed during the Great Terror. Some of these people ultimately became members of the post-Stalin Soviet Politburo, the highest organ of the Communist Party, including such future leaders as **Nikita Khrushchev** and **Leonid Brezhnev**. For these men, who had started their careers as ordinary workers, the Soviet Union was truly a dictatorship of the proletariat!

Even with the support of the communist worker elite, however, Stalin's system of planned heroism and mass terror might well have disintegrated had it not been for the enormous changes in the international environment wrought by World War II. When Adolf Hitler invaded the USSR in June 1941, Soviet forces were hardly able to resist; within months, the Nazis were at the gates of both Leningrad and Moscow. However, before the conquest of the Soviet Union was complete, the Russian winter began to set in, and the German soldiers found themselves quite unprepared for the extreme cold.

Soon fresh troops from the east came to reinforce Moscow. By December, when the United States entered the war after the Japanese attack on Pearl Harbor, the pressure on the Nazis was increasing. Fighting between Soviet and Nazi troops continued for three more years, and ultimately the USSR lost more than 20 million people in the conflict. However, by the end of 1943, the tide had turned decisively against Hitler, and by 1945, Red Army troops met Allied troops in Berlin in triumph.

After the Soviet victory in World War II, Stalin insisted that his policies of the 1930s had been vindicated. After all, the giant steel mills, cement plants, and weapons factories set up in the First Five-Year Plan had played a crucial role in the Soviet war effort; without rapid industrialization, the Nazis might actually have conquered Russia. Stalin could now claim – despite his genocidal policies – that he was a great Russian patriot who had defeated an alien invader of the motherland. Finally, at the conclusion of the war, Soviet troops occupied most of Eastern and Central Europe, including the eastern portion of Germany. Within three years, Stalin had imposed both Leninist one-party rule and Stalinist collectivization and planning on these unfortunate nations. If one accepted Stalin's definition of socialism then, it followed that Stalin was the first person who had successfully created an international "socialist commonwealth," one that even included part of Marx's homeland. World War II – or, as the Russians still refer to it, the "Great Fatherland War" – thus greatly solidified the legitimacy of Stalin's regime and led many ordinary citizens to embrace a "Soviet" identity for the first time.

Until his death in 1953, Stalin continued to defend the system he had created – and to use terror to silence his real and imagined opponents. Toward the end of World War II, entire peoples whom Stalin accused of being disloyal, such as the Crimean Tatars, the Volga Germans, and the Chechens, were deported to Siberia and Central Asia. After the war was over, the arrest of supposed capitalist spies continued; even the relatives of prominent Politburo members were sent to the gulag. Meanwhile, Stalin promoted a "cult of personality" in the Soviet media and arts that constantly trumpeted the dictator's supposed genius as an architect, as a poet, as a military commander, as a linguist, and so on. Shortly before his death, Stalin was preparing to launch a new terror campaign against so-called enemies of the people – this time including Politburo doctors, whom he accused of plotting to poison the leadership, and, even more ominously, Soviet Jews, who he claimed were part of a global Zionist conspiracy against him. Fortunately, Stalin died in March 1953, before he could act on these ideas.

FROM STALIN TO GORBACHEV

Stalin's successors were faced with a dual legacy. On the one hand, by 1953 the USSR was a global superpower. Its industrial production had become sufficiently large to allow it to compete militarily with the capitalist West; by

1949 it had also built its first nuclear bomb. Newly decolonized and developing countries looked to the Soviet Union as a counterweight to the power of the West and in some cases as an ally whose institutions should be emulated. The Western powers themselves had just emerged from decades of world war and global depression – phenomena Marx had predicted would result from capitalism's "inner contradictions" – and it would be some time before analysts were sure that democratic capitalism in Europe could be revived and sustained.

On the other hand, the fundamental problems of Leninist party politics and Stalinist planned economics remained. Years of dictatorship and terror had killed off much of the popular enthusiasm that had once existed for heroic efforts to build socialism. Bribe taking and black-market activity on the part of Soviet officials had already become a way of life. Problems with economic waste and inefficiency, worker absenteeism and alcoholism, and poor-quality production had become more severe. Clearly, something had to be done to address the growing cracks in the foundation of the Soviet superpower.

Again, the post-Stalin leadership analyzed and responded to these problems in a way they thought was consistent not only with their own personal interests but also with the basic outlines of the Soviet socialist identity. First, every Soviet leader after Stalin's death in 1953 agreed that the days of mass, indiscriminate terror in Soviet society must end. Stalin's last secret-police chief, Lavrentii Beria, was himself executed by the end of the year, millions of people were freed from the gulag, and the most extreme forms of Stalin worship ceased. The post-Stalin leadership also agreed that the next stage in building socialism somehow had to involve the creation of a truly socialist culture that would inspire ordinary workers and peasants to contribute their energies to the further development of Soviet institutions voluntarily. There was, however, no clear consensus on how to do this.

From 1953 until 1985, leadership struggles again centered on debates among what we can now recognize as Right, Left, and Centrist strategies concerning how to create a "socialist way of life" without Stalinist terror. Supporters of the "Right" strategy during this period, such as Georgii Malenkov, the first post-Stalin prime minister, argued that Soviet socialism must abandon revolutionary crusades in economic and foreign policy and instead promote efficiency within enterprises and high-quality production for ordinary consumers. This advice, however sensible from our perspective, struck most party officials and Stalinist planners as a direct attack on their interests and as a departure from the revolutionary ideals of Marxism and Leninism.

By 1954, Malenkov's authority had been eclipsed by Communist Party leader Nikita Khrushchev. Khrushchev advocated the opposite of Malenkov's policies, calling for a revolutionary advance toward communism as rapidly as possible. In a secret speech to the party elite in 1956, Khrushchev sought to inspire mass revolutionary sentiment by exposing the abuses of the Stalin period as "deformations" of socialism that would never be permitted again. This speech was followed by a "de-Stalinization" campaign involving a significant easing of censorship over the media and the arts. Khrushchev called on the Soviet people to participate in a whole series of economic campaigns to set records in corn planting, milk and meat production, and chemical manufacture; he even revised the party program to include a timetable according to which Marx's original vision of "full communism" would be attained in the USSR by 1980! He also pursued a risky and often reckless foreign policy, threatening the West with nuclear missile attacks if it did not agree to Soviet demands. Such "leftist" policies led to administrative chaos at home and military embarrassments, such as the Cuban missile crisis, abroad. In 1964, Khrushchev was ousted in a Politburo coup.

From 1964 until 1982, Leonid Brezhnev presided over an orthodox Marxist-Leninist Politburo that resisted any reform of Soviet institutions – and, besides supporting various pro-Soviet regimes in the developing world, did very little else. Brezhnev's leadership arrested vocal dissidents and tightened censorship to prevent open criticism of the regime, but it largely turned a blind eye to private disaffection, corruption, and black-market activity. Party officials and state bureaucrats were rarely fired, and the Soviet elite began to age, and ultimately to die, in office. The planning system, now lacking either mass enthusiasm or fear as incentives for the fulfillment of production targets, sank into stagnation and decline. By the mid-1970s, the Soviet economy became dangerously dependent upon energy exports and sales of vodka. The disastrous Soviet military intervention in Afghanistan in 1979, combined with the declaration of martial law to suppress the independent Solidarity trade union in Poland in 1981, exposed the growing vulnerabilities of the Soviet army and the Warsaw Pact alliance of Leninist regimes in Eastern Europe. Meanwhile, such leaders as Margaret Thatcher in Britain and Ronald Reagan in the United States were calling for a much more aggressive foreign policy to confront the Soviet "evil empire" (to use Reagan's term). Finally, from 1982 until 1985, a veritable parade of dying general secretaries of the Communist Party – Brezhnev, Yuri Andropov, and Konstantin Chernenko – made the USSR an international joke.

It was under these dire global and domestic circumstances that the party elite decided to entrust the key position of general secretary to the 54-year-old **Mikhail Gorbachev**. Upon his promotion to the leadership in March 1985, a furious debate ensued among Western Sovietologists. The "totalitarian" school, which insisted that the Soviet system was still in essence a regime based on terror, tended to see Gorbachev as merely a more polished representative of Soviet tyranny and warned the West to remain vigilant. "Modernization" theorists, who claimed that the USSR had become a developed, modern society not unlike the United States, saw Gorbachev's leadership as a final break with the Stalinist past and hoped for a new era of peace and cooperation between his regime and the West.

In effect, each side assumed that Gorbachev knew what he was doing but did not believe what he was saying. The totalitarian interpretation of Gorbachev assumed that he knew how to revitalize the Soviet economy in order to produce a more technologically advanced and efficient communist challenge to the West but did not believe his own promises of reform and democratization of the Soviet system. The modernization interpretation of Gorbachev assumed that he knew how to eliminate the corruption, misman-agement, and ideological rigidity of the Brezhnev period but did not believe his own constant assurances that he was a Leninist who hoped to revive the ideals of the October Revolution. In fact, Gorbachev believed what he was saying but did not know what he was doing. When he told the world that he was a "Leninist reformer," he meant exactly that. As for what reformed Leninism in the Soviet Union would eventually look like in practice, however, he had no concrete idea.

How could Gorbachev really believe in Leninism as late as the 1980s? Gorbachev had been promoted his whole life for espousing this ideology. He had come of age politically during the successful and painful struggle against the Nazis and had been a teenager during the triumphant emergence of the Soviet Union as a global superpower. As a young man, he was given the Order of the Red Banner of Labor for his "heroic" work as a combine operator on a collective farm. Largely as a result of this award, he was admitted to the prestigious Moscow State University Law School. In his twenties, he became a party official, and by his thirties he had been appointed the first party secretary in Stavropol, an agricultural region in southern Russia. Because of Stavropol's strategic location on the way to various Black Sea and Caucasus mountain resorts, Gorbachev got to know almost every significant Soviet leader, including Brezhnev, Andropov, and Chernenko. By 1978, at the age of 47, he had been promoted to the Politburo as secretary of agriculture, in part because his sincere enthusiasm for Leninism and socialism had impressed his somewhat jaded elders.

Thus, by the time he became general secretary, Gorbachev was one of the few people in the USSR who still truly believed in Leninist ideology. People's enthusiasm for participation in the Communist Party and for heroic plan fulfillment, Gorbachev insisted, could be rekindled – but only if he found some way to eliminate the corrupt, petty bureaucracy that had blocked popular initiative during what he called the "era of stagnation" under Brezhnev. His first step was to purge hundreds of old party bureaucrats. By 1986, Gorbachev had already dismissed or retired almost 40 percent of the Central Committee and felt strong enough to launch his dramatic campaign for perestroika, or restructuring.

Perestroika consisted of three basic elements: glasnost, democratization, and "new thinking" in foreign policy. Glasnost, or openness, meant greater disclosure of people's criticisms of the Soviet past and present in newspapers, television, and films. This campaign got off to a rather ambiguous start when, in April 1986, the Chernobyl nuclear power plant in Ukraine exploded, spewing radioactivity over much of Eastern Europe; the Soviet government hid this information from its citizens for a full three days after the event. However, by the fall of 1986, the quantity and quality of published revelations about Soviet history and current Soviet society began to increase markedly. The release in December 1986 of the famous Soviet nuclear physicist and dissident Andrei Sakharov, who had been sent into internal exile for his public denouncement of the Soviet invasion of Afghanistan, demonstrated the seriousness of Gorbachev's break with Brezhnevite forms of censorship. After 1987, the scope of glasnost widened to include every conceivable topic, including Lenin's terror during the civil war, the horrors of collectivization, and even the dictatorial nature of Communist Party rule itself.

Democratization also began slowly, with vague calls to reinvigorate the system of soviets that had been subordinated to the party hierarchy since the Russian civil war. By 1988, however, at the Nineteenth Party Conference, Gorbachev announced that genuine multicandidate elections would be held for a new Soviet Congress of People's Deputies to replace the old rubber-stamp Supreme Soviet. To be sure, Gorbachev attempted to guarantee the continued leading role of the Communist Party, reserving a third of the seats in the new 2,250 seat congress for "public organizations" under direct party control. Moreover, in many electoral districts, local party bosses still ran unopposed, as in the times of Stalin and Brezhnev. Nevertheless, the national elections held in the spring of 1989 generated many serious, competitive races between reformers and party conservatives that galvanized Soviet society.

Finally, Gorbachev's campaign for new thinking in foreign policy announced a turn away from attempts to build client regimes in the developing world, a campaign to reduce tensions with the capitalist West, and, most significantly, an end to the Stalinist subordination of countries in the communist bloc. Since the end of World War II, Soviet leaders had been able to preserve Leninist rule in Eastern Europe only through repeated military interventions, including Khrushchev's invasion of Hungary in 1956, Brezhnev's invasion of Czechoslovakia in 1968, and the Soviet-supported declaration of martial law in Poland in 1981. Now, one of Gorbachev's spokesmen announced that the old "Brezhnev doctrine" of military intervention had been replaced by the "Sinatra doctrine": the former communist satellite states would be allowed to "do it their way." Again, early reaction to this announcement was skeptical, both in the West and in Eastern Europe. In 1989, the seriousness of new thinking was tested when Solidarity candidates won every possible seat but one in new elections for the Polish Parliament. When Gorbachev did nothing to prevent the creation of the first non-Leninist government in the communist bloc, liberal democrats and nationalists throughout the region moved to gain their own independence. By the end of the year, revolutions against Communist Party rule had succeeded in every single country of the former Warsaw Pact.

Gorbachev's perestroika, then, was every bit as revolutionary as its author had intended – but not with the results he had expected. Within three years of the launching of the campaign for restructuring, both the identity and the institutions at the core of Leninism had disintegrated. Instead of inspiring a new faith in socialist ideas as Gorbachev had hoped, glasnost made the history of communism appear to be a long and bloody tragedy. Democratization, designed to remove corrupt Brezhnevite bureaucrats in order to make space in the system for more enthusiastic socialists, instead destroyed Lenin's "party of professional revolutionaries" altogether. New thinking, which was supposed to allow the USSR to compete with capitalism more effectively by discarding the coercive methods of past foreign policy, resulted in the rapid disintegration of the Soviet empire.

By 1990, the spiraling loss of party control produced two further unanticipated results: an economic crisis and a nationalist resurgence. Economically, Gorbachev's perestroika had done surprisingly little to change the fundamental elements of the Stalinist planning system other than to permit small-scale cooperatives in the service sector and limited joint ventures with foreign capitalists. The breakdown of party authority by 1990 meant that producers no longer had any reason to obey the orders of the planning bureaucracy. Those who simply hoarded raw materials or manufactured goods, then sold or traded them on the black market, could not be punished in the absence of an effective central-party dictatorship. As soon as some people stopped deliveries of goods to Gosplan, however, other enterprises found themselves without necessary supplies; they were also then forced to hoard whatever they had and barter with their former suppliers. Outright theft of enterprise resources also became commonplace; in some cases, corrupt party officials even shipped valuable minerals out of the country for hard currency and had the proceeds placed in Swiss bank accounts. As a result of the breakdown of the planning system, goods began to disappear from store shelves all over the country.

At the same time, nationalism began to fill the gap left by the discrediting of Marxism-Leninism. In many ways, it is ironic that the system of Soviet republics created by Lenin and Stalin to deal with the multiethnic nature of Soviet territory had actually reinforced national identity in the USSR. Peoples living in the republics had been allowed to preserve schools, museums, and cultural institutes promoting their native traditions and languages but had been ruthlessly subordinated to Moscow politically and economically. The Baltic republics of Estonia, Latvia, and Lithuania had in fact been independent countries until 1940, when Stalin annexed them to the USSR after having made a secret deal with Hitler to divide Eastern Europe. After the revolutions of 1989 in East-Central Europe, people in the republics began to demand greater autonomy and, in the case of the Baltics, outright independence. These trends were further fueled by elections to the Supreme Soviets of the 15 republics in 1990. In each of these campaigns, advocates of greater republican autonomy outpolled representatives of the Soviet communist center; even those who did not really want full republican independence often voted for "sovereignty" as a way of protesting Gorbachev's ineffective leadership. By the end of 1990, however, the disintegration of the USSR had become a very real possibility.

That possibility became a reality because of **Boris Yeltsin**'s mobilization of a powerful movement for national independence within Russia itself. Yeltsin had originally been brought to Moscow by Gorbachev in 1986 to be the city's party boss and a candidate member of the Politburo. Yeltsin, born the same year as Gorbachev, shared the latter's belief that Soviet socialism had grown stagnant and corrupt. He won the hearts of Muscovites by criticizing party conservatives, making surprise televised visits to inspect shops suspected of profiting on the black market, and talking with ordinary people on the streets wherever he went. In October 1987, however, Yeltsin made the mistake of attacking conservative Politburo members in a party meeting – thus violating Lenin's decades-old prohibition on "factions" within the party. He was drummed out of the Politburo and given the dead-end job of USSR deputy minister of construction.

The elections for the USSR Congress of People's Deputies in the spring of 1989, however, revitalized Yeltsin's political career. Running on a platform of greater democracy and marketization, Yeltsin gained 90 percent of the votes in his Moscow electoral district. Together with Sakharov, he formed a movement of Congress deputies committed to the end of one-party rule and reintegration with the West. Such a reintegration, Yeltsin argued, could be achieved only if Russia attained greater autonomy from the Soviet Union and took control over its own political and economic life. Yeltsin's embrace of this distinctive anti-Soviet Russian nationalism attracted even some conservatives to his side, including the Afghan war hero General **Alexander Rutskoi**. By the summer of 1990, Yeltsin had quit the Communist Party, and in February 1991 he called on Gorbachev to resign. In June 1991, Yeltsin, with Rutskoi as his vice-presidential candidate, easily won popular election to the new post of president of the Russian Federation – the first time in history that a Russian leader had been democratically elected.

Faced with the potential secession of the Soviet republics, the disintegration of the Soviet economy, and the emergence of a powerful Yeltsin-led opposition in Russia itself, Gorbachev tried desperately to hold the regime together. In May 1991, he negotiated a new "union treaty" with the newly elected leaders of those republics – or at least the nine still willing to talk to him. But on August 19, 1991, the day before the treaty was to take effect, conservative Leninists within the leadership mounted a coup against Gorbachev as he vacationed on the Black Sea. The heads of the KGB, the defense ministry, and the interior ministry announced that Gorbachev was "too sick to continue" in office and proclaimed the formation of a "State Committee for the Emergency Situation" that would lead the country for an unspecified period. However, the coup attempt was ineptly planned and executed. Gorbachev refused to cooperate with the coup plotters, as they had apparently hoped he would. Meanwhile, Yeltsin made his way to the Russian "White House," the building housing the Russian Congress, where over a hundred thousand Muscovites had gathered to protest the coup. He climbed on top of a tank and declared his uncompromising opposition to the coup plotters. At that moment, he became, in essence, the new leader of Russia.

Key units of the KGB and military defected to Yeltsin's camp. The coup unraveled shortly thereafter. Interior Minister Boris Pugo committed suicide; the other leaders of the coup were arrested. Yeltsin announced Russia's recognition of the independence of the Baltic states; he also banned the Communist Party of the Soviet Union, branding it a criminal organization. Gorbachev returned to Moscow on August 22, but he appeared to be totally out of touch with the changed situation in the country, quoting Lenin and defending the Communist Party at a televised press conference. Gorbachev continued to try to preserve what was left of the Soviet Union, but Yeltsin and other leaders of the national republics soon committed themselves to full independence. On December 1, 1991, over 90 percent of the Ukrainian population voted for national independence in a referendum; a few days later, the leaders of Russia, Ukraine, and Belarus announced the formation of a new, decentralized **Commonwealth of Independent States** to replace the USSR. On December 25, 1991, Gorbachev, bowing to the inevitable, resigned as leader of the Soviet Union, thus ending the 74-year history of the Leninist regime.

Interests, Identities, and Institutions in Postcommunist Russia

THE LENINIST LEGACY AND POST-SOVIET INTERESTS

When the Soviet Union was officially declared dead in December 1991, most Western governments and many analysts understandably greeted the news with euphoria, predicting that Russia would join the prosperous, democratic West in short order. Unfortunately, Westerners tended at the time to underestimate the enormous structural problems that would inevitably face new democratic and market-oriented governments in Russia and other former Soviet republics. As we emphasize throughout this textbook, institutions inherited from the past can exert a powerful influence on politics in the present. This was especially true in the postcommunist world, which was saddled with the legacy of a particularly brutal ideological, political, and socioeconomic tyranny that had endured for decades. Moreover, former communist countries now found themselves exposed to competition from technologically advanced capitalist countries. The economic gap between Russia and the West in 1991 was, if anything, even greater than it had been in 1917.

It was extremely unlikely, then, that a rapid "transition to democracy and markets" in Russia would take place without reversals, inasmuch as the elimination of Soviet institutions often contradicted the interests of the people who had previously lived under them. It is unsurprising that those institutions most costly for individuals to abandon proved the most difficult to destroy. For this reason, Soviet institutions decayed in the same order as they were originally created: first Marxist ideology, then Leninist party politics, and finally, only very slowly, Stalin's planned economy.

Marxist ideology was the easiest to abandon, and it died soon after the collapse of the regime. Indeed, in the immediate aftermath of the August coup, popular disgust with the ideological language of the old regime was so widespread that labeling oneself a Leninist or even a socialist was tantamount to committing political suicide – as Gorbachev soon discovered. Mainstream Russian politicians strove to outdo one another with professions of opposition to communism. Even those who still called themselves communists largely stopped referring to Marx, Engels, and the global proletarian revolution. Even more significantly, the sudden disappearance of Marxism-Leninism left in its wake an almost total ideological vacuum; in contrast with the Soviet period, the politics of short-term material interest now blocked all efforts to articulate a new post-Soviet national identity.

In response to this situation, Yeltsin and his advisers became convinced that there was no alternative to adopting liberal capitalist ideology. However, whereas liberals in other postcommunist countries could claim – with some justification – to be returning to national traditions suppressed under Soviet rule, liberalism in post-Soviet Russia appeared to many as a capitulation to the West. As the post-Soviet crisis continued, anti-Western sentiments in Russian society understandably strengthened, and those in search of consistent ideological visions often gravitated toward radically antiliberal figures.

This brings us to the second legacy of Leninism, that of one-party rule. Again, the initial effect of Yeltsin's banning of the Communist Party of the Soviet Union (CPSU) in the days after the August coup was to encourage widespread formal defection from that organization. However, leaving the party was potentially far more costly than disavowing Marxist-Leninist ideology. Because Communist Party officials had monopolized every significant position of power in society, right down to the shop-floor level, membership in alternative political organizations could hardly deliver comparable benefits in the short run. For this reason, formal withdrawal from the CPSU was, in most cases, followed by a scramble to cement key personal ties and to maintain access to economic resources inherited from one's days as a communist functionary.

It was therefore somewhat comical to see early post-Soviet Russian politicians accuse their opponents of being communists, since almost all of them had been members of the CPSU in the recent past. This is not to deny that a very real degree of political pluralism emerged after 1991, especially compared with Soviet times. However, the legacy of one-party rule continues to be a serious obstacle to the formation of genuine, alternative grassroots organizations and mass political parties in the Russian Federation. Indeed, long after the collapse of the USSR, throughout Russia one could still find former party bureaucrats ruling over their local fiefdoms as they did under Leninist rule.

A final political legacy of Leninism was the inheritance of administrative boundaries that tended to worsen, rather than ameliorate, ethnic conflicts. The borders of the Russian Federation, like those of the other Soviet republics, had been drawn up by Stalin with little concern for nationalist sensibilities. More than 20 million ethnic Russians lived outside the new Russian state and were now suddenly inhabitants of foreign countries. Meanwhile, the Russian Federation itself contained dozens of "ethnic republics" and "autonomous districts" formally set aside for regional non-Russian ethnic groups, and although most of these regions seemed content to remain part of Russia, others, in particular Chechnya, mounted their own drives for national independence. As a result, popular acceptance of the existing boundaries of the state was weak, and several prominent opposition figures called for restoration of at least part of the old Soviet empire.

The most burdensome institutional legacy of the Soviet system, however, was the residue of the Stalinist planned economy. All over Russia and the other former Soviet republics – indeed, all over the postcommunist region – an enormous rust belt of outdated factories continued to produce goods that few consumers wanted, to poison the surrounding environment, and to waste scarce energy and other resources. Enterprises that had for decades been judged solely according to their ability to overfulfill plan targets – or at least fake it – were poorly prepared to compete in a market economy, especially in the global high-tech environment of the 1990s. Unfortunately, Stalinist factories employed tens of millions of people and under the Soviet system had distributed a whole range of welfare benefits, including child care, recreational facilities, housing, and even food. The loss of one's factory job meant the disappearance not only of one's salary but also of one's social safety net. Blue-collar workers, former Soviet managers, and the local party officials who had formerly supervised them thus formed a natural lobby against any rapid transition to competitive capitalism.

The legacy of Stalinist collectivization of agriculture reinforced this anti-market lobby. The brutal methods used to create *kolkhozy* and *sovkhozy* during the 1930s had drained the countryside of its most knowledgeable and productive farmers; the poor services and supplies found in rural regions had inspired most young people to leave the villages for the cities. The remaining 30 million Russians living in rural areas at the end of the Soviet era were primarily elderly, poorly skilled, and culturally conservative. They, too, were hardly prepared for the establishment of a capitalist farming system.

Along with the sheer weight of inefficient agricultural and industrial sectors in the post-Soviet Russian economy came a more subtle problem, namely, the absence of most of the market institutions now taken for granted in advanced capitalist societies. The USSR, for example, had never created a functioning real estate market because private ownership of land was banned; a decade after the Soviet collapse, there was still no consistent legal basis for land ownership in Russia. Nor did the Soviet economy possess anything like a capitalist financial system. The Soviet ruble was never freely tradable for currencies such as the U.S. dollar or Japanese yen; its value was set artificially by state bureaucrats. Soviet banks, instead of making careful investment and loan decisions based upon calculations of profit and loss, simply funneled resources to those enterprises the planners directed them to support. Stock and bond markets were also nonexistent under Soviet rule, and those operating in the early years of the Russian Federation were prone to wild speculative swings. Finally, the Soviet judiciary was not trained in the enforcement of legal property rights, and it has been difficult to get post-Soviet Russian courts to uphold business contracts in a consistent manner.

Thus, decades of Leninism had generated huge institutional obstacles to a smooth reentry into the Western capitalist world. Nonetheless, Yeltsin and his supporters chose what might be termed a revolutionary, rather than evolutionary, approach to Westernizing Russia. With the support of Western political leaders and economic advisers, they launched an all-out drive to reintegrate Russia into the global economy. Predictably, the results fell far short of expectations.

YELTSIN AND THE DESIGN OF POST-SOVIET INSTITUTIONS

During the autumn of 1991, Boris Yeltsin fought successfully against conservative nationalists and supporters of Gorbachev who wished to preserve the USSR. In this struggle, he maintained the enthusiastic support of the Russian Congress of People's Deputies that had been elected in 1990. The Congress voted in November to grant Yeltsin special emergency powers for one year in order to deal with the extraordinary political and economic crisis resulting from the Soviet Union's collapse. On New Year's Day, 1992, the Russian Federation became, along with the rest of the former Soviet republics, an internationally recognized independent state; Yeltsin declared himself Russia's first prime minister.

Immediately, Yeltsin used his emergency powers to implement a policy of rapid marketization popularly known as **shock therapy**. To administer this policy, he named a 35-year-old economist, Yegor Gaidar, as his deputy. The theoretical assumption behind shock therapy was that unless Russia made immediate moves toward capitalism, it would remain stuck in a hopeless halfway house between the old Stalinist system and the new global market economy. In theory, shock therapy would be painful in the short run but better for Russian society in the long run. Gaidar's plan, drawn up in close consultation with Western advisers and the International Monetary Fund (IMF), contained three key elements: price liberalization, monetary stabilization, and privatization of state property.

The argument for freeing prices was hard to refute. For decades, the Soviet planners had kept prices for energy, housing, consumer goods, and basic foodstuffs artificially low in order to prevent public protest. Such low prices made it unprofitable for anyone to produce these goods, except on the black market. Letting prices rise was arguably the only way to induce entrepreneurs to deliver food and basic goods to markets in time to prevent starvation during the cold Russian winter. But the end of price controls was bound to cause social unrest.

Price liberalization was announced on January 2, 1992. Within days, prices had doubled and even tripled; by the end of the year, they were over 17 times higher. The effect was to wipe out most people's savings. An elderly person who had painstakingly saved 10,000 rubles – a significant sum in the Soviet era – by 1993 found that her fortune was worth approximately $10. On the positive side, goods did reappear in shops throughout the country; the old Soviet phenomenon of people lining up for blocks to buy scarce consumer goods was now a thing of the past.

Fighting inflation required attention to the second key element of shock therapy, monetary stabilization – controlling the money supply in order to make the ruble a strong, convertible currency like the U.S. dollar. This turned out to be easier to do in principle than in practice. By the spring of 1992, Soviet factories and collective farms everywhere were struggling to pay for supplies at vastly higher prices than before. Russian managers called up their old friends in the Congress of People's Deputies in Moscow to demand that money be sent to help enterprises pay their bills. By May, the Central Bank of Russia had begun to issue new rubles day and night to subsidize failing enterprises. Instead of achieving monetary stabilization, Russia was flooded with money; as a result, inflation remained extremely high. The alternative, however, was to shut down an enormous number of huge factories and farms and to fire the millions of workers who worked in them.

In theory, of course, unemployed workers should have been able to find new jobs at more efficient start-up companies generated by capitalist competition. But new companies could not easily emerge in a country still owned almost entirely by the state. Thus, the third element of shock therapy, privatization of property, was seen as crucial to the entire reform effort. The privatization drive was led by Gaidar's close ally and friend, Anatoly Chubais. In late 1992, privatization "vouchers" were issued to every man, woman, and child in Russia; they could either use them to bid on state enterprises put up for sale at privatization auctions or sell them for cash. The idea was to build a mass base of support for the new capitalist economy by giving everyone at least a small share of the proceeds of the sale of Soviet properties. Unfortunately, few ordinary Russians had much of an idea of what to do with their vouchers. Many people invested them in bogus "voucher funds," the organizers of which simply cashed in all their vouchers and fled the country. An even greater problem was that much of Soviet state property was doomed to produce at a loss under market conditions – so why bid on it? After a few showcase privatization auctions, the voucher campaign bogged down.

Chubais now engineered a compromise proposal. According to a "second variant" of privatization worked out with leaders of the Russian Congress, 51 percent of the shares of a company could simply be handed over to its existing management and workers, with the rest being divided between the state and any interested outside investors. More than two-thirds of Russian enterprises chose this form of privatization – which, in effect, amounted to a simple declaration that former Stalinist factories were now private property, although they were run by the same people, and with the same workforce, as before. In this way, Yeltsin, Chubais, and Gaidar could claim that, within two years, two-thirds of the Russian economy had been privatized; underneath the surface, however, inefficient Soviet production methods remained largely in place.

The collapse of the Soviet Union and the inconsistencies and mounting social unrest associated with the shock-therapy program quickly turned a majority of Congress deputies against Yeltsin's Westernization drive. Yeltsin's own vice-president, Alexander Rutskoi, now forged an alliance with the parliament's leader, Ruslan Khasbulatov, in opposition to Yeltsin and Gaidar. At the Sixth Congress of People's Deputies in December 1992, a majority refused to confirm Gaidar's reappointment as prime minister. Yeltsin's emergency powers had by then expired, so he was forced to appoint a compromise candidate, **Viktor Chernomyrdin**. Chernomyrdin was the former head of the state natural gas monopoly, Gazprom, and shared the basic economic views of the factory managers clamoring for an end to shock therapy. At the same time, Chernomyrdin was rumored to have become a multimillionaire through profits from exports of gas to Western Europe. In practice,

Chernomyrdin tried to be a centrist, calling for an "end to market romanticism" but not a reversal of market reforms.

Chernomyrdin's appointment as prime minister did not end the growing tensions between Yeltsin and the Congress. Rutskoi and Khasbulatov now openly called for the creation of a new government led by the Congress and its executive body, the Supreme Soviet. In April, Yeltsin turned to the public, sponsoring a nationwide referendum on his leadership and economic policies, and asking whether early elections should be held for the president and/or the parliament. The results showed that Yeltsin's public support remained, at this stage, remarkably strong, with a majority even supporting the basic economic policies of the past year. The opposition in the Congress, however, continued to press for Yeltsin's ouster.

During the summer of 1993, a form of dual power emerged. Both the president and the parliament issued contradictory laws and decrees; both sides had drawn up new constitutions for the Russian state. Given the administrative chaos in Moscow, Russia's 89 regions and ethnic republics began to push for even greater autonomy, withholding taxes and resources and often insisting on the primacy of regional laws over central laws. Fears that Russia would disintegrate like the Soviet Union became increasingly widespread. In September, Yeltsin brought the crisis to a head by announcing the disbanding of the Supreme Soviet and Congress. The parliament responded by declaring Yeltsin's presidency null and void and declaring Rutskoi as the new Russian leader. The possibility of civil war loomed. On October 3, extremist supporters of the Congress tried to take over the main television station and mayor's office in Moscow. Yeltsin then decided to order a military assault on his enemies.

More than 150 people were killed in the attack on the Russian White House in October 1993. There was a sad symbolism in watching Yeltsin order the shelling of the same building where he had courageously defied the Soviet coup plotters just two years earlier. After October 1993, the impression that "democracy" was merely a disguise for naked presidential power became widespread among disaffected groups in Russian society.

The destruction of the Russian Congress did, however, allow Yeltsin to design and implement a new constitution in December 1993 (just barely approved by Russian voters – at least officially). The Russian constitution, like democratic constitutions elsewhere, formally divides political power among the legislative, judicial, and executive branches. The legislature is bicameral. The lower house, the **State Duma**, consists of 450 deputies. From 1993 through 2003, half of them were representatives of national parties selected on the basis of proportional representation (PR) and half were representatives of local electoral districts; beginning in the 2007 Duma election, all deputies are selected through PR. The 178 members of the upper house, the **Federation Council**, represent the governors and regional legislatures of each of Russia's federal regions. The judicial branch is led by the Constitutional Court, empowered to rule on basic constitutional issues; the Supreme Court, the country's highest court of general appeal; and the Supreme Arbitration Court, the highest body within Russia's separate system of commercial courts. However, the 1993 Russian constitution gives by far the greatest share of political power to the president. The Russian president is the commander in chief of the armed forces, appoints the prime minister, and even has the right to issue presidential decrees with the force of law, as long as they do not contradict existing legislation. Moreover, if the State Duma refuses to confirm the president's choice for prime minister three times or votes no confidence in the government twice, he can dissolve the lower house and call new elections.

Notwithstanding the overwhelming powers of the presidency, Russian elections after 1993 have had genuine political significance. Even in the first elections to the State Duma in December 1993, Russian voters were able to express their alienation from those responsible for the shock-therapy reforms of the preceding two years. Despite highly visible state support, Gaidar's political party, Russia's Choice, attained only 15.5 percent of the party-list vote – the parliamentary seats allocated according to proportional representation. Meanwhile, the two other most successful parties were led by antiliberal ideologues. A full 23 percent of the electorate chose the Liberal Democratic Party of Russia (LDPR) farcically named, considering that it was led by **Vladimir Zhirinovsky**, a flamboyant ultranationalist who promised to lower the price of vodka, shoot criminals on the spot, and invade the Baltic states and the Middle East. An additional 12 percent of the voting public chose **Gennady Zyuganov**'s Communist Party of the Russian Federation (CPRF), which called for the resuscitation of the Soviet Union – not because of any lingering faith in Marx's communist workers' utopia but in order to rebuild Russia as a great power. The remainder of the Duma was split among smaller parties that managed to surpass the 5 percent barrier to party-list representation – such as the more moderate promarket party Yabloko (Apple), led by economist **Grigory Yavlinsky**; the Agrarian Party, representing collective farms, and the Women of Russia Party, which emphasized problems of unemployment and abuse facing many Russian women – and independent deputies elected in local electoral districts.

A new constitution and elections did not eliminate Russia's continuing economic problems, however. The government did gradually manage to get inflation under control, primarily by stopping the printing of rubles. But factory managers throughout the country responded to the cutoff of subsidies by resorting to barter and by ceasing to pay their workers for months at a time. Eventually, mounting "wage arrears" to Russian workers, state employees, and soldiers grew into an intractable social problem. Small businesses, meanwhile, were strangled by a combination of arbitrary state taxation, corrupt bureaucrats demanding bribes, and interference by local "mafias" demanding protection money. Foreign and domestic investment remained at a very low level, and the overall gross domestic product (GDP) continued to decline. Taxation to cover government expenditures became increasingly difficult because many people (understandably) did their best to hide their incomes. The government began to rely on revenues from the privatization drive, which continued to favor well-connected elites. By 1995, a handful of billionaires – popularly known as the **oligarchs** – had gained control of most of the country's energy and mineral resources, banks, and mass media.

Moreover, although the new constitution contributed to a temporary stabilization in relations between Moscow and the various regional governments of the Russian Federation, the danger of state disintegration remained. Yeltsin was soon forced to conclude a series of separate treaties with restive regions, such as oil-rich Tatarstan and the diamond-producing republic of Sakha in the Far East. Then, in December 1994, hard-line advisers persuaded Yeltsin to reassert Moscow's authority over the regions by invading the rebellious republic of Chechnya. The invasion quickly escalated into a full-scale war that killed tens of thousands of ordinary citizens – including many elderly ethnic Russians who could not escape the Chechen capital of Grozny in time. But the war only succeeded in further stiffening Chechen resistance to Russian rule. The utter failure of the campaign in Chechnya demonstrated clearly that the Russian military, like the rest of the government, was in a state of near-total demoralization and ineffectiveness.

Given Russia's continuing decline – and Yeltsin's growing health problems and increasingly erratic behavior – it is perhaps unsurprising that parliamentary elections in 1995 once again favored antiliberal forces. That voters were confronted with a long, confusing ballot listing 43 competing parties did not help matters. This time, Zyuganov's CPRF was the biggest vote-getter, attaining 22 percent of the PR vote. Zhirinovsky's LDPR still polled a disturbing 11 percent. The only two other parties to exceed the 5 percent barrier were Yavlinsky's Yabloko, with 7 percent, and a new pro-government party called Our Home Is Russia, led by Prime Minister Chernomyrdin, which managed to attain only 10 percent of the party-list vote despite an expensive government-sponsored media campaign. Gaidar's party dropped below the 5 percent barrier and won just a few single-member district seats. Meanwhile, because of the absurdly large number of competitors on the ballot, a majority of Russian voters voted for parties that did not get any Duma seats at all.

The first post-Soviet presidential campaign in Russia, in 1996, thus began with Yeltsin's political future in grave doubt. In February, polls showed that only 6 percent of Russians supported the Russian president, whereas over one-quarter supported his Communist challenger, Zyuganov. With the fate of

Russia's weak democratic-capitalist regime hanging in the balance, however, Yeltsin mounted a remarkable comeback. He traveled throughout the country, energetically shaking hands, handing out money to pay late pensions and wages, and even dancing to a rock band. Yeltsin's campaign was financed by a huge infusion of cash from the IMF, which delivered the first installment of a $10 billion loan to Yeltsin's government, and by the oligarchs, who were terrified that their newly privatized companies would be renationalized in the event of a Communist victory. The oligarchs also flooded Russian newspapers and television with political advertising portraying Zyuganov as a tyrant who would reimpose totalitarian rule. Zyuganov, meanwhile, made such fears seem realistic by praising Stalin as a great Russian leader and declaring that the USSR still legally existed.

In the first round of the presidential elections in June 1996, Yeltsin got 35 percent of the vote to Zyuganov's 32 percent. In third place with 15 percent was General **Alexander Lebed**, who called himself a "semidemocrat" and promised to restore "truth and order." Yavlinsky managed fourth place with 7 percent of the vote, and Zhirinovsky came in fifth with 5 percent. Five other minor candidates polled less than 2 percent each – including Mikhail Gorbachev, supported by a minuscule 0.5 percent of the electorate.

Russian electoral rules require a runoff between the top two vote-getters in the first round of presidential elections if no candidate attains a majority. Thus, voters now faced a stark choice between Yeltsin and Zyuganov. The oligarchs continued their media campaign, portraying the election as a decision between freedom and totalitarianism. Lebed decided to support Yeltsin in return for an important government post. Zyuganov himself repeated his standard themes, blaming the IMF, the West, and Yeltsin for the ruin of Russia and calling for the restoration of Soviet power. In early July, Yeltsin completed his comeback, gaining 54 percent of the vote versus 40 percent for Zyuganov (with 5 percent of voters declaring themselves "against both").

Yeltsin's reelection meant that the flawed democratic-capitalist institutions he had established after 1991 in Russia would endure at least a while longer. However, powerful postcommunist interest groups, including many blue-collar workers, collective farmers, pensioners, military men, and anti-Western intellectuals, continued to oppose Yeltsin's regime. Moreover, the perpetual crises, violence, and economic decline of the early post-Soviet period had alienated even Yeltsin's own supporters among the urban, educated middle class, most of whom in 1996 had in essence voted against Zyuganov and a return to communism, rather than for the aging and erratic president. Indeed, a few days before his reelection, Yeltsin had suffered a severe heart attack; he was barely able to attend his own inauguration ceremony and was only sporadically active afterward. The president's incapacitation set the government adrift while its political, economic, and regional challenges mounted.

Elections for regional governors in 1997 – though marking an important extension of Russian democracy – tended to strengthen further the power of Russia's regions as the capacity of the central government decayed.

In the spring of 1998, during one of his infrequent periods of political activity, Yeltsin made one last effort to rejuvenate market reforms. He unexpectedly fired Chernomyrdin as prime minister, replacing him with Sergei Kiriyenko, a 35-year-old ally of Gaidar, Chubais, and other liberal "young reformers." However, the underlying structural problems in the Russian economy were by this point too severe to fix. Given continued economic stagnation, decreasing confidence on the part of foreign investors, poor tax collection, declining world oil prices, and an increasingly unmanageable debt burden, Russia's budget deficit became unsustainable. The IMF tried to help Kiriyenko's government, delivering almost $5 billion in late July, but within a few weeks this loan had been exhausted in a failed attempt to prop up the weakening ruble.

On August 17, Kiriyenko suddenly announced a devaluation of the ruble and a 90-day moratorium on government debt payments. A deep financial crisis ensued. Inflation soared to almost 40 percent for the month of September alone, dozens of banks failed, and foreign investors left Russia in droves. Yeltsin fired Kiriyenko but then inexplicably proposed to replace him once again with Chernomyrdin. Besides Chernomyrdin's own party, no major faction in the Russian Parliament would go along. After tense negotiations, all sides agreed to support the compromise candidacy of Foreign Minister **Yevgeny Primakov**, a Soviet academic specialist on the Middle East and former chief of Russian foreign intelligence. On September 11, 1998, Primakov was overwhelmingly confirmed as Russia's new prime minister. The constitutional order had been preserved.

Unfortunately, the endemic uncertainties of Russian politics continued. Only seven months after Primakov's promotion, another nearly disastrous battle between the president and the Parliament erupted when Zyuganov's Communist Party initiated impeachment proceedings against Yeltsin. Although more moderate political forces seemed unlikely to support some of Zyuganov's most extreme claims – for example, that Yeltsin had committed "genocide" against the Russian people by launching the shock-therapy program – the vote to impeach the president for unconstitutional actions in launching the war in Chechnya looked too close to call.

But on May 12, 1999, just three days before the impeachment vote in the Duma, Yeltsin suddenly dismissed Primakov as prime minister, proposing to replace him with Interior Minister Sergei Stepashin. Now a full-scale constitutional crisis loomed. According to the text of the 1993 Russian constitution, the Duma would be disbanded if it failed to confirm Stepashin as the new prime minister on a third vote; yet, at the same time, the constitution also forbade the president from dissolving the Duma if it voted for impeachment.

Faced with the very real possibility that Yeltsin would take advantage of the constitution's ambiguity to declare a state of emergency rule – and worried that they would lose their parliamentary perks and privileges as a result – the Duma majority backed down. The vote to impeach Yeltsin failed, and Stepashin was later easily confirmed as prime minister.

Even this was not sufficient to make the increasingly isolated president feel secure, however. In early August, two new threats to Yeltsin's regime emerged. First, Primakov and the powerful mayor of Moscow, **Yuri Luzhkov**, announced the formation of a new political party supported by many of Russia's most powerful regional governors, the Fatherland–All Russia Bloc, which would compete against parties supported by the Kremlin in the December 1999 Duma elections. Then, Chechen extremists led by Shamil Basaev and the Islamic fundamentalist Khattab invaded the neighboring ethnic republic of Dagestan, proclaiming their goal to be the creation of an Islamic state in southern Russia. Yeltsin fired Stepashin, who appeared to have been taken by surprise by these events, and replaced him with the dour, 46-year-old former KGB spy Vladimir Putin, who headed the KGB's successor organization, the Federal Security Service (FSB). Yeltsin also announced that he considered Putin to be his heir and that he hoped that Russians would rally around him as the 2000 presidential elections neared. Remarkably, despite Putin's almost total political obscurity at the time of his appointment, this is exactly what happened.

The key event propelling Putin into the top position in Russian politics was the outbreak of the second war in Chechnya in the fall of 1999. Although rumors of a renewed Russian assault on the breakaway republic had been swirling for some time, the final decision to launch a full-scale invasion was reinforced by shocking events in September: terrorist bombings of apartment buildings in the suburbs of Moscow and in the southern Russian city of Volgodonsk that killed nearly 300 Russian citizens. Putin's government immediately blamed these bombings on the Chechen rebels led by Basaev and Khattab, whipping up an understandable public outcry for revenge – although doubts about who was really responsible for the terrorist attacks remain.

The Russian military counterattack on the Chechen rebels soon escalated into an all-out invasion of the Chechen republic. Putin now declared his intention to wipe out the Chechen "bandits" once and for all. The resulting conflict, like the first Chechen war, led to the deaths of thousands of innocent Russian and Chechen civilians and the near-total destruction of much of the region, including the capital city of Grozny, which was finally taken by Russian troops in February 2000. Once again, the Chechen resistance fighters fled to the mountainous southern part of Chechnya, from which they continued to launch bloody attacks on Russian forces.

The emotionally charged political environment generated by the new Chechen war could not help but affect the outcome of the 1999 Duma elections. A new pro-Putin party known as Unity, made up of various regional leaders and state bureaucrats, was hastily thrown together in October; it ended up gaining 23 percent of the party-list vote. Zyuganov's nationalist KPRF did very well, attaining 24 percent of the party-list vote and 46 seats in single-member districts. The Union of Rightist Forces, including famous "young reformers" such as Gaidar, Kiriyenko, and Chubais, also received an endorsement on television from Putin; as a result, they, too, did surprisingly well, attaining 8.5 percent of the party vote. Meanwhile, pro-Kremlin television mounted a sustained mudslinging campaign against Primakov and Luzhkov; as a result, the Fatherland–All Russia Party performed well below early expectations, with just over 13 percent of the vote. Finally, Yavlinsky's Yabloko Party – the one political force publicly critical of the war in Chechnya – barely squeaked past the 5 percent barrier, as did Zhirinovsky's LDPR.

This popular endorsement of Putin and his policies reassured Yeltsin that he could now leave the political stage with no fear that he or his circle of intimates would later be investigated or prosecuted, as had been continually threatened by the communists and their allies. On New Year's Eve, 1999, Yeltsin stunned the world with the sudden announcement of his early resignation as Russia's president. As specified in the Russian constitution, Prime Minister Putin now became acting president as well, and early elections for the presidency were scheduled for March 26. Given Putin's war-driven popularity and the limited time available for his opponents to campaign against him, his victory was certain.

THE PUTIN ERA

When Vladimir Putin was formally elected as Russia's president in March 2000, he inherited a corrupt government, an imbalanced economy, and a demoralized society. A new defeat in Chechnya, he claimed, might under such circumstances lead to the final disintegration of the country. Thus, the central priority for President Putin was the rebuilding of the Russian state. Pursuit of this goal would involve a reformulation of Russia's political identity and major reforms of its institutions – changes that, inevitably, had important effects on the organization of Russian social interests.

Putin's conception of Russian national identity can be summed up in one of his most frequently used slogans: *gosudarstvennost'*, or loyalty to the state. In Putin's view, a general lack of state-oriented patriotism, and a desire to pursue only short-run selfish interests, played a key role in undermining the global power of the Soviet Union and in weakening the coherence of Russia's post-Soviet institutions. His conception of *gosudarstvennost'*, designed to combat the decline of patriotism, contained three main elements. First, Putin claimed that victory in Chechnya, and the final suppression of "banditry" and "terrorism" emanating from the southern borders of Russia, would lead to the resurrection of Russia as a global great power; he even declared that the stabilization of the Caucasus was his personal mission. Second, Putin called for the restoration of what he termed the "vertical of power" linking Kremlin leaders to state officials throughout Russia's vast territory: Dutiful obedience to one's superiors was supposed to replace the political and social free-for-all of the Yeltsin era. Third, Putin expressed intense suspicion of independent social forces that opposed the Kremlin, arguing that in many cases such forces represented foreign interests trying to weaken Russia from within.

Putin's efforts to rebuild Russians' trust in the state had some positive initial impact. Public-opinion polls during Putin's first term showed that ordinary Russians were more optimistic about the country's future than at any time in the 1990s. At times, however, Putin's efforts to restore loyalty to the state, and to stifle political criticism, recalled the secrecy and political conformity of the Soviet era. In August 2000, for example, the Kursk nuclear submarine sank after a failed test of a new torpedo, killing all 118 men on board; Putin, who was on vacation at the time, remained silent about the crisis for days, while the head of the Russian navy blamed the accident on a collision with an American sub. By December 2000, Putin – over the strenuous objections of liberal lawmakers – had moved to restore the Soviet-era national anthem (with new, noncommunist lyrics) and, for the Russian military, the red flag of the USSR (without the Marxist-Leninist hammer and sickle). A shadowy new youth organization called Moving Together began to organize mass pro-Putin rallies, and to criticize "unpatriotic" authors, in many Russian cities. Still, Putin's calls for state patriotism did not constitute the resurrection of any full-blown political ideology like the Marxism-Leninism of the past; indeed, Putin's political worldview remained in many respects both vague and flexible.

Along with Putin's efforts to resurrect Russian patriotism came a series of reforms designed to rebuild Russian state and economic institutions. To prevent further disintegration of central authority over the regions and republics of the Russian Federation, Putin initiated a series of federal reforms in May 2000: The 89 subjects of the federation were now regrouped into seven new federal districts, headed by appointed "supergovernors" answering directly to the president; regional governors and parliamentary heads were removed from their seats on the Federation Council and replaced with unelected representatives generally more supportive of the Kremlin; and new legislation allowed the Russian president to dismiss regional governors if they acted "unconstitutionally." To streamline economic policy, Putin during his first presidential term reduced the income tax to a flat rate of 13 percent and the corporate tax to 24 percent, introduced a new land code allowing – for the first time in Russia's history – the legal buying and selling of both urban and agricultural land, and introduced a new labor code weakening the power of Russia's trade unions and making it easier to hire and fire workers. The judicial system, too, was reformed: trial by jury was introduced on a limited basis; judges' salaries were raised in order to lessen the temptations of corruption; and, reversing both tsarist and Soviet-era practices, defendants were now officially to be considered innocent until proven guilty beyond a reasonable doubt.

Such policies convinced many analysts and business investors that Putin was at heart a Westernizer, continuing in the same basic spirit as the architects of shock therapy but with more decisiveness and competence than his predecessor Yeltsin. However, the antiliberal and authoritarian elements of Putin's *gosudarstvennost'* were also evident early in his presidency. In particular, Putin launched an attack on the oligarchs that seemed to focus solely on those billionaires who had the temerity to oppose the Kremlin; other pro-Putin oligarchs were allowed to keep and even expand their business empires. In June 2000, Vladimir Gusinsky, owner of the main independent television station, NTV, along with several liberal newspapers and magazines, was jailed on embezzlement charges. He was released only after pledging to give up control of NTV to Gazprom and soon fled the country. Then Putin's government opened up an investigation concerning powerful oligarch Boris Berezovsky, who had been the primary financial backer of both Yeltsin and later Putin himself during the late 1990s. Berezovsky, seeing the writing on the wall, gave up his seat in the Duma and also fled to Great Britain. Such attacks on oligarchs were generally quite popular among ordinary Russians, most of whom thought of these "robber barons" as thieves profiting from the poverty of the masses; simultaneously, Putin's policies sent a threatening signal to other businessmen, journalists, and opposition figures. At the same time, FSB agents also began to hassle, detain, and in some cases imprison independent journalists, scholars, and leaders of nongovernmental organizations (NGOs).

For Putin to rebuild the Russian state, however, not just identity and institutions would be important – he would have to appeal to important interest groups in Russian society as well. In this respect, he clearly benefited from his extraordinarily good economic timing. The post-Soviet depression of the 1990s came to an end in 1999, just as Putin entered the political arena, and Russia's GDP grew strongly every year of his presidency, in large part because of profits from oil and gas exports. Putin used this windfall to balance the budget, repay Western debt, and – most importantly for ordinary people – to eliminate most of the wage arrears that had accumulated under Yeltsin. Still, in order to attack the interests of oligarchs, regional governors, and opposition politicians simultaneously, Putin had to promote the interests of a more specific social group willing to back him in tough battles. Here he largely turned to friends and associates within the secret police and, to a lesser extent, the military. Five of the seven new supergovernors, for example, were FSB or military generals. In March 2001, Putin's FSB colleague and close friend Sergei Ivanov was appointed defense minister. By the end of Putin's first term, according to analysts Olga Kryshtanovskaya and Stephen White, at least one-quarter of the Russian government elite had military or security backgrounds, and their number continued to rise steeply after that.

A final factor that was crucial in shaping the contours of Putin's Russia is the new global context generated by the terrorist attacks on the World Trade Center and Pentagon in the United States on September 11, 2001, and the subsequent global war on terrorism launched by U.S. President George W. Bush. Surprisingly for many, 9/11 and its aftermath led initially to much closer relations between the United States and Russia; indeed, Putin was the first foreign leader to telephone the White House to express his condolences after the attacks, and he pledged his full support for the war on terror. In many respects, in fact, the U.S. response to 9/11 only reinforced Putin's general political line: He, after all, had argued all along for a more decisive and forceful response to "Islamic terrorism." Putin's position was reinforced further as Chechen rebels continued to launch major terrorist attacks throughout his first term in office – most spectacularly, the seizure of over 900 hostages at a downtown Moscow musical theater in October 2002, an event that ended in tragedy when well over a hundred hostages died from the effects of a poison gas used by the Russians to incapacitate the hostage-takers. Given the new global environment, Western official criticism of continuing Russian brutality in Chechnya became significantly more muted. In the end, the U.S.-Russian "strategic partnership" declared after 9/11 failed to live up to initial high expectations, as the two countries began to quarrel over trade issues, U.S. plans to build a missile defense system, the expansion of NATO (the North Atlantic Treaty Organization) to include the Baltic states, and, especially, the U.S. decision to invade Iraq in March 2003. But general Western support for Putin's political approach continued through the end of his first term, helping him maintain the backing of many liberals and Westernizers within the Russian elite.

By the end of 2003, Putin had become so dominant over his political opponents that there was little if any doubt he would win a second term. Indeed, a kind of miniature cult had emerged around the president. In one popular song, a female singer complained that she wished she could find "a man like Putin," who would not lie, drink, or break his promises. A government-sponsored Web site for children, www.uznai-prezidenta.ru, displayed photos of a smiling president Putin and his black dog. In a manner reminiscent of Soviet times, television news began to feature Putin's daily activities, no matter how trivial, as the lead story every evening. And even independent public-opinion polls continued to show Putin's popularity rating in the 70–80 percent range.

Given this political milieu – and the Kremlin's active efforts to ensure political loyalty – it is perhaps not surprising that the elections of 2003–2004 were far less competitive than those of the Yeltsin era. The campaign for the State Duma got off to a troubling start when, in October 2003, oligarch Mikhail Khodorkovsky – then Russia's richest man, and the key funder of the liberal Yabloko Party and the Union of Rightist Forces, as well as a backer of Zyuganov's Communists – was arrested by masked FSB police at an airport in Siberia and charged with embezzlement and tax evasion. Khodorkovsky's imprisonment not only deprived these opposition parties of crucial monetary resources but also made both the liberals and the Communists look like the pawns of an unpopular robber baron. State-run television also did its best to promote the pro-Kremlin United Russia Party; opposition politicians found it extremely difficult to compete for news coverage. In the end, the party of power received 37.6 percent of the party-list vote; counting single-member district seats and defections from other parties and factions, United Russia controlled over 300 seats – that is, a two-thirds majority in the new Duma. Zhirinovsky's LDPR, capitalizing on rising nationalist sentiment, rebounded to 11.5 percent, whereas KPRF support was cut in half compared with 1999, to just 12.6 percent. The new pro-Kremlin nationalist Motherland Party, cobbled together just a few months before the election to draw votes away from the Communists, did surprisingly well, attaining 9 percent of the vote. Meanwhile, both liberal parties failed to break the 5 percent barrier for Duma representation and won only a handful of seats, leaving their political future very much in doubt.

With Putin enjoying near-total dominance over the Parliament, and with no credible political opposition, his reelection in March 2004 was a foregone conclusion. Indeed, even a few weeks before the election itself, Putin moved to replace his prime minster, Mikhail Kasyanov – a holdover from the late Yeltsin era who had been openly critical of the Khodorkovsky arrest – with the more pliable bureaucrat Mikhail Fradkov, saying that he wanted voters to know what sort of government he planned for his second term. Both Zhirinovsky and Zyuganov refused to run against Putin at all and named obscure subordinates to campaign on their parties' behalf. Another presidential candidate even told voters that he himself favored Putin's reelection! In the end, Putin received 71.9 percent of the vote, compared with just 13.8 percent for his closest challenger, Nikolai Mikhailovich Kharitonov of the Communist Party of the Russian Federation.

Despite Putin's increasing personal power, his second term in office got off to a very difficult start. On the first day of the new school year, September 1, 2004, Chechen rebels took hundreds of schoolchildren, parents, and teachers hostage in the southern town of Beslan; more than 340 were killed when terrorist explosives were detonated in advance of a rescue attempt by FSB troops. Putin's response to the Beslan tragedy was once again to strengthen the power vertical: He abolished elections for regional governors, who would henceforth be appointed by the president. Soon afterward, Putin's attempts to help elect the pro-Russian candidate Viktor Yanukovich in Ukraine's November 2004 presidential elections backfired when evidence of serious electoral fraud generated massive popular demonstrations in Kiev. This "Orange Revolution" forced the Ukrainian authorities to hold new elections in December which were won by the pro-Western presidential candidate, Viktor Yushchenko. In January 2005, Putin's efforts to eliminate Soviet-era welfare policies, such as free subway rides for World War II veterans and heavily subsidized prescription drug benefits for the elderly, generated large-scale national protests. Meanwhile, the trial of oligarch Mikhail Khodorkovsky dragged on and on; after a year and a half in prison, he was formally convicted and sentenced to a nine-year term for embezzlement in May 2005. Finally, the situation in Chechnya and the rest of the North Caucasus continued to deteriorate: pro-Putin Chechen President Akhmad Kadyrov was assassinated by Chechen rebels while attending a parade to celebrate the Soviet victory over the Nazis on May 9, and in October, attacks on police stations by Islamist and anti-Putin militants in nearby Kabardino-Balkaria were suppressed at the cost of over 100 lives. All of these developments caused deep concern in the West about the future direction of Russian politics.

Yet by 2006, many of these troubling trends in Russian politics had seemingly been reversed – at least temporarily. Most significantly, surging prices for oil and natural gas on world markets, along with the continuing recovery of Russian light industry and services, now fueled a true economic boom in Russia affecting not only Moscow and St. Petersburg, but also most other cities throughout the country. By the end of the year, Russia had paid off its entire debt to foreign countries ahead of schedule and had declared the ruble a convertible currency like the euro and the U.S. dollar. Russian foreign currency reserves, levels of foreign investment, and the Russian stock market index all hit record levels. And while levels of inequality between Russia's new rich and the population of rural areas and poorer cities remained a source of intense social discontent, the organized protests of pensioners against Putin's welfare policies had died down completely. The year 2006 also saw a major shift in the fortunes of Russia's campaign to subdue resistance in Chechnya and the North Caucasus. The young Ramzan Kadyrov, who took over de facto control over Chechnya from his father after the latter's asssasination, managed to restore a degree of order in the republic (even if this order depended on widespread fear of Kadyrov's increasingly powerful personal militia). Then in July, Shamil Basaev, the mastermind of the most brutal terrorist attacks on Russia since the initial 1994 Russian invasion of Chechnya, was killed in an explosion, leaving the Chechen rebels without effective leadership.

Given Russia's continuing economic success combined with the stabilization of the situation in Chechnya, Putin's sustained popularity ratings during his second term – approaching or exceeding 80 percent in most reputable polls – were hardly surprising. Paradoxically, however, Putin's increasing support at home was now accompanied by increasingly vocal Western criticism of the authoritarian direction of Russian politics. Signs of renewed authoritarianism in Russia were indeed quite clear by 2006. A new law requiring the reregistration of Russian nongovernmental organizations approved by Putin in January 2006 appeared to target primarily those NGOs with ties to the West, those focused on preserving democratic freedoms in the Russian Federation, and those devoted to taboo topics such as promoting Russian-Chechen reconciliation. The state's control over major sectors of the economy, too, was growing rapidly, as the remnants of Khodorkovsky's Yukos, other major energy assets, and even large Russian manufacturing concerns were swallowed up by various Kremlin-controlled conglomerates with strong ties to the FSB. As the parliamentary elections of 2007 and the presidential elections of 2008 approached, a whole series of changes to Russian electoral laws were adopted, seemingly designed to ensure more effective control by the Kremlin over the results – including the abolishing of all single-member district seats in the State Duma, which would henceforth be elected purely by proportional representation; the raising of the threshold for party representation in the Duma from 5 percent to 7 percent of the electorate; the elimination of the previous option to vote "against all" parties on the ballot; and the abolishing of all minimum voter turnout requirements for the election to be considered valid. Such maneuvering raised the inevitable question, both in Russia and in the West, of whether Putin himself would actually step down as Russia's leader as scheduled in March 2008 – as the president had repeatedly promised to do in a variety of public settings – or find some legal or semi-legal way to continue in office after all.

By this point, a disturbing disconnect had emerged between a Russian public that, by and large, approved of Putin's course and had few concerns about the increasing centralization of state power, and Western opinion leaders who wished to punish Putin in some way for his betrayal of democracy. In such an environment, the sense among many Russians that the West was conspiring to bring Russia to its knees – perhaps to counter Russia's economic rebound and renewed international prominence – remained widespread. Western critics of Putin who decried his efforts to rebuild the power vertical seemed to wish a return to the Yeltsin era – one perceived by the vast majority of Russian citizens as a time of chaos, economic disaster, and international humiliation. Precisely when Putin had decided to ignore Western economic advice and recentralize the Russian state, it seemed, Russia's economy began to skyrocket; so why should anyone in Russia listen to Western criticism of Putin now? The gap between Russian and Western perceptions became obvious to everyone in November 2006, when a prominent FSB defector and critic of Putin, Alexander Litvinenko, was poisoned at a fancy London hotel after he somehow ingested highly radioactive material at a meeting with two Russian businessmen. While much of the Western media directly blamed the Kremlin for Litvinenko's murder, the Putin administration along with many ordinary Russians claimed the entire affair to be a conspiracy organized by anti-Putin forces to blacken Russia's image.

The widespread feeling among Russians that their country stood entirely alone against the world greatly aided Putin's efforts to manage the problem of leadership succession at the end of his formal second term as Russian president. As the December 2007 parliamentary elections approached, the Kremlin further stepped up its efforts to harass or intimidate independent political groupings of all sorts, portraying them as agents of hostile foreign powers. Both of Russia's liberal parties, the Union of Rightist Forces and Yabloko, now found it nearly impossible to gain access to state-controlled television or even to obtain permits to hold political meetings. An opposition group known as The Other Russia, led by former chess champion Garry Kasparov and novelist and radical activist Eduard Limonov, mobilized anti-Kremlin rallies in several Russian cities, but these were quickly dispersed by police. In the meantime, the pro-Kremlin United Russia party was showered with positive media coverage, and huge advertisements appeared all over the country promoting the party of power as the vehicle for realizing "Putin's Plan." The result of this highly uncompetitive campaign was another triumph for United Russia, which received 64 percent of the vote and more than two-thirds of the seats in the Duma. Zyuganov's Communists received 12 percent, while Zhirinovsky's LDPR attained 8 percent, as did another new pro-Kremlin party, Fair Russia. Once again, liberal parties were shut out of the parliament entirely. Armed with this convincing show of popular support, Putin now formally announced his choice of successor – Dmitry Medvedev, a 42-year-old lawyer who had worked with Putin since the 1990s, ultimately rising to the positions of Gazprom chairman and deputy prime minister. Medvedev then announced that if elected president, he in turn would nominate Putin as his own prime minister – a post that Putin soon afterwards promised to accept. On March 2, 2008, Medvedev predictably trounced his three nominal opponents for the Russian Presidency – Zyuganov, Zhirinovsky, and the little-known Andrei Bogdanov – receiving more than 70 percent of the popular vote.

Institutions, Interests, and the Search for a New Russian Identity

By the end of the 1990s, it was clear to everyone that the dream of a rapid transformation of postcommunist Russia into a liberal-capitalist country like the United States was just that – a dream. From the perspective adopted in this textbook, which emphasizes the long-term impact of institutions created at critical junctures in a country's history and the specific social interests that these institutions generate, the initial failure of market economics in Russia should not have been surprising. After all, the political and economic institutions of the Soviet Union were designed by men committed to destroying global capitalism. The all-powerful Communist Party was supposed to train new "professional revolutionaries" to conquer the world bourgeoisie, but it degenerated into a giant, corrupt bureaucracy entangled with a vast network of secret police. Those who had benefited from their positions in the party hierarchy were thus rarely interested in establishing new institutions that would strictly enforce norms of democratic citizenship and the rule of law. Soviet industrial cities were supposed to be heroic sites for revolutionary production but decayed into polluting, outmoded factory towns. They were thus ill-suited for the task of producing consumer goods according to Western standards of efficiency.

Despite the burdensome legacy of its communist past, the collapse of the Soviet Union in 1991 – like the collapse of tsarism at the beginning of the century – marked another critical juncture in Russia's history during which new institutions promoting new interests could be established (see Table 7.1 at the end of the chapter). Indeed, despite all of the country's well-publicized problems, Russia did manage during the 1990s to establish the first democratic regime in its long history. Even if Russia's democracy remained rife with state corruption, undermined by abysmal economic performance, and threatened by vocal antiliberal movements, this accomplishment should not be dismissed.

The Putin era has seen a return to sustained economic growth, a resurgence of Russia's influence in the international arena, and a partial restoration of the coherence of the state. At the same time, however, Putin has presided over a serious erosion of many of Russia's early democratic achievements, and even the fate of the 1993 Russian constitution itself now seems uncertain. Moreover, in the wake of 9/11, Russia finds itself in a new global context that remains highly threatening, with continued turbulence and uncertainty on nearly all of its borders. Where is Russia headed now?

Russia's future depends not only upon the nature of its institutions and interests. It depends also upon the outcome of Russia's search for a new state identity, now that both Marxism-Leninism and "revolutionary" capitalism have failed. Indeed, with the military still largely unreformed, growing international tensions between Russia and its neighbors over trade and energy issues, the potential for renewed terrorist attacks by insurgents in the North Caucasus, and widespread popular distrust of all political parties and movements, the Russian Federation remains an unconsolidated state prone to sudden political shocks – a terrifying prospect given Russia's substantial stockpiles of chemical, biological, and nuclear weapons. Russia's collapse, however,

TABLE 7.1. Key Phases in Russia's Political Development

Date	Regime	Global context	Interests/identities/ institutions	Developmental path
1690–1917	tsarist empire	Russia as great power on periphery of capitalist West	landowning aristocracy/"divine right" monarchy/feudal state	autocratic modernization
1917–1928	Soviet Russia/USSR	World War I, collapse of tsarist empire, civil war, postwar isolation	revolutionary intellectuals and workers/Marxist ideology/Leninist one-party rule	party control over key industries, toleration of market production
1929–1945	USSR	Great Depression, rise of Nazism in Germany, World War II	Stalinist secret police and "heroic" workers/Marxism-Leninism/planned economy	rapid industrialization, brutal collectivization, prison labor, military buildup
1945–1984	USSR	Cold War with United States, anti-Soviet rebellions in Poland and Afghanistan	corrupt party and state elites/"superpower" socialism/stagnating planned economy	enforcement of status quo, military expansion in developing world
1985–1991	USSR	military buildup in West, disintegration of Soviet bloc and USSR	reformist intellectuals/ "socialist renewal"/ institutional disintegration	"perestroika" (unintended self-destruction of Leninism)
1991–1999	Russian Federation	Russia as fading power on periphery of triumphant capitalist global system	former party and state elites and local "mafias"/search for new Russian identity/weak democracy	"shock therapy," corrupt capitalism
1999–present	Russian Federation	Russia tries to rebuild its great power status in context of global war on terrorism	Putin loyalists and security services/pragmatic patriotism/ increasing authoritarianism	increasing state intervention in economy combined with dependence on energy exports

appears highly unlikely, given Putin's success in reversing the institutional chaos of the Yeltsin years and the strong sense among almost all citizens of the Russian Federation that "Russia," in some form, must be preserved.

But which Russia? The liberal capitalist Russia originally envisioned by Gaidar and his allies has been largely discredited by the Yeltsin-era economic crisis. Zyuganov's nostalgic communist version has little appeal for younger, educated Russians, and the KPRF is a fading political force. Zhirinovsky's neoimperialism, despite the LDPR's continuing presence in the Russian Duma, seems unlikely to become a serious mass movement. More explicitly pro-Nazi and anti-Semitic politicians are trying to convert disgruntled youths and soldiers to their cause – but ever since Hitler's invasion in World War II, "fascism" has been deeply unpopular in Russia. Nor do any of Russia's other leading political figures – including Putin and Medvedev – have a clearly developed new definition of "Russia." As long as Putin, Medvedev, and their team remain popular and the Russian economy continues to grow, the Kremlin's efforts to rebuild the Russian state might appear relatively successful. But there continue to be serious factional rivalries among the Russian elite, and new domestic or international challenges could quickly erode popular support for the regime. The one thing that can be predicted with confidence, then, is that we have not seen the final chapter in Russia's painful transition from Soviet rule.

BIBLIOGRAPHY

Baker, Peter, and Susan Glasser. *Kremlin Rising: Vladimir Putin's Russia and the End of Revolution*. New York: Scribner, 2005.

Breslauer, George. *Khrushchev and Brezhnev as Leaders: Building Authority in Soviet Politics*. London and Boston: Allen and Unwin, 1982.

Brown, Archie. *The Gorbachev Factor*. Oxford and New York: Oxford University Press, 1997.

Conquest, Robert. *The Great Terror: A Reassessment*. New York: Oxford University Press, 1991.

Conquest, Robert. *The Harvest of Sorrow: Soviet Collectivization and the Terror Famine*. New York: Oxford University Press, 1987.

Dunlop, John B. *The Rise of Russia and the Fall of the Soviet Empire*. Princeton, NJ: Princeton University Press, 1993.

Fish, M. Steven. *Democracy from Scratch: Opposition and Regime in the New Russian Revolution*. Princeton, NJ: Princeton University Press, 1995.

Fitzpatrick, Sheila. *The Russian Revolution*. Second edition. Oxford and New York: Oxford University Press, 1994.

Hanson, Stephen E. *Time and Revolution: Marxism and the Design of Soviet Institutions*. Chapel Hill: University of North Carolina Press, 1997.

Hoffmann, David. *The Oligarchs: Wealth and Power in the New Russia*. New York: Public Affairs, 2002.

Jowitt, Ken. *New World Disorder: The Leninist Extinction*. Berkeley: University of California Press, 1992.

Kotkin, Stephen. *Armageddon Averted: The Soviet Collapse, 1970–2000*. Oxford: Oxford University Press, 2001.

Kryshtanovskaya, Olga, and Stephen White. "Putin's Militocracy." *Post-Soviet Affairs* 19, no. 4 (October 2003): 289–306.

McAuley, Mary. *Russia's Politics of Uncertainty*. Cambridge: Cambridge University Press, 1997.

McFaul, Michael. *Russia's Unfinished Revolution: Political Change from Gorbachev to Putin*. Ithaca, NY: Cornell University Press, 2001.

Putin, Vladimir V., with Nataliya Gevorkyan, Natalya Timakova, and Andrei Kolesnikov. *First Person: An Astonishingly Frank Self-Portrait by Russia's President*. New York: Public Affairs, 2000.

Remnick, David. *Resurrection: The Struggle for a New Russia*. New York: Random House, 1998.

Shevtsova, Lilia. *Putin's Russia*. Washington, DC: Carnegie Endowment, 2003.

Solnick, Steven. *Stealing the State: Control and Collapse in Soviet Institutions*. Cambridge, MA: Harvard University Press, 1998.

Stoner-Weiss, Katherine. *Local Heroes: The Political Economy of Russian Regional Governance*. Princeton, NJ: Princeton University Press, 1997.

Yeltsin, Boris N. *The Struggle for Russia*. New York: Random House, 1994.

Yeltsin, Boris N. *Midnight Diaries*. New York: Public Affairs, 2000.

Zaslavsky, Viktor. *The Neo-Stalinist State: Class, Ethnicity, and Consensus in Soviet Society*. Armonk, NY: M. E. Sharpe, 1994.

IMPORTANT TERMS

Leonid Brezhnev leader of the Communist Party of the Soviet Union from 1964 until his death in 1982. He presided over an orthodox Marxist-Leninist regime that became more and more politically corrupt and economically stagnant over time.

Chechnya an ethnic republic that declared its independence from the Russian Federation in September 1991. In December 1994, Yeltsin launched a disastrous full-scale military attack on Chechnya in which tens of thousands of Chechens and Russians were killed. This first war was settled in the summer of 1996, but the political status of the republic remained unresolved. A second Chechen war broke out in the fall of 1999.

Viktor Chernomyrdin prime minister of the Russian Federation from December 1992 until March 1998. Chernomyrdin, the former head of the Soviet natural gas ministry, was originally promoted as a compromise candidate after the refusal of the conservative Russian Congress of People's Deputies to reconfirm Yegor Gaidar as prime minister. Later, he became the leader of the pro-regime Our Home Is Russia Party and, under Putin, Russia's ambassador to Ukraine.

collectivization Stalin's policy of creating "collective farms" (*kolkhozy*) and "state farms" (*sovkhozy*) throughout the Soviet countryside, supposedly in order to build socialist agriculture. This policy led to the deaths of millions of peasants through political violence and famine, and it created an enormously inefficient agricultural system.

Commonwealth of Independent States (CIS) the loose association of former Soviet republics formed in December 1991 to replace the USSR. It was officially created at the Belovezh Forest meeting of Boris Yeltsin, president of the Russian Federation, and the presidents of Ukraine, Belorussia (Belarus), and Kazakhstan. The CIS has been largely ineffective since the collapse of the Soviet Union.

democratic centralism the central institutional principle of Leninist political organization. According to this principle, "democratic" debates among party members are allowed only until the party leadership makes a final decision, at which point all members are obliged to implement the orders of their superiors without question.

Federation Council the upper house of the Federal Assembly. The Federation Council has since 2001 been made up of representatives appointed by the governors and regional legislatures of all of Russia's federal regions and republics.

five-year plan the basic organizing framework of Stalinist economic institutions. Beginning with the First Five-Year Plan of 1928–1932, all industrial and agricultural production in the USSR was regulated by monthly and yearly output targets given to each manager and worker. Bonuses went to those managers and workers who overfulfilled their plan targets to demonstrate their revolutionary zeal.

Mikhail Gorbachev leader of the Communist Party of the Soviet Union from 1985 to 1991. Gorbachev tried to reverse the stagnation of the Brezhnev era by launching a policy of "revolutionary restructuring" (perestroika) that called for open criticism of the past, greater democracy, and "new thinking" in foreign policy. The result was the wholesale disintegration of Leninist political institutions and Stalinist economic organizations, leading to the collapse of the USSR.

gulag the Russian abbreviation for "chief directorate of labor camps." The gulags were a vast network of labor camps, set up by Lenin and greatly expanded by Stalin, that were used to imprison millions of people who were suspected of opposing the Communist Party and its policies.

Nikita Khrushchev leader of the Communist Party of the Soviet Union from shortly after Stalin's death in 1953 until 1964. Khrushchev endeavored to reinvigorate Soviet socialism by means of a series of "revolutionary" economic campaigns in agriculture and industry and also attacked Stalin's terror. This "leftist" strategy, however, only produced general administrative chaos, and Khrushchev was ousted in a Politburo coup.

Alexander Lebed popular general who came in third in the 1996 presidential elections, after which he became the head of the Security Council. After having settled the first war in Chechnya, Lebed was fired by Yeltsin. In 1997, he was elected governor of the vast Krasnoyarsk region in Siberia. In 2002, he was killed in a helicopter crash.

Vladimir Lenin Russian revolutionary and the author of *What Is to Be Done?* Lenin insisted on strict "professional revolutionary" discipline among Marxists. In 1917, Lenin led the October Revolution and founded the Soviet regime in Russia.

Yuri Luzhkov mayor of Moscow and leader of the Fatherland Party which merged with Putin's Unity Party to form the pro-Kremlin party, United Russia. Luzhkov built a mini-empire through his control over business activities in Russia's capital city and became one of the country's most influential politicians.

Karl Marx nineteenth-century German intellectual, the coauthor (with Friedrich Engels) of the *Communist Manifesto* and the author of *Capital*. Marx provided the main theoretical inspiration for the later movement to create a socialist society in Europe.

New Economic Policy often abbreviated NEP, the economic program adopted by Lenin in 1921 in the wake of the social devastation caused by the Russian civil war, which he saw as a "strategic retreat" from the ultimate goal of building socialism. The NEP allowed for the reestablishment of markets for agricultural products and legalized small-scale trade in the cities, but the Soviet state retained control over the major industries, and one-party rule was strengthened.

oligarchs the group of a dozen or so bankers and industrialists who took advantage of the rapid privatization of Soviet property to amass huge personal fortunes. During the 1990s, this group controlled most of Russia's most powerful media, banks, and raw-material companies. President Putin launched a crackdown on those oligarchs who openly opposed his regime.

Yevgeny Primakov former academic adviser to Gorbachev and later head of the Foreign Intelligence Service and foreign minister. Primakov was appointed prime minister in a compromise between Yeltsin and the communist-led Duma after the financial crisis of August 1998; he was then fired as the communists tried to impeach Yeltsin in the spring of 1999.

provisional government the temporary government of former parliamentarians that ruled Russia after the fall of the tsarist empire in February 1917. This ineffective body failed to stabilize the revolutionary situation in the country and was overthrown by Lenin's Bolshevik Party in October.

Vladimir Putin first appointed prime minister by Yeltsin in August 1999, he was then elected as Russia's president in 2000 and 2004. Putin attained high popularity among Russians for his prosecution of the war in Chechnya, his restoration of economic and social stability, and his efforts to restore the power of the Russian state.

Alexander Rutskoi general during the Soviet war in Afghanistan, and Yeltsin's vice-president from 1991 to 1993. He originally supported Yeltsin's Russian nationalism against Gorbachev's conception of "socialist reform" but later broke with Yeltsin when the president agreed to break up the USSR and tried to implement capitalism in the Russian Federation. Rutskoi was a leader of the opposition in the Russian Congress in 1993.

shock therapy policy of rapid transition to capitalism officially adopted by Boris Yeltsin in January 1992. In theory, shock therapy was supposed to involve the simultaneous liberalization of all prices, privatization of state property, and stabilization of the Russian currency. In reality, the program was implemented only haphazardly, generating disastrous economic and social results.

socialism in one country Stalin's slogan advocating the defense of Marxism-Leninism within the USSR alone, despite the absence of a global worker revolution in response to the Bolshevik Revolution of 1917. This phrase was used to denounce opponents like Trotsky and Zinoviev, and to justify Stalin's policies of rapid industrialization and collectivization of agriculture.

soviets a word that means "councils" in Russian. It refers to the spontaneous groups of workers and soldiers that formed in the chaotic social situation under the provisional government. Lenin saw these bodies as the seeds of the future communist society, and for this reason he declared the country a "soviet regime" after his party seized power. Until Gorbachev came to power, however, the soviets remained politically powerless and wholly subordinate to the party.

Joseph Stalin the unrivaled leader of the Communist Party of the Soviet Union from 1928 to 1953. Stalin rose to power in a bitter and prolonged struggle with Trotsky, Bukharin, and Zinoviev after Lenin's death. He then implemented a policy of rapid industrialization and mass terror designed to build "socialism" in peasant Russia as quickly as possible – at the cost of tens of millions of lives.

State Duma the lower house of the Federal Assembly, the Russian parliament created in the constitution of 1993. The Duma has 450 members. Until 2007, half of them were selected by proportional representation on party lists and half of them were elected in single-member districts. From 2007 forward, the entire Duma will be elected by PR.

Grigory Yavlinsky leader of the Yabloko (Apple) movement, so named after the initials of its three founders. He argued that capitalism in Russia must be implemented by means of democratic and uncorrupted state institutions rather than via shock therapy.

Boris Yeltsin the first democratically elected president of Russia. He organized the movement to declare the Russian Federation an independent country and thus to destroy the USSR. In 1993, he violently disbanded the Russian Congress of People's Deputies and introduced the new Russian constitution. After winning reelection in 1996, Yeltsin experienced increasing health problems, and his power gradually diminished. He resigned on December 31, 1999.

Vladimir Zhirinovsky leader of the so-called Liberal Democratic Party of Russia (LDPR). Zhirinovsky and his party argue for an ultranationalist solution to Russia's postcommunist problems, envisioning an eventual expansion of Russia to the Indian Ocean. In practice, however, Zhirinovsky has often voted in support of the government in return for political and financial support.

Gennady Zyuganov leader of the Communist Party of the Russian Federation (CPRF). Zyuganov and his party argued for the restoration of "Soviet power," including the reconstitution of the USSR. The ideology of the party, however, is much more oriented toward great-power nationalism than toward original Marxism or Leninism.

STUDY QUESTIONS

1. Should Russia today be classified as a developed industrial society comparable to Britain, France, or Germany? Why or why not?

2. Was Lenin's conception of a revolutionary one-party regime consistent with Marx's vision of communism, or was it a betrayal of Marx's dream of worker liberation?

3. What were the main reasons for the rise of Stalin and his policies of mass terror? Would you blame primarily the ideals of communism, the institutions of Leninism, the interests of Stalin and his supporters, or the global context in which the Soviet Union was situated?

4. Does the failure of Gorbachev's perestroika demonstrate that the Soviet system in the 1980s was unreformable? Or could some alternative strategy for reforming communism have succeeded in revitalizing the institutions of the USSR? What is the relevance, if any, of Deng Xiaoping's reforms in China to the Soviet case?

5. Should social scientists have been able to predict the disintegration of the Soviet bloc? What explains the remarkably poor track record of Western scholars in making predictions about the future of the Soviet Union and Russia?

6. Compare and contrast the problem of ethnic conflict in the Soviet Union and in the Russian Federation. Do you think that the Russian Federation will eventually break up into smaller countries as the Soviet Union did? Or could Russia instead expand to include some of the former Soviet republics?

7. Was Russia's post-Soviet economic crisis caused by the failure of Yeltsin's shock-therapy program or was it simply due to the legacy of Stalinist socio-economic institutions? Might some alternative strategy for building capitalism in post-Soviet Russia have been more successful?

8. Are capitalism and democracy in conflict in postcommunist Russia, or do they instead reinforce each other?

9. In 1917, the tsarist empire collapsed, and Lenin's radical Bolshevik Party came to power soon after. In 1918, the German empire collapsed, and within 15 years the Nazi Party came to power. Is there any chance that a radically antiliberal party like Lenin's or Hitler's will eventually triumph in post-Soviet Russia as well? Why or why not?

10. Would you expect the next generation of Russian politicians to be more successful at institution-building than was the generation reared under communism? Why or why not?

11. If you were a Russian voter, would you support or oppose Vladimir Putin? Would you support or oppose Dmitry Medvedev he designated as his favored successor?

CHAPTER EIGHT

China

Yu-Shan Wu

Introduction

China has one of the world's most ancient civilizations, dating back more than 3,000 years. It is easy for political scientists studying China to emphasize its uniqueness, as Chinese culture, language, political thought, and history appear quite different from those of any of the major Western countries. Modern Chinese history was obviously punctuated with decisive Western impacts, but the way China responded to those impacts is often considered to be uniquely Chinese. Furthermore, Chinese political leaders themselves frequently stress that they represent movements that carry uniquely Chinese characteristics. China, it seems, can only be understood in its own light.

When put in a global and comparative context, however, China loses many of its unique features. Imperial China, or the **Qing dynasty**, was an agricultural empire when it met the first serious wave of challenges from the West during the middle of the nineteenth century. The emperor and the mandarins (high-ranking Chinese officials) were forced to give up their treasured institutions grudgingly after a series of humiliating defeats at the hands of the Westerners. This pattern resembled what occurred in many traditional political systems when confronted with aggression from the West. From that time on, the momentum for political development in China was driven by global competition and the need for national survival. China differed from other cases in the developing world mainly in the immense dimensions of the country, not in the nature of its response.

As in other developing countries, different political forces in China competed for power as the country faced international challenges. Those different political forces represented distinct interests, developed alternative identities, and proposed competing institutions. The outcome of their competition shaped the developmental path of China, and that outcome was, in turn, contingent on the international environment in which China found itself.

As previous chapters have noted, late developers tended to put more emphasis on the state's role in development. Thus, from Britain to France, Germany, and ultimately Russia, one finds an increasingly coercive state accumulating scarce capital to fuel economic growth. British liberalism was translated into strategic investment in France, state sponsorship in Germany, and total state control under the name of communism in Russia. Following this logic, one could safely predict that China would follow a development strategy that puts a much stronger emphasis on a developmental state than would a typical Western liberal model.

"Developmental state" in the German (and Japanese) or in the Russian sense? This is the major difference between the **Kuomintang** (**KMT** or nationalist) regime that ruled China from 1928 to 1949 and the Communist regime that established the **People's Republic of China** (**PRC**) in 1949 and has ruled the country since then. The global European and Japanese challenge forced the Chinese to adopt new institutions with greater governing capacity and, at the same time, offered models for the Chinese to emulate. The KMT opted for the German model, whereas the **Chinese Communist Party** (**CCP**) chose the Soviet model. The KMT and the CCP represented two different interests, upheld nationalism and communism as their respective identities, and established authoritarian and totalitarian regimes, respectively. Though both are undemocratic in nature, a totalitarian regime controls and mobilizes the society to a much greater extent than an authoritarian regime. In short, the international challenge to China brought about two distinctively different developmental models, as represented by the KMT and the CCP, and the interests, identities, and institutions of these two dominant political forces.

During the post-1949 period, mainland China experienced first **Mao Zedong**'s totalitarianism, followed by rapid economic and political reform under **Deng Xiaoping**, and then a consolidation staged by **Jiang Zemin** and **Hu Jintao**. On the island of Taiwan, to which the KMT and its followers had fled after 1949, the KMT experienced a less turbulent and more linear development toward Western liberal capitalism and an increasing attenuation of its authoritarian model, leading ultimately to the adoption of democratic institutions. Viewed from a historical perspective, irresistible forces have compelled both the CCP and the KMT to adapt to the world market and play by the rules. Global competition first compelled the Chinese to establish a strong state for the initial push of industrialization on both sides of the Taiwan Straits and then pressured them to tinker with the market when the state proved ineffective at sustaining growth. Markets and private property then nurtured social demands for political tolerance and a cultural shift away from collectivism to individualism, thus undermining authoritarian rule in both mainland China and Taiwan. Taiwan has already conformed to that pressure for democracy, partly because of the strong influence of the

United States, on which Taiwan has been totally dependent, whereas mainland China remains opposed to democratic change, but with increasing difficulty.

In short, global challenges, foreign examples, and reliance on outside sponsors (in the case of Taiwan) shaped the political institutions of China. It is impossible to recognize or understand Chinese political development without first grasping the fundamental forces that influence China from outside its borders. Chinese responses to the world do carry certain characteristics that one does not easily find in other developing countries. However, the impetus and momentum for those responses and the general directions they took are quite understandable in a global and historical context. In the following discussion, we will trace the political development of China during modern times from the Qing dynasty to Deng's reform and subsequent development. Our focus will be on mainland China, but we will also make comparative references to Taiwan, an alternative Chinese society that has taken a different developmental route.

Historical Background

Imperial China was a static system. Dynasties came and went, but the basic outlines of China's patriarchal social structure and absolutist-monarchical political institutions remained unchanged from the Han dynasty (206 B.C. to A.D. 220) until its collapse at the beginning of the twentieth century. Authoritarian control by head of the family in the private realm was mirrored by the absolutist rule of the emperor in the public domain. Confucianism, a way of thought developed by the Chinese philosopher Confucius around 500 B.C. that laid emphasis on social order, was enshrined as the state ideology and emphasized filial piety and loyalty to the emperor as the ultimate virtues. A sophisticated examination system recruited intellectuals into the government based on their mastery of Confucian classics. Technological innovations and successful human organization made it possible for the Chinese dynasties to expand into great empires that often dominated neighboring tribes and nations in East Asia. Up until the Yuan dynasty (1229–1305), when China had Mongol rulers, the Middle Kingdom, as the Chinese referred to their country, was the envy of many Europeans.

China's ancient civilization, however, proved to be a mixed blessing for the Chinese people when the real challenge came in the form of the arrival of Westerners. Equipped with guns and steamers, Westerners began their exploitation of China's vast markets on a mass scale in the mid-nineteenth century, pioneered by British opium dealers. This could not have come at a worse time. China was then in the middle of the Qing (also known as the Manchu) dynasty. Following the pattern of all established dynasties, the Qing emperors during that period were not great rulers but neither were they weak enough to be overthrown easily. Had the Qing emperors at the time been as ambitious and capable as their forefathers (such as Kangxi, Yongzheng, and Qianlong), China would have had a much better chance of rejuvenating itself while confronting the Western powers. Had they been totally weak, then the dynasty might have fallen and a new one come to power, as had happened in Chinese history more than two dozen times. Because the Manchu dynasty was in the middle of its dynastic cycle, ruled not by the vigorous founding emperors but by their mediocre successors, it could not come up with an effective response to the challenge posed by the West but was able to drag on in decline for yet another half-century before it was buried amid lost wars, unequal treaties, depleted national wealth, and a disintegrated social fabric. During this agonizing period of national humiliation and attrition, the deep-rooted sense of superiority of the Chinese elite gradually gave way to a realization that China was actually inferior to the West, not only in military might but also in institutions and even in culture.

The Manchu dynasty was ultimately overthrown in 1912 by a revolutionary movement led by **Sun Yat-sen**, a U.S.-trained doctor from the Guangdong province. The **Republic of China** (**ROC**) was then founded. Sun's ideal was to transform China into a modern, democratic, and affluent country that could repel foreign invasion and offer the Chinese people a decent life. Sun and his colleagues were at the time mainly inspired by the Western model and hoped China could evolve into a liberal democracy. However, political turmoil ensued, as no political-military force was able to prevail in China's postimperial era. Yuan Shikai, a Qing general turned president, attempted to restore imperial rule and make himself emperor. He was forced to curtail his ambition when beleaguered by defecting generals and Sun's comrades, who swore to protect the new republic.

After Yuan's death in 1916, China split into warring territories controlled by warlords of various kinds. Foremost were Zhang Zuolin in Manchuria and northern China, Wu Peifu in the Yangtzu area, and Sun Chuanfang in the southeast provinces. For his part, Sun established the KMT in 1919, expecting to rely on the support of China's urban intellectuals. He then sought Soviet support from his base in the southern province of Guangdong and accepted Moscow's advice to establish the Whampoa Military Academy for the training of an officer corps loyal to his ideas, foremost of which were the **"Three Principles of the People"** – nationalism, democracy, and people's livelihood – a kind of democratic socialism with distinct Chinese characteristics. General **Chiang Kai-shek** was then appointed commander of the academy and charged with producing a highly indoctrinated revolutionary army for the KMT. Although still holding the liberal model as the ultimate goal, Dr. Sun now envisioned a strong state to fulfill his ideal. This change of mind is important in that the KMT had opted for a nonliberal strategy in state-building. However, whether the KMT would choose a German-style statist model or a communist model was unclear at the time because the two tendencies were competing for dominance in the party.

General Chiang succeeded in building a revolutionary army committed to Sun's ideas, but only with heavy infiltration by the communists, who followed an order from Moscow to join Sun's KMT and develop the CCP's influence inside the KMT apparatus and military establishment. Sun died of liver cancer in 1925, leaving a heavily divided KMT. Chiang then launched a northern expedition to expand the KMT's territory and shed communist influence. The initial thrust north was successful, and in early 1926 the KMT army was able to control the provinces south of the Yangtze River. Chiang established his power base in Nanjing and Shanghai, on the east coast of China, while the KMT Left and their communist allies set up a separate center in Wuhan in central China. Chiang then purged the communists in territories under his control, while the left-wing elements of the KMT and the communists were finding their relations strained because they could not agree on how to deal with Chiang. Finally, the communists were forced out of the KMT and began organizing peasant riots against Chiang's government in the countryside hitherto dominated by the landowning gentry class. In the end, Chiang was able to suppress the communist uprisings, subjugate the left-wing KMT factions, and complete his conquest of northern China. He established a nationalist government in Nanjing, the capital of the Republic of China. The country was unified.

The communists became rebels in China's mountainous areas, which they called the "Soviet regions." They tried to find support in China's tenant farmers, who had long been yearning for land through a land-redistribution scheme. Moscow's influence loomed large at the time. A Chinese Soviet Republic was established in Jiangxi province and later became a target for Chiang's "annihilation campaigns." In 1934, the communists' main base in Jiangxi was attacked, and they were chased across the south and southwest provinces of China by the pursuing KMT army. This desperate retreat was what the communists would later call the "**Long March**." Ultimately, the retreating communist forces founded a new base in Yan'an, a remote town in the north of China. There the KMT offensive was finally thwarted, for the nationalist government faced a much more serious challenge from Japan's military incursions at that time. During the Long March, Mao Zedong was able to grasp first military and then political leadership of the CCP by criticizing and ousting those Chinese communists trained in Moscow. In Yan'an, Mao firmly established his personal leadership.

The period from 1928 through 1936 is considered the golden years of the KMT's rule in China. Industry grew, commerce expanded, and foreign trade surged. China might have taken a different route from what it actually did had it not been for an all-out Japanese invasion and the ensuing Sino-Japanese War, which totally devastated the country. As it turned out, the communists were able to appeal to nationalism and generate strong support among Chinese intellectuals, who grew increasingly critical of Chiang's concentration on crushing the communist insurgency. In December 1936, Chiang was kidnapped by the son of a Manchurian warlord and, although he was finally released, the nationalist government was forced to shift its priority from mopping up the communists to preparing for war with Japan.

On July 7, 1937, Japan launched an all-out attack on the Chinese army guarding Peking (Beijing). China and Japan entered into a protracted and devastating eight-year war. The Japanese had built a powerful war machine that dwarfed China's fragmented and poorly equipped army. Chiang's strategy was to "trade space for time," and the KMT troops went into a large-scale retreat. As the war dragged on and the Japanese military was spread thin in China's vast territory, the KMT army was able to hold its defense line, while the CCP found great opportunities to expand in rural China, which the KMT vacated and the Japanese failed to penetrate. As it turned out, the Sino-Japanese War decisively altered the balance of power between the KMT and the CCP so that at the end of the war the communists were in control of north China and, with the help of the Soviets, Manchuria.

The nationalist government was not prepared to fight a civil war with the communists after eight years of fighting with the Japanese. Most people simply wanted peace and were unwilling to support the KMT's war effort. Corruption and inflation cost the nationalists their traditional urban support, whereas communists were successful in mobilizing peasants with their land-reform programs. In the end, the nationalist troops were demolished in several decisive campaigns, and Chiang Kai-shek led millions of KMT loyalists to the island of Taiwan, a territory retroceded to the ROC by the Japanese after World War II. On October 1, 1949, the People's Republic of China (PRC) was formally established in Beijing, while the ROC migrated to Taiwan. There has been no peace treaty between mainland China and Taiwan since then, and the Chinese civil war technically has not ended to this date.

The civil war was significant in shifting China's developmental strategy. During the republican period, the KMT basically pursued a statist development model, which had technocratic capitalism, authoritarian political control, and exultation of nationalism as its major components. Even though one finds traditional elements and emphasis on Confucian teachings in the KMT's ideology, the system established by Chiang was modeled on those of Germany and Japan. It was not totalitarian, as the KMT lacked the capacity to penetrate deeply into the rural grassroots, and had to share power with the gentry class, urban bourgeoisie, and international capital. Religious leaders, intellectuals, and underworld gangs also exercised great influence. The KMT attempted to monopolize the mass media but was unable to do so. Those weaknesses were fully exploited by the communists. With the defeat of the KMT, China moved into a new developmental stage characterized by

Soviet-style institutions and, later on, Maoist frenetic movements, mobilization campaigns of extreme intensity.

The reason that the KMT opted for the German or Japanese model was simple. China was facing a crisis of national survival. It was only natural for the ruling elite to emphasize the importance of concentrating power in the hands of the leadership and guiding national development from the top. However, as the nationalist leaders came primarily from the middle and upper classes of Chinese society, they had no appetite for radical social revolutions as championed by the communists. The nationalists appealed to Chinese nationalism to gain legitimacy and criticized the communist notion of a class struggle. This strategy proved successful in their initial competition with the communists, inasmuch as the latter's radical land-redistribution program antagonized the landowning class while failing to mobilize genuine peasant support. Also, it can be argued that the rise of communist power during the Sino-Japanese War was a direct result of the CCP's shift from blatant class struggle to peasant nationalism. The nationalists' social background further suggests a deep commitment to many traditional values, such as filial piety (abiding respect for parents and ancestors), and the rich cultural legacies of China. For the communists, however, those values were dispensable as long as they stood in the way of rapid modernization.

During the first half of the twentieth century, international competition and national survival forced the Chinese elite to choose an effective modernization model. The liberal, statist, and communist models, as exemplified by Britain, Japan, and the Soviet Union, were particularly appealing to the urban intellectuals, the KMT, and the CCP, respectively. These were the interests on which the identities of liberalism, nationalism, and communism were formed. Three distinctively different institutions would flow naturally from the three interests and identities. The triumph of the urban intellectuals would bring about a Western-style democracy. The victory of the KMT would install a modernizing authoritarian regime. The success of the CCP would establish a totalitarian party-state. As it turned out, the liberal intellectuals lacked the organizational means to realize their ideas. The British model never had a real chance.

China's choice, then, was narrowed down to two models: authoritarian statist or communist. When the CCP won the civil war in 1949, China's fate was sealed. There was going to be a series of stormy movements aimed at thoroughly transforming the society based on the communist model. The CCP's interest was reflected in the communist identity and a totalitarian institution – the Communist Party. On the separate island of Taiwan, however, the KMT kept the statist model alive and managed to produce an economic miracle based on private enterprise and government control of the market. The main identity on Taiwan was nationalism, and the key institution was an authoritarian state. In later years, Taiwan's statist model was attenuated by the rise of an affluent middle-class society and the dominant influence exercised by the United States, which preferred the liberal-democratic model.

As Taiwan gradually moved to liberalism, mainland China experienced a shift from the communist model to the statist model that Taiwan had exemplified in the past. The driving force for such a fundamental change stemmed from the inherent defects of the communist, and particularly the Maoist, developmental model, which proved inadequate in the face of economic and military competition. As we will see, the destructive Cultural Revolution transformed the minds of the party cadres and turned them into modernizing technocrats. They became keenly aware of the deficiencies and atrocities of the old model. The CCP regime began moving toward the KMT's statist model. Communism was gradually being replaced by nationalism as the national identity, and the totalitarian regime was being transformed into an authoritarian state. With the relaxation of political control, the adoption of an "open-door policy" to the outside world, and the introduction of the market and private property, reform in China has even rekindled a liberal-democratic tendency rooted in the republican period, as demonstrated in the Tiananmen Square protests in June 1989 when Beijing's college students allied themselves with workers and citizens in order to stage a massive, one-month sit-in for political freedoms in the heart of the capital. During that month, there were several massive demonstrations that involved more than a million participants, an unprecedented phenomenon in communist China. However, the ease with which this pro-democracy movement was suppressed shows that liberal roots had not been thoroughly established in China. The current economic reform, however, may ultimately bring about an affluent middle-class society heavily influenced by international liberalism and eventually turn China institutionally toward liberalism, as happened earlier in Taiwan.

Some words on mainland China's relations with Taiwan are in order here. As its experience of governing mainland China gradually moved into Taiwan's past and Taiwan adopted a liberal political model, relations between the two sides remained tense and the United States found itself as involved as ever in the conflict across the Taiwan Strait. Since 1949, several armed conflicts have erupted in the Taiwan Strait, and the United States has acted as Taiwan's guardian, thwarting invasion from the mainland with a strong commitment to the security of Taiwan. In 1979, changing strategic calculations by the United States caused a shift of Washington's formal diplomatic recognition from the ROC to the PRC as the legitimate government of China. However, Taiwan still received a security guarantee from the United States through the Taiwan Relations Act, which helped the island wade through the political turbulence of the 1980s. **Chiang Ching-kuo**, Chiang Kai-shek's son, lifted martial law and allowed the formation of the opposition party, the Democratic Progressive Party, before his death in 1988. Ching-kuo was succeeded by Lee Teng-hui, who further democratized Taiwan's political system by holding a full-scale parliamentary election in 1992 and a direct presidential election in 1996. As it turned out, democratization in Taiwan produced a strong tendency toward independence (as demonstrated by replacing the name Republic of China with Republic of Taiwan and permanently separating Taiwan from mainland China) that since the mid-1990s has challenged the "one China" commitment held dearly by both the KMT and the CCP in the past. Tension ran high and threatened to engulf the United States in a cross-Strait war on several occasions, most noticeably during the 1995–1996 missile crisis, making the Taiwan Strait one of the most volatile hotspots in international politics at the turn of the twenty-first century. The election of the blatantly pro-independence Chen Shui-bian from the Democratic Progressive Party as the ROC's tenth president in 2000 further fueled the cross-Strait tension. The core of the conflict resides in Chen's professed plan to rewrite Taiwan's constitution, and to apply for United Nations (UN) membership under the name of Taiwan, acts widely understood as hallmarks of declaring permanent legal separation of the island from the Chinese mainland. Such a possibility prompted Beijing to seek help from Washington to rein in Chen's ambition and to co-manage the crisis in the Taiwan Strait. The strategic interaction among the United States, mainland China, and Taiwan thus is critical to the stability of the region, and to whether Washington can successfully handle the rise and challenge of China on a global scale.

Developmental Stages of the Communist Regime

Because political power in the PRC has been highly concentrated in the hands of a small group of communist leaders, and particularly in the hands of the paramount leader (Mao Zedong from 1949 to 1976 and Deng Xiaoping from 1978 to 1997), China's post-1949 political development can best be understood in terms of the ideas and policies of its top leaders. However, this does not mean that individuals determined China's political development by dint of their personalities and particular political inclinations. As strong as Mao's and Deng's influence on the political process may have been, they nevertheless reflected underlying forces that propelled a communist regime through the kinds of different developmental stages that one can also find in the Soviet Union and other communist countries. In this sense, both Mao and Deng (and Jiang Zemin and Hu Jintao, who succeeded Deng) were more representative of the underlying trend than they were creators of such a trend. As we have seen in the Russian example from Lenin to Brezhnev, the developmental stages of a Leninist regime can be characterized as (1) the initial transformation aimed at remaking the society; (2) the reform backlash; and (3) the conservative consolidation. The logic behind these stages is simple. The communists, as true believers in their utopian ideas, tend to act on the

ideology when they seize political power. This is the period of great transformation and revolutionary politics: Private property is confiscated; markets
are abolished; a centrally planned economy is erected; and a forced-draft
industrialization drive is launched. At this stage, one usually finds a tyranni-
cal despot concentrating all political power in his hands and terrorizing his
subjects into total subservience. Elaborate party networks, an all-powerful
secret police apparatus, and gigantic state enterprises are created, and a totalitarian party-state comes into existence. However, after years of traumatic
totalitarian rule, a reform period is bound to emerge. Totalitarianism trauma-
tizes not only ordinary people but also a ruling elite whose fate is tied to the
whim of the totalitarian despot, who launches repeated political campaigns
to "purify" the party. The whole nation yearns for relief from economic deprivation and treacherous politics. Thus, one finds a relaxation of state control
over the economy in the form of "perfecting the planning system" or "market
socialism," a withdrawal of secret police from their most blatant intrusion
into citizens' private lives, and a diminution of the party's omnipresent control of cultural expressions of the society. A more benign ruler succeeds the
despot, but usually not until the despot dies a natural death, as in the case
of Khrushchev succeeding Stalin and Deng succeeding Mao. The party-state
then comes to a truce with the society.

The reform backlash does not last long, however, as the very liberal policies characterizing this period breed further social expectations and threaten
to undermine the communist regime. What follows then is usually a conservative technocratic regime that does not embark on any major institutional initiatives or structural political reform but clings to the status quo
and gives it a conservative twist. The mission is no longer radical transformation of the society or desperate redressing of the excesses of totalitarianism
but rather entrenchment and consolidation. The leaders at this consolidation stage might keep or even deepen certain aspects of the reform stage,
particularly on the economic side, but their overall mentality is conservative
and their paramount goal is stability. The elite maintained political stability,
through economic performance and an all-embracing coercive apparatus. In
the Soviet Union and most of Eastern Europe, this period was embodied
in the rule of Leonid Brezhnev and like-minded communist leaders, such as
Gustav Husak of Czechoslovakia. In the following analysis, we see that China
moved into the consolidation stage with the death of Deng Xiaoping and the
political ascendancy of the technocrat par excellence, Jiang Zemin, as the
new top leader of the CCP in 1997. The succession of Jiang by Hu Jintao in
2002 further consolidated this trend, for the latter was a technocrat ruler just
like his predecessor.

Despite all the developmental similarities between the Chinese and Soviet
experience, it should be pointed out that significant differences remain.
First, consolidation and stability were pursued in China through dynamic

equilibrium, with periodic replacement of senior leaders, whereas the Soviet and Eastern European communist regimes pursued the same goals through static equilibrium, without rejuvenation of top leadership. Second, the Chinese economic reform went far beyond what the Soviets had attempted, or ever imagined. Under Deng, market reform was introduced and private property crept back. Under Jiang and Hu, private entrepreneurship was exalted. Today, one can picture mainland China as a huge newly industrializing country (NIC). In many respects, China resembles the preceding NICs such as South Korea and Taiwan, only that it is much larger. China has developed into a post-totalitarian capitalist developmental state, combining features from the Soviet and East European experience and developmental traits of the East Asian NICs. The combination of constituent elements from these two highly divergent models and regions would make the Chinese developmental case unique, were it not for a similar development in Vietnam. In sum, the historical communist regimes in Europe and today's China are two distinctive types of consolidating leadership, although the paramount goals of political stability and regime preservation remain the same in both.

The Maoist Period: Totalitarianism

We begin our analysis with Mao Zedong, the totalitarian despot. Mao rose to power when he assumed command of the Red Army at the Zunyi conference in 1935 on the Long March. Prior to that meeting, Mao had been dominated by a group of Moscow-trained communists. Mao understood that there was no hope for the communists to establish power bases in China's cities. The size of the working class there was too small and their revolutionary consciousness too underdeveloped. Instead, the Chinese communists had to rely on the peasants. This meant that the CCP had to adopt a strategy of "encircling the cities from the countryside" and tailor its programs to the needs of the peasants; that is, redistributing land instead of creating communes. Mao's idea was in serious conflict with the Soviet experience, which relied heavily on the workers in the cities for vital support. It was not until the KMT's fifth annihilation campaign, which swept the communists from their Jiangxi base, that Mao grasped a golden opportunity to unseat his Moscow-trained rivals and assume military leadership. He then put his strategy into practice. This realistic shift of strategy, when combined with the Japanese invasion, contributed greatly to the CCP's resurgence as a serious contender for power during the post–World War II period.

Mao's greatest contribution to the communist movement was, of course, leading the party to the defeat of Chiang Kai-shek in the civil war and establishing the People's Republic of China in 1949. The 1950s witnessed a great transformation of Chinese society. The traditional gentry elite was purged.

Social hierarchy in the rural areas was smashed. The business class in the cities was deprived of its properties. A Soviet-style command economy characterized by state economic units under the control of the central bureaucracy was installed with the help of Soviet advisers. The end of the civil war brought about a golden opportunity for national reconstruction. Women were given equal status with men and emancipated from their traditional subjugation in the family. One witnessed great social mobility. Although the nationalist government initiated many social reforms before 1949, its inability to penetrate into the depths of Chinese society limited the effectiveness of its reforms. Under the communists, traditional society was turned upside-down for the first time in China's multithousand-year history. All of this happened under heavy Soviet influence. In 1950, Mao paid a tribute to Stalin in Moscow when he made his first visit to a foreign country and signed a treaty of friendship between the PRC and the Soviet Union. To the outside observer, especially to politicians in the United States, it appeared as if there was now one large, unified communist bloc that extended from Berlin to Beijing.

It was only a matter of time, however, before the Chinese and the Soviets would compete for influence in the world communist movement. Mao was, after all, the leader of China, one of the five permanent members of the UN Security Council (although the seat was at that time still held by the Republic of China in Taipei), the world's most populous nation, and a country proud of its ancient civilization. It would be difficult to imagine a subservient China bowing to the interests of the Soviet Union in the name of a world communist movement. During the 1950s, Mao developed his own ideas about how to govern China and conduct Beijing's relations with other countries in the world.

This struggle for dominance in the world communist movement led to an outright acrimonious split after Stalin's death and the criticism of Stalin in the Soviet Union under Khrushchev's rule. Mao launched a series of verbal attacks on Soviet "revisionism," seeing in Nikita Khrushchev a weak, willing traitor who flirted with the world's arch-capitalist nation, the United States. Determined to shed Soviet influence, Mao in the late 1950s urged the party to adopt a uniquely Chinese modernization strategy, which would prove disastrous for the nation.

Mao's experience with the Chinese civil war, in which the ill-equipped communist fighters had overpowered the KMT's huge army, convinced him that spiritual mobilization was the key to success. As China was short of capital, Mao found the abundant Chinese labor a ready substitute. Mao believed that people could be mobilized through political campaigns modeled on revolutionary action. This idea was a natural extension of Mao's wartime strategy, which had relied on China's huge peasantry. The result was a policy that Mao called the "**Great Leap Forward**." The apex of the campaign was the creation of the gigantic People's Communes, which presumably embodied the communist ideal. Communes were large in scale, collectively owned, and were composed of several production brigades, which were subdivided into production teams. They organized production activities, distributed revenues, performed governmental functions, and took care of social welfare. In the heyday of communization, rural markets were abolished, prices were set by the state, and private property was eliminated in the countryside. The commune experience had little economic rationality and was imposed on the country at the whim of Chairman Mao. The result of this experience was a total disruption of agricultural production that ended in an unprecedented man-made famine during which some 30 million Chinese people died. Mao was forced to the second line by his pragmatic colleagues, such as Liu Shaoqi, Deng Xiaoping, and **Chen Yun**, but the "great helmsman" refused to accept his political downfall and made a revengeful comeback by launching the Great Proletarian **Cultural Revolution** that ravaged the nation for a whole decade (1966–1976).

Mao's comeback tilted the balance between the party and the state. Prior to 1949, the CCP had an extensive party organization that performed regular government functions in the communist-controlled areas. The party was initially led by a **general secretary**, then by a chairman. The CCP practiced the "democratic centralism" of a typical Leninist party, which meant, in practice, the concentration of power in the hands of a supreme party leader. After the establishment of the People's Republic, the communists began to build a set of state institutions and gradually shifted administrative power to the newly founded government bureaucracies. This process of "normalization" coincided with Beijing's "leaning toward the Soviet Union" and demonstrated, at the time, China's earnest effort to build a society modeled on the well-established Soviet system.

In September 1949, the party began to set up a Central People's Government as the highest organ of state power. Mao was elected its chairman. Under it was the Government Administrative Council headed by **Zhou Enlai**. After the 1954 constitution was promulgated, a National People's Congress was created to serve as the parliament. The Government Administrative Council became the **State Council** and was responsible to the people's deputies. Zhou Enlai continued to serve as the premier. This arrangement resembled the governing structure of a typical communist country. The Communist Party remained the ultimate source of power and legitimacy. The leader of the party, Chairman Mao in the Chinese case, ruled supreme. The head of government was usually the second most powerful figure in the party-state as long as that position was not taken by the party leader himself.

There was an ill-defined division of labor between the party and the government, with the party initiating policies and guaranteeing their political correctness, and the government implementing those policies. The military also played an important role at this initial stage of the People's Republic.

From 1949 to 1952, military administrative committees directly controlled 20 provinces. The power of the generals, however, was curbed by Mao when the political and economic situation of China stabilized. Mao himself headed the party's Central Military Commission (CMC) and directed the People's Liberation Army in that capacity. The government's control of the military (both the People's Revolutionary Military Commission and the National Defense Council) was totally overwhelmed by the party CMC. A firmly established tradition in the PRC is for the party to "command the guns" and for the leader of the party to head the party CMC. The party's control over the military was also guaranteed by recruitment into the party of all officers above the rank of platoon commander, setting up political commissars and political departments in the army, and establishing party committees at the regiment level and above.

The party, the government, and the army are the three power pillars in the PRC. In Table 8.1, we see that it is not always easy to figure out the real paramount leader simply by looking at the official positions held by China's top politicians. The general rule seems to be that the paramount leader always controls the party CMC. This held true until Deng formally gave that position to Jiang at the end of 1989 while still running the show from behind the scenes. That anomaly did not occur during Mao's reign from 1949 to 1976, however, when he was both **chairman of the Central Committee of the Chinese Communist Party** and chairman of its Central Military Commission. That is to say, Mao directly controlled the party and the military. The government was left in the hands of Zhou Enlai, who had risen to the CCP's top leadership earlier than Mao. The 1959 promotion of Liu Shaoqi to state chairman was not an insignificant move, for even though the PRC's head of state was a titular position, Liu's advancement was widely considered to be a sign that Liu, as a moderate, was in line to be Mao's successor, which would have been consistent with the de-Stalinization campaign unfolding in the Soviet Union. However, Liu's assumption of the state chairmanship proved ominous in view of Mao's vengeful rearguard actions that followed his blunders in the Great Leap Forward. These kinds of power struggles, inherent in communist leadership succession, became entangled with international competition and ideological dispute within China.

Mao's rupture with Khrushchev proved fatal to China's state-building efforts, as he began to whip up local support for his Great Leap Forward and People's Communes. Mao abhorred Soviet-style technocratism and overconcentrated state planning. In 1958, Mao began to delegate very significant power to party officials (cadres) in running the economy; this set China apart from the Soviet Union and Eastern European countries, which had a more centrally controlled economy under communist rule. Even though China underwent several rounds of "decentralization-recentralization" in the following years, it never went back to the original planned-economy model

TABLE 8.1. China's Top Leaders and Their Positions

	President[a]	Prime Minister	Communist Party Leader	Chairman of Party CMC	Paramount Leader
1949 Oct.	Mao Zedong	Zhou Enlai	Mao Zedong	Mao Zedong	Mao Zedong
1959 Apr.	Liu Shaoqi				
1968 Oct.	Dong Biwu				
1975 Jan.	Zhu De				
1976 Feb.		Hua Guofeng (acting Feb.–Apr. 1976)			
1976 July	Song Qinglin (acting)				
1976 Oct.			Hua Guofeng	Hua Guofeng	Hua Guofeng
1978 Mar.	Ye Jianying				
1978 Dec.					Deng Xiaoping
1980 Sept.		Zhao Ziyang			
1981 June			Hu Yaobang (Party Chairman)	Deng Xiaoping	
1982 Sept.			Hu Yaobang (General Secretary)		
1983 June	Li Xiannian				
1987 Jan.			Zhao Ziyang		
1987 Nov.		Li Peng			
1988 Apr.	Yang Shangkun				
1989 June			Jiang Zemin		
1989 Nov.				Jiang Zemin	
1993 Mar.	Jiang Zemin				
1997 Feb.					Jiang Zemin
1998 Mar.		Zhu Rongji			
2002 Nov.			Hu Jintao		
2003 Mar.	Hu Jintao	Wen Jiabao			
2004 Sept.				Hu Jintao	Hu Jintao

[a] The PRC's president is the state chairman when that position exists (i.e., from 1954 to 1975 and from 1983 on). In the absence of a state chairman, it was the chairman of the National People's Congress who took on the function of the head of state.

that the Soviet advisers had helped China to build during the 1950s. This historical legacy of a decentralized system was later hailed as a unique Chinese advantage for implementing market reform during the 1980s. However, institutionally, the most important development during the 1958 decentralization was the shift of power from state technocrats to party cadres, which was reminiscent of the revolutionary years when they had had an important mission.

Mao's experiment proved disastrous and temporarily diminished his power. As a result, the short interlude between the Great Leap Forward and the launching of the Cultural Revolution saw a temporary revival of state institutions. The stormy politics of the Cultural Revolution, however, again dampened the vitality of government agencies and returned power to party cadres. Mao launched campaigns against the "small clique of capitalist-roaders in power" who were often found in government institutions. Revolutionary committees took the place of the local governments, and direct military control was instituted to curb the excessive infighting among Red Guard zealots, militaristic groups of students who had been sent to monitor and brutalize government critics and "class enemies," whom Mao himself had unleashed. The normal politics of the 1950s was replaced by the stormy movements of the 1960s. State institutions were attacked, government officials were purged and sent to reeducation camps in China's remote provinces, and millions of intellectuals were humiliated and condemned to forced labor. For Mao, this was a "class struggle." The simple fact remained that Mao did his best to undermine the very institutions that he helped establish during the first decade of the People's Republic.

Even though Mao vehemently attacked the Soviet Union in the ideological battle between the two communist giants, his basic position and policies did not deviate from orthodox Stalinism. As a matter of fact, he based his attacks on Khrushchev's leadership on its betrayal of the original ideals of communism. During the decade of the Cultural Revolution, the personality cult of Mao was carried to absurd lengths. The chairman was hailed as a great hero in all walks of life. He was the greatest military genius, a brilliant and accomplished poet, and a swimmer who broke the world's record. Bountiful harvests could be assured simply by reading the "little red book" that recorded the chairman's words. Children were taught not to love their parents but to love Chairman Mao. The whole world was said to admire this great leader of China. Mao actually ruled by terror, exercising it even against his chief lieutenants (most notably State Chairman Liu Shaoqi and Party General Secretary Deng Xiaoping). Public denunciations and beatings at mass rallies were substituted for Soviet-style show trials, with equally fatal consequences for the accused. The Red Guards were Mao's invention, for he lacked organizational means to defeat his opponents in the party-state hierarchy. As a result, the chairman was able to unleash abundant social anger at the regime after the traumatic Great Leap Forward campaign and the resulting famine, directing it toward his intraparty enemies. The devastation was greater than in the Soviet Union, where purges and power struggles were conducted in a more "orderly" manner. On the economic front, Mao mercilessly mobilized China's resources to pursue heavy industrialization, and

TABLE 8.2. Share of Investment by Industries, 1953–1978

Years	Agriculture	Light industry	Heavy industry	Other industries
First Five-Year Plan (1953–1957)	7.1	6.4	36.2	50.3
Second Five-Year Plan (1958–1962)	11.3	6.4	54.0	28.3
1963–1965	17.6	3.9	45.9	32.6
Third Five-Year Plan (1966–1970)	10.7	4.4	51.1	33.8
Fourth Five-Year Plan (1971–1975)	9.8	5.8	49.6	34.8
1976–1978	10.8	5.9	49.6	33.7

Source: Lin Yifu, Cai Fang, and Li Zhou, *Zhongguo de qiji: fazhan zhanlue yu jingji gaige* (China's Miracle: Developmental Strategy and Economic Reform) (Hong Kong: Chinese University Press, 1995), p. 56.

both agriculture and light industry that directly affected the livelihood of the population were severely neglected (Table 8.2). The developmental priorities were thus the same as in the Soviet Union, although Mao's strategy of spiritual mobilization and absolute egalitarianism were quite counterproductive in the long run. In short, Mao's rule in China was a classical case of totalitarianism, characterized by massive ideological indoctrination, the personality cult of the leader, rule by terror, a state-run economy geared toward heavy industrialization, and disregard of consumers' needs in economic planning. In many respects, Mao's practices were even more excessive than Stalin's.

Deng Unleashes Reform

The conflict between Mao and his political enemies in the leadership was a fight between the leftist radicals and the pro-stability technocrats, between the movement-oriented party and order-conscious state. Here one finds the conflict between two interests (cadres versus technocrats), two identities (revolution versus development), and two institutions (party versus state). With the death of Mao and the political demise of the ultraleftists, a new force emerged that advocated market reform and political relaxation. Those reformers then competed with the technocrats for supremacy. This reform force was easily recognizable when one refers to the post-Stalinist Soviet Union and Eastern Europe. In China, the artificial suppression of the reform momentum during Mao's years meant that when it was finally unleashed, the reform in China came with a vengeance.

The pro-stability technocrats constituted a significant political force in the PRC after the 1950s. However, throughout the Maoist era, they were suppressed by the leftists. Their early leader was Liu Shaoqi, Mao's designated successor. Liu was an organizational man who favored orderly development of the country's economy in the manner of Soviet-style five-year plans. He abhorred the anarchy that Mao's endless campaigns brought about. With regard to basic economic policy, Mao's "red" line insisted on breathtaking growth through ideological movements, whereas the "expert" line of Liu's technocrats emphasized the need for balanced development and allowed modifications of the system in order to improve performance. This "line struggle" was elevated by Mao to the height of "class struggle," and repeated movements were launched from above to ensure that Mao's line was in command.

As the Soviet and Eastern European experiences demonstrate, totalitarianism is but a stage in the development of Leninist regimes. Stabilization of the political process and turning to economic reform to improve performance seem to be a natural tendency. In the PRC, however, Mao's political genius and his overwhelming prestige in the party-state artificially delayed the end of totalitarianism. In the 1960s and 1970s, Mao mustered all his vigilance to guard against having the CCP slip into Soviet-style revisionism as in the Khrushchev and Brezhnev eras. As a result, the Chinese communist regime delayed its reform stage until the death of its despotic ruler.

Reform was inevitable, however. Mao's revolutionary politics and stormy economic campaigns provided few benefits to either the population at large or to the ruling elite, who were in constant fear of being Mao's next target and were forbidden to enjoy a decent material life. China's economy was on the brink of collapse by the time of Mao's death, suffering from the inefficiencies and rigidities of a socialist planned economy and the irregularities of Mao's unpredictable ideological campaigns. Persistent poverty seriously undermined the regime's legitimacy, particularly when the population compared China's economic plight with the high-speed growth of neighboring countries in East Asia. On the international front, Mao's radical politics at home antagonized the Soviet Union while forestalling a genuine rapprochement with the United States. Being at odds with both superpowers put the country in a dangerous position internationally. In these circumstances, Beijing's leaders were acutely aware of the fact that a backward economy and a predominantly rural society could not support China's ambition to compete on the world stage. The discrimination against students from the propertied classes, the absolute demand for equality but not quality, the disdain for intellectuals, and the glorification of manual labor at the expense of formal education devastated the school system and left a whole generation of Chinese youth uneducated. Even the military was indoctrinated in the virtue of the people's war, exulting in ideological correctness and willpower at the expense of absolutely necessary military modernization. China's immense potential to become a great nation in the world was suffocated by Mao's ideology and the endless internal strife perpetuated by it. It became obvious to all but the most radical faction in the CCP elite that things had to change and that reform was necessary to save both the country and the leaders themselves. In order to survive both domestically and internationally, China had to restructure its system and shed the debilitating aspects of Mao's totalitarianism.

The fact that China resisted the advent of reform longer than most other socialist countries foretold the vengeance with which reform would ultimately come. As it turned out, Deng Xiaoping transformed the Chinese economic system much more thoroughly than Nikita Khrushchev did the Soviet Union's. In terms of politics, the personality cult and ruthless persecution of comrades were denounced in reform-era China, much as they had been during periods of reform in the Soviet Union and Eastern Europe. Obviously, this is not democratization but relaxation in a post-totalitarian society, as witnessed by Deng's continued insistence on the leading role of the Communist Party. Stability now hinged on material benefits that the communist regime delivered and on a widespread sense of improvement on the previous decades of impoverishment and rule by terror.

Mao's legacy was dismantled bit by bit. One month after Mao's death in September 1976, the **Gang of Four** (including Mao's wife, Jiang Qing, and three other ultraleftist leaders) were arrested. Two years later, at the historic **Third Plenum of the CCP's Eleventh Central Committee** held in December 1978, the interregnum leader Hua Guofeng was defeated by Deng Xiaoping, and the reform era was ushered in (see Table 8.3 at the end of the chapter). With the ultraleftists dislodged from power, a schism developed in the anti-Hua coalition. The radical economic reformers, led by Deng and his handpicked lieutenants **Hu Yaobang** (general secretary of the party) and **Zhao Ziyang** (premier), did not see eye to eye with the technocrats, led by Chen Yun. Although Deng's reform project was a reaction to totalitarian excesses, one can nevertheless find a similar mentality between the ultraleftists and the radical reformers. They all took a pro-growth stance as opposed to the technocrats' pro-stability line. Mao, Hua, and Deng were all proponents of high growth, although they resorted to different means for achieving that same goal: Mao with his Great Leap Forward, Hua with his Great Leap Westward, and Deng with his market reform. The determination of those Chinese communist leaders to achieve super growth had a lot to do with their realization that China was backward and that extraordinary means were necessary for the country to compete effectively in the world. It was under this "surpassing mentality" that the strategic goal of doubling the PRC's industrial and agricultural production by the year 2000 was set at the Twelfth Party Congress in 1982, when the era of reform formally began.

The technocrats thought otherwise. For them, stability of the system was a paramount consideration. Led by Chen Yun in the post-Mao era, the technocrats stressed the need for balanced development, limited spending, and measured growth. After the death of Mao and the short interlude of Hua Guofeng, the technocrats' line temporarily gained dominance in Chen Yun's "adjustment" policy, designed to curb the rash and unbalanced investment surge under Hua's Ten-Year Plan. But Chen's line was in command for only five years (1979–1983). It was then swiftly replaced by Deng's pro-growth marketization drive, implemented by the new prime minister, Zhao Ziyang. With the country on the road to reform – that is, with Deng in command – the technocrats found themselves circumvented, although continuing struggles between the reformers and technocrats testified to the resilience of the latter. Vested interests were also involved in this factional conflict, as inland provinces, production ministries, planning agencies, state enterprises, and other heavily subsidized sectors of the economy naturally loathed radical market reforms, whereas coastal areas, light industries, local governments, and those sectors benefiting from reform measures supported expansion and deepening of the reforms. In this case, ideals and interests were intertwined.

Several economic cycles during the 1980s shaped the balance of power between the pro-growth reformers and the pro-stability technocrats. As a rule, the reformers fueled the economy with expansionary monetary policies and liberalization. High growth was pursued at the expense of macrostability. Under Deng, one saw the failed People's Communes farming system abolished and a realistic household-responsibility system instituted that combined compulsory state procurements with peasant discretion over above-quota produce. Prices of agricultural products increased. Rural markets revived. Township and village enterprises mushroomed. In the cities, one first saw the emergence of millions of small individual businesses (getihu) and then the rapid development of hitherto unthinkable private enterprises. The state enterprises were also reformed, first by raising the profit–retention ratio and then by a contract scheme that resembled the household-responsibility system in the countryside. A tax-for-profit reform was launched in 1983–1984 that was designed to provide level ground for healthy competition. Various kinds of ownership reforms were tested after 1986, culminating in the introduction of stock shares and their free trade in newly opened stock markets. An open-door policy invited a huge inflow of foreign capital that provided timely funding for the rapid growth of the Chinese economy. Indirect foreign investment also surged as international lenders designated China as a promising market. According to the World Bank, China's annual per capita GDP (gross domestic product) growth reached an average of 8 percent between 1978 and 1995. Only South Korea and Taiwan grew at comparable rates (at 6.9 percent and 6.3 percent respectively).

It is not surprising that high growth brought about inflation and a trade imbalance, as happened in 1985, 1988, and 1993–1994. With wide fluctuations of the economy came episodes of political unrest, the most serious of which were the Beijing Spring of 1986–1987 and the Tiananmen pro-democracy movement of 1989. The first incident brought down the then Secretary General Hu Yaobang and the second one Hu's successor, Zhao Ziyang. The **Tiananmen incident** was a tragic confrontation between student demonstrators demanding political liberties and a communist regime heavily divided between reformers and hard-liners. It showed the destabilizing effect of Deng's reforms, the limits of which were not clearly defined by Deng himself. In an atmosphere of increasing economic liberties and political relaxation, it was only natural that young students would grow impatient with the regime's authoritarian style and demand structural political reforms. Economic mismanagement of the time provided an immediate impetus, while the signs of intraregime schism further emboldened the student activists. The Tiananmen incident was started when students memorialized the death of Hu Yaobang, a bona fide reformer in the regime, and refused to leave the Tiananmen Square in front of Beijing's Forbidden City. The stalemate between the pro-democracy students, whose numbers on the square surged, and the regime continued until Deng ordered a ruthless crackdown and soldiers fired at the unarmed demonstrators on June 4, killing hundreds or thousands of them. The picture of a brave lone man standing in front of an approaching tank column, daring them to run him over, was broadcast around the world and has become the single most powerful image of the Tiananmen suppression. It became clear that once the regime was able to mend its internal division (ousting Zhao, the sympathizer in this instance), the post-totalitarian state found it easy to quell whatever resistance and protest that the young dissidents of China were able to mount against it. However, the fact that the Tiananmen protest did happen and that tanks had to roar and shots be fired in the center of the capital city to quell it demonstrates how Deng's reforms had disturbed political stability in China. From the regime's point of view, obviously reform had gone too far, and something had to be done to prevent the recurrence of another Tiananmen protest.

In the aftermath of Tiananmen, General Secretary Zhao was replaced by Jiang Zemin, a technocrat from Shanghai. In an overall environment of regimentation, the technocrats regained some power, silencing the society with mass arrests and show trials, reimposing strict control over mass media, and launching ideological war against China's peaceful evolution into a "bourgeois democracy." Economically, they reduced investment and tightened the monetary supply, particularly against the nascent private sector. Further reform measures were put on hold. In this way, stability was restored but only at the expense of growth. Seeing his reform enterprise in a quagmire, Deng made a breakthrough tour to the south, from where he relaunched a reform drive. With Deng's active intervention, the reformers resurged and snatched power from the technocrats. The economy entered a high-growth phase again, starting a new cycle.

During the course of relaunching the reform, Premier Li Peng was reprimanded by Deng for his overconservative goal of 6 percent annual growth for the Eighth Five-Year Plan period (1991–1995). After the southern tour, Deng was temporarily triumphant, and the Chinese economy registered double-digit growth rates for four consecutive years. Soon, however, the economy overheated and a new policy of "macroadjustment" came into vogue. The person in charge of this limited austerity program was **Zhu Rongji**. Zhu was widely considered Deng's favorite to succeed Li Peng as the prime minister. This should not blur the fact that there was no substantial difference between him and Li or Jiang. Jiang, Li, and Zhu are all technocrats with a good educational background, and they all consider stability a paramount goal at the PRC's current stage of development. They may belong to different power blocs and may compete vehemently for ascendancy in the post-Deng period, but they are not pro-growth zealots in the mold of the old patriarch. The desperate, extraordinary period of supergrowth has come to an end with the phasing out and, ultimately, the death of Deng. To summarize, Deng's rule in China has left a legacy of unprecedented growth that lifted the largest number of people out of poverty in human history. It also brought about unprecedented economic volatility and political instability. Unparalleled openness to the outside world and increasing influence from the West were accompanied by the creeping return of many traditional aspects of Chinese society, such as the unequal treatment of women in rural areas. Economic reform also enhanced regional disparities and inequalities between the cities and the countryside. In short, growth and openness were gained at the expense of equality and stability.

In comparative terms, Deng's strong reaction to Mao's line was not unlike Khrushchev's reform after the death of Stalin. Both carried a movement mentality and focused on institutional innovations. Even though the economic reform of Dengist China went far beyond the scope of the limited market and reorganizational experiments of the Soviet Union under Khrushchev, the prevalent ethos and the impact of radical reform were similar in the two cases. Both the Soviet Union and the PRC were plunged into constant institutional flux by their reform leaders, and powerful technocratic interests were violated.

In the Soviet Union, Khrushchev was ultimately deposed by a rebelling technocracy led by Leonid Brezhnev, the technocrat par excellence, who then ruled with his colleagues in a self-perpetuating **Politburo** for 18 years during the most stable and immobile period of Soviet history. In mainland China, on the other hand, Deng was able to sustain the reform's momentum through his prestige and masterful maneuvering among central and provincial interests. However, technocratic consolidation was a natural tendency for a mature communist regime, just as reform was inevitable after the rule of a revolutionary tyrant, which explains the conservative triumph during the retrenchment period of 1988–1991. And yet, the advent of the technocratic age in China was artificially thwarted by Deng, who, in his famous southern tour of 1992, single-handedly relaunched hypergrowth reform and brought mainland China out of its conservative retrenchment at one stroke, despite opposition by most of his technocratic lieutenants. That phenomenal achievement of Deng, however, should be viewed as the last gasp of radical reform rather than the beginning of a new reform era. At Deng's death, China was ready for entry into the next stage of development: technocratic consolidation.

Jiang Zemin, Hu Jintao, and Neoconservatism

In China, new developmental stages seem to await the physical death of the leader who dominated the earlier stage. For a while, Jiang was considered an opportunist who shifted his opinions to suit the political needs of the time. Thus, his various speeches made in the immediate post-Tiananmen period of 1989–1991 were characterized by the themes of "anti-peaceful evolution" and "socialism or capitalism?" These were ideological themes and were in tune with the conservative backlash of the moment. Within a few years, however, Jiang suddenly became a champion of pro-growth economic reform and stressed repeatedly the need to "prevent the resurgence of the left line." The contrast is sharp but can be explained in terms of Deng's strong pressure on him. After Deng was disabled by poor health (particularly after 1994), however, Jiang began to reveal his innate preferences. "Stability in command" became the regime's motto. Through various administrative and macroeconomic policy instruments, the overheated growth and the accompanying inflation of 1993–1994 were effectively curbed, and the leadership engineered, in 1996, a "soft landing" of the economy that successfully brought down annual inflation to 6.1 percent (from 21.7 percent in 1994 and 14.8 percent in 1995). Economic imbalances were redressed without undue austerity and loss of growth. And yet, with all the good news, Jiang still insisted on stability in early 1997, not succumbing to the temptation of raising the economic growth rate in the year of a party congress. This cautious approach suggests that stability was indeed a paramount consideration for the new secretary general.

Jiang's commitment to stability was also reflected in his insistence that politics should be in command. Initially launched in September 1995, Jiang's slogan of "mindful of politics" became a nationwide campaign in 1996, embraced first by an ardent People's Liberation Army. The purpose of this old-style political campaign was to raise party cadres' political consciousness, something that had become increasingly difficult as economic reform progressed. In this context, Jiang ordered a suppression of the Falungong religious cult, which had been attracting great numbers of practitioners within

China and many believers around the world. The cult was originally approved and applauded by the communist regime for its combination of apparently innocuous religious beliefs, spiritual and body exercises, and healing techniques. Soon the ability of Falungong to recruit members from party, government, and military organizations, and to mobilize supporters to stage protests against the regime, terrified Jiang and his associates and led to a large-scale suppression that shocked the world. The underlying cause of the regime's overreaction was its obsession with absolute political control of the society. Put together, one finds that during Jiang's reign, the "soft landing" was to pursue economic stability, while the "mindful of politics" campaign and the suppression of Falungong (let alone continued repression of democracy-movement activists) were designed to ensure political stability through strict control. Both themes testified to the importance of stability in Jiang's mind.

Jiang's rule officially ended at the Sixteenth Party Congress, held in 2002. He was succeeded by Hu Jintao as secretary general. The following year, Wen Jiabao replaced Zhu Rongji as premier. Jiang still held the chairmanship of the party's Central Military Commission and exercised great influence from behind the scenes until September 2004, when he handed over the military command to Hu. The new Hu-Wen regime is not significantly different from the Jiang-Zhu regime in that both are dominated by technocrats with stability at the top of their agendas. Specifically, the new fourth-generation leadership is keenly aware of the danger of an overheated economy and is determined to crush any political opposition. They differ from Jiang's third-generation leaders only in their younger age, lesser experience, higher educational credentials, and lower prestige. In the Seventeenth Party Congress held in October 2007, one witnesses the continuation of the Hu-Wen regime and the appointment of the fifth-generation leaders Xi Jinping and Li Keqiang into the ruling Politburo Standing Committee, apparently to succeed the current leadership when they phase out in 2012. Compared with their predecessors, Xi and Li are even younger, less experienced, better educated, and less prestigious. Xi is a chemical engineer by training, but later received a Ph.D. degree in law. The son of a revolutionary veteran, Li was promoted to the party's chief of Shanghai in 2004. Li heads Liaoning, a northeastern province of China, after rising within the hierarchy of the Chinese Communist Youth League, the power base of Hu Jintao. Li holds an M.A. degree in economics and a Ph.D. degree in law, both from the prestigious Peking University. Xi and Li are the first top leaders of China to have received Ph.D. degrees. The standard profile of the fifth-generation leaders suggests that China remains entrenched in the stage of technocratic consolidation.

Jiang and Hu (and the new appointees to the Seventeen Party Congress's Politburo) should be viewed less as unique personalities than as representatives of two generations of technocrats who rose to positions of leadership after the rule of revolutionaries (the Maoists) and radical reformers (the Dengists). The new technocratic rulers wielded much less power than their predecessors. Deng was certainly less powerful than Mao, but in many respects these two men were still comparable. The difference between Deng and his successors was much more striking. Except in the area of education, the third- and fourth-echelon leaders led by Jiang and Hu are dwarfed by Deng in all forms of power resources, such as experience, military support, charisma, will to power, vision, self-confidence, and contribution to the establishment and maintenance of the regime. As a result, the personal imprint of Jiang and Hu on Chinese politics and society is markedly lighter than that of Mao or Deng.

Declining personal authority and increasingly technocratic rule seem to be an evolutionary regularity for communist regimes. From a comparative point of view, communist regimes naturally evolved from the stage of totalitarianism, through reform, to technocratic rule. The totalitarian ruler (for example, Stalin or Mao) launched political and economic campaigns to transform the society. The horrendous human costs that such transformation entailed forced the second-generation rulers to seek a truce with the society and terminate the rule of terror. Material improvements and political relaxation ensued. However, the reformers, in their zeal to redress the excesses of totalitarianism, often went too far, creating instability with constant institutional restructuring and risking the regime's political control over the society. The cadres' huge vested interest was also undermined. All of this prompted reactions from the technocrats.

Just as the reformers naturally acted against the extremes of revolutionary enthusiasm, the technocrats by their nature sought to bring about stability (on both the individual and regime levels and in both political and economic senses), which had been undermined by radical reform measures. In form, this seemed like a partial return to totalitarianism, but in essence the emergent technocratic rule was a conservative backlash against both revolution (the first stage) and reform (the second stage). The purpose of the regime was no longer to remold the society, or to redress the atrocities of the past and catch up with the world, but simply to keep things as they stood, particularly to keep the communist regime in power. This was what the Brezhnev era meant in the Soviet Union.

The same development has dawned on China. The death of Deng Xiaoping and the political ascendancy of Jiang Zemin signified the advent of the technocratic era. Jiang and his colleagues of the third-generation leadership had more formal and technical education than their predecessors. Hu and the fourth-generation leadership in turn received even higher education than Jiang and his associates. All of those people were products of an established technocratic system and not its creators or builders. Their experience was typically concentrated on one functional area, and that usually was not military affairs. As technocrats, Jiang, Hu, and their comrades sitting on the CCP's Politburo were intrinsically more interested in preserving the status quo and pursuing stability than exploring new reform frontiers. In this sense, whether it was Jiang or any other technocrat to succeed Deng is not really important, as communist technocratic rulers basically behave in similar ways. They have a realistic understanding of the popular desire for material betterment, they loathe destruction in the name of revolution and the institutional flux brought about by radical reform, and they want to absorb Western technology and capital, but they abhor pluralistic ideas and democracy. When faced with a choice between economic development and political stability, they would overwhelmingly opt for the latter. The contrast with Russia's choice under Gorbachev of democratization before economic reform could not be more apparent.

The advent of a technocratic era has been fostered by the country's economic development. The urgency under which Deng pursued his reform programs has diminished over time. Mainland China's annual economic growth rate averaged 9.5 percent over 18 years (1979–1996), and the size of its economy is predicted to surpass that of the United States in the early twenty-first century. The desperate need to grow at breathtaking speed has been reduced. At the same time, the anxiety over the grave costs accompanying rapid growth has increased. The link between a heated economy and political disturbance has been recognized by the ruling elite, with Tiananmen serving as a vivid reminder. Because growth is more or less taken for granted, the paramount consideration is naturally stability, both economic and political. This developmental feature plays into the hands of the technocrats, who treasure stability as the primary policy goal of the regime. Thus, when Jiang outlined his blueprint for governing China, he treated stability as a precondition for development and reform, a lesson he said he had gained only with painful experience. In this regard, Hu and Wen followed in Jiang's footsteps, putting a brake on economic growth whenever there is a sign of overheating.

Besides evolutionary necessity and economic prosperity, there is a third major reason that links the Jiang and Hu regimes to stability. As has been mentioned, the new leaders were much weaker than their predecessors (Jiang being much weaker than Deng, and Hu in turn being much weaker than Jiang). This means that their ability to initiate and implement new policies against the entrenched interests – ministerial, military, regional, and others – was much smaller than when Mao or Deng ruled. Stability, then, was the default outcome, the result of inaction.

The post-Deng era is characterized by technocratic rule and stability. Power struggles increasingly take a purely factional form, in which political leaders clash not over ideological lines, or a pro-growth versus pro-stability development strategy, but over personal power and prestige. Very much like Brezhnev, Jiang and Hu were first among equals in their respective cohort, rather than a strongman like Mao or Deng. Certainly the PRC's economy grows much faster than its erstwhile Soviet or Eastern European counterparts, and China's political control is a bit looser, but the pro-stability technocratic mentality is the same in post-Deng China as in the Soviet Union under Brezhnev. Nothing appeals to party cadres, state officials, and managers of state enterprises more than job security, and nothing attracts communist leaders in a post-ideological age better than a secure political career. Here lies the appeal of stability. Communist technocrats were suppressed in both the revolutionary and reform periods, for Mao and Deng were committed to transformation of the society, albeit in opposite directions. With Jiang and Hu acting as the core of the leadership, pro-stability technocrats in the PRC finally have their way.

Although consolidation and technocratic rule are common to the evolution of the Soviet/Eastern European and Chinese communist regimes, there are differences in the ways in which stability was pursued in the two cases. First, the Soviet planned economy under Stalin was not as discredited as Mao's improvised economic models. Consequently, the Soviet and Eastern European economic reforms concentrated on perfecting the existing system and/or limited market socialism, whereas the Chinese reform moved beyond those schemes and embraced large-scale marketization and privatization. The Chinese reform model was particularly influenced by the East Asian NICs (South Korea, Taiwan, Hong Kong, and Singapore) surrounding China. These countries practice developmental capitalism characterized by a growth-oriented authoritarian system, an autonomous economic bureaucracy, cooperation between the pubic and private sectors, and an export expansion strategy. When China started its reform in the late 1970s, the gap between its command economy and developmental capitalism appeared unbridgeable. In the 1980s, Deng spearheaded the introduction of the market without endorsing the revival of private enterprises, hence socialist market economy. After Tiananmen, however, the communist regime realized the utter importance of economic performance for its political survival, and began tearing down the last ideological defense against capitalism. Private enterprises were openly encouraged and legally protected. At the same time, one still saw the state's visible hand behind the rise of new industries and enterprises. The communist state designates strategic industries, manipulates resource allocation, and practices industrial policy. In this way, China has grown more and more like its NIC neighbors by adopting developmental capitalism. Socialism as an ideal has been closeted, although still paid lip service, while the mechanism of totalitarian control is maintained and refined. In this sense, one can characterize China as a post-totalitarian capitalist developmental state. This model is similar to the Soviet experience only on its post-totalitarian side.

Developmental capitalism is derived from the East Asian NIC experience and has little to do with the trajectory of a Leninist regime. In short, one finds in the Chinese case a blending of two distinctive models: post-totalitarianism from the Soviet Union and Eastern Europe, and developmental capitalism from East Asia.

Another major difference between the Chinese model and the Soviet/ Eastern European experience resides in the retirement policy of party and government officials. The Soviet/Eastern European model was characterized by static equilibrium, allowing a secure political career for cadres and job security for managers. The Chinese model, on the other hand, aimed at securing reasonable growth (although not to the extent of inviting inflation) to guarantee stability or dynamic equilibrium. This means enterprises are under constant market pressure and no managers enjoy tenure. Because preservation of the communist regime is the ultimate goal, economic dynamism is coupled with tight political control. Here one finds the ostensible discrepancy of economic reform and political conservatism. These two phenomena, however, are a logical pair for preserving the rule of the Chinese party-state under technocratic rule. In order to invigorate all levels of political leadership, the Chinese even designed a system of generational replacement whereby senior leaders were retired when they reached a certain age set for specific levels of posts in the party-state hierarchy. Thus, for example, the retirement age for the provincial and ministerial cadres is set at 60, and the age limit for top party leadership is 70. There are exceptions, of course, to those rigid retirement rules, including Jiang's continued presence at the party's Central Military Commission until September 2004. However, forced rejuvenation of the ruling apparatus with the generational replacement principle has become a hallmark of Chinese technocratic rule and sets it apart from the petrification of leadership in the former Soviet and Eastern European communist regimes.

In sum, the Chinese technocratic rule that emerged from Mao's stormy revolutionary politics and Deng's precarious reformism is more open and more adaptable to changing domestic and international environments than its Soviet and Eastern European predecessors. This being said, however, one still needs to recognize that the current Chinese leadership consists of technocratic rulers who are primarily interested in preserving the party-state's monopoly of power with coercion and economic performance, just like their erstwhile European comrades. They are pragmatic, authoritarian rulers separable from the first (revolutionary) and second (reform) leaderships by great differences in age, experience, values, and educational background. Chinese communism has matured into a variant of the East Asian developmental state that is constantly shedding the communist features and adopting the statist ones. However it changes, it remains staunchly authoritarian and undemocratic.

Will China Become Democratic?

Although the communist regimes developed through concrete stages within the basic one-party structure, this does not mean that democratization is impossible in the long run. However, academic discussion on this issue is usually shaped by the current situation, thus projecting into the future a fixed picture of the present.

Discussion of China's political future after the Tiananmen Square protests of 1989 has shifted focus with the apparent increased stability of the communist regime. Although in the immediate wake of the Tiananmen crisis a complete breakdown of the system was predicted, with the consolidation of the post-1989 power structure, less dramatic scenarios have been presented. Among the latter one finds a revival of the neoauthoritarianism theme, which depicts mainland China's future in the light of the East Asian capitalist-authoritarian model, Taiwan and South Korea in particular. Some scholars argue that, although direct democratization is unlikely and even undesirable, a two-step transition through an intermediary phase of enlightened authoritarianism toward the ultimate destination of democracy should be welcomed. China's introduction of competitive (though not multiparty) elections at the village level is seen, from this perspective, as a particularly encouraging sign, which shows mainland China gradually evolving toward political pluralism following Taiwan's model. Since 1949, local economic and political experiments have been used as the basis from which to reorganize China. The introduction of democratically elected villagers' committees thus carries significance far beyond its immediate impact in the rural areas. A dual power structure has been created in which the villagers' committee is developing into a democratic executive apparatus to manage day-to-day politics, while the party branch has come to be responsible for general policy, and it intervenes if "necessary" by using its ties to township or county governments. Optimists predict that power would gradually migrate from the party branch to the villagers' committee and bring the countryside closer to genuine grassroots democracy. Experiments have been conducted that extend competitive elections up to the township level, a sign for further optimism. Finally, there are experiments with democratic election of local party bosses, so that democracy can be pursued without undermining the party's power base. These optimistic opinions are a variant on the theme of the time-honored modernization theory, which predicts a universal pluralistic outcome for authoritarian systems undergoing rapid economic development.

Among the less dramatic scenarios is a reprise of the neoconservatism theme that popped up during the retrenchment period in the early 1990s. In the more rigid political and economic atmosphere after the Tiananmen protests, especially in light of the difficulties facing Russia after its democratic transition, this neoconservative theme emphasizes order and stability and harkens back to traditional values, as opposed to the radical reforms of the previous decade. Neoconservatism argues that social progress is best accomplished through a gradual reform of society. It eschews revolution and the sudden overthrow of government. It is asserted that historically in China progress was always made gradually. Revolutionary ruptures from the past without exception begot disasters, as shown in Mao's Great Leap Forward, the Cultural Revolution, and the Tiananmen protests. Neoconservatives generally support the regime and predict long-term stability under the current system. Which scenario of the three (regime breakdown, neoauthoritarianism, or neoconservatism) is most likely to be China's future? In order to answer this question, we have to move back to the big picture and read again the country's historical trajectory.

China's political development has always been heavily influenced by the global context in which the country found itself. The emergence of the nationalists and communists as the competing political forces in China was embedded in the country's desire to regain its power and rightful place in a challenging international environment. The KMT and the CCP adopted different developmental models from abroad to revive China. Because the KMT regime lost the civil war and has been highly dependent on the United States, its development on Taiwan witnessed a gradual shedding of the statist system and an adoption of liberal-democratic institutions. The mainland moved into a comparable point in Taiwan's past when it realized that the Soviet/Maoist system was totally ineffective for China to compete in the world and for the communist regime to hold onto power. It has decisively shifted to a statist model, with post-totalitarian authoritarian politics and developmental economic policies, and this new model has specific implications that favor the growth of liberalism.

Global competition will force China to maintain its openness to the world and sustain its market reforms. But China will not soon become a democracy. In the short run, the legitimacy of the regime will be buttressed by superb economic performance. In the long run, rapid economic development will nurture social forces that are difficult to contain in an authoritarian political environment, even with the regime keeping post-totalitarian control mechanisms. When China reaches a stage at which economic growth inevitably slows down while at the same time the structural changes go deep enough to arouse strong political participation for liberalization, then the pressure for democracy will greatly increase. As China is not as dependent on a liberal hegemony as Taiwan is, the route toward democratization will take much longer and will encounter greater difficulties. Nevertheless, the possibility of China's becoming a liberal, democratic system should not be dismissed under its current image of a successful, post-totalitarian, developmental state.

China (including Taiwan) made a historical detour away from the original pursuit of liberal democracy in the early days of the Republic of China, through the choice of statist authoritarianism (from the founding of the ROC to the mid-1980s) or communist totalitarianism (post-1949 PRC) as the major development strategy, and finally to the adoption of the liberal formula (Taiwan) or a gradual approach to it (mainland China). China's developmental trajectory has been, to a large extent, determined by a challenging international environment that forces different political actors representing different interests to respond. Urban intellectuals, the KMT, and the CCP spoke for different class interests, opted for different identities, and developed different institutional preferences. The lack of organization and power by the urban intellectuals doomed their effort to bring about a liberal democracy in China in the early years of the republican period. The authoritarian model that the KMT chose was imposed on the country before 1949 but was then transplanted to Taiwan when the KMT lost the civil war to the communists. American pressure and international competition later persuaded the KMT to embrace liberal democracy and abandon its authoritarian past. The Democratic Progressive Party's political ascendancy and the election of its presidential candidate, Chen Shui-bian, in 2000 and 2004 ended the KMT's half-century rule and testify to the democratic maturity of the ROC. On the Chinese mainland, the CCP's 1949 victory foretold the inauguration of a communist-totalitarian regime modeled on the Soviet Union. Ensuing economic disasters and the pressure of international competition prompted the leadership to embrace the authoritarian model (the post-totalitarian variant), but not until the death of Mao Zedong. The natural tendency toward pluralism inherent in market reforms has already planted seeds of political liberalization in China, even though that tendency is now being resisted by a technocratic regime that treasures stability more than anything else and holds fast to its vested interests.

In short, as in other developing countries, different political forces in China competed for ascendancy as the country faced international challenges. Those different political forces represented distinct interests, developed alternative identities, and proposed competing institutions. The outcome of their competition shaped the developmental route of China, and that outcome was, in turn, contingent on the international environment in which China found itself. The momentum for political development in China has derived from its quest for national survival and the rigors of global competition. China differed from other cases in the developing world mainly in the immense dimensions of the country, not in the nature of its response. As such, China's political development can be best understood from a global and comparative perspective, and it is also from this perspective that one can evaluate the possibility of China becoming a democracy in the future.

BIBLIOGRAPHY

Dittmer, Lowell. *China's Continuous Revolution: The Post-Liberation Epoch, 1949–1981*. Berkeley: University of California Press, 1987.

Dittmer, Lowell, and Yu-Shan Wu. "The Modernization of Factionalism in Chinese Politics." *World Politics* 47, no. 4 (1995): 467–494.

Fewsmith, Joseph. *Dilemmas of Reform in China*. Armonk, NY: M. E. Sharpe, 1994.

Friedrich, Carl J., and Zbigniew K. Brzezinski. *Totalitarian Dictatorship and Autocracy*. New York: Praeger, 1963.

Gerschenkron, Alexander. *Economic Backwardness in Historical Perspective*. Cambridge, MA: The Belknap Press of Harvard University Press, 1962.

Gold, Thomas. *State and Society in the Taiwan Miracle*. Armonk, NY: M. E. Sharpe, 1986.

Johnson, Chalmers. *Peasant Nationalism and Communist Power*. Stanford, CA: Stanford University Press, 1962.

Jowitt, Ken. "Inclusion and Mobilization in European Leninist Regimes." *World Politics* 28, no. 1 (1975): 69–96.

Jowitt, Ken. "Soviet Neotraditionalism: The Political Corruption of a Leninist Regime." *Soviet Studies* 35, no. 3 (1983): 275–297.

Lee, Hong Yung. *From Revolutionary Cadres to Party Technocrats in Socialist China*. Berkeley: University of California Press, 1991.

Lowenthal, Richard. "Development Versus Utopia in Communist Policy." In Chalmers Johnson, ed. *Change in Communist Systems*. Stanford, CA: Stanford University Press, 1970.

Lowenthal, Richard. "The Post-Revolutionary Phase in China and Russia." *Studies in Comparative Communism* 14, no. 3 (1983): 191–201.

Meaney, Constance Squires. "Is the Soviet Present China's Future?" *World Politics* 39, no. 2 (1987): 203–230.

Nathan, Andrew. "A Factionalism Model for CCP Politics." *China Quarterly* 53 (1973): 34–66.

Shirk, Susan. *The Political Logic of Economic Reform in China*. Berkeley: University of California Press, 1993.

White, Gordon. *Riding the Tiger: The Politics of Economic Reform in Post-Mao China*. Stanford, CA: Stanford University Press, 1993.

Wu, Yu-Shan. *Comparative Economic Transformations: Mainland China, Hungary, the Soviet Union, and Taiwan*. Stanford, CA: Stanford University Press, 1994.

Wu, Yu-Shan. "Jiang and After: Technocratic Rule, Generational Replacement and Mentor Politics." In Yun-han Chu, Chih-cheng Lo, and Ramon H. Myers, eds. *The New Chinese Leadership: Challenges and Opportunities after the 16th Party Congress*. Cambridge: Cambridge University Press, 2004.

Zheng, Shiping. *Party vs. State in Post-1949 China: The Institutional Dilemma*. Cambridge: Cambridge University Press, 1997.

TABLE 8.3. Key Phases in China's Political Development

Time period	Regime	Global context	Interests/identities/ institutions	Mode of development
1644–1911	Qing dynasty	expansion of Western imperialism	imperial rulers vs. modernizers/ Confucianism/ traditional authoritarian institutions	sporadic reform
1912–1928	Republic of China (rise and fall of warlordism)	rising Japanese imperialism	warlords, KMT, CCP/traditionalism, nationalism, communism/warlord regimes	country in disunity
1929–1949	Republic of China (KMT authoritari- anism)	rising Japanese imperialism and outright invasion	KMT vs. CCP/nationalism vs. communism/ authoritarian developmental state	authoritarian development
1949–1978	People's Republic of China (Maoism)	Cold War	CCP/revolutionary Marxism-Leninism- Maoism/totalitarian state	totalitarianism
1978–1997	People's Republic of China (Dengism)	end of Cold War and globalization	Reforming CCP/socialism with Chinese characteristics/ post-totalitarian party-state, provinces	authoritarian capitalist development
1997–present	People's Republic of China (post-Deng)	globalization	neoconservative CCP/Chinese nationalism/nationalist party-state, provinces	authoritarian capitalist development
1949–1987	Republic of China (on Taiwan, party-state)	Cold War	KMT and business interests/Chinese nationalism/ authoritarian development state	authoritarian capitalist development
1987–present	Republic of China (on Taiwan, democratic)	globalization	pro-unification and pro-independence interests /liberal- democratic values, Taiwanese nativism/state and parties	liberalism and growing Taiwanese nationalism

Note: Rule separates mainland China from Taiwan.

IMPORTANT TERMS

chairman of the Central Committee of the Chinese Communist Party the paramount leader of the CCP from the Seventh Party Congress of April 1945, when that position was instituted, to September 1982, when that position was abolished. Three persons have assumed that position: Mao Zedong, from April 1945 until his death in September 1976; Hua Guofeng, from October 1976 to June 1981, when he resigned at the Sixth Plenum of the Eleventh Central Committee; and Hu Yaobang, from June 1981 to September 1982, when the Twelfth Party Congress abolished the chairmanship.

Chen Yun an important leader in the Chinese Communist Party who was particularly powerful during the First Five-Year Plan period (1953–1957) and during the adjustment period that followed Mao's disastrous Great Leap Forward. Chen was a worker with no formal education when he joined the communist movement. After the founding of the People's Republic of China, Chen became the most important cadre in charge of economic construction. He was purged during the Cultural Revolution but was rehabilitated when Deng Xiaoping came to power in 1979. He then resumed the leading role in directing China's economic reconstruction during 1979–1983. After 1983, he quarreled seriously with Deng and the radical market reformers, insisting on a "birdcage economy," by which he meant that the market should be given somewhat of a free hand, but still within broad parameters set by the state. Chen represented the pro-stability technocrats.

Chiang Ching-kuo son of Chiang Kai-shek, and his successor. He was sympathetic to the communist cause when he was young and spent 12 years in the Soviet Union. Because of his father's anticommunist policy, Ching-kuo was kept as a hostage by Stalin and prevented from returning to China. After his eventual return in 1937, Ching-kuo became an able lieutenant to his father. After the ROC's displacement to Taiwan, Ching-kuo headed the China Youth Corps, the political department in the national army, and the defense ministry. He finally became the premier in 1971 and succeeded his father as the KMT chairman in 1975 and ROC president in 1978. Ching-kuo led Taiwan through the turbulent 1970s, when the ROC faced international isolation and global economic recession. Toward the end of his rule, Ching-kuo initiated political reforms and lifted martial law in 1987. He died in 1988.

Chiang Kai-shek the KMT's supreme leader, who succeeded Dr. Sun Yat-sen in 1926. Chiang led the Northern Expedition to unify China in 1928 and purged the communists from the KMT. He was forced to stop his annihilation campaign against the communists after the Xi'an incident of December 25, 1936, when Chiang Kai-shek was kidnapped. Chiang then led China's resistance war against the Japanese to victory but was defeated by the communists in the civil war that followed. He then led the nationalist government to Taiwan and ruled the displaced ROC in the island country until his death in 1975.

Chinese Communist Party (CCP) founded in 1921 as a part of the international communist movement. From the very beginning, the CCP was heavily influenced by the Communist International, the international organization of Communist Parties founded by Lenin in 1919. Its organization, guidelines, and leadership were to a great extent determined by Moscow. In 1922, the CCP members were instructed by the Soviets to join Dr. Sun Yat-sen's KMT to form a united front against the warlords, powerful individuals who had seized control of land through military might. This KMT-CCP collaboration was short-lived, as the death of Sun and the launch of the Northern Expedition, the military campaign led by Chiang Kai-shek in 1927 intended to unify China under KMT rule, caused an open split between Chiang Kai-shek and the communists over leadership in the revolutionary movement. The communists then organized riots in the rural areas and saw their bases annihilated by the KMT army one by one. The incoming Japanese invasion saved the CCP, as Chiang was not able to concentrate on mopping up the communists. Under the leadership of Mao Zedong, the CCP was able to mobilize peasant nationalism, and it defeated the KMT after the surrender of Japan. The CCP then founded the People's Republic of China in 1949 and it remains the ruling party in China.

Cultural Revolution Great Proletarian Cultural Revolution, the great political upheaval in the PRC that lasted for a decade (1966–1976). Touched off by Mao's effort to regain political influence after the disastrous Great Leap Forward, the Cultural Revolution was ostensibly aimed at uprooting the traditional Chinese culture that was accused of undermining the communist revolution. The concrete targets were party cadres, state officials, and intellectuals whom Mao and the radicals found threatening to their power. Liu Shaoqi, Mao's designated heir and state chairman; Deng Xiaoping, the CCP's secretary general; and many other prominent leaders were purged. During the revolution, the state was paralyzed, the educational system destroyed, and production seriously disrupted. Young students were recruited into the Red Guard brigades and dubbed "rightful rebels" by Chairman Mao. They finally came into serious conflict with the army and were expelled to the countryside for correction. The Cultural Revolution brought unimaginable damage to China, but, paradoxically, it also laid a solid groundwork for the post-Mao reforms, as the disrupted planned economy of China proved much more conducive to market reforms than the more rigid economic system in the Soviet Union and Eastern European socialist countries.

Deng Xiaoping paramount leader of the Chinese Communist Party from 1979 to 1997. Deng was originally a lieutenant to Mao and was appointed the CCP's general secretary in 1956. He was purged during the Cultural Revolution but rehabilitated in 1973, purged again in 1976, and rehabilitated again in 1977. Deng was a pragmatist; thus, he opposed Mao's ultraleft line, which caused his downfalls. However, with the death of Mao, Deng was able to gain political ascendancy and directed China toward a structural economic reform. The inefficient People's Communes were abolished, a limited market economy was introduced, foreign capital was invited, stock markets were opened, special economic zones were set up, industrial ownership rights were restructured, and people's living standards were significantly improved. Deng's economic liberalism, however, does not mean that he was pro-democracy, as witnessed by his order to crush the pro-democracy movement in Tiananmen Square in 1989. Deng died in 1997.

Gang of Four four ultraleftist leaders who were most prominent under Mao Zedong during the Cultural Revolution period. The four were Jiang Qing, Mao's wife and a Politburo member; Yao Wenyuan, Mao's son-in-law and a Politburo member; Vice Chairman of the CCP Wang Hongwen; and Vice Premier Zhang Chunqiao. They formed a faction against the old cadres, such as Liu Shaoqi, Zhou Enlai, Deng Xiaoping, and Chen Yun. After Mao's death in September 1976, the Gang of Four attempted to seize party leadership but was thwarted by Hua Guofeng. They were arrested in October and put on trial for high treason.

general secretary the top leader of the Chinese Communist Party. From the Fourth (January 1925) to the Fifth Party Congress (April 1927), Chen Duxiu was the general secretary of the CCP. After the KMT purged the communists, Qu Qiubai, Xiang Zhongfa, Chin Bangxian, and Zhang Wentian assumed that position successively before Mao Zedong discarded it at the Seventh Party Congress in 1945 and led the CCP as chairman of its Central Committee. However, the Eighth Party Congress reinstituted the title of general secretary and elected Deng Xiaoping to fill the position, which was reduced to that of chief lieutenant to the party chairman and in charge of the secretariat, rather than that of the party's paramount leader. After Deng's purge during the Cultural Revolution, the position was again abolished. At the Twelfth Party Congress of 1982, Hu Yaobang was elected general secretary, ostensibly the top job in the CCP, as the chairmanship had been abolished, but Hu was still beholden to Deng, who was then the paramount leader of the party. Finally, Zhao Ziyang (October 1987) and Jiang Zemin (June 1989) were elected general secretary under Deng's auspices. With the death of Deng, general secretary again became the most important position in the party, a situation that changed when Jiang retired at the Sixteenth Party Congress in 2002 but managed to keep the post of chairman of the party's military commission. The new secretary general, Hu Jintao, had been designated Jiang's successor by Deng when the old patriarch was still alive. With the partial succession of Jiang by Hu in 2002, the new secretary general was nevertheless still beholden to his predecessor, until Jiang's full retirement in 2004. Hu was reelected secretary general at the Seventeenth Party Congress in 2007.

Great Leap Forward Mao's greatest economic adventure. During the First Five-Year Plan period (1953–1957), the PRC adopted the Soviet model and built a centrally planned economy to boost economic growth. Toward the end of that period, serious bottlenecks developed and Mao was impatient. His solution was to mobilize human labor through ideological agitation and plunge the whole population into production campaigns. The goal was to surpass Europe and the United States in industrial production. The Great Leap Forward brought unprecedented famine and the death of three million Chinese people.

Hu Jintao secretary general of the CCP since the Sixteenth Party Congress of November 2002 and president of the People's Republic of China since the Tenth National People's Congress of March 2003. Hu assumed the post of chairman of the powerful Central Military Commission of the party in September 2004. Hu was designated Jiang's successor by Deng and promoted to the all-powerful Politburo Standing Committee at the Fourteenth Party Congress in 1992 as its youngest member. Prior to his transfer to the PBSC, Hu was a graduate of the prestigious Tsinghua University and trained as a water-conservancy engineer. He spent a great amount of time serving in leading posts in China's remote provinces of Gansu, Guizhou, and Tibet, and he headed the Communist Youth League of China. He is the core of the fourth-generation leadership and a quintessential technocrat.

Hu Yaobang one of Deng Xiaoping's major lieutenants during the reform era, whose death in 1989 touched off unprecedented massive demonstrations for political reform in Tiananmen Square. Hu first succeeded Hua Guofeng as the CCP's chairman in 1981; then, at the Twelfth Party Congress in 1982, he was elected secretary general of the party. From 1982 to 1986, Hu faithfully executed

Deng's reform policies and earned himself a liberal reputation. However, Deng considered Hu too soft toward dissident intellectuals, and in January 1987 he was removed from the position of general secretary.

Jiang Zemin former secretary general of the CCP and successor to Zhao Ziyang. Jiang was the CCP's Shanghai party secretary when the Tiananmen incident broke out in June 1989. He was chosen to replace Zhao Ziyang because he had been successful in combining economic reform with a tough political stance against "bourgeois liberalism" in both December 1986 and June 1989 without resorting to force. Jiang's strengths also included his being an outsider and not beholden to any of Beijing's entrenched factions. He took the position of chairman of the party's military commission in November 1989, and he was elected president of the PRC in 1993. After the death of Deng Xiaoping in February 1997, Jiang's leading position in the CCP became indisputable. He was replaced by Hu Jintao as secretary general at the Sixteenth Party Congress of November 2002. His other positions in the government and in the army were also taken over by Hu in the next two years.

Kuomintang (KMT) or Chinese Nationalist Party, the ruling party in the Republic of China until May 2000. The KMT had its precedents in *Xingzhonghui* (Society for Regenerating China) and *Tongmenghui* (Society of Common Cause), the two revolutionary organizations aimed at overthrowing the Qing dynasty. After the founding of the ROC, Dr. Sun Yat-sen first transformed *Tongmenghui* into a parliamentary party, the Nationalist Party, and then remade it into the Chinese Revolutionary Party when he saw no hope of practicing democracy in a China plagued by warlord politics. In 1919, Dr. Sun again transformed the Chinese Revolutionary Party into the Chinese Nationalist Party (Kuomintang, KMT) and then in 1924 reorganized it on the Soviet model. The new KMT was equipped with a centralized party organization, special departments targeting specific groups in the population, and the National Revolutionary Army. After the death of Dr. Sun, Chiang Kai-shek became the paramount leader of the KMT and, in that capacity, dictated politics in the ROC. When the ROC was displaced to Taiwan in 1949, Chiang continued to lead the KMT-ROC party-state until his death in 1975, after which his son Ching-kuo assumed the party's leadership. In 1988, Ching-kuo died and Lee Teng-hui took over. Lee Taiwanized the KMT and led the party to victory in all of the major elections on the national level after having successfully democratized the ROC. The March 2000 presidential election defeat of the KMT's candidate, Lien Chan, threw the party into disarray. That debacle was repeated in the March 2004 presidential election in which Lien was for a second time defeated by his DPP (Democratic Progressive Party) opponent, Chen Shui-bian. The KMT remained the major opposition party in the ROC.

Long March the retreat of the communist forces of Mao Zedong from the nationalist army after the annihilation campaign of 1934. After the communists had been purged from the KMT in 1925, the CCP organized riots and set up many "Soviet regions." The KMT then launched five annihilation campaigns against them. In 1934, the largest Soviet region in Jiangxi was overrun by the KMT troops, and the communists were forced to flee from their base with the nationalist army in hot pursuit across southwest China over the most difficult terrain with the most hostile environment. After the Long March, Mao's forces ultimately settled in Yan'an of Shan'xi Province.

Mao Zedong leader of the Chinese Communist Party from 1935 until his death in 1976. Mao espoused an unorthodox strategy of revolution in China that emphasized the importance of the peasants and land reform and the need to "encircle the cities from the countryside." That strategy at first found no favor with the party leaders, but after the Moscow-sponsored leadership had failed to thwart the KMT's onslaught in 1934 and the whole party had been forced to flee, Mao captured the military leadership at the Zunyi Conference in 1935. Mao's strategy brought about the CCP's victory over the KMT, and he became the party chairman. After the founding of the People's Republic of China, Mao continued to apply his guerrilla-warfare strategy to economic development, causing the famine and destruction of the Great Leap Forward. His refusal to give up power was followed by his launch of the Cultural Revolution, which threw China into a decade of political chaos. Mao died in 1976.

People's Republic of China (PRC) the socialist country founded in 1949 and ruled by the Chinese Communist Party. The PRC has had five paramount leaders of the country and the CCP since its founding: Mao Zedong (1949–1976), Hua Guofeng (1977–1978), Deng Xiaoping (1979–1997), Jiang Zemin (1998–2004), and Hu Jintao (2005–). During Mao's rule, the PRC had a totalitarian regime. Since Deng, however, the country has gradually shifted to an authoritarian system.

Politburo the organ in the Chinese Communist Party where the real power resides. The CCP follows the Soviet model in its power structure. Ostensibly, the Party Congress is the source of ultimate power in the party. However, under the practice of Lenin's "democratic centralism," the real power migrates to the Central Committee, which the Congress elects, and then to the Politburo, which the Central Committee elects. The Politburo is headed by the general secretary and is composed of the highest-ranking officials from the party and the government. The Politburo has a Standing Committee, which assumes the power of the Politburo when it is not in session. The current (Seventeenth Party Congress) Standing Committee of the Politburo is composed of nine members: Hu Jintao, Wu Bangguo, Wen Jiabao, Jia Qinglin, Li Changchun, Xi Jinping, Li Keqiang, He Guoqiang and Zhou Yongkang. These people are the most powerful leaders in the PRC.

Qing dynasty the last imperial dynasty in China (1644–1911). The Qing dynasty was founded by the Manchus, who originally lived in the northeastern part of China outside the Great Wall (Manchuria). In the middle of the seventeenth century, they invaded the Ming Empire to the south, captured the capital city of Beijing, and established their own rule all over China. The original emperors of the Qing dynasty – Kangxi, Yongzheng, and Qianlong – were able rulers who contributed greatly to the consolidation of the Manchu reign in China. When the Western powers arrived, however, the Qing dynasty was already showing signs of decline but was able to survive military defeats at the hands of foreigners, unequal treaties, domestic rebellions, and a bankrupting economy for the next 80 years. In 1911, the Qing dynasty was overthrown by a revolutionary movement led by Dr. Sun Yat-sen.

Republic of China (ROC) the country founded in 1912 by Dr. Sun Yat-sen. The ROC suffered from warlord politics and did not reach genuine political unification until after the Northern Expedition (1925–1928) led by Chiang Kai-shek. After the communists defeated the nationalists in the Chinese civil war, the ROC retreated to Taiwan, an island province off the eastern coast of China. From the

1950s to the 1980s, Taiwan was an authoritarian country with a thriving market economy. Since the late 1980s, its political system has been democratized.

State Council the central government of the People's Republic of China. The State Council's predecessor was the Government Administrative Council, headed by Zhou Enlai, which was set up in 1949. After the 1954 constitution was promulgated, the Government Administrative Council became the State Council, and Zhou remained the premier until his death in 1976. The State Council is headed by the premier, who is usually the second most important person in the PRC.

Sun Yat-sen the founding father of the Republic of China, who led a revolutionary movement to overthrow the Manchu (Qing) dynasty in 1912. When the ROC disintegrated into warring regions, Dr. Sun founded the Kuomintang (KMT), built a power base in the southern province of Guangdong, and began inviting Soviet advisers to his camp. He died in 1925 before China was unified under the KMT.

Third Plenum of the CCP's Eleventh Central Committee the historic party meeting held in December 1978 that ushered in the reform era in post-Mao China. At the meeting, Deng Xiaoping saw his political influence greatly expand as his lieutenants were elected to the Central Committee, and his line, the "four modernizations," was substituted for Mao's "treating class struggle as the major link." Hua Guofeng's authority as paramount leader was undermined with the institution of a collective leadership. The CCP's historians treat the Third Plenum as the turning point in the party's development. It signifies the shift from the totalitarian stage to the reform stage in China's post-1949 political development.

Three Principles of the People Dr. Sun Yat-sen's political philosophy of nationalism, democracy, and people's livelihood, with the last principle denoting a pragmatic program that emphasizes the combination of private entrepreneurship and active state involvement in economic development. This doctrine is by nature a liberal program for reconstructing China. It is enshrined in the constitution of the Republic of China.

Tiananmen incident the massive student pro-democracy movement of June 1989 and its brutal suppression. Deng Xiaoping's reforms during the 1980s opened up China to the world, but rapid economic growth was accompanied by omnipresent corruption and rising expectations for greater political liberties. Fluctuations in the economy fueled public dissatisfaction, and students became inspired by Western, especially U.S., democracy. Hu Yaobang's death and the visits to China by U.S. President George Bush and the Soviet communist party leader Mikhail Gorbachev also came into play. The convergence of these factors in the summer of 1989 brought Beijing's college students to the streets and to Tiananmen Square, demanding fundamental political reforms. After a protracted stalemate between the students and the authorities that lasted for a month, martial law was declared and the troops moved in on June 4. Great casualties running in the thousands were reported.

Zhao Ziyang one of Deng Xiaoping's major lieutenants, who from 1983 to 1989 was mainly in charge of economic reform. Zhao succeeded Hua Guofeng as premier in 1980. After the purge of Hu Yaobang in 1987, he was promoted to general secretary of the CCP. His "soft" attitude toward the students in the summer of 1989 cost him his job. After the June 4 suppression of the pro-democracy movement, Zhao was replaced by Jiang Zemin.

Zhou Enlai China's prime minister from 1949 to January 1976. Zhou was a senior CCP leader who directed the political department at Whampoa Military Academy in 1924–1925, that is, during the first KMT-CCP collaboration. Zhou was very close to the Communist International but was wise enough to side with Mao Zedong at the Zunyi Conference in 1935, at which Mao took military leadership of the party. After 1949, Zhou became prime minister of the new government, a position he held until his death in 1976. Zhou is remembered for his restraining influence on Mao during the Cultural Revolution period and for his diplomatic sophistication outside China. In 1973, Zhou rehabilitated Deng Xiaoping, a move that later proved critical in bringing the totalitarian phase of China to an end after the death of Mao.

Zhu Rongji Chinese prime minister from 1998 to 2003. Zhu was a technocrat by training who rose in Beijing's state hierarchy until his critical tendency got him into trouble during the 1957 antirightist campaign, after which he was purged. Deng Xiaoping's political ascendancy brought Zhu back to the official arena, and he advanced rapidly until he was mayor of Shanghai. There he executed Deng's plan to build China's most important window to the world. He was promoted to vice premier during Deng's famous Tour to the South that relaunched economic reform following the conservative retrenchment period of 1988–1991. In March 1988, he was elected premier to replace Li Peng.

STUDY QUESTIONS

1. What kind of developmental strategy did the Kuomintang take on the Chinese mainland? Was it an effective response to the international challenge that China faced at that time?

2. Dr. Sun Yat-sen originally attempted to build China on the liberal model. Why and how did he abandon that model?

3. How was the first KMT-CCP collaboration formed and dissolved?

4. How did the Japanese invasion and the Chinese civil war alter China's developmental strategy?

5. Discuss the similarities and dissimilarities between political development in the PRC and in the Soviet Union.

6. Explain China's post-1949 political turbulence in terms of the conflict between the party and the state and in terms of the shift from transformation to reform.

7. How did Deng Xiaoping's reform agenda conflict with Chen Yun's emphasis on stability in the post-Mao period?

8. How do you place Taiwan's democratization in the general framework of China's political development?

9. Discuss the possibility of China's democratization.

10. Was China unique in its response to international challenges during the twentieth century?

STOP AND COMPARE

EARLY DEVELOPERS, MIDDLE DEVELOPERS, AND LATE DEVELOPERS

If it makes sense to group Britain and France as early developers and Japan and Germany together as middle developers, comparativists feel that it makes even more sense to group Russia and China together as late developers. Not only did both countries industrialize only in the twentieth century, but both also experienced communist revolutions and have lived with the long-term burdens of communist economic and institutional development. While Russia cast off its communist political institutions and ideology in 1991, it continues to search for a viable path into the capitalist world. Moreover, after initially moving in the direction of democracy after 1991, in the past five years Russia's rulers have become increasingly authoritarian. China, on the other hand, has retained its communist political structures but has done so while rapidly introducing capitalist economic institutions in important parts of the economy. These are the ironies that we examine in the case of the late developers.

LATE DEVELOPERS: RUSSIA AND CHINA

Compared with its European neighbors, Russia entered the twentieth century as a politically and economically backward country. As the core region of the tsarist empire, Russia had neither a constitution nor a working national parliament. Instead, Russia's tsar, Nicholas II, ruled as his father and grandfather had – as an autocrat unchecked by the power of law or political opposition. The privileged nobility served the tsar and lived in a moral and political universe separate from that of the masses of powerless and impoverished peasants. Nor did Russia have a consolidated sense of its own nationhood; one look at a map was enough to see that the empire consisted of well over one hundred different ethnic groups and languages. Its economy was still primarily agricultural, despite some serious efforts to modernize agriculture and initiate industrialization in the latter part of the nineteenth century.

311

In fact, several of Russia's earlier rulers had attempted modernizing reforms. Peter the Great (1680–1725) had introduced modern technologies acquired in the West and had even built a new capital city, St. Petersburg, on the Gulf of Finland, replete with the best Italian and French architecture of the day, as a tangible symbol of Russia's Western orientation. Catherine the Great (1762–1796) had welcomed significant elements of Enlightenment rationalism and European thinking into imperial administration. Alexander II had freed the peasant serfs in 1861 with the intention of unleashing the social energies of ordinary Russians in order to harness them for economic development and military competitiveness.

The problem with all of these reforms, however, was the deep ambivalence Russia's rulers felt toward them. The tsars wanted the military and technological advances that reforms and economic development might bring, but they feared the kinds of social and psychological changes in the population that occurred in France and ultimately led to revolution. Over time, as the rest of Europe was democratizing, this contradiction grew more intense: Military competitiveness required economic development; economic development entailed adopting Western technologies, methods, and ideas; but Westernization appeared to lead inexorably toward some kind of political liberalization – something that all tsars resisted until the very end.

Even within Russian society, there was ambivalence about embracing the experience of the West. During the nineteenth century, some parts of the intelligentsia wanted to preserve distinctive Slavic traditions and were thus dubbed "Slavophiles." Others looked to the West and hoped one day to force a rupture with the nobility, who dominated political life, and the Orthodox church, which dominated the spiritual life of Russia – and were thus labeled "Westernizers." The Westernizers themselves were split between those who wanted liberal democracy and those who wanted a distinctively socialist form of industrial modernity. Yet even among the socialists, there was a further split. The Mensheviks wanted to come to power democratically and the Bolsheviks wanted a revolution and to construct a communist society. Which path Russia would ultimately take became the burning question of the nineteenth and early twentieth centuries.

The Russian Revolution of November 1917, led by Lenin and his Bolsheviks, answered this question for the better part of the twentieth century. Although the Bolsheviks wanted to build a new kind of society, they still had to build this society in a world of hostile countries, and they were thus confronted with some of the same challenges that faced their tsarist predecessors. How could a first-rate military be built on the resources of a less-than-second-rate economy? Unlike their tsarist forebears, however, the Bolsheviks faced a further dilemma. How could all of this be done without capitalist markets and be made into something called "socialism" or "communism"? Lenin died too early to deal with these questions, but his successors were forced to deal with little else.

Lenin's successor, Stalin, undertook what some comparativists have called a second revolution and created distinctive communist economic and political institutions in the successor to the Russian empire, the Soviet Union. The Communist Party became the sole ruler of the country, agriculture was collectivized, and the economy was transformed into a command economy, planned and administered from Moscow (which, perhaps tellingly, had become the new capital after the revolution). The net result of the revolution was to create a totalitarian dictatorship that succeeded in rapidly industrializing the country and creating a huge military-industrial complex. As we now know, this could only be accomplished at a tremendous price in terms of lost lives and wasted resources. After Stalin's death, successive Soviet leaders, once again like the Russian tsars of earlier eras, sought ways to improve the economy and compete with the West without dismantling the distinctive communist political and social order.

The last Soviet leader, Mikhail Gorbachev, undertook what was perhaps the most important set of communist reforms. He too failed, but implemented important political changes (his economic programs were utter nonstarters) that permitted society to mobilize against the Communist Party. In 1991 the Soviet Union broke up and Russia emerged as a smaller but formally democratic state. Once again, however, in some respects Russia finds itself in the position it was in before it embarked on the failed communist experiment – a country that is trying to catch up to the West using institutions, methods, and ideas not of its own design. The added burden, however, is that the legacy of the Lenin-Stalin system has made democratic and capitalist transformation exceedingly difficult for Russia's postcommunist leaders. With so many obstacles to successful transformation, Russian politicians have been tempted to cast aside democratic institutions altogether in favor of a return to more familiar hierarchical and authoritarian forms of political rule.

Like Russia, China also experienced a communist revolution. But China continues to be ruled by a Communist Party that has overseen a stop-and-go series of economic reforms over the last 15 years that have led to spectacular rates of economic growth, accompanied by new social tensions. The reasons for the divergence in experience between the two countries are to be found in the very different legacies of the global past.

Comparativists are quick to point out that unlike Russia, which had always viewed itself as embedded within the broader European culture, China has always understood itself as culturally distinct from Europe. And for good reason, too. Chinese culture is far older than Europe's, and for centuries China remained isolated from the outside world. Under successive Confucian rulers China had managed to create an impressive form of bureaucratic rule based on an educated elite. These rulers were not subject to democratic control, but they did face the threat of overthrow if the mandarin and gentry elite felt that they had lost the "mandate of heaven" to govern their country.

The imperial order lasted for centuries but was ultimately destabilized by its encounters with the industrialized West. Over the course of the nineteenth century, the Western powers forced China to open a number of its port cities to foreign merchants and trade. Chinese imperial bureaucrats brought this access into question in 1842, when the British were forbidden to market opium to the Chinese population. In response, the British successfully waged war and secured for the next century foreign domination of China's economically important coastal regions. British imperialism in the region ultimately paved the way for Japanese imperialism, which culminated in the Japanese invasions and atrocities of the 1930s and 1940s.

Military pressures and internal fragmentation brought down the last Chinese emperor in 1911. Initially, after the emperor's departure, China was united under an alliance of the Nationalist Party (the Kuomintang) and the Chinese Communist Party (CCP), but the alliance collapsed in 1927 in a bloody rupture between the two partners. The CCP, although it was nominally a Marxist party and thus could be expected to look for support among the urban proletariat, fled to the countryside where it worked closely with the peasant masses and perfected its unique contribution to revolutionary theory: the conduct of a guerilla war. The leader of the CCP, Mao Zedong, established his base in the countryside among the disaffected and the outlawed. Faced with increased military pressure from the Kuomintang, in 1933 thousands of Communists abandoned their base in Jiangxi to begin their Long March of 7,000 miles, a forced retreat that decimated the ranks of the party (only 8,000 of the original 100,000 arrived at the end) but also provided a formative, steeling experience for the Communist elite.

At the end of World War II in 1945, the Japanese fled the country and the civil war between the Nationalists and the Communists resumed. With the support of the majority of the peasants, who in fact constituted the vast majority of all Chinese, the CCP won the war in 1949 and the Nationalists were forced to flee to the island of Taiwan. The People's Republic of China was proclaimed on October 1, 1949. The CCP could look to the Soviet Union for a model to emulate, but they could easily look to their own "heroic" past to justify carving out their own path. Although important aspects of the Soviet model were adopted, the CCP under Mao's leadership pursued policies that were at times much more radical than in the Soviet Union (the Great Leap Forward and the Cultural Revolution). After Mao's death in 1976, the reformist-direction branch of the party emerged dominant, and under Deng Xiaoping's leadership the CCP ushered in several waves of successful marketizing economic reforms and a broad opening to international market forces. At the same time, the party has retained tight control over political life and has forestalled any move toward democracy. The comparison with the Soviet communist experience is highly instructive. Whereas the Soviet Communist Party fell because it democratized before it marketized, part of the secret of the Chinese Communists' capacity to retain control has been their willingness to marketize their economy without democratizing their politics.

Yet, after much dissatisfaction with the democratic politics in the 1990s, Russia's political elite under President Vladimir Putin turned back to its much older and more embedded traditions of top-down rule. Communism has not returned, but by the time of the presidential election of 2008 Russia appears to be much more of an authoritarian country than a democratic one. As long as energy prices remain high and export earnings can subsidize living standards, Russia's population seems content to revert to some form of state-led market economic development. In short, as the first decade of the twenty-first century draws to a close, the Chinese model seems to have won out and the two great countries of the Eurasian landmass have ended up at basically the same place despite having taken different initial paths after the demise of communist central planning.

STOP AND COMPARE

PART FOUR

EXPERIMENTAL DEVELOPERS

UNITED STATES OF AMERICA

Tijuana

Ensenada

Ciudad
Juárez

Gulf of California

Guaymas

Chihuahua

M

Topolobampo

Nuevo Laredo

La Paz

Monterrey

Matamoros

*Gulf of
Mexico*

E

Durango

X

Mazatlán

I

San Luis Potosí

Tampico

Cancún

Puerto Vallarta

León

Tuxpan

Mérida

*Gulf of
Campeche*

Guadalajara

C

PACIFIC

Mexico City ⊛

Veracrus

O

Manzanillo

OCEAN

Lázaro Cárdenas

Oaxaca

Coatzacoalcos

BELIZE

Acapulco

*Gulf of
Tehuantepec*

GUATEMALA

MEXICO

| 0 | 100 | 200 | 300 | 400 | 500 miles |
| 0 | 100 | 200 | 300 | 400 | 500km |

CHAPTER NINE

Mexico

Anthony Gill

Introduction

January 1, 1994, will be remembered as an important date in Mexican history. As Mexicans celebrated the beginning of the new year, two events occurred that marked profound changes in the country's political development and would eventually lead to a significant shift in the country's balance of political power. First, the **North American Free Trade Agreement** (**NAFTA**) took effect. This treaty integrated Mexico's economy more closely with those of the United States and Canada, marking the end of a nearly seven-decade strategy of sheltering Mexico from the vagaries of global markets. Pressures from international investors and trading partners to create greater economic openness dramatically affected (and continue to affect) Mexico's domestic institutions and day-to-day politics. The day's second memorable event made this readily apparent. As Mexico's President **Carlos Salinas de Gortari** was celebrating the new year and the implementation of NAFTA at a cocktail party, he received word that a major guerrilla insurgency had erupted in the southern Mexican state of Chiapas. A revolutionary organization known as the **Zapatista National Liberation Front (EZLN)** (or Zapatistas) was demanding greater political participation and a solution to the dire economic plight of poor rural farmers.

That the guerrillas attacked on the same day NAFTA took effect was no accident: The Zapatistas considered Mexico's increased integration into the world economy a threat to the economic well-being of the majority of Mexico's rural population, most of whom are of indigenous origin. Once considered to be part of Mexico's national identity – a blend of pre-Columbian and Spanish heritage – the majority of Zapatista supporters asserted their ancient cultural origins as part of a subnational identity that divided Mexico along racial and ethnic lines.

The insurgency also shook the foundations of Mexico's political institutions, long considered one of the developing world's most stable polities. The Zapatista rebellion highlighted a growing trend in contemporary Mexican politics – the rise of political instability and the breakdown of one-party rule. Throughout 1994, Mexico witnessed a rash of political assassinations, including that of the ruling party's presidential candidate. Protests against the government, rare before 1980 but on the increase since the mid-1980s, became almost daily occurrences. Social turmoil alarmed many international and domestic investors, who began to withdraw their money from the country. By the end of the year, Mexico had undergone a major economic crisis that further exacerbated social tensions. The impact of this conflict was felt internationally. Fearing that other countries in Latin America would experience similar socioeconomic problems, foreign businesses scaled back their economic connections to the region, increasing unemployment and affecting the economic policies in such countries as Argentina, Brazil, and Colombia. As many Mexicans fled to the United States in the hope of finding better economic opportunities, anti-immigration pressure influenced election results in California, Texas, and other states. Clearly, the international environment has played an important role in shaping the domestic political identities, institutions, and interests of Mexico. Likewise, Mexico's developmental path has equally affected the politics of countries abroad.

To many comparative political scientists, the events of 1994 indicated a profound change in Mexican politics, culminating in the election in 2000 of the first opposition-party candidate to be elected president of Mexico. Throughout most of the twentieth century, a single party – the **Institutional Revolutionary Party** (**PRI**) – dominated Mexican politics. Although Mexico was technically a representative democracy with regular elections throughout the past century, the PRI dominated nearly all elected offices, tightly regulated social organizations, and dampened real political competition. To the extent that the PRI was able to promote rapid economic growth and rising standards of living, the party retained popular support among the citizenry. This popular support translated into an unprecedented level of political stability. Whereas most other countries in Latin America were experiencing turbulent oscillations between democratic and authoritarian rule, or facing serious revolutionary challenges, Mexico had maintained a peaceful transfer of power among national and local rulers since 1920, longer than a number of European countries, such as Germany and Italy.

The socioeconomic and political turmoil of the 1990s eventually culminated in the election of **Vincente Fox**, the first candidate from an opposition party – the **National Action Party** (**PAN**) – to win the presidency since the 1920s. Moreover, it was Mexico's first peaceful transition of presidential power to an opposition leader since the late 1800s. And, for the first time in eight decades, the dominant Institutional Revolutionary Party (which existed under different names during its history) no longer held a clear majority in the national legislature. These results marked a crucial point in the country's political development and were hailed internationally as a major step toward a competitive, multiparty democracy. Mexicans continued taking further steps down this path with clean legislative elections in 2003 and a tightly contested presidential election three years later. In the 2006 election, the PAN's candidate inched past the leader of the leftist coalition not associated with the traditionally dominant PRI, signaling that the one-party system of the past is now likely buried. Despite this movement toward competitive democracy, most of the socioeconomic problems that beset Mexico during the last two decades of the twentieth century persist, and new political dilemmas have emerged. In a political system that in the past encouraged a strong presidency, Vincente Fox found himself constrained by a limited term in office, no clear majority in the legislature, and a bureaucracy that is still staffed by members of the PRI who have no clear interest in seeing him succeed. Whether, and how, Mexico is able to overcome these obstacles will have a profound effect on the governing institutions of Mexico for decades to come. In light of this turbulent history, this chapter addresses the following questions: How was Mexico able to maintain such a high degree of political stability over the past century? Why did this political stability come under such intense pressure during the 1990s, and what factors led to the breakdown of single party rule? Will there continue to be a peaceful transfer of power between rival political parties at all levels of government, or will political and social chaos ensue? Answers to these questions will tell us more about Mexico's political history and help us to understand how the global context shapes domestic interests, identities, and institutions and how these give rise to varying types of developmental paths.

Historical, Social, and Ideological Origins

As seen in Chapter 1 of this text, political systems evolve from the choices and actions of earlier political actors. Previous institutional arrangements, entrenched interests, philosophical mind-sets, and the international environment help fashion a country's contemporary political institutions and social identity. Reflecting on the past is thus crucial for understanding the present. For Mexico, the obvious point of historical departure starts with the Spanish Conquest in 1521 (see Table 9.1 at the end of the chapter). This does not imply that indigenous societies had no role in shaping political and social arrangements in the Western Hemisphere. Several pre-Columbian social and political structures were adopted by the Spanish conquerors (conquistadors) to subjugate the indigenous populations. Indigenous cultures also play a complex role in shaping Mexican political identities (for example, in the way they view themselves in relation to the polity). In part, Mexicans pride themselves on a general identity that blends the country's Spanish and indigenous heritages. Yet, indigenous populations have not been fully incorporated into national life. The difficult economic problems facing these communities, particularly in southern Mexico, continue to promote social tensions. Nonetheless, when tracing the history of Mexico's contemporary political landscape, one can see that the forceful imposition and near-total dominance of Spanish institutions make the conquest a conventional starting point.

The Colonial Period

The roots of the contemporary Mexican political system date back to the sixteenth-century invasion by Spanish conquistador Hernan Cortes. With his defeat of Aztec emperor Montezuma in 1521, Spain's distinct style of colonial governance prevailed over the territory of New Spain for exactly three centuries. The colonial period had three important effects on modern Mexican political life. First, it laid the ideological bedrock of **corporatism**, the core philosophical framework guiding Mexican political life. Corporatism refers to a system of government wherein the state officials are viewed as being responsible for closely regulating and coordinating various economic and social groups within society including businesses, labor unions, agrarian co-operatives and even cultural groups. Second, the centralized and top-heavy political structures established by the Spanish monarchy provided comparatively little opportunity for self-governance in the colonies, resulting in political instability and an all-out war for power following independence in 1821. Third, labor relations and landholding patterns established during the colonial era set the stage for future economic and political problems.

The cultural framework that came to dominate Mexico's national political identity emanated from the intersection of a strong religious tradition (Catholicism) and a political philosophy (corporatism). This line of thinking viewed society as an organic whole: Individuals belonged naturally to a variety of functional social groups (for example, craft guilds, clergy, aristocracy). Although each of these groups may have dissimilar interests, all are needed for the harmonious operation of society. It stands to reason that the interests of the entire body politic should come before the interests of any particular component. Politically speaking, the needs of the state take precedence over the specific desires of any single group or individual within the state; groups exist to serve the state, not vice versa.

The institutional impact of this worldview was a statist, patrimonial style of government. For the body politic to function properly, so the argument ran, a centralized entity needed to mediate any potential conflict between social groups. The most effective way to do this is to have the state determine which interest groups are socially vital and then regulate their operation. Rather than allowing for the autonomous, grassroots organization of individuals with distinct interests, the state itself organizes, grants legitimacy to, and absorbs these groups into the decision-making apparatus of society. It also has a tendency to promote rigid class distinctions while downplaying the possibility of social mobility.

Corporatism, in the Mexican context, reflects a "top-down" strategy of interest aggregation, a process directed by the state wherein political leaders determine what groups receive official recognition and how they operate. Contrast this with the bottom-up approach of classic liberalism, in which spontaneously formed interest groups emerge and function autonomously. This latter philosophy, a product of the English Enlightenment, emphasizes individual (not group) rights and views competition among autonomously organized interests as healthy for the economy and polity. The fact that Spain tried to keep its colonies isolated from such ideological influences had a long-term impact on Mexico's political identity and institutional design. Yet despite the predominance of this corporatist ideology, Mexican politics could not remain completely immune to liberal ideas. The struggle between the corporatist and liberal worldviews is an ongoing theme in Mexican political history and is still playing itself out today.

In terms of social interests, the primary motivation driving colonization was the enrichment of Spain, particularly in relation to its European rivals. Although mineral wealth (for example, silver) was highly prized, the Spanish crown also taxed other economic production (for example, cotton and sugar), with the goal of increasing royal wealth. Given the distance between the crown and the colonies, ensuring the proper amount of revenue flow back to Madrid was a difficult task. Colonists had a competing interest in keeping as much wealth as possible for themselves, and thus they tried to hide their wealth from royal tax agents. The political institutions established to govern the colonies reflected an attempt to minimize the problem of wealth extraction for Spain.

The colonies were also governed with an eye toward ensuring that local officials remained strictly loyal to the crown. Only individuals born in Spain were appointed to the highest levels of colonial government. Each official served a specified term and then returned to Spain. Inasmuch as poor administration was punished on return, the rotation of colonial officials in this manner ensured a high degree of loyalty. To enhance it further, the monarchy conducted regular audits of colonial administrators. The Catholic Church was also under the control of the king and was used to keep watch over both colonial officials and citizens (specifically by the Holy Office of the Inquisition). Although relatively complex in nature, the system of colonial administration was far from perfect. The social structure of the community often dictated that even high-ranking officials court the favor of the colonists. Because it was difficult to supervise the behavior of colonial officials completely, corruption was common and, up to a point, even tolerated by Spain.

Despite tight control by Spain, colonists were granted a limited degree of self-governance. Municipal councils (**cabildos**), staffed primarily by individuals born in the colonies, administered the day-to-day activities of town life (for example, issuing building permits). These local councils later became the locus for the independence movement. However, it is important to note that the *cabildos* were relatively isolated from one another and were in no position to provide unified national leadership. Therefore, when Spain eventually did withdraw from Mexico, no strong centralized institutions existed to replace the colonial administration. The inevitable result was that the post-independence period would be one of substantial political uncertainty and instability.

The final consequence of the colonial period for the contemporary era relates to the pattern of land tenure and the resulting social-class relations. To encourage the conquest and settlement of New Spain in the mid-1500s, the Spanish monarchy had granted large tracts of land to conquistadors and the Catholic Church. These land grants typically included access to the labor and tribute of indigenous communities. The result of this pattern of land tenure and labor relations was the creation of a rigid class structure and a serious maldistribution of wealth that closely paralleled racial cleavages: **criollos** (individuals of pure-blooded Spanish descent) typically have occupied the upper classes, *indigena* the lowest classes, and mestizos (mixed blood) in between. As the indigenous population has tended to be concentrated in southern Mexico, economic and political tension has had a strong geographic component to it. Under such conditions, trying to construct a fair and just governmental system that represents the interests of all Mexicans and creates a common national identity has proven to be an enormous challenge. With criollos claiming higher economic status than the *indigena*, interest-based conflict has frequently inspired clashes over cultural identity.

From Independence to Revolution

INDEPENDENCE AND THE ERA OF THE CAUDILLOS

Comparative political scientists understand that seemingly distant international events can have very important effects on domestic political arrangements. Mexican decolonization is a prime example. Both material interests and ideological influences emanating from abroad provoked the separation of Mexico from Spain. The seeds of Mexican independence were sown during the seventeenth-century decline of Spain. With the Spanish fleet unable to seal off New Spain from foreign ships (primarily French and British), contraband trade increased. Colonists began to get a taste for economic life beyond

Spain's exploitative system. In 1700, a new royal dynasty, the Bourbons, attempted to reverse Spain's imperial decline. The central goal of the Bourbon Restoration was to rebuild Spain's influence in European affairs. Achieving this meant extracting greater amounts of revenue from the Americas. To this end, Charles III (1759–1788), the most influential Bourbon monarch, initiated a series of economic and political reforms. He promoted intracolonial trade, which spurred economic activity and increased Spain's colonial tax revenue. The king also tightened administrative control over the colonies by introducing a more rigorous bureaucratic arrangement borrowed from France. The plan was an overall success, and the colonial economy boomed. Despite their resentment over the effective collection of higher taxes, most colonists benefited economically from the reforms. Nonetheless, political tensions erupted as many of the Spanish bureaucrats sent to administer the king's affairs replaced or marginalized local administrators. Just as in the U.S. War of Independence, "taxation without representation" stirred discontent with Spain among the Mexican populace.

The final series of events that sparked the drive toward independence had their origins in Europe. In 1808, French troops invaded Spain and imprisoned Charles IV (1788–1808). Confusion reigned as to who had final authority in the colonies: the deposed king? the king's colonial administration? the local *cabildos*? A small number of criollos influenced by European liberalism and the U.S. and French revolutions declared independence. Colonists loyal to the crown immediately quashed this liberationist movement and arrested all involved. A more significant challenge came in 1810 from two renegade Catholic priests – Padres Miguel Hidalgo and José Maria Morelos. Following a severe economic crisis in 1809, they rallied a significant peasant army around the symbolic banner of the **Virgin of Guadalupe** – an apparition of the Virgin Mary seen by an indigenous man in 1531. Given the dark, indigenous complexion of the Virgin, this apparition became one of the most important symbols of Mexican nationalism, reflecting the country's unique blending of European (Catholic) and indigenous cultures. The lower-class rebellion inspired by Hidalgo and Morelos, who were eventually captured and executed, lasted nearly five years. Many landholders and urban criollos, fearing a radical peasant rebellion, allied with the royalists. This caused independence to be delayed by a decade.

The path toward independence followed a circuitous route. Once French troops had withdrawn from Spain, Ferdinand VII (reigned 1808, 1814–1833) took the throne and increased military assistance to New Spain in a relatively successful effort to extinguish lingering separatist forces. However, just when it appeared that the independence movement had been defeated, events in Spain intervened to turn the tide. Under pressure from the Spanish Parliament, Ferdinand VII endorsed a liberal-inspired constitution in 1820. Frightened that similar liberalizing tendencies would infect New Spain, many conservative, pro-royalist forces abandoned their support of the king and opted for Mexican sovereignty. Mexico's independence thus had a decidedly conservative, antiliberal tinge. Instead of a liberationist movement promoting the democratic ideal, the newly separated Mexican state declared itself a constitutional monarchy under the reign of Emperor Augustin de Iturbide (who abdicated in 1823, returned to the throne in 1824, and was assassinated in 1824).

The monarchy did not last long. Several events conspired to bring it to an end in 1823. First and foremost was a serious economic crisis facing the new nation. Eleven years of war had destroyed most of the revenue-producing assets in Mexico, including mines, livestock, and cropland. The financial capital and entrepreneurial skill needed to restart the economy had fled to a safer haven in Spain. War casualties had depleted the source of skilled labor. Lacking a strong economy and tax base, the government found itself bankrupt. Even if the economy had been able to jump-start itself, the state lacked the institutional capacity to collect taxes. Because central administrative authority was largely in the hands of Spaniards at the turn of the nineteenth century, this bureaucratic capacity vanished when those officials fled. The paucity of internal transportation networks further meant that centralizing control over an expansive territory would be an impossible task. Attempts to rein in autonomous localities met with fierce resistance. Unable to raise revenue, the new regime could not finance basic governmental functions, including the salaries of military officers and troops. Criticism of the monarch grew rapidly, forcing him to resign in 1823 under the threat of a military coup and civil war.

Iturbide's abdication marked the beginning of a cycle of political instability known as the "era of the **caudillos**." (Caudillos were independent military leaders who commanded localized armies.) The most famous (perhaps notorious) was **Antonio López de Santa Anna**, who ruled Mexico directly nine times and manipulated the choice of the presidency on numerous other occasions. The pattern of political instability during this period followed a typical cycle: A sitting president would discover the government was bankrupt and be forced to cut back on military expenditures, including salaries and troop levels. With a stagnant economy, unemployed soldiers and officers were unable to find work. Discontent spread rapidly among the military, provoking a coup d'état. The new president would find himself in the same situation as the previous one and the cycle would be repeated.

All told, there were roughly 50 separate administrations from 1821 to 1860. This was hardly the environment for any single model of government, let alone democracy, to flourish. Nor was this a suitable context for the forging of a national identity, although the long-term effect of this chaos was a preference for more corporatist (in contrast with liberal) forms of government. The anarchic nature of this period allowed for the rise of local political bosses (**caciques**), who firmly resisted attempts to centralize national authority in any meaningful sense. To this day, the "culture" of the caciques persists, as current administrations have difficulty implementing policies without first considering the interests of local power brokers.

International pressures aggravated Mexico's political chaos. Foreign powers could easily take advantage of the country's weakened domestic position. Primary among these foreign interlopers was a young, expansionist United States. Settlers from the United States began occupying the Texas region in 1821, the year of Mexico's independence. Although Texans were technically citizens of Mexico, efforts by Mexican authorities to make them accountable to central rule led the settlers to call for secession. Tensions escalated as U.S. settlers quickly outnumbered native Mexicans. Domestic U.S. pressure to annex Texas eventually provoked a war in 1846. With Mexico in political disorder, the United States won the war and roughly half of Mexico's national territory (extending from present-day Texas to California and Washington State).

The United States was not the only foreign power to play a role in complicating Mexico's political development. Several European powers, most notably France, also intervened. Financial interests were at the heart of the conflict. With the national treasury essentially empty from the first days of independence, various Mexican administrations had found it difficult to make restitution for damage done to foreign property during the wars of independence. Nor could the government repay foreign loans used to fund day-to-day administrative operations. In 1861, the Mexican government, facing a serious fiscal crisis, suspended payment on foreign debts owed to Britain, France, and Spain. These three powers responded by occupying Mexican ports to collect customs duties as repayment. French ambitions, however, extended beyond this action. Emperor Louis-Napoleon Bonaparte opted for an all-out invasion of the country and installed an Austrian aristocrat, Ferdinand Maximilian Joséph, as president. The French intervention lasted for three years (1864–1867) until Mexican armed forces prevailed in ousting Maximilian. Such intervention only aggravated the country's political instability, retarding the creation of viable political institutions.

THE ASCENDANCY OF LIBERALISM

Foreign occupation and war were not the only international influences to shape the Mexican polity. An ideological "invasion" also proved decisive in Mexico's political history. Along with increased contraband trade in material goods during the latter half of the eighteenth century, new ideas began to filter into the region. Increased contact with Britain, France, and the United States following independence further exposed many Mexican elite to new streams of political thought. The philosophies of the English Enlightenment and French Revolution, with their emphasis on citizens' liberties and rights, contrasted with conservative, corporatist thought that gave primacy to the state over the individual. Throughout the nineteenth century and for the first several decades of the twentieth, the struggle for a national political identity involved the efforts of liberals to graft their ideological beliefs onto a culture heavily influenced by medieval Catholicism.

The conflict between liberalism and corporatism resulted, during the 1800s, in a bloody contest between two factions – **Liberals** and **Conservatives**. The former sought to build a political system based upon many of the same precepts as the U.S. Constitution. Mexico's first constitution (1824) divided national government among three branches – legislative, executive, and judicial. A bicameral legislature further balanced the geographical interests of states (two senators per state) with representation based on population (one deputy per 8,000 people). The document also promoted a federalist system that distributed power away from the capital, Mexico City, and toward local governments. Subsequent constitutions of 1836, 1857, and 1917 were based on this earlier document and kept a preference for liberal political institutions. Liberals also favored moving Mexico toward a more secular society and pursued anticlerical reforms to restrict the Catholic Church's cultural, political, and economic power. Conservatives, alternatively, preferred centralized government based upon a strong executive. Their philosophical identity owed more to the corporatist thought of medieval Catholicism than to the English Enlightenment. It was their defense of the Catholic Church that most differentiated Conservatives from their Liberal counterparts.

Although the political instability of the 1800s took on the veneer of a great battle between competing worldviews, the ideological basis for conflict during this period should not be overestimated. Interest-based struggles over personal power prompted constant turnover in presidential administrations. Politics became a "winner-take-all" game; daily survival in office took precedence over achieving long-term philosophical goals. Over time, Liberals and Conservatives became virtually indistinguishable in their economic policy preferences, with both favoring export-oriented growth and trade relations with Europe and the United States. Politically, Liberals abandoned their federalist pretensions and opted for centralized government, which allowed them to rule a large territory more effectively. This was most evident during **La Reforma** (1855–1876), when Liberals finally dominated their Conservative rivals. Dominance did not imply political stability, however. This period included a major civil war (1858–1861) and the French occupation of 1864 to 1867. The most prominent politician during this period was **Benito Juárez**, a pure-blooded Zapotec Indian who demonstrated that although upward mobility was very difficult for the indigenous, it was not impossible. (Juárez's heritage is often championed as evidence of the strong indigenous influence in Mexico's cultural identity.) Juárez, a Liberal, realized that Mexico needed a strong, centralized government to end the internecine warfare that had torn the country apart since independence. He concentrated power in the presidency against his own liberal principles calling for a strong legislature. In doing this, Juárez became the first president to complete a constitutionally prescribed term in office (1867–1871) and provided the country with its most stable governance to date. This lesson was not lost on future leaders. Ruling Mexico meant maintaining centralized political institutions. Under Juárez's presidency, business investment became a reasonably safe activity and the economy began to show signs of growth.

THE PORFIRIATO

President Juárez's successful completion of his presidential term raised the hope that a stable rule of law had finally arrived in Mexico. Unfortunately, personal hostilities erupted during Juárez's next term in office, which ended prematurely with his natural death. The resulting succession crisis gave way to a harsh dictatorship under Porfirio Díaz from 1876 to 1911, a period known as the **Porfiriato**. Although ruthless, the dictatorship did have a beneficial side. For 35 years, Mexico experienced unprecedented political stability and economic growth, bolstered by a favorable global context. Industrial growth in Europe and the United States fueled demand for raw materials. Rising commodity prices boosted Mexico's domestic economy and helped fill state coffers. Government tax revenue, along with U.S. and British foreign investment, was used to build Mexico's infrastructure. Railroads were built, ports modernized, and the national bureaucracy expanded. Because Britain had no interest in expanding its empire into the Americas, and the United States was pursuing a policy of relative isolation, direct foreign intervention in Mexican affairs was minimal. Expansionary desires of other countries were kept in check by the Monroe Doctrine, a U.S. policy designed to prevent European encroachment into the Americas.

Porfirio Díaz also left his mark on Mexico's political landscape. He was the first of Mexico's rulers to unify Mexico effectively under central authority for any extended period. He accomplished this by means of shrewd manipulation of military appointments, the buying off of local political bosses (caciques), and the creation of a separate police force directly loyal to his authority. Despite ideological loyalty to the liberal constitution of 1857, which provided for a strong legislative branch, Díaz further concentrated institutional power in the executive branch. Since that time, the Mexican president has enjoyed political power above and beyond what is legally prescribed.

The Porfiriato's final legacy was to establish a style of rule that has been used to guarantee political stability to the present day – ***pan o palo***, the rule by "bread or club" – meaning the dual use of patronage and coercion. With increased revenues flowing into the treasury during the economic boom, Díaz bought the loyalty of various towns and constituencies. Important members of the elite received lucrative positions in the governmental bureaucracy in exchange for their support. Hence, Díaz earned his legitimacy not by appealing to the will of the majority but by being able to deliver the goods. The liberal goal of popular sovereignty gave way to the corporatist manipulation of political support. Alternatively, those individuals or groups not willing to cooperate with the policy directives of the president were dealt with by the heavy hand of the police.

Although dissent was not permitted, it could not be entirely prevented. The economic prosperity of the late 1800s gave rise to a new set of middle-class interests. Although generally pleased with the economic management of the country, middle-class professionals began demanding greater political participation, something that their brethren in other Latin American countries were enjoying at that time. With Díaz nearing his eightieth birthday, many anticipated that the dictatorship would soon end and lead to a liberalization of Mexican politics. Díaz himself heightened these expectations by announcing in 1908 that he would not run for office in 1910. Positioning began in earnest for the upcoming presidential campaign, with Francisco Ignacio Madero as an early favorite. As the election neared, Díaz changed his mind and Madero found himself in prison for mounting an effective opposition campaign. Díaz's rigged electoral victory in 1910 unleashed the **Mexican Revolution**.

Politics in the Twentieth Century: Revolution and Institutionalized Rule

THE MEXICAN REVOLUTION

The Mexican Revolution began as another conflict over presidential succession, something to which Mexicans had grown accustomed. The ideological rhetoric of the initial rebellion mirrored the liberal leanings of the 1800s, with a call for representative democracy coupled with checks and balances on executive power. Early on, revolutionary leaders attempted to institutionalize the classic liberal tenets contained in the 1857 constitution. However, the Mexico of 1910 was very different from what it was just 30 years earlier. New social classes, such as urban labor, had arisen, and existing ones (especially the rural peasantry) had grown politicized. These groups brought to the political arena a new set of interests – a desire for higher wages, better working conditions, social welfare, and access to arable farmland – that political institutions needed to capture. A new global ideological climate also shaped the course of the revolution; in Europe, socialist ideals began to challenge the underlying logic of liberal capitalism. The Russian revolutions of 1905 and 1917 provided further examples that the peasantry and urban labor were becoming a major force for social change and could not be ignored in any new political arrangements. Many of those participating in the revolution wanted not only liberal political institutions but also major social reforms aimed at bringing the lower classes into a ruling coalition. Such demands radicalized the revolution and gave form to the resulting **Constitution of 1917** and the corporatist institutions it would spawn.

With the disappearance of Díaz's effective system for holding the country together, internal chaos again reigned. The initial coalition that brought Madero to power began unraveling. Accusing Madero of failing to carry out his promised social reforms, a rebel from southern-central Mexico, **Emiliano Zapata**, declared war on the Liberal administration. An attempt to suppress this rebellion by relying on one of Díaz's former generals backfired, and Madero was overthrown in a counterrevolution supported by the Catholic Church and the U.S. government. Another faction, led by Venustiano Carranza (northern Mexico's governor and a landholder), toppled this counterrevolutionary regime with the help of Zapata. Unhappy with Carranza's reluctance to implement progressive policies, Zapata's forces marched on Mexico City and forced a number of radical reforms that resulted in the drafting of a constitution in 1917. This new constitution included provisions for workers' rights to unionize, exclusive national ownership of mineral wealth, and communal land redistribution. These provisions represented a step beyond classical liberalism's preference for individual rights and established a basis for a modern corporatist system that gave the state enhanced powers in regulating social conflict. Much of the contemporary political strife in Mexico relates to efforts by recent presidents to rescind these social duties and move the country back to a more liberal framework.

The consolidation of the modern Mexican state began in 1920, the year typically viewed as the end of the revolutionary transition. That year marked the beginning of the peaceful transfer of power between presidential administrations and the return of political stability. The decade from 1924 to 1934 saw the emergence of another presidential strongman, Plutarco Calles. Calles became the first president to implement the revolution's most radical promises, including the distribution of nearly eight million acres of land to communal farms (*ejidos*) and the organization of labor into government-sponsored unions. Other social policies, including increased wages, better sanitation, and health programs, were also implemented. All of this was made possible by a relatively strong global economy that allowed Mexico to increase its exports of raw materials and attract foreign investment.

Despite the progressive social policies undertaken by Calles, the actual political working order that emerged was far from the liberal-democratic ideals contained in the 1917 constitution. Dissidents were jailed and the press censored. Calles's governing strategy closely resembled the *pan o palo* methods of Porfirio Díaz. Indeed, the heavy reliance on patronage networks by a centralized presidency to win social support and legitimacy is one of the main reasons Mexico's political system remained stable and free from military intervention from the 1920s to the present. Coercion (*palo*) became less needed as time wore on because rapid economic growth guaranteed that the patronage strategy (*pan*) would work effectively. In effect, the legacy of the revolutionary era was the forging of a new mode of governance for Mexico – one that synthesized the basic political elements of liberalism (for example, elections, popular sovereignty) with the corporatist mode of operation (that is, top-down social organization, increased political centralization). Although corporatism came to dominate liberalism, the blend of these two forms of government represented a political system that was uniquely Mexican.

THE REVOLUTION INSTITUTIONALIZED

The figure most credited with shaping the Mexican political system into what it is today is **Lázaro Cárdenas**. As president from 1934 to 1940, he institutionalized the corporatist philosophy of government. However, the revolutionary process had radically transformed the philosophic basis of corporatism. The corporatism of the nineteenth century was inherently conservative and exclusionary, seeking to preserve the socioeconomic organization of a bygone colonial era. Political participation by those other than the landed elite was strictly forbidden, and class relations remained static. The corporatist philosophy underlying Cárdenas's political arrangements, on the other hand, was progressive and inclusionary. It sought to transform Mexico into a modern industrial nation by organizing, coordinating, and controlling the social groups that would build the nation. Government would be pro-worker and pro-peasant. The state would try to tame the ravaging effects of "raw capitalism" and build a nation free from foreign influence. Under Cárdenas, Mexico had finally achieved a strong national identity based on a unique blend of liberalism, corporatism, and socialist ideas.

Economically, Mexico's international position prescribed a more state-centric approach to development than the Anglo-American model of capitalism. Being an industrial latecomer placed several constraints on the country's ability to achieve a modern economy. Most of what Mexico wanted to produce domestically was already being produced more efficiently in the United States and Europe. Mexican entrepreneurs were at an inherent disadvantage because domestic consumers would invariably prefer less costly, higher-quality goods manufactured abroad. No incentive existed to engage in entrepreneurial activity unless the state stepped in to guarantee businessmen domestic markets (via protective tariffs) or to subsidize their production costs. It is ironic that providing business with domestic markets meant creating a consumer base for manufactured goods because this, in turn, meant promoting higher wages for urban and rural workers, a situation that businesses try to avoid in order to protect their profits.

The political tumult that ravaged the country for nearly a century meant that there was little private capital to provide the impetus to build factories.

Given the high start-up costs of building heavy industry in the mid-twentieth century, few Mexican citizens had the financial capacity to invest in large-scale industry. As in other cases of late development, such as Russia and China, the state would become the main vehicle for raising and investing capital. Mexico's industrialization was promoted extensively by a combination of state-owned enterprises and state subsidization of preferred industries. Overall, this general economic strategy was known as **import-substituting industrialization (ISI)**. The component parts of ISI included high import tariffs on manufactured consumer goods, financial subsidies to private business, overvalued exchange rates (to reduce the costs of producer imports), and state ownership of industries with high capital costs (for example, electrical power and steel). Unionization and higher wages were promoted and a welfare system created to provide a consumer base for domestically produced goods. Import-substituting industrialization was common throughout Latin America and other parts of the developing world (for example, Iran) during the mid-twentieth century and was largely a reaction to the Great Depression and World War II, when these countries were cut off from the manufactured goods traditionally provided by Europe and the United States. Although ISI policies were designed essentially to promote autarkic development, the lack of domestic capital inevitably meant courting foreign investment.

The Revolutionary Party, created under President Calles, became Cárdenas's institutional vehicle for achieving political stability and industrialization. The Mexican Revolutionary Party – later renamed the Institutional Revolutionary Party (Partido Revolucionario Institucional, known by its Spanish acronym, PRI) – was created as an autonomous entity to mobilize the population in support of Cárdenas's reformist agenda. Cárdenas structured the party around three organizational pillars, each representing an important social sector: (1) the Mexican Workers' Confederation (CTM), representing urban industrial labor; (2) the National Peasant Confederation (CNC), representing rural workers and the *ejidos*; and (3) the National Confederation of Popular Organizations (CNOP), composed of white-collar professionals, government bureaucrats, and small entrepreneurs. Each of these organizations was given representation in the policy-making apparatus of the party and, hence, the government. (The PRI was the only party to hold national office from 1934 to 2000.) However, because the party's top leaders chose the officials of these organizations, the PRI became the epitome of inclusionary corporatism. The ruling party organized societal interest groups from the top down, and political loyalties were based on "corporate," not geographic, identities. Autonomous groups that arose over the years were absorbed into the corporatist structure, ensuring that the government maintained tight regulatory control over popular interests.

A fourth organizational body, representing the armed forces, was also created. Cárdenas's early incorporation of the military into the party proved crucial to ensuring his immediate political survival. By currying the favor of officers and troops with substantial pay raises, educational opportunities, and other benefits, he prevented his rivals from using the army to plot against him. More importantly, these actions institutionalized civilian control over the armed forces, something historically rare in Latin America. In large part, Cárdenas's actions during the 1930s prevented Mexico from falling prey to the intermittent coups and military dictatorships that plagued South America for most of the 1960s and 1970s. The military reforms proved so successful that when the PRI disbanded the official organization representing the military in 1940, no military revolt ensued.

The institutionalization of labor, the peasantry, and the middle class into the ruling party became the crucial defining feature of Mexican politics for the next six decades. By connecting each social sector to the party, Cárdenas ensured enormous popular support for the PRI and set the stage for a single-party state. Relying more on *pan* (patronage) than *palo* (coercion), Cárdenas won the long-term loyalty of the Mexican lower classes. He dramatically improved urban working conditions and promoted the unionization of more than a million workers. During his presidency, roughly one in three Mexicans benefited from land reform involving nearly 50 million acres. The majority of land went to communal *ejidos*, which received privileged loans and technology from the government, further ensuring their political support. Finally, the incorporation of government bureaucrats, teachers, and lawyers into the PRI meant that the state and the Revolutionary Party would become virtually indistinguishable.

Cárdenas also instituted many of the political practices that became standard fare over the next several decades: He extended the presidential term to six years. The president, as head of the PRI, would nominate his successor. Patronage benefits to privileged groups, controlled almost exclusively by PRI officials, increased in the months preceding a national election. Government-organized labor received higher wages, business groups were granted subsidies, and public works projects sprang up in rural communities. This increased spending prompted a period of inflation leading up to the election. Following national elections, the outgoing president would undertake deflationary policies so that the new president could begin his term with the task of rebuilding the economy. In many respects, this pattern represented a classic "political business cycle" of inflation and recession, determined by the electoral calendar.

Cárdenas also institutionalized a number of other political practices that made the Mexican system uniquely stable. Retiring presidents left office quietly and avoided interference in political matters. Power continued to be concentrated in the presidency; the Senate and Chamber of Deputies served as a rubber stamp for the policies of the executive. Although the CNOP, CTM, and CNC were supposed to be involved in the policy-making process, they fell under the increasing dictate of party leaders. Government and party officials decided when and where labor could strike or make demands on employers. Assistance to rural communities was conditioned on unswerving support of the PRI. Reasonably fair elections were held, but real political competition was minimized. All of this combined to ensure the electoral dominance of the PRI and gave the state a quasi-authoritarian flavor. Although outsiders may be quick to criticize the lack of effective democracy in Mexico, it should be remembered that the institutionalization of one-party rule in Mexico gave the country something it had long lacked – political stability. This in turn provided the basis for rapid and sustained economic growth until the 1980s.

The final legacy of the Cárdenas era was his reaction to the international political and economic environment. Mexico had always been at the mercy of foreign powers, either militarily or economically. This changed during the 1930s. The 1938 nationalization of 12 foreign-owned oil companies not only signaled a country seeking to control its own economic development but also was a high point in the creation of a Mexican national identity. Antiforeign (particularly anti-U.S.) sentiment increased noticeably. The economic policies of ISI were a natural extension of this growing nationalism as Mexico sought to become industrially self-sufficient. Despite being located adjacent to the world's foremost superpower, the Mexican government exercised a substantial degree of autonomy in its economic and foreign policy. Mexico became a leading member of the nonaligned, developing nations during the Cold War and frequently criticized U.S. foreign policy in Latin America.

The reforms of the Cárdenas era were politically and economically successful, and they benefited from a favorable international climate. When manufactured imports from Europe and the United States slowed to a trickle during the Great Depression and World War II, Mexican industry developed to fill the supply gap. The war also created a high demand for oil and other primary commodities in the world market. Political stability further boosted the domestic economy, and the country entered an era of unprecedented growth known as the "**Mexican Miracle**" (circa 1940–1980). Gross domestic product grew at an average annual rate of over 6 percent, an unprecedented feat in Latin America. Accounting for population growth, per capita income increased approximately 3 percent per year. Within two short decades (1950–1970), living standards doubled.

Presidential succession continued peacefully for the next six decades, and the PRI held onto the major institutions of power. Although much of the PRI's dominance can be attributed to its control over important government resources and manipulation of patronage to loyal constituents, the party's popularity was also due to the nation's strong economic performance. The Mexican single-party system maintained a high degree of popular legitimacy. This is not to say that economic gains were distributed evenly. Over time, the actual policies of the government began to deviate from its revolutionary rhetoric and the redistributive legacy of Cárdenas. Large private industries

not included in the 1930s corporatist arrangement gained an increasingly privileged position among policy makers. Contrary to the nationalist intentions
of ISI, Mexico increasingly depended on foreign investment to fuel economic
growth. Nonetheless, economic growth and political stability became mutually reinforcing. As long as the economy stayed healthy, the PRI was able
to "buy" the support of most major social groups, and a politically dominant
PRI ensured a stable social environment that was attractive to domestic and
foreign investors. Despite outward appearances of durability, however, the
corporatist system built under Cárdenas was fragile. If either the economy
or the PRI faltered, the political system as a whole would become vulnerable
to crisis. This is exactly what happened during the 1980s and 1990s. Fortunately, unlike the collapse of other civilian regimes throughout Latin America
that ended in military dictatorships from the 1960s to the 1980s (Chile, for
example), Mexico managed to deal with its political and economic crises with
a peaceful transition to an opposition party in the year 2000.

THE FORMAL INSTITUTIONAL STRUCTURE OF MEXICAN POLITICS

At this point, it is worthwhile to review the general institutional structure of
Mexican politics in the late twentieth century. These institutions were largely
laid down in the 1917 constitution, although they have undergone some modifications since the 1970s. As noted earlier, Mexican politics between the
1920s and the late 1990s was determined by the informal politicking that
went on within the dominant PRI. With single-party rule and the president
and his close advisers controlling the party, most of the formal constitutional
rules of politics held little sway. The Mexican Congress was largely a rubber
stamp for presidential decrees, and the judiciary served to bolster executive dominance by posing little challenge. However, with the breakdown of
the corporatist control of the PRI and the rise of real electoral competition,
the rules establishing these governing institutions will undoubtedly take on
greater importance.

The 1917 constitution provided Mexico with a federalist and presidential
form of government similar in structure to the U.S. Constitution, although
with important procedural differences. First, in keeping with the historical
regional fragmentation of the country, Mexico is divided into 31 states,
and each state has a relative degree of autonomy in setting policy relevant to regional interests. Second, political power was divided among three
branches – executive, legislative, and judicial – each of which was to retain
institutional autonomy from the others. The president initially was to be
elected by popular vote every four years, although this provision was modified
under President Lázaro Cárdenas to extend to a six-year term. The memory
of Porfirio Díaz dominating the presidency for an extended period of time
created a strong desire to impose a strict, one-term limit on the president.
Unlike the case in the United States, the Mexican political system does not

have a provision for a vice-president. In the event that the president is unable to fulfill his term in office, the national legislature (Congress) is empowered to appoint an interim president, with a call for a new general election if the president is incapacitated during the first two years of his term. If the president's incapacitation occurs in the final four years of his tenure, the appointed interim president will serve the remainder of the term.

The national legislature, known as the Congress, is divided into two chambers – the Chamber of Deputies (lower house) and the Senate (upper house). Members of the former are elected for three-year terms via two methods of election. Three hundred members of the Chamber of Deputies are elected via plurality rule (first past the post) in single-member districts. The remaining seats are selected via proportional representation with a provision guaranteeing seats to any party able to garner at least 2.5 percent of the vote. Initially, only 100 seats were to be selected in this manner, but bowing to increased pressure for representation by minority parties, the number of seats allocated by this method was expanded to 200 in 1986. The Senate originally consisted of two senators from each state and an additional two from the federal district of Mexico City. A 1993 constitutional reform doubled the number of senators to 128. This reform again represented a concession to minority parties who were calling for greater representation in a system dominated by the PRI. Currently, three of the senators from each state are elected via plurality rule, and the fourth seat is guaranteed to the minority party receiving the highest number of votes. Both deputies and senators are restricted to serving only one term in office.

Finally, the judicial branch of government was designed originally to be an autonomous check on the legislative and executive branches of government. Twenty-six judges, appointed by the president and confirmed by the Senate, sit on the Supreme Court and serve lifetime terms. Despite this guaranteed tenure, a norm developed wherein all Supreme Court justices would proffer their resignation following a presidential election, allowing the new president to retain the justices he desired and appoint any new people from his political coterie. A series of federal circuit courts exist below the Supreme Court, and judges within these courts are appointed by the Supreme Court. Not surprisingly, the courts did not function according to institutional design; instead of being a check on government abuses, the judicial system only served to strengthen and legitimize a top-heavy presidential system.

The Crisis of Corporatism during the Late Twentieth Century

Mexico's political development since the 1980s, defined by the historical tension between liberalism and corporatism, has been a battle of interests as well as identities. Following decades of social turmoil, top-down corporatist institutions proved best at reducing political conflict and promoting rapid industrialization. In turn, the Mexican Miracle financed the corporatist system. But miracles rarely last forever. Political stability and economic growth gave rise to new social interests and demands for a liberalized political system. Addressing these demands was easy when the economy was strong and government resources plentiful. However, changes in the world economy during the 1970s seriously limited state access to the resources needed to keep patronage-based corporatist arrangements intact. With the PRI finding it financially difficult to fulfill its corporatist obligations, groups that were once loyal constituents began organizing independently and seeking help from new political parties. The ruling party's rule is no longer guaranteed, and corporatism is giving way to demands for political liberalization. How Mexico negotiates its transition from a single-party, corporatist state to a liberal-pluralist democracy, if it does so at all, is the central problem facing the country today.

ORIGINS OF THE CRISIS

Mexico's political foundation began to show cracks during the late 1960s. Just as economic growth during the late 1800s gave rise to new social interests that prompted the Mexican Revolution, the Mexican Miracle created new social interests that demanded reform of the country's corporatist institutions. Among these new demands were greater autonomy for local governments, the ability to organize groups independent of government ties, and alternative (non-PRI) political representation. Such demands appeared first in the wealthy industrial and ranching states of northern Mexico. The central government's corporatist policies worked against northern interests by directing patronage resources away from them and toward the more populous central and southern regions. Defending their economic interests meant promoting electoral competition; if PRI power were challenged in the region, the central government would be required to respond to northern interests. In 1965, candidates from the center-right National Action Party (Partido Acción Nacional, PAN) won two mayoral elections in the prosperous state of Baja California, Norte. The ruling PRI, unfamiliar with such a challenge, nullified the elections, marking the first time that fraudulent tactics were used openly to retain power. Political liberalization might favor the industrial north, but it was not in the interests of the ruling party. Corporatism still trumped liberalism.

University students also began to call for political change. A booming economy created an expanding middle class; more youths were attending college and expecting professional careers. However, the closed political and economic system of the time could not adapt to meet these heightened expectations of a rapidly expanding population. Frustration among students ensued. Inspired by campus unrest in the United States and Europe, they began to agitate for expanded civil liberties. These protests boiled over just before the opening of the 1968 Olympic Games in Mexico City. The spark was a brawl among high school students that prompted local government officials to call riot police in a massive show of force. Police overreaction enraged students, who then demanded police reform and expanded civil liberties. The well-organized student protesters eventually mobilized the largest antigovernment rally in Mexican history, involving some 500,000 people. Unfortunately, a two-month series of protests ended with government troops firing on demonstrators in the **Tlatelolco** district of Mexico City, killing more than 100 civilians (and perhaps upward of 400). The Tlatelolco massacre showed that popular support for the corporatist political system was waning.

By the early 1970s, the economy also began to show signs of stress. Import-substitution industrialization encouraged inflation, currency overvaluation, and a serious balance-of-payments crisis. Inflation ate away at the real wages of most Mexicans. More importantly, the corporatist institutions designed to give workers and small farmers a voice in government (for example, the CTM and *ejidos*) increasingly became a way to repress their demands. The government discouraged workers from striking and implemented policies favoring business interests. The government also promoted large-scale, capital-intensive farming for export, which markedly slowed the pace of land redistribution between 1940 and 1970. Disaffected peasants responded by invading private lands. Contrary to nationalist rhetoric, foreign investment gained a noticeable presence in the economy, causing resentment among local workers and small businesses.

The social unrest of the late 1960s challenged Mexico's corporatist system but did not break it. President Luis Echeverría (1970–1976) responded to this discontent by increasing wages, distributing more land to the rural poor, and permitting the autonomous organization of labor. His administration also allowed limited civil protests. Bowing to pressure for increased political representation, Echeverría's successor, José López Portillo, enacted legislation in 1977 that guaranteed opposition parties 100 seats in the Chamber of Deputies based on proportional representation. These reforms represented a limited "democratic opening" and raised expectations for future liberalization.

The corporatist system survived due in large part to the oil crisis of the 1970s. Mexico, an oil-exporting nation, benefited from the dramatic rise in petroleum prices beginning in 1973. Revenue from the state-owned petroleum industry flowed into the national treasury, where it was used to alleviate economic hardship caused by a global economic slowdown. Additionally, the flood of Middle East "petrodollars" on world financial markets allowed the Mexican government to borrow abroad. Increased government revenue prompted more state intervention in the economy as the state began to nationalize hundreds of firms. In turn, the expansive economic reach of the government provided more avenues for distributing patronage in the form of jobs, preferential loans for favored businesses, and subsidies to important rural clientele. Because Mexico's political stability was built upon the PRI's extensive patronage networks, oil revenue and foreign loans bolstered the survival of the corporatist system during a time of growing popular discontent.

POLITICAL CHALLENGES IN THE 1980s AND 1990s

The same global economic system that provided the financial liquidity to keep corporatism afloat during the 1970s served to undo the system during the 1980s and 1990s. Relying upon oil revenue and foreign loans to buy domestic political support was at best a temporary solution for Mexico's socioeconomic ills. Loans required repayment, and reliance on petroleum for the bulk of government revenue was an inherently risky strategy. Two international events during the late 1970s and early 1980s made this strategy unworkable and sent shock waves through Mexico's political system. First, to combat soaring inflation at home, the U.S. Federal Reserve raised interest rates between 1979 and 1982. Rates on international loans followed suit, dramatically increasing Mexico's debt obligation. Concurrently, the world market experienced an unexpected oil glut and prices dropped precipitously. With roughly two-thirds of Mexico's foreign revenue coming from petroleum exports, government income fell sharply just as international financial obligations increased. Facing a massive outflow of economic resources, Mexico devalued its currency, reducing the value of the peso relative to other currencies, announced it was suspending payment on its international debt, and nationalized the country's banking system.

Business and consumer confidence disintegrated rapidly. International loans dried up and domestic investment slowed to a standstill. Mexico, like many countries in the developing world, entered its worst economic recession in more than a century. Total domestic production declined by 4.2 percent in the year following the devaluation and debt moratorium. Real wages tumbled by over 25 percent between 1980 and 1987. Unemployment and underemployment soared. With the economy in decline, government revenue (collected from taxes as well as oil) shrank noticeably. Although halting payment on international loans would seem a reasonable response to the domestic crisis caused by a shortage of government revenue, this solution was not feasible. Defaulting on its loans would have entailed severe economic sanctions from the world community, including the denial of loans in the future. Over the next several years, Mexico renegotiated repayment of its foreign debt, thus averting a major default and restoring partial confidence in the economy.

Part of the debt-negotiation agreement required the implementation of a series of austerity measures designed to control inflation and reduce the fiscal deficit. A radical reduction in government spending ensued. Jobs and wages in the government bureaucracy were trimmed. The government privatized hundreds of state-owned enterprises, which were used in the past to reward union supporters with high-paying jobs. Making these firms competitive meant slashing salaries and positions. Privatization thus struck at the heart of one of the central institutional pillars of corporatism – industrial labor. The peasantry felt the pinch of austerity as well. In order to generate foreign exchange with which to pay back foreign loans, the PRI began to promote agricultural exports. Government policy favored the most efficient, export-oriented farmers, typically those with large, capital-intensive plantations. *Ejidos* typically did not meet this need, and policy turned against their interests. Again, a traditional clientele of the corporatist system felt the brunt of the international economic crisis. A Mexico that had once tried to gain independence from the vagaries of the world market was now more than ever at its mercy.

THE POLITICAL CONSEQUENCES OF ECONOMIC CRISIS

Events in the economy profoundly affected the Mexican political sphere. The loss of government revenue placed severe restrictions on government spending. This undermined the ability of the PRI to manipulate patronage networks to ensure popular support. Discontent that had been brewing since the late 1960s erupted during the mid-1980s. A strong civil society began to emerge at the grass roots, a trend contrary to the corporatist philosophy of top-down organization. The growth of civil society received an unlikely push from a series of major earthquakes in 1985 that killed more than 10,000 residents of Mexico City. The massive destruction left a cash-strapped government paralyzed. Foreign assistance poured in, but what really mattered most was the autonomous creation of thousands of small community organizations that assisted in rescue and cleanup efforts. These organizations sowed the seeds from which independent political-action groups took root. For the first time since the modern corporatist system was constructed, a complex network of nongovernmental social groups emerged to challenge the hegemonic authority of the PRI.

The self-assertion of an autonomous civil society affected electoral politics. In 1983, members of the opposition National Action Party (PAN) won a significant number of municipal posts in the northern states of Chihuahua and Sonora. It is interesting to note that whereas one would expect leftist parties to make the greatest gains from labor discontent, PAN occupied the center-right and advocated an economic platform similar to the PRI's current neoliberal policies. National Action Party candidates won these elections because they were the only opposition party with significant organizational strength to mount an independent attack aimed at loosening the PRI's hold over the government. Most left-wing parties had been previously co-opted by the PRI through links to labor unions. Officials in those parties accepted this situation in exchange for token positions at various levels of administration. In other words, the leftist leadership owed its existence to the PRI and thus had little incentive to challenge the ruling party's authority. Only PAN had sufficient leadership that remained independent of the PRI.

PAN's electoral success went beyond organizational strength. It also signaled growing dissatisfaction with the PRI. Because northern Mexico is wealthier and more industrially developed than the central and southern states, PAN's success made it apparent that business interests were becoming increasingly unhappy with a PRI-dominated government. Furthermore, the preference for PAN indicated that there was more to the electoral discontent than strictly pocketbook matters; the electorate wanted real political choice and a greater say in government. The top-heavy corporatist model was facing a serious challenge from the grass roots.

The extent of popular unhappiness became clear during the presidential election of 1988. The handpicked PRI candidate, Carlos Salinas de Gortari, won the presidency with only 50.5 percent of the vote, a slimmer margin than for any previous PRI candidate. Cuauhtemoc Cárdenas, son of the former president and the representative of a loose coalition of left-wing parties, came in second with 30.9 percent. The PAN candidate, Manuel Clouthier, finished third with 16.7 percent. This in itself signified a substantial defeat for the one-party state. In reality, Salinas may have actually lost the election. Electoral irregularities marred the election, including a power outage that affected the computerized ballot counts. As political competition grew throughout the 1980s, the PRI increasingly resorted to electoral fraud to retain important seats. Although the true totals from the 1988 election may never be known, it is enough to say that this election had a lasting impact on the Mexican polity. The Mexican corporatist framework that had brought an era of unprecedented political stability for Latin America could no longer be sustained in its present form. The 1990s thus initiated a transitional period for the Mexican state.

INTERESTS, IDENTITIES, AND INSTITUTIONS AT THE END OF THE TWENTIETH CENTURY

As the 1990s came to a close, Mexico found itself struggling with one of the central political themes of its past – the tension between liberal and corporatist forms of government. Whereas this conflict was resolved for most of the century in favor of a corporatist one-party state, the crises of the 1980s and the rise of an autonomous civil society made liberal-pluralism (a system of private interest articulation outside of government control) a viable contender as the organizing principle of Mexican political life. Economic globalization and the collapse of the socialist model of development have pushed economic policy in the direction of laissez-faire policies. President Carlos Salinas de Gortari (1988–1994) stepped up the pace of privatization begun by his predecessor, Miguel de la Madrid (1982–1988). Under pressure to attract foreign capital and cultivate new export markets, Salinas also gave the central bank greater autonomy and entered into an expansive free-trade agreement (NAFTA) with the United States and Canada. His successor, **Ernesto Zedillo**, continued on the same economic path, although Zedillo was more adventurous when it came to introducing liberalizing political reforms. Salinas's policy of economic liberalization under a one-party state was reminiscent, in some ways, of similar reforms undertaken by Mikhail Gorbachev in the Soviet Union – so much so that the Mexican reforms were given the name "Salinastroika." But, as Gorbachev found out, economic liberalization unleashes powerful forces in society. New interests are created, institutions transformed, and identities reshaped.

The economic crises of the 1980s and the resulting laissez-faire (**neoliberal**) policies remade political interests in ways not seen since the Mexican Revolution. Definite winners and losers emerged. The most extreme example has been in the southern state of Chiapas, where a guerrilla insurgency burst onto the scene in 1994. With land becoming increasingly concentrated in the hands of a few large-scale farmers, *ejidos* found it exceedingly difficult to sustain a living, and grievances against the government grew. In 1992, President Salinas revised Article 27 of the 1917 constitution, which was the cornerstone for earlier land-redistribution programs. The new article made privatizing *ejido* lands easier. Peasants seeking to have their concerns addressed were frequent targets of violent attacks by the state police and private paramilitary groups supported by large landholders. The implementation of NAFTA in 1994 further threatened the interests of *ejido* farmers, as it favored large-scale agricultural exporters over small-scale communal farms. With their economic livelihood at risk, many peasants found it worthwhile to join the Zapatista National Liberation Army (EZLN). As of this writing, the EZLN and the Mexican government remain deadlocked over a variety of issues that affect peasant interests, including land redistribution, human rights, effective political representation, and electoral fraud.

The Zapatista movement is not only about economic interests. Because many of the peasants in Chiapas are of direct Mayan ancestry, the movement has asserted strong indigenous claims. Mexican nationalism plays little, if any, role. In fact, the insurgency in Chiapas has demonstrated the difficulty in forging a single Mexican identity. In societies where economic class divisions map closely onto racial and ethnic cleavages, ethnic identity is bound to be closely associated with interest-based politics. How the central government treats the descendants of pre-Columbian inhabitants has become a central policy issue in a country that has largely ignored such concerns for nearly five centuries. Indigenous communities are now identifying themselves as distinct groups within the Mexican polity and demanding to have their voices heard in the central government. This implies a greater respect for civil liberties (for example, freedom of association) and the ability of indigenous groups to freely elect government officials who represent their interests. The rise of a strong indigenous identity thus creates pressures for political liberalization.

The political legacy of the 1990s has been the emergence of real electoral competition, one of the central features of a liberal-democratic polity. With the PRI losing its ability to deliver patronage to its core constituencies because of fiscal restraints on state spending and an ambitious program of privatization and government downsizing, many of those interests tied tightly to the party in the past have sought new avenues of representation. Nongovernmental organizations have appeared as a new force in society. Political participation also has been channeled into two major opposition parties – the National Action Party (PAN) and the **Democratic Revolutionary Party (Partido Revolucionario Democrático, PRD)**. The latter was forged from a coalition of leftist parties and disaffected members of the PRI in the early 1990s. It has attracted mostly members of the urban and rural working class and poor, although significant portions of lower-income voters remain tied to the traditional patronage networks of the PRI. Political infighting has also weakened the PRD. During the 1994 presidential elections, the PRD candidate – Cuauhtemoc Cárdenas (a former member of the PRI) – won only 17 percent of the vote in a reasonably clean election. Nonetheless, by the late 1990s, the PRD had scored a number of important victories at the local level, including winning the mayoral seat of the nation's capital.

The PAN has been the most consistent threat to the PRI's political hegemony. Representing upper-income interests, the PAN has tapped into domestic business disapprobation with many of Salinas's and Zedillo's economic policies. Although it seems odd that domestic businesses would be dissatisfied with laissez-faire policies, it must be remembered that many of these businesses benefited from the high tariffs and government subsidies of the 1960s and 1970s, and these businesses were not prepared to compete internationally. Neoliberal policies took many of these benefits away, although overall they have helped to create a friendlier environment for foreign investment. It is ironic that the PAN champions many of the same neoliberal policies as the PRI. In this respect, much of the support for the PAN can be viewed more as a search for an alternative political voice than as a desire to shift the economic policies of the state. This voice has found a forum, as PAN candidates have won numerous local offices and captured key gubernatorial positions in several northern states.

The increase in electoral competition affected two of the country's primary political institutions – the national legislature and the PRI. Power still remains highly concentrated in the presidency, and the executive branch remains

under the control of the PRI. However, in 1997 the PRI lost majority control of the Chamber of Deputies (equivalent to the U.S. House of Representatives). Previously, the PRI had enjoyed majority representation in both the Chamber of Deputies and the Senate, making the Congress a rubber stamp for executive decisions. This pattern was reinforced by the fact that the PRI Party leadership chose each legislator, which meant that the president had a strong influence over the career paths of politicians. In some respects, this resembled parliamentarianism in reverse – the leading party executive chose legislators rather than vice versa. Results from the 1997 midterm elections earned opposition parties a combined majority in the Chamber of Deputies for the first time in the twentieth century. Although the PRI still controls the Senate and can play divide and conquer among the deputies to ensure a winning legislative coalition, the presence of a majority opposition in the lower house has forced the PRI to engage in negotiation and compromise, both steps toward more pluralistic interest representation. With opposition parties in general agreement on the need for further electoral reforms, this environment bodes well for continued political liberalization. Political liberalization, in turn, raises the prospects for greater representation for opposition parties in the Congress and for a stronger legislative branch. Although it is still too early to tell, the classic liberal notion of checks and balances may become a reality in the near future.

Increased political competition and social pluralism have shaken the dominant party itself. Within the party elite, a debate rages over how to manage the economic and political turmoil engulfing Mexico. The faction that emerged as dominant since the 1980s represents a more reformist line of thinking. Known as the **técnicos** (technocrats), they hearken from the bureaucratic side of the PRI. Presidents Salinas and Zedillo are members of this faction. Both were educated in U.S. universities and earned their political stripes by working their way through the Mexican bureaucracy rather than by winning seats in local and regional government. The *técnicos* began occupying high-level offices during the 1980s, when the economic crisis called for policy makers with specific expertise in managing domestic and international macroeconomic affairs. The ascendance of *técnicos* gave rise to a competing faction within the PRI called the **dinosaurios** for their hard-line, traditional corporatist stance.

The split within the PRI created an interesting and fluid pattern of alliances. The primary intraparty cleavage related to economic policy. Whereas the *técnicos* favored neoliberal economic reforms to modernize Mexico's economy, the *dinosaurios* preferred the old formula of state-directed growth and opposed both the privatization of industries and NAFTA. This put the *dinosaurios* in policy agreement with the PRD. The *técnicos* found policy allies in the center-right PAN. Despite their differences, both the *técnicos* and *dinosaurios* strongly desired that the PRI hold onto political power. Political

survival tended to take precedence over economic policy disagreements, and both factions were involved significantly in vote tampering during the 1980s. The transparency of electoral fraud, especially at the local level, only fueled further dissatisfaction with the ruling party and intensified public cries for electoral reform.

Whereas President de la Madrid (1982–1988) represented a transition between the hard-line *dinosaurios* and the *técnicos*, Carlos Salinas de Gortari firmly identified himself with the latter. Following his narrow electoral victory in 1988, Salinas surprised many analysts by charting a course independent of the *dinosaurios*. It was believed that this would be a dangerous strategy for a man who needed as much internal party support as he could muster. Nonetheless, his institutional reengineering had a lasting impact on the Mexican polity, and he most likely will be remembered as a pivotal character in Mexico's political history. Salinas was credited with disassembling many of the PRI's traditional patronage networks. Realizing that *dinosaurio* power rested in those channels, he cut funds for favored programs and dismissed important union officials. Still needing social support for his presidency, however, Salinas created the Solidarity Program, a new set of patronage networks that circumvented many of the local political bosses who remained loyal to the *dinosaurios*. President Zedillo continued this tradition through a similar set of programs. The end result was to destroy almost completely the traditional pillars of support holding up Mexico's corporatist system, which had ensured political stability in the past.

Constitutional reforms undertaken in 1992 further changed Mexico's political landscape by removing some of the most radical elements of the revolutionary constitution. Without recourse to the revolutionary ideals of the past, a new legitimating formula needed to be found. Although Salinas and the *técnicos* hoped that economic growth would boost support for the PRI, they realized that economic restructuring would pay dividends too far off in the future. Discontent with the country's economic situation was increasing, especially among the traditional corporatist allies of the PRI – labor, the peasantry, and middle-class bureaucrats. Both presidents Salinas and Zedillo sought to restore the PRI's legitimacy by championing political reform. Salinas began the process of promoting electoral reforms that would allow opposition parties a fair chance at winning office. Secret balloting was guaranteed to prevent voter intimidation, and ballot counts came under greater scrutiny. Salinas further cracked down on local PRI officials who engaged in electoral fraud, although enforcement of this policy typically favored the PAN, not the PRD. Given that the *técnicos* and PANistas shared a similar economic policy agenda, capitulating to their electoral victories was a more palatable solution than allowing PRD victories. Fraud continued against PRD candidates, leading to violent clashes between protesters and police. Despite ideological disagreements, however, leaders of the PAN and PRD found it

in their mutual interest to cooperate and press for more electoral reforms. The PRI still controlled access to state financial resources and public media outlets, giving it a significant electoral advantage.

Political reform was put to the test in 1994. The growing rift within the PRI erupted in violence. In March, Luis Donaldo Colosio, a *técnico* and Salinas's handpicked presidential successor, was assassinated on the campaign trail. Although the crime was pinned on a young garage mechanic, it was widely suspected that members of the PRI's *dinosaurio* faction had masterminded the plot. Several months later, the secretary general of the PRI (and brother-in-law of the president) was gunned down. Salinas's own brother was arrested as the prime suspect. Such high-level political violence had a profound effect on Mexican politics. To ensure free and fair elections and deflect further accusations of fraud, an independent electoral commission was established to monitor voting practices. International observers also were invited to oversee national balloting. As a result, Mexico's 1994 presidential elections were the most honest in nearly two decades, a triumph for liberal-pluralism.

The PRI's Ernesto Zedillo, another young *técnico*, won the election with a plurality of the vote (48.8 percent), and the ruling party hung onto a narrow majority in the Chamber of Deputies. The victory came at a severe cost for the country, however. To win popular support amid growing political turmoil, the PRI inflated the Mexican economy throughout most of 1994, making it easier to pay off needed constituents with government projects and providing a general feeling of economic prosperity in the country. The government also issued a large quantity of short-term government bonds to boost the confidence of foreign investors, who were growing increasingly nervous about the spreading political violence (including the Zapatista uprising). However, faced with rapidly declining foreign currency reserves, the incoming Zedillo administration was forced to devalue the Mexican peso. Traditionally, hard economic choices had been made by the outgoing president, thereby allowing the incoming president to avoid public hostility. Former president Carlos Salinas de Gortari, however, was pursuing a bid to become the president of the newly created World Trade Organization, based on his success in negotiating NAFTA. He refused to devalue the peso, knowing that such action would reveal weakness in his administration's monetary policy. When Zedillo finally attempted a controlled devaluation, speculator pressure pushed the currency into a spiraling freefall. Inflation soared and government actions to stem rising prices plunged the economy into another major recession, just as it had a decade earlier. Salinas further challenged the informal norms of Mexican political life by criticizing the Zedillo administration's handling of the economic crisis. Zedillo countered by investigating the former president's financial dealings. In a unique turn of fate for a former Mexican president, Salinas exiled himself abroad, fearing arrest should he return to Mexico. Such an unprecedented situation clearly signals that the Mexican political system is no longer operating as it has in the past, although the future shape of the polity is still unclear.

Pressured by a severe recession, a stalemated guerrilla insurrection, and growing international skepticism about Mexico's business climate, Zedillo was forced to speed up the political reforms begun under Salinas. The center-piece of these reforms was an electoral reform package implemented in 1996. Among its many provisions, the new laws provided for greater public financing of campaigns and media access for all parties. The plan also eliminated party membership based upon group ("corporate") affiliation. This measure effectively eliminated the basis for corporatist interest representation that had been the bedrock of Mexico's political system for most of the twentieth century. Perhaps more important was the strengthening of the Federal Electoral Institute and the Federal Electoral Tribunal in 1996. The former institution, composed of an independent citizen advisory board, is charged with the duty of monitoring all federal elections to minimize fraud. The Tribunal serves as a court to investigate all electoral irregularities and prosecute individuals engaged in electoral malfeasance. Initially created in 1990, both entities were given full independence and a permanent footing by President Zedillo in 1996. Since introducing these reforms, most observers of Mexican politics agree that the incidence of fraud, although still present, has been greatly reduced. Finally, President Zedillo departed from the traditional practice of the *dedazo*, the selection by the president of a successor. Instead of the sitting PRI president naming his successor, an open primary would be held to determine the presidential candidate of the party. This move was geared largely toward ensuring that the PRI's candidate would be vetted by the voting public and, hopefully, possess greater popular appeal and legitimacy during the general election.

Implementing these reforms has not been easy. Regional PRI caciques continue to manipulate local politics, subverting the implementation of the new laws. A once hegemonic party facing real political competition for the first time can be expected to bend or break rules in order to stay in power. Nonetheless, the reforms have shown some success in guaranteeing a more open political process. The 1997 midterm elections for the national legislature gave opposition parties their first combined majority in the Chamber of Deputies. Both the PAN and PRD made substantial gains in local elections, culminating in the historic victory of Vincente Fox in the 2000 presidential election. Despite his rather unassuming personality, overshadowed by the controversial Carlos Salinas de Gortari before him and the animated Vincente Fox who followed, Ernesto Zedillo should really be remembered as one of the most influential Mexican presidents of the twentieth century, perhaps rivaling Lázaro Cárdenas in importance. Ironically, his being perceived initially as a weak president who was not threatening to entrenched interests in the PRI may have granted him the political space in which to undertake these bold political reforms. And as the tumultuous twentieth century came to a close, he could rest assured that his decisions helped to initiate a new era in Mexican politics.

Competitive Democracy in Twenty-First-Century Mexico

Just as January 1, 1994, will be remembered in Mexican history for its high political drama, so will the date of July 2, 2000, when the PRI went down to defeat in presidential elections. Polls just weeks before the election showed a dead heat between the PAN's candidate, Vincente Fox Quesada, and the PRI's candidate, Francisco Labastida. Although no one assumed that the PRD's candidate, Cuauhtemoc Cárdenas, would win the election, his presence certainly represented a wild card in the race. Mexican citizens held their breath as election results came in. It was feared that a narrow victory by the PRI would raise doubts about the integrity of the electoral process and might provoke social chaos. Alternatively, some feared that if the PAN (or PRD) won by a slim margin, the military might intervene and declare a coup. Although in hindsight such fears appeared overblown, they were nevertheless real at the time. Fortunately, Vincente Fox emerged as the clear victor in the contest, winning 42.5 percent of the vote compared with Labastida's 36.1 percent.

Fox's success at the ballot box certainly resulted from two decades of growing pressure for political change and the liberalizing political reforms championed by Ernesto Zedillo. But an interesting question still presents itself: Why, with the Mexican economy struggling for more than two decades, did the citizenry decide upon a candidate who represented a continuation of the neoliberal economic policies of the new *técnicos* (such as Salinas and Zedillo) instead of the PRD's candidate, who promised a return to a more statist/corporatist approach to economic policy? If anything, the results of the 2000 election signaled that the Mexican populace was hungrier for political change than economic change, and Vincente Fox, as a dynamic campaigner, represented the most viable option for an opposition victory. Moreover, there is no reason to suspect that greater state intervention will be demanded by a population in times of economic crisis. The economic revolutions of Ronald Reagan and Margaret Thatcher were enormously popular among the working classes in the United States and Britain, and more recently neoliberal reforms in New Zealand have garnered widespread support. Even in Chile, the privatization of the social security system has proven to be a political winner. Although academics have often assumed that the interests of economically distressed populations would naturally favor increased state intervention of the nature that the PRD was promising, the results of the Mexican election proved otherwise.

But the reasons for Fox's victory went beyond the policy preferences of voters. At a time when popular support for the PRI was rapidly eroding, the PAN had the strongest political organization and a historical identity that crossed various socioeconomic barriers. Founded in the 1920s, the original aim of the PAN was not so much to win elections as it was to educate Mexicans about civic engagement. This approach represented a long-term strategy in influencing the political landscape and made perfect sense after it was realized that the PRI was the overwhelmingly dominant player in the electoral arena. The PRI initially appealed to an odd mix of socially conscious Catholics and small- and medium-sized-business owners. Both of these groups were excluded from the corporatist pillars established under the Cárdenas regime. As the Mexican Miracle provided a robust economy wherein even small- and medium-sized businesses thrived, the latter group drifted away from the PAN, leaving a number of Catholic lay intellectuals in charge of the party. Influenced by the socially progressive thinking of Pope Pius IX (1846–1878) and the Second Vatican Council (1962–1965), the PAN had a noticeable leftist identity during the 1950s and 1960s. However, as the economy soured during the 1970s and the more interventionist policies of President Echeverría alienated the business community, small-sized business owners began returning to the PAN, moving the party leadership in a more rightward direction in terms of economic policy. Moreover, with the PRI's support beginning to erode among the middle class, the PAN began to focus on a strategy of winning local elections. Focusing primarily on a platform of greater political liberalization, the PAN managed to create a somewhat broad-based ideological umbrella that was comfortable both for the progressive Catholics and neoliberal business interests. The PAN developed an extensive grassroots campaign network that was rather unified in its purpose and, as noted earlier, paid off during the 1980s and 1990s with some significant electoral victories in local elections.

One could contrast this institutional organization with the PRD, which did not come together as a formal political party until the late 1980s and consisted largely of a splintered coalition of leftist parties, each with their own separate organizations, personalities, and ideologies. Although Cuauhtemoc Cárdenas, as the son of the famous Mexican president and a high-profile defector from the PRI, presented a figure to rally around in the 1988 elections, the organizational inexperience and disparate interests within the PRD did little to help them build national momentum. Granted, the PRD was capable of winning local elections (particularly in the southern states that were home to the poor and the indigenous peoples), where their organization was more cohesive, but translating these successes to a national level proved more elusive.

The PAN also benefited enormously from the vibrant personality of Vincente Fox. His story as a self-made business executive, moving from delivery driver for Coca-Cola through the ranks of the company's sales force, and eventually becoming the CEO of Coca-Cola's Mexican subsidiary, gave him the aura, rightfully deserved, of economic success. His towering height and polished speaking skills also added to his reputation as a strong leader. Finally, and perhaps most ironically, Fox apparently fell victim to electoral fraud at the hands of the PRI while running for the governorship of Guanajuato in 1991. This case made Fox a national celebrity and guaranteed his election as governor of the state in 1996. His national profile, combined with his political ambition, made Fox the ideal candidate for the PAN in the 2000 presidential campaign. His optimistic energy contrasted greatly with the more dour and pessimistic campaign style of Cárdenas and, in a new era where opposition candidates were granted greater access to the popular media, this enhanced the electoral edge of both Fox and the PAN Party in general.

The peaceful transition of power to Vincente Fox certainly represented a major step toward competitive multiparty democracy in Mexico. Most observers would now agree that the 2000 election set the stage for a new era of clean and competitive elections. Indeed, the 2003 midterm elections for the Chamber of Deputies were once again hailed as being reasonably free from corruption. Although the PAN lost a substantial number of seats in the Chamber of Deputies and the PRI and PRD gained seats, all of this represents the normal vagaries of democratic politics. With an economy in recession, it was normal to expect that the party holding the presidency would lose seats. The 2003 elections demonstrated that the electoral process continued to function as it should and the main political parties seemed to be adjusting well to a new political environment.

The next major challenge to emerge during this new era of competitive democracy came in the closely contested presidential elections of 2006. Like the 2000 presidential election in the United States, the Mexican presidential contest was decided by a razor-thin margin of roughly 244,000 votes out of nearly 42 million ballots cast, a difference of less than sixth-tenths of a percentage point. Perhaps more importantly, the victor – **Felipe Calderón Hinojosa** (of the PAN party) – captured only 35.89 percent of the vote, while his closest challenger – Andrés Manuel López Obrador (of a tripartite coalition of leftist parties led by the PRD) – won 35.31 percent. Third place went to the PRI's candidate; who managed only 22.26 percent of the vote. Ironically, it wasn't so much the strength of the PAN that led to the PRD's defeat as it was fragmentation among the Left. Patricia Mercado, the candidate from a small leftist Peasant Alternative Party, garnered 2.7 percent of the vote, which probably would have gone to López Obrador and moved him past Calderón. The PAN remained a relatively unified force on the political Right while continued factionalization among the Left limited the effectiveness of the PRD at the national level.

In terms of what the 2006 election – both presidential and legislative – meant for the Mexican polity, several observations can be made. First, electoral democracy in Mexico is proving to be resilient. Despite a series of protests, minor violence, and a mock inauguration by the petulant loser of the presidential election, the PAN's Felipe Calderón was allowed to don the sash of the Mexican presidency with the majority of Mexicans accepting him as the legitimate winner. While some irregularities and charges of voter fraud were present during the election, the independent Federal Electoral Institute – created in the 1990s – and a number of international observers rated this election as remarkably clean and fair. Political protests (some violent) did erupt, but by the end of 2006 it appeared as if the vast majority of Mexico's citizens accepted the official results. Fears of military intervention that were rumored during the 2000 election proved groundless once again, as civilians successfully determined the shape of the government. Second, the political Right continued to show surprising strength in an era where left-leaning populists were making significant gains elsewhere in Latin America. Although the market-oriented Calderón won only a slim plurality of the presidential vote, the PAN won 206 seats in the House of Deputies, giving it a near majority in the 500-seat lower house. While the PRD's leftist coalition also picked up 63 seats to bring its total to 160, the PAN has a greater likelihood of building a legislative majority coalition by attracting some of the PRI's 121 deputies. As of 2006, the PAN also held a plurality of 52 seats in the 128-member upper house (Senate) of the Mexican Congress, with the PRI holding a three-seat advantage over the PRD, with one seat allocated to a minor party. Third, the electoral breakdown between the PAN and PRD continued to show significant geographic cleavages, with the former party retaining strength in the more developed and industrial north, while the PRD (and other leftist parties) continued to secure popularity among the poorer and agrarian-based southern states.

Finally, what is perhaps most interesting about the 2006 elections is the significant decline of the PRI as a political force in Mexico. In addition to marshaling only 22 percent of the electorate for its presidential candidate, the PRI lost more than 50 percent of the seats it held in the House of Deputies in the three short years between 2003 and 2006. And whereas the PRI held a 60-seat plurality in the Senate, it only captured 39 seats in 2006. The reasons for this collapse remain debated among scholars. Surely the divisions among the *técnicos* and *dinosaurios* that appeared in the 1980s play a role in weakening the party, although many from the old guard have been passing from the scene. The image among the electorate of the PRI being a remnant of the past and a source of bureaucratic corruption may also account for its declining popularity. Uncovering the real reasons for the PRI's faltering position will remain a task for scholars in the coming years. Nevertheless, it is unlikely that the PRI will disappear from the political arena altogether. It will likely become an interesting wild card in the competition between the more ideologically distilled parties of the Left and Right. Adjusting to its role as just one of three or more parties in an electorally competitive system will undoubtedly take some time.

Despite the encouraging democratic gains made over the past two decades, the political future is not unequivocally promising for Mexico. Several problems remain, many of which are directly related to the institutional structures that were developed during the twentieth century to deal with problems of the nineteenth century. Preeminent among the institutional problems facing Mexico is the term limit placed upon the president and members of Congress. In the past, with one dominant party and a system that gave the greatest power to the president, the president was able to get his legislative agenda passed quickly. Concerns over a single-term limit were ameliorated by the fact that the president would choose his successor and determine the political fortunes of others within the party, making almost all legislators willing to give the president what he wanted. Although one could rightly argue that this system was too dictatorial and could lead to bad policy outcomes, it also allowed for rapid government decision making in times of crisis. The situation in the early twenty-first century is very different. With a president highly restricted in his ability to name his successor, legislators have less incentive to cooperate on policy making with the president. This problem was exacerbated by the specific relationship that Vincente Fox had with his own PAN Party. Being a relative newcomer to the political arena, only getting involved in politics in the decade before he was elected president, Fox had very few loyal connections to PAN members, and many of his initial policies were not to the liking of PAN legislators. Attempts to negotiate a settlement with the Zapatistas by demilitarizing Chiapas early in his administration were met with resistance not only by the PRI but members of his own party as well. A similar situation arose when Fox tried to reform Mexico's complicated and rather archaic tax structure. Major policy successes during Fox's six-year term were rare and the economy lumbered on at a sluggish pace. With few gains to be made on the domestic front, Fox turned his attention toward foreign policy, with a major goal being an immigration policy with the United States that would allow a greater number of Mexicans to work there temporarily and repatriate needed foreign currency.

The policy gridlock witnessed under the Fox administration also resulted from the mixed electoral system that selects the national legislature. Although plurality voting in single-member districts tends to push the political system to a two-party outcome, the presence of proportional representation in deciding a significant portion of the Chamber of Deputies still encourages minority parties. This has resulted in there being no definitive majority party in the legislature since 2000.

The electoral incentives for a multi-party system at the legislative level invariably have an impact upon presidential elections as was noted in the 2006 election. With small parties having a chance to pick up a handful of seats in the House of Deputies (or within local governing bodies such as states or municipalities), there are incentives for each of these parties to field a presidential candidate to maintain national visibility. While any of the three major parties – PAN, PRI, or PRD – could craft a coalition with any of these parties, such coalitions remain unstable over the long term. And as noted the fragmentation of the Left makes coalition formation more important for the PRD and creates a handicap for its candidates at the federal level. How Mexicans will manage their party system in the coming years and decades remains to be seen. At least in the short term, it looks as if the country will continue with three major parties while a series of smaller parties will come and go around the fringes of the electoral spectrum. And irrespective of which party can control the presidency and legislature, the presence of an entrenched bureaucracy that was responsible for running Mexico's state-led economy during the previous century continues to be a difficult obstacle for civilian rulers to overcome. Efforts by President Fox to reform the system proved largely futile and without the heavy hand of the PRI to guide the bureaucracy as it had following Lázaro Cárdenas, the problem of corruption remains endemic and difficult to combat.

The problem of corruption is not merely a political conundrum. Bureaucratic corruption also places a significant drag upon the economy as government resources are not used in an economically rational and efficient manner and business entrepreneurs become less willing to invest in the economy. While NAFTA presented Mexico with a great many opportunities to diversify its economy, global economic competition from countries such as China has placed new pressures on the Mexican economy. The privatization of many industries beginning in the 1980s, including the creation of an autonomous central bank, helped to boost the economy, but the heavy hand of the state combined with corrupt bureaucracies continue to prevent Mexico from reaching its full economic potential. The result has been a high unemployment rate that creates incentives for many Mexican citizens to seek work in the United States. With limited political opportunities to reform the economy domestically, President Fox focused his attention on opening the border with the United States and supporting a guest-worker program that would both alleviate some of the unemployment pressure in Mexico while allowing Mexican migrants to repatriate much needed foreign currency. In turn, however, political demands within the United States to end or limit the migration of workers from Mexico have created a potential point of conflict, which may sour trade relations between the two countries if not addressed to the satisfaction of both, a task that may prove politically intractable.

Finally, the Zapatista movement that burst onto the scene in January of 2004 as a response to Mexico's economic alliance with the United States remains a symptom of many of Mexico's political and economic ills. While the Zapatistas pose little military threat to the government, they do serve as a reminder of the great political and economic inequities in the country. Much of Mexico's wealth and political power still is found in the more industrialized northern states and the nation's centrally located capital. Attempts by the EZLN and their allies to develop greater political autonomy for the southern region, particularly in states such as Oaxaca and Chiapas, have proven moderately successful and the federal government appears to be paying more attention to the economic development of the southern rural region. However, until greater economic opportunity, both in terms of agriculture and industry, can be guaranteed to that region, political tension – as reflected in recent elections – and questions about fair and equal representation will remain. While the controversy over the razor-thin presidential election of 2006, which included some allegations of fraud, was resolved relatively peacefully there is no guarantee that social chaos will not erupt anew in the future. Like many other countries discussed in this text, Mexico's path toward democracy has not been without problems or controversy, but it is encouraging that the country remains one of the more resilient polities in Latin America.

Conclusion

The Mexico that we see today is an artifact of its past. The legacy of political violence during the 1800s and early 1900s paved the way for a quasi-authoritarian, corporatist regime. Foreign intervention in Mexican affairs complicated the country's search for political stability and gave the country's policies a decidedly nationalist and autarkic tone. But the world economy could not be ignored. Despite attempts to free itself from dependency on the world economy, Mexico found itself more dependent upon the good graces of the international financial community by the late 1970s. The economic crisis of the 1980s prompted Mexicans to rethink not only their economic development strategy but also their political system. Grassroots demands for greater political representation prompted a movement away from a one-party corporatist state and toward a multiparty pluralist democracy.

All of this history has shaped the interests and identities found within Mexico today. Moreover, Mexico's position in the international arena has combined with these interests and identities to shape its current political landscape. Mexico's long-standing tradition of corporatism has created strong interests in society that expect government patronage. Unionized labor has come to expect job security and wages that support an increasing standard of living. Rural campesinos (farm laborers), particularly in the south, have come to expect a certain level of stability that the constitutionally mandated *ejido* system provided. And both small and big businesses (in both the industrial and agricultural sectors) have demanded subsidies and tariff protection to shield them from international competitors. Meeting these basic economic interests was possible when the Mexican economy was growing by leaps and bounds.

Those days ended in the early 1980s when Mexico became saddled with an expanding international debt and a sharp loss in export revenues. Although the international economy changed, societal interests in Mexico did not. The PRI could no longer meet the societal demands that had become part of the institutional and ideological fabric of Mexican society. With a shrinking economy, the various sectors (labor, agriculture, and industry) found their demands in direct competition with one another. Mexico's corporatist identity – the ability to develop economically based on the harmonious balance of competing social interests – was also torn apart. Recognizing that the PRI could no longer deliver upon past corporatist privileges, citizens began to demand more organizational autonomy from the government and a greater say in political decision making.

This conflict of interests also appeared to tear at another aspect of Mexico's national identity. Whereas Mexican heritage had often been presented as a distinct mix of two cultures – Spanish and indigenous (Aztec and Mayan) – it has become increasingly apparent since the 1980s that economic inequity closely mirrored racial and ethnic divisions within society, which in turn reflected geographic patterns. Criollos maintained their historic position at the top of the socioeconomic ladder, whereas indigenous populations languished at the bottom. As noted at the beginning of this chapter, this long-standing problem became evident to the world on January 1, 1994, when a guerrilla insurgency composed mainly of impoverished indigenous farmers placed a damper on the festivities of a New Year's Eve party attended mostly by criollos and well-to-do mestizos. These insurgents proudly identified themselves as being of Mayan ancestry, and far from simply demanding reintegration into past corporatist arrangements, they announced their desire for greater political independence and the ability to freely choose their political representatives. It is interesting to note that these demands demonstrated that the struggle between corporatism and liberalism was not just a historical artifact but a present reality.

At the dawn of the twenty-first century, Mexico finds itself on the verge of a new era of liberal democracy with competitive multiparty elections. Demands for greater political participation during the early 1800s resulted in independence from Spain, although many among the governing elite sought to keep the top-down political arrangements of the colonial era. Similar cries for political reform were heard during the Mexican Revolution a century later. Although significant changes did result in a general rise in economic

TABLE 9.1. Key Phases in Mexico's Political Development

Time Period	Regime	Global context	Interests/identities/institutions	Developmental path
1521–1821	colonialism–strict control of Spanish America by crown; Spain discourages autonomous government in colonies, although some local control granted	rise and decline of the Spanish Empire; Napoleonic Wars and occupation of Spain, combined with growth of liberalism in Spain, prompt independence movement	strong landed elite (*latifundistas*)/monopolistic Catholicism and mestizo culture develop (Virgin of Guadalupe represents fusion of European colonial culture and indigenous culture)/ colonial authoritarian control	mercantilism – raw material exports from colonies to Spain; finished goods imported to colonies from Spain; tight regulation over domestic colonial economy; colonial manufacturing discouraged
1820s–1876	era of the caudillos – period of political uncertainty, instability, and internecine warfare punctuated by foreign economic and military intervention; battles between Liberals and Conservatives	growth in European economic influence (primarily British and French); U.S. territorial expansion leads to war and loss of Mexican territory	geographically located strongmen seek power/weak nationalism develops and grows/intermittent authoritarianism at national level; local caudillos rule regionally	economic chaos – political instability discourages economic investment and fosters government fiscal crises; export-led growth based on primary goods in latter period
1876–1911	Porfiriato – "liberal dictatorship" of Porfirio Díaz; expansion of middle class	direct foreign economic and military interference wanes	export agriculture and mining/growing liberal sentiment/centralized authoritarian rule	export-led growth – economic stability and growth prompts initial industrialization

(continued)

TABLE 9.1 (continued)

Time period	Regime	Global context	Interests/identities/ institutions	Developmental path
1910–1920	Mexican Revolution – begins as succession crisis, but radicalized by lower-class social movements and leftist political ideologies; general political chaos	general non-interference in Mexican affairs, U.S. isolationist, and Britain's presence in Western Hemisphere waning	geographic strongmen seek power; rise of peasantry and working class as political force/growing socialist/ redistributive sentiment/ intermittent dictatorial rule	economic chaos – economic activity severely limited by political chaos
1920–1982	state-led corporatism – one-party rule based on incorporation of social groups into government structure; creation of extensive patronage networks	growing U.S. influence in Latin America; Great Depression and movement toward economic openness among industrialized nations	labor, peasantry, and large business closely integrated with state/corporatism/highly centralized state and one-party rule	"Mexican Miracle" and import-substitution industrialization; restriction of imports of manufactured finished goods; increasing government intervention in economy
1982–2000	decline of corporatism – movement toward greater political openness and party competition; rise of civil society; new model of governance still uncertain	third world debt crisis and end of Cold War	rise of bureaucratic *técnicos* and decline of influence of labor and peasantry/ disillusionment with one-party rule and corporatism/gradual decay of one-party rule; opposition parties begin to win local elections	neoliberalism – promotion of free trade (NAFTA) and less government regulation of economy
2000– present	continued growth of multiparty democracy and decline of the once-dominant PRI	increased globalization and competition from Asian countries; immigration to U.S. becoming a hotly contested issue	non-PRI parties show continued success in local and federal elections	continuation of free market policies although state continues to play large role in economy

well-being, governing structures continued to leave little room for popular participation at the grass roots of society. The changes taking place today are reminiscent of those earlier eras. However, the contemporary world in which Mexico operates is, in many ways, smaller than it was before. With international investors demanding a liberalized economy, and with labor and capital mobility more fluid than ever, the Mexican government has less leeway in determining its economic policy. Yet the urgency to rekindle economic growth will affect the country's social stability. The new neoliberal course pursued since the 1990s will undoubtedly affect the interests of important political players and reshape the national character of Mexican society. As in previous centuries, the new shape of politics will play out over time. Interests and identities are not set in stone. Although it is too early to predict what the political outcomes will be, this ever-shifting global environment offers a wonderful opportunity to understand the complexities of comparative politics.

BIBLIOGRAPHY

Bulmer-Thomas, Victor. *The Economic History of Latin America since Independence*. Cambridge: Cambridge University Press, 1994.

Camp, Roderic Ai. *Politics in Mexico: The Democratic Transformation*. Fourth ed. New York: Oxford University Press, 2002.

Cardoso, Eliana, and Ann Helwege. *Latin America's Economy: Diversity Trends and Conflicts*. Cambridge, MA: MIT Press, 1992.

Chand, Vikram K. *Mexico's Political Awakening*. Notre Dame, IN: University of Notre Dame Press, 2001.

Cothran, Dan A. *Political Stability and Democracy in Mexico: The "Perfect Dictatorship"?* Westport, CT: Praeger, 1994.

Eckstein, Susan. *The Poverty of Revolution*. Princeton, NJ: Princeton University Press, 1988.

Eisendstadt, Todd A. *Courting Democracy in Mexico: Party Strategies and Electoral Institutions*. Cambridge: Cambridge University Press, 2004.

Fuentes, Carlos. *A New Time for Mexico*. Berkeley: University of California Press, 1997.

Gill, Anthony. "The Politics of Regulating Religion in Mexico: The 1992 Constitutional Reforms in Historical Context." *Journal of Church and State* 41, no. 4 (1999): 761–794.

Gill, Anthony, and Arang Keshavarzian. "State Building and Religious Resources: An Institutional Theory of Church–State Relations in Iran and Mexico." *Politics and Society* 27, no. 3 (1999): 430–464.

Grayson, George W. *Mexico: From Corporatism to Pluralism?* Fort Worth, TX: Harcourt Brace, 1998.

Hamilton, Nora. *The Limits of State Autonomy*. Princeton, NJ: Princeton University Press, 1982.

Hansen, Roger D. *The Politics of Mexican Development*. Baltimore: Johns Hopkins University Press, 1971.

Meyer, Michael C., and William L. Sherman. *The Course of Mexican History*. Fourth ed. New York: Oxford University Press, 1991.

Middlebrook, Kevin J. *The Paradox of Revolution: Labor, the State, and Authoritarianism in Mexico*. Baltimore: Johns Hopkins University Press, 1995.

Morris, Stephen D. *Political Reformism in Mexico: An Overview of Contemporary Mexican Politics*. Boulder, CO: Lynne Rienner, 1995.

Ruvio, Luis, and Susan Kaufman Purcell, eds. *Mexico under Fox*. Boulder, CO: Lynne Rienner, 2004.

Skidmore, Thomas E., and Peter H. Smith. *Modern Latin America*. Fourth ed. Oxford: Oxford University Press, 1995.

Wiarda, Howard J. "Toward a Framework for the Study of Political Change in the Iberic-Latin Tradition: The Corporative Model." *World Politics* 25 (1973): 206–235.

Womack, John, Jr. *Zapata and the Mexican Revolution*. New York: Vintage Books, 1970.

IMPORTANT TERMS

cabildos town councils established during the colonial period that served as the basis for the independence movement.

caciques political bosses who control local government and are relatively autonomous from the federal government. Co-opting these individuals has been a main concern in the centralization of political authority in Mexico.

Felipe Calderón Hinojosa the second non-PRI president elected since the 1920s. Calderón is a member of the PAN (National Action Party) and committed to a pro-business, market-oriented economic platform.

Lázaro Cárdenas president of Mexico from 1934 to 1940. He was responsible for institutionalizing the corporatist form of government and bringing labor, agricultural workers, and industry under the control of the state.

caudillos political strongmen during the 1800s who frequently controlled their own armies and dominated local politics. Their presence made centralized political authority difficult to establish during the nineteenth century and led to decades of political instability.

Conservatives loose-knit political party during the 1800s that represented the interests of the agricultural sector while being opposed to industrialization and democratic reforms.

Constitution of 1917 constitution of the Mexican Revolution that promoted radical agrarian reform and workers' rights. It would become the legal basis for Lázaro Cárdenas to redistribute land and nationalize Mexico's oil industry.

corporatism (Mexican) an ideology derived from medieval Catholic thought that sees the polity as an organic whole and seeks to minimize social conflict via central government organization of competing interests in society. In its institutionalized form, the government organizes and directs urban and rural labor unions as well as professional organizations.

criollos individuals of pure-blooded Spanish heritage born in Mexico. The economic and political elite tend to be from this racial class.

Democratic Revolutionary Party (PRD) a leftist political party formed after the 1988 presidential election by defectors from the PRI in order to offer an electoral alternative to the dominant party.

dinosaurios a faction of the ruling PRI Party in the last two decades of the twentieth century. Its members want to maintain corporatist forms of economic and political organization.

ejidos communal farms that originated in pre-Columbian indigenous societies and were promoted in the 1917 constitution. Lázaro Cárdenas established a number of them during the late 1930s as a way of distributing land among indigenous populations and poor farmers (found mostly in southern Mexico).

Vincente Fox victor of the 2000 presidential election from the PAN (National Action Party) and a former businessman. The first candidate from an opposition party to win the presidency since the Mexican Revolution.

import-substituting industrialization (ISI) the dominant economic policy of Mexico from the 1930s to the early 1980s, designed to industrialize the nation. According to this general economic strategy, high import tariffs are imposed to stimulate domestic production of consumer goods.

Institutional Revolutionary Party (PRI) the dominant ruling party of Mexico since the 1920s. Although it originated as a center left party, it has drifted toward the center-right since the 1980s.

Benito Juárez a liberal reformer in the mid-1800s who sought to promote land reform, centralize political authority, and modernize Mexico.

La Reforma a period in Mexican political history (ca. 1855–1876) during which liberal political forces predominated over their conservative rivals and began implementing economic and political reforms designed to bring Mexico closer to the policies and forms of government of the United States and Northern Europe. This represented the first time since the end of colonialism that a consistent governmental plan appeared, even though this era was beset by civil war and a foreign occupation.

Liberals a loose-knit political party during the 1800s that represented urban interests and promoted increased trade ties with Northern Europe and the United States.

Antonio López de Santa Anna the most important caudillo in Mexico during the nineteenth century, who intermittently served as president.

mestizos individuals of mixed Spanish and indigenous heritage. They represent the mingling of two different cultures into a distinct Mexican identity.

Mexican Miracle a period from 1940 to the 1980s (with the apogee from 1950 to 1970) wherein rapid industrialization promoted high levels of economic growth and improved living standards. This era gave rise to a new middle class with rising expectations that were restricted by the government's inability to satisfy these demands during the last two decades of the twentieth century.

Mexican Revolution the period from 1910 to 1920 wherein a major civil war among various factions eventually led to a set of radical social programs, namely labor rights and land reform, being included in the constitution of 1917 and eventually implemented under Lázaro Cárdenas during the 1930s.

National Action Party (PAN) a center-right party established in the mid-1900s as a challenge to PRI dominance. It won some critical local elections during the 1980s and 1990s that pushed Mexico toward greater political liberalization.

neoliberalism a policy that emphasizes free trade, privatization of industry, and a reduction in government intervention in the economy. This strategy was pursued by Presidents Salinas and Zedillo during the 1980s and 1990s.

North American Free Trade Agreement (NAFTA) an international treaty that lowered trade barriers among Mexico, the United States, and Canada. The centerpiece of President Salinas's neoliberal economic strategy, it was implemented on January 1, 1994, the same day that the Zapatista National Liberation Army initiated its guerrilla insurgency.

pan o palo literally meaning "bread or club," the phrase that refers to two common forms of political power in Mexico. *Pan* (bread) denotes the use of political patronage to buy political support, whereas *palo* (club) implies the use of coercion.

Porfiriato the period from 1876 to 1910 during which caudillo and dictatorial President Porfirio Díaz ruled Mexico. This was the first time since colonial days that Mexico was unified under central rule for a significant period; it was also a time of strong economic growth that gave rise to new social classes and, eventually, the Mexican Revolution.

Carlos Salinas de Gortari Mexican president from 1988 to 1994. He reversed decades of corporatist and ISI policies in favor of a neoliberal economic agenda. His economic liberalization prompted calls for political liberalization at the end of the twentieth century.

técnicos a faction within the ruling PRI that rose to prominence in the 1980s by promoting neoliberal economic reforms. Typically trained in U.S. and European universities, the members are in conflict with the *dinosaurios*, who favor corporatist policies.

Tlatelolco site of a massacre in 1968 where more than 100 protesters were killed by state police. The protest signaled that the long-standing legitimacy of the PRI's corporatist rule was wearing thin, especially among students and the middle class.

Virgin of Guadalupe a symbol of Mexico's unique national identity that blends European Catholicism with indigenous images. It represents the appearance of the Virgin Mary before an indigenous boy during the colonial period and has since been used as a rallying point for Mexican nationalism.

Emiliano Zapata the leader of a revolutionary army during the Mexican Revolution. He demanded greater rights for indigenous rural workers in southern Mexico, including a substantial land reform that eventually became a centerpiece of the 1917 constitution.

Zapatista National Liberation Army (EZLN) a guerrilla army that appeared in the southern Mexican state of Chiapas in 1994 following the implementation of NAFTA. Like their earlier revolutionary namesake, Emiliano Zapata, the Zapatistas, as they are known, demanded land reform, economic justice, and freer political representation for the poor indigenous communities.

Ernesto Zedillo president of Mexico from 1994 to 2000. He oversaw an extension of neoliberal reforms and promoted greater political liberalization, including the first-ever presidential primary election in Mexican history.

STUDY QUESTIONS

1. Mexico has prided itself on its unique blend of Spanish and indigenous heritages. Not only did the Spanish conquistadors adopt a number of indigenous traditions and symbols, but Spaniards and indigenous people also physically intermingled, forming a mestizo (mixed-blood) ethnic group. Nonetheless, economic and political power remains highly stratified along class lines, with criollos holding the most powerful positions, the indigenous population inhabiting the lowest economic classes, and the mestizos falling in between these two groups. Tensions among these groups spilled over most recently during the Zapatista uprising in southern Mexico, with the guerrillas being composed mostly of indigenous, non-Spanish-speaking individuals. How might this ethnic/racial stratification affect the ability of Mexicans to craft a single national identity? As long as this stratification exists, is it possible to speak of "one Mexico"? What actions might the government take to alleviate the problems created by these socioeconomic and ethnic divisions?

2. Political instability was one of the main features of Mexico during the 1800s. What factors led to and exacerbated this political instability? (Consider a comparison with the United States, which won its independence from colonial powers four decades earlier.) What were the short- and long-term consequences of this era of political instability? Consider how this era both shaped the interests of various actors in society and affected the nation's political consciousness.

3. A common problem faced by political rulers during the colonial and postcolonial periods was how to govern distant geographic regions that had incentives not to obey central authority. Even today, the Mexican president has difficulty implementing policies in isolated regions, such as the state of Chiapas. Local political bosses (caciques) retain a great deal of power over local populations. How have political leaders dealt with this problem throughout Mexican history? What types of policies could the current Mexican government develop to bring local caciques in line with national policy?

4. The revolutionary Constitution of 1917 promised radical changes in land tenure and workers' rights. Many of these proposals were implemented by Lázaro Cárdenas during the late 1930s, but enthusiasm for continuing these programs has since waned. Why has this been the case? Is it possible to maintain policies that support communal farms (*ejidos*) and government-sponsored labor unions in an increasingly globalized world economy?

5. Consider the name of the Institutional Revolutionary Party. Looking at Mexico's history, why do you think this name was chosen? To what extent can a revolution be institutionalized? To what extent has the PRI remained a revolutionary force in Mexican society? Now consider the name of the Democratic Revolutionary Party. Why do you suppose this name was chosen? If the PRD gains power, do you expect to see it evolve similarly to the PRI? Discuss.

6. Mexican corporatism brings various social actors (for example, labor, business professionals) into an officially sanctioned ruling coalition. While guaranteeing certain privileges for these groups (for example, job security for unionized labor and subsidies for businesses), it also limits such freedoms as choosing when to strike or how to allocate capital. Discuss the advantages and disadvantages of such arrangements. Since the 1980s, there has been a move by some groups to obtain greater autonomy from the government. Why? Consider the role of the economic crisis in the 1980s and its effects on government revenue.

7. Mexico's general economic strategy from the 1930s to the 1980s (known as import-substituting industrialization) was to isolate itself from the world economy by imposing high tariffs on imported consumer goods and limiting foreign investment in the economy. Although it was successful in generating rapid economic growth in the short term, this plan has created some long-term problems. Discuss. To what extent is it possible for Mexico to isolate itself from the world economy today? What possible effects might increased economic integration (e.g., NAFTA) into the global economy have on domestic politics?

8. There is a popular saying in Mexico that describes the country as follows: "So far from God; so close to the United States." What role has the United States (and other foreign countries) played in shaping Mexican politics? How has this role changed over the past 200 years? What does NAFTA have to say about changing relationships among the countries of North America? Is the relationship between the United States and Mexico only a one-way street, or has Mexico influenced the domestic politics of its northern neighbor?

9. Both Presidents Salinas and Zedillo faced the difficult task of promoting economic growth and political democracy while maintaining the PRI in political power. What are some of the difficulties in balancing these competing interests? How has the pursuit of these different goals affected the PRI itself? To what extent does the pursuit of economic liberalization and liberal democracy conflict with Mexico's long-standing identification with a corporatist philosophy?

10. Many observers of Mexican politics argue that Mexico's transition to a liberal democracy will not be complete until there is a new party in charge of the executive branch. Consider the results of the 2000 and 2006 presidential elections. Would you agree that Mexico has made a successful transition to a stable democracy? Was the ability to overcome a controversial election, decided by 0.58 percent of the vote, an encouraging sign for the Mexican polity? Or was the 2006 election indicative of more political turmoil to come in a multiparty democracy where the executive (president) cannot garner a majority of the vote nor secure a legislative majority in the Congress? What possible institutional changes would you suggest, if any, to the Mexican political system to make it more fair, democratic, and/or stable?

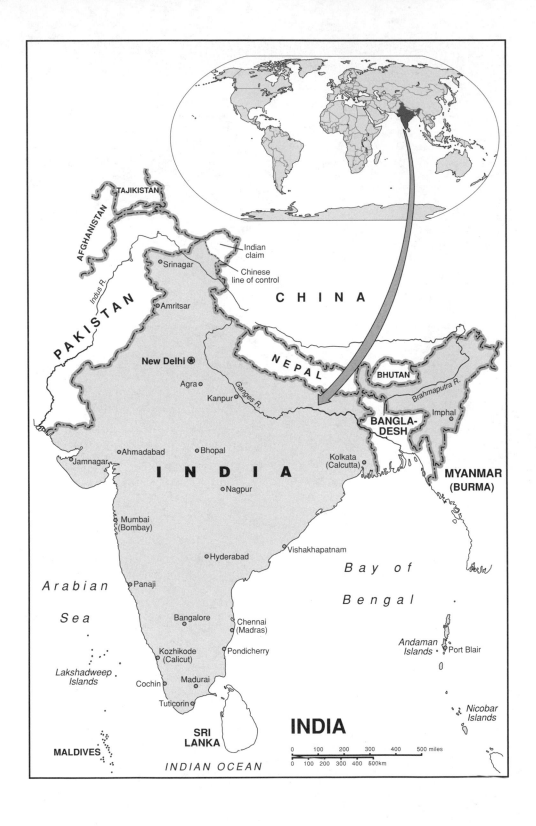

INDIA

CHAPTER TEN

India

Rudra Sil

Introduction

For most of the first four decades after its independence in 1947, India was led by the **Congress Party**, which descended from the independence movement once led by **Mohandas K. (Mahatma) Gandhi** and was committed to a vision of a modern, industrialized, secular state. The party that led India into the twenty-first century, however, was the **Bharatiya Janata Party (BJP, or the Indian People's Party)**, which descended from political and social organizations committed to redefining Indian national identity in terms of **Hinduttva** (Hindu culture and civilization). Under the leadership of the BJP, India held a series of underground nuclear tests in 1998 and proclaimed itself a member of the nuclear club, setting off joyous celebrations throughout the country and prompting rival Pakistan to launch its own nuclear tests. The following year, Indian troops ousted Pakistani-backed militants from Kargil in Indian-held Kashmir (the Himalayan region claimed by both India and Pakistan), spurring another round of celebrations accompanied by emotional tributes to the "Kargil martyrs." Soon after, India's population passed the one billion mark, triggering still more national euphoria as India closed in on China for the dubious distinction of being the world's most populous country. Following the terrorist attacks of September 11, 2001, in the United States, given Al Qaeda's stated support for Muslim insurgents in Kashmir, India became a key player in the international war on terror, but it also reaffirmed its independent posture by refusing to join the U.S.-led coalition that invaded Iraq. And, with its huge pool of scientific talent and an economic growth rate surpassing 8 percent in 2003–2004, India began to receive international recognition as an emerging global economic power and a new hub for high-tech research and development.

Given this string of achievements, it did not come as a surprise when the BJP's leaders called for early elections in 2004 and initiated a public relations campaign triumphantly dubbed "India shining." What did come as a surprise was the result of the election. The BJP and its allies saw their share of seats in the Parliament drop dramatically from 56 percent to 35 percent, while the bloc formed by the Congress Party managed to outgain the BJP bloc to form a new coalition government with the backing of leftist parties that had garnered nearly 12 percent of the parliamentary seats. In retrospect, it is clear that the BJP had underestimated the economic frustrations of India's large pool of poor voters, especially in the rural areas where nearly two-thirds of the country's population still reside. It is to this pool that the Congress Party and the leftist parties had appealed, attacking the BJP for catering to the wealthy and neglecting the plight of the poor. It was true that the Congress Party had been primarily responsible for initiating economic liberalization during the early 1990s, and it was equally true that a Congress government was not about to abruptly shift economic policies that were generating high growth. But, the fact remains that the party that lost power in 2004 did so at a time of impressive economic growth and rising international stature, whereas the new ruling coalition came to power by promising new measures to improve the lot of the rural poor, whose economic plight was only magnified by the BJP's "India shining" campaign.

What does this turn of events tell us about the evolving interplay of identities, interests, and institutions in postcolonial India? How can India's economic liberalization be sustained in a parliamentary democracy featuring over 600 million potential voters, the vast majority of whom are engaged in agriculture? Why does the fourth largest economy in the world attract the interest of global multinational firms in high-tech sectors while simultaneously witnessing an epidemic of suicides among farmers crushed by the burden of debt and poverty? What accounts for the continued political salience of identities based on **caste**, region, and religion even as new kinds of interest groups and social movements have proliferated rapidly? Why, after several decades of political independence and sustained industrialization, did Hindu nationalism seemingly become a powerful force during the mid-1990s, only to become seemingly irrelevant in 2004? And, more broadly, what do the political, economic, and social transformations in India since the early 1900s tell us about the challenges and opportunities facing postcolonial nations striving to sustain political order and economic growth in a changing global order?

This chapter will help you make sense of these questions in the course of tracing the shifts in India's developmental path from the arrival of colonialism through the post–Cold War era. The first section will discuss the emergence of a South Asian civilization comprised of numerous social identities, the arrival and effects of British colonial rule, and the rise of Indian nationalism. The second section will examine the developmental path taken by India during the 1947–1984 period when, in the midst of the Cold War, India's leaders sought to define a "third way" that combined democratic political institutions and a state-led program of autarkic economic development. The third section will trace the shifts in India's developmental path accompanying the end of the Cold War, including the arrival of a new era of coalition politics, the evolving significance of long-standing cultural identities, India's experience with economic liberalization, and the emergence of new kinds of interest groups and social movements.

Pre-Independence India: Civilization and Empire to Colonialism and Nationalism

The term "India" has its origins in one of the world's great ancient civilizations that developed in the Indus Valley region to the northwest of present-day India (in the southern part of present-day Pakistan). The Indus Valley civilization, which is thought to have emerged as early as 4000 B.C., flourished around 2500–2000 B.C., developing its own system of culture, language, irrigation, municipal administration, and even intercity communications networks. This civilization seems to have gone into decline by 1500 B.C., just as a distinct population of Indo-Aryans arrived on the Indian subcontinent, ushering in a new era in the making of South Asian civilization.

CIVILIZATION AND EMPIRE: THE SOURCES OF IDENTITY AND UNITY IN SOUTH ASIA

One of the great divides in Indian society has its roots in the settlement of the lighter-skinned Indo-Aryans in the northern and central plains of the Indian subcontinent. The newly transplanted population spread across the subcontinent, developing a series of languages that were loosely related through their common roots in ancient Sanskrit. The darker-skinned Dravidians, who were native to the subcontinent, became concentrated in the southern part of India. Although the physical differences between Indo-Aryans and Dravidians have been exaggerated by British anthropologists and historians, the descendants of Dravidians continue to constitute a distinct ethnic group, encompassing one-quarter of the population of present-day India. As we shall see, this ethnic divide has played a significant role in Indian electoral politics and center-periphery relations.

The shared identity of Dravidians is reinforced by the fact that they speak languages that are not derived from Sanskrit, upon which most northern Indian languages are based. Each of the four main Dravidian languages today serves as an official state language in the south (for example, Telegu in Andhra Pradesh and Tamil in Tamil Nadu). Most other languages spoken in India have common roots in ancient Sanskrit, but no single language can be identified with a majority of India's population. The official languages of several states in northern India are not spoken much outside of those states (for example, Bengali in West Bengal and Punjabi in the Punjab). Of the languages spoken by significant populations in different states, the most common is Hindi, the main indigenous official language. Constructed by standardizing popular local variants, Hindi is spoken by 36 percent of the population spread over the north-central states called the "Hindi belt" (for example, Bihar, Uttar Pradesh, and Haryana). Other significant languages include English, which has the status of an official language and is regularly used for government documents as well as in several major newspapers. Although spoken by only about 5 percent of the total population, the proportion is much higher in urban areas and has been increasing steadily since the time of independence. Also spoken commonly across regions is Urdu, the primary language for nearly half of the Muslims in the country. The use of Urdu dates back to the arrival of Central Asian Islamic groups and combines most of the vocabulary of Hindi with an Arabic script. As we shall see later, these linguistic differences have acquired a political significance given the nature of state boundaries in India.

In spite of the formation of diverse linguistic communities, from the time of the Indo-Aryan settlement of the Indian subcontinent, a common civilization began to take shape in the northern and central plains. This process was intensified through the formation of empires under powerful princes who managed to conquer several regional kingdoms in different parts of the subcontinent. Soon after Alexander the Great's invasion stalled in India, the first major empire in South Asia was founded by Chandragupta Maurya in 326 B.C. His empire eventually stretched from the Indus Valley region to all but the most southern part of the subcontinent. Subsequent rulers (for example, the Gupta kings, A.D. 320–550, and King Harsha Vardhana, A.D. 606–647) would also establish large empires that contributed to the expansion of administrative bureaucracies as well as closer economic and political ties among the diverse regions of the subcontinent. In addition, the tributary relationships established between the emperor's court and the regional provinces provided a model for later empires, including the British colonial empire.

These periods of dynastic rule also contributed to the flowering of a recognizable Hindu culture throughout much of the Indian subcontinent. The main beliefs, deities, rituals, and spiritual philosophy identified with Hinduism can be traced back to the writing of two major texts (the *Vedas* and the *Upanishads*) in northern India between the eighth and fifth centuries B.C. With the formation of progressively larger empires from the fourth century B.C. onward, an increasingly recognizable set of religious beliefs and practices – such as the belief in reincarnation and the rituals of *puja* (the worship of gods and deities) – came to be manifested among Hindus across the Indian subcontinent. This process gained momentum during the fourth and fifth centuries A.D., when priests and scholars under the patronage of the Gupta dynasty rulers helped to mold a more standardized expression of Hinduism. By the eighth century, the process spread to the southern regions of India as Dravidian princes, poets, and religious scholars began to accept and promote Hindu beliefs and practices. The result was not a unified religious doctrine upheld by a central religious authority (as in the case of Catholicism), but in everyday life, many of the beliefs and practices associated with Hinduism were recognizable across different regions throughout the Indian subcontinent.

Caste is another key aspect of social life that was recognizable across South Asia. As a way of organizing work and ordering social life, the Indian caste system was not fundamentally different from social hierarchies prevalent in Europe during the Middle Ages. What made the Indian caste system distinctive was the fact that families associated with different traditional occupations were ranked on a hierarchical scale of "purity." Those who were able to read Hindu scripts (written in Sanskrit) and perform Hindu rituals came to be regarded as a higher-status (more "pure") category of **Brahmins** (priests). Rulers, court officials, and soldiers constituted the second category in the caste hierarchy. They were followed by merchants and traders, peasants and artisans, and, finally, "untouchables," who performed menial tasks considered "unclean" or "impure." These categories, however, were too broad to serve as sources of shared identity across regions. What really counted was membership in one of the specific subdivisions (*jati*) of the five general caste categories *within a given region* (usually a cluster of nearby villages). In everyday life, it was one's *jati* that marked one's inherited occupational and social status; it was *jati* that determined the rules, habits, and obligations of individuals; and it was *jati* that defined the pool of eligible marriage partners within a region. Although the tasks, rules, obligations, and relative positions of a given *jati* varied across regions, in all cases, work and society were organized in terms of a fixed hierarchy within which there was no opportunity for upward mobility or intermarriage.

Many Indian leaders and scholars (including Mahatma Gandhi) have not viewed the caste system as an intrinsic feature of Hinduism. However, the fact that social organization and religious practice were so thoroughly fused for so many centuries contributes to the perception – both in India and abroad – that the caste system is inseparable from Hinduism. This also accounts for the fact that caste communities have remained an important source of identity and division throughout contemporary India even after the caste system was formally abolished by the Indian constitution after independence. At the same time, this source of division paradoxically facilitated the crystallization of a South Asian civilization by making the social structures of diverse communities recognizable throughout India. In fact, the basic structure of the caste system later influenced the social organization of many Muslim and **Sikh** communities in India.

Now, we turn to the origins of the religious cleavage between the Hindu majority, which accounts for more than 80 percent of the Indian population, and the significant Muslim minority, which accounts for about 11 percent. (The remainder consists of Sikhs, Christians, Buddhists, and members of other religions.) The Hindu–Muslim divide has its origins in raids carried out by Muslim groups from the Arabian peninsula and Central Asia into the northern plains of India. Some of these groups attempted to convert local populations and eventually settled down. A more significant and lasting Muslim presence in India came about with the arrival of an Afghan Muslim prince named Babur, founder of the Moghul Empire (1526–1757). Babur's grandson, Akbar (1556–1605), followed in the footsteps of the Mauryan and Gupta empires, extending Moghul control through most of the Indian subcontinent. As in the case of earlier empires, a centralized administrative machinery coexisted with tributary relations with several layers of provincial and regional rulers who retained their titles and some autonomy as long as they paid tribute to the emperor in Delhi. Under Akbar, Islam gained a permanent foothold in South Asia and led to the establishment of new Muslim settlements as well as a spate of conversions. At the same time, Akbar adopted aspects of Hindu political thought, included Hindus in his court in Delhi, treated Hindu scholars with respect, and abolished many policies that discriminated against Hindus. In this tolerant atmosphere, Akbar won the respect of Hindu princes while Muslim artists and scholars came to be appreciated by Hindu cultural elites. This period of relatively peaceful coexistence between Hindus and Muslims suggests that the relationship between the two groups is not inherently a conflictual one, and that the outbreaks of Hindu–Muslim violence during and after colonialism have many complex causes.

In sum, between 1500 B.C. and A.D. 1700, a number of sociocultural cleavages emerged throughout the Indian subcontinent: between northern Indo-Aryans and southern Dravidians, between different linguistic communities, between different caste groups, and between the majority Hindus and religious minorities such as Muslims and Sikhs. Yet, it is important to remember that for all the emphasis placed on social divisions in India, there was a centuries-old civilization that had evolved and spread through most of the Indian subcontinent well before the establishment of British colonial rule. The use of Sanskrit as a common language for priests and literati, the spread of recognizable religious beliefs and practices across regions, the emergent similarities in social organization across diverse communities, and the establishment of tributary rule and bureaucratic administration during various empires all provided a common frame of reference for people in different parts of South Asia. Although this may not have been sufficient to preempt every kind of social conflict, it did serve to distinguish South Asian civilization from the tribally based local communities scattered across sub-Saharan

Africa, giving India's future leaders more of a foundation for building a modern nation-state.

THE ENCOUNTER WITH THE WEST: BRITISH COLONIAL RULE, 1757–1947

Although contact with "foreign" cultures (for example, Persians and Afghans) was nothing new to South Asia, the arrival of British traders marked South Asia's first significant encounter with the West. As the Moghul Empire went into decline during the seventeenth century, the British East India Company, a large trading company officially backed by the British government, began to establish trading stations in coastal towns such as Bombay (now Mumbai) in the west and Calcutta (now Kolkata) in the east. The regional rulers in these areas signed agreements with the British East India Company partly to enhance their own political and economic position vis-à-vis neighboring provinces and the Moghul court in Delhi, but they could not foresee the long-term consequences of the trading concessions that they gave the British. Eventually, a Bengali prince realized that the agreements were giving the British increasing economic control over his region and he set out to evict the British. However, his troops were decisively defeated by British troops at the Battle of Plassey (1757). Partly as a result of disunity among India's provincial rulers and partly as a result of superior military technology, the British rapidly proceeded to defeat dozens of other regional armies and by 1840 had established their own colonial empire throughout the subcontinent.

Initially, British colonialism proceeded through indirect rule. This system functioned through a series of alliances with regional princes who kept their titles, possessions, and local authority in exchange for supporting British administrators and their economic interests. This informal colonial empire would become a more formalized system of direct rule after a major 1857 rebellion launched by Indian guards trained by the British. The Sepoy Mutiny began as a spontaneous reaction to the discovery that animal grease from pigs (hated by Muslims) and cows (sacred to Hindus) was being used in rifle cartridges, but it soon became an organized campaign supported by some Indian princes to end Britain's political and economic control in their regions. After violently suppressing the mutiny, the British established direct rule over most of India (but maintained indirect rule in a few of the less troublesome provinces such as Kashmir). Direct rule still depended on cooperation from Indians serving as soldiers and administrators, but now Queen Victoria was crowned the ruler of India, a viceroy was appointed to rule India directly on her behalf, and British governors and local officials were appointed to maintain local order. During the next ninety years (1857–1947), the impact of British rule became more pronounced as India became "the jewel in the crown" for an expanding British empire that stretched from Hong Kong to East Africa.

The *political* legacy of British colonialism was twofold: the establishment of institutions that would be adapted by a postcolonial Indian nation-state and the heightening of mistrust among groups identifying with different castes, regions, and religions. With regard to political institutions, one of the most important bodies created by the British was the civil service, which assisted in the administration of the colony and would later provide the foundation for the Indian Administrative Service (IAS), the backbone of modern Indian bureaucracy. After World War I, the British also proceeded to establish national and regional assemblies consisting of elected representatives in order to create a semblance of legitimacy for the colonial administration. Of course, these assemblies had no real legislative power and had little say over the most important policies and laws introduced by the British viceroy. However, they did provide an institutional basis for parliamentary democracy in postcolonial India. Also, as part of direct rule, the British systematized the division of labor between central and provincial administrations, providing a bridge from the tributary system set up by various empires to the institutions of modern Indian federalism. Although these institutions were not set up with an independent nation-state in mind, they did provide a foundation for the political system that is still in evidence in contemporary India.

A more problematic political legacy of British colonialism is its differential treatment of various groups, which is most clearly evident in the deliberate strategy of "divide and rule." Even during the period of indirect rule, the British had taken advantage of the fact that native elites in different regions could be made to compete with each other for status or influence. During the period of direct rule, upper-caste Hindus (especially Brahmins), because of their relatively high level of literacy, were recruited into the colonial administration in disproportionate numbers. This left the much larger lower-caste groups with fewer opportunities for upward mobility and made some suspicious of political leaders drawn from upper-caste backgrounds. But the most divisive legacy of colonialism stems from the manipulation of tensions between the Hindu majority and Muslim minority in order to justify British colonial administration in South Asia. The best example is the 1905 partition of Bengal in eastern India into a predominantly Muslim eastern half (today the nation of Bangladesh) and a predominantly Hindu western half (today the Indian state of West Bengal, which borders Bangladesh). Although Hindus constituted 40 percent of the population in eastern Bengal and Muslims constituted 20 percent in western Bengal, and although the populations in both parts spoke Bengali, the British claimed that the partition was necessary to administer the region more efficiently. Although many Muslims may have welcomed the opportunity to constitute a majority in a separate province, the partition was consciously designed to stifle a nationalist movement that was gathering steam in Bengal and causing great concern for the British viceroy at the time, Lord Curzon. Ironically, the partition had the unintended effect of spurring greater activism across India and giving more impetus to the budding independence movement.

British *economic* policies had a more profound and widely felt impact on the interests and identities of different segments of the Indian population. Karl Marx once wrote that British colonialism was a progressive force in India because it helped to dismantle feudalism and expedite the formation of capitalism (which had to precede socialism). Indeed, throughout British India, colonial economic activities contributed to new mining and construction, the building of new factories and machinery, and the construction of an extensive network of transportation and communication, including what is today one of the world's largest railroad systems. This led to the first sustained exposure for thousands of Indians to industrial production and factory life. A small Indian middle class and a somewhat larger working class also emerged as a result of the increase in British economic activities in India, setting the stage for class divisions that would cut across preexisting cleavages based on caste, region, and religion.

These were significant changes for a society that was overwhelmingly agrarian, but Marx may have underestimated the negative effects of British colonialism on Indian economic development. Throughout the two centuries of colonial rule, the original motives that had brought the British East India Company to the subcontinent remained very much in play. Much of the infrastructure set up by the British was designed not to boost indigenous industrial growth but to facilitate the extraction of valuable resources and the transportation of British-manufactured goods to distant markets. The participation of the indigenous Indian middle class in production and distribution was controlled and restricted; for example, the British imposed limits on textile production by Indian-owned factories because their products were in competition with the more expensive textiles imported from British factories. The nascent working class was severely exploited as the British took advantage of cheap labor as part of their continuing industrial expansion. The expanded production of cash crops took away land and labor from subsistence agriculture, intensifying poverty and hunger among the rural population. The British also established monopolies on the production of key necessities (even salt) in order to make the native population dependent on the colonial economic apparatus. Thus, although the British did help to create a new infrastructure for industrial production in India, they also contributed to "misdevelopment" because the economic institutions of colonialism were intended to facilitate the exploitation of resources and markets rather than to support India's industrialization. Postcolonial India's economic problems would have many and complex causes, but the economic legacy of colonialism is certainly one of them.

The *social* impact of colonialism affected far fewer people but proved to be most significant in the eventual weakening of British rule. This social impact was mainly evident among educated, urban, mostly Hindu intellectual elites who attended British schools and universities in increasing numbers. These elites encountered new literature and new social movements, as well as Western political ideologies such as nationalism, liberalism, and socialism. The effect of this exposure came to be evident toward the end of the nineteenth century in vigorous debates among Indian intellectual elites in response to British social reforms aimed at institutionalizing English common law and eliminating certain egregious local customs (such as the practice in Rajasthan of wives throwing themselves on the funeral pyres of their husbands). Also worth noting is the use of the English language, which not only provided an alternative medium for communication among elites from different regions but also enabled these elites to express themselves articulately to foreign audiences. The significance of these changes for the development of Indian nationalism cannot be understated. In fact, one of the ironies of British colonial rule is that its dependence on an English-speaking Indian elite paved the way for the emergence of a new political class that would lead the movement for Indian independence.

THE RISE OF NATIONALISM AND THE MOVEMENT FOR INDEPENDENCE

The organization that led India to independence, the **Indian National Congress** (**INC**), was established in 1885. The founding members, the majority of whom were educated Brahmins from relatively wealthy families, did not initially challenge British rule. Their two original purposes were to expand the representation of Indians *within* the British colonial administration and to debate the merits of various Hindu traditions in light of social reforms initiated by the British. However, the British rejection of even the most moderate demands, together with the outcry over the aforementioned partition of Bengal, spurred the INC to embrace the goal of independence (*swaraj*) in 1906.

The evolution of the INC into a mass nationalist movement, however, did not happen until the arrival of Mohandas Karamchand Gandhi (referred to as "Mahatma," or "Great Soul"). Gandhi had gone to Britain to be trained as a lawyer and then spent several years challenging discriminatory British policies in South Africa. Upon his return to India in 1915, Gandhi quickly became a popular leader of the INC. Most significantly, Gandhi managed to attract the attention of lower-caste Indians in the countryside. To demonstrate to India's mostly rural population that the INC was more than an exclusive club of educated upper-caste urbanites, Gandhi chose to live as most villagers did and traveled throughout the countryside to document economic difficulties and social injustices brought about by colonialism.

Gandhi focused on the points that united Indians from different religions, regions, castes, and classes. He emphasized the power of a universal inner truth that all human beings shared, while appreciating the distinctive spirituality shared by all Indians despite their diversity. He also emphasized the more universal aspects of Hindu philosophy, such as its spiritualism, while attacking specific beliefs and practices that served to divide communities by caste or religion. This was not an easy synthesis for many Indians to grasp. Some Hindus worried that Gandhi was diluting the core tenets of Hinduism, whereas Muslims saw his philosophical positions as relevant mainly for Hindus. Nevertheless, by emphasizing the negative economic and cultural consequences of British colonial rule for members of all castes, regions, and religions, Gandhi was able to draw millions of previously apathetic South Asians into the campaign for independence.

It was Gandhi's strategy of nonviolent noncooperation that did the most to attract the attention of the rural masses as well as the international community. This strategy, which was later replicated by Martin Luther King, Jr., during the U.S. civil rights movement, served two purposes. First, it directly disrupted British colonial administration and its economic activities, which depended on the cooperation of the native population. Second, it demonstrated to the Indian masses that their strength lay in their numbers and their will rather than in the acquisition of arms. For example, Gandhi and the INC orchestrated a major nationwide boycott of British cloth in 1920–1921 during which millions of Indians burned cloth manufactured in Britain and began to wear white homespun cotton; in just one year, the value of foreign clothes imported into India was cut nearly in half. Even today, most Indian politicians continue to wear white homespun in public as a sign of their patriotism. Similarly, Gandhi's "salt march" caught the attention of Indians everywhere as he led hundreds of his followers on a 200-mile trek to the sea to make salt on the beaches; this was in defiance of a British law prohibiting Indians from manufacturing salt and requiring them to pay taxes on salt manufactured in factories. Also noteworthy are two campaigns that began in Bengal but spread rapidly to other parts of the country: a student boycott of British-run schools and colleges and a boycott of British-run courts by scores of well-known lawyers who gave up lucrative practices (including Motilal Nehru, the father of India's first prime minister).

Most INC members followed Gandhi, renouncing violence in favor of continued reliance on the tactic of nonviolent noncooperation. The one leader who opted for more direct action, Subhas Chandra Bose, was elected president of the INC for a brief period in 1938 but left to organize the Indian National Army (with German and Japanese assistance) to fight British rule. Whether this army might have eventually become an effective instrument for ending British colonialism is not clear, given the outbreak of World War II. Nor is it clear whether colonial rule would have ended when it did in the absence of the impact of World War II on Britain's own economy and infrastructure. What is clear is that the INC campaign of nonviolent noncooperation made it increasingly difficult and costly for the British to maintain the existing system of colonial administration.

On August 15, 1947, British colonial rule formally ended, and two independent nations emerged: India and Pakistan. Gandhi himself had hoped for a unified nation that would include all Hindus and Muslims, but now that independence was at hand, the unity of the nationalist movement was giving way to competing interests. Although some Muslims supported the idea of a unified India, others simply did not trust the Hindu-dominated INC, fearing that their interests as a minority would be ignored. Mohammad Ali Jinnah, an INC member who helped found the Muslim League in 1920, insisted on a separate Pakistani nation and would become its first leader. On the other side, several Hindu organizations that had supported the INC campaign for independence now devoted themselves to promoting traditional Hindu ideals and symbols that they felt had been diluted by Gandhi's efforts to court Muslims. Fearing civil war, Gandhi agreed to a plan that would form a separate nation, Pakistan, in parts of the subcontinent where Muslims constituted a majority: a western part corresponding to the borders of present-day Pakistan and an eastern part corresponding to eastern Bengal (which would secede in 1971 to form the present-day nation of Bangladesh). During the partition, millions of people left their old homes to migrate to find new homes, while thousands died in bloody clashes between frustrated Hindus and Muslims. Eventually, the violence subsided, and in India the INC leaders set out to draft a new constitution. The Indian constitution, based on principles of democratic federalism and English common law, went into effect on January 26, 1950.

India's "Third Way": Political and Economic Development in the Cold War Era

The global context within which India emerged as an independent nation helped to shape India's self-image in world affairs, its political system, and its development program. The influence of Western political doctrines and institutions, the appeal of the Soviet model of rapid industrialization, and the Cold War between the two superpowers all contributed to a distinctive developmental path Indians proclaimed to be a "third way." This path was identified with neutrality in the Cold War, a steadfast commitment to secularism, and a "mixed" strategy of development that combined elements of both capitalism and socialism. This third way came to represent an appealing mixture for the dozens of new nations becoming independent in the 1950s and 1960s, most of which joined India in forming the "nonaligned movement" to proclaim their neutrality in the Cold War. It is true that few of the new nations were able to remain neutral given their security concerns in an era of superpower competition; indeed, India would later sign a "treaty of friendship" with the Soviet Union as Pakistan sought closer ties to the United States. However, India's generally independent foreign policy and its conscious effort to balance elements of capitalism and socialism made it a model for many developing countries and gave Indians a sense of identity and pride within the international order during the years of the Cold War. But what distinguished India from most other newly independent countries was a set of stable political and legal institutions that has now remained more or less intact for over five decades.

THE MAKING OF A SECULAR NATION: POLITICAL AND LEGAL INSTITUTIONS

After independence, the Indian National Congress (INC) reconstituted itself as the Congress Party but was without many of its most distinguished former leaders. Gandhi was assassinated in 1948 by a Hindu fanatic. Bose, who had advocated armed confrontation with the British and had envisioned a centralized one-party Indian state, is thought to have died in a plane crash after his anticolonial army was disbanded. Sardar Patel, a prominent Congress Party leader who envisioned an industrialized India in which Hindu traditions would be preserved, died of natural causes. Thus, **Jawaharlal Nehru** found himself to be the party's undisputed leader and the nation's first prime minister (1950–1964). Much more so than Gandhi or Patel, Nehru embraced an unequivocally modern worldview. This included a commitment to science and technology, a faith in the capacity of technocratic planning to deliver both economic growth and social justice, and, above all, a belief that a secular, democratic nation-state could function for all citizens regardless of caste, region, and religion.

"Secularism" generally implies that public life should be governed by the rule of law as evident in a written constitution and legal codes (and not by traditional customs, religious texts, or hereditary privileges). As such, the term applies both to the United States and the Soviet Union. In the Indian context, however, secularism acquired a more specific meaning in opposition to "communalism." Aside from the formal equality of all citizens before the law, secularism in India implies that politics should revolve around the interests of individuals rather than of groups identified by the communal ties of caste, region, or religion. Significantly, this understanding of secularism incorporates the principle that minorities and previously disadvantaged groups should be granted special privileges until the playing field becomes more level for all citizens. Thus, the caste system was abolished by law. A system of "**reservations**" (India's version of affirmative action) was instituted to help members of the lowest caste groups gain entry into educational institutions and employment, and India's Muslims and other religious minorities (but not the Hindu majority) were granted the special right to observe certain religious laws and attend religious schools.

India's parliamentary democracy was based mainly on the British Westminster model. This system has remained more or less unchanged since India's independence and continues to function in an orderly fashion. The legislative branch is bicameral. The focus of national politics is the lower house of the Parliament, the Lok Sabha. Elections for the lower house are held every five years unless the ruling party chooses to call early elections or unless defections from the ruling coalition result in no party being able to command a majority. Of the 545 members in Parliament, 543 are candidates winning a plurality of votes in single-member districts (a first-past-the-post system), and two special members are appointed by the president. The upper house of the Parliament, the Rajya Sabha, consists of 250 members elected for fixed six-year terms, with one-third standing for elections every two years. Most members are elected by the parliamentary assemblies of the states and territories constituting India, but 12 are appointed by the president on the basis of special considerations or expert knowledge. Like the British House of Lords (but not the U.S. Senate), the primary function of the upper house is not to independently make laws but to approve existing laws and provide continuity and stability through changing governments; given these functions, the upper house can never be dissolved.

The prime minister is usually the leader of the party or coalition that holds a majority in the lower house of the Parliament. He or she serves as the head of the government and is the focal point of national politics, being responsible for appointing cabinet ministers, launching new initiatives or programs, and making important decisions with regard to key domestic and foreign policy issues. The president, the head of state, is usually a nominee of the victorious party in Parliament but is formally elected to a five-year term by an electoral college that gives votes to each member of Parliament and weighted votes to all members of the state assemblies (to ensure reasonable representation of each region). The president often is not a career politician but an individual with significant personal accomplishments (for example, in science or literature) who is thought to stand above political conflicts as a symbol of unity and order throughout the republic. At the state level, the triad of the national parliament, prime minister, and president are replicated in the triad of the state assembly, the chief minister (leader of the ruling majority in the state assembly), and a governor appointed by the Indian president (often at the behest of the prime minister) to ensure that public order, the rule of law, and the constitution are upheld at the state level. Table 10.1 lists the prime ministers and presidents of India to date.

The first-past-the-post electoral system used at both the national and state levels means that a larger, better-organized party can convert narrow margins in popular votes into a disproportionately large share of seats in the

TABLE 10.1. Government Leaders of India, 1950–Present

Prime Ministers	Presidents (Heads of State)
1950–1964: Jawaharlal Nehru, Congress[a]	1950–1962: Rajendra Prasad
1964–1966: Lal Bahadur Shastri, Congress[b]	1962–1967: Sarvapalli Radhakrishnan
1967–1977: Mrs. Indira Gandhi, Congress-I	1967–1969: Zakir Hussain[h]
1977–1979: Morarji Desai, Janata Party	1969–1974: Varahagiri Venkata Giri
1979–1980: Chandra Shekhar, Janata Party	1974–1977: Fakhruddin Ali Ahmed[i]
1980–1984: Mrs. Indira Gandhi, Congress-I[c]	1977–1982: Neelam Sanjiva Reddy
1984–1989: Rajiv Gandhi, Congress-I[d]	1982–1987: Giani Zail Singh
1989–1991: V. P. Singh, Janata Dal	1987–1992: Shri R. Venkataraman
1991–1996: N. P. Narasimha Rao, Congress-I	1992–1997: Shankar Dayal Sharma
1996–1997: Deve Gowda, Janata Dal/UF[e]	1997–2002: Shri K. R. Narayanan
1997–1998: Inder Gujral, Janata Dall/UF	2002–present: A. P. J. Abdul Kalam
1998–2004: Atal Behari Vajpayee, BJP/NDA[f]	
2004–present: Manmohan Singh, Congress/INC[g]	

Prime ministers are selected by party forming government after Parliament elections; prime ministers in office for less than one month are not included.
[a] Died in office 1964.
[b] Died in office 1966.
[c] Assassinated while in office, 1984.
[d] Lost elections, but assassinated during campaign for next elections in 1991.
[e] Janata Dal and allies renamed "United Front" (UF) in 1996–1998.
[f] BJP and allied parties also called "National Democratic Alliance" (NDA).
[g] Congress-I now renamed Indian National Congress (INC).
[h] Died in office, 1969.
[i] Died in office, 1977.

Parliament or the state assembly. In the course of the system's first four decades, only the Congress Party was sufficiently large and organized to be able to benefit from this. In the first three elections (1952, 1957, and 1962), for example, the Congress Party managed to capture more than 70 percent of the seats in the national parliament without once gaining a majority of the popular vote (see Table 10.2). During this period, the Congress Party also controlled the state assemblies in most states. This led to the characterization of India's political system as a "**dominant-party system**," with the Congress Party holding sway over national politics and several smaller national or regional parties acting as "parties of pressure" to lobby Congress Party leaders or mobilize public opposition to particular Congress Party policies.

A dominant-party system, however, is a far cry from one-party rule (as with the PRI in Mexico). Elections were fairly contested by parties espousing vastly different platforms, leadership transitions were generally orderly, and the rule of law was upheld for most of India's existence as an independent republic. More telling is the fact that the parties of pressure, as well as a host

TABLE 10.2. Congress Party's Parliamentary
Majorities, 1952–1984

Year	Popular vote (%)	Seats in Parliament (%)
1952	45	74
1957	48	75
1962	46	73
1967	41	54
1971	44	68
1977[a]	35[a]	29[a]
1980	43	67
1984	48	79

[a] 1977 elections held after ending of "emergency rule" declared
by Indira Gandhi in 1976; Janata Party coalition forms
government 1977–1980.

of new regional parties, eventually became better organized during the 1960s
and 1970s, cutting into the Congress Party's share of parliamentary seats
and taking control of several state assemblies. And, when the era of Congress
Party dominance in national politics came to an end in the late 1980s, this
was not the result of any electoral reform or external pressure; it was simply the predictable result of the growth of other parties and the reduction in the Congress Party's size and unity. These facts suggest that the
dominant-party system was mainly a result of the initial advantages that the
Congress Party had in the form of the leadership, reputation, and organizational base inherited from the independence movement once led by Mahatma
Gandhi.

India's founders also adopted an independent judiciary headed by a
national Supreme Court. This body consists of a chief justice and 25 justices who are formally appointed by the president but are usually chosen by
the prime minister in consultation with sitting members of the court. As in the
United States, the Indian court's main purpose is to interpret the constitution
and ensure civil liberties. However, its prerogative of judicial review has been
hampered at times by numerous constitutional amendments introduced in
Parliament, notably Amendment 42 (1976), which prohibits the court from
reviewing changes introduced by constitutional amendment. The court also
suffered a temporary loss of reputation for failing to oppose the suspension
of several constitutionally guaranteed rights during the 18-month period of
"**Emergency**" rule in the mid-1970s. Compared with courts in other postcolonial settings, however, India's courts have generally functioned in a fair,
nonpartisan manner and have been able to safeguard the basic spirit of the
constitutional and legal order.

THE MAKING OF INDIAN FEDERALISM AND
CENTER-PERIPHERY RELATIONS

To deal with India's diverse regions, a federal republic was set up, with a central government in New Delhi sharing powers with the governments of each of the 14 states and 6 territories existing at that time (now 28 states and 7 territories). Certain policies are primarily in the jurisdiction of state governments (for example, rural policy, municipal projects, and educational curricula), whereas others are primarily in the jurisdiction of the central government (for example, defense, foreign policy, and national economic planning and related budget transfers to states). Although this division of labor between center and state is essentially similar to that found in federal systems elsewhere, other features of Indian federalism emphasize the primacy of the center and the integrity of the nation as in unitary states (states in which power is concentrated in the center and not shared with other levels of government) such as France or Japan.

Consistent with the views expressed by James Madison and Alexander Hamilton in *The Federalist Papers*, India's founding leaders (notably Nehru and B. R. Ambedkar, the chair of the committee that drafted the constitution) were seeking to balance the imperatives of states' rights and state-level governance with the preservation of national unity in the face of conflicts within or among states. In the case of India, however, the latter challenge took precedence given the Hindu–Muslim riots that accompanied independence, the conflict with Pakistan over Kashmir, and fears of destabilizing secessionist movements. As a result, the Indian constitution was more explicit in asserting the unity and primacy of the central government than is the U.S. Constitution. For example, India's constitution treats the union as indestructible but allows the national parliament to alter the boundaries of its constituent units. Moreover, in contrast with the United States, the Indian national government (and not the state governments) retains the residual powers of legislation and can preempt any state legislation that contradicts a parliamentary act or federal law. In addition, Article 356 establishes "**President's Rule**" when serious disturbances are reported by a state's governor. Since independence, the article has been invoked on dozens of occasions, sometimes for valid reasons but sometimes on shaky grounds for the purpose of ousting uncooperative state legislatures.

Another distinctive feature of Indian federalism is the manner in which state boundaries are defined. The 1956 States Reorganization Act originally established 14 states and 6 territories with boundaries corresponding to populations predominantly speaking a particular regional language. Prime Minister Nehru did not wish to encourage the provincialism of the Congress Party's regional leaders, but he encouraged the nation to adopt the States Reorganization Act in the interest of stability. In any case, he expected the central government to play the dominant role in India's development as a unified modern nation. Yet, by institutionalizing differences between linguistically defined regions, the States Reorganization Act ended up establishing a principle that has since been invoked to carve out a number of new states. In fact, in the five decades since the adoption of the States Reorganization Act, the number of states doubled from 14 to 28! Thus, in contrast with the United States, conflicts in center-periphery relations and competition among states are reinforced by the identities shared by members of the linguistic groups corresponding to respective state boundaries.

India's distinctive brand of federalism has produced three patterns of center-periphery politics in India. First, the most complicated cases involve the very few states or territories where a non-Hindu group constitutes a majority. In these cases, dramatic, even violent, social movements have sprung up at various points with the aim of securing autonomy. This is evident in the state of Punjab (where Punjabi-speaking Sikhs constitute 51 percent of the population), the state of Jammu and Kashmir (which is the only Indian state with a Muslim majority and encompasses the disputed area of Kashmir), and the northeastern territories (which are economically underdeveloped and inhabited by tribal populations that are ethnically distinct). Although there are also political parties that have sought to gain control of a state assembly on behalf of the non-Hindu majority (for example, the Akali Dal in the Punjab), violence has been evident in all three regions since the time of Nehru. The threat posed by this violence has varied, however. Conflicts in the Punjab largely subsided after reaching a peak during the 1980s; conflicts in the northeast have been sporadic and relatively small scale; and conflicts in Jammu and Kashmir have been an ongoing problem since the time of independence, a situation that has been complicated by Pakistan's support for Muslim militants in Kashmir.

A second pattern of center-periphery politics involves the emergence of regional political parties that claim to represent the distinctive interests of the dominant majority in a linguistically defined state. This pattern is most common in the southern states, where much of the population is identified as Dravidian and where the main state languages are distinct from those with roots in Sanskrit. For example, two major parties have dominated politics in the state of Tamil Nadu since the 1960s: the Dravida Munnetra Kazhagam (DMK) and its splinter party, the All-India Anna DMK (AIADMK). These parties can be traced back to a powerful regional movement during the 1940s and 1950s that aimed at reducing the influence of northern (Indo-Aryan) culture in southern India and even called for an autonomous state of "Dravidastan." Rather than continue to press for autonomy, however, these parties have participated within the framework of Indian federalism, focusing on controlling their respective state assemblies and capturing a block of seats in the national Parliament.

The third pattern of center-periphery politics involves the operation of national parties as de facto regional parties. Such parties have platforms that publicly outline national priorities rather than promote the interests of any one state, but the fact that they come to power in one state makes them behave much like the regional parties in the south in the course of center-periphery bargaining. With the decline of Congress Party dominance in national politics, this pattern has become more prevalent, with some parties splitting off from national parties to seek influence among some large bloc of voters in a particular state (for example, the Samajwadi Party in Uttar Pradesh). The longest standing example of this pattern is the **Communist Party of India–Marxist**, or CPI-M, in the state of West Bengal. Although formally dedicated to Marxist ideology, which regards class divisions as more significant than national or ethnic ones, this party took over the West Bengal assembly from the Congress Party in the 1960s. Although it originally focused on working-class interests and land reform in gaining power, the CPI-M has proven remarkably flexible in adapting to changing times, with much of its continuing appeal resulting from its role as a steadfast defender of Bengali interests. Long after the fall of communism in Eastern Europe, the CPI-M stands as a rare example of a Communist Party that has been able to gain and maintain power in one state within the framework of democracy and federalism (although, like the Chinese Communist Party, it has been adopting more market-oriented policies in the past decade to make West Bengal competitive with other states in the course of economic liberalization).

THE INDIRA GANDHI ERA: POPULISM, PATRONAGE POLITICS, AND THE "EMERGENCY"

After Jawaharlal Nehru's death in 1964, Lal Bahadur Shastri emerged as the new leader of the Congress Party and the next prime minister of India. Shastri had not been a unanimous choice to begin with, and his untimely death just two years into his term (in 1966) left the Congress Party scrambling once again to reach consensus on a new leader who could lead it to victory in the 1967 elections. That leader turned out to be **Indira Gandhi** (daughter of Nehru and not directly related to Mahatma Gandhi), primarily because her lineage was seen as an asset to the Congress Party's public image in the upcoming elections. Given her inexperience, however, she was expected essentially to serve as a figurehead for the more established party bosses. In the 1967 elections, the Congress Party's popular support declined to a low of 41 percent, but it was able to capture a majority of seats in the Parliament. Indira Gandhi was named prime minister, becoming one of the first women to head a national government.

Once in power, Indira Gandhi surprised the party bosses by announcing her own policy agenda and elevating individuals personally loyal to her at the expense of the older party elites. The rift between Indira Gandhi and the old bosses became so deep that the Congress Party split into two distinct parties: One, following Mrs. Gandhi, reconstituted itself as Congress-I, (henceforth referred to as Congress), inherited the bulk of the old Congress Party's grass-roots membership, and is considered the main successor to the original Indian National Congress. The other, Congress-O (for "organization"), was formed around several of the old party bosses who now joined the opposition. As the successor to the independence movement, the Congress Party had been able to build an extensive organizational framework that cut across national, state, and local levels. Given the split with some of the party bosses, Indira Gandhi now had to find ways to shore up her own base of support.

One strategy was evident in a concerted effort to mobilize the masses directly by means of populist appeals to the economic interests of peasants and workers, who had not seen their positions improve much during the first two decades after independence. In areas where Mrs. Gandhi no longer had reliable local allies to deliver "**vote banks**" (blocs of votes obtained by a candidate as a result of deals made with leaders of a local caste or village community) during critical elections, she needed a new message that she could take directly to a new, larger vote bank – the hundreds of millions of impoverished lower-class and lower-caste voters, especially those in the rural areas. This message took the form of a national antipoverty campaign with promises to boost agricultural production while not giving in to the interests of large foreign companies. This message resonated with India's lower classes and castes, enabling Mrs. Gandhi's Congress Party to capture over two-thirds of the seats in Parliament during the elections of 1971. Also worth noting is that Mrs. Gandhi began to rely more heavily on appeals to Indian national pride to buttress her populist posture. This was evident not only in the framing of her protectionist policies (economic nationalism) but also in the cultivation of nationalistic fervor accompanying the 1971 war with Pakistan (in which India provided military support to successfully aid the secession of Bangladesh).

A second strategy that Mrs. Gandhi used to offset the loss of the former Congress Party bosses had to do with building a new base of Congress-I cadres through a distinctive brand of patronage politics. With her demonstrated ability to capture a parliamentary majority and her popularity soaring after the victory over Pakistan, Mrs. Gandhi had no trouble attracting new recruits to Congress-I while regaining the support of former Congress Party activists who had initially joined Congress-O. But what became strikingly apparent during this process was Mrs. Gandhi's active personal involvement in the appointment and promotion of key party leaders. Increasingly, these personnel decisions were based not on demonstrated competence or loyalty to the Congress Party as a whole but on the basis of personal loyalty to Mrs. Gandhi in exchange for her political patronage. She and her advisers regularly reviewed personnel files to identify and reward politicians who were loyal to Mrs. Gandhi, while taking note of those who might challenge her authority. Although patronage politics was nothing new to India, Mrs. Gandhi's emphasis on personal loyalty resulted in a more hierarchical web of patron-client networks centered on the prime minister and her closest advisers.

During the mid-1970s, this approach served to further alienate Mrs. Gandhi's opponents and led to a serious crisis that almost undermined India's political and legal institutions. During 1974, some of the older Congress Party bosses (Congress-O leaders) and other opposition leaders joined together to accuse Mrs. Gandhi of corruption and campaign violations. One of these leaders, J. P. Narayan, once a devout follower of Mahatma Gandhi, organized frequent protests and even called upon the army to oust the prime minister. The Indian army, noted for its noninterference in civilian politics, did not intervene. Mrs. Gandhi, however, felt that her opponents had gone too far, and she responded by declaring a national emergency. The next 18 months (1976–1977), referred to simply as "the Emergency," represented the only period during which postcolonial India appeared to function more like an authoritarian regime than a parliamentary democracy. Many of the opposition leaders were arrested for their part in the campaign against Mrs. Gandhi, selective censorship was introduced, and some parts of the constitution were temporarily suspended. At the same time, in contrast with typical dictators in authoritarian regimes, Mrs. Gandhi had come to power via the electoral process rather than through a military coup, she did not seek to dismantle opposition parties or rewrite the constitution, and she promised and called a new round of national elections, stepping aside when her party lost in those elections.

In the 1977 election, Mrs. Gandhi hoped that the voters would understand her actions and that her Congress Party would retain its power, given its sheer size. However, these elections marked the first time that the Congress Party was unable to gain a parliamentary majority. Instead, the new government was formed by the **Janata Party**, an umbrella organization composed of a wide array of opposition parties, including the Congress-O. Just as the first-past-the-post electoral system had previously enabled the Congress Party to convert pluralities of popular votes into a majority of seats, the Janata Party managed to convert 43 percent of the popular vote into 55 percent of the seats in Parliament. The result demonstrated that the Congress Party's previous electoral dominance was partly a result of a fragmented opposition that, when united, proved capable of unseating it. At the same time, the dominant-party system remained intact because the Janata Party was little more than a hastily formed coalition of parties with quite different interests and ideologies, with no single party capable of defeating Congress in national elections. Opposition to Mrs. Gandhi proved sufficient to enable the Janata Party to engineer a victory following her controversial actions during the Emergency, but it was not sufficient to enable it to stay in power for a full term. The diverse elements constituting the Janata Party found little common ground when it came to specific policies for reducing central planning or attacking the problems of poverty and inequality. Moreover, the two Janata prime ministers (Morarji Desai, 1977–1979, and Charan Singh, 1979–1980) had neither the reputation nor the personal appeal of Mrs. Gandhi. As a result, the 1980 elections saw Indira Gandhi stage a spectacular comeback, with her Congress capturing two-thirds of the seats in the national Parliament.

Following her return to power, Mrs. Gandhi sought to consolidate her political base by more frequently invoking Hindu nationalist themes, although still officially committed to the secularism of her father, Jawaharlal Nehru. This tactic was intended to boost her personal popularity by appealing to as large a segment of the Indian population as possible. Predictably, however, this also triggered fears among India's religious minorities, sparking a militant movement for greater autonomy in the Punjab (where there was a Sikh majority). In her efforts to quell militants seeking an independent "Khalistan," Mrs. Gandhi ordered the army to storm the Sikh Golden Temple at Amritsar (where the militants had holed up). This sparked violent Hindu–Sikh riots and provided the main motivation for her assassination at the hands of her own Sikh bodyguards on October 31, 1984.

INDIA'S "MIXED" STRATEGY OF ECONOMIC DEVELOPMENT, 1950–1984

India's development strategy was set in motion under Jawaharlal Nehru and was influenced by the global context in which it was conceived. National economic priorities were influenced by the level of wealth and technology evident in the West. The program for achieving those goals was simultaneously influenced by the vitality of entrepreneurship evident under Western capitalism and by the dramatic achievements engineered by socialist planners in the USSR during the 1930s and 1940s. This led to the emergence of another component of Nehru's third way: a "mixed" strategy of economic development.

As part of this strategy, the principle of private property was respected, and private economic activity was encouraged in some sectors. However, half of the gross domestic product (GDP) was supposed to be accounted for by a large public sector managed according to Soviet-style "five-year plans." This public sector, consisting of thousands of large state-owned factories, mainly concentrated on heavy industry (that is, the large-scale production of major industrial goods along with major infrastructure projects such as coal mining, power stations, railroads, and so forth). Private firms were selectively authorized to participate in heavy industrial production, but most tended to be concentrated in the production of agricultural and light industrial (or consumer) goods. Moreover, the public and private sectors were protected and regulated by the Indian government so that they could contribute to the expansion of industrial production while being shielded from competition against firms from more advanced industrial countries. The assumption was that because colonialism and economic backwardness had made the playing field uneven, a postcolonial economy could not hope to catch up to that of its former colonizers without state protection and coordination of domestic industry and without tight restrictions on foreign imports. The Indian government also upheld laws that prevented public-sector workers from being fired, provided generous welfare benefits for public-sector employees, guaranteed protection for trade-union members, and established a progressive system of taxation.

Under Nehru, this mixed development strategy did enable native industrialization to take off but did not make any significant strides toward closing the gap between India and the advanced industrial economies of the West. In addition, some serious problems with the strategy became evident during Nehru's last few years in office. In spite of Nehru's personal commitment to improving the lot of the lower classes, his fixation on rapid industrialization and the priority given to heavy industry neither helped to reduce poverty and socioeconomic inequities nor brought tangible benefits to the masses whose expectations had been ratcheted up after the euphoria of independence. Even more problematic was the continually low level of investment in the agricultural sector, which left millions of villagers perilously close to the threshold of subsistence. As a result, when severe droughts struck during the early 1960s, there was not enough of a cushion to prevent famine in many parts of the countryside. In light of these problems, Nehru's successors would have to make some adjustments, albeit within the framework of India's strategy of mixed development.

First, a new consensus emerged on the importance of addressing chronic food scarcity for India's rapidly growing populace. Nehru's successors believed that one key reason for the famines of the early 1960s was the inadequacy of channels for distributing surplus grain. To remedy this, in 1965 the government set up the "public distribution system," a network of thousands of shops through which surplus grain from high-yield agricultural regions would be redistributed throughout the country at controlled prices to be monitored by state governments. This system played a major role in alleviating the problem of hunger among the poorest peasants throughout rural India, and the scaling back of this program in recent years is thought to be one reason why some of India's poorer farmers have suddenly found themselves in a precarious position even as the country's economy continues to grow at an impressive rate.

The other part of the solution was India's "**green revolution**." Under Indira Gandhi, the government encouraged the use of new varieties of seed, new methods of fertilization, and new techniques of crop rotation. Although the green revolution targeted regions with good soil and irrigation and tended to benefit relatively wealthy farmers, the total increase in agricultural production was dramatic and made India self-sufficient for the first time. While the green revolution and the public distribution system did not put an end to poverty and malnutrition, the combination of the two measures did help to bring an end to starvation-related deaths by sharply raising food production and guaranteeing access to cheap foodstuffs for poorer citizens nationwide. Between 1965–1966 and 1983–1984, India's food production more than doubled from 72 million tons to over 150 million tons.

A second set of changes was evident in increased state control over the economy, manifested in greater protectionism and greater regulation of the private sector. With developing countries becoming a dominant majority in the United Nations by the early 1970s, India joined a group of 77 such countries that passed a United Nations resolution calling for a "new international economic order." Although it was not enforceable, the document reflected the proponents' common view that free trade would effectively perpetuate the exploitation of former colonies unless protectionist measures were allowed to boost native manufacturing capabilities and create a level playing field. In keeping with the spirit of this movement, Indian banks and some key firms were nationalized, and new restrictions were imposed on multinational corporations, prompting many to leave. Moreover, the domestic private sector came to be more thoroughly regulated through the expansion of the "**license raj**," the requirement that private firms with assets above a certain threshold secure a government license to manufacture, export, or import goods in several key sectors. These measures were designed to protect Indian firms from foreign competition and boost native industrial production, but it also increased the government's leverage over large private-sector firms, benefiting some while stifling others.

On the whole, India's strategy of mixed development during the 1950–1984 period did not generate anything resembling the rapid economic growth seen in the East Asian newly industrialized countries (NICs) during the same period. Given its burgeoning population, India's per capita growth rate remained low, and comparatively little progress was made in reducing the rate of poverty. With economic pressures mounting, corruption became a more serious problem. Bribery became a part of everyday life, and government funds for special programs often ended up in the pockets of local officials. The license raj also contributed to the growth of corruption, enabling those who were politically connected or willing to offer bribes to obtain licenses more expeditiously, while others faced endless delays caused by bureaucratic red tape. The licensing system also conferred certain benefits on established firms – many of which became inefficient in the absence of competitive pressures – while stifling the growth of newer firms that were potentially more efficient. Among the working class, organized workers in the public sector had secure jobs and little incentive to be productive, whereas most of India's workers (including a sizable contingent of child laborers) continued to toil under poor working conditions for low wages. Poverty was still widespread, with nearly half the rural population officially considered below the poverty level. Sharp differences also emerged between states and regions in the levels of growth, poverty, and literacy.

Yet, it is important to bear in mind that the economic legacies of colonialism and the initial advantages held by advanced industrial countries in the world economy combined to make it difficult for most postcolonial nations to achieve any dramatic results during the first decades after independence. Against this background, India's mixed economy did make some important strides that should not be ignored. Between 1950 and 1984, the real gross domestic product gradually tripled. Over this period, total food-grain production also tripled, with wheat production growing nearly sixfold. In industry, coal production went up fourfold, steel production went up more than sixfold, electricity generation rose more than twentyfold, and India developed indigenous automobile and airplane manufacturing facilities. There were also significant improvements in health and literacy, as average life expectancy rose from just 30 years at the time of independence to nearly 55 by 1984, while the rate of adult literacy rose from under 20 percent to nearly 50 percent over the same period. Although India continued to depend on substantial foreign aid, the per capita rate of borrowing was much lower than in other developing countries, and foreign debts were generally repaid as scheduled. Given the more rapid growth accompanying liberalization since the early 1990s, one might argue that much more could have been achieved during the 1950–1984 period with less government intervention and more open markets; at the same time, India's growth since the early 1990s might not have been possible at all without first establishing a secure base for domestic industrial manufacturing, without solving the problem of food scarcity, without the marked improvements in basic health and literacy, and without keeping foreign debt from spiraling (as it did in Latin America).

India Shining? Institutional Dynamics, Resilient Identities, and Evolving Interests in the Post–Cold War Era

The end of the Cold War coincided with a marked shift in the development path that India had been following for four decades since independence. With the decline of communism as a viable alternative model, the significance of, and pride associated with, being a leading nation of the developing world began to decline. Suddenly, dozens of countries were scrambling to redefine their national interests, identities, and strategies within an increasingly interdependent global economy that was clearly dominated by the advanced industrial capitalist countries. Within this changing global context, India's democratic institutions and federal system remained stable and have enjoyed a measure of legitimacy that is uncommon in postcolonial nations in the Middle East or Africa. However, the political dynamics within these institutions became more fluid and more "decentered" as more local actors found new ways to influence political outcomes. Core identities related to caste or religion remained politically salient, but the way in which they influenced politics became more subtle. India cautiously embarked upon economic liberalization, progressively becoming a more significant actor in the global economy. In response to these changes, the interests of different groups became varied, and new social movements began to tackle such problems as women's rights and environmental degradation.

STABLE INSTITUTIONS AND COALITION POLITICS IN THE WORLD'S LARGEST DEMOCRACY

Following Indira Gandhi's assassination in 1984, her elder son, Rajiv, reluctantly agreed to lead Congress (his younger brother was being groomed for this role but had died in a plane crash). **Rajiv Gandhi** led his party to a landslide victory in the 1984 elections as it captured 79 percent of the parliamentary seats. The results appeared to point to the continuing appeal of both the dominant-party system under Congress and the Nehru dynasty (which had now provided three generations of leadership spanning Jawaharlal Nehru, his daughter Indira Gandhi, and his grandson Rajiv Gandhi). As it turns out, however, the election outcome was heavily influenced by the wave of sympathy following Mrs. Gandhi's death. In the six national elections held over the following two decades, Congress remained an important player but was never again able to secure a majority in Parliament without the aid of other parties. In fact, the 1984 elections marked the beginning of a transition to a new, more fluid era of coalition politics in which it has become commonplace for leading parties to form a government with allies and coalition partners. ("Allies" refers to parties that campaign alongside a leading national party and agree in advance to support its agenda in the Parliament; "coalition partners" refers to parties that offer outside support to a leading party and its allies to help construct a ruling majority but without subscribing to the party's political agenda.) This has forced larger parties to broaden their appeal while generating new opportunities for dozens of smaller parties to join coalitions and bargain for greater influence. Table 10.3 provides an overview of the performance of the leading parties in each of the national parliamentary elections held between 1989 and 2004.

Upon becoming prime minister in 1984, Rajiv Gandhi set out to fulfill a campaign promise to uproot corruption in the government. However, his own administration soon became ensnared in a corruption scandal involving accusations of officials accepting bribes in exchange for offering contracts to a Swedish defense firm (Bofors). The Congress Party's huge majority in

TABLE 10.3. Election Results during the Era of Coalition Politics, 1989–2004

Year	Party	Popular vote (%)	Seats in Parliament (%)
1989	Congress	39	38
	Janata	18	28 (forms government)
	BJP	11	16
	Others[a]	32	18
1991	Congress	37	45 (forms government)
	BJP	20	24
	Janata	11	11
	Others[a]	32	20
1996	Congress	29	26
	Janata and allies (UF)[b]	29	32 (forms government)
	BJP and allies	24	34
	Others[a]	19	8
1998	BJP and allies[b]	36	46 (forms government)
	Congress and allies[b]	26	26
	Janata and allies (UF)[b]	21	18
	Others[a]	17	10
1999	BJP and allies (NDA)[b]	41	55 (forms government)
	Congress and allies[b]	34	25
	Others[a]	25	20
2004	Congress and allies (INC)[b]	35	40 (forms government)
	BJP and allies (NDA)[b]	35	35
	Left parties[c]	8	11
	Others[a]	22	13

[a] "Others" include regional parties winning national parliamentary seats as well as national parties or splinter parties that are not part of alliances and that individually receive less than 10% of parliamentary seats. For 1999 and 2004, this includes former members of the Janata-led alliance that did not join the alliances formed by the Congress Party or BJP.

[b] UF refers to the "United Front" alliance formed around the Janata Party in 1996. ND refers to the "National Democratic Alliance" (NDA) set up by the BJP and its allies in 1999. INC refers to the "Indian National Congress," the name of the former independence movement taken by Congress and its allies in 2004.

[c] The two largest "left parties" are the Communist Party of India-Marxist (CPI–M) and the Communist Party of India (CPI), but there are dozens of other communist or socialist parties, including the Revolutionary Socialist Party (RSP) and the All-India Forward Block. These are counted among "others" in 1989, 1991, and 1999 and as part of the United Front coalition in 1996 and 1998. They are listed separately for 2004 because they independently won 11% of the contested seats and offered crucial outside support to form the new Congress-led government.

Parliament allowed Rajiv Gandhi's administration to serve out the full five-year term, but the fallout from the Bofors scandal and the growing trend toward coalition politics caused Congress's share of parliamentary seats to plummet from 79 percent to 38 percent during the 1989 elections. Although no other single party won more seats, Congress's opponents banded together once again under the umbrella of the Janata Party (this time using the Hindi term Janata Dal) and managed to form a ruling coalition with the backing of several smaller parties, including an emerging Hindu nationalist party called the Bharatiya Janata Party (BJP, or Indian People's Party).

The new Janata Party government came to be led by Prime Minister **V. P. Singh**, an ardent critic of Rajiv Gandhi's administration. Singh is noted for his support for the work of a national commission, the **Mandal Commission**, which identified several new caste-based categories for consideration under an expanded system of reservations. However, the Singh government was not able to do much beyond approving the report because its unwieldy coalition broke up by the end of 1990 under the strain of the different interests and ideologies of its members. Especially significant here was the coalition's dependence on support from the BJP, which was led by upper-caste Hindus and was on a campaign to mobilize public support for its distinctive agenda of promoting *Hinduttva*. In 1990, a key BJP leader (future home minister **Lal Krishna Advani**) was arrested for exhorting his countrymen to take down a mosque and rebuild a Hindu temple that had supposedly stood at the same spot to honor the Hindu demigod Rama. Given Singh's own secularism and his full support for Advani's arrest, the BJP withdrew its support from the government, leaving the Janata Party without a majority in the Parliament. New elections were temporarily staved off because Congress was willing to offer outside support to the Janata coalition but only after a new prime minister was named in place of Singh, who had been a longtime thorn in Congress's side. However, this coalition proved to be short-lived, as Congress used the time to prepare for fresh elections that would be called as soon as it withdrew its support of the Janata coalition in 1991. The Janata-led government of 1989–1991 demonstrated that the new era of coalition politics would prove to be a complicated one, requiring careful negotiations among parties of different sizes that represented the interests of different regions, classes, castes, and religious groups.

Congress began campaigning during the 1991 elections with hopes that it would return to its dominant position after its rule had been temporarily interrupted by a fragile coalition. But, unlike Mrs. Gandhi's triumphant return to power in 1980, there would be no second term for her son. On May 21, 1991, as Rajiv Gandhi left behind his security cordon to go into the crowds as part of a more open campaign strategy, a young woman set off a massive bomb strapped to herself. The group involved in Rajiv Gandhi's assassination was linked to an organization operating in Sri Lanka with the intention of establishing greater autonomy for the Hindu Tamil minority there. During the 1980s, rather than side with the Tamils in the name of Hindu solidarity, Rajiv Gandhi had offered troops to help the Sri Lankan government maintain stability. He did so because he viewed the Tamil separatists' demands in Sri Lanka as analogous to unacceptable demands for regional autonomy by militant separatists in India (for example, Sikh militants pursuing an autonomous "Khalistan"). Thus, although Rajiv Gandhi's assassination was orchestrated by a group operating in Sri Lanka, he essentially fell victim to the same dynamic that had claimed his mother's life six years earlier: Both sought to uphold the principle of a unified nation-state in the face of separatism, and both were assassinated by members of separatist groups.

After a brief respite to allow for Rajiv Gandhi's funeral, the elections resumed and another wave of sympathy helped the Congress Party to form the new government under **Narasimha Rao** (1991–1996), the first Congress Party prime minister to come from outside the Nehru dynasty in nearly a quarter of a century. Significantly, however, Congress was unable to secure a majority of seats in the Parliament and found itself in the unfamiliar position of having to woo coalition partners. Anyone paying attention to the other parties' performances, however, might have been surprised that the party finishing second in the 1991 elections was not the Janata Party but the BJP, the Hindu nationalist party that had forced the collapse of Singh's cabinet and now held nearly one-quarter of the seats in Parliament. The coalition under Rao, led by Congress, proved stable enough to serve out its full five-year term. However, when the next election was held in 1996, it was the BJP that won the largest bloc of seats (34 percent) in Parliament. The more loosely organized Janata-led alliance finished second with 32 percent of the seats. Congress ended up with its worst result ever, totaling just 26 percent of the seats in Parliament.

The BJP's rise and the politics of identity are examined in more detail later, but what is worth noting here is how the BJP's emergence as a powerful new national party further increased the fluidity of coalition politics in India. To prevent a BJP-led coalition from forming the new government in 1996, the Congress Party agreed to offer outside support to the alliance led by the Janata Party. Given the history between Congress and Janata, however, the so-called United Front coalition government collapsed after going through two prime ministers (Deve Gowda and Inder Gujral) in as many years. This paved the way for fresh elections in 1998, and this time the BJP and its allies won a decisive victory with 46 percent of the seats in Parliament and managed to form a majority coalition by courting several smaller parties. When new elections had to be called after the defection of a key coalition partner, the BJP and its allies, referring to themselves as the "National Democratic Alliance" (NDA), went on to control 56 percent of the parliamentary seats, while Congress's share dropped to a new low at 25 percent. Unlike Congress, which was not used to coalition politics and had only courted a handful of allies, the BJP aggressively set out to strike deals to make regional parties not just coalition partners but integral members of the ruling alliance. One of the most significant of these was the Telegu Desam Party, from Andhra Pradesh, which had historically attacked the central government for favoring the interests of the Hindi belt states in northern India. Now, ironically, Telegu Desam found itself in an alliance with the BJP, which had owed its rise to the same Hindi belt states.

Without having to depend on outside support from uncommitted parties, the BJP was able to remain in power until 2004 under the leadership of Prime Minister **Atal Behari Vajpayee**. Initially, given the BJP's assertive brand of Hindu nationalism, the Vajpayee cabinet was viewed with some anxiety. This was understandable given the strident nationalist rhetoric that some BJP leaders continued to embrace publicly. For the most part, however, Vajpayee and the BJP's national leadership proved to be pragmatic in their approach and did not break sharply with what previous governments had done. Although there was some talk of amending the constitution, the dynamics of alliance-building and coalition politics made it obvious that this effort would be a waste of time. The BJP's economic policies essentially continued along the path of liberalization initiated during the late 1980s. The BJP's decision to launch nuclear tests in May 1998 shocked many, but these tests were only possible then because the preparations had been well under way during the previous Congress government. The BJP's decision to join the U.S.-led war on terror in the aftermath of the 9/11 attacks was consistent with past leaders' efforts to secure international backing for the suppression of militants in Kashmir, and the decision *not* to join in the U.S.-led coalition's invasion of Iraq was consistent with India's fiercely independent foreign policy posture since independence. And the common threat posed by Islamic militants and terrorists even provided new momentum toward the normalization of relations with Pakistan and China. On the whole, as we saw in the introduction to this chapter, the BJP's rule at the center came to be associated not with ardent fundamentalism but with a sober approach in domestic and foreign policy that helped to produce high economic growth and increase India's stature as an emerging global power. These achievements were the basis for the BJP's triumphant "India shining" public relations campaign.

Thus, the verdict of the 2004 elections came as a surprise to many. Many had expected a small reduction in the BJP's share of parliamentary seats as a result of communal riots that broke out in BJP-controlled Gujarat in 2002. But few had expected that the populist appeals to the rural poor by Congress would enable it to form a new majority coalition in the parliament. The Congress victory was unusual in two regards. First, it was being led by the Italian-born widow of Rajiv Gandhi, **Sonia Gandhi**, whose foreign birth did not seem to trouble millions of rural voters as much as the BJP thought it would. Second, Sonia broke with tradition in that, although remaining party leader, she declined the post of prime minister in favor of the internationally respected economist **Manmohan Singh**. Also surprising was that Congress's ruling majority came to depend on outside support from leftist parties, which pulled off one of their strongest showings to date by capturing over 11 percent of the parliamentary seats nationwide. All in all, this was the Left's best performance in over a decade, and it occurred when its chief nemesis, the BJP, appeared so confident of its performance that it had called for elections several months early. The Congress Party not only managed to attract a much wider range of allies than before but also garnered significant support in BJP strongholds such as Gujarat and Maharashtra (where the BJP had thoroughly defeated Congress in 1999). These results showed that the BJP leadership failed to anticipate how its "India shining" campaign would serve to magnify the social inequities and economic hardships still afflicting India's poor. At the same time, just as it would have been a mistake to deem Congress irrelevant after its defeats in the previous three elections, so, too, would be any premature dismissal of the BJP, which, after all, managed to finish dead even in popular votes with the alliance led by Congress.

Thus, the 2004 elections revealed that the decline of Congress dominance is not the same thing as the demise of the party, and that, even in defeat, the BJP showed that it was here to stay. The Janata Party, although it provided a common front for Congress opponents and played a role in ending Congress dominance, was never a unified organization to begin with, and its constituent elements increasingly began to be run as independent parties or as allies of the BJP or Congress. As a result, it appears that Indian politics is now dominated by two well-organized national parties, Congress and the BJP. Even without allied parties, the candidates from these two parties accounted for nearly half the seats in 2004. At the same time, it would be a mistake to see this as a two-party system in the making, as neither party is likely to be in a position to form a government without allies and coalition partners. In 2004, the Congress-led bloc's 40 percent share of parliamentary seats and the BJP-led bloc's 35 percent share both depended on dozens of allies, most of which individually received less than 2 percent of the seats in Parliament but without which Congress's and the BJP's share of seats would have been just 26 percent and 21 percent, respectively. This means that regional parties and smaller national parties, far from receding, now have even greater reason to focus on local constituencies to ensure some representation in Parliament given their value as potential allies and coalition partners. This also means that, whatever their ideological commitments, both Congress and the BJP will have to be pragmatic in their approach in order to attract a wide range of voters, allies, and coalition partners.

THE EVOLVING POLITICS OF CASTE AND RELIGION IN CONTEMPORARY INDIA

In light of the resilience of identities that emerged centuries ago on the Indian subcontinent, it is worth taking a closer look at the role that caste and religion have continued to play in the post–Cold War era. Ironically, although India's secular political institutions do not recognize caste practices or Hindu religious institutions as having any legal standing in public life, the efforts to institutionalize special considerations for lower-caste groups and religious minorities have had the effect of giving cleavages based on caste and religion a new political significance as electoral politics has become more competitive in a changing international environment.

During the last quarter of the twentieth century the link between occupational structures and caste hierarchies has been steadily weakened. India's Hindu political elites, once dominated by the upper castes, are now from a much more varied background, with several lower-caste politicians rising to national prominence. India's business elites now extend beyond the Hindu merchant caste and include members of other caste groups and non-Hindu minorities. Also, India's laboring classes are comprised of members of all caste groups. Nevertheless, caste-based identities are still relevant in everyday social relations, as is evident in the still high rate of within-caste marriages, the formation of community associations, and the continuing role of Brahmins in the performance of Hindu rituals. Within the context of contemporary politics, the significance of caste continues to be manifested in two ways.

First, there is the mobilization of electoral support through local caste communities. In the past, regional Congress Party candidates often received an entire block of votes from members of local caste communities in exchange for promises to advance the interests of these communities. With the rise of coalition politics, such "vote banks" are no longer clearly bounded because there are now multiple candidates promising varied social goods and because electoral preferences reflect not only caste-based interests but also a variety of class-based, regional, or individual interests. Nevertheless, caste-based identities remain available as an important basis for political mobilization, especially because many of the regional and splinter parties, whether they officially claim to represent certain caste groups or not, have been focusing on strengthening their standing among particular castes in a given state. Moreover, many candidates have been making direct appeals to members of their own caste communities. These trends have had an especially significant impact in boosting the political relevance of the more numerous lower-caste communities, catapulting several low-caste leaders into national prominence.

Second, the politics of caste is evident in responses to the government's efforts to expand the system of reservations for lower castes. It will be recalled that reservations refer to quotas in education and employment to enable the upward mobility of lower-caste groups. This includes the "scheduled castes" (encompassing the 20 percent of the population labeled "untouchables" and a number of marginalized tribal groups), which are eligible for a wide range of special privileges, including access to education, government, and public-sector employment. In addition, various strata of peasant or artisan caste groups (roughly 25 percent of the population) are considered "other backward castes" and receive a somewhat narrower range of privileges with smaller quotas in education and employment. As in the case of "affirmative action" in the United States, India's system of reservations has been the subject of much debate, with many upper-caste Hindus voicing concerns about the utility and fairness of the reservations system. This opposition has become even more vocal as a result of the release in 1990 of the Mandal Commission Report, which identifies a lengthier list of caste groups to be considered for some form of preferential treatment under the label of "other backward castes." Implementing the recommendations of this report would result in nearly half the jobs in the government or public sector being set aside for members of certain castes, but given that upper-caste Hindus represent less than one-fifth of the population, this would have only had a slight impact on opportunities for most upper-caste groups. Nevertheless, the government's approval of the Mandal Report in 1990 provoked some stunning reactions, ranging from the suicide of several upper-caste students to large numbers of upper-caste individuals changing their names to acquire lower-caste surnames. These dynamics suggest that the reservations system, although contributing to the upward mobility of lower-caste individuals, has ended up making Indians simultaneously more conscious of caste distinctions and more calculating in terms of the impact of caste-related social policies on their individual interests. As we will see, tensions over caste-based affirmative action would also play a role in strengthening the BJP's appeals to Hindu nationalism during the 1990s.

The BJP, formally established under that name in 1984, had its roots in the immediate post-independence period, when a small political party, the Jan Sangh, was formed with the support of the **Rashtriya Seva Sangh (RSS)**. The RSS itself was a key Hindu social organization that was created in 1925 to preserve and promote Hindu traditions. Although it joined the INC's struggle against British colonialism, after independence it steadfastly opposed the Congress Party's secular vision in favor of the revival of pride in *Hinduttva*, the values and ideals of a centuries-old Hindu civilization. The RSS criticized Congress-led governments for disregarding the values and interests of India's Hindu majority while granting special privileges and considerations to Muslims, Sikhs, and Christians. The RSS became especially strong in Hindi-speaking states across northern and western India, cultivating ties to various social and political organizations and holding weekly meetings devoted to discussions of nationalist-religious ideology. In the 1970s, the RSS began to coordinate its activities with the **Vishva Hindu Parishad (VHP)**, which was also promoting *Hinduttva* among Hindus worldwide. With the emergence of the BJP in 1984, the RSS and VHP teamed up to put their organizational and financial resources at the disposal of the party in the hopes of eventually overcoming Congress Party dominance. At the time, however, the BJP's appeal was primarily limited to upper-caste groups who embraced the idea of *Hinduttva* for its own sake. This was not a particularly large social base for a party aspiring to one day lead a country as diverse as India.

The BJP's subsequent rise to power during the 1990s would be the result of three intersecting factors. First, the BJP was able to expand its core constituency of upper-caste Hindus by empathizing with the latter's anxieties over the Mandal Commission's recommendations for expanded quotas for lower-caste groups. An increasing number of upper-caste communities, whether or not they had given much thought to the place of *Hinduttva* in India's national identity, came to see the BJP as a viable alternative to secular parties that seemed to be going too far to accommodate the lower castes at the expense of upper castes. With the BJP's visibility rising, the 1991 elections brought it 20 percent of the popular vote. This made the BJP a significant national party, but two other factors were necessary for the BJP to build a broad enough base of support to form a government.

The second factor was the BJP's ability to fill the need for redefining India's national identity in the post–Cold War era. With India's place in the international system no longer tied to being a leader of the developing world, the BJP was prepared to offer a compelling substitute: the renewal of a millennia-old Hindu civilization that would retain its distinctiveness while propelling India's ascent in a new world order. The Congress Party's continued emphasis on secularism held some appeal for many cosmopolitan citizens, but without the aura of the independence movement and the status as a leader among postcolonial nations, Congress had difficulty constructing an inspiring vision of India's place in the world. For a newly emerging class of self-confident professionals, both in India and abroad, the BJP was able to provide such a vision.

The third factor was the most significant: The BJP was able to attract the attention of a large segment of lower-caste voters throughout rural India by drawing attention to the privileges accorded to religious minorities at the expense of the majority Hindu population. Severing the historical association between Hindu civilization and caste hierarchies, the BJP's leaders focused public attention on the imbalance between the rights of Hindus and religious (mostly Muslim) minorities, pointing out that members of other religious groups were accorded special privileges (such as Muslim citizens' right to selectively follow Islamic law and attend Islamic schools). These issues were driven home by the drama surrounding the destruction of the Babri mosque in Ayodhya at a site where a temple honoring the demigod Rama had been razed by Muslim invaders five centuries ago. Although the BJP's General Secretary Advani had been arrested in 1990 for exhorting Hindus to take down the Babri mosque, in December 1992, BJP supporters and cadres from the RSS and VHP did just that. This sparked a huge uproar and resulted in several days of Hindu–Muslim rioting in cities throughout India while catapulting the issue of *Hinduttva* into the national spotlight and capturing the attention of Hindu lower castes. In the 1998 elections, the BJP managed to win 40 percent of the lower-caste vote while also garnering substantial support from big business, urban workers, student groups, and educated professionals working in high-tech sectors.

While these dynamics suggest that communal identities were mobilized in different ways during the era of coalition politics, it is also important to note that the BJP's share of the popular vote never exceeded the total share held by Congress and other parties committed to secularism. Moreover, the challenges of maintaining alliances and coalitions gave impetus to the pragmatic wing of the party, led by Atal Behari Vajpayee (prime minister from 1998 to 2004). In its profile of former prime ministers, the Office of the Prime Minister of India refers to Vajpayee as a leader who is at once a "champion of women's empowerment and social equality" *and* a leader who "stands for an India anchored in 5000 years of civilizational history, ever modernizing, ever renewing, ever re-engaging itself." Vajpayee, perhaps to the chagrin of hardcore RSS activists, managed to craft a formula that linked the unifying aspects of Hindu civilization to modern India's national greatness and international standing, which, in turn, were linked to further progress in economic liberalization and scientific and technological advancement. This message resonated with India's ambitious business elites, students, and white-collar professionals, and even enabled Vajpayee to recruit a few Muslim political leaders into the BJP alliance.

At the state and local levels, however, BJP leaders' often strident rhetoric of Hindu revivalism has often drowned out the more inclusive themes emphasized by the party's pragmatic wing. This has tended to generate anxiety among religious minorities, sometimes fueling communal riots between Hindus and Muslims. The most troubling event in this regard occurred in the state of Gujarat in 2002. Hundreds of Hindus were returning from a trip to Ayodhya (where they had gone to show support for the building of the Rama temple) when the train they were on was set on fire in the state of Gujarat, killing dozens. For the next several days, Hindus went on a rampage, attacking Muslims and burning their homes and shops. Even after the rioting had subsided, sporadic attacks continued for weeks. In the end, hundreds of Hindus and nearly two thousand Muslims were dead, and ten thousand people were left homeless. The chief minister of Gujarat, the BJP's Narendra Modi, was seen by some as either failing to act quickly to end the violence or consciously exploiting the riots to consolidate Hindu support ahead of his reelection. (He went on to win the election decisively.) Although Vajpayee condemned the violence as an isolated incident that needed to be investigated, the BJP as a whole lost credibility among some groups for its poor handling of the Gujarat riots, giving more ammunition to Congress and other secular parties during the 2004 election.

However, although the BJP's victories in 1998 and 1999 should not be viewed as evidence that the forces of communalism were on the rise, the 2004 election results should not be interpreted as evidence that secularism has now prevailed. It is true that the BJP lost some support as a result of its handling of the Gujarat riots, but the BJP did win 35 percent of the seats in Parliament and matched Congress in terms of the popular vote. It is also worth noting that Congress's populist campaign not only unseated the BJP but also ousted a once popular regional incumbent party in Andhra Pradesh (Telegu Desam). Although formally an ally of the BJP in national politics, this party's appeal had rested not on *Hinduttva* but on its emphasis on boosting Andhra Pradesh's position within India through faster liberalization and promotion of the information technology sector. This suggests that Congress's successes in 2004 had less to do with its secularism and much more to do with its populist appeal to the frustrated urban underclass and the rural poor. In fact, taken together, the elections since the mid-1990s suggest that the salience of the battle between communal and secular forces can vary significantly depending on the immediate concerns of voters at the time of a particular election. In the turbulent years immediately following the end of the Cold War, perhaps the need to redefine India's place in the world amplified the BJP's emphatic elevation of *Hinduttva*. Subsequently, however, the BJP's trumpeting of economic achievements without acknowledging the continuing difficulties facing hundreds of millions of voters gave the edge to Congress's message of poverty alleviation and social justice. In this respect, the results of the 2004 elections are comparable to the results of national elections in several Latin American countries that have brought left-of-center candidates to power during the 2002–2006 period (in Bolivia, Brazil, Ecuador, and Nicaragua, for example).

ECONOMIC LIBERALIZATION IN A GLOBAL AGE: ACHIEVEMENTS, PROBLEMS, AND PROSPECTS

During the 1980s, under the pressure of mounting foreign debt, many countries throughout the developing world abandoned import-substituting industrialization and opted for market-oriented reforms, partly as a condition for new "structural adjustment" loans from the World Bank and the International Monetary Fund. Following the demise of communism in Eastern Europe, the push for market reforms accelerated worldwide and was marked by the liberalization of trade, privatization of many state-owned enterprises, and increased foreign investment. Although a major borrower, India had maintained a low level of per capita foreign debt and had consistently managed to service the debt in a timely manner. Thus, economic liberalization in India began without the same sense of crisis or the same level of external pressure that accompanied economic reforms elsewhere in the developing world.

Under Rajiv Gandhi's leadership (1984–1989), although there was no dramatic initiative to indicate that India had embarked upon a new developmental path, a new consensus began to take form among India's economic bureaucrats and business elites. With the Soviet Union and China both reconsidering the efficacy of central planning, and with other developing countries adopting reforms to make their economies more competitive, it was time to consider more fundamental changes to the Nehruvian model of a state-managed mixed economy. The clearest signal of this emerging consensus came in the form of changes in the licensing system by: (1) raising the asset threshold that determined whether a company needed a government license, and (2) permitting companies with licenses to manufacture certain products to manufacture upgraded versions of those products without procuring a new license. In effect, this meant that there were now fewer "barriers to entry" for new firms and that a wider range of existing companies could now expand their activities without going through the long and corrupt process of obtaining a license. These changes were modest, but they marked the beginning of a new era of economic development that has proceeded steadily along the path of liberalization through several changes of government.

The V. P. Singh government (1989–1991), although an ardent critic of Congress, continued to support further economic liberalization, linking the attack on corruption to a critique of the government's role in the economy. When the Congress Party returned to power, the cabinet of Narasimha Rao (1991–1996) was able to engineer further steps to accelerate economic liberalization. Licensing requirements were relaxed even further to allow for the growth of the private sector, and imports were liberalized more significantly as new incentives began to attract more foreign investment to India. Even state governments under leftist parties (for example, Kerala and West Bengal) had to embrace market-oriented policies in order to attract investment and keep up with expanding economic opportunities and activities in neighboring states. The process of reform was still quite gradual and featured many obstacles. There remained what some refer to as "barriers to exit" in that it was still illegal to shut down state enterprises, even if they were insolvent, and that several laws still protected major firms from going bankrupt despite mounting losses. With fears of a backlash from public-sector employees, most state-owned enterprises were not privatized right away. In sectors with significant workforce reductions, the government's effort to retrain laid-off state workers through the National Renewal Fund proved to be costly. And import tariffs, although declining, still remained relatively high, prompting foreign multinational companies to invest in countries where liberalization and privatization had occurred more rapidly. But the progress in liberalization made during the early 1990s was significant, building momentum for increasing rates of economic growth without triggering any major social catastrophes such as a spike in unemployment or hyperinflation.

After Congress lost the election in 1996, the Janata government of 1996–1998 and the BJP government of 1998–2004 continued to move forward along the course of liberalization. Under these governments, the central administration pursued unpopular reform measures by strategically coordinating with international financial institutions. In contrast with countries on which the World Bank and the IMF imposed specific conditions for further loans, India's central government actually worked with these organizations to identify conditions that corresponded to policies it wanted to enact. This enabled the government to characterize unpopular policies as unavoidable steps that were necessary to secure the cooperation of international financial institutions. Under the BJP, the government took one of the boldest steps to date in seeking to revise labor laws to remove restrictions on employers in relation to the dismissal of redundant workers and the signing of short-term contracts. The BJP also continued to court foreign investors and support the development of the high-tech sector. Thus, although often portrayed as a party preoccupied with India's past, the BJP showed that it was willing to take the necessary steps to accelerate economic growth and promote science and technology, viewing these as essential to India's ascendance in the international arena.

These policies, engineered in an incremental fashion over more than a decade, have begun to pay dividends. The average rate of economic growth during the 1990s climbed to six percent per year, nearly double the rate of annual growth seen during the 1970s. In the 2006–2007 fiscal year, India's GDP grew at a rate of 9 percent, making it one of the world's fastest-growing economies. And, unlike economies that have depended on particular sectors for growth, India's GDP growth has come from all sectors, ranging from agriculture and manufacturing to services and information technology. Not surprisingly, foreign companies have come to recognize that the Indian middle class, no matter how small it is relative to the population as a whole, represents a huge market compared with most other national markets worldwide. Past investments in higher education have also begun to pay off in the form of a huge pool of highly educated English-speaking professionals whose scientific training and computer skills are now in high demand. This is most clearly evident in the rapid expansion of the high-tech sector of the economy, which regularly exports software programs to the West, and in the proliferation of research and development centers established by such global corporate giants as IBM, Intel, Nokia, and Google.

Critics, however, point to a number of problems. One is the growth of social inequalities, as is evident in the wide income differential between urban and rural residents, increasing disparities among states, and a greater concentration of national wealth in the hands of the richest segments of the population. Poverty remains a serious problem, with 250 million people below the official poverty line established by the government, and this figure does not include the hundreds of millions who are not counted as poor but are close to the poverty line. Especially worrisome is the fact that the poverty is extreme among some segments of the population, most notably among rural populations in regions where protracted droughts have occurred and soil quality has been deteriorating. With the scaling back of government subsidies, the public distribution system has been significantly truncated to target only the most impoverished groups, leaving unprotected millions of farmers who were slightly above the subsistence threshold. It is among this group that we find the first reports of starvation-related deaths in India in nearly two decades.

Another worrisome trend in rural India has been a virtual epidemic of farmer suicides over the past several years. In 2003, the year preceding the Congress's surprising victory over the BJP, over 17,000 farmers committed suicide according to government statistics published later. The trend has continued unabated, prompting Manmohan Singh to promise a $156 million package of aid to the most suicide-prone regions along with a vast expansion of mechanisms for rural credit. This surprising phenomenon reflects some of the unintended consequences of India's economic liberalization. Thanks to the lowering of barriers to foreign direct investment, large numbers of peasants have come into contact with giant multinationals offering, for a not unsubstantial price, new varieties of genetically modified seeds with promises of dramatically increasing the yield of particular crops. In order to acquire these new seeds, farmers have had to borrow heavily, often from local moneylenders charging high interest rates, thereby taking on large debts they had hoped to repay by selling off the sharply increased surplus yields they were led to expect. The problem was that the new seeds produced only a marginal increase in the crop yield and, according to some sources, reduced the richness of the soil. In the meantime, millions of farmers had given up their previous practice of relying on crop diversification and rotation, while finding themselves sinking toward the subsistence threshold and being unable to repay their debts. The combination of these dire circumstances is what has driven tens of thousands of farmers to escape the crushing and shameful burden of unpaid debts by taking their own lives. Although addressing this problem has been a high priority for Manmohan Singh's government, whether this tragic epidemic will be subdued remains to be seen.

At the same time, when considering the ramifications of economic liberalization elsewhere in the developing world, the picture in India is not so bleak (see Table 10.4). The official poverty rate of 25 percent of the population, even if it understates the real magnitude of the problem, reflects a significant drop from the 40 percent poverty rate of the 1980s. This reduction in the poverty rate offers cause for some hope, especially when contrasted with the current 40 percent poverty rate in Mexico and Iran and the 50 percent poverty rate in South Africa. Inequality may be rising, but the overall level of social stratification in India is comparatively low. The richest 20 percent of India's population controls six times the share of national income controlled by the poorest 20 percent, which is lower than in the United States (where the ratio is 9) and much lower than in Mexico (where the ratio is 17) and South Africa (where the ratio is 34). Moreover, new strategies are becoming apparent for coping with rural poverty without having to put the brakes on the growth of the high-tech sector of the Indian economy. In the state of Karnataka, for example, hundreds of computer kiosks have been set up throughout rural areas where farmers previously lacked access to crucial

TABLE 10.4. Economics and Social Development Indicators, ca. 2000–2006

Category	India	Selected countries
GDP/rank (purchasing power parity, billion U.S. $), 2006	4247/3	U.S.: 13202/1; China: 10048/2; Japan: 4131/4; Iran: 592/21; Mexico: 1202/12; Russia: 1705/10; S. Africa: 567/23
GDP per capita/rank (purchasing power parity, U.S.$), 2005–2006	3802/118	U.S.: 43223/4; China: 7722/86; Japan: 32530/20; Iran: 8535/79; Mexico: 11369/63; Russia: 12178/59; S. Africa: 13018/56
Share of labor force in agriculture (%) in 2000	60	U.S.: 2; Japan: 5; China: 50; Iran: 30; Mexico: 20; Russia: 12; S. Africa: 30
Human development indicator rank (countries ranked, based on life expectancy, infant mortality, poverty, inequality, literacy, etc.), 2006	126	Norway: 1; Japan: 7; U.S.: 8; Mexico: 53; Russia: 65; China: 81; Iran: 96; S. Africa: 121
Life expectancy at birth 2000–2005 [1970–1975 average]	63.1 [50.3]	U.S.: 77.3 [71.5] Japan (highest): 81.9 [73.3] China: 71.5 [63.2] Russia: 65.4 [69.7] South Africa: 49.0 [53.7]
Population below poverty line (%) (based on official government data)	25	U.S.: 12.7; China: 10; Iran: 40; Mexico: 40; Russia: 25; S. Africa: 50
Ratio of richest 20% to poorest 20% (by share of national income or consumption)	5.7	U.S.: 9.0; Japan: 3.4 (best); Iran: 9.7; Mexico: 17.0; Russia: 10.5; S. Africa: 33.6
Literacy of adults over 15 (%), 2003 [and ratio of female to male literacy]	60% [0.82]	U.S., Japan, Russia: > 99 [1.0]; China: 86 [0.98]; Mexico: 91 [0.99]; Iran: 77 [0.95]; S. Africa: 86 [0.98]
Public spending on debt servicing (as percentage of GDP, 1998–2000)	1.9%	China: 2.1; Iran: 4.4; Mexico: 7.9; Russia: 5.6; S. Africa: 3.8
Annual population growth rate (%) projected for 2001–2015 [and average rate, 1975–2001]	1.3 [2.0]	U.S: 1.0 [1.0]; Japan: 0.0 [0.5]; China: 0.6 [1.3]; Mexico: 1.2 [2.0]; Iran: 1.4 [2.7]; Russia: -0.6 [0.3]; S. Africa: 0.0 [2.1]

Sources: World Bank, *World Development Indicators 2006* (Washington, DC); United Nations, *Human Development Report 2003 & 2006* (New York); International Monetary Fund, *World Economic Outlook Database* (April 2007); *CIA World Factbook 2004* (Washington, DC).

services because of poor roads and inadequate communication links. These kiosks allow farmers to access computerized databanks where millions of land deeds have been recorded, helping to reduce the incidence of land fraud. For those without access to sophisticated medical facilities, these kiosks help local medical providers obtain updated medical information and send data to urban doctors who can run laboratory tests. In addition, farmers can now directly purchase seed and fertilizer at wholesale rates online rather than going through middlemen, who may charge exorbitant fees for their services. Of course, it remains to be seen whether such initiatives can be replicated in other states, whether they can boost the standard of living for the 250 million Indians living in poverty, and whether they can help bridge the widening gaps in living standards across classes, regions, and sectors.

THE DIVERSIFICATION OF SOCIAL FORCES: LABOR, WOMEN, AND ENVIRONMENTAL GROUPS

The growing fluidity of electoral politics and the liberalization of the economy have propelled an increasingly diverse array of interest groups that cut across long-standing cleavages based on caste, region, and religion. Several of these groups are at the forefront of India's integration into the global economy. India's business elites are sophisticated, well educated, attentive to international trends, and strategic in their pursuit of new opportunities both within India and abroad. India's economic reformers rely heavily on the advice of native scholars who are well trained in macroeconomics and thoroughly familiar with the dynamics of international trade and global financial markets. Younger members of the urban middle class are hooked into satellite television, carry cell phones, and regularly surf the Internet, absorbing certain common topics of discussion, lifestyles, and consumption patterns found worldwide. However, these groups, although more visible to outside observers, constitute only a small fraction of India's huge population. Hence, to understand the challenges facing the country in the coming century, it is necessary to consider the evolving interests of some of the less visible segments of Indian society: the laboring classes, women, and grassroots environmentalists.

India's working class represents a heterogeneous social category with significant variation across different segments. The 10 percent of the workforce that is organized into trade unions is primarily concerned with maintaining the level of job security, workplace benefits, and social recognition of workers in larger firms, especially in the public sector. Historically, Indian trade unions have been fragmented because they are joined together in federations that subscribe to different ideologies and are allied with competing political parties. The unions that support the BJP, for example, reject the socialist principles embraced by unions linked to the leftist parties. However, the increasing fluidity of coalition politics, together with the common threat of workforce reductions in the public and private sectors, has given rise to increasing coordination across union bodies. This has been evident in strikes and protests to challenge the privatization of certain enterprises and to preserve the job security, wage levels, and social benefits associated with public-sector employment. However, given the challenges facing unions worldwide and the very small segment of the Indian workforce that is unionized, there is little reason to expect that India's unions will emerge victorious in their confrontation with business.

For the hundreds of millions of laborers in the "informal sector" who are not organized, the challenges are quite different. The informal sector includes millions of workers in agriculture, industry, and the service sector who are employed without formal contracts on a casual basis. Although some workers in the informal sector have made the most of their opportunities, for the majority, the lack of contracts and adequate legal protection has translated into long working hours, low hourly wages, and miserable working conditions. The World Bank and the International Monetary Fund still insist that aggregate economic growth will *eventually* bring about the alleviation of poverty and inequality, but for those facing extreme poverty, waiting may not be an option. Thus, it is not surprising that the most impoverished segments of the laboring classes have been responsive to populist criticisms of incumbent politicians accused of representing the wealthy and neglecting the poor. Some have even looked to radical social movements – some organized around revolutionary ideologies (for example, the radical socialist Naxalite movement), others around the predicaments of specific tribal or lower-caste groups (for example, the Telengana movement in Andhra Pradesh). Although still confined to the margins of political life, such groups may quickly grow in size if no public action is taken to alleviate the hardships of the poorest segments of the workforce. As a whole, workers in the informal sector constitute a large underclass of have-nots that has a far more pressing interest in eradicating poverty and reducing inequality than in basking in India's growing importance in the high-tech sector.

The majority of India's women, too, are facing new challenges as a group. India has traditionally been a patriarchal society, with men dominating the decision making in most communities and women often confined to the domestic sphere. Today, the gender gap in India, although smaller than before, remains significant, with men continuing to be disproportionately represented in higher education, public office, and the organized workforce. Nevertheless, in comparison with other postcolonial developers, it is noteworthy that women's participation in the Indian political system has been steadily growing over the past century. Women's involvement in the nationalist movement, the arrival of universal suffrage in connection with parliamentary democracy, the increase in the literacy rate for women and girls, and the rise of Indira Gandhi and other women to prominence in national politics all helped to gradually increase the visibility of women in the public sphere. This is evident in the increasing number of female voters and candidates in electoral politics, in feminist movements spearheaded by urban middle-class women who have set out to challenge patriarchal attitudes, and in the proliferation of nongovernmental organizations (NGOs) that provide credit to support women's independent economic activities or campaign to end violence against women (especially physical abuse or murder related to dowry disputes). Since the 1990s, India's integration into the global economy has brought new challenges for women, especially those in poorer families, who have been negatively impacted by reduced public spending on programs targeting women. At the same time, the social dimension of globalization has enabled Indian women's groups to form transnational alliances as they seek to expand their political clout and create new opportunities for themselves in the public realm. The diverse forms of women's activism in India may not evolve into a Western-style feminist movement, but nor can it be expected to given the distinctive experiences of Indian women. What is more important is that increasing numbers of Indian women, regardless of their religion, caste, or language, are coming together to challenge practices that restrict their options, limit their upward mobility, or endanger their lives.

Environmental activists also have become more visible in the public sphere, with growing fears that the quest for economic growth will further accelerate environmental degradation. In the 1970s and 1980s, environmental movements were made up of relatively poor people focused on the protection of their own communities and habitats in the face of particular developmental projects. The "Chipko" ("Embrace the Trees") movement, for example, was launched in the early 1970s when a group of poor hill people in northern India stood between trees and loggers' saws in order to prevent the loggers from destroying the forests that constituted their habitats. During the late 1980s, several communities in western India banded together to form a campaign to protest against the construction of a massive dam on the Narmada River; the protest gained enough international attention to get the World Bank to withdraw financial support for the project and led the Indian government to change the original blueprint for the dam. These movements have gained national and international attention, providing the impetus for a rapid proliferation of environmental activism that features NGOs such as the Green Future Foundation as well as cross-regional citizens' groups such as the National Alliance of People's Movement. The environmental movement in India today is now a heterogeneous one, with some groups coordinating with environmental advocacy groups worldwide and others continuing to focus on the immediate habitats of local communities.

Conclusion

Under Prime Ministers Nehru and Mrs. Gandhi, India's national identity remained secular and tied to its self-conception as a leader of the developing world on the international stage. India's political institutions functioned well compared with those in many other experimental developers, but the Congress Party's initial advantages produced a "dominant-party system" in which other "parties of pressure" could not yet compete on the national stage. A "mixed" economy with a large public sector became firmly entrenched. Mrs. Gandhi introduced her own distinctive brand of politics and her own economic initiatives, but these took place within the institutional framework and program of development initiated by Nehru during the 1950s. During this period, many scholars and leaders – indeed, Nehru himself – thought that preexisting sources of collective identity were atavistic, and the national political elite maintained a secular vision of modern India.

Since the mid-1980s, however, the changes in the global order have been accompanied by a fundamental shift in India's developmental path (see Table 10.5 at the end of the chapter). India's political system has remained stable, but with the growth of new parties and platforms, a more fluid era of coalition politics is now under way. With the growth of the BJP, Congress no longer dominates, and both parties depend on alliances or coalitions involving dozens of regional and splinter parties. In the process, new interests and strategies have emerged, while preexisting identities linked to caste and religions have taken on a new significance as a basis for political mobilization. This has been accompanied by a move away from a mixed economy, with economic liberalization accompanied by greater integration into the global economy. This shift has, in turn, produced new groups of winners and losers, with the latter thus far being a more significant portion of the electorate. These transformations mean that India's leaders in the twenty-first century will have to demonstrate considerable political skill if they wish to maintain the delicate balance between social forces pulling in different directions – between cosmopolitan secularists and those identifying with centuries-old civilizational ideals; between a majority Hindu population and Muslims and other religious minorities; between upwardly mobile lower-caste groups and anxious upper-caste groups fearful of losing access to educational and employment opportunities; between an urban elite that is seizing new opportunities in the information technology sector and a rural population that constitutes over 60 percent of the population but accounts for just one-quarter of India's GDP; and between those trumpeting India's achievements in science, technology, and industry and those concerned with environmental degradation, labor standards, and the gender gap in economic opportunities.

India's leadership will also have to be nimble in balancing the interests of their domestic and international constituencies. Immediately following the 2004 elections, the Bombay Stock Exchange, the country's largest stock market, initially experienced a sharp drop because of fears of a retreat from market reforms. The fears soon subsided, and the stock market stabilized with the naming of former Finance Minister Manmohan Singh as the new prime minister. However, these fluctuations reveal the challenge of managing a nervous international audience in a fast-moving global economy. Had foreign investors continued to flee India, they would have been effectively penalizing hundreds of millions of voters for casting their ballots in line with their interests and values. They would also have been triggering an economic downturn on the basis of unsubstantiated assumptions: Many of those who were concerned over a Congress victory in 2004 had also worried when the BJP gained power in 1998. In 1998, some of these foreign investors did not see the link between the BJP's vision *of Hinduttva* and its ambitious hopes for elevating India's place in the world; in 2004, they did not consider that the victorious party, although it had embraced a populist platform, was the same party that had set economic liberalization in motion. Thus, in marked contrast with leaders in authoritarian countries such as China or "superpresidential" political systems such as Russia, leaders in parliamentary democracies such as India must constantly balance the threat of exit by foreign investors (if they seek to appease voters clamoring for social justice) with the threat of electoral defeat at the hands of the voters (if they adopt policies perceived as catering to business elites and foreign investors). Thus far, Indian politicians have proven themselves up to the task, but whether they can continue to handle this challenge over the long run remains to be seen.

Finally, it is worth noting that, in the face of adversity and skepticism, India's institutions have proven to be durable, enjoying a measure of legitimacy not often seen in postcolonial countries. This legitimacy is most clearly evident in voter turnout, which is considerably higher than in the United States. It is also evident in the behavior of all kinds of political parties, ranging from Hindu fundamentalists to Marxist-Leninists, who have generally behaved responsibly once in power. Thus, without minimizing the social problems and conflicts that continue to plague India today, it is necessary to acknowledge the robustness of the institutions that have somehow managed to reconcile the complex web of identities and interests that has emerged across India. The real test for these institutions, however, may still lie ahead as this nation of over one billion people continues to grow in population while its leaders simultaneously attempt to combat poverty, preserve its rich cultural heritage, and elevate its position in a changing global order.

BIBLIOGRAPHY

Basu, Amrita. *Two Faces of Protest: Contrasting Modes of Women's Activism in India.* Berkeley: University of California Press, 1992.

Bayley, Susan. *Caste, Society and Politics in India.* Cambridge: Cambridge University Press, 1999.

Bery, Suman, Barry Bosworth, and Arvind Panagriya, eds. *India Policy Forum, 2005–2006.* Two Volumes. New Delhi: Sage, 2004 (Volume 1) and 2006 (Volume 2).

Bose, Sugata, and Ayesha Jalal. *Nationalism, Democracy and Development: State and Politics in India.* New York: Oxford University Press, 2003.

Brass, Paul. *The Politics of India since Independence.* Cambridge: Cambridge University Press, 1994.

Carras, Mary C. *Indira Gandhi: In the Crucible of Leadership.* Boston: Beacon, 1979.

Chakraborty, Bidyut. *Forging Power: Coalition Politics in India.* New York: Oxford University Press, 2006.

Chanda, Asok. *Federalism in India.* London: Allen and Unwin, 1965.

Chhibber, Pradeep. *Democracy without Associations: Transformation of the Party System and Social Cleavages in India.* Ann Arbor: University of Michigan Press, 1999.

Chibber, Vivek. *Locked in Place: State Building and Late Industrialization in India.* Princeton, NJ: Princeton University Press, 2003.

Cohen, Stephen. *India: Emerging Power.* Washington, DC: Brookings Institution Press, 2002.

Corbridge, Stuart, Glyn Williams, and Manoj Srivastava. *Seeing the State: Governance and Governmentality in India.* Cambridge: Cambridge University Press, 2005.

Dalton, Denis. *Mahatma Gandhi.* New York: Columbia University Press, 1993.

Dasgupta, Jyotirindra. *Language, Conflict and National Development.* Berkeley: University of California Press, 1970.

Frankel, Francine. *India's Political Economy, 1947–2004: The Gradual Revolution.* New Delhi: Oxford University Press, 2005.

Ganguly, Sumit. *The Crisis in Kashmir: Portents of War, Hopes for Peace.* Woodrow Wilson Center Press Series. Cambridge: Cambridge University Press, 1999.

Gopal, Sarvepalli. *Jawaharlal Nehru: A Biography.* New Delhi: Oxford University Press, 1984.

Guha, Ramachandra. *The Unquiet Woods: Ecological Change and Peasant Resistance in the Himalaya.* New Delhi: Oxford University Press, 1991.

Hasan, Zoya, ed. *Parties and Party Politics in India.* New York: Oxford University Press, 2002.

Jaffrelot, Christophe. *The BJP and the Compulsions of Politics in India.* New York: Oxford University Press, 2000.

Jaffrelot, Christophe. *India's Silent Revolution: The Rise of the Lower Castes.* New York: Columbia University Press, 2002.

Jalal, Ayesha. *Democracy and Authoritarianism in South Asia.* Cambridge: Cambridge University Press, 1995.

Jenkins, Rob. *Democratic Politics and Economic Reform in India.* Cambridge: Cambridge University Press, 1999.

Jenkins, Rob, ed. *Regional Reflections: Comparing Politics Across India's States*. New York: Oxford University Press, 2004.

Jha, Raghbendra. *Indian Economic Reforms*. New York: Palgrave Macmillan, 2003.

Kapur, Devesh, and Pratab Bhanu Mehta. *Public Institutions in India: Performance and Design*. New York: Oxford University Press, 2006.

Kohli, Atul. *Democracy and Discontent: India's Growing Crisis of Governability*. Cambridge: Cambridge University Press, 1990.

Kohli, Atul, ed. *The Success of India's Democracy*. Cambridge: Cambridge University Press, 2001.

Kothari, Rajni. *Politics in India*. Boston: Little, Brown, 1970.

Muller, Anders Riel, and Raj Patel. *Shining India? Economic Liberalization and Rural Poverty in the 1990s*. Oakland, CA: Food First/Institute for Food and Development Policy, 2004.

Nehru, Jawaharlal. *An Autobiography*. New Delhi: Oxford University Press, 1980.

Pandey, Gyanendra. *Remembering Partition: Violence, Nationalism and History in India*. Cambridge: Cambridge University Press, 2001.

Parekh, Bhikhu. *Gandhi*. New York: Oxford University Press, 1997.

Perkovich, George. *India's Nuclear Bomb*. Berkeley: University of California Press, 2001.

Robb, Peter. *A History of India*. New York: Palgrave, 2002.

Rudolph, Lloyd, and Susanne Rudolph. *In Pursuit of Lakshmi: The Political Economy of the Indian State*. Chicago: University of Chicago Press, 1987.

Sengupta, Bhavani. *Rajiv Gandhi: A Political Study*. New Delhi: Konarak Publishers, 1989.

Sinha, Aseema. 2005. *The Regional Roots of Developmental Politics in India: A Divided Leviathan*. Bloomington: Indiana University Press, 2005.

Srinivas, M. N. *The Dominant Caste and Other Essays*. New Delhi: Oxford University Press, 1987.

Subramanian, Narendra. *Ethnicity and Populist Mobilization: Political Parties, Citizens and Democracy in South India*. New York: Oxford University Press, 1999.

Talbot, Ian, and Gurharpal Singh. *Region and Partition: Bengal, Punjab and the Partition of the Subcontinent*. New York: Oxford University Press, 1999.

Van der Veer, Peter. *Religious Nationalism: Hindus and Muslims in India*. Berkeley: University of California Press, 1994.

Varshney, Asutosh. *Democracy, Development and the Countryside: Urban–Rural Struggles in India*. Cambridge: Cambridge University Press, 1995.

Varshney, Asutosh. *Ethnic Conflict and Civic Life: Hindus and Muslims in India*. New Haven, CT: Yale University Press, 2003.

Wilkinson, Steven. *Votes and Violence: Electoral Competition and Ethnic Riots in India*. New York: Cambridge University Press, 2006.

Wolpert, Stanley. *A New History of India*. Fifth edition. Chicago: University of Chicago Press, 1997.

TABLE 10.5. Key Phases in India's Political Development

Time period	Regime	Global context	Interests/identities/ institutions	Developmental path
Pre-1757	empires, kingdoms	invasion and settlement	emergence of race, caste, religious, and regional identification, tributary systems, local autonomy, competition between localities	diffusion of some shared administrative, social, and cultural practices
1757– 1947	British colonialism	European imperialism	indirect rule with princely states, but more direct rule from 1857, nascent urban commercial interests, Parliament and courts established, spread of national identity led by Indian National Congress	early industrialization with "misdevelopment" (promotion of cash crops and limits on local capital)
1947– 1984	Congress Party dominance	Cold War and nonaligned movement	caste-based "vote banks," peasant and working-class interests, federalized democracy, with residual powers left to center	state-dominated import-substitution industrialization, with 1970s green revolution
1984- present	coalitional politics with two major parties	post–Cold War globalization, with entry into "nuclear club"	rise of Hindu nationalism (BJP), lower-caste mobilization grows, business interests gain ground, new social movements emerge, political institutions stable, but with more subnational units and regional parties	incremental process of liberalization, with selective privatization (accelerated after 1991)

IMPORTANT TERMS

Lal Krishna Advani leading figure in the BJP, who served as the home minister in the 1998–2004 BJP government. He was noted for his public advocacy of the destruction of the Babri mosque in Ayodhya, for which he was once arrested.

Bharatiya Janata Party (BJP, or the Indian People's Party) a political party that has its roots in past Hindu fundamentalist organizations and gradually became a major political force during the 1990s on the strength of its glorification of *Hinduttva* (see term).

Brahmins Hindu priests, considered to be the most "pure" of the caste groups and uniquely qualified to read scriptural texts and perform Hindu religious ceremonies.

caste the generic term employed to mean a fivefold occupational and social hierarchy ranging, in decending order of "purity," from Brahmins (see term) and warriors to merchants/traders, peasants/artisans, and "untouchables." Should be distinguished from the term "jati," which is used to identify groups of families belonging to a subcategory of a caste within a particular region or community.

Communist Party of India–Marxist (CPI-M) the most significant leftist party in India, notable as a rare case of a communist party that gained power through elections. It has maintained continuous control over the state assembly of West Bengal since the 1960s.

Congress Party the political party that grew out of the Indian National Congress (INC) and held power for most of the first five decades after independence. Later referred to as Congress-I (for Indira Gandhi), which split with the less significant Congress-O (for "organization") in 1967. Since the 1990s, Congress and its allies have been using the original pre-independence appellation (INC).

dominant-party system the term employed to characterize India's political system as a result of the Congress Party's steady control over Parliament for all but one election between 1952 and 1984. Not an authoritarian system but rather the combined result of India's "first-past-the-post" electoral system and the initial advantages inherited by the Congress Party.

Emergency an 18-month period from late 1975 to early 1977 when Indira Gandhi suspended parts of the constitution and arrested opposition leaders in response to her opponents' calls for the army to remove her from power for alleged campaign violations.

Indira Gandhi daughter of Jawaharlal Nehru, and prime minister of India (1967–1977, 1980–1984). Identified with the rise of patronage politics, the green revolution, a populist antipoverty campaign, the "Emergency" (see term), and the assault on Sikh militants in the Punjab. Assassinated by Sikh bodyguards in 1984. No direct relation to Mohandas K. Gandhi.

Mohandas K. Gandhi (Mahatma, or "Great Soul") British-educated   lawyer who became the de facto leader of the Indian nationalist movement. Noted for his opposition to the caste system and for nonviolent civil-disobedience campaigns that helped to mobilize grassroots support for independence. Assassinated in 1948 by a Hindu fanatic.

Rajiv Gandhi elder son of Indira Gandhi. He became prime minister of India (1984–1989) following Indira's assassination. His administration took the first steps toward economic reform. Following the Congress Party's defeat in 1989, Rajiv was assassinated while campaigning for the 1991 elections.

Sonia Gandhi Italian-born wife of Rajiv Gandhi. Initially stayed out of politics, but then led the Congress Party to victory in 2004, although declining the post of prime minister.

green revolution the campaign during the early 1970s to promote the use of new seeds and new methods of fertilization and crop rotation in order to boost agricultural production. Helped to make India self-sufficient in food production.

Hinduttva a term popularized by the BJP and some Hindu nationalist social organizations to emphasize the distinctiveness and greatness of Hindu civilization and to make this civilization the basis for defining India's national identity.

Indian National Congress (INC) an organization that emerged in 1885 and became the main force for the independence movement. Turned into the Congress Party after independence.

Janata Party/Dal a loosely organized party that includes several diverse components that claim to share a common platform that emphasizes reduced planning, local self-reliance, poverty alleviation, and redistribution of wealth. Originally called the Janata Party, this party has formed three separate coalition governments (1977–1979, 1989–1991, and 1996–1998), none of which has lasted a full term.

license raj an aspect of India's statist economy in which private-sector firms above a certain asset threshold had to obtain a government license to produce, import, or export goods. Has been steadily scaled back since the mid-1980s as part of economic liberalization.

Mandal Commission Report a report approved in 1990 that identifies a long list of groups as "other backward castes" that would qualify for preferential treatment through India's system of "reservations" (see term).

Jawaharlal Nehru leading figure in the Indian National Congress and India's first prime minister. He is identified with a "third way" of development that rejected alliances with the superpowers while combining aspects of Western-style capitalism and Soviet-style planning.

Narasimha Rao prime minister of India (1991–1996) who led the Congress Party after Rajiv Gandhi's assassination. His cabinet sped up the pace of economic liberalization.

President's Rule the rule stipulated in Article 356 of the Indian constitution whereby the president can authorize intervention by the central government in states thought to be experiencing extraordinary political or social unrest. Has sometimes been invoked on shaky grounds to oust uncooperative state assemblies.

Rashtriya Seva Sangh (RSS) a Hindu social organization created in 1925 to preserve and promote Hindu traditions. Together with the VHP (see term), it helped mobilize support for the BJP.

reservations the term used by Indians to refer to India's "affirmative action" system for increasing the representation of lower-caste groups in educational institutions and the public sector.

Sikhs followers of the Sikh religion, who constitute a slim majority in the state of Punjab. Sikh militants waged a struggle for a separate "Khalistan" nation during the 1980s, but the conflict has since subsided.

Manmohan Singh prime minister of India following the Congress Party's surprising electoral victory in May 2004. Formerly minister of finance in the 1991–1996 Congress government.

V. P. Singh prime minister of India under the Janata government of 1989–1991. Noteworthy for efforts to check corruption and expand system of "reservations" (see term).

Atal Behari Vajpayee BJP leader who served as prime minister of India from 1998 to 2004. Identified with pragmatic wing of the BJP.

Vishva Hindu Parishad (VHP) a worldwide organization of Hindus committed to promoting *Hinduttva* (see term). Constitutes a major social base and source of funding for the BJP.

vote bank a bloc of votes for a particular candidate delivered by members of a given community (usually a local caste group or a village) as a result of deals brokered between the candidate and the community's leaders.

STUDY QUESTIONS

1. What were the various sources of collective identity in South Asia prior to British colonialism? Why have these cleavages generated less collective violence than we find in postcolonial Africa?

2. In what ways did British colonial administration affect the prospects for political and economic development in postcolonial India?

3. Why was Mahatma Gandhi's leadership important to the success of the Indian National Congress? What were the strengths and limitations of his strategy of nonviolent noncooperation?

4. What institutional characteristics distinguish Indian democracy and federalism from democracy and federalism in the United States?

5. In what respects did Nehru's India represent a "third way" of political and economic development? How did successors modify his approach from the 1960s to 1970s?

6. What were the sources of the Congress Party's dominance between the 1950s and early 1980s? What trends characterize the transformation of India's electoral politics since the late 1980s?

7. What do the BJP's electoral victories in 1998–1999 and the Congress Party's victory in 2004 suggest about the dynamics of coalition politics and about the salience of identities based on caste or religion?

8. What factors account for the rise in India's position in the international economic order? To what extent can this rise be attributed to market reforms during the 1990s as opposed to investments in science and education during the previous three decades?

9. Which groups appear to be the main winners and losers in the process of economic liberalization? Why did tens of thousands of farmers commit suicide in rural India during the first several years of the twenty-first century?

10. How have global economic, social, and political processes affected the interplay of identities, interests, and institutions in post–Cold War India?

CHAPTER ELEVEN

Iran

Vali Nasr

Introduction

At the turn of the twentieth century, Iran embarked on a path to development that was typical of many late developers. Iran's experience, however, has proved to be unique. Development was accompanied by ideological conflicts that culminated in a religiously inspired revolution in 1979. In the process, a modernizing monarchy gave place to the theocratic and revolutionary politics of the **Islamic Republic of Iran** (the official name of Iran since the revolution). As populism changed the character of the economy and **Islamic ideology** (a political doctrine based on **Islam**) transformed Iranian society, its norms, institutions, and, for a time at least, pursuit of its interests were subsumed under preservation of identity. Since the revolution, the nature of development has been complex, revealing modernizing impulses tempered by the pressures of Islamic ideology. Beyond its ideological and institutional particularities, the Islamic Republic shares many of the characteristics and problems of populist authoritarian regimes elsewhere in the developing world: a bloated public sector, mismanagement, and corruption.

There are three distinct and yet interrelated periods in Iran's modern development: the early and later **Pahlavi** (the dynasty that ruled Iran from 1925 to 1979) periods; those of **Reza Shah Pahlavi** (1925–1941) and **Muhammad Reza Shah Pahlavi** (1941–1979); and the Islamic Republic (1979–present). There is greater continuity between the first two periods, under the Pahlavi monarchs, although there are notable differences as well. The Reza Shah period coincided with the rise of the modern Iranian state and started the process of development. The Muhammad Reza Shah period continued in the footsteps of the first period but accelerated the pursuit of modernization. Development under the second Pahlavi monarch was, moreover, conditioned by different global influences and domestic sociopolitical identities and interests. The Islamic Republic has been distinct from the earlier periods in its ideological orientation and in many aspects of its economic policies and political characteristics. Above and beyond their differences in ideological orientation or policy choices, the three periods are similar in the dominant role of the state in development. The basis of Iran's path in the modern world is to be found in the historical circumstances in which Iran first embarked on development.

The Global Context and the Rise of the Modern Iranian State

Iran is among the handful of developing countries to escape direct colonialism but not the impact of imperialism. Throughout the nineteenth century, the ruling Qajar dynasty (1796–1921) was unable to resist Western imperialist penetration; nor could it stave off the gradual loss of territory and control over national assets to foreign powers. This provided the context for the rise of the modern Iranian state and the path to development that it would follow (see Table 11.1 at the end of the chapter).

Also important was the pivotal role of the monarchy during the nineteenth century. The monarchy was important to imperial powers who wished to maintain a captive and weak center in Iran. As a result, imperial powers provided strategic support to the monarchy and helped thwart significant challenges to its authority. The broader powers of the monarchy were rooted in the dominant social position of the feudal aristocracy and tribal leaders, who sustained monarchical authority at the center, even as they resisted taxation and defended their autonomy. Of equal importance was the role of the religious establishment. Throughout the nineteenth century, the clergy resisted domination by the monarchy and defended the rights of the nation before imperialist interests that often worked through the monarchy. Still, at a more fundamental level, the clergy defended the sociopolitical position of the monarchy, just as the monarchy protected the socioeconomic interests of the clergy. The nature of relations among the state, the elite, and the religious establishment would change over time, with important consequences for Iran's pattern of development.

Concentration of power in the monarchy occurred at a time of weakening of the ruling political establishment as a whole, in large part caused by pressures that were brought to bear on Iranian society and Iran's body politic by imperialism. The concentration of power in a decaying central government led to circumstances in which neither the state nor social forces enjoyed countrywide domination. This, in turn, produced a crisis for monarchical absolutism. Eventually the monarchy found itself on the defensive against a strong constitutionalist movement that included the intelligentsia – who were the conduit for European constitutionalist ideals – elements of the religious establishment, the urban poor, and aspiring members of the bureaucracy and the emerging middle classes. The Constitutional Revolution, as this movement and the resultant 1906 constitution came to be known, placed limits on the power of the monarchy and vested much of its authority in a parliament. This would be the first serious attempt to alter the balance of power between the state and society. It produced a period of democratic rule in Iran, which proved to be short-lived. By the end of the first decade of the twentieth century, Iranian democracy had begun to lose ground to authoritarian tendencies.

The rise of democracy did not produce stable governing coalitions or well-organized and effective political parties. Democracy intensified political competition in the central government, just as it weakened the hold of the central government over the country, leading to palpable fears of the country's disintegration. This, along with the collapse of law and order, rampant corruption, and deteriorating economic conditions, limited the prospects for democratic consolidation. Elected governments proved to be just as pliable in the face of imperialist pressure as had absolutist monarchs before 1906. It had further become evident that democracy would not produce rapid modernization. Hence, those social forces that supported the Constitutional Revolution with the hope of bringing both political and economic modernization to Iran were confronted with a zero-sum choice – democracy or socioeconomic modernization. Many opted for the latter, believing that a strong central state would better protect fundamental rights to life and property, the integrity of national borders, and national rights before imperialist demands.

In the meantime, the Anglo-Russian rapprochement of 1907 made the division of Iran between the two world powers a distinct possibility, placing greater pressure on the democratic order. This possibility would continue to haunt Iranians until the Bolshevik revolution of 1917 drove a wedge between Russia and the West. Thenceforth, the British would once again take an interest in strengthening the central government in Iran. However, by then, the democratic order had been seriously damaged. Consequently, the domestic and foreign efforts to shore up the central authority and the increasing demands for effective modernization and development within Iran – which had first been pursued through the Constitutional Revolution – would now lead to a regime change. The result would be a new political order that would draw heavily on the institutional framework of the absolutist era. Iran would thus embark on its path to development by reconstituting the pre-1906 political institutions.

The Reza Shah Period and the Beginnings of Development, 1921–1941

The crisis of democracy ended with a military coup in 1921 that was led by Reza Khan (later Reza Shah Pahlavi) in alliance with dissident civilian politicians and intellectuals. Reza Khan quickly consolidated power and in

1925 ascended the throne. The coup ushered in a new period in Iran's history, during which national boundaries became institutionalized, the country committed itself to development, and its interests, identity, and institutions became defined and entrenched. In many ways, the fundamental characteristics of the modern state and the defining elements of its path to development were outlined during this period.

Reza Shah's monarchy was concerned with two separate but interrelated objectives: first, to assert the power of the central government and limit regional autonomy – that is, to ensure law and order and guarantee the territorial integrity of the country; and second, to develop Iran, understood at the time to mean social modernization and industrialization. The first objective required the establishment of a strong military, and the second objective required the construction of modern bureaucratic institutions. The realization of both objectives required an increase in state revenue and the mobilization of financial resources through taxation, greater regulation of the economy, and attempts to increase the proceeds from oil production and export. Both objectives would in time broaden the state's ability to formulate and implement coherent policies and to reach into society. The two objectives were the most important examples of the state's provision of "public goods" (that is, things that people want but that no individual or group of individuals can provide) in a society where such a concept was largely absent. The provision of these public goods had popular support and helped the state to expand its role in the society and economy and to organize resources and people effectively. In fact, reshaping identities and value systems in order to better provide those goods became central to the state's conception of its own function.

Reza Shah was largely successful in realizing both objectives. His military campaigns defeated separatist movements and subdued autonomous regions and rebellious warlords. In the process, he asserted the primacy of the central government and laid the foundations for strong centralized control of the country. Still, this did not end the obsession with territorial integrity, which at key junctures would translate into xenophobic nationalism but would otherwise further serve to strengthen state control and nudge Iran in the direction of absolutism. Historically, military-bureaucratic absolutism in Europe had facilitated the mobilization of resources in the face of threats to borders. The same process was evident in Iran as well. Hence, early on, the modern Iranian state developed authoritarian tendencies in response to international and domestic military threats and the need to mobilize resources to respond to them.

The goal of economic development led the state to extend its control over the economy to mobilize resources for industrialization. Following the examples of Germany and Japan during 1921–1941, the state established the first industries, invested in infrastructure, and tightened its hold over customs, banking, and foreign trade. The result was a form of state-led capitalism in which the state would see to industrialization, just as it would manage the day-to-day affairs of the economy, although it would provide a role for the private sector.

The objective of economic development both required and promoted administrative and social reform. Reza Shah supported the rise of modern bureaucratic institutions, a new judiciary, and the reform of public health and education. Students were sent abroad, and modern educational institutions were established in Iran. In addition, new administrative procedures and secular civil and penal codes were adopted.

Reza Shah was convinced that making Iran strong and fostering its economic development would require fundamental changes in the country's identity and social relations – an ambitious project of cultural engineering that required a coherent state ideology. The state secularized the judiciary and the educational system, and it restricted the powers of the clergy. It mandated the change of traditional dress to Western dress and promoted secular values. In so doing, it hoped to make popular culture compatible with the requirements and goals of development. In place of Islam, the state promoted nationalism, defined in terms of pre-Islamic Iranian identity. Such an identity would be secular and would provide an ideological foundation for both monarchical power and rapid development. The change in identity was also intended to inculcate discipline in the population as a prelude to development. It was then believed, largely because of imperialist propaganda, that Iranian cultural beliefs could not promote discipline and the values that are necessary for a modern society. Secular nationalism would remedy that problem. In all of this, Reza Shah was deeply influenced by the examples of Germany and Japan, and of **Kemalism** (a model of development based on secularism, nationalism, and state dominance in socioeconomic matters) in Turkey. Global context thus shaped interests, identities, and the relation between the two.

The concern with identity as a necessary prerequisite for successful development would become a hallmark of state-society relations in Iran. In Iran, the two dominant markers of identity are Islam and Iranian nationalism. The two have at times reinforced one another and at other times have represented different political ideals. Iranians became Muslim pursuant to the Arab invasion of Iran in the seventh century. As such, Islam has always been viewed by Iranian nationalists as the invader's faith. Iranians are unique among the early civilizations that converted to Islam in that they did not adopt the Arabic language and culture. This has created tensions between Iran's nationalism and its faith. Iranian **Shia** Islam is a minority sect in Islam that is distinguished from the majority Sunnis in that it believes that the descendants of the Prophet (whom Shias refer to as Imams) were the legitimate successors to the Prophet and that today the clergy (*ulama*, the highest-ranking among whom the Shias call **ayatollah**) serve as their representatives and as such exercise authority over the Shias. The Shias were always a suppressed community, and they did not exercise power until 1501, when a Shia monarchy made the faith the official religion of Iran. Shias differ from Sunnis in matters of faith much as the Eastern Church differs from the Western Church in Christianity. That Iran became the seat of Shi'ism gave the country its own unique attachment to Islam, which has always distinguished it from the Arab world and as such underscored the uniqueness of Iranian identity – setting it apart from the rest of the Muslim world.

Islam and Shi'ism have always played an important role in defining Iranian identity. However, with the advent of the modern state, emphasis was placed on secularism, which demanded separating Islam from Iranian nationalism. In place of Islam, Iranians were to identify themselves with their ethnicity and language, which as secular concepts were seen to be more compatible with modern nationalism and developmentalism. Iranian nationalism never replaced Islam, nor were the complex relations between the two ever completely resolved. Rather, from Reza Shah's regime to that of the Islamic Republic, identity featured importantly in state policy. The preoccupation with questions of identity – and hence issues such as music, dress, popular beliefs, and the cultural outlook of the individual – became important in defining the public good and setting the agenda for development. The legacy of the state's cultural policies continues to influence state-society relations in Iran to this day, and hence debates about development begin with struggles over identity.

Giving the state the means to govern effectively was expensive. In fact, how it dealt with financial needs shaped, to a significant degree, the nature of state power. Since the beginning of the twentieth century, Iran received royalties from the **Anglo-Iranian Oil Company**, a British company that managed oil production in southern Iran. Efforts to increase royalty payments to the Iranian government proved futile, which forced the state to rely more on tax revenue. Tax farming – a system in which local officials' incomes are tied to the amount of taxes they manage to collect – and other forms of unsystematic revenue collections were replaced with a centralized taxation system. The state also turned to foreign advisers to streamline Iran's financial system. Foreign expertise helped the state to extract resources from society and develop plans for economic development; it did not, however, altogether resolve the financial problems confronting the state. Financial constraints encouraged the state to monopolize power in order to increase its ability to extract resources from society and to negotiate more effectively with foreign commercial interests over royalties.

That a strong state did in fact rise in Iran at this time and that it did so despite significant financial constraints and resistance to central control, and in contravention of foreign interests, is noteworthy. It has been generally accepted that the rise of states is directly correlated with war making, and that societies that experience wars or significant social dislocation are more prone to produce strong states. The rise of the modern Iranian state during the 1920s was closely tied to the military campaigns that consolidated the central government's hold over the country and occurred amid the significant hardships – for example, economic hardship, famine, disease, social strife, and civil war – that Iranians endured during the first two decades of the twentieth century. The campaign to centralize power and defend the territorial integrity of the country had broad support among many social groups, notably those who had also been the main support for democracy. This allowed Reza Shah to tie the defense of the integrity of state borders to his own consolidation of power. It also allowed his regime to avoid compromises with various social actors – the feudal elite, tribal leaders, and merchants – in order to mobilize resources for the military campaigns.

During the 1920s, local power in Iran was strong but unorganized. It was, moreover, dissociated from politics at the center, and in some cases was supported by, and integrated with, foreign interests. It therefore did not serve as a source of support for the Parliament during the turbulent years of the democratic period or during the period of regime change in the 1920s. The subsequent weakening of democratic institutions such as the Parliament during the period of regime change meant minimal oversight by the Parliament of the administrative and financial activities of state leaders. Consequently, power accumulated at the center, and absolutist tendencies grew unbridled.

The growing dominance of the monarch combined with the social changes that development entailed created tensions in Iranian politics. In the first place, Reza Shah had been prevailed upon by the clergy to become a monarch, whereas in reality his regime was a "republican monarchy." No sooner had Reza Shah become king than he embarked on secularization and modernization and also abolished the hereditary titles of the aristocracy. In addition, his campaign to assert centralized control over the country pitted the state against local leaders. He thus moved away from those elite groups and social classes that had until then served as the pillars of the monarchy – the elite, the religious establishment, and tribal leaders – and was looking instead to the new middle classes to bolster his regime. The Reza Shah period thus changed the social base of the ruling order. In the economic arena, the same trend was evident. Traditional tradesmen and commercial interests became alienated from the state as it extended its control over the economy. The change in the social base of the monarchy would prove consequential. Disenchanted elite groups, the religious establishment, and small merchants and traders would form the basis of the anti-Pahlavi oppositional coalition. This coalition would eventually serve as the backbone of the revolution of 1979.

Initially, Reza Shah allied himself with the new middle classes to take on the elite, local leaders, and the clergy. The new middle classes were then receptive to modernization, secularization, and the nationalist identity that Reza Shah promoted in lieu of Islam. The alliance between the new middle classes and the monarchy, however, failed to provide the state with a countervailing base of support because these classes were not ideologically committed to the monarchy. As the pace of modernization increased, tensions in the monarchy's relations with the new middle classes grew. By the 1930s, many in these classes were joining pro-democracy and various leftist organizations.

Development spearheaded the rise of modern bureaucratic agencies. At the outset, the bureaucracy supported Reza Shah. Over time, however, he became wary of the rising power of the bureaucracy and purged it of its principal leaders. By exercising more control over the bureaucracy, Reza Shah precluded the possibility that the bureaucracy would develop as a legal-rational institution independent of the control of the monarchy. The Iranian state from this point forward would display many characteristics of what comparativists sometimes term *patrimonialism*, in which power is concentrated in the ruler, whose exercise of authority is only partially influenced by legal and administrative procedures.

In sum, during this period, the global context – in the form of imperialism and the German-Japanese model – combined with the state's need to safeguard territorial integrity and pursue development to shape interests, identity, and institutions in a manner that empowered the state and hence ensured its domination over Iranian politics.

The Democratic Interregnum, 1941–1954

The pattern of development that began in 1921 was interrupted by World War II. The Reza Shah state fell victim to changes in the broader international environment. The western Allies were keen to use Iranian territory for supplying the Soviet Union against Germany, and for this it was imperative that they maintain control over Iran. Reza Shah's constant bickering with British oil companies, combined with Iran's reliance on Germany for a number of public projects, had made the British wary of him. The Allies demanded that Iran declare neutrality and expel all German citizens, that Reza Shah abdicate, and that the Iranian military disarm. In 1941, Reza Shah was replaced on the throne by his son, Muhammad Reza Pahlavi (known in the West as "the **Shah**"). Foreign intervention thus ushered in a new era in Iranian politics that was characterized by greater openness and new possibilities for state-society relations. Still, foreign intervention did not decisively reshape Iranian politics – rearranging its institutions and altering the balance of power among them – in the manner that the United States would do in Germany and Japan after the war. The British retained the monarchy and did not change the country's constitution or the balance of power among the various social and political actors. That the monarchy would in later years emerge once again as a dominant force in an all-powerful state was therefore not very surprising.

Still, Reza Shah's departure opened the political process and created alternate developmental paths. During the war, political groups that had been suppressed by Reza Shah – liberals, leftists, and the clergy – organized and established a place for themselves in the political arena. The Parliament, which since 1921 had steadily lost ground to the monarchy, was empowered and once again occupied center stage. The political opening suggested that Iran could develop along democratic lines and that power might permanently shift from the monarchy to the Parliament, devolving in the process from state institutions to a broader spectrum of social and political actors. By 1954, however, domestic problems combined with changes in the global context to end the democratic opening.

The 1941–1954 period witnessed an intense struggle over the definition of political identity in Iran. The outcome of that struggle would be important for the fate of democracy. Some of the political forces that became dominant during the 1941–1954 period were illiberal. Communist, fascist, and religious groups and parties operated in the open political process but were not committed to democracy. In fact, their activities would serve as the pretext for once again vesting the state – and the institution of the monarchy – with greater powers.

Most important in this regard was the communist Tudeh (Masses) Party. Closely allied with the Soviet Union, the Tudeh Party posed a strong challenge to the ruling order and Western interests in Iran. The party was active among the middle classes, labor, intellectuals, and students, mobilizing these social groups in defense of social justice. It subscribed to the cult of Stalin and did not favor democracy. The Tudeh Party's ambiguous role in the Soviet Union's attempt to separate two provinces in northern Iran after World War II helped create both popular and Western support for strengthening the political center, which ultimately weakened the Tudeh Party and, in the process, the budding democracy.

The resurgence of religion in politics was equally significant. Religious forces were keen to roll back the secular policies of the Pahlavi state and to institutionalize their role in society and politics. To this end, they became active in the political arena, but not with the aim of strengthening democracy. Both the communists and religious forces weakened democracy by engaging in agitational politics: demonstrations, strikes, and sit-ins in the case of the Tudeh Party, and political assassinations in the case of religious activists. By creating political uncertainty, disruptions, and social tensions, the two groups made the task of democratic consolidation difficult and helped the monarchy enlist foreign support for its campaign to consolidate power.

Most damaging to democracy was the oil crisis of 1951–1953 and its link with Cold War politics. The dispute over royalties with the Anglo-Iranian Oil Company, which had begun during the 1930s, eventually culminated in an impasse during 1951–1953. As the British company refused to accommodate Iran's demands for higher royalties, nationalist feelings were aroused and they dominated Iranian politics. The monarchy, the military, and some in the business community favored a low-key approach, believing that a confrontational attitude would not favor Iran. Because of British intransigence, however, Iranians demanded more. The popularly elected nationalist prime minister, **Mohammad Mossadeq**, and his National Front Party capitalized on the public mood and nationalized the assets of the Anglo-Iranian Oil Company in Iran in 1953. The decision was widely popular within Iran and was supported by the Tudeh Party and religious activists as well.

Britain responded by cutting Iran out of the oil market. The Iranian economy collapsed, causing social tension and political radicalism. The palpable fear of a communist takeover changed the political alignment that had dominated Iranian politics. The clergy, worried about communism, switched sides, as did key segments of the middle classes, commercial interests, and elements of the nationalist elite. This political realignment facilitated concerted action between the monarchy and the Iranian military in close cooperation with the United States and Britain. The result was a military coup that toppled the National Front government, ending the democratic interregnum and restoring the monarchy to power. The 1941–1954 period had seen the possibility of alternate identities – Islamic, secular, democratic – shaping state-society relations and Iranian politics developing along a different path. By 1954, however, those possibilities were no longer present. Foreign intervention first interrupted and then led to the resumption of the state's development in the direction first instituted by Reza Shah. Interests, identities, and ultimately institutions were reshaped by the changing global context.

Resurrection of the Pahlavi State, 1954–1963

The 1954–1963 period was one of consolidation of monarchical power. Relying on the military, and with crucial financial and technical assistance from the United States, the monarchy went on the offensive against its opponents. The National Front Party and the Tudeh Party were banned. The military and bureaucracy were purged of their sympathizers. The campaign also weakened the institutions of civil society and ultimately the Parliament, dimming the prospects for democracy. Cold War considerations led the United States to support these developments in Iran and to help train Iranian military and intelligence agencies to protect the state, which was viewed as a bulwark against communism and the southward expansion of the Soviet Union.

Financial aid helped buoy Iran's economy and generated support for the ruling order. The consolidation of power under the monarchy would commit the state to a largely economic vision of development. The spirit of this posture was captured in the Shah's statement: "When the Iranians learn to behave like Swedes, I will behave like the king of Sweden."

The single-minded pursuit of development – the public good whose provision would justify state authority from this point forward – required further streamlining the organization of resources and people, the imperatives that had also propelled the expansion of state authority under Reza Shah. This led the state to reformulate its relations with agrarian elites, who had to this point remained close to the monarchy; the religious establishment, with which the monarchy had only a tenuous alliance; and the middle classes, which were the main agents and beneficiaries of development, although they were not committed to the monarchy. The consequences of these reformulations would determine the course of Iran's subsequent development.

Economic Growth and Authoritarianism, 1963–1979

Between 1959 and 1963, the Pahlavi state had to weather a number of challenges, the resolution of which both necessitated redoubling its commitment to development and created greater room for pursuing it. The political rumblings occurred at a time when the United States began to waver in its unconditional support of the Pahlavi state and viewed some form of reform in Iran as necessary to limit communist influence in the country. The change in the U.S. attitude was parlayed into momentum for wide-scale reform.

In the meantime, an austerity package prescribed by the International Monetary Fund, which included a cut in government spending and devaluation of the currency to discourage imports, brought on a severe recession during the 1960–1962 period. The perceived threat to the ruling order convinced state leaders that they could not afford prolonged economic crises. Oil revenue, even despite modest increases ($555 million in 1963–1964, comprising 12 percent of the GNP), would not remedy the crisis or satisfy development needs. Hence, reform would have to go hand in hand with, as well as help spur, economic growth. The state began to see its objective of development as integral to sociopolitical reform. This vision culminated in the "White Revolution" of 1963, the term coined to upstage the Left and its promise of "Red" revolution.

The White Revolution was a package of sweeping reforms that aimed to change the structure of societal relations in Iran and to enable more effective resource mobilization in the service of development. The most important initiatives were land reform, the enfranchisement of women, and the provision of greater rights and a greater share of industrial profits to industrial labor.

Through the White Revolution, the state was hoping to institutionalize its hold over the middle classes and among those social groups that might serve as the base of support for an effective communist movement, including the poor, the peasantry, and industrial labor. These reforms, so the argument ran, were necessary for effective development. They would modernize Iranian society, changing it in ways that would help industrialization.

The White Revolution was a risky venture because the principal losers in the reforms – the landed elite and the clergy – had in the past served as sources of support for the monarchy, whereas the support of the modern middle classes for monarchy had at best been tenuous. The Shah was falling into the same trap that his father had, vesting his political fortunes in a social class whose loyalties ultimately would not rest with the monarchy. In addition, given the Pahlavi state's pro-industry bias, it did not cultivate a base of support among the peasantry that it was enfranchising. Industrial labor, meanwhile, did not as yet possess sufficient power to act as a significant source of support for the monarchy; and if they were to become a force, the monarchy was unlikely to claim their allegiance for long. More immediately, however, the state would rely on the rising power of the bureaucracy, which itself was being modernized from within. The bureaucracy was committed to development and to that end joined in a ruling alliance with the monarchy. In effect, the state reformulated its links with society and also defined the shape of its opposition. The landed elite, the clergy, and the "liberal Left," all of whom opposed the White Revolution or viewed it as the means through which the state might devour their base of support, gravitated toward a united antistate stance. The restoration of power to the monarchy thus reconstituted the oppositional alliance that had first surfaced during the earlier Reza Shah period.

The first expression of this opposition was the protest movement led by the cleric **Ayatollah Ruhollah Khomeini** in 1964. The protest was strongly antistate, but its immediate concern was with the White Revolution. Khomeini characterized the enfranchisement of women as "un-Islamic." He also rejected land reform as a violation of Islamic protection of property rights. The protest movement brought together the landed elite, the religious establishment, and the liberal Left. The first two groups opposed specific points of the White Revolution, whereas the liberal Left viewed the entire reform package as a threat to its political position and had a vested interest in its failure. The White Revolution sought to change the social structure, in opposition to which the liberal Left had mobilized support, and to render the Left's political programs obsolete.

The protest movement failed. The state's agenda of social reform and rapid economic development thus unfolded unencumbered. Still, the protest movement had the effect of committing the state to a greater use of force in contending with the opposition. This in turn led to the consolidation of the anti-Pahlavi forces into a more coherent alliance under the unified leadership of the clergy and the liberal Left. Such thinkers as **Ali Shariati** actually began to formulate a socially conscious religio-ideological perspective that could consolidate an anti-Shah alliance. This opposition would in time become increasingly violent and would, in turn, face greater violence from the state. From this point forward, the security apparatuses of the state, most notably the secret police, **SAVAK**, would use repressive measures, including detentions and torture, to subdue the opposition. The opposition produced radical communist and Islamist urban-guerrilla organizations, escalating anti-state activities to the level of armed conflict and acts of terror. The radicalization of the opposition and the state's use of violence in suppressing it polarized Iranian politics and gradually concentrated power in a limited number of state institutions – most notably its security apparatuses – and in the monarchy.

Economically, however, the 1960s was a period of relative success. Land reform, the overhaul of the bureaucracy, and the weakening of the Parliament allowed economic managers to pursue growth aggressively and with greater freedom from outside influence. The result was an industrial transformation, producing growth rates that were unmatched in Iran's history. The gross domestic product (GDP) for this period grew at an average of 9.2 percent per year, and industrial growth rates averaging 15 percent per year were among the highest in the developing world. At the same time, the central characteristics of the economy changed as it acquired medium and heavy industries and a modern private sector.

Economic development in Iran during the 1960s was based largely on **import-substitution industrialization (ISI)**. Although ISI produces rapid growth rates early on and helps kick-start industrialization, it also poses political and economic challenges down the road. As we saw in the chapters on Mexico and India, ISI places emphasis on capital-intensive industries and hence leads to the neglect of small-scale production and the agricultural sector. It can lead to uneven development, overurbanization, and income inequality. It also puts pressure on government finances and the balance of trade, just as it augments state control of the economy. It was partly to address problems born of ISI that Iran decided to support the oil-price hikes of **OPEC** (the Organization of Petroleum Exporting Countries) during the 1970s.

The rise in oil prices ($958 million in 1968–1969, comprising 18 percent of Iran's GNP, in contrast with $20 billion in 1975–1976, representing 35 percent of the GNP) removed financial pressures from the state and allowed it to spend more freely on various industrial and social projects. It is interesting to note, however, that higher oil prices augmented the challenges before the Shah. They adversely affected the pattern of economic development as the state deepened ISI, but did so with decreasing efficiency. Although the Iranian economy performed well during the 1970s, it veered off the path toward viable industrialization and market development and eventually faced serious crises.

The oil boom created bottlenecks in the economy and led to wasteful spending on grandiose projects. Iran spent billions of dollars on infrastructure and industrial projects. It also spent huge sums on war material and public enterprises of questionable economic value. All of this eroded trust in the management of the economy. The rapid pace of growth also created social dislocation, cultural confusion, and new political demands with which the state was unequipped to contend. In addition, the newfound wealth encouraged corruption and speculative financial activities. This adversely affected public morale and skewed popular perception about the meaning and intent of entrepreneurial activity. The oil wealth also raised expectations – so much so that the state not only was unable to gain political support for acquiring the new wealth but also found itself falling short of fulfilling growing expectations.

The Iranian state began to face political problems associated with "**rentier states**," that is, states in which income that is external to the productive capacity of the economy accounts for the lion's share of state revenue. Rentier states are generally politically weak because the state derives little if any of its income from the population and, as a result, does not devise ways to increase revenues through taxation. Nor does it negotiate with the population in order to increase society's contribution to state revenue. Instead, rentier states invest in distributive mechanisms and, having developed a relationship of distribution and patronage with their populations, do not develop meaningful links with society. The population does not credit the government for the generation of wealth, although it expects more from the government in terms of distribution of wealth. Popular support remains contingent on a continued flow of "rent."

As oil income came to dominate the Iranian economy, the Pahlavi state began to face a serious political crisis. On the one hand, its developmental agenda had concentrated power in the state and the monarchy and isolated both from other social groups. On the other hand, the state justified its course of action in terms of provision of a public good: development. Between 1946 and 1979, the state had changed the character of the economy in a fundamental fashion from agriculture to industry. Public planning, urbanization, industrialization, diversification, and infrastructural and human capital investments had produced sustained change and growth. The increase in oil wealth, however, denied the state the ability to claim credit for its economic achievements. It undermined the state's developmentalist claims as it depicted development as synonymous with oil revenue, rendering redundant the political apparatuses that the Pahlavi monarchs had argued were necessary for realizing development. All of this pushed an already narrowly based state to the brink of collapse. The resultant political tensions erupted in

1977, culminating in the Islamic Revolution of 1979 that toppled the Pahlavi state.

The global context proved important at this juncture as well. The revolution unfolded at a time of change in Iran's relations with the United States. Jimmy Carter, the U.S. president, was unwilling to provide unconditional support to the Shah's regime and instead strongly advocated political reform in Iran. The new U.S. approach created confusion in the Iranian state and emboldened the opposition.

The opposition to the Pahlavi state consisted of liberal and pro-democracy forces, the Left, and religious activists, but it increasingly adopted a strongly Islamic character, especially after Ayatollah Khomeini – then in exile in Iraq – assumed its leadership. Khomeini used his position of authority to put forward a particularly revolutionary and antistate reading of Islam and used its symbols to mobilize the masses. Khomeini also built on the traditional role of Shia clerics, arguing that given their knowledge of religion, they must rule politically if the society was to be Islamic, just, and prosperous. His religio-political crusade was therefore directed at constructing a theocratic form of government.

Khomeini's arguments – which were published as *Islamic Government* were part of a broader movement of revolt against secularism, and the state institutions that represented and promoted it, that was defining politics in the Muslim world at the time. Across the Muslim world, thinkers such as Khomeini were rejecting the modern state as a failure. They argued that it had failed to bring about genuine development or resolve regional crises such as the Arab–Israeli conflict, and most importantly it had failed to reverse the palpable decline of Muslim worldly power before that of the West. These thinkers captured the frustration of those whom development had left behind and those who lamented the weakness of Muslim states on the world stage when they argued that, rather than empower Muslims, the modern state had merely trampled on their culture by promoting secularism and marginalizing Islam in public life. These thinkers argued that the problem in the Muslim world was secularism and its protector and promoter, the modern state. Far from being the solution to sociopolitical problems and agents of positive change, the modern state had cut Muslims off from the roots of their power – their religion. Therefore, it would be by dismantling the secular state and erecting in its place an Islamic state that Muslims would find the path to development. For these thinkers and activists, Islam provided the blueprint for a perfect government that would be built on Islamic law and the model of the Prophet of Islam's rule during the religion's early years in the seventh century. Their vision of the Islamic state was revolutionary and utopian, rejecting the existing social and political systems and promising a perfect order in their place. Their challenge to the state was not only socioeconomic – as was the case with the Left – but also cultural. The Shah's regime – with its pro-Western secularism – and Khomeini's challenge to it in many regards epitomized the politics of Islamic activism and served as the opening battle between Islamic activism and the secular state that has defined Muslim politics since 1979.

The success of Islamic activism in Iran was not entirely a matter of ideology. In promoting his cause, Khomeini strengthened the alliance between the religious establishment and the Left that had been in place since 1964. Khomeini successfully managed to keep the opposition focused on overthrowing the Shah, while postponing the resolution of ideological disagreements and cultural tensions between the religious and secular opposition to the Shah to the postrevolutionary period. His presence on the political scene, however, made religious identity central to politics. In so doing, Khomeini and the revolutionary forces rejected the developmentalist secularism of the Pahlavi state. The revolution owed its success, in large part, to the fact that this stance did not create tensions in the ranks of revolutionary forces, segments of which were politically at odds with the Pahlavi state but shared in its secularism and were themselves products of the Pahlavi state's social engineering. As a result, the revolutionary movement in Iran in 1979 was politically uniform but culturally and socially eclectic in that it had both Islamist and secular-liberal and leftist elements in it.

The revolution itself unfolded rather rapidly over the course of a mere 18 months. It fed on a set of cascading events that converged to overwhelm the Shah's regime, which failed to react adroitly to the challenge before it. These events were: wide-scale street demonstrations, the mobilization of religious institutions and activists, labor strikes, the disappearance of the democratic middle, and the collapse of the military. The first three events had the effect of including larger numbers of people in the revolution, producing a degree of popular mobilization that overwhelmed state institutions. The latter two events ensured that the state would not respond effectively to the mobilization, guaranteeing the success of the revolution.

Throughout 1977 and 1978, a growing number of Iranians joined street demonstrations to ask first for political reform and later for regime change. The Shah's government proved unable to contend with the demonstrations either through a show of force in the streets or by giving in to demands for reform. The growing religious tenor of the demonstrations that was facilitated by the growing political importance of a network of mosques, seminaries, and religious organizations soon provided a backbone to the demonstrators and helped tie their demands to the larger ideological arguments that were put forth by Khomeini. The popular mobilization reached a critical stage when it led to labor strikes, which included not only government workers but also employees of critical industrial sectors such as oil and electricity, whose walkouts were of more than symbolic importance and impacted the economy directly.

There were then two forces capable of dealing with the mobilization: the first were the pro-democracy politicians who were associated with the National Front Party of the 1950s; and the second was the military. The first could contain and manage the mobilized social force, and the second could have suppressed them. The democratic middle failed to play its historic role, partly because it would not reach an agreement with the Shah on how to deal with the mobilization and partly because it decided not to challenge Khomeini or the Left. The military was not deployed in an effective way during the early months of the agitations when it could have changed the outcome. It was not until the Shah had left Iran in February 1979 that the military decided to flex its muscles, only to find that its window of opportunity had already been closed.

In the end, the Shah's failure to divide the opposition along ideological and cultural lines precluded the possibility of negotiations between the monarchy and the liberal Left over a transfer of power. The result was that the political situation continued to radicalize in favor of the religious element in the revolutionary coalition. This did not bode well for democratic development in Iran in 1979. In the end, the Pahlavi state collapsed because of the Shah's inability to contend with political challenges at a critical juncture. The Pahlavi state had in effect become reduced to the Shah, and his inaction meant that despite the broad coercive power available to the state, it would not survive.

With the fall of the Shah in 1979, the evolution of state authority and function took a new turn. However, despite significant changes in the way in which the state and the economy work in the Islamic Republic, the balance of power between state and society, and the role of the state in socioeconomic change, cannot be understood separately from what occurred during the Pahlavi period. Despite the regime change, ideological shift, and radical social transformation, the path down which the Pahlavi period set Iran continued to shape its subsequent development.

The Revolutionary Era, 1979–1988

The collapse of the monarchy in February 1979 ushered in a new era in Iranian politics. The ideological force of the revolution suggested that the working of the state, the role of interests, and the centrality of identity in development were all likely to change. The revolution promised an axial shift in Iranian politics that would occur in a changing global context.

The immediate aftermath of the revolution was a period of great fluidity during which the old order was dismantled and revolutionary forces began to leave their imprint on the state and society. Revolutions destroy certain social classes, alter state bureaucracies, and thus make other paths of development possible. In Iran, however, the revolution did not produce a strong state but took over an existing one and adapted it to its ideology. The central role of the state in development thus remained unaffected. As a result, the postrevolutionary state displayed continuity with the past as well as change from it.

Revolutionary forces purged supporters of the old order from various state institutions, public and private organizations, and economic enterprises, and the revolution quickly produced institutions of its own. Revolutionary courts and committees and the **Revolutionary Guards** were organized to serve the functions of the judiciary, the police, and the military. Just as the rise of the Pahlavi state had been closely associated with the creation of the Iranian military, the rise of the new revolutionary state was closely tied to the emergence of these new institutions. Although initially formless and disorganized, the new institutions wielded a great deal of power. In time, their presence would create confusion in the state, as the purview of activities of the old military, police, and judiciary would overlap with those of the newly formed revolutionary committees, guards, and courts.

The liquidation of the old order, however, was only a prelude to larger struggles over defining the new order. With the success of the revolution, Ayatollah Khomeini became the undisputed leader of Iran. His supremacy only thinly disguised the intense conflict that was being waged over the definition of the new order. With the triumph of the revolution, the political concord of the disparate groups in opposition to the Shah began to unravel. The liberals, the Left, and the clergy now competed to determine Iran's future.

In March 1979, Iranians voted in a referendum to replace the monarchy with an "Islamic Republic." The term was coined by Khomeini, but it symbolized the struggle among the various factions of the revolutionary alliance over the identity of the regime that was to rule Iran. Throughout 1979, the struggle became more pronounced in the debates over the new constitution. The resulting document envisioned the Islamic Republic as a modern state with all of the constitutional and organizational features of such a state. It provided for a parliament, a judiciary, and an executive branch. It delineated the powers of each through a system of checks and balances. But the constitution also made Islamic law supreme. It furthermore recognized Khomeini's position as that of the supreme leader of the revolution (office of **Vali-e Faqih**, or "supreme guardian-jurisconsult"), an office whose occupant would not be elected, would not be accountable to any authority, and would have total veto power over all government decisions and policy making. This arrangement subjugated the political to the religious in state affairs. It also made identity central to the question of state authority, above and beyond economic and social interests.

The outcome of the constitutional process suggested that the religious element, led by Khomeini, had gained the upper hand. His domination became more apparent as the revolutionary regime demanded greater popular observation of Islamic strictures, especially those concerning women's dress. Religious elites also mobilized support among the lower middle classes and the poor – groups with close ties to the religious establishment – to marginalize the modern middle classes, who served as the social base of the liberal Left. With the victory of the religious hard-liners in this conflict, the number of clerics in high political offices grew dramatically.

The final consolidation of power in the hands of the religious element came in 1981–1982. Although Islamic activists had already gained the upper hand, it was the global context in the form of the **hostage crisis** in 1979–1980 (when a group of militant "students" took over the U.S. embassy in Tehran and held its American personnel hostage for months on end) and the **Iran-Iraq War** (1980–1988) that facilitated their complete domination. These events diverted popular attention in Iran, and international attention abroad, from domestic power struggles. In addition, both events created a siege mentality that bolstered the popularity of the religious leadership, who could claim to be defending Iran from American and Iraqi aggression. In this climate, the liberal Left was portrayed as U.S. stooges, and resistance to a greater role for Islam in society was depicted as a Western ploy to destabilize the revolution.

With the purge of the liberal Left, the revolution became a distinctly Islamic affair. Revolutionary zeal and concern with identity would henceforth define the nature and function of the state. As in the formation of the Pahlavi state under Reza Shah, the Islamic Republic likewise justified its power in terms of the provision of a public good, except that the public good presented by the Islamic Republic was to be greater Islamization of society and politics rather than economic development. The Islamic Republic was not interested in rolling back the state's control over society or its ability to penetrate and control it. It, too, believed in a domineering state. In fact, the leadership of the Islamic Republic aimed at expanding rather than contracting the state's control of society.

As in the early Pahlavi state, the Islamic Republic engaged in social engineering as a prerequisite for the realization of its public-policy agenda. It, too, became directly concerned with the dress, music, and cultural outlook of Iranians. It instituted tight control of both the public and private arenas, and viewed social engineering as central to successful policy formulation and implementation. The state's understanding of its function and powers, in some respects, reflected significant continuities with the Pahlavi period.

The centrality of Islamic ideology to state policy made identity and revolutionary fervor central to the flow of politics and the relations between the state and society. That fervor, in turn, continued to unfold in the context of the Iran-Iraq War during the 1980s. The war, caused by border disputes and Iraqi leader Saddam Hussein's expansionism, was one of the most costly and devastating of the latter part of the twentieth century. During the course of the eight-year war, some one million Iranians lost their lives. Iran temporarily lost control of parts of its oil-rich province of Khuzestan and incurred significant damage to its urban centers, agriculture, and industrial infrastructure. It was able to turn the tide of the war only at a tremendous human cost. The need to mobilize support and resources for the war pushed the state to emphasize ideology and the revolutionary values that are associated with it. The successful use of ideology in mobilization for war helped entrench revolutionary zeal and identity in lieu of socioeconomic interests in Iranian politics. Consequently, throughout the 1980–1988 period, the workings of the state remained closely tied to the pursuit of Islamization. This, in turn, committed Iran to a confrontational foreign policy and shifted power to the more radical elements in the state leadership. Khomeini supported this trend because it bolstered his power in Iran and served his ambitions to influence regional and international politics.

Ideological zeal also shaped politics and economics in the Islamic Republic. The Islamic Republic has been different from the Pahlavi state in that despite greater state domination of society, it has avoided personalized rule. Even when Khomeini was at the helm, power was spread among the clerical leaders, who were unified through a patronage network that connected the religious leadership at the center to clerical power brokers. The clerical establishment was committed to the Islamic Republic and to Khomeini's leadership. In fact, Khomeini quickly inculcated group interest in a politically active clergy, thus tying their political ambitions and social position to the fortunes of the Islamic Republic. The clerical leadership ruled collectively – acting as a dominant class – distinguished from the general population by dress and education. The uniform commitment to the Islamic Republic and Khomeini's ideology, however, did not eliminate struggles for power, differences over policy, and disagreements over ideological interpretation among the religious activists and the clerical leadership.

The clerical leadership did not produce a satisfactory way of managing these political debates and conflicts. Before the revolution, there had existed no dominant revolutionary party, as had been the case in Russia or China before their communist revolutions. Iran's revolutionary movement was not ideologically and culturally uniform, further limiting the development of a dominant revolutionary organization either before or immediately after the revolution. This revolution, then, turned out to be the first modern revolution to lack a "**vanguard" party**.

In the absence of a formal organization to manage struggles of power and debates over policy among state leaders, factional politics came out into the open. In the 1980s, three notable factions emerged within the Islamic Republic. The first favored a relaxation of revolutionary vigilance and stabilization of economic relations. Its members came to be known as the "moderates." Those identified with the second faction favored a continuation of revolutionary fervor but at the same time wished to promote a mercantile economy and the right to private property. They came to be known as the "conservatives." The third faction favored a strong anti-Western policy and the export of the revolution, as well as state control of the economy and limited rights to private property. It came to be known as the "radical" or "hard-line" faction and was responsible for much of the excesses of the Islamic Republic in foreign policy and for the expropriation of private property during the first decade of the Islamic Republic. The Iran-Iraq War and Iran's confrontational foreign policy helped the radical faction, whose members were closely allied with the Revolutionary Guards and oversaw Iran's support for revolutionary activism in the Muslim world. The revolutionary fervor espoused by this faction served the aims of mobilizational politics. Although the hard-liners had only a small base of support, mainly in the Revolutionary Guards and in the lower-middle and lower classes, they wielded much power in the government and were supported by Ayatollah Khomeini throughout the 1980–1988 period. The hard-line faction owed its power to its role in mobilizing support for the war and for the Islamic Republic's foreign policy. That power, derived from the global context in which Iran found itself, worked to increase state domination of the economy and promoted centralized economic planning.

The three factions existed only informally. There has been no actual organization, charter, rules, or platforms to define membership; nor are there any grassroots movements or party structures. The factions have functioned as informal circles within the revolutionary elite, with ill-defined and often changing boundaries. The factions have, however, become protoparty structures, especially because they have shaped electoral results directly.

Struggles for power among these factions occurred for the most part in the Parliament, in various consultative forums, in government agencies, in **Friday Prayer** sermons, and in the media. Whereas debates over foreign policy were restrained, in economic matters the differences were pronounced and the debates were acrimonious. Most notably, the radical faction clashed with the two other factions over the right to property and the legal protection of mercantile activities, both of which were eventually accepted by the revolutionary government.

Factionalism dominated politics in Iran throughout the 1980s. It greatly influenced the distribution of power between the president and prime minister on one side and the Parliament on the other. It also influenced the state's relations with society. More importantly, it influenced the working of the economy and determined the extent to which interest or identity would shape the state and its policies.

The revolution changed the course of economic development in Iran significantly. The political turmoil of the revolution (1977–1979), subsequent domestic political crises, legal uncertainties following the collapse of law and order, the meting out of revolutionary justice, debates over property rights, the "brain drain" (the exodus of educated people), the war with Iraq, and international isolation after the hostage crisis all acted to retard the rate of growth. The revolution also radically altered the perceptions of socioeconomic interest and the nature of development. The leftist elements in the revolution viewed economic development under the Pahlavi state as misguided, capitalistic, and, hence, doomed to failure. The religious element was uninterested in development as such and favored replacing it as a national goal with Islamization. Khomeini set the tone in this regard when he commented that "economics is for donkeys" – that is, only Islamization matters. The pursuit of interest, he maintained, should be made subservient to identity.

After 1979, therefore, economic development occupied a less prominent place in the priorities of state leaders. To the extent that there was an economic policy in the early years, it was heavily influenced by Marxist models that had been tried in a number of developing countries. Hence, soon after the revolution, the government nationalized the financial institutions, major industries, and business ventures of those who had been close to the Pahlavi state. By 1998–1999, the state owned 80 percent of the Iranian economy, relegating the private sector to small-scale economic activities.

The expansion of the state's control of the economy in time served political ends because the state could distribute jobs to its most ardent supporters. The growth of the public sector also produced new avenues for corruption in the bureaucracy and the political leadership. The net result of this was significantly reduced efficiency. Between 1978 and 1988, the GDP fell by 1.5 percent per year. Put differently, in 1988, the GDP stood at 1974 levels. Industry experienced six years of negative growth. Rapid population growth produced high levels of unemployment, which in 1988 exceeded 30 percent. The weak private sector was unable to create enough jobs to absorb the surplus labor. The government throughout the 1980s addressed the problem by providing employment in the public sector, which by 1988 accounted for one-third of all jobs. In the meantime, oil income fell. The share of oil revenue as a percentage of GDP fell from 30–40 percent in the 1970s to 9–17 percent in the 1980s as production levels fell from 5.6 million barrels per day to between 2.2 and 2.9 million. The government increased the rate and scope of taxation, but the economy depended on oil revenues, which continued to account for 85 percent of hard-currency earnings.

By 1988, the economic impact of the war with Iraq, international isolation and economic sanctions, and a growing population and declining production presented the Iranian economy with a serious crisis. Shortages in consumer goods had produced a thriving black market that skewed economic interests and the distribution of resources, further reducing efficiency. In addition, the growth of the public sector did not eradicate poverty. By weakening the private sector, it did reduce income inequality. But standards of living, especially of the urban poor, did not improve substantially. Inflation and unemployment had effectively undermined the radicals' populism.

Although during the 1980–1988 period economic hardships could be blamed on the Iran-Iraq War, the conclusion of the war denied the state that excuse. The scope of the economic crisis facing the state now posed serious political challenges. Interests could no longer be easily made subordinate to ideological concerns and the rhetoric of identity politics. Change thus became imperative.

The Post-Khomeini Era, 1988–Present

In 1988, the Iran-Iraq War ended with Iraq's unequivocal victory. The following year, Ayatollah Khomeini died. These two events had a profound effect on politics in the Islamic Republic. The defeat in the war was a psychological blow to the revolutionary elite. It diminished their legitimacy and reduced the utility of their ideological politics. The population became less tolerant of sacrifices demanded of them, especially because eight years of such sacrifices had ended in an ignoble military defeat. Khomeini's passing from the scene made it more difficult for the ruling order to resist change. As the state began to yield to pressure for change, its policy making became more pragmatic, reflecting a greater concern for interests over identity.

After Khomeini died, the president, **Ayatollah Ali Khamenei** (a member of the conservative faction), became supreme leader, and the speaker of the Parliament, **Ayatollah Ali Akbar Hashemi-Rafsanjani** (a member of the moderate faction), became president (1988–1997). The ascendance of the two suggested an alliance between the conservative and moderate factions to marginalize the radical faction. The immediate consequence of Khamenei's and Rafsanjani's assumption of power was the streamlining of the workings of the offices of supreme leader and president. These changes were followed by constitutional reforms that, among other things, integrated revolutionary committees and courts and the Revolutionary Guards with the police, judiciary, and the military, respectively. The Rafsanjani administration also vested greater powers in the bureaucracy and reduced the influence of ideological politics in its day-to-day work. These efforts once again made economic development a central concern of the state and a justification for its power. The post-Khomeini era thus saw the revival of the Pahlavi conception of the state. These changes did not, however, altogether resolve problems of governance in the Islamic Republic. Most importantly, the position of the supreme leader limited the power of the president and continued to tie the political system to ideological politics.

The Iranian legislature wields extensive power and limits the scope of the presidency. This is because of the complexities of the political relations of the ruling elite. From the outset, the Islamic Republic did not have the institutional means to distribute power among its various elements and factions. The function that should have been performed by internal party elections was thus performed by general elections. As such, the Islamic Republic itself functions as a party with regular and free elections among "Islamic" candidates. The ruling order has viewed the voters as party members, mobilized through mosque networks and ideological propagation, and the Parliament as a "**Central Committee**" of sorts. Still, the regularity of general elections has helped institutionalize the place of the Parliament, the Islamic Consultative Assembly, in the Islamic Republic. Hence, the requirement of deciding over the distribution of power within the ruling regime, and the absence of institutional mechanisms to do so outside of the public arena, by default introduced electoral politics and parliamentary behavior to Iran.

General elections and parliamentary practices, despite all their limitations, have brought about a certain degree of pluralism in the essentially theocratic structure of the Islamic Republic. This means that although Iran is an authoritarian state, far more of its political offices are distributed on the basis of elections – albeit limited elections – and its Parliament wields far more effective power than comparable bodies in the Arab world. In fact, one observes two contradictory tendencies working themselves out in the Islamic Republic: on the one hand, the concentration of supreme power in an ideological state; and on the other, democratic practices that are being given significant, if limited, scope for expression within a power structure governed at its apex by a clerical leadership.

It is important to note that elections in the Islamic Republic have not been entirely open in that there are strict limits on which candidates are allowed to participate. However, once the list of candidates has been set, the elections have been generally free. This has to do with the combination of the institutional restriction and procedural freedom that characterizes the structure of the Islamic Republic. The state possesses an authoritarian control over society, but the state itself is complex and made up of powerful factions that continuously vie with one another for control. Although the state has been successful in eliminating from the electoral process all those who challenge its fundamental ideological vision, it has not been able to eliminate those who, while sharing this vision, nonetheless challenge various aspects of policy making. Elections are therefore real insofar as they determine the relative influence of the various power centers at the top. They are less than real, however, in that they do not allow for any genuine change in the distribution of power within society nor alter the composition of the leadership of the state.

The importance of the elections and the Parliament increased in the post-Khomeini era because Khomeini's passing from the scene intensified factional rivalries. Khomeini's death also increased interest in electoral politics, which reached its climax in the presidential elections of 1997. The intensification of the factional rivalries has in effect nudged the Islamic Republic in the direction of electoral politics and vested greater powers in its representative institutions.

Also important in this regard has been the growing role of economic considerations and, more generally, interests in policy making. Rafsanjani assumed his presidency at a time of economic crisis in Iran. He proposed to reform the Iranian economy and also change the policy-making environment to better reflect economic interests and pragmatic considerations. His government proposed an extensive privatization program, investment in infrastructure, introduction of free-trade zones, relaxation of currency restrictions, and the attraction of expatriate entrepreneurial talent. The proposals were designed to generate growth through effective state management of the economy, an interesting return to the Pahlavi state's developmentalist approach.

The reform initiative enjoyed some success. Investment in infrastructure increased, management became more efficient, and as a result the economy began to grow again. In this regard, the institutional and industrial developments of the Pahlavi period were extremely useful to the economic policies of the Islamic Republic. Nevertheless, more fundamental reforms proved difficult. The government faced stiff resistance to privatization from the bureaucrats and the myriad quasi-private foundations that manage state-owned enterprises, as well as from labor – and the power brokers who had used public-sector jobs for patronage – who feared the loss of jobs. As a result, privatization meant the transference of the ownership of public-sector industries to state-controlled foundations and cronies of the regime. In this way, the state retained control of the industries, even though technically it had privatized them.

The bureaucracy's attempt to assert its autonomy in economic policy making also faced resistance, as it would have reduced kickbacks and patronage, along with profits made by merchants and black marketers. This resistance translated into support for the conservative faction in subsequent elections and pressure to prevent Rafsanjani from running for a third term in 1997.

In the end, Rafsanjani's economic initiative suffered as a consequence of the tightening of Western sanctions against Iran. New efforts to isolate Iran internationally and stop its support of terrorism during the 1990s led to a collapse of the Iranian currency and a decline in the rate of economic growth. The consequence of change in the global context was a heightened debate over Iran's future. Should economic interests continue to be sacrificed in the pursuit of ideological goals, or should Iran subordinate its commitment to identity politics in favor of economic growth? Although there is strong support for continuing Iran's commitment to Islam and the values of the revolution, the scope of economic crises facing the state has prevented complacency in the economic policy-making arena. By 1998, 65 percent of Iran's population was under 21 years of age, the unemployment rate stood at 40 percent, inflation was at 300 percent, and the GDP growth rate lagged behind the population growth rate. Without ending Iran's international isolation as well as undertaking domestic economic reform, Iran could face a political crisis, which could threaten the ruling order and its revolutionary values more seriously than would pragmatism.

By the mid-1990s, revolutionary values and ideological politics came under attack from an unexpected quarter – a resurgence of the secular values of the Pahlavi period. The Islamic Republic has enforced a strict cultural code in Iran. The "Islamization" of society has extended beyond the public sphere and has sought to transform the private lives of Iranians as well. Women's dress, music, public programs, school texts, publications, and all manners of cultural, social, and educational activities have been subject to state control. This state policy has generated unhappiness and opposition.

The Pahlavi state, too, had sought to transform its citizens, secularizing as well as modernizing them as a prelude to development. Its collapse in 1979, however, has diverted scholarly attention from the extent to which it was successful in transforming Iranian society. In 1979, there existed a peculiar circumstance wherein the Pahlavi state was weak politically but quite strong culturally. The fact that its secular subjects did not have the same political outlook as the rulers weakened the state. The new Islamic Republic, on the other hand, enjoyed far more political appeal among the middle classes than it did cultural support. The Islamic movement in Iran triumphed politically in large measure because it was able to divide secular Iranians along political lines. The Pahlavi state's political failure, however, should not be read as evidence of its cultural irrelevance because the underlying cultural impact of Pahlavi policies continues to be a major force in Iranian society. Its continued salience is attested to by the inability of the Islamic Republic to establish uncontested cultural hegemony in Iran two decades after the revolution and also by the fact that prerevolutionary cultural attitudes have increasingly served as the starting point of important dissenting tendencies in the political arena. Those social groups that continue to live by the norms of the past may be out of power but they remain nonetheless potential contenders for power.

The Islamic Republic was never able to win over the secular social stratum or eliminate it. It could merely suppress it. Islamic clerics imposed new laws and regulations on the population, largely by force. For instance, new attire for women was imposed after several large demonstrations, one of which drew more than a million woman protesters into the streets in 1979. Since then, the strict women's dress code has been enforced brutally by the Revolutionary Guards.

The "**Cultural Revolution**" in 1980 "cleansed" educational institutions of all those who did not subscribe to Islamic ideology. As far as the liberal Left element within the revolutionary movement itself was concerned, the

Islamic Republic eventually resolved that inherent anomaly in the alliance that brought it to power. After an open struggle for power in 1979–1981, the Islamist element in the revolutionary alliance purged the secular liberal Left element.

Secular Iranians, among them prominent professionals and intellectuals, were forcibly marginalized, but they remained important as they shifted their activities to the private arena and the important sphere of civil society. In fact, this social stratum has acted in a fashion similar to those groups who spearheaded the uprising in the name of civil society against Eastern European communist states. The refusal to abide by state ideology at the popular and even personal levels has challenged the domination of Islamic ideology and is forcing changes on the ruling regime. The cultural influence of the Pahlavi era has continued and remains dominant at the personal level among the middle classes. Since the early 1990s, economic crises and problems of isolation have constricted the ruling regime and weakened its hold over society. Creeping pragmatism in policy making has, moreover, made the secular middle classes and the values they espouse the vanguard force for a decisive movement of political resistance. That economic growth both needs and will empower this social stratum has made it difficult for the Islamic Republic to resist its influence.

The Presidential Elections of 1997

All of these factors coalesced to determine the outcome of the presidential elections of 1997. These elections were the first to involve a transfer of power at the level of the presidency during the post-Khomeini era. Given the debates over the relative importance of identity and interests in state policy, the elections were viewed as decisive. Early on in the election campaign, the nominee of the conservative faction emerged as the front-runner. The faction had a strong base of support among small businessmen and in the political apparatus of the Islamic Republic, and it also had the backing of Ayatollah Khamenei. In addition, the conservatives posed as a force for continuity, and to some extent retrenchment, of the values and norms of the Islamic Republic. They held to a conservative line on social and cultural issues and supported the thrust of Iran's anti-Western foreign policy. In this way, they differed from President Rafsanjani, who had favored easing the strictures that govern social and cultural practices, and who had tried – albeit with little success – to reduce tensions between Iran and the Western powers.

What appeared to be the conservatives' unchallenged march to the presidency, however, soon became a closely contested race with **Ayatollah Mohammad Khatami**. Khatami did not represent any of the rival factions but appealed to the moderate faction and its followers. In addition, his promise of relaxing the state's ideological vigilance also gained him a following among women, youth, and the secular elements. In many regards, Khatami's platform and following greatly resemble those of Gorbachev in the Soviet Union. Khatami, too, believes in the promise of the revolutionary ideology and hopes that once that ideology is freed from the authoritarian control of the state through reform measures, it will fulfill its promise of progress and prosperity. Many who followed Khatami (again, similar to Gorbachev in Russia) did not share his belief in the promise of revolutionary ideology but liked the implications of his reform proposals.

The intensity of the factional rivalry guaranteed the openness of the elections and paved the way for greater freedom of expression in the media. The election itself, held in May 1997, proved to be nothing short of an earthquake in Iranian politics. Most observers had expected Khatami to do well but thought that in the end the conservatives would win. This did not come to pass. Khatami won the elections with an overwhelming majority of the vote – 70 percent (some 20 million votes). The defeat of the conservative faction was total and humiliating. Iranians had taken the elections seriously and had voted convincingly in favor of fundamental changes in the nature, structure, and workings of the Islamic Republic. Many saw the elections as a referendum on the Islamic Republic and, at the very least, as a referendum on how its existing leadership ought to understand its mission and relations with society. The vote was also one for interests over identity in the workings of the state.

The election results had important implications. First, this was a unique case in the Middle East: A head of state stepped down from power at the end of his term of office and peacefully handed over power to a successor elected through constitutional means. The transition of power from Rafsanjani to Khatami has therefore been of tremendous significance in itself. Second, the large turnout – some 30 million, an overwhelming majority of the eligible voters – meant that Iranians of all political persuasions had taken the elections seriously and decided to voice their views and demands within the political process rather than outside of it. This means that the electoral process has become institutionalized in the Islamic Republic and has become the most important means of integrating various social groups into the political system. It is no longer an artificial appendage to the Islamic state but is very much part of the fabric of its politics.

Khatami's campaign speeches were peppered with references to "democracy," "civil society," "women's status," "rule of law," and "dialogue between civilizations." He in particular emphasized "civil society" and championed the cultural freedoms and legal protections that empower it. As such, Khatami gave new direction and energy to the demand for reform. The decision by so many to use the ballot box to promote change has also strengthened the Islamic Republic, as those who have been unhappy with its achievements have chosen to participate in it rather than opt out of it. The elections and the transition of power have the potential to include greater numbers of Iranians within the Islamic Republic. However, to do so successfully, the Islamic Republic must accommodate a broader set of sociopolitical demands, and most notably move farther away from ideological politics and the values of the revolution. This generated democratic expectations on which Khatami now had to deliver.

The elections of 1997 had caught the leadership of the Islamic Republic off guard. This led to a short-lived "Prague Spring" in Iran during which significant freedom of expression in the press and certain relaxations in control of social behavior gave new impetus to demands for change. These demands began to take an increasingly secular orientation as the new cultural opening mobilized the Iranian middle class, which now became a new force in Iranian politics. This new political constituency was no longer merely satisfied with debating Islam and began to demand fundamental political reforms.

Khatami's campaign promised to address those demands and by so doing create a bridge between reformers inside the regime – who were attached to its ideological foundations – and the larger constituency for reform. His ideal of "Islamic civil society" captured this objective. His success in this endeavor would have transformed the Islamic Republic but would have kept it in control of the process of change. However, his failure has instead created a rift between reformers within the Islamic Republic's ideological fold and political reformers in the larger society, and clearly pitted the latter against the Islamic Republic.

Within a year after Khatami assumed office, the supreme leader, Ayatollah Ali Khamenei, began to use the judiciary and the Council of Guardians (a watchdog institution that is dedicated to protecting the ideological foundations of the Islamic Republic), and his allies in the media, the Parliament, and various government agencies, to stifle reform. Khatami repeatedly lost ground to these conservative forces in showdowns over legislation, freedom of the press, the rule of law, and individual rights. His more reform-minded ministers were pushed out of government, and some were tried and incarcerated. From the time that Khatami assumed office in 1997 until January 2004, the Council of Guardians vetoed 111 of his 297 legislations. Faced with strong resistance to change, Khatami and his lieutenants and supporters began to speak about instituting limits to theocracy and advocated the rule of law and the protection of individual rights.

These developments shifted the focus from calls for rational government to demands for democratization. However, Khatami shied away from openly breaking with the theocratic core of the Islamic Republic. He would not endorse fundamental constitutional changes and proved unwilling to openly challenge Khamanei's authority. On a number of occasions, he threatened the supreme leader with resigning, and on one occasion with not running for reelection in 2001; but each time he backed away from an open breach with Khamanei and his conservative allies.

More importantly, Khatami continued to declare fealty to the theocratic constitution of the Islamic Republic, which runs counter to his support for "civil society" and the "rule of law." As such, at the end of the day, Khatami's rhetoric went no further than advocating better management of government. Khatami's capitulations to Khamanei have attested to his reluctance to step beyond the bounds of the constitution of the Islamic Republic. This in turn has severely limited his ability to continue to lead the popular demand for democracy that his own electoral success had unleashed.

Khatami's dilemma has, however, had a cathartic effect on the democracy debate. By failing to reconcile the demands for change with the reality of the Islamic Republic, Khatami relinquished control of the democracy debate to voices outside the regime. The debate moved to the streets, where, for instance, student demonstrations became a leading voice in demanding fundamental changes to the structure of the Islamic Republic. Student demonstrations during the summer of 1999 to protest the closure of some reformist newspapers, in November 2002 to protest against a death sentence for alleged blasphemy imposed on a university lecturer, and in 2003 to demand greater political rights have not only posed direct challenges to theocracy but also confirmed the shift in focus of the struggle for reform from the high circles of power to the society and to those who want constitutional change and secular democracy. Popular demands for change have further mobilized secular intellectuals and activists associated with civil-society institutions and universities as well as journalists, who initially rallied in support of Islamic reform.

The ideal of the reformists is not Islamic democracy but secular democracy. This involves placing limits on the exercise of state power and creating legal institutions and a system of checks and balances that guarantee individual and social rights. This trend found greater impetus when the 2003 Nobel Peace Prize was awarded to a leading advocate of individual rights, Shirin Ebadi. However, the democracy movement in Iran today lacks clear leadership. The Khatami presidency has failed to provide that leadership, and secular political activists and the students have yet to fill the void.

In the meantime, the ruling establishment has a different path of development in mind. The supreme leader and the conservative leadership look to the Chinese model of reform: economic change and opening to the world with little or no political reforms. They believe that the Soviet transition to democracy under Gorbachev was not a success; rather, it is the Chinese path to change that holds true promise. The conservative leadership is now looking to roll back gains made by pro-democracy forces under Khatami – following a "Putin" strategy, referring to the creeping authoritarianism in Russia under Vladimir Putin. With that aim in mind, the conservative Council of

Guardians prevented many pro-reform candidates from participating in the parliamentary elections of 2004, producing a conservative Parliament ahead of the presidential elections of 2005, in which a conservative victory can give the conservatives complete domination over the political power structure as well as the scope and extent of political reforms.

The Presidential Election of 2005

In June 2005 Iranians went to the polls to choose **Mahmoud Ahmadinejad** as the country's sixth president and the first since 1981 not to hail from the ranks of the clergy. The election marked the second transfer of presidency in the post-Khomeini period. It proved to be the most intensely contested since the 1979 revolution, and the first to go to a second round of voting. Close to 30 million (62 percent of the electorate of 47 million) voted in the first round on June 17, and over 27 million (60 percent of the electorate) voted in the second round on June 24.

The election produced dramatic results. It brought to power a hard-line conservative populist whose election confirmed the conservative consolidation of power, and stood in marked contrast to the popular choice in 1997. The election also marked a shift away from the middle class and its youth culture, which had become increasingly important since 1997, to the lower class and its grievances. The presidential campaign was one of the most dynamic and innovative in Iran's history. It brought to the fore intense debates over various conceptions of government and social organization, economic development, and foreign policy. The campaign witnessed experimentation with new language and styles of politics, using methods that were openly borrowed from campaigns in the West. The election result, however, opened new fissures in Iranian politics and raised new questions about the pursuit of development and the prospects of democracy.

The impact of privatization and the extent of private-sector growth in Iran in the 1990s had largely been absent in political discussions. However, in Iran, as was also the case in Eastern Europe or Latin America, privatization had led to economic disparities that translated into support for populist platforms at the polls. In 2005 the demand for reform was upstaged by the lower-class revolt at the ballot box. In the campaign hard-line candidates adopted a populist platform directed at the urban poor and disadvantaged areas of the country.

The reformist platform continued to promise political change, cultural freedoms, civil society activism, and improvement in the status of women. It targeted the urban middle class, virtually ignoring the poor. It argued that participation in the elections was the only way to prevent a reversal of gains made during the Khatami period and sustaining the momentum for reform.

Reformist candidates did not, however, provide a compelling argument for why they would fare better than Khatami in achieving these goals, in particular because conservatives were now far more powerful and better organized than they had been in 1997. As such, reformist candidates faced difficulty in attracting disillusioned pro-democracy forces that had called for a boycott of the elections to join the process.

The reformists did not initially have to compete with hard-line conservatives. Far more important were pragmatic conservatives, such as the former president Rafsanjani, who to varying degrees straddled the boundaries between reformism and conservatism, and who put forward new political programs that confounded the reformist platform.

Expectation of victory after the parliamentary elections of 2004 had intensified competition among conservative candidates – hailing from various conservative factions and the Revolutionary Guard – to differentiate their respective positions, and also to broaden their appeal to the conservative vote bank, as well as to other voters. The competition led to divergent political paths. Whereas hard-liners turned to the poor for support, pragmatic conservatives looked to the middle class. It was pragmatic conservatives who were targeting the reformist constituency that captured most attention early on and looked most promising in the opinion polls. Conservative pragmatists presented new ideas, and more significantly introduced a new style to politics that used secular and youthful themes, pop music, and stylish dress along with colorful advertising. The pragmatists did not reject reform, but rather redefined it. They did not advocate a return to theocracy, revolutionary values, or militant foreign policy – in fact their campaigns were largely secular in tone and notably silent on Islamic issues – but rather pragmatic domestic and foreign policies that although lacking in democratic intent nevertheless promised change. They combined the promise of economic growth, better living standards, accountable and strong government, and engagement with the outside world with a strong appeal to Iranian nationalism. The central theme in pragmatists' arguments was the promise of a "strong government" that would solve social problems, bring about development, and maintain order. Strong government was defined in terms of competence and the capability to get things done. More important, it meant a government that would be able to work with the Supreme Leader and hence avoid the kind of gridlock that characterized the stand-off between Khatami's reformist administration and the conservative leadership. This was an argument that also favored Ahmadinejad, who was expected to fare well with the hard-line conservative Parliament. The pragmatic conservatives in effect promised government reform rather than political reform, arguing that this approach would more quickly and directly impact economic problems.

The intense rivalry of conservatives showed that despite their opposition to reform they have nevertheless internalized certain democratic forms, and in particular looked to public opinion and elections to settle struggles of power. Absence of a democratic state therefore has not precluded contestation of power.

In the first round the pragmatic conservative Rafsanjani won 21.2 percent of the vote, followed by hard-line conservative Ahmadinejad with 19.2 percent. The reformists garnered most votes, but those votes were divided among several candidates – and some went to pragmatic conservatives – denying reformists a place in the run-off election. The outcome of the first round quickly changed the tenor of the campaign and its central issues. Rafsanjani's campaign continued to reflect middle-class demands for cultural opening and political reform. He was endorsed by reformist intellectuals and politicians in an effort to prevent an Ahmadinejad victory, which was seen by them as a return to war fundamentalism and the militancy of the early years of the revolution – characterized by reformists as the "Talibanization" of Iran – and also a turning back on the economic reforms, which since 1989 had restructured the economy but had benefited the private sector and the middle class. Shocked by the emergence of class politics, the reformist-pragmatic conservative alliance put forth a defensive campaign, hoping to rally the middle class to stop Ahmadinejad, thus underscoring the ideological and class divisions that had surfaced in the first round of voting. The dilemma facing reformists and pragmatic conservatives was that in an election now focused on socioeconomic grievances their candidate epitomized the wealth and corruption that the lower class was mobilizing against.

Ahmadinejad's stealth campaign now came into the open. Posing as an outsider and a man of the people, he promised to fight corruption and the political and economic domination of the clerical leadership – the first generation of the revolution – and to redistribute wealth to the poor. He touted his record as mayor of Tehran, promising effective, accountable, and transparent government. To his detractors he promised a future that was modeled on Iran's past: militant Islamic socialism and a Third Worldist foreign policy. His platform appealed to the urban poor and the disadvantaged provinces, who had gained little from privatization strategies and look nostalgically to state control of the economy in the 1980s. He subsumed his hard-line ideological position under a populist platform, and as such created a popular base of support for conservative rule. After he became president he outlined a strident anti-Western foreign policy built around a defiant rejection of Western demands that Iran curb its nuclear program, and virulent attacks against Israel. Using populist rhetoric at home and anti-Westernism abroad Ahmadinejad sought to consolidate power in the presidency – hoping that hard-line conservatives equipped with populist rhetoric could accomplish what reformists failed to do. Beyond populism, nationalism, and anti-Westernism, Ahmadinejad's presidency is likely to serve as another chapter in the power struggle between the Iranian presidency and the Supreme Leader.

The 2005 presidential elections entrenched competitive politics in conservative ranks, and compelled them to fight for control of the middle in Iranian politics. These were the most closely fought presidential elections in Iran's history, which were taken particularly seriously by conservatives and their constituency. These were also the first presidential elections in which the candidates' image and message were shaped by the need to garner votes and the realization that to do so politicians must reflect the demands of their constituencies.

The election confirmed the continued popularity of reformism, but also showed the growing importance of socioeconomic issues. These issues divided the electorate along ideological and class lines, and also brought home the complex question concerning the role of elections in promotion of democracy. The conservatives themselves became divided over these issues as was evident in the turn of some to populist politics and others to pragmatism and courting reformists.

The outcome also compelled reformists to regroup and reformulate their position to reflect changes that the election has brought about. The reformists were blindsided by the depth of socioeconomic disgruntlements. Lacking a united platform or a strong candidate they failed to mount an effective campaign and to adequately organize the electorate. They expected to win – a high turn-out would favor them – but the election denied them that advantage. In this election, in the words of one prominent reformist editor, "reformism lost to democracy." The challenge before pro-democracy forces now is to build a cohesive movement, and relate the demand for change to socioeconomic grievances – building bridges between middle and lower classes.

Looking back at developments since 1988, one can conclude that greater pragmatism has restored the state to its central role in the management of society, politics, and the economy in the name of economic development, as in the earlier Pahlavi era. Nevertheless, the possibility of greater democratization of politics suggests that beyond restoration of power to the state and greater attention to the pursuit of economic growth and development, Iranian politics may be developing along a new trajectory. Whether elections will evolve beyond settling struggles for power among ruling factions into a broad-based democratic system or whether the state will be able to regain control will depend on changes in the relative power of the state and society as well as the relative importance of interests and identity in shaping institutions and, ultimately, Iran's developmental path. The pace and scope of economic reform will influence those changes in turn. These considerations have already spurred much thinking about the role that civil-society institutions, the private sector, and other foundational features of democracies must play in the political maturation of the Iranian state. The relations of power that have defined Iranian politics over the course of much of this century will most likely also influence the process of change.

Conclusion

At the beginning of the twentieth century, there existed little in the form of interests, identity, or institutions in the Iranian polity to provide an impetus for development or to chart a path for that process. It was the global context at the time that imbued the Iranian political process with interests and set the country on its path to development. Those interests, in turn, influenced identity and shaped institutions to give form to the modern Iranian state. Iran looked to Germany and Japan – and also Turkey – as models to follow, and so invested in strong state institutions and promoted a secular national identity. As state institutions expanded, they defined interests and identity in order to serve the state's objectives in the economic and the political arenas. Thus, early on in the process of development, the global context and interests that emerged from it shaped Iran's identity and institutions, guaranteeing the central role of the state in that process.

A changing global context in subsequent years, along with crises that are inherent in development, altered the state in important ways but would not change the state's dominant role in society and politics. Even the Iranian Revolution did not reverse this trend. The revolution placed more importance on identity – articulated in Islamic terms – in charting the country's developmental path. It changed some old institutions and produced some new ones, but it did not change the role of the state in economic development. The case of Iran shows that the interaction among interests, identities, and institutions – as militated by changes in the global contexts and imperatives of the domestic scene – is more fluid early on in the development process but becomes increasingly less so over time. As institutions grow in size and reach, they become more rigid. Although institutions continue to respond to the global context and reflect the influence of interests and identity, they do so with greater infrequency and seldom in major ways. The size and power of the state thus become more important in determining the course of development than do interests and identity, the impact of which must now happen through institutions rather than separate from them.

In many ways, the domination of institutions that emerged through Iran's experiment with development – producing a strong and centralized state – accounts for the fact that Iran has been unable to achieve the end goal of democratic capitalism. Still, in major and minor ways, the global context has shaped interests, and through them identity and institutions, to present Iran with new development possibilities. At the dawn of the twenty-first century,

Iran has yet to arrive at democratic capitalism. However, history has shown that even strong institutions – such as the eighteenth-century French monarchy, nineteenth-century Meiji Japanese feudalism, and the twentieth-century Soviet Union – change in response to global pressures. Given the changes in economic and political life in Iran during the early years of the twenty-first century, the possibility of realizing that goal is not as remote as it may have been only a short while ago.

BIBLIOGRAPHY

Abrahamian, Ervand. *Iran Between Two Revolutions*. Princeton, NJ: Princeton University Press, 1982.

Akhavi, Shahrough. *Religion and Politics in Contemporary Iran: Clergy-State Relations in the Pahlavi Period*. Albany: SUNY Press, 1980.

Amuzegar, Jahangir. *Iran's Economy under the Islamic Republic*. London: I. B. Tauris, 1993.

Arjomand, Said A. *The Turban for the Crown: The Islamic Revolution in Iran*. New York: Oxford University Press, 1988.

Azimi, F. *Iran: The Crisis of Democracy*. New York: St. Martin's Press, 1989.

Bakash, Shaul. *The Reign of the Ayatollahs: Iran and the Islamic Revolution*. New York: Basic Books, 1984.

Bakhtiari, Bahman. *Parliamentary Politics in Revolutionary Iran: The Institutionalization of Factional Politics*. Gainesville: University Press of Florida, 1996.

Dabashi, Hamid. *Theology of Discontent: The Ideological Foundation of the Islamic Revolution in Iran*. New York: New York University Press, 1993.

Ehteshami, Anoushiravan. *After Khomeini: The Iranian Second Republic*. New York: Routledge, 1995.

Elm, Mostafa. *Oil, Power, and Principle: Iran's Oil Nationalization and Its Aftermath*. Syracuse, NY: Syracuse University Press, 1992.

Ertman, Thomas. *Birth of Leviathan: Building States and Regimes in Medieval and Early Modern Europe*. Cambridge: Cambridge University Press, 1997.

Ghani, Cyrus. *Iran and the Rise of Reza Shah: From Qajar Collapse to Pahlavi Rule*. London: I. B. Tauris, 1998.

Gheissari, Ali, and Vali Nasr, *Democracy in Iran: History and the Quest for Liberty*. New York: Oxford University Press, 2006.

Karshenas, Massoud. *Oil, State and Industrialization in Iran*. Cambridge: Cambridge University Press, 1990.

Katouzian, Homa. *The Political Economy of Modern Iran, 1926–79*. New York: New York University Press, 1981.

Kurzman, Charles. *The Unthinkable Revolution in Iran*. Cambridge, MA: Harvard University Press, 2004.

Looney, Robert. *Economic Origins of the Iranian Revolution*. New York: Pergamon Press, 1982.

Migdal, Joel S., Atul Kohli, and Vivienne Shue, eds. *State Power and Social Forces: Domination and Transformation in the Third World*. Cambridge: Cambridge University Press, 1994.

Schirazi, Asghar. *The Constitution of Iran: Politics and the State in the Islamic Republic*. London: I. B. Tauris, 1997.

Skocpol, Theda. "Rentier State and Shi'a Islam in the Iranian Revolution." *Theory and Society* 11, no. 3 (May 1982): 265–283.

Takeyh, Ray. *Hidden Iran: Paradox and Power in the Islamic Republic*. New York: Times Books, 2006.

TABLE 11.1. Key Phases in Iran's Political Development

Time period	Regime	Global context	Interests/identities/ institutions	Developmental path
1921–1941	autocratic monarchy foreign occupation	European imperialism World War II	authoritarian institutions landed and tribal elite, ethnic and regional forces, and authoritarian forces	state-building state collapse
1941–1954	constitutional monarchy and parliamentary democracy	European imperialism	democratic, Islamic, and communist force and authoritarian institutions	democratic institution-building
1954–1963	autocratic monarchy	Cold War	landed elite, authoritarian institutions	state-building
1964–1979	autocratic monarchy	Cold War	bureaucratic and industrial elite; authoritarian institutions	state-building and centralized economic development
1979–1988	revolutionary theocracy	Cold War	lower classes and revolutionary institutions	state important
1988–1997	autocratic republican and theocracy	globalization	revolutionary institutions, mercantile and bureaucratic forces	state-building and economic development
1997–present	autocratic theocracy and reformist presidency	globalization/ war on terror	authoritarian institutions, civil society, mercantile forces	state-building, economic development, and democratic institution-building

IMPORTANT TERMS

Mahmoud Ahmadinejad Iran's president since 2005.

Anglo-Iranian Oil Company the British company that owned the concession to excavate, process, and export Iran's oil until 1954.

ayatollah literally meaning "sign of God," the title of the highest-ranking religious leader in Shia Islam. He has the authority to interpret religious law and to prescribe proper personal, social, and political behavior.

Central Committee the central decision-making body in a communist party structure.

Cultural Revolution attack by the revolutionary forces on Iranian universities and intellectuals in 1980 in order to purge them of liberal and leftist elements and to force conformity with revolutionary values. This term originated in China during the purges of the 1960s.

Friday Prayer congregational Muslim prayer on Fridays. In the Islamic Republic, it has been used as a political forum to propagate government views and mobilize the masses in support of government policies.

Ayatollah Ali Akbar Hashemi-Rafsanjani revolutionary leader, speaker of the Parliament, and president between 1988 and 1997. He introduced the first efforts to reform the Islamic Republic.

hostage crisis the crisis initiated in November 1979 when radical students took U.S. diplomatic personnel hostage at the U.S. embassy in Tehran, demanding the handover of the Shah to Iran and recognition of Iran's grievances against the United States for its role in the 1953 coup and support of the Shah. The hostages were released in January 1981 after 444 days.

import-substitution industrialization (ISI) a strategy for industrialization that became popular in the developing world after World War II. It advocates beginning industrialization by producing finished goods and then expanding the scope of the process by moving to intermediary and primary industrial goods and using protectionism to favor the young industries. It has been associated with several economic and political problems.

Iran-Iraq War an intense war between Iran and Iraq between 1980 and 1988 during which Iraq first occupied parts of Iran but then was compelled to defend its own territory against Iranian offensives. The most bloody and costly war since World War II, it ended with Iran's defeat.

Islam a monotheistic religion and the world's second-largest faith, with more than one billion followers.

Islamic ideology a political doctrine with views on society and government that are drawn from a puritanical understanding of Islam. Advocating that politics should be subservient to religion, it was the guiding ideology of the religious faction of the revolution.

Islamic Republic of Iran the official name of Iran after the revolution. It attests to the centrality of Islam to statecraft since 1979.

Kemalism a model of development that emerged in Turkey during the 1920s. Named after the Turkish president Mustafa Kemal, its most important features were secularism, nationalism, and a domineering role for the state in socioeconomic change.

Ayatollah Ali Khamenei revolutionary leader, president, and currently supreme leader of Iran. He has been associated with the anti-reform faction since 1997.

Ayatollah Mohammad Khatami Iran's president from 1997 to 2005. He spearheaded efforts to liberalize the Islamic Republic.

Ayatollah Ruhollah Khomeini the chief architect and leader of the revolution of 1979, who ruled Iran as supreme leader between 1979 and 1988.

Mohammad Mossadeq the nationalist prime minister at the time of the 1953 coup. He nationalized Iran's oil industry and led the drive for limiting foreign influence in Iran and for instituting democracy in the country.

OPEC Organization of Petroleum Exporting Countries, a cartel formed in the late 1960s to strengthen the position of oil producers in the international market. It pushed for higher oil prices during the 1970s.

Pahlavi the name of the dynasty that ruled Iran between 1921 and 1979.

Muhammad Reza Shah Pahlavi the second Pahlavi monarch, who ruled between 1941 and 1979.

Reza Shah Pahlavi the founder of the Pahlavi monarchy and the initiator of Iran's development during the twentieth century. He ruled between 1921 and 1941.

rentier state a state that earns an overwhelming proportion of its income from sources outside of its domestic economic activity. Such states become autonomous from the society and rely on distributive mechanisms to assert authority. That, in time, will erode their legitimacy.

Revolutionary Guards an ideologically committed militia that was formed after the revolution to perform the functions of the police and the military.

SAVAK Iran's intelligence agency between 1954 and 1979. It was responsible for contending with the opposition and was associated with the Pahlavi monarchy's human-rights violations.

shah "king" in Persian.

Ali Shariati an intellectual who blended Marxist ideology with Islamic teachings to produce a potent ideology of revolutionary change in Iran during the 1970s.

Shia a branch of Islam that is dominant in Iran. It places great authority in its religious leaders and values sacrifice in the path of justice.

Vali-e Faqih literally meaning the "supreme guardian-jurisconsult," it is a position that was put forward by Ayatollah Khomeini to embody his belief that it is religiously mandated for Shia clerics to rule in the political arena. This view justified the religious nature of the revolution and the constitutional setup of the Islamic Republic.

vanguard party a party that spearheads a revolution.

STUDY QUESTIONS

1. How has change in identity influenced Iran's development?
2. How has the revolution altered prospects for democratic capitalism?
3. What are the most important turning points in Iran's development?
4. Was there a greater chance for democratic development in 1977 or in 1997?

5. Has identity been important in Iranian institutional change? If so, how?

6. Does the pursuit of interests produce a more sustainable development path than pursuit of identity?

7. Can religious identity sustain secular state institutions and serve developmental goals?

8. How important is the location of Iran to its path of development?

9. In what ways can the global context influence Iran's development from this point forward?

SOUTH AFRICA

CHAPTER TWELVE

South Africa

Michael Bratton

Introduction

As one of the world's youngest democracies, South Africa seeks to escape a bitter political legacy. During the second half of the twentieth century, its white minority government systematically built a powerful, militarized state around institutions of racial oppression. Starting even earlier, the discovery of minerals enabled the development of an industrial economy, which thrust Africans and the descendants of European settlers into close contact in the country's burgeoning urban areas. Predictably, political conflicts erupted between blacks, who provided labor, and whites, who benefited from economic growth. Because the old regime was dead set against political change until the late 1980s, the struggle over **apartheid** (as extreme racial segregation was called in South Africa) seemed destined to end in a cataclysm of violence.

That a bloodbath was averted was one of the most remarkable stories of an eventful interlude of global democratization. Against the odds, political leaders from both sides (but especially the visionary **Nelson Mandela**, president of the **African National Congress**) came to recognize that the long-term interests of South Africa's deeply divided communities were inextricably intertwined. Through tough negotiation and painful compromise, hardheaded opponents forged an elite pact, albeit against the backdrop of popular mobilization, that allowed the country to hold an open election and to install the country's first democratic government in 1994. The world welcomed this transition as marking both the end of colonial rule in Africa and the burial of the last twentieth-century government based on myths of racial supremacy.

The years that followed in South Africa have seen a flurry of political innovation. New institutions and policies have been designed to redress the exclusions and inequities of the past. But difficult questions remain about the viability of the new order. Do South Africans from different social backgrounds acknowledge their interdependence? Can the government redistribute wealth to blacks without inducing white flight? Does the government have the capacity to deliver the benefits promised in South Africa's expansive new constitution? And, perhaps most importantly, given the absence of a democratic heritage and the omnipresence of crime and HIV-AIDS, what are the prospects for consolidating democracy?

The Global Historical Context

The southernmost tip of Africa, a dry region rich in mineral resources, has supported small hunting and gathering communities from the time that humans first trod the earth. From about 2,500 years ago, the indigenous Khoisan peoples were gradually joined by **Bantu**-speaking African migrants from the north, who introduced herding, crop cultivation, and iron production. As these groups intermingled, they formed a succession of small-scale chieftaincies, which, due to the relative abundance of land, had little need to establish standing armies or other state institutions.

Southern Africa became less isolated from the rest of the world in the late fifteenth century when – at about the same time that Spain was dispatching Columbus to the Americas – Portuguese mariners rounded the Cape of Good Hope in search of an eastward route to India. Succeeding the Portuguese as the world's top trading power during the seventeenth century, the Dutch founded the first permanent European settlement there. From the beginning, the **Cape Colony** was run along lines that established the foundations for modern South Africa: the forced annexation of land and the coercion of labor. This economic system, together with sexual liaisons between white burghers, Malay slaves, and native blacks, gave rise to a complex society stratified along racial and class lines.

The ascendancy of Britain as a global power was marked in Southern Africa by its annexation of the Cape Colony in 1806 and the arrival of English settlers on the frontier of the eastern Cape in 1820. At this time, the colony remained predominantly rural, though its economic importance to Britain remained as a way-station for trade rather than as an agricultural exporter. The population clustered into four main groups: the English, the **Afrikaners** (Dutch descendants who had developed their own Africanized culture and dialect), the Cape **Coloureds** (an emerging community of mixed-race people), and the indigenous **Xhosa** (on the eastern frontier). Political conflicts over land rights between these groups gave rise to demands for government. At the same time, agitation against slavery by English missionaries drove many Afrikaners to trek northward in an effort to escape the reach of regulation.

The first colonial administrations were autocratic: former military officers drawn from the ranks of the English aristocracy were appointed as colonial governors. An important political precedent was set in 1853, however, when Britain allowed the establishment of an elected legislative council. Henceforth, the country's political evolution would diverge from India's, whose elected institutions were not set up until almost a century later. Instead, the Cape Colony came to more closely resemble Canada (and later Australia and New Zealand), where Britain gradually granted self-government to a small but dominant group of white settlers. Although the first franchise was color-blind – it granted the vote to any adult male who owned property or earned a salary – Africans and Coloureds were effectively excluded from political life because they were poor.

As in other settler colonies (including the United States), contacts with white immigrants were devastating for indigenous peoples. Even during the rule of the Dutch East India Company, the Khoisan hunters and herders of the western Cape had been decimated by European diseases like small-pox and measles. By the mid-nineteenth century, Bantu-speaking groups as far north as the Limpopo River had lost their land, crops, and livestock to European invaders. Foreign conquest was not achieved by strength of num-bers – blacks have always greatly outnumbered whites in South Africa – but by the technological superiority of a metropolitan industrial economy that could mass-produce firearms. This is not to say that conquest occurred easily; instead, it was punctuated by hard-fought wars of resistance launched by the Xhosa in the eastern Cape in the 1840s, the **Zulu** in Natal in the 1850s, and the Sotho, the Venda, and the Pedi in the interior highlands in the 1860s. The Zulu, who themselves had earlier brutally repressed neighboring groups, cultivated the identity and organization of a warrior nation throughout much of the nineteenth century.

Initially, four separate settler states were formed in the territory now known as South Africa. Apart from the Cape, the British controlled Natal, a sec-ond colony on the eastern seaboard, to which they imported laborers from colonial India (mainly Hindu but also Muslim) to develop sugar plantations and railways. Christian missionaries were particularly active in Natal, estab-lishing schools and hospitals that attracted displaced Africans into modern-ized lifestyles. On the high-altitude savanna, Afrikaner stock-farmers set up two agrarian republics based on the institutions of individual land title and an armed citizenry. The Orange Free State was a constitutional republic run by an elected assembly of white males under a semblance of legality, whereas the Transvaal was a much more rough-and-ready state held together by roving commandos. The political and religious leaders of these republics constructed a historical mythology of the Afrikaners as a chosen people who had thrown off the bonds of the British Empire and founded their own promised land.

While British colonies and Boer (Afrikaner farmer) republics had distinct origins, they nonetheless shared a patrimonial ideology that reduced the rela-tions between the races to those of master and servant. For their part, the

African peoples of the region ultimately proved more resilient than the aboriginal populations of the Cape. Shunted into crowded rural areas, they adjusted to an emerging capitalist economy by growing crops for sale to the settlers (both on their own land and as sharecroppers), providing labor on white commercial farms, and adopting not only Christianized religions but tastes for Western consumer goods. The presence of missionaries, labor recruiters, and tax collectors in the African territories further reduced the influence of hereditary chiefs, whose authority already had been undermined by conquest and colonization.

The Path of Development

The economic growth of the region reached a major turning point in 1870 with the discovery in the interior of the world's richest deposits of gold and diamonds. The resultant mining boom generated glittering profits for investors in Britain, Europe, and North America and, by the turn of the century, firmly integrated Southern Africa into a global capitalist economy. Industrialization was accompanied by urbanization. Waves of English-speaking immigrants from around the world and African migrant laborers from as far north as modern-day Mozambique, Tanzania, and Zambia converged on the boom towns of Kimberley and Johannesburg. From the outset, the industrial economy was constructed on racial lines. Whites were awarded skilled jobs with high wages and supervisory responsibilities while black laborers were poorly paid and housed in spartan, male-only barracks. The joint-stock companies that dominated the mining sector found common cause with the colonial governments in controlling the flow of labor by introducing "pass" laws, which ruled that no unemployed African could stay in an urban area without a valid identity document.

Political conflicts intensified over the country's newfound wealth. Despite deep differences between Boer and Briton, the colonists united to crush the last remnants of African resistance. Aided by intelligence reports from the Afrikaners and factionalism in the Zulu royal family – but not without significant military losses – an armed British expedition finally subdued the region's most powerful African kingdom in 1879. The Zulu monarchy was abolished and Zululand was divided into 13 weak parts under appointed chiefs. At the same time, Britain was determined to wrest political control of the goldfields from the Afrikaners in the Transvaal; after several unsuccessful attempts at annexation, it resorted to all-out war to guarantee imperial supremacy. The South African War (1899–1902) pitted an orthodox British army of almost half a million soldiers against a mobile guerrilla force. A British victory was achieved only when Boer farms were burned to the ground and families were herded into disease-ridden camps, humiliations that rankled long after the war was over.

A postwar peace settlement unified the region politically and gave birth to the modern state of South Africa. The constitution of the **Union of South Africa** in 1910 contained several principles that profoundly shaped the course of subsequent events. First, the constitution adopted a British Westminster model in which Parliament was supreme within a unitary state (that is, with a single center rather than a federation). In the absence of a separation of powers, the political party that controlled Parliament enjoyed largely unchallenged control. Second, the plural culture of the new state was acknowledged when English and Dutch (later supplanted by Afrikaans) were recognized as official languages of equal status. Finally, and most importantly, blacks (that is, Africans, Indians, and Coloureds) were denied a share of political power. The franchise laws of the former colonies remained in place, entirely excluding blacks from government in the new provinces of Transvaal, Orange Free State, and Natal. Voting rights for blacks were protected in the relatively more liberal Cape Province; in practice, however, blacks never accounted for more than one-seventh of the electorate and never elected one of their own to parliamentary office.

Instead, white settlers set about consolidating control of a large and potentially affluent African state whose autonomy from the mother country was further strengthened when the British Parliament abandoned legislative oversight in 1934. The period of the white-run Union (later Republic) of South Africa can be divided conveniently into two periods: first under anglicized Afrikaners (1910–1948) and later, momentously, when Afrikaner nationalists took over (1948–1994). Public policies during these periods differed in degree rather than kind; both aimed at racial segregation. The post-1948 apartheid regime, however, extended the separation of the races to a deranged extreme by drawing biological distinctions between people and institutionalizing racial discrimination into the structure of the state.

Two countervailing forces offset these political developments. On the one hand, the expansion of the industrial economy required the creation of a stable urban workforce, which brought the races into close economic interdependence. At the same time, the enactment of discriminatory laws was matched at each stage by the emergence of new and gradually more militant forms of black resistance, starting with the formation in 1912 of the organization that became known as the African National Congress (ANC).

One of the first steps of the Union government was to pass a Native Lands Act (1913) that prohibited Africans from buying or leasing farms designated for whites. The effect of this legislation – and of accompanying "hut" taxes – was to force peasants into wage labor as farm workers or miners. As for the urban areas, the state gave legal effect to customary color bars; for example the Industrial Conciliation Act (1924) denied Africans the right to engage in collective wage bargaining. And in 1936, the Natives Representation Act removed Africans from the ordinary voters' rolls in the Cape Province even as white women were being enfranchised nationwide. These indignities fueled campaigns for legislative reform by a small elite of educated Africans – clergy, lawyers, and teachers – who had begun to rally under the ANC banner. They also prompted strikes led by the Industrial and Commercial Workers Union (formed in 1928), even though labor actions had been ruled illegal. Indeed, despite segregation, Africans continued to pour into towns, surrounding the prim, white, middle-class suburbs with proletarian squatter settlements that teemed with discontent.

The Second World War (1939–1945) divided the white community. Many Afrikaners were distressed that South Africa entered a European conflict on the side of Great Britain, leading extremists in their midst to openly express sympathy for Nazi ideas of racial purity. For their part, most English-speakers welcomed a chance to mobilize South Africa's resources in support of the Allied war effort, which resulted in the rapid buildup of the country's coal, iron, and garment-manufacturing industries. Seeking to extend economic expansion after the war and recognizing the growing reliance of the economy on black labor, the United Party government of Jan Smuts suggested modest reforms to improve African wages and working conditions. But even these timid steps prompted a right-wing backlash. In the 1948 election, the electorate swung toward the **National Party**, which won a narrow victory in part because rural voting districts were overrepresented. The government of D. F. Malan came to power at a time when ideas were gaining currency in the Afrikaner churches and secret societies about apartheid (literally, apart-ness). A monstrous social experiment to create a government of racial institutions was about to begin.

The Apartheid Experiment

The National Party government began by packing the state apparatus – the army, the police, the civil service, and the publicly owned railways – with its own supporters. It ensured that Afrikaners became the prime beneficiaries of agricultural and educational subsidies and of public construction contracts. Thus was state power used to enable social mobility for a population that had always resented the greater economic wealth of the English-speakers. These developments, along with the duplication of public services for segregated communities, meant that the state in South Africa became large, interventionist, and riddled with patronage.

As the basis for apartheid, the government classified every citizen under the **Population Registration Act** (1950) into one of four racial categories: African, Coloured, Indian, or white. New laws were introduced to prohibit sex and marriage between people of different races; the authorities even went so far as to break up existing mixed-race families. Under the Group Areas Act (also 1950), black urban neighborhoods like Sophiatown in Johannesburg and District Six in Cape Town were bulldozed and their inhabitants dispersed. Every public facility was segregated – from bus and train stations and drinking fountains to parks, cinemas, and beaches – by means of demeaning "Whites Only" signs. A Bantu Education Act (1953) effectively abolished mission schools for Africans, replacing them with substandard public institutions. Bent on removing every vestige of political rights for people of color, the National Party did to Coloured voters in 1956 what the United Party government had earlier done to African voters: removed them from the common electoral rolls.

But the architect of apartheid, Hendrick Verwoerd (prime minister, 1958–1966) had an even grander vision that called for the complete geographical partition of the races. Under the Bantu Homelands Constitution Act (1957), Africans were stripped of citizenship, expelled from the choicest parts of the country (and from 87 percent of its total land area) and consigned to ten, scattered, ethnic "**homelands**." The implementation of this scheme – which included nominal political independence for unviable entities like Transkei and Bophutatswana – amounted to the largest forced movement of population anywhere in the postwar world. Because the impoverished homeland administrations could neither generate employment nor deliver basic services, relocation exacted a harsh toll of malnutrition, disease, and death.

The government's policy of "separate development," however, flew in the face of the reality that South Africa had become an economically integrated society. By 1980, at the peak of apartheid's ethnic cleansing, more than half of the nonwhite population continued to reside in towns, where blacks – 6.9 million Africans, 2 million Coloureds, and 700,000 Indians – together outnumbered 4 million whites.

Urban dwellers rejected the official fiction that Africans belonged in rural backwaters under the tutelage of "tribal" chiefs. Instead, a new generation of young leaders like Walter Sisulu, Oliver Tambo, and Nelson Mandela recommitted the African National Congress (ANC) to multiracial democracy. In 1955 the ANC's Freedom Charter declared that "South Africa belongs to all who live in it, black and white, and that no government can justly claim authority unless it is based on the will of the people." The charter's mix of liberal values (freedom of speech, the right to vote, equality before the law) with more socialist ideas (free education and health care, public ownership of mines and industry), reflected the ANC's openness to various political tendencies. Other liberation movements – like the South African Communist Party (SACP, formed 1921), the Pan-Africanist Congress (PAC, formed 1959), and the Black Consciousness Movement, (which coalesced in the 1970s around the ideas of Steve Biko) – sounded more radical or Africanist themes.

Resistance to apartheid started out peacefully in civil disobedience: modeled on Ghandian principles of nonviolence, the antiapartheid movement first took the form of the burning of passes or defiance of other discriminatory laws. In response, the police gunned down 67 demonstrators in the urban township of **Sharpeville** in 1960 and banned the ANC and PAC. Deprived of all opportunity to organize peacefully, resistance leaders had little choice but to take up arms. The military wings of the PAC and ANC – later known as the Azanian Peoples Liberation Army (APLA) and Umkhonto we Sizwe (MK, or the Spear of the Nation) – embarked on bombing campaigns against state installations like electricity switching stations and post offices. Convicted for authorizing such attacks, Mandela and Sisulu were incarcerated under life sentences on Robben Island, a prison off the coast at Cape Town, in 1964. There followed a long hiatus while the resistance movement gathered strength again, punctuated by a wave of strikes led by increasingly militant black workers' organizations in 1973, and by a youth uprising in Soweto (Johannesburg's black South Western Townships) in 1976. The school children employed black-consciousness ideas to challenge the use of Afrikaans as a medium of instruction. Within a year, however, the police had arrested, beaten, and killed their hero, Steve Biko.

By the 1980s, apartheid entered a crisis born of its own contradictions and of new pressures emanating from a changing world. Internally, the economy suffered from recession, currency inflation, and the excessive costs of administering a maze of oppressive social controls. As white professionals began to emigrate and blacks bore the brunt of a second-rate education system, the country encountered shortages of the skills necessary to operate its increasingly sophisticated economy. Then the National Party was rocked by scandal over misappropriated public funds that forced the resignation of Prime Minister John Vorster. His successor, P. W. Botha, pursued a mixed strategy of repression and reform. On the one hand, he enhanced the powers of the presidency at the expense of the cabinet, drew military men into government through a State Security Council, and used the police as agents of local government. On the other hand, he tried (unsuccessfully) to co-opt Indians and Coloureds into their own separate legislatures and local government councils under a revised 1984 constitution. By 1986, Botha even authorized the repeal of selected "petty" apartheid laws in recognition of the fact that blacks now lived permanently in the heart of all major metropolitan areas.

Botha's strategy did not work because it continued to ignore majority political aspirations. It was overtaken by events as Africans in the urban townships and industrial workplaces took matters into their own hands. By the end of the 1970s, trade unions had won the right to organize legally and strikes were occurring at unprecedented rates. In 1983, a **United Democratic Front (UDF)** of trade unions, churches, civic organizations, and women's and youth groups coalesced to protest the new constitution. The UDF, considered by many to be a front for the banned and exiled ANC, completely disrupted urban local government through an orchestrated campaign of service and consumer boycotts, although, too often, the resultant void of authority was quickly filled by intimidation and violence. Faced with open popular resistance – symbolized by the *toyi-toyi* dance performed en masse at political funerals – the Botha government had no answer except to deploy the army in a nationwide State of Emergency in June 1986.

Internationally, South Africa was becoming increasingly isolated. Long gone were the halcyon days of the 1960s and 1970s when international investors were attracted by a stable business climate. Gone too was the political support of U.S. President Richard Nixon, who had concluded on the advice of Foreign Secretary Henry Kissinger that white settlers had a long-term future in Southern Africa and were a valuable bulwark against communism. The fall of settler regimes in Mozambique, Angola, and Rhodesia (now Zimbabwe) on South Africa's northern borders removed the country's buffer from black Africa.

In place of these allies, South Africa faced an increasingly hostile Organization of African Unity (the international body of black African states) and Commonwealth (the association of former British colonies, many from Asia and Africa, from which South Africa had withdrawn in 1961 when it declared itself a republic). The United Nations was clamoring for South Africa to surrender its mandate over neighboring Namibia, to withdraw its troops from Angola, and to immediately dissolve apartheid. The Jimmy Carter administration in the United States came out openly for majority rule and, in 1986, the U.S. Congress overrode a veto by President Ronald Reagan in order to impose comprehensive economic sanctions against South Africa. The inflow of investment capital turned into an outflow. Not only at home, but also abroad, the South African state had become a pariah.

An Unexpected Transition

As political attitudes hardened on all sides, a race war seemed inevitable. Yet nothing that had gone before prepared South Africans for what was to follow. Recognizing that further violence would devastate Africa's most productive economy, the leaders of the country's opposing political forces stepped back from the brink. Driven by their own intertwined interests, they unexpectedly forged a peaceful passage that granted black majority rule in return for a continued place for whites in South Africa's bright economic sun. Against the backdrop of the end of the Cold War, South Africa made a sudden transition to multiracial democracy in the mid-1990s.

Events in the 1980s created the climate for negotiation and compromise. Cut off from flows of international capital, the economy began to shrink, driving the South African government to seek rehabilitation within the Western world. The collapse of communism in the Soviet Union and Eastern Europe deprived the ANC of its main sources of political, financial, and military support. Because both sides therefore lacked the means to win an outright military victory, each began to see virtue in coming to terms. Thus political contacts were initiated: openly among white businessmen, Afrikaner intellectuals, and the ANC leaders in exile and, secretly, between government officials and political prisoners within the country. These encounters reassured the government that Nelson Mandela would not insist on a winner-take-all solution and would respect minority (that is, white) rights. Soon after acceding to leadership of the National Party, **Frederick Willem (F. W.) de Klerk** decided to gamble on political reform while Afrikaners still enjoyed a measure of control over the political situation. On February 2, 1990, he announced that Mandela would be released, banned parties could resume political activities, and negotiations for an inclusive new political order would begin. Nine days later, in the glare of global television coverage, Mandela walked free.

Negotiations over the country's political future began at the end of 1991 when delegates from the government, the ANC, and 17 other political organizations, including leaders from the ethnic homelands, gathered in the Convention for a Democratic South Africa (**CODESA**). Some political parties held back: leftist black power movements like the PAC continued to favor armed struggle ("one settler, one bullet"); and conservative groups, like the **Inkatha** Freedom Party (IFP), which appealed to Zulu traditionalists, launched attacks on ANC supporters with the covert connivance of the South African security forces. CODESA and the multiparty forums that followed were "on-again, off-again" affairs, regularly breaking down in the face of violent incidents (like the massacre of shack dwellers at Boipatong in 1992 and the 1993 assassination of the popular Communist Party secretary general, Chris Hani). Ironically, however, the ever-present specter of escalating disorder repeatedly helped to drive the parties back to the negotiating table.

At issue in negotiations was the shape of the new political order. The two major parties could agree on a few basic points – one person, one vote; an independent judiciary; and the reintegration of the homelands – but on little else. Whereas the ANC insisted on a unitary state, the NP (at first) and IFP (throughout) favored federalism. Whereas the ANC wanted majority rule, their opponents called for a rotating presidency and minority vetoes. These differences were ultimately resolved through a series of behind-the-scenes pacts: a political pact to share power in a government of national unity (**GNU**) for five years; an economic pact to guarantee property rights and civil service positions and pensions; and a military pact to extend amnesty to individuals on all sides who confessed to politically motivated crimes. While these deals were struck largely as a result of the self-regarding calculations of South African elites, the international community kept nudging the peace process forward with promises of diplomatic recognition, aid, and investment.

The multiparty negotiating forum of 1993 eventually produced a transitional government, an interim constitution, and a timetable for the country's first open elections. The interim constitution was modeled on a variety of sources – German, American, and Indian, among others – but, more than anything, it reflected the art of the possible in South Africa's complex society. It was a quasi-federal document with a strong central government that provided for 9 provincial legislatures and 11 official languages. It imported conventional ideas from abroad like proportional representation, according to which seats were allocated in the national and provincial assemblies according to the share of the electoral votes won by each political party. But it was original in its provisions for a GNU, whereby parties also obtained seats in a coalition cabinet based on their share of the vote.

The election was scheduled for April 27, 1994. From the outset, the campaign was fraught with uncertainty. Inkatha and the far-right Conservative Party announced that they would not take part because the new constitution did not provide autonomy for either a Zulu kingdom or an Afrikaner republic. As a result of growing armed clashes between supporters of the IFP and the ANC, a state of emergency was declared in the Natal province. Chief **Mangosuthu Buthelezi**, the leader of rural Zulus, was effectively sidelined from negotiations by Mandela and de Klerk. In return, he appeared willing to risk civil war and to sacrifice South Africa's transition to democracy in pursuit of personal political ambitions and his people's regional interests. Eventually realizing that the transition would occur without him, however, Buthelezi ended his brinkmanship barely one week before the election by announcing that the IFP would take part.

In the event, the 1994 election in South Africa was a celebration, both solemn and jubilant, of a momentous historical shift. For the first time ever, South Africa's diverse peoples participated as political equals in the democratic ritual of choosing their own leaders. The election brought an end to 350 years of settler colonial rule and, with it, the perverse idea that the right to self-government was the preserve of some races but not others.

To be sure, South Africa's founding election did not run entirely smoothly: Voters had to wait in long lines to cast their ballots, some for several days; and the result in the Zulu heartland probably owed as much to an elite political bargain as to a valid vote. Nevertheless, the high voter turnout (86 percent of all adults) and the peacefulness of the polls throughout the country enabled the Independent Electoral Commission to declare the election "substantially free and fair." The ANC won a solid majority (63 percent of the vote), followed by the National Party and the IFP (20 percent and 11 percent respectively), each of which secured control of at least one provincial legislature (in the Western Cape and Kwazulu-Natal respectively). These three parties formed a Government of National Unity with Nelson Mandela as president and F. W. de Klerk as his second executive deputy. Against all expectations, these farsighted and level-headed leaders – who deservedly shared the 1992 Nobel Peace Prize – had averted revolution, created a culture of compromise, and – unexpectedly – pulled democracy out of the hat.

The Socioeconomic Structure

Despite the drama of the democratic transition, change in the political sphere was offset by socioeconomic continuities. South Africa's first elected government inherited a society and economy whose population was mutually estranged, not only in terms of race, but also by wealth and well-being. The economy had never been designed to serve a black majority – including a vast, impoverished underclass – that now clamored for jobs, houses, and education. Could South Africans from different social backgrounds emerge from a bitter political conflict and put old divisions behind them? Whereas whites tended to see the democratic transition as the end of a difficult process of change, blacks rather saw it as just a beginning.

South Africa has always been a predominantly African country, though official policies acknowledged this only after 1994. According to the 2001 census, the total population is almost 45 million persons, of whom some 79 percent classified themselves as African, 10 percent as white, 9 percent as Coloured, and 2 percent as Asian. The most common mother tongues are Zulu (24 percent), Xhosa (18 percent), and dialects of Sotho (17 percent), followed by Afrikaans and English (13 and 8 percent, respectively). While South Africans are relatively literate and unusually multilingual, many people have received poor-quality schooling and remain uncomfortable using English, the country's main language of government and business. Yet, over one-half live in towns (at least 54 percent) and the urban areas are growing at more than twice the rate of the nation as a whole (5 percent versus 2 percent).

With the largest and most complex economy on the African continent and a gross national product (GNP) per person of US$3,630 in 2004, South Africa is a middle-income country. It features bustling cities with gleaming skyscrapers, modern highways filled with fancy German and Japanese automobiles, and vast irrigated farms employing the latest agricultural technologies. Indeed, the country's stock of physical infrastructure (roads, railways, harbors, power grids, and water networks), financial institutions (banks, insurance companies, a stock market), and business and technological skills is solid. After stalling in the late 1980s and early 1990s, the economy revived after 1994: Over the next three years the GNP grew at a rate exceeding population growth for the first time in two decades and speeded up further after 2000. Foreign debt remains low and inflation is under control. Importantly, because the South African economy was capable of financing socioeconomic development from domestic resources, the government had little need for aid or loans from international donors.

Set against these advantages, however, are poverty and inequality. At least one-third of economically active South Africans lack a formal job, with unemployment being highest among young people, women, and Africans. The average monthly wage of an employed African (about US$350) is barely above the amount needed for the subsistence of a low-income household. Thus, poverty haunts not only the unemployed, but also many families with wage earners. Among the African population, one-quarter lacks access to safe drinking water, almost one-half has only minimal sanitation, and three in ten (more in rural areas) are without electricity. The most common living conditions for the poor are either a single-roomed hut in an isolated rural backwater or, more commonly, a homemade shack in a garbage-strewn, peri-urban, informal settlement.

Thus, grinding poverty coexists alongside brazen displays of wealth. Among countries that keep reliable records on the gap between the "haves" and the "have-nots," South Africa ranks as one of the most unequal societies in the world, perhaps second only to Brazil. The poorest 20 percent of households earns just 3 percent of the country's income whereas the richest 20 percent earns fully 63 percent. According to the Human Development Index of the United Nations, the lifestyle enjoyed by white South Africans is equivalent to that of New Zealanders, whereas black South Africans live under conditions similar to their counterparts in Congo-Brazzaville. Asians and Coloureds fall somewhere in between.

HIV, the virus that causes AIDS, has spread alarmingly in South Africa. By 2004, 20 percent of adults aged 25 to 49 were living with the virus or the disease, and the country had a larger number of infected persons than any country in the world at that time. While all classes of society are affected, the poor and women are disproportionately stricken. An average South African's life expectancy fell by 10 years (from 63 to 53 years) between 1991 and 2002, and is projected to fall much further (to 38 years) by 2010. Some 13 percent of South African children have already lost one or both parents.

Severe deprivation and inequality, combined with a legacy of brutal politics, have bred crime and social violence. South Africa's murder rate – 65 deaths per day in 1997 – probably leads the world; other manifestations include gang warfare, organized cash-in-transit heists, and illegal international trade in drugs, guns, and diamonds. The government claims that it has reduced crime but the facts are mixed: While some offenses like murder may be falling, others like burglary and armed robbery continue to climb. Conventional wisdom connects crime with joblessness, but this economic interpretation does not explain the linkage between crime and violence. Here it is necessary to remember that South Africa's seemingly smooth political transition was actually very turbulent. Both the security forces and some antiapartheid activists adopted tactics of intimidation and vigilantism. A gap in authority opened up between a repressive state and an ungovernable citizenry, into which large numbers of weapons have continued to flow as a result of conflicts elsewhere in the region. Thus, fear of crime is pervasive among South Africans both black and white.

Scholars have engaged in heated debates about whether South African politics are better understood in terms of social identities like ethnicity (including race) or with reference to the interests of economic classes. What is important, however, is that race and class significantly overlap in South Africa; in social science terminology, social and economic cleavages tend to reinforce rather than cross-cut. To the extent that apartheid was an integrated system that used racial classification not only to exert political control (over blacks), but also to accumulate wealth (for whites), it resulted in particularly deep and lasting divisions.

Thus apartheid's legacy of race-based material inequality remains the starting point for any analysis of the dynamics of the country's contemporary politics. The inherited socioeconomic structure has profoundly shaped the design of political institutions in the country's new constitution. Inequality between the races remains a potentially explosive source of political instability that could still turn South Africa into yet another failed multiethnic state. And the capacity of elected governments to deliver social justice has already become the standard by which many South Africans evaluate the merits of democracy.

Contemporary Political Identities

To what extent, then, are contemporary South African politics shaped by social identities, particularly race, but also other aspects of ethnicity? Is it possible to build a shared sense of nationhood in this deeply divided, multicultural society?

Nelson Mandela staked his political career on the proposition that the country belongs to all its people. He used his considerable moral authority to promote a vision of "reconciliation" in which South Africa's diverse groups forego revenge and live peacefully side by side in a "rainbow nation." To this end, the first GNU cabinet was truly multiracial, being made up of 16 Africans, 8 whites, and 6 Indians or Coloureds. The transition spawned new symbols of national unity such as a multi-colored flag and an anthem that melds the favorite hymns of the old and new regimes. In this sports-mad country, citizens of all races demonstrate their patriotism by enthusiastically embracing these symbols at national soccer and rugby matches. And in public-opinion surveys, more than 90 percent of respondents say they feel "proud" to call themselves "South Africans."

Nevertheless, the same surveys show that most citizens still also identify with narrow subcommunities. Even as they profess newfound commitments to nonracialism, South Africans still behave politically as if they belong to racial and language blocs. In important respects, for example, national elections are a kind of "ethnic census": in 1994, fewer than 3 percent of whites cast ballots for the (black-led) ANC and fewer than 5 percent of Africans chose the (white-led) National Party. The fact that two-thirds of Coloured and Indian voters sided with white-led parties suggests that these communities also felt racial distance from Africans and were concerned about the consequences of majority rule. These concerns center on the potential for monopolization of the electoral process by one demographic group. Because black Africans constitute some 70 percent of the electorate, and because about 75 percent of them vote for the ANC, the ruling party would seem to enjoy a permanent, built-in majority. With a dominant ruling party and a fragmented opposition, it is difficult to see how South Africa can attain a turnover of governments in the near future. This aspect of democracy would require the realignment of voter support away from its present racial structure.

Indeed, the salience of race in South African politics has hardly declined since 1994. The government ordered that racial categories be restored in the collection and reporting of official data, arguing that this was necessary to address existing inequities. Also introduced were policies of affirmative action to create job opportunities for disadvantaged groups, which, while encouraging the much-needed transformation of institutions throughout society, also helped to keep consciousness of ethnicity alive. Race relations are marred by harsh stereotypes: Many South African whites believe that their black counterparts lack the technical capacity to operate a complex economy and government; aware of these prejudices, many blacks are overly sensitive to criticism, tending to dismiss even constructive dissent as racism. Thus have debates between the government and the opposition – especially in Parliament and in the press – too often lapsed into a defensive exchange of epithets.

To South Africa's advantage, however, the industrial economy long ago brought blacks and whites together in workplaces across the country and now, increasingly, into residential proximity in the major cities. Economic integration therefore continues to dissolve the mutual isolation of the two main racial communities. Some minority groups, however, remain clustered in their own areas: for instance, 83 percent of the Coloureds live in the Cape provinces, especially around Cape Town, and 78 percent of Asians live in Kwazulu-Natal, especially in Durban. In these cases, geographical concentration has probably helped minorities to avoid being shut out from politics entirely. In the long run, however, any party that wishes to govern at the national level in South Africa must attract black votes.

Ethnic interpretations of South African politics should not be pushed too far, however. The struggle over the allegiance of the Zulu people is not a simple tribal conflict. Instead, the Zulu are internally split; while rural folk have been attracted to the Inkatha Freedom Party (which borrows Zulu cultural symbols like assegais, shields, and leopard skins), many urban Zulus support the ANC. Political killings in the countryside have usually arisen when ANC adherents have sought to mobilize support back home, only to invoke a counter-reaction from Inkatha traditionalists who perceive a threat to the power and status of the *Amakhosi* (chiefs). While the level of political violence between the IFP and the ANC declined in Kwazulu-Natal after 1994, it rose again as 1999 elections approached. Persistent clashes prompted the top leadership of the two parties to reopen negotiations, including talk of a governing alliance. To ease tensions and demonstrate trust, Mandela appointed IFP leader Buthelezi not only as minister of home affairs but also as acting president during the former's absences from the country.

Both Zulu and Afrikaner nationalists now seem to recognize that their communities' separation from the South African state is both undesirable and impractical. Instead, they have turned their attention to preserving languages and cultures. Under the interim constitution, Afrikaans was downgraded from one of two official languages and, when the terms of a permanent constitution were being negotiated in 1996, language rights became a critical issue. Afrikaner leaders sought to portray the ANC's multicultural project as an effort to subjugate linguistic minorities (including Zulu-speakers and Afrikaans-speaking Coloureds). Thus racial and ethnic differences were bridged by shared cultural concerns. Again, Mandela bent over backward to accommodate differences, recognizing that extremists among cultural minorities could constitute a threat to the stability of the political system if not incorporated within it.

Other potential bases for political identity include religion and gender. As elsewhere in Africa, religious movements that combine Christian and indigenous beliefs have strong popular appeal. The largest voluntary association in the country is the **Zion Christian Church**, which has more active members than the ANC or the trade-union confederation. This independent religious movement advocates traditional African values like *ubuntu* (community) and differs from the governing party's positions by opposing abortion and gay marriage and favoring the death penalty. Here, religion serves not so much to mobilize people into politics as to encourage withdrawal from a secular world that is seen as excessively materialistic, corrupt, and competitive. The social conservatism of many South Africans also expresses itself in the suppression of women. Whether in Afrikaner, Zulu, or Xhosa families, the older males dominate and try to confine women to the domestic sphere. Disrespect for females is expressed in disturbingly frequent incidents of domestic violence and rape, the latter an especially frightening prospect in a society where HIV-AIDS is rampant. Encouraged by guarantees against sexism in the **South African Constitution**, but set back by weak implementation, women in South Africa have yet to make a reality of gender equality.

Finally, while overt racial discrimination is no longer socially acceptable, new forms of exclusion are arising. Even as a new South African identity takes shape, nationalism reveals a darker side. Xenophobia (fear of the "other") is on the rise as hundreds of thousands of political refugees and economic migrants from other parts of Africa (especially from unstable Zimbabwe) have streamed into the country since the democratic transition. In the context of an economy that cannot generate enough employment for local entrants into the labor market, foreigners are too often blamed for job shortages, diseases, and criminal activities for which they are not responsible. Attacks on strangers are on the rise. And political tolerance – both within South Africa's diverse citizenry and between citizens and outsiders – remains in short supply.

Contemporary Political Interests

If the development of an industrial economy helped to dissolve divisions between the races, then it also helped to create social classes. At the same time as South Africans have tried to shrug off the ethnic labels imposed by apartheid, they have devised new forms of political solidarity based on economic interests. As in other capitalist economies, class conflict in South Africa revolves mainly around the divergence of interests between business and labor.

Under apartheid, the government and private companies got together to prohibit African workers from joining trade unions, engaging in collective bargaining, or going on strike. But a large, semiskilled, industrial workforce with the power to bring economic production to a halt could not be contained indefinitely. Escalating wildcat strikes in the metal, textile, and chemical industries forced government and employers alike to officially recognize African trade unions in 1979 and to acquiesce to the formation of a federated Congress of South African Trade Unions (**COSATU**) in 1985. By 2000, 460 registered trade unions had a total membership of about 3.5 million, about half of whom were affiliated with COSATU. At first, the unions focused on securing better wages and working conditions, refusing to align themselves with any political movement. With the advent of COSATU, however, organized labor entered the "national democratic struggle" under the leadership of the ANC.

As in Poland and Zambia, the labor movement was a key actor in South Africa's late twentieth-century transition to democracy. In 1991, COSATU successfully pushed for amendments to the Labor Relations Act that established mediation procedures for settling industrial disputes. When political negotiations over the country's future began to break down in 1992, COSATU orchestrated the "rolling mass action" (marches, stoppages, and stay-aways) that backed up the ANC's bargaining positions. And, in 1994, when the ANC announced lists of candidates for national and provincial parliaments in the GNU, the names of 70 COSATU leaders were included.

Because the labor movement played a crucial role in building support for the ANC's electoral victory, COSATU expected the new government to adopt labor-friendly policies. In practice, however, worker interests were not always protected, in part because the ANC had also developed close ties with private capital. Contacts grew from tentative overtures between business and political leaders in the late 1980s to substantial corporate contributions to the ANC's election campaigns after 1994. In the intervening period, entrepreneurs had set up projects to uplift the poor, brought together diverse interest groups to discuss options for the future, and sponsored research on policies for the postapartheid era. By the time Mandela put together the national unity government, it seemed only natural that he would seek guidance from Harry Oppenheimer – former chairman of Anglo-American Corporation, South Africa's largest conglomerate – about appointments to key economic portfolios in the cabinet.

Though learning occurred on both sides, contacts with business interests – both domestic and international – transformed the ANC's approach to economic policy. The party had long preferred a socialist strategy based on the "seizure" of the "commanding heights of the economy," such as land, industries, and banks. Even as Mandela was released from prison in 1990, he reiterated the movement's commitment to nationalization of the means of production and the redistribution of wealth. But moderate voices within the ANC began to question whether it was advisable to grab property and raise taxes in an era of mobile international capital. By late 1991, on a visit to the United States, Mandela reassured corporate executives, the World Bank, and U.S. President George H. W. Bush that nationalization was no longer in the cards. Instead, the ANC declared that economic growth was the best means for addressing poverty, which in turn was only possible if private companies – local and foreign – felt confident enough to invest.

In revising its economic strategy the ANC did not completely jettison a role for the state. After all, the new government announced a Reconstruction and Development Policy (**RDP**) that envisaged socioeconomic "transformation" through public investments in education, housing, health care, electricity, and other basic amenities. The fact that the RDP was originally a COSATU blueprint is evidence that popular, working-class interests remained critical in shaping ANC thinking. But the RDP never really addressed and was unable to satisfy citizens' (and the unions') most pressing demand: jobs. To this end, the government introduced an orthodox macroeconomic policy framework in 1996 known as GEAR (for Growth, Employment and Redistribution). Following market principles and reflecting fiscal discipline, GEAR sought to accelerate South Africa's annual economic growth rate to 6 percent by reducing budget deficits, deregulating the economy, and selling off selected state-owned enterprises. By 2006, GEAR had been supplemented by a program known as ASGISA (Accelerated and Shared Growth Initiative for South Africa) to refocus attention on poverty alleviation via public works, service delivery, and welfare payments. Since South Africa will host the 2010 soccer

World Cup planners hope that the construction of sports stadiums and transport and tourism infrastructure will help to boost investment, growth, and jobs.

The South African government thus finds itself at the fulcrum of class conflict. It must perform a delicate balancing act between rival political interests. How can it satisfy the expectations of the downtrodden for improved living standards without at the same time driving away the capital and skills needed to make the economy grow? In search of solutions, the government built on the country's experience with negotiation and compromise. It established a bargaining forum called the National Economic Development and Labour Council (**NEDLAC**) in which workers, employers, and the state discuss proposed legislation before Parliament enacts it. NEDLAC represents what political scientists call corporatism: an institutional arrangement that channels conflicting interests into a process of cooperative decision making. Because corporatism allows extra weight to groups who are more powerful than their mere numbers would allow, it has led to economic policies in South Africa that are more business oriented than most ANC supporters would like. But, even as trade has been liberalized and government budgets have been reined in, COSATU has managed to prevent the introduction of labor market reforms, ensure the introduction of a minimum wage, and slow down plans for the privatization of public enterprises. Through this judicious mix of policies, overt class conflict has been averted.

The government can also afford to make economic adjustments without losing too much political support, however, in part because the class structure is changing. As race barriers weaken, a black middle class is emerging. In the decade before 1994, the personal disposable income of Africans increased by more than 35 percent, while the disposable income of whites dropped slightly. Since 1994, a new African elite has eagerly embraced moneymaking and American-style consumption, perhaps because private enrichment was so long denied them. Responding to legislation requiring "employment equity" and "black economic empowerment," the private sector has created new opportunities for previously excluded people to advance in their careers and to purchase stocks, shares, and even entire companies. As a result, income inequality is proving resistant to change and has risen to almost the same level within the black community as for the society as a whole.

Even the working class is not immune from the allure of the market. The median wage of unionized workers is more than double the median for nonunionized counterparts, indicating that trade unionism in South Africa is scarcely a movement of poor people. COSATU's member unions have established profit-making companies and invested worker retirement funds in stock holdings. Trade-union leaders now sit on the boards of major corporations, including in the deeply conservative mining sector. These movements in the class structure have unsettled relations within the trade unions and between unionized workers and the unemployed. Politicians and labor leaders face charges that they have "sold out" to capitalism and calls have started for a new political party of the left. The more militant members of COSATU see their own organization as the vehicle for such a party, openly urging the unions to split from their political alliance with the ANC.

As South Africans come to reject ethnic labels in favor of class identities – in a 2002 survey, just as many people saw themselves in terms of occupation as of race – a foundation is being laid for civil society. Voluntary associations and social movements have always thrived in South Africa, as has an independent press. Whereas, in the past, dissenters organized resistance outside the bounds of conventional politics, today they partake in the democratic process as forceful advocates on a range of single-issue policies, especially employment, land reform, and HIV-AIDS. In 2001, for example, protests by the Treatment Action Campaign (TAC) forced reluctant pharmaceutical firms to reduce the price of antiretroviral drugs and the government to grudgingly begin a drug distribution program.

Democratic Political Institutions

The purpose of government institutions is to provide authoritative decisions that resolve political conflicts among opposing identities and interests. To govern ("rule") is to issue decisions ("rulings") that are codified in law ("rules") that must be obeyed by everyone. Under an authoritarian regime (like the old apartheid system), citizens reluctantly comply with the commands of government institutions because they fear that the state will unleash violence against them if they do not. Under a democratic regime (such as South Africa since 1994), citizens grant compliance more willingly because they regard elected institutions as having been legitimately installed. Ideally, a good government is both responsive to popular demands and effective at enforcing its own policy decisions.

Several key institutions are essential to a democracy. These include a constitution with a bill of rights, a separation of governmental powers, a regular cycle of open elections, and a vibrant and autonomous civil society. Each of these (sets of) political institutions is examined in the section that follows. And special mention is made of two bodies – the **Constitutional Court** and the **Truth and Reconciliation Commission** (**TRC**) – that have made distinctive contributions to South Africa's development as a democracy.

The South African Constitution of 1996 is both liberal and social democratic. Widely praised internationally, it was produced by the GNU's Constituent Assembly and is the jewel of the first government's political accomplishments. As well as a full gamut of civil and political liberties (for example, to freedom of speech and association and to voting), the constitution's bill of rights also includes wide guarantees of access to food, water, education, health care, and social security. Certain offsetting provisions reflect South

Africa's unique history: Freedom of expression is qualified with prohibitions on hate speech; rights to cultural heritage are allowed only to the extent that they do not infringe the rights of others; and property rights do not preclude the possibility of redistribution (for example, through affirmative action and land reform). Adopted by an overwhelming parliamentary majority, the constitution has won broad acceptance throughout society. Given the generosity of its promises, however, it has yet to prove fully enforceable.

As in other countries, the constitution of South Africa lays the foundation for the rule of law. It requires a measured separation of central government powers, assigning these conventionally to legislative, executive, and judicial branches of government. It is unconventional, however, in the relative balance ascribed to the executive and legislature, resulting in a democratic system that is neither presidential nor parliamentary, but a hybrid of the two. On one hand, the constitution (rather than Parliament) is supreme. And the constitution provides for an executive president who enjoys extensive powers of appointment and decision making. On the other hand, the president is not elected directly but by the National Assembly from among its own members. The president must select cabinet members from the assembly and dissolve the government if faced with a "no confidence" vote. Because of these formal limitations, the South African chief political executive looks on paper more like a Commonwealth prime minister than the unconstrained "super-president" commonly found in other African republics.

In practice, however, the ANC's large working majority in Parliament has compromised the separation of powers by allowing the executive to control the legislature. In South Africa, the Parliament is bicameral, meaning that it has two houses: the National Assembly and the National Council of Provinces, both currently based in Cape Town. Parliament has been active, passing an average of over 100 laws in each of its sessions, which together have reversed the thrust of apartheid legislation. But all bills originate from the president's office or from other executive departments, rendering the legislature the weakest and most passive of the three branches of government. Major decisions on economic policy – like the shift of emphasis from service delivery under the RDP, to job creation under GEAR, and to public welfare under ASGISA – are made within the executive branch and without much consultation with MPs. Nor are parliamentary checks effective. For example, during 2001, the ANC blocked an effort by Parliament's Standing Committee on Public Accounts to investigate a massive corruption scandal in the Ministry of Defense over a U.S. $5 billion arms deal.

So far, the judiciary has been more independent than the legislature. A Constitutional Court, which has final say on fundamental legal matters, rejected the draft constitution until provisions were included to strengthen the rights of individuals, the autonomy of provincial governments, and public oversight by watchdog agencies. Although being careful to frame its judgments narrowly, the court has already tilted the scales in favor of social justice: In landmark rulings in 2001 and 2002, it directed that the state must provide drugs to combat mother-to-child transmission of HIV and that the homeless have a right to state-provided housing. In so doing, the courts have required that the executive justify its policies and demonstrate that its policies point toward the realization of socioeconomic rights. Even while dragging its feet on implementation – for example by only slowly rolling out antiretroviral drugs – the executive branch has ultimately respected these rulings. A commitment to a rule of law is all the more remarkable given that the judiciary is the least "transformed" branch of government: elderly white judges held over from the previous regime continue to serve on the higher courts.

Because South Africa's recent past was marred by gross violations of human rights, the new order included special institutions to deal with this legacy. Again to international acclaim, the new government established a Truth and Reconciliation Commission (TRC) under the supervision of Archbishop Desmond Tutu, another Nobel Peace Prize winner. The TRC was charged with three tasks: to uncover the truth about the abuses of apartheid; to offer amnesty to those who confessed to politically motivated crimes; and to make reparations to victims. The commission sought to resolve South Africa's past problems of political violence without causing an escalating spiral of punishment and revenge. Armed with the stick of subpoena power and the carrot of amnesty, it was easily the most powerful commission of its kind ever created.

Several thousand victims testified before the TRC's public hearings, which provided a chance for those who had suffered in silence at last to be heard. A stream of low-level apartheid functionaries also came forward to admit, in chilling detail, how they served as the covert hit men and torturers of the old order. The commission also delved into the misdeeds of the liberation movements, including abuses in former ANC training camps and the alleged involvement of Winnie Madikizela-Mandela (then Nelson's wife) in several murders in the late 1980s. The TRC's extraordinary achievement was to cast a spotlight on the inner secrets of the apartheid years, making denial difficult and reducing the likelihood that its horrors can ever recur.

By the time the TRC issued its final report in 2003, however, it faced criticism from across the political spectrum. Unconfessed perpetrators from all political parties cried foul. Because senior figures like former prime minister P. W. Botha and IFP leader Mangosuthu Buthelezi refused to testify, the truth remained obscure about state-sponsored killings and the civil war between the ANC and the IFP in Kwazulu-Natal. The families of victims also expressed anger at a process that opened old wounds and offered minimal compensation and little succor afterward. Indeed, the TRC confirmed that truth does not always lead to reconciliation. The graffito scrawled on an underpass – "Tutu has made them confess, now we will kill them!"– surely represents an extreme view, but it nonetheless captures the missing element: justice. For many South Africans, the righting of wrongs will require more than criminal justice for official perpetrators; it also requires a meaningful measure of social justice that involves broad sacrifices from apartheid's beneficiaries.

In the context of persistent social divisions, the political institutions of democracy, including multiparty elections, offer one way forward. By 2004, South Africa had conducted three national multiparty contests and introduced a system of elected local government. All these elections were professionally and peacefully conducted to the point that free and fair electoral competition must now be regarded as a routine norm of South African politics. In a survey conducted in 2005, some 82 percent of the population – and a higher proportion of blacks – preferred to "choose leaders through regular, honest and open elections" than to "adopt other methods."

In both the interim and new constitutions, South Africans opted for an electoral system based on proportional representation (PR), which seemed like an appropriate choice. In contrast to the previous, constituency-based, winner-take-all system that had helped the (Afrikaner) National Party rise to power, rules of proportionality now ensure that all voices are heard. In practice in South Africa, however, PR has also created new problems. Because candidates for legislative office are not chosen by local districts, but are selected by their parties to run on a national electoral list, citizens have found it difficult to hold MPs accountable. And, in 2003, the ruling party blocked proposed electoral reforms that would have introduced smaller, multi-member constituencies, thus allowing voters to clearly identify their representatives. As such, a "representation gap" has emerged between voters and political elites.

The government was no longer constitutionally bound to share power with minority parties, although the ANC again chose to offer cabinet seats to the IFP in 1999 and the New National Party (NNP) in 2004. The second national elections in 1999 marked the dissolution of the GNU and the completion of the country's transition to a multiparty democracy, which now featured a government in power and an out-of-power opposition. With each passing election, the majority party's hold on the electorate has grown ever more secure: the ANC increased its share of votes to 66 percent in 1999 and 70 percent in 2004. In so doing, it induced parliamentarians from the NNP (the former party of apartheid) to first "cross the floor" in 2003 and to then dissolve their party in 2005. The ANC thereby gained outright control of all nine provincial legislatures, and cemented a two-thirds majority in the national legislature, sufficient to change the constitution. Its nearest competitor, the white-led Democratic Alliance, won just 12 percent of the vote in 2004. In short, the ANC faces no serious electoral competitor.

Rather than regarding these lopsided developments as an unwelcome harbinger of one-party rule, however, many citizens apparently see the ANC as the country's best bet for reducing the gap between the "haves" and the "have-nots." To be sure, voter turnout was down in 2004 (to about 75 percent of registered voters, and smaller percentage of all eligible adults), perhaps because supporters of opposition parties stayed home, thinking that their vote would hardly count. But the ANC, having delivered in good part on promises to improve popular access to housing, electricity, water, health care, and pension services, can convincingly portray itself as the representative of the impoverished majority. Even the widespread eruption of popular protests in 2005 against slow service delivery in South Africa's worst slums did not seriously dent the ANC's margin of victory in 2006 local government elections. But these events did tend to confirm that South Africans judge the consolidation of democracy in terms of the satisfaction of material expectations, an issue to which we return at the end of this chapter.

Bureaucratic State Institutions

When South Africans refer to "government" (or **Pretoria**, the city where most government offices are found) they usually mean the executive. The executive is the branch of government charged with running the country between elections. It comprises the president, the deputy president, the cabinet, and all government ministries and departments. The Department of Finance (in consultation with an independent Financial and Fiscal Commission that oversees the distribution of revenues to provincial and local governments) is responsible for drawing up the national budget. Within the executive branch, the Policy and Advisory Services unit within the Presidency and the budget planners within the Treasury have centralized the most power.

From the outset, President Nelson Mandela concentrated on solving high-profile political problems and performing the presidency's ceremonial duties; he delegated policy making and routine administrative decisions to Deputy President Thabo Mbeki. In a smooth leadership succession in 1999, the ANC prepared the country and the world for Mandela's retirement and ensured Mbeki's ascent to the presidency. While South Africans may never love the technocratic Mr. Mbeki as much as they do the charismatic Mr. Mandela, the former has proved a capable steward of the economy, restoring a measure of investment and growth and, in 2007, securing the first public budget surplus in a generation. But Mbeki has played a less sure hand in political and social affairs. By pulling power into the president's office and appointing loyalists in the provinces (techniques for sidelining rivals), he has often alienated rank and file members within the ANC. And by disputing whether HIV causes AIDS and failing to challenge dictator Robert Mugabe in neighboring Zimbabwe, he has caused citizens and outsiders alike to question his judgment.

At the time of writing, South Africans were beginning to debate heatedly the next presidential succession, which is an untested procedure in any new democracy. Mbeki's term as party president expires at the end of 2007 and he is constitutionally prohibited from seeking a third term as national president in 2009. In 2005, Mbeki fired the heir apparent, Jacob Zuma, from the national vice-presidency as the latter became implicated in the scandal about bribes for arms contracts. But the case was thrown out of court – as was an unrelated charge of rape – releasing Zuma to resume his political career. Because Zuma draws support from both the ANC's left wing of trade-union allies as well as from his more conservative Zulu co-ethnics, and because he never surrendered his post as vice-president of the party, the populist Zuma remains the strongest contender to succeed managerial Mbeki at the helm of both the party and the state. Given the ANC's electoral dominance, its candidate is virtually assured of election to the national presidency.

Much like the legislature, the executive branch of government in South Africa is strongly influenced by the majority political party. The top organs of the ANC – its National Congress, National Executive Committee (NEC), and National Working Committee (NWC) – lay down the policies for the government to follow. The NEC is the party's highest policy-making body between party congresses and the NWC is responsible for the day-to-day running of the organization. Most importantly, because almost all cabinet ministers also serve as ANC officeholders, party ideas regularly find their way into government policy. But, if ANC activists aim to blur the line between the executive and the party, senior civil servants seek to define it clearly. The directors-general (DGs) of government departments – the senior civil servants who provide professional advice and management – are appointed by the president but are sometimes able to influence policy in their own right. Similarly, insofar as government programs are funded by foreign aid, international donors insist on technical requirements that counterbalance the party's political weight.

Precisely because modern governments control considerable resources – like budgets, expertise, and coercion – the potential always exists for abuses of power. This threat increases to the extent that the ANC government aims to accumulate and centralize authority in order to radically "transform" society. Certainly, South Africa's previous National Party government was highly secretive, an impulse that still guides bureaucrats today; and a culture of corruption took deep root in the former homeland governments that have been incorporated into current provincial administrations. A 2005 public opinion poll revealed that more than one out of five South African citizens think that "most" public officials are corrupt and that one-half thinks that government is performing poorly at "combating corruption." A string of scandals reported in the national press – not only the spectacular arms deal, but more mundane violations like the illegal sale of drivers' licenses, nonexistent "ghost workers" on the state payroll, and violations in contract tendering procedures – suggests that there is substance behind popular perceptions.

On paper, South Africa's constitution provides plentiful antidotes to the abuse of executive power. A Human Rights Commission is charged to redress violations and educate the citizenry; a public protector receives citizen complaints about lax or unfair administration; and an auditor-general reports to legislatures on executives' use of taxpayer money. At first, the ruling party sought to expand these ample provisions for public oversight, for example by passing a model code of conduct for parliamentarians. With the passage of time, however, the ANC has backed off from these early commitments to transparency, for instance by stalling on an Open Democracy Bill that would provide freedom of information about the work of government. And, in practice, the operations of all public watchdog agencies have been limited by budgetary constraints imposed by the Ministry of Finance; none functions comprehensively at the provincial or local levels, where most abuses occur. If such institutions cannot be sustained, executive accountability may be difficult to obtain in this new democracy.

At the heart of executive authority is the coercive power of the state. Under apartheid, the South African government used the state security apparatus – the army, the police, and the intelligence services – not only against neighboring countries, but against its own people. Since 1994, the role of the army has been redefined (it is now charged to guard against external threats and to keep peace in regional conflicts) and the defense budget has been slashed in favor of social spending. A smaller South African National Defense Force (SANDF) has been built by combining selected elements from the old regular army and the armed wings of the guerrilla movements. While not entirely eliminating racial tensions over promotions and salaries, the merger helped the executive to establish civilian control over the military, greatly reducing the possibility of an illegal coup (seizure of power).

More troublesome are the intelligence services and the police, which still contain elements uncommitted to the new political order, some of whom have indulged in disruptive dirty tricks. Citizens have not forgotten that the South African Police Services (SAPS) were used as paramilitary shock troops to impose order during the township uprisings of the 1970s and 1980s. The police are widely distrusted by South Africans of all races because they lack professional training (for example, in crime control and community relations) and because their ranks have not been fully purged of racists and criminals. This lack of public confidence is not alleviated by a justice system that regularly fails to convict offenders. Instead, prosecutors are overworked, witnesses are inadequately protected, hearings are endlessly postponed, and many badly prepared cases are thrown out of court. As such, the government is widely regarded as soft on crime and unsympathetic to the plight of ordinary people who fear the depredations of increasingly brazen and violent criminal gangs.

Which brings us to the biggest challenge faced by the new South African government: building institutional capacity. As stated earlier, governments must be effective at implementing their own policies and at eliciting citizen compliance. In short, they must govern. The first decade of the new South Africa was a productive interlude of progressive reform in which popular policies were enacted in almost every governmental sector. But amid the welter of policy papers, a nagging question remains: Is the executive branch equipped to ensure proper implementation?

The task of building what the ANC calls a "developmental state" in South Africa is complicated by the complex structure of government. In order to accommodate the country's social diversity, the constitution establishes three tiers of government: the national, the provincial, and the local. Each tier has responsibility for particular public functions. Whereas the national government is responsible for tasks like defense and most taxation, the provinces take the lead on health and education among other things; for their part, local governments must deliver a range of municipal services like street cleaning, road maintenance, and waste disposal. Each tier has a legislative body (provincial parliament or local government council) and an executive body (a provincial executive council or a municipal/district administration). Simply staffing all these units of government when the majority population lacks relevant education and experience is only the start of the capacity building challenge.

Generally speaking, the state apparatus tends to perform less well as one moves from well-established institutions at the political center to new and untested structures in the locality. And yet, South Africa's great social needs arise primarily among poor populations at the grassroots level. The new government therefore is trying to take on an expanded range of services to mass populations at the same time as revising public policies and constructing new delivery institutions, often from scratch. As one politician put it, this is akin to moving the furniture into a new house before you have finished building it.

Even at the political center, civil servants sometimes lack the management and technical skills necessary to run a modern state, leading to a heavy reliance on external consultants. The South African Revenue Service (SARS) has shown improvement in collecting income, corporate, and sales taxes, for example by meeting revenue targets in 2004. But customs control at international airports and harbors leaves much to be desired. Basic middle management skills are scarce at the provincial level, where 57 percent of the public budget is actually expended. As a result, provincial ministries responsible for education and health have been unable to meet goals of providing universal service coverage ("education and health for all"). Although many previously disadvantaged South Africans have obtained school places or preventive health care for the first time, the quality of such services is falling. In the localities, life goes on much as before; established suburban areas enjoy a full range of modern services but too many informal settlements endure without paved roads, running water, and electricity.

On the surface, the problems of institutional capacity would appear to be financial. In about one-third of urban townships and rural areas, the local authorities cannot collect enough revenues to cover the costs of delivering basic services. Provincial governments are unable to fully spend their annual budgets or to adequately monitor the use of funds that they do actually disburse. But the vacuum of governmental authority is fundamentally political, originating in unresolved struggles from the apartheid era. For example, many township dwellers still continue to resist payment of fees and taxes for services delivered by local councils, even though these bodies are now democratically chosen. And in some rural areas, traditional leaders and their followers refuse to recognize the authority of elected councilors, whom they regard as interlopers in the jurisdiction of chiefs. Thus, among South African citizens, the legitimacy of democratic institutions is far from universally accepted.

Conclusion: Consolidating Democracy?

The long-term challenge in South Africa is to consolidate recent achievements of peace, prosperity, and democracy. Even though the country's transition from authoritarian rule was led by bold political initiatives, the health of its fragile new institutions will hinge on subsequent economic and social developments. The emergence of a new black business class and the continuing influence of unionized workers will limit the extent to which the government can fully address mass welfare needs. Yet satisfying the material interests of disadvantaged identity groups in the context of an AIDS crisis is key to the country's future. As President Mandela stated when opening Parliament in 1998, "our performance should be judged above all on whether our programs are positively affecting the lives of the most vulnerable sections of society."

In this task, the South African government faces numerous knotty dilemmas. By way of conclusion, we will consider just six. Can the economy grow fast enough to enable a redistribution of wealth and opportunity? Can institutions be de-racialized at the same time as effectively delivering services? Can crime be aggressively fought within a human rights regime? Can political and economic progress continue if citizens are incapacitated by epidemic disease? Can South Africa avoid developing a one-party dominant party system, along with the political pathologies that this system has wrought elsewhere in Africa? And, finally, can democratic institutions function well if citizens are not strongly attached to democracy? The ways in which these paradoxes are resolved will determine the kind of economy, society, and polity that South Africa will attain in the future.

First, can the economy grow fast enough to enable redistribution? South African political leaders are bound to be preoccupied with economic growth, a prerequisite for creating enough jobs to ease chronic black impoverishment. Yet the formal sector's ability to generate employment has slumped, with mining, manufacturing, and agriculture all recently experiencing net job losses. Foreign investment was at first slow to arrive in South Africa, was disrupted during the Asian financial crashes of 1997–1998, and only recently has helped generate growth above 4 percent from 2005 to 2007. While jobs are now being created, the stubbornly high unemployment rate has strengthened the hand of critics (like COSATU and the Communist Party) who call for the state to play a larger role. Ironically, however, the more the state intervenes in the economy, the less competitive South Africa becomes in attracting essential private investment from both domestic and international sources. Such are the narrow policy options available to a government whose economy reentered the world marketplace at a moment when capital had become highly mobile.

Second, can public institutions be de-racialized at the same time as effectively delivering services? The South African government is trying to "downsize" a bloated bureaucracy while also "transforming" it (that is, making it more socially representative and responsive). Some ministries and departments have been virtually paralyzed by clashes between old-order officials and new civil service recruits, often in disputes over affirmative action. Such logjams contribute to the crisis of institutional capacity that has slowed South Africa's post-transition development. Malaysia's experience suggests that preferences for formerly disadvantaged groups can be implemented with little conflict in a context of a rapidly growing economy. But where job opportunities remain limited, affirmative action implies real losses to the formerly advantaged, leading those with marketable skills to seek opportunities abroad. Already, South Africa has lost too many doctors, accountants, and engineers whose talents are vital to the country's progress.

Third, can the government fight crime and respect human rights at the same time? Because democratization imposes limits on the use of state power, it relaxes controls over society. People who previously feared state repression are freed to engage in new pursuits, both legal and illicit. In South Africa, evidence is rising that former combatants from the apartheid conflict – both regular soldiers and guerrillas – are applying their war skills to careers in violent crime. Criminals of all types are taking advantage of the ANC's progressive policies, like the abolition of the death penalty and guarantees against arbitrary arrest and detention. Lacking confidence that the state will punish wrongdoers, citizens in South Africa are increasingly taking the law into their own hands. The response varies across social groups: In the wealthy enclaves, people retreat behind the protection of private security guards; in poorer communities, they resort to vigilante action. Quite regardless of whether the government cracks down, crime threatens to undermine many of the gains of democratization.

Fourth, HIV-AIDS also threatens to reverse many of the country's recent economic and political gains. Because the pandemic strikes young people in the prime of their lives, it strips valuable human capital from the workforce and the electorate, and weakens the capacity of today's generation to pass on skills and knowledge to the next. The South African Bureau for Economic Research predicts that HIV will reduce the country's economic growth rate by .5 percent for each year over the next decade. And the Independent Electoral Commission, among many other political and economic institutions, recognizes that it will have to replace many of its experienced staff, while still continuing to provide a high quality service. While we do not know for sure that declining electoral turnout is attributable in part to AIDS, it stands to reason that sick people, caregivers, and young people disillusioned with the government for delaying treatments are unlikely to be enthusiastic voters.

Fifth, elections in democratic South Africa have entrenched the ANC's hold on power. This dominant political party now effectively controls all levers of executive and legislative authority and it possesses a large enough parliamentary majority to potentially water down the checks and balances embodied in a rule of law. Absent a future realignment of voters along nonracial lines or the breakaway of a labor-led black opposition to the left – both unlikely events – the ANC's electoral dominance is assured for the foreseeable future. From this unassailable position, an insulated ruling party has few incentives to respond to popular demands for political accountability. Instead, ANC leaders may be tempted to change the rules of the game to cover up corruption or to squelch political dissent. So far, the constitution remains sovereign but, as long as South Africa lacks the counterweight of a viable political opposition, constitutional rule will remain tenuous.

Finally, can democracy ever be consolidated in the absence of a supportive political culture? Observers have hailed the impressive array of democratic institutions embodied in South Africa's new constitution. But the behavior of citizens reveals low levels of political tolerance among competing social groups and strong popular attachments to antidemocratic political traditions. Certainly, there is little in South Africa's political history – whether in Zulu chieftaincy, the apartheid state, or exiled liberation movements – that nurtured democratic commitments. We should not be surprised, therefore, that South Africans do not value democracy intrinsically, that is, as an end in itself: Just one-quarter of respondents in a national survey associate democracy with civil and electoral rights. Instead, South Africans tend to regard democracy instrumentally, as a means to other ends: Almost one-half associate it with jobs, education, and housing. And a similar proportion of citizens say they would be willing to give up elections for a leader who would provide these material goods.

Thus South Africa has a distance to travel before its formal political institutions are transformed into a living, breathing democracy. Those who expect democracy to deliver social and economic equality may be sorely disappointed. All that democracy bestows is political equality. It does not guarantee that disparities of social and economic status will be redressed, though, comparatively, democracies have a slightly better track record at redistributing wealth than do authoritarian regimes.

A culture of democracy is not a lost cause in South Africa. There are at least two hopeful signs. The first is that South Africans are likely to remember that democratization restored to people of all races the human dignity that apartheid denied. This they will not surrender easily. The second is that, when push came to shove, South Africans of widely differing backgrounds resorted to negotiation and compromise to find their way out of the country's deepest political crisis. One must therefore be confident that, in building new political institutions, South Africans will recognize afresh that, however divided their identities, their interests are inexorably connected.

BIBLIOGRAPHY

Butler, Anthony. *Contemporary South Africa*. New York: Palgrave Macmillan, 2004.

Cling, Jean-Pierre. *From Isolation to Integration: The Post-Apartheid South African Economy*. Pretoria: Protea Book House, 2001.

Friedman, Steven. "South Africa: Building Democracy after Apartheid." In E. Gyimah-Boadi, ed., *Democratic Reform in Africa: The Quality of Progress*. Boulder, CO: Lynne Rienner Press, 2004. Chapter 10, pp. 235–261.

Friedman, Steven, and Doreen Atkinson, eds. *The Small Miracle: South Africa's Negotiated Settlement*. Randburg: Ravan Press, 1994.

Gibson, James, and Amanda Gouws. *Overcoming Intolerance in South Africa: Experiments in Democratic Persuasion*. New York: Cambridge University Press, 2003.

Johnson, R. W., and Lawrence Schlemmer, eds. *Launching Democracy in South Africa: The First Open Election, April 1994*. New Haven, CT: Yale University Press, 1996.

Lodge, Tom. *South African Politics: From Mandela to Mbeki*. Cape Town and Johannesburg: David Philip Publishers, 2003.

Mandela, Nelson. *Long Walk to Freedom: The Autobiography of Nelson Mandela*. Boston, Little Brown, 1994.

Mattes, Robert. "South Africa: Democracy without the People?" *Journal of Democracy* 13, no. 1 (January 2002): 22–36.

Natrass, Nicoli. *The Moral Economy of AIDS in South Africa*. New York: Cambridge University Press, 2004.

Price, Robert. *The Apartheid State in Crisis: Political Transformation in South Africa, 1975–1990*. New York: Oxford University Press, 1991.

Seekings, Jeremy, and Nicoli Natrass. *Class, Race, and Inequality in South Africa*. New Haven, CT: Yale University Press, 2005.

Thompson, Leonard. *A History of South Africa*. New Haven, CT: Yale University Press, 1995.

TABLE 12.1. Key Phases in South Africa's Political Development

Time period	Regime	Global context	Interests/identities/ institutions	Developmental path
until 19th century	small-scale chieftaincies, European outposts	European trade with Asia; slavery and forced labor	access to plentiful resources/ emergence of mixed races/limited institutional reach	imperial trade
1806–1853	Cape Colony (authoritarian, colonial)	colonial annexation; seizure of land; wars of conquest and resistance	struggles over land/construction of racial identities/British governors	early state-building and expansion
1853–1910	self-government by white settlers (authoritarian, oligarchic)	Industrial Revolution; discovery of minerals; influx of migrant populations	control of gold and diamond fields/ racial and ethnic warfare/elected legislative councils for whites only	consolidation of settler states
1910–1948	Union of South Africa (authoritarian, segregated)	World Wars I and II; globalization of industrial production	capitalist firms versus African workers/English- versus Afrikaner- speakers/exclusive parliamentary democracy	political unification; economic integration but social segregation
1948–1994	Republic of South Africa (authoritarian, apartheid)	United Nations; liberation wars; decolonization	growing labor unrest and organization/ Afrikaner versus African nationalism/ separate unequal institutions, police state	ethnic cleansing; state capitalism
1994– present	Republic of South Africa (democratic)	globalization of capital markets; global wave of democratization	persistent economic inequalities/ interdependence of racial groups/liberal constitution, majority rule	multiparty democracy; market capitalism

IMPORTANT TERMS

African National Congress the political party that led the struggle for majority rule in South Africa.

Afrikaners people of mainly Dutch extraction who comprise a distinctive linguistic subculture within the white community.

Amakhosi traditional tribal chiefs, for example of the Xhosa and Zulu.

apartheid an oppressive system of racial segregation that denied political and economic equality to blacks.

Bantu a language group that includes Zulu and Xhosa; formerly used by the apartheid regime as a general designation for Africans.

Mangosuthu Buthelezi president of the Inkatha Freedom Party, whose supporters are mainly rural Zulu.

Cape Colony the first outpost of white settlement, located in the southwest of present-day South Africa.

Coloureds the South African term for persons of mixed race; an identity group in their own right.

CODESA a multiparty forum convened in 1991 to negotiate the political future of the country.

Constitutional Court the supreme court, charged with deciding constitutional issues.

COSATU the national confederation of trade union organizations, politically affiliated with the ANC.

F. W. de Klerk the last Afrikaner president, known for releasing Mandela and negotiating a handover of white power.

GNU the Government of National Unity, formed as a coalition of the parties who won the most votes in the founding election of 1994.

homelands impoverished rural areas to which Africans were banished under apartheid, supposedly to govern themselves.

Inkatha a movement of Zulu traditionalists, represented by its own political party, the Inkatha Freedom Party.

Nelson Mandela president of the African National Congress and first national president of majority-ruled South Africa. Widely respected as the father of racial reconciliation in South Africa.

Thabo Mbeki Mandela's successor as national President; took office in July 1999.

National Party right-wing political party supported mainly by Afrikaans-speakers that came to power in 1948 and proceeded to implement apartheid.

NEDLAC a bargaining forum for discussion of policy proposals among the business, labor, and governmental sectors.

Population Registration Act the legislative foundation of apartheid, by which the South African people were classified into racial groups.

Pretoria administrative capital of the country; shorthand for "government."

RDP the Reconstruction and Development Policy of 1994, which envisaged rapid socioeconomic "transformation" of the lives of poor people.

Sharpeville site of a massacre of peaceful protesters in 1960 and a commemorated landmark of anti-apartheid resistance.

South African Constitution ratified in 1997, this document promises a wide range of long-denied political, social, and economic rights to the citizens of South Africa.

Truth and Reconciliation Commission (TRC) (established 1995) was charged to investigate the human rights abuses of apartheid.

Union of South Africa formed 1910, this confederation of former colonies defined the geographical boundaries of the modern South African state.

United Democratic Front a social movement of community organizations that confronted apartheid policies during the 1980s.

Zion Christian Church a mass-based, socially conservative, independent religious movement.

Xhosa an African language group concentrated in the Eastern Cape Province.

Zulu a centralized African kingdom found in Kwazulu-Natal Province.

STUDY QUESTIONS

1. What were the historical origins of South Africa's identity groups. When, where, and how did they first come into mutual contact?

2. Describe the new political interests that emerged as a consequence of industrial development in South Africa. On whose terms, and how, were differences of interest first resolved?

3. Apartheid has been described as a "system of institutionalized racism." What were its key institutions?

4. Trace the course of political resistance to racial segregation in South Africa from its beginnings to the release of Mandela in 1990.

5. What explains the failure of apartheid and the unexpected success of the democratic transition? Consider both socioeconomic developments within South Africa and influences from abroad.

6. In South Africa's deeply divided society, which are more important: political identities based on race or the economic interests of social classes?

7. In what sense do elections in South Africa take the form of an "ethnic census"? How does this tendency square with an emerging popular attachment to "South African" identity?

8. How are the divergent interests of business and labor addressed in contemporary South Africa? Identify key institutions.

9. From a comparative perspective, what is new and distinctive about the political institutions created in South Africa since 1994?

10. How are South Africa's current challenges – creating jobs, building state capacity, and controlling disease and crime – derived from its past?

EUROPEAN UNION

0 100 200 300 400 miles
0   200   400   600 kilometers

ICELAND

Norwegian Sea

NORWAY

SWEDEN

FINLAND

RUSSIA

Volga R.

Helsinki

Stockholm

Tallinn

ESTONIA

ATLANTIC OCEAN

North Sea

Baltic Sea

Riga

LATVIA

DENMARK

Copenhagen

LITHUANIA

Vilnius

IRELAND

Dublin

UNITED KINGDOM

Celtic Sea

London

NETH.

Amsterdam

BELG.

Brussels

Berlin

GERMANY

Warsaw

POLAND

BELARUS

Dnieper R.

UKRAINE

Paris

Seine R.

LUX.

Rhine R.

Prague

CZECH REPUBLIC

SLOVAKIA

Bratislava

Danube R.

MOLDOVA

FRANCE

SWITZ.

Vienna

AUSTRIA

Budapest

HUNGARY

ROMANIA

Bucharest

Black Sea

SLOVENIA

Zagreb

CROATIA

BOS. & HERZ.

SER. & MONT.

BULGARIA

Sofia

PORTUGAL

Lisbon

Madrid

SPAIN

Corsica

ITALY

Rome

MONT.

MAC.

ALB.

GREECE

TURKEY

Sardinia

Mediterranean Sea

Sicily

MALTA

Crete

Athens

Nicosia

CYPRUS

TUNISIA

ALGERIA

LIBYA

EGYPT

Nile R.

CHAPTER THIRTEEN

The European Union

Paulette Kurzer

Introduction

Students of political science are the first to admit that the European Union is an implausible construct. From our long tradition of scholarship, we know that sovereign states guard their government authority and independence zealously. So why would mature democracies agree to effectively reduce their policy independence and compromise their national sovereignty by transferring many areas of decision making to a supranational organization? Why would countries tie their hands by entering into one of the world's most dramatic examples of economic and political integration?

While the European Union (EU) is not a regular state, it shares many features of nation-states. On the one hand, it has no policing powers and it cannot fall back upon a judiciary to punish those who disobey its laws. It does not possess the legal right to employ coercion. It is also deprived of the legal authority to dictate defense and military policy. On the other, many functions associated with sovereign nation-states fall within the competence of the EU. Moreover, EU law is supreme and takes precedence over national law.

Therefore, the EU is a rare mix of a state and an international organization. It does not meet the traditional definition of a nation-state because it lacks core responsibilities and legal rights, which are considered central aspects of national sovereignty. It cannot employ the use of force to enforce compliance with its laws. It does not possess a proper defense and security dimension. It is not based on a distinct political system and its geographic boundaries have grown by leaps and bounds. Its citizens, moreover, are more diverse linguistically, culturally, and politically than what we usually observe in traditional nation-states. It counts 23 official languages when language is one of the principal instruments for forging a common identity.

In short, the EU resembles a federal regime where different policy domains are concentrated at different levels of governance. Some areas of decision making have remained in the hands of the member governments. Welfare and retirement programs, schooling and education, planning and zoning, public services and public sector are all under the purview of the member states. Environment, consumer protection, agriculture, market regulations, food safety, monetary policy, and regional aid are transferred in their totality or partly to the EU.

The aim of this chapter is to explain how and why mature democracies voluntarily agreed to transfer an ever larger array of specific policy domains to the supranational level. It concludes by examining some of the current challenges faced by the European Union.

The Origins of Regional Integration

A few years after the end of World War II, toward the late 1940s, European leaders had to square three major challenges: (1) how to keep communism and Soviet power at bay, (2) how to expedite economic recovery and secure political and social stability, and (3) how to handle the Federal Republic of Germany.

After the disasters of the Great Depression and World War II, a consensus emerged among Western leaders that economic prosperity was a powerful weapon against right-wing nationalist populism. Moreover, economic prosperity would also beef up the state capacity of West European countries, necessary to withstand the threat of Soviet aggression. Thus, economic growth and then redistribution were high on the agenda. The question was what to do about Germany, which occupied a geo-strategic position in Europe, and was its largest country and most important economy. Most European countries, and France in particular, felt decidedly ambivalent about a strong, dynamic Germany, which could pose a threat to their security.

Against this background, European integration emerged as a plausible solution. Here was a way to restrain both German nationalistic/authoritarian tendencies while promoting economic growth and bolstering Europe's military defense simultaneously. Regional integration presented itself as the most convenient strategy to accelerate economic growth as well as control the economic rise of Germany. Economic integration accompanied trade liberalization and expansion of export markets would bolster economic growth and manufacturing capacity. Second, regional integration would contain and moderate unpleasant forms of nationalism that had been so central in the emergence of the Nazi regime. It was thought that if regional integration turned out to be a real success, citizens' allegiance would shift from the nation state to European supranational organization, and ferocious militarism would be a thing of the past.

The architects of European integration also held on to the idea of **spill-over**. Although the thrust of integration focused on economics, eventually officials and politicians would have to cooperate politically to address new challenges. Market integration would lead to pressures to seek greater political coordination and elites would be forced to venture beyond economics into politics. In the end, at some future date, increased political cooperation would spur the creation of a federation of European states.

Moreover, the founders of the European Union offered regional integration as a solution to the question of what to do with Germany. Americans pushed for the full rehabilitation of Germany so that it could be part of the Western defense alliance. France would have preferred a weak fragmented Germany, which would pose no threat to its peaceful existence. It resisted the idea of a resurgent, economically dynamic Germany. Yet an economically self-sufficient Germany with limited military capabilities was a strategic necessity to keep Soviet aggression at bay and create a West European defense system. It followed that European institution building was seen as a way to placate French concerns about a resurgent Germany, manage the previous sources of tension and conflict in the European heartland, and promote economic growth and thereby political and social stability.

Looking back, therefore, there were compelling reasons why six nations ratified a treaty that transferred some policy functions to a supranational organization. The original six countries were France, West Germany, Italy, Belgium, the Netherlands, and Luxembourg (Benelux). In 1950 they signed a treaty establishing the **European Coal and Steel Community** (ECSC), which laid out provisions for a single market for coal and steel through the gradual elimination of tariffs and other barriers to trade. The ECSC went into operation in 1951. Britain was invited to participate but the Labour government had ambitious plans for their nationalized coal and steel industries while generally the British political class preferred to preserve its ties with the Commonwealth and the United States.

Though its goals were modest, the ECSC was a success and government leaders decided in 1955 to explore further options by creating a common market for other industries and atomic energy. This exploration led to the **Treaty of Rome**, signed in 1957 by the six governments. The treaty established two bodies: the **European Economic Community** (EEC) and the European Atomic Energy Commission. As before, it called for the elimination of all internal tariffs and the creation of common external tariffs over a period of 12 to 15 years. In 1967, the EEC and Euratom were merged and formed the European Community (EC).

The founders of European integration expressed the hope that increased economic interdependence would stimulate greater political coordination and cooperation. They felt sure that the endless demands to sort out economic, financial, legal, and social issues associated with the building of a common market would require extensive political deliberations and tactical compromises. They speculated that economic integration would bring the people of Europe to "ever closer union." The Treaty of Rome left many details blank and unspecified. Yet the assumption of many of its early promoters was that this was the first step toward a federal Europe. It was the final chapter of a horrific story in which internecine quarrels among European countries caused worldwide destruction.

Evolution of the European Union

Until the final wave of enlargement in 2004, the evolution of the EU mirrored the efforts of France and Germany to find a middle ground. They constituted the twin engines of integration because once they agreed on an issue or project, other countries usually came around and accepted the compromise. France and Germany held divergent ideas about regional integration, each representing an approach or opinion prevalent in the rest of Europe. If they were able to reconcile their differences, other countries felt assured that their interests would be protected as well.

The Treaty of Rome was based on such a bargain. By the mid-1950s, Germany had emerged as an economic powerhouse with a highly competitive export sector. German leaders were eager to export to the rest of Europe and for this reason were keen to push for trade liberalization. The French preferred to protect their agricultural sector and nurture their ties to former colonies by giving them access to the European market. The French were less enthusiastic about trade liberalization. The agreement they struck consisted therefore of opening the European/French market to German manufactured goods while the EEC market became accessible to French agricultural products and those of its former colonies. The economic bargain was underpinned by specific political calculations as well. The French political elite hoped to use the EEC to project ambitious foreign policy goals for itself and Europe. The German leadership sought to rehabilitate and normalize the Federal Republic of Germany by participating in an international venue. The Italians hoped to check the influence and appeal of the Left and to push modernization of different regions. The small states felt vulnerable surrounded by much larger economies and preferred to deal with their powerful neighbors in a multilateral context. Nevertheless, it was the deal struck between Germany and France that made it possible to proceed with a common market. Germany obtained free access to neighboring markets while France received support for an ailing and oversized agricultural sector. As part of the bargain, the heads of state agreed to create a **Common Agricultural Policy (CAP)**, which opened trade to agricultural goods while simultaneously designing a price support program to ensure a decent standard of living for its farmers (of which France had many). In return, tariffs on manufactured goods were abolished.

In 1973, after difficult negotiations, the United Kingdom, Ireland, and Denmark joined the EC. The enlargement, however, was plagued with difficulties and rancor. By the time Britain joined it was desperate to share the economic benefits of regional integration. For a long period of time, Britain had spurned the EC club, disliking its supranational framework and preferring to align itself with former colonies and the United States.

Alas, this scenario did not play out in ways in which the British had envisioned membership in the EC. By 1973, when Britain finally joined, the world economy was absorbing the first shock of steeply increased oil prices, while the immediate economic advantages of trade liberalization had been exhausted. Growth rates shrunk virtually everywhere. As the decade of the 1970s unfolded, advanced industrialized countries increasingly struggled with large trade deficits, growing budget deficits, and a chaotic international economy.

From the beginning, therefore, the British harbored resentments against European institutions. Britain's economy did not get a boost from membership because international trade slowed down in the wake of increased turmoil in currency markets and a more challenging global economic climate. Moreover, because the British had been in a rush to accede, they had failed to strike a very hard bargain and became, ironically, a large "net contributor" to the EC budget. In their haste to accept the conditions of membership, they did not pay much attention to the financial costs of the common agricultural policy, which was the biggest spending program of the EC. Because of its colonial history, Britain had always imported foodstuff from its dependent territories. Its own agricultural sector was minimal and barely benefited from the generous payments made by the EC. Thus, Britain was one of the poorer countries yet it paid more into the EC budget than it received back in terms of subsidies, financial aid, or regional development.

The first enlargement was therefore an unhappy experience and associated with economic uncertainty, an increase in protectionist posturing, growing budget deficits and unemployment, and sharpened diplomatic squabbling. Although the European institutions survived intact, they showed little life in the late 1970s and early 1980s.

Out of this bleak period grew one of the most innovative dynamic initiatives. The best way to understand the extraordinary turnaround was the depth of the crisis and the growing alarm expressed by observers and politicians alike that in the absence of bold thinking the EC might disappear. At the same time, national governments had pursued their own solutions to bring down high inflation, high unemployment, and growing budget deficits with little success. The national approaches had not yielded much improvement and the realization dawned that the EC countries faced very similar dilemmas, which could mean that a collective response might be more effective than divergent national strategies. The new awareness that Europe might hold the key to solving the economic crisis of welfare states also reflected two other developments. The question of Britain's budget contribution was resolved in 1984 by granting it a rebate that returned money to the British Treasury. In addition, in 1986, three new member states had joined, putting pressure on the institutions and member states to revisit the functioning and governance of the EC. Greece, Spain, and Portugal were poor countries that required substantial aid and transfer payments, but they were also enthusiastic Europeanists. They encouraged fresh thinking about the relationship between the different EC institutions, but also added a new dose of energy and focus to regional integration.

Originally, the Treaty of Rome had called for the free movement of goods, services, people, and capital. In the mid-1980s, heads of state agreed to move forward with this program and approved in 1985 the White Paper on Completing the Internal Market, which listed nearly 300 measures to meet the original goals outlined in the Treaty of Rome, namely the creation of a genuine single market. The measures would result in the free movement of goods, persons, services, and capital, and give birth to an area without internal boundaries.

The **single European market** and the **Single European Act** (SEA) reflected a combination of pressures, stemming from enlargement and the need for institutional reforms as well as the challenges of globalization. Supporters of the internal market made alarming statements that Europeans could choose survival or decline. Survival meant strengthening the European economy by pooling the combined resources of the member states. The white paper of the European Commission, the executive branch of the EU, laid out a timetable of eight years to achieve the end goal of a stronger, more competitive European economy (1985–1992). It is the task of the European Commission to submit legislative proposals (such as the white paper) to the member states and its proposals must in turn be approved by the Council of ministers, which represents the governments of the member states.

What were these measures? Of the nearly 300 measures, the bulk concentrated on physically removing cross-border formalities, of developing common European standards and norms, and of harmonizing value added and excise taxes. In sum, it amounted to a very ambitious scheme to liberalize and deregulate different aspects of the European economy.

Because this grand program was to be completed in a relatively short time frame, it included amendments to the Treaty of Rome. The Single European Act (in force since 1987) introduced **qualified majority voting** in the **Council of ministers**. The Council of ministers votes on proposals drafted by the European Commission and is the intergovernmental voice of the EU. It wields both legislative and executive powers and is thus one of the main actors in the European Union. Until the Single European Act, most legislative proposals required unanimity. Since the Council represents the national interests of member states, qualified majority voting was introduced in order to expedite the implementation of single market measures. Prior to this, member states had enjoyed a veto power to block any piece of legislation. Since unanimity would obviously greatly slow down, if not put an end to, the single market project, the member states agreed to accept a qualified majority vote for matters not considered too sensitive. Unanimity would continue to govern fiscal policy, border controls, workers' rights, and the movement of people. Because member states could be outvoted, the Single European Act extended the powers of the European Parliament in order to broaden the democratic foundation of the EC.

As officials in Brussels and the state capitals worked feverishly on meeting the deadlines of the single European market, momentous geo-political shifts transformed the very foundation of the EC. The withdrawal of the Soviet Union from Central and Eastern Europe put both German unification and further enlargement on the agenda. The Treaty of Rome specified that a country eligible for membership should fulfill two minimum requirements: be part of the European continent and history while embracing liberal democracy and market capitalism. The redrawing of the European map and the possibility of ten or more additional member states led to another **intergovernmental conference** to revisit the amended Treaty of Rome and account for the changes taking place right under their nose. The **Treaty of European Union** (TEU) was negotiated in 1991 and was ratified by all member states in 1993. The summit took place in Maastricht and the treaty is also called the Maastricht treaty.

The TEU formally designated the EC as the European Union and introduced a new structure of three **pillars** with different levels of integration. The first and largest pillar, the **Community pillar**, consisted of single-market legislation, agricultural and fishery policy, external commercial policy, competition, customs cooperation, regional funds, visa, asylum, immigration, and other areas in which supranational initiatives and action make sense: environmental protection, food safety, and development aid. Legislative proposals would be decided by mostly qualified majority vote. The second pillar contained **common foreign and security policy** and remained under the purview of national leaders. The third pillar, renamed **Police and Judicial Cooperation in Criminal Matters** (it used to be Justice and Home Affairs) covered cooperation in criminal justice and internal security (policing, transnational crime, money laundering, terrorism). It also remained under the control of national elected leaders. In 1999, the civilian component of judicial cooperation was moved to the European Commission and the EU governs issues related to visas, asylum, immigration, displaced persons, and other policies related to free movement of people. After 2009, and once the new **Lisbon treaty** is ratified, all judicial matters will be transferred to the EU and the pillar will cease to exist. The most surprising outcome of the summit meeting was the agreement to go ahead with the single currency. The pledge to launch the single currency symbolized the centrality of the Franco-German partnership. France insisted on more control over monetary policy by handing it over to a **European Central Bank** and away from German monetary authorities, while Germany insisted on more political integration. The result was the increased cooperation of the member states on internal and external security in return for a European monetary policy.

In the wake of the collapse of the Soviet Union, three small and prosperous countries joined the EU in 1995: Austria, Finland, and Sweden. Norway held a bitterly fought referendum and a slim majority voted against membership. Switzerland preferred to preserve its neutral status and declined membership application.

At a summit meeting in Copenhagen in 1993 the heads of state of the member states issued a statement that the EU would be willing to accept new applications from candidate states if they met four criteria: They needed stable political and legal institutions, they had to have a functioning market economy, they had to accept and adopt the body of legislation produced by the EU, and they could only join if their accession did not destabilize the EU and the process of integration. In 1994, Hungary and Poland had applied for membership, and by 1997 all eight Central and Eastern European countries, plus Malta and Cyprus, had expressed interest in membership.

Realizing that it was just a matter of time before the EU-15 would become EU-27, the member states convened another intergovernmental conference in 1997 to address the inevitable enlargement. But this summit was highly contentious and did not produce any serious amendments and reforms. It was decided to postpone any hard decisions to a later summit scheduled for 2000 in Nice (in France). The Nice treaty, however, was another fiasco and plagued by quarrels. However, it finalized the accession of the candidate members and it outlined provisional plans for reforms of institutions so they could function more effectively with as many as thirty members, including the possibility of enacting a constitution.

In 2004, a large wave of new members acceded to the EU. In January 2007, Romania and Bulgaria joined. The last major expansion added 30 percent to the population but only 9 percent in GDP because most of the new member states are considerably poorer than the EU average. Table 13.1 shows that many of the new member states are small in size because 6 out of the 12 have a population of fewer than 4 million. And all of them have a GDP (gross domestic product) per person lower than the average of EU-25. If the average of the European Union of 25 member states is set at 100, the richest newcomer is Cyprus with an average GDP 12 points less than the EU-25.

TABLE 13.1. Economic and Demographic Statistics for EU-27 (2007)

Member state	Population (millions)	GDP per person[a]
EU-27	494	100
EU-15		108
Austria	8.1	123.3
Belgium	10.4	118.2
Bulgaria	7.3	34.2
Czech Republic	10.2	76.1
Cyprus	0.7	88.3
Denmark	5.4	122.6
Estonia	1.4	65
Finland	5.2	113.1
France	59.6	107.3
Germany	82.5	110
Greece	11.0	84.9
Hungary	10.1	69.7
Ireland	4.0	139.2
Italy	57.3	99.4
Latvia	2.3	52.3
Lithuania	3.5	55
Luxembourg	0.4	257.1
Malta	0.4	69.7
Netherlands	16.2	126.1
Poland	38.2	51.1
Portugal	10.4	69.8
Romania	22.3	35.8
Slovenia	2.0	83.6
Slovakia	5.4	59.4
Spain	40.7	98.1
Sweden	8.9	116.1
United Kingdom	59.3	117.2

[a] GDP is measured in purchasing power parities. EU-25=100. Figures are forecasts.
Source: Commission of the European Union. Eurostat: GDP per Capita in PPS. 2006

This last wave of enlargement therefore will prove to be by far the hardest in terms of absorbing these societies in the EU and it has moved the EU from an organization of mostly wealthy prosperous countries to a much more diverse polity in numerous ways.

The Institutions

The European Union is shaped by two conflicting forces, each of which negotiates and maneuvers to gain the upper hand. At one end of the integration pole stands the European Commission, the engine of European integration.

At the other end are the nation-states represented by heads of governments, national cabinet officials, and civil servants. The history of European integration can best be captured by describing it as a tug of war between the supranational complex of organizations (the European Commission and the European Parliament) fighting against the natural instincts of the Council of ministers to retain as much autonomy and authority under national control. At various times, the Commission gains the upper hand over the Council, while at other times the heads of state successfully put a brake on further supranational institution building. Mediating between the triangular relationship between Commission, Council, and Parliament is the European Court of Justice, which interprets and defends European law.

THE COMMISSION

The European Commission located in Brussels is the executive center of the EU and has four tasks. First, it has the exclusive right to propose legislation. This legislation comes in two forms: directives and regulations. A **directive** is a collective legislative act of the European Union which requires member states to achieve a particular result without dictating the means of achieving that result. European **regulations** apply to all member states and are automatically in effect because they do not require any implementing measures. Directives normally leave member states with a certain amount of leeway as to the exact rules to be adopted and they are only binding in those member states to whom they are addressed. In practice, directives are usually addressed to all member states. Regulation becomes European law without requiring adoption by national legislatures.

Second, the Commission oversees the adoption of community law and policy into national law. For this, it relies greatly on national agencies to report back on the execution of EU directives and regulations. Since it is the guardian of the treaties, it can bring noncompliant member states and private actors before the European Court. Its third task is to guarantee administration and implementation of European law. Finally, the staff of the Commission represents the EU in international venues and is the public face of Europe.

It employs approximately 20,000 people. Of these, around 6,000 are the real Eurocrats who draft recommendations, rules, and laws. Another several thousand work in the language/translation services because every piece of major legislation must be translated in 23 original languages. At the head of each service or department (**directorate general – DG**) stands a **commissioner**. This man or woman is nominated by the home government and is approved by a qualified majority vote in the Council. They serve renewable five-year terms. Once they are approved, they swear an oath of allegiance to the EU and are not supposed to take instructions from the home governments.

The commissioners form a college and they meet regularly to deliberate on key decisions. The college is led by a president, who is appointed by the heads of state. The **president of the European Commission** is the public face of the EU and he or she presides over commission meetings, coordinates, sets the agenda, and provides leadership and moral support to the vast multilingual staff. The term of the president runs five years, with the possibility of renewal. The previous president of the Commission was the center-left Italian politician Romano Prodi (2000–2004). The current president is **José Manuel Barroso**, who is a center-right politician from Portugal.

Once the Commission is in place and the president and commissioners are nominated and approved, the real work begins. The Commission works on the principle of collegiality and the agenda of each DG is a collective decision taken by the entire college. Each commissioner is expected to participate in general affairs and events of the Commission. Commissioners are assisted by a cabinet or personal staff who do most of the legwork and prepare the commissioner for weekly meetings with the college of commissioners and with the administrative staff of bureaucrats. Cabinets play an important role and exercise considerable influence.

There are 27 commissioners, one for each member state, although its size will be curbed after 2014, when member states will have to forgo the right to appoint a commissioner each and positions will be rotated equally among two-thirds of member states. Assuming that nobody else will join, the number of commissioners will be limited to 18. This decision was taken because there are not enough policy responsibilities for 25, 27, or 30 chiefs, while the collegial spirit is hard to preserve in a large group of diverse participants.

Commissioners can design legislative proposals only in areas set aside for supranational decision making. Its prerogatives have gradually expanded from agriculture, competition law, and common external trade policy to the single market, regional development aid, environmental policy, research and development, social funds for disadvantaged regions, food safety, and consumer protection. The TEU introduced the concept of **subsidiarity** by stipulating that community action was justified only in areas where the objectives could not be achieved by the member states themselves. Under this formula, in the 1990s the Commission received several new areas for policy action such as public health, education and training, and consumer protection.

THE COUNCIL

Alongside the Commission stands the Council of ministers. Often in competition with the Commission, the Council of ministers represents the national interests of the member states. Formally, it has four responsibilities. The Council develops large strategic visions set out during European summits or intergovernmental conferences (IGC) held at least twice a year, in December and June. These visions often shape the agenda for years to come. The

Commission tends to frame legislation to meet the goals of the broad agenda outlined during the intergovernmental conference.

The Council also signs all international agreements and formulates defense and security policies while it signs off on all accession agreements. It also meets to discuss world affairs of political and geographic importance to the EU. The Middle East may be on the agenda, or relations with the United States. Third, the Council decides the budget and major legislation. It selects the president of the Commission, which is an arduous and difficult process in which the interests of small and large member states are balanced against the need to have ideological representation of the main political trends in European politics. Finally, it covers matters related to internal security, which fall outside the first community pillar and have remained under the control of national governments.

The Council actually consists of two institutions. When the heads of state gather to discuss major themes during an IGC, we speak of the **European Council**. The European Council deliberates on larger issues, the budget, the geopolitical situation, and determines the appointment of the new president of the Commission. The meetings of the European Council are grand affairs, often held in fancy resort towns with fine scenery, good food, and plenty of expensive alcohol. The IGC meeting is held in the country which holds the presidency of the council, which rotates every six months. The European Council should not be confused with the Council of Europe, which has 46 members and includes all countries in Europe. Since 1989, its main job has become to be human rights watchdog for Europe's post-communist democracies.

The Council of ministers and the European Council are the intergovern-mental part of the EU. They articulate and defend the national interests of the member states. The composition of the regular council varies with the policy terrain or issue. Frequency of meetings also varies in relation with the salience of a policy issue. Ministers of tourism may meet three times a year to discuss areas of importance related to tourism. By contrast, ministers of the environment may meet monthly to strategize how to arrest the increase of greenhouse gases. Each meeting is chaired by the relevant cabinet minister of the presiding member state. The Council also implements and executes EU policy. The Commission does not have the administrative staff to over-see EU directives and regulations. This is delegated to the national capitals. Members of the Council usually head a ministry or department which is in charge of implementing laws and regulations. The Council administers both the implementation of rules and the disbursement of funds.

The bulk of the work of senior cabinet officials is in the home country. Much of the groundwork is therefore completed by permanent delegates from the national capitals to Brussels who are intimately familiar with the portfolio and viewpoint of the politicians back home. **COREPER** is the

Committee of Permanent Representatives, which supplies information, feedback, and support to the Commission while developing its legislation and reports back to national capitals with advice and suggestions. Civil servants sit on the COREPER and they facilitate ongoing contacts between Brussels and national capitals. Because the Commission consults with the officials sent by national ministries to Brussels, by the time that the legislation arrives on the desk of the council members, it has been vetted, discussed, scrutinized, and debated by the member states exhaustively.

The Council demonstrates the continued power of the states. However, it has lost some of its powers with the ratification of the Single European Act in 1987. All commission proposals become law only after they have been passed by the Council. Until 1987, most decisions had to be unanimous giving each member state veto power. The unanimity rule repeatedly paralyzed the decision-making process and it would have buried single market legislation. At an IGC in 1985, the European Council introduced treaty amendment by permitting qualified majority voting for all proposals except the most dramatic and sensitive initiatives. Table 13.2 tallies the votes assigned to each country roughly in correspondence with its population size. Since attention must be paid to the fact that laws cannot defy the wishes of a sizable minority of member states and cannot be imposed against the expressed will of the majority of EU citizens, the current formula therefore speaks of a qualified majority vote.

The total number of votes in the EU-27 is 345 and the qualified majority threshold is 255 votes out of 345, that is, 73.91 percent. A blocking minority must marshal 90 votes. The system tends to overrepresent the smaller countries to keep large states from running the show, yet it is impossible to pass legislation without the support of two or three big countries.

In the late 1990s, with enlargement looming, a large number of European leaders agreed to reconsider the basic principle of weighted voting. In 2001, politicians decided to revisit the institutional structure of the EU and to combine and streamline close to 80,000 pages of rules, directives, treaties, and amendments. The Convention on the Future of Europe produced a fully fledged proposal for a **Constitutional Treaty** for Europe in 2004. The ratification of the Constitutional Treaty failed after both French and Dutch voters said no during a popular referendum.

Nevertheless, the Constitutional Treaty proposed a completely new system of qualified majority voting known as "double majority," reflecting the ideals of a union of states and people. It would have been based on the majority of member states and the majority of the population of the European Union. All member states would receive one vote out of respect that they are equal, yet it also would take into consideration the different population sizes. Therefore the double majority system defined a majority as a vote in which at least 55 percent of the states representing at least 65 percent of the total EU

TABLE 13.2. Seats in Parliament and Votes in Council

	Seats in EP	Votes in council	Population (in millions)
Belgium	24	12	10.4
Bulgaria	18	10	7.3
Czech Republic	24	12	10.2
Denmark	14	7	5.4
Germany	99	29	82.5
Estonia	6	4	1.4
Greece	24	12	11.0
Spain	54	27	40.7
France	78	29	59.6
Ireland	13	7	4.0
Italy	78	29	57.3
Cyprus	6	4	0.7
Latvia	9	4	2.3
Lithuania	13	7	3.5
Luxembourg	6	4	0.4
Hungary	24	12	10.1
Malta	5	3	0.4
Netherlands	27	13	16.2
Austria	18	10	8.1
Poland	54	27	38.2
Portugal	24	12	10.4
Romania	35	14	22.3
Slovenia	7	4	2.0
Slovakia	14	7	5.4
Finland	14	7	5.2
Sweden	19	10	8.9
United Kingdom	78	29	59.3

Note: Countries are arranged according to their formal name in the original language.

population (493 million) supports a proposal. The Lisbon treaty (agreed upon in 2007) confirmed that the new voting rules would be phased in between 2014 and 2017, after which a majority in the Council carries if 55 percent of the countries, representing 65 percent of the overall EU population, say yes. For the most part, in the past, the Council sought to achieve a consensus and shunned rounds of voting, although this might change with the greater heterogeneity in the EU and the extension of new policy areas falling under qualified majority voting.

THE EUROPEAN COURT OF JUSTICE

The European Court of Justice (ECJ) is located in Luxembourg and has greatly contributed to the metamorphosis of the modest EEC to a state-like EU. The Court has 27 judges – each member state appoints one judge for a renewable six-year term – and it is supported by eight advocates general (the number will rise to nine once the new Lisbon treaty will have been ratified by all member states). For the most part, the judges meet in separate and smaller chambers unless a case intersects with a significant treaty issue. Advocates general review cases and provide legal opinion to the judges, which are often adopted by the Court. But principled cases of fundamental legal importance go directly to the Court.

The ECJ has the right of judicial review over the interpretation of the EU treaties and over the secondary legislation (directives and regulations) issued by the Commission and approved by the Council. Legal cases arrive at the court through two different procedures. **Direct actions** relate to EU law and actions taken by member states and EU institutions. The judges can rule on whether the actions of national governments, private actors, and EU institutions are consistent with the obligations set out by treaties and EU secondary law. Usually, a direct-action case involves an infringement proceeding brought by the Commission or a member state against another member state for noncompliance. Direct action is supposed to ensure enforcement of EU law, although member states routinely ignore direct-action rulings since the political and economic consequences of noncompliance are minimal.

The second procedure is called **preliminary reference**. National courts submit queries on how an EU law applies. The ECJ responds without giving detailed instructions on how to implement the EU law, directive, or regulation although it elaborates on the legal principles behind its reasoning. Local or national judges decide on how to proceed once the ruling is published. Originally, preliminary reference was meant to provide private individuals with access to the ECJ to challenge the actions of EU institutions. Over time, it has grown into a powerful tool for the Court to expound on the legal principles of EU treaties and legislation.

Preliminary references account for the majority of cases brought to the ECJ and national governments find it much harder to ignore a ruling based on a preliminary reference than a direct action. The reason is that national courts are in charge of enforcing decisions stemming from preliminary references since they ultimately use the rulings of the ECJ to decide how to resolve the legal conflict that prompted the preliminary ruling in the first case. Under preliminary reference, national judges decide whether national law or action is compatible with EU law once they obtain a judgment from the ECJ. Politicians face high political costs if they do not comply with informed decisions of their national court. Thus the preliminary ruling carries broader reach because it ties national courts to the ECJ and constrains national governments.

The ECJ has gradually expanded its role, although it was mostly dormant during its first five years of existence. In 1963, in a landmark case (Case 26/62, *Gend en Loos v. Nederlandse Administratie der Belastingen*), the ECJ was asked to rule on the question of whether individuals or firms could invoke rights based on EEC law even if the national government had not adopted such a law. Thus the question was whether European law vested corporate entities and private citizens with rights not recognized by national law. The six judges at that time responded that EEC law was autonomous and carried "**direct effect**" on individuals and corporate entities. Because of that, EU law governed citizens through national courts.

In 1964, a second landmark case (Case 6/64, *Costa v. ENEL*) arrived when the arbitration court in Milan (Italy) submitted a query on how to resolve a direct conflict between national/Italian law and treaty obligations. The judges in this case replied that member states willingly accepted the constraints imposed by European law and transferred a limited amount of sovereignty to EEC institutions with the result that EEC law should be granted primacy over national law. This ruling established the **doctrine of supremacy** in that European law takes precedence over national law.

Both rulings were controversial and member states challenged them. However, over time the rulings produced other rulings with similar implications and contributed to the emergence of a legal order that is closer to the American federal system than centralized state systems of France and the United Kingdom.

National courts became important allies of the ECJ enabling it to construct a legal space. Thanks to their queries under the procedure of preliminary reference, the judges were able to render important judgments on general principles. The ECJ could also rely on national courts to enforce the interpretation of EU law stemming from the preliminary reference. In the beginning, national judges were reluctant to adopt the role of "enforcer or guardian" of EU law but eventually they saw some real benefits in aligning themselves with the ECJ. Ironically, preliminary reference enlarged their independence because it permitted national courts to exercise judicial review over national policy, an option that many national judiciaries missed in centralized state systems.

For national governments, the costs and consequences of ignoring directives, regulations, and ECJ rulings are minimal. Ultimately, neither the Commission nor the Court can oblige national courts and governments to adopt European law. The Commission maintains a list of violators and hopes to name and shame them, but there are modest political costs and hardly any economic ramifications if national authorities disregard infringement procedures. The ECJ is aware that its reach is limited and it restrains itself when it senses that the mood is frosty and governments are unlikely to agree with court judgments. Like the Commission, its weight fluctuates in accordance with the overall integrationist ambiance in the EU and its capitals.

THE EUROPEAN PARLIAMENT

During the first two decades of its existence, the European Parliament (EP) was a docile extension of national governments and voted according to the preferences of the home country. In 1979, the first direct elections were held to the European Parliament although it continued to play a subordinate role in EU institution-building and policy expansion. Once the SEA went into effect, the EP increased its powers. Elections are held every five years during the same week in June. The current parliamentary session lasts until the next election in 2009.

The **Treaty of Nice** (2001) capped the size of the EP to 750 from 786. The Lisbon treaty of 2007 added one extra seat for the president of the EP in order to give Italy one extra vote in the EP and the new distribution of seats will enter into force before the next election in 2009. Table 13.2 shows the current number of seats allocated to each member state based on its population size. Since the Lisbon treaty incorporated the Treaty of Nice articles on the size of the European Parliament, it also stipulates that the minimum number of seats per member state should be six to ensure that all major political trends will have a chance of gaining representation in the thinly populated states while the maximum will be set at 96.

Political candidates run in the member state on a national party ticket. There are no Euro political parties that field candidates across different political jurisdictions. However, once elected, members of the European Parliament (MEPs) become affiliated with political families or groups and seek out the group to which they belong ideologically. All MEPs from social democratic parties belong to the Party of European Socialists (218 seats). The Christian democratic parties are grouped in the European People's Party and are the largest family with 277 members. The third important group – Alliance for Liberals and Democrats for Europe – brings liberal, free-market parties together (106 seats).

All tasks and functions are distributed according to the size of the party groupings. The political groups negotiate and bargain about committee assignments, office staff, office space, agenda lists, and so forth. The leaders of the political groups manage the voting in EP and make sure that their members are aware of an important vote and the position taken by the group. Because political affiliation outweighs nationality, the political blocs form a cohesive voting block.

Members of the EP serve in committees, which produce reports and position papers, and prepare the vote on the relevant issues. The EP has around 24 committees covering relevant policy and political issues. Thus, there is a committee for the environment, public health, and food safety, which has 63 members and a staff of 10. Its main counterparts in the European Commission are DG Environment and DG Health and Consumer Protection. Because committees have large membership, they often set up sub-committees.

The European Parliament has come a long way from a forum for discussion by national delegates appointed by national parliaments. In the original conception of the Treaty of Rome, the European Parliament was divested of any real power and influence. It had only consultative powers and the Council would take into consideration Parliament's opinion. Europe's legislative body had no legislative power. In the 1970s, it received the right to deliberate on the Community's annual budget. As the EU took over more and more policy areas, it became increasingly obvious that the institution suffered from a "**democratic deficit**." To remedy this, the Single European Act (1987) introduced cooperation procedures so that the EP could propose amendments to single market legislation.

The architects of the SEA realized that the powers of the EP had to be increased after the Commission received greater responsibilities and many decisions would be taken by qualified majority voting in the Council. The legitimacy of the EU was literally at stake. Nevertheless, the reforms contained in the SEA were far too thin to redress the deficit. Therefore, in 2001 and 2004, the powers of the EP were expanded and streamlined with the result that the EP now has **codecision** powers. The Commission must submit a proposal to the EP and Council for consideration. Under codecision, the EP has the right to approve or reject the proposal. It codecides with the Council, literally. If it rejects the proposal, it can suggest amendments or announce its intention to reject the measure all together. If Parliament proposes amendments, and the Council disagrees, it must negotiate with the EP to hammer out a common position in a special conciliation committee. If they can find a common ground, the joint text is submitted to Parliament, where it can be approved or rejected by an absolute majority. The text also passes if Parliament fails to vote on it or fails to vote it down within six weeks. Council and Parliament each receive the right to read and discuss a proposal twice.

In the course of several intergovernmental conferences, Parliament has also gained the right to give its voice on the application of candidate countries, on important international treaties, on constitutional changes in the European Central Bank, and on multiyear funding of important aid funds (Structural and Cohesion funds). It also has the right to approve the installation of a new commission and to question the budget.

Nevertheless, although the EP has steadily acquired more powers, it is a weak version of its counterparts in the member states. It cannot vet the appointment of individual commissioners and it can only remove an entire commission in a vote of censure that requires a two-thirds margin. It can scrutinize the whole budget but it cannot reject separate items. Above all, the European Parliament suffers from low respect and poor reputation.

Some of the factors that have contributed to its lowly status are beyond its control. Unfortunately, a deal struck among heads of state has meant that its plenary meeting hall is located in a postmodern structure in Strasbourg whose offices and meeting rooms appear to be empty and devoid of activity; this is because most of the action takes place in Brussels, where the MEPs hold committee meetings and hearings, and interact with other European institutions. Its administrative staff is housed in Luxembourg. MEPs travel back and forth from Brussels to Strasbourg, which is both a waste of time and funds.

Not surprisingly, voters regard European elections as second-order national elections and the outcome often says more about national political developments than events in the EU. European political life and decisions are subordinate to the issues and concerns of the voters at home and voters routinely vote for candidates from opposition parties in order to express dissatisfaction with the incumbent government. In the meantime, citizens spend little time following and understanding parliamentary debates on European legislation in the EP. Accordingly, voter turnout is low as many voters stay home during elections. Remarkably, voter apathy is especially strong in the 10 new member states, where less than 40 percent of the electorate bothered to vote in 2004.

The European Parliament has acquired increasing power and leverage in order to close the gap between the extensive policy authority granted to the unelected Commission and democratic principles of participation and accountability characteristic of the political system of EU member states. But low participation rates and public dissatisfaction question this strategy of legitimizing the expansion of EU competencies by bolstering the legislative power of the EP. At the core of the dilemma is of course the absence of a European political culture, sustained by Euro political parties that foster a Euro political discourse. The idea of a Euro-wide election campaign is hard to fathom when a political party would have to address electorates in 23 different languages.

For the most part, European voters perceive events unfolding at the Euro level through purely national lenses and organizations. Euro parliamentary debates lack the clarity and resonance that inform national parliamentary discussions, which, moreover, tend to cover issues of direct relevance to the voter. Thus, the European Parliament grew from a toothless debating club for semiretired politicians to a legislative assembly with decision-making authority on a par with the Council, but it has not succeeded in transcending public apathy, linguistic diversity, divergent political traditions, and its distance from the daily concerns of the voter. It will have to connect with the voter before it can emerge as a true voice of the people of Europe.

Interests

From this discussion, the obvious conclusion is that the EU is neither a nation-state nor an international organization like the United Nations. It is more than an international organization because European rules, regulations, and laws supersede national law while European institutions acquired many of the trappings and features of national administration and governance agencies.

At the same time, it is not a nation-state since much of political life unfolds in the national arena, key areas remain beyond its control, and heads of state, representing the national interests of the member states, shape many of its policies.

By far the most underdeveloped areas are electoral politics and civic participation. Political and economic elites struck bargains and deals that gradually expanded policy competencies from national to European institutions. Yet the public has been absent in the building of European institutions. The European Parliament has not become a terrain for settling Euro conflicts because its structure is not conducive to public participation.

However, as the Commission and Parliament have become more involved in market regulations, environmental and consumer protection, technical standards, and opening of protected firms and industry sectors, interest groups and lobbyists have proliferated and become entrenched in the Euro-policy process.

At the Euro level, interests do not organize around class (labor unions), ethnicity (disadvantaged minorities), or religion (Catholic church, Muslim organizations). At the EU level, such new social movements are absent because it does not define family law or civil partnerships, which remain safely lodged in the hands of national governments. The EU regulates and reshapes market relations so interest groups reflect that particular focus of the EU. The dominant type of interest group that has emerged in the wake of the Europeanization of legislation mirrors the functional specialization of the Commission. Producer groups are prominent players and scores of industry sectors, firms, and business groups rushed to establish a European presence in Brussels to defend their interests, to influence the outcome of the deliberations, and to inform its members of future Euro developments.

The target of all this lobbying energy is both commission officials and EP committee members. Many business groups and professional associations recognize that so many rules and regulations are decided in Brussels that they need to be there. They often design a three-pronged strategy. They consult with national civil servants who assist the Commission with the drafting of legislative proposals, they approach sympathetic members of the European Parliament serving on relevant committees or subcommittees, and they knock on the doors of commission officials to gain access to information and influence. What makes this process slightly different from similar activities in the national theater is that many officials and Euro politicians welcome the lobbying efforts of private-sector agents. In fact, they rely on the feedback and input of interest lobbyists to grasp the limits of what can be achieved, how to calculate the varied costs of different proposals, and how to assess the depth of resistance to certain initiatives. Interest groups are a key part in the process of legislation and institution-building.

The staff size of the Commission is modest considering the complexity of the drafting legislation applicable across 27 distinct national jurisdictions. For the Commission, it does not make sense to squander time on frivolous, futile proposals so it seems safest to invite feedback, advice, or information from umbrella organizations. Interest groups are therefore partners of the Commission, although often adversarial partners since they are not necessarily on the same wavelength and may seek to obstruct European regulations or impose their version of the rules. Likewise, MEPs rely on lobbyists and associations to understand the trade-offs of competing initiatives and proposals.

Most of this lobbying is performed by professionals who speak for economic or producer interests. The Commission and Council, committed to bridging the "democratic deficit," have expressed concern about the lopsided influence peddling in Brussels. Producers possessed ample representation. Consumers were barely visible.

To shed the impression that economic integration is all about nurturing the competitive advantages of big business, both the Council and Commission actively encourage civic organizations to become supranational Euro federations and participate in the policy deliberation process. With the help of funding and subsidies, hundreds of nongovernmental organizations (NGOs) have appeared in Brussels and lobby the Commission and EP. Even more so than the economic interests, NGOs occupy a contradictory space as both partner and adversary of the Commission and EP. They are partners because they provide input on suggestions for measures and initiatives. By the same token, they are adversaries in that they criticize the Commission on matters where the European process fails, misses, or goes too far.

Civic organizations are a relatively new phenomenon in Brussels. Yet their independence is somewhat compromised by the fact that most of them receive generous funding from the Commission to maintain a European umbrella federation. In some cases, European subsidies account for half the budget of a NGO. Although it would appear that many of them feel free to assert themselves and criticize the Commission, they are still beholden to particular officials who decide on funding renewals.

In short, over time, the Commission and European Parliament have attracted the attention of many business groups, firm associations, professional federations, civic action groups, and nongovernmental organizations. There are thousands of registered lobby and interest groups in Brussels. The Commission (with the approval of the Council) releases funding to encourage the formation of consumer groups or civic organizations to balance the dense representation of producer interests. But many NGOs are cumbersome constructions and dependent on the Commission for funding. In short, their presence is unlikely to close the "democratic deficit."

What Has Been Accomplished

Over the decades, the EU has become involved in an ever larger circle of policy activities. In all federal systems (the United States, Canada, Australia) different levels of governance cover different policy areas and carry different responsibilities. In the EU, the split is between national and Euro/supranational. The organization of the EU reflects that division of authority. The Commission has exclusive decision-making power on external commercial policy, agriculture, environment, internal market, and single currency. National governments control social welfare programs, tax policy, health care, and education. Then, there is a third set of policies in which responsibility is shared. Aspects of internal security (asylum, immigration, policing), consumer protection, and public health are supposed to be coordinated by both levels. In 1991 (during the TEU negotiations), it was decided that the lowest level of government was always the appropriate decision-making level. Only areas of policy intervention that involved a fair amount of international coordination and oversight should be delegated to the European Commission (that is, subsidiarity). The first successful Euro policy was the Common Agricultural Policy, which underpinned the original pact to ratify the Treaty of Rome.

THE COMMON AGRICULTURAL POLICY

The structure of the Common Agricultural Policy (CAP) is very complex and has been a major source of global trade disputes. Its twin goals are to support the livelihood of farmers and protect the European economy from cheaper agricultural commodities grown in countries with more suitable climate, better soil conditions, and more land such as the United States, Brazil, and Argentina. The Commission guarantees prices by promising to buy products which do not sell on the open market. Prices are set to reflect the cost of living of farmers in different regions in the EU and are set relatively high to provide adequate income for farmers. Food prices in Europe are therefore higher than what they could have been if there had been no CAP. The Commission often ends up having to fulfill its pledge and buy up surplus foodstuff, which it has to transport and store. It then tries to sell surplus grain, milk, or wine abroad at lower prices in order to get rid of its inventory. The dumping of agricultural commodities has been an enormous source of aggravation and friction for more efficient exporting countries like the United States and Canada because the dumping lowers the price for these products on the global market and cuts into the profit margins of foreign farmers.

In the 1990s, under international and fiscal pressure, the Commission extracted concessions from member states with sizable farming/food sectors to reduce the income support scheme to minimize its disruptive impact on global agricultural trade. Over the years, reforms have indeed decreased the surpluses and reduced the CAP's share in the total EU budget from three-quarters to half. Price guarantees have been lowered to discourage overproduction, which not only led to huge surpluses but also hurt local ecology and caused pollution of groundwater and soil. Currently, the CAP supplies direct payments to farmers if they produce less or reduce their herds or convert part of their holdings into eco-habitat for tourism or wildlife. Nevertheless, it is the largest funding program of the EU.

THE SINGLE EUROPEAN MARKET

Regional integration is best understood as a lengthy attempt to achieve market integration. The underlying motive has been economic. The Treaty of Rome called for the removal of barriers against the free movement of goods, labor, capital, and services, which necessitated the adoption of a common external commercial policy and a watchdog to guarantee that the member states would play fair and square by introducing competition (antitrust) policy. By the 1960s, most member states had removed tariffs on industrial goods and opened their markets to foreign trade. However, the lifting of tariffs on goods faltered in the 1970s when international economic conditions deteriorated and governments increasingly revived semiprotectionist measures to protect struggling manufacturing firms and industrial sectors.

In the 1980s, as economic growth decreased, unemployment increased, and budget deficits exploded, many governments became ever more creative in finding ways to protect domestic actors from international trade. The removal of tariffs on manufactured goods simply generated a whole new system of protectionism that was more insidious and harmful. Discriminatory trade practices only worsened after the late 1970s once the global economy resulted in closure of core manufacturing industries in the EC.

The Single European Act and single European market (SEM) grew out of concern for the future of the EC, the weaknesses of the European economy, and the fact that governments were adopting nontransparent trade barriers to shelter domestic actors from export losses and import competition.

The Commission's 1985 white paper came to the rescue as it set out new goals and priority. It emphasized market liberalization and deregulation. The objective was to give firms greater room to innovate, grow, develop, and become global competitors. Alongside the transparent economic aims of the white paper, the Commission also envisioned greater political integration. In part greater political coordination was required to formulate new rules at the Euro level to ensure the completion of the single market program. The Commission required additional powers to issue complementary legislation in competition, consumer protection, food safety, research and development, which meant that national governments had to transfer some powers to European institutions.

Undoubtedly, the SEM project was massive. By the end, nearly 1,500 different measures were drafted and proposed. The core objectives of the SEM can be summed up as easing market access, competition, and market functioning. Market-access measures included the physical removal of border controls and mutual recognition of certification and licensing of service providers and professionals. It also resulted in the relaxation of residence requirements for EU citizens. Examples of easing competition are withdrawal of state aid for failing industries and firms, and greater vetting of mergers and acquisitions. It also produced rules to establish a European vocational training certificate. Proposals that fall under the heading of market functioning are standardization of technical requirements in telecommunications and EU standard for ATM bank cards. It also led to European corporate law so that firms could easily move from different national jurisdictions without incurring great transaction costs.

Many of the measures proposed by the Commission under the aegis of the single market borrowed from a principle first promulgated by the ECJ in a case of Cassis de Dijon (Case 120/78 *Rewe-Zentral AG v. Bundesmonopolverwaltung fur Branntwein*). The background of the case involved the difficulties that a German importing company encountered when it tried to market the French Crème de Cassis de Dijon in its home country. The German federal authorities declared that the liqueur did not meet the high alcohol content requirements for liquor or the low alcohol content requirements for beer. Citing health concerns, the German Monopoly Administration for Spirits prohibited the sale of the cassis liqueur. The German importing company took the case to the European Court of Justice citing a restriction on the free movement of goods and basically claiming that the health restrictions were a form of trade suppression. The European Court of Justice struck down the German import prohibition. It decided that the German authorities had not demonstrated an urgent need to bar this liqueur. Instead, the judges concluded French standards should prevail in Germany and that the principle of mutual recognition of national standards should govern most of the differences and divergences in national standards. In short, the ECJ proclaimed that if the beverage was safe for French it was safe for Germans!

The ruling gave the European Commission an opportunity to develop the principle of "**mutual recognition**." Ultimately, the principle implies that any national law with reasonable policy goals, such as environmental conservation, health, and so on, should be tolerated within the EC. Rather than imposing common rules for determining whether a product complies with the descriptive characteristics and norms of each individual member state, the Commission freed itself from this impossible task and declared that products approved by a regulatory agency of one member state can be legally marketed throughout the Community. The only task of the Commission was to determine minimum standards across a wide range of similar products. Harmonization was no longer the final goal because the free movement of goods and services did not require harmonization but rather recognition.

The single market has not been the final answer to slow growth and lagging international competitiveness. But it has certainly addressed the fragmented nature of the European economy and the tendency to coddle selected firms and industries. Compared to two decades ago, European firms have become more competitive and the EU has become an attractive destination for foreign direct investments. European consumers pay lower prices on a range of products and services thanks to liberalization of previously protected industries and sectors. Many European firms have become serious global players. However, as in any process of rationalization and liberalization, the creation of the single market created winners and losers. Furthermore, many of the economic regulatory adjustments were taken without the active participation of political parties and wide variety of interest groups with the result that the changes wrought by increased openness to markets and global competition have left deep dissatisfaction and insecurity. European economics have undergone an amazing transformation yet it was without open debate and mostly achieved through technical regulations bypassing parliamentary debate. The impact of liberalization and deregulation has also varied as some economies were more adept at absorbing the challenges than others. Countries with a more liberal version of market structures dealt with the demands of liberalization easier than tightly organized economies with comparatively large state intervention. Thus, the United Kingdom was well positioned to take advantage of the new regulatory standards. But France and Italy have struggled and have not fully come to terms with the economic changes.

A SINGLE CURRENCY

For the Commission, it was a truism that the single market project was not complete without a single currency. How can we speak of a single market if goods are priced in 15 or 25 different currencies? The SEM concluded its list of measures with a reference to the creation of a single currency. Commission officials made it clear that currency differences concealed inefficiencies, undermined the ability of the consumer to compare prices, and hampered the free movement of goods and services. However, a single currency challenges the core definition of what it means to be a sovereign nation-state. The main task of governments is to spend money that they collect in taxes. Politics is about the distribution of resources. Governments would not be in a position of authority if they did not control the national purse. Elected officials manage macroeconomic policy together with central banks, which are independent from the political system. They set interest rates and thus determine the price of money. In turn, interest rates determine the cost of borrowing capital and influence how much governments spend on public programs. If interest rates are low, governments can borrow more. If interest rates are high, it is more costly to borrow both for governments and private agents.

The question therefore is why national governments would ever agree to the idea of a single currency with the resulting loss in monetary autonomy and policy independence?

The short and simple answer to this question is that national governments had lost their ability to set policy independently from the strongest, most stable economy in the EU, namely Germany. Central bankers followed the decisions made by their German counterparts and set interest rates according to what was best for the German economy. They were no longer able to fine-tune monetary policy in response to the particular needs of the domestic economy.

This situation emerged in the wake of the success of the **European Monetary System**. In 1978 five of the EC-12 (France, Italy, Denmark, Benelux, Germany) agreed to form a zone of monetary stability in a world of fluctuating exchange rates and decided to fix their exchange bilaterally. The European Monetary System (EMS) had two remarkable features. It came with a "fake" currency, the **ECU**, which was used as an accounting unit to enable companies and public agencies to avoid exchange rate costs. More importantly, each EMS-member government was obliged to stabilize its currency value with respect to the value of a basket of EMS-member currencies, namely the ECU. Each country's currency had a weight in the ECU that was proportional to that country's trade within the EC. An autonomous shift in the external value of any EMS-member currency changed the value of the ECU and therefore imposed exchange-rate adjustment obligations on all members of the system. However, the burden of adjustment mostly fell on the currencies of smaller or weaker economies. By definition, the system was asymmetrical in its operation. A shift in the external value of the currency of a major member of the EMS (such as the German mark) had a greater effect on the external value of the ECU than had the same percentage disturbance to the external value of the currency of a less important member (for example the Belgian franc). It therefore imposed greater exchange-rate adjustment responsibilities on the smaller members. Many of the EMS countries welcomed this asymmetrical burden because it was the price they paid for exchange-rate stability with their main trading partners (including France and the German Federal Republic).

Eventually, many smaller currencies decided to shadow German fiscal and monetary policies, since that would minimize the need for exchange rate adjustments. By the mid-1980s, virtually all EMS currencies were following German monetary policy to avoid inflation rates higher than that of Germany and unwanted, although needed, exchange-rate realignments. Eventually, all the EMS currencies shadowed the German mark and national monetary authorities followed the lead of the German central bank. Of course, the latter made policy based on West German economic conditions and often the decisions taken by the German authorities did not suit the needs of other EMS countries.

Thus, when the Commission revived the idea of creating a common currency, by the early 1990s, quite a few countries were ready for that momentous change. There was plenty of resentment of having to follow in the footsteps of German macroeconomic policy and a single currency would greatly dilute the weight and influence of the German central bank, which would be one of many participating central banks.

During the Treaty on European Union negotiations in 1991, **Economic and Monetary Union** (EMU) was incorporated into the amended treaty. Countries received an opt-out clause if they did not want to participate and Britain and Denmark decided to withdraw from the negotiations. The heads of state adopted the commission guideline to demand strict convergence criteria so that unstable financial countries would not be eligible. Participants were supposed to record modest budget deficits (3 percent of GDP), manageable public debt (60 percent of GDP), and inflation and interest rates within the average of the three best-performing economies. The Commission report also set out the blueprint for the new European Central Bank, which would be independent from the political class and be endowed with a strong commitment to price stability. The time line designated January 1997 as the date on which the member states and the Commission would determine who is eligible, and January 1999 would be the start of EMU.

The schedule had to be pushed back and the euro went into circulation on January 2002. Eleven currencies participated: Denmark, Sweden, and the United Kingdom stayed out (Luxembourg used the Belgian franc). The euro has had a shaky start as it first fell by over 25 percent but then recovered and increased against the dollar after 2005. The euro is used as a reserve currency and a wide range of corporate and government bonds are denominated in euros. Increasingly, oil exporting countries, China and Japan, and other countries with large trade surpluses are diversifying and reducing their dependence on the dollar by buying euros.

The single market and single currency have been the EU's most significant achievements. The euro symbolizes the crowning achievement of regional integration at the expense of national sovereignty. Its adoption grew out of several developments and calculations. First of all, most of the European countries were no longer in control of their "monetary destiny," which was decided in Frankfurt. Second, they felt strongly it was better to have a European central bank in control of their monetary destiny than German officials at the German central bank. The single currency has terminated for once and for all any pretense of monetary independence. Yet it freed the participating currencies from the whims of the German central bank.

This raises the question why the Germans would ever have agreed to EMU when they ran Europe's monetary regime? Here, political factors played a major role. Unification stirred all kinds of worries about a resurgent strong Germany more interested in its Eastern borderlands than the EU. Germany was the largest net contributor to the EU, it possessed the largest economy, and it played an active role in European integration. What if its attention and interests wandered eastward and it lost interest in the EU? Its partners expressed their concerns in many different ways and the German federal government felt great pressure to demonstrate that it would never abandon regional integration and would always remain committed to its Western allies (and especially France). Former chancellor Helmut Kohl therefore agreed to the creation of a single currency. The Germans sacrificed a treasured symbol of their postwar record of political and economic stability to reassure its European partners that it would remain committed to the EU. Since the EMS did not constrain German monetary policy, the German authorities had to make the largest sacrifices. They did so for the sake of the future of Franco-German partnership. The Germans agreed to give up their stable currency and in return the French agreed to accept greater political integration, which for them was an additional guarantee that the Germans would continue to be committed to regional integration.

Conclusion: Future Challenges

So much has been accomplished in the last 20 years. The list of achievements would include the absorption of nearly 20 additional members, the single market, European Monetary Union, and the first serious attempts to formulate a European foreign and defense dimension as well as increased integration in justice and policing. Nevertheless, the mood in Europe is somber and the EU is experiencing some of its greatest self-doubts. Why would these incredible achievements be a source of ambivalence and uncertainty?

To understand this contradiction it is useful to talk of what has not been accomplished, and why.

Much of the process of integration was driven without any clear end objectives in mind. This was partly by design since the architects of Europeanization differed on the basic contours of the future EU. From the beginning there was a tension between federalists, who aimed for the creation of a federal Europe, and intergovernmentalists, who viewed the whole project as a way to strengthen Europe against global pressures, against the rise of American and Asian competition, and against marginalization of the European state system. Political leaders left the end objectives vague because they knew that they disagreed fundamentally on the question of how much political integration should occur. They found common ground in the idea of economic integration, increasingly aware that the fragmented national economies of Europe could not hope to compete against the much larger unified markets of the United States, Japan, and now China.

Yet the focus on market integration and expansion of EU competencies resulted in the Europeanization of national polities and a loss of national autonomy and independence. Extensive economic integration could only succeed if politicians agreed to increase the regulatory powers and legislative mandate of the Commission and the European Parliament. Moreover, the benefits of regional integration were built on adjustments and reforms that frequently entailed difficult sacrifices and trade-offs that generated short-term losses and pain. For example, EMU is a tremendous success. However, to get there, many governments had to cut back public spending because they had to bring down high budget deficits to meet its fiscal criteria.

During these years, voters were not part of the discussion and Europe was only mentioned when politicians were looking for an easy scapegoat to avoid an electoral backlash against spending retrenchment and social program cutbacks. The common mantra across Europe was that the Commission forced austerity programs onto reluctant national governments and that voters ought to blame Brussels. Yet when deregulation of protected industries brought down prices, politicians took the credit.

Not surprisingly, many EU citizens are currently questioning the utility of regional integration and institution-building. Many EU citizens are confused, to say the least, about what the end goal is and where it is going, and why. What they have heard repeatedly is that Brussels imposes conditions that challenge treasured policy regimes. Because there has been no honest debate on why institution-building required many painful adjustments, citizens find it hard to rationalize why they should endorse institutional reforms in the EU.

The lack of civic involvement and public debate was a tactic adopted by the leadership from the beginning. In the 1950s, the reasoning was that the people of Europe were not ready to transfer policy competences to a supranational authority. Later, national leaders continued to avoid public and open deliberations because many of the initiatives were highly technical and esoteric. Academics and central bankers felt strongly that it was futile to consult voters about the exact details of economic and monetary union when their own knowledge and familiarity with central bank objectives and monetary policy was limited. Observers spoke of the permissive consensus, so called because the public seemed to go along with whatever was suggested. Operating under the assumption that citizens were more or less on the same wavelength, elites could pretend that the electorate had given them a mandate to negotiate the next phase in institution-building.

This is to say that regional integration deliberately discouraged the public's involvement out of fear that the nationalist sentiments of the people might thwart the attempts to create a European community. Later a sense of complacency convinced leaders to keep the public in the dark since it appeared that the people were on the same page as the governing elite.

The end result is a lack of Euro identity. With that, the EU's legitimacy is incomplete because people's attachment to Euro institutions is thin. European law is accepted and recognized thanks to the respect accorded to national courts, which have been reliable interpreters of ECJ judgments. Public legitimacy also comes from the allegiance expressed by national institutions to the EU. However, EU citizens remain embedded in the value system and norms shaped by the experiences of their national polity. Political identification with the EU is extremely modest.

There is nothing new here except that enlargement puts enormous pressure on institutions originally designed for a community of six members in 1957. National leaders vowed in 2001 to make the EU "more democratic, more transparent, more efficient" by opening up summit negotiations and by pushing institutional reform. Years later these promises have come to naught in part because citizens voted down a constitutional treaty in 2005 that contained many of the reforms to manage a more heterogeneous EU.

The leaders of the EU went back to the drawing board and transformed the constitutional treaty into the Lisbon treaty, claiming that this treaty was simply an amendment to existing treaties, and should not be subjected to a national referendum. However, the Lisbon treaty more or less adopted all the reforms initially proposed by the constitutional treaty and introduces a whole set of innovations that will determine the operation of the EU for years to come. The new treaty, as I indicated above, introduces a simpler voting system, reduces the size of the Commission and European Parliament, extends majority voting to areas such as criminal justice and police cooperation, creates a full-time president of the European Council (representing the national leaders), and it also establishes the post of a EU foreign minister who will have their own diplomatic service and represent the EU in venues such as the United Nations. The treaty also gives legal force to the Charter of Fundamental Rights and permits national parliaments some say over legislation if at least half of national parliaments demand changes.

The truth of the matter is therefore that the Lisbon treaty is the sort of document over which EU citizens should have a say. Yet European leaders do not trust their voters and prefer to revert back to the previous strategy of cramming in a long list of steps to strengthen the EU while pretending that these reforms are just another set of amendments and only beautify or beef up existing rules and agreements. European leaders figure that voters may again turn down a treaty so they seek to avoid a referendum. Yet if they do not consult voters directly about the new direction and reforms of the EU, the whole process will continue to face a shortage of legitimacy and accountability.

Thus, 50 years after it all began, the EU is at a crossroads, faced with difficult choices. It succeeded in creating a single market and a new currency. European coordination across a whole array of policies has increased (environment, food safety, public health, asylum, regional development, fisheries, agriculture, and so on). However, vast changes in governance and policy authority at the state and Euro level have not been accompanied by parallel trends at the societal/political level. How to address this dilemma is something that has eluded national and European leadership for now. They will have to think of a solution if the EU is to succeed with 27 divergent member states.

BIBLIOGRAPHY

Bulmer, Simon, and Christian Lequesne, eds. *The Member States of the European Union*. New York: Oxford University Press, 2005.

Commission of the European Communities. *"Completing the Internal Market," White Paper from the Commission to the European Council* (Milan, 28–29 June 1985).

Culpepper, Pepper, Peter Hall, and Bruno Palier. *Changing France: The Politics that Markets Make*. New York: Palgrave Macmillan, 2006.

Davies, Norman. *Europe: A History*. New York: Oxford University Press, 1996.

Dedman, Martin. *The Origins and Development of the European Union, 1945–95*. New York: Routledge, 1996.

Dehousse, Renaud. *The European Court of Justice: The Politics of Judicial Integration*. New York: St. Martin's Press, 1998.

Dimitrakopoulos, Ioannis. *The Changing European Commission*. Manchester: Manchester University Press, 2004.

Falkner, Gerda. *Complying with Europe: EU Harmonisation and Soft Law in the Member States*. New York: Cambridge University Press, 2005.

George, Stephen. *An Awkward Partner: Britain in the European Community*. New York: Oxford University Press, 1994.

Gowland, David. *Reluctant Europeans: Britain and European Integration, 1945–1998*. New York: Longman, 2000.

Hayes-Renshaw, Fiona, and Helen Wallace. *The Council of Ministers*. New York: Palgrave Macmillan, 2006.

Hix, Simon. *The Political System of the European Union*. New York: Palgrave Macmillan, 2005.

Hooghe, Liesbet. *The European Commission and the Integration of Europe: Images of Governance*. New York: Cambridge University Press, 2001.

Hösli, Madeleine. *The Euro: A Concise Introduction to European Monetary Integration*. Boulder, CO: Lynne Rienner Publishers, 2005.

Jacobsson, Bengt. *Europeanization and Transnational States: Comparing Nordic Central Governments*. New York: Routledge, 2004.

Kurzer, Paulette. *Markets and Moral Regulation: Cultural Change in the European Union*. New York: Cambridge University Press, 2001.

Lodge, Juliet. *The 2004 Elections to the European Parliament*. New York: Palgrave, 2005.

Martin, Andrew, and George Ross, eds. *Euros and Europeans: Monetary Integration and the European Model of Society*. New York: Cambridge University Press, 2004.

Menz, Georg. *Varieties of Capitalism and Europeanization: National Response Strategies to the Single European Market*. New York: Oxford University Press, 2005.

Pollack, M. *The Engines of European Integration: Delegation, Agency and Agenda Setting in the EU*. Oxford: Oxford University Press, 2003.

Robyn, Richard. *The Changing Face of European Identity*. New York: Routledge, 2005.

Ross, George, *Jacques Delors and European Integration*. Cambridge: Polity Press, 1995.

Schmidt, Vivien. *Democracy in Europe*. New York: Oxford University Press, 2006.

Stone Sweet, Alec. *The Judicial Construction of Europe*. New York: Oxford University Press, 2004.

TABLE 13.3. Key Phases in the European Union's Political Development

Year	Event
1951	Creation of the ECSC (Belgium, Luxembourg, the Netherlands, France, Germany, and Italy join)
1957	Treaty of Rome signed by ECSC members
1967	Creation of EC
1972	First enlargement concluded
1973	Denmark, Ireland, United Kingdom join
1981	Greece admitted
1985	Single European Act passed
1986	Single European Market launched (project 1992)
1986	Portugal and Spain admitted
1991	Treaty of Maastricht signed (with section on EMU)
1995	Austria, Finland, Sweden join
1997	Treaty of Amsterdam negotiated
1998	Benelux, France, Germany, Italy, Spain, Portugal, Greece, Ireland, Austria, Finland form EMU
2001	Treaty of Nice signed
2002	Euro launched
2004	Ten new members join EU (Cyprus, Czech Republic, Estonia, Hungary, Latvia, Lithuania, Malta, Poland, Slovakia)
2005	Constitutional Treaty voted down in France, Netherlands
2007	Bulgaria, Romania join
2007	Slovenia joins EMU
2007	Lisbon treaty agreed at Lisbon summit

IMPORTANT TERMS

José Manuel Barroso president of the European Commission (2004–2009).

codecision Parliament may amend and block legislation in those policy areas that fall under its mandate, which currently make up about three-quarters of EU legislative acts. The EP and Council must agree on an identical text before any proposal can become law.

commissioner serves in the Commission and heads a department or division called directorate general. Commissioners are appointed by home governments but swear allegiance to the EU. There are 27 commissioners.

Committee of Permanent Representatives (COREPER) ambassadors or civil servants from home governments of the member states who generally prepare the council agenda, and negotiate minor and noncontroversial matters, leaving controversial issues for discussion by the Council.

Common Agricultural Policy (CAP) a system of agricultural subsidies and programs. It represents about 44 percent of the EU's budget in 2005. These subsidies work by guaranteeing a minimum price to producers and by direct payment of a subsidy for crops planted. It formed the basis for a Franco-German agreement to establish the EEC.

common foreign and security policy the second area of policy making in the EU, referring to foreign policy and military matters. Most decisions require council unanimity vote and the involvement of the Commission and Parliament is limited. Decisions are based on intergovernmental cooperation.

Community pillar the first and largest policy area of the EU and includes economic, social, and environmental policies. All decisions are taken by qualified majority vote in the Council of Ministers. Decisions are based on supranational principles.

Constitutional Treaty was signed by the member states in late 2004 and was in the process of ratification until French and Dutch voters rejected the treaty in June 2005 in referenda. The failure of the constitution to win popular support in these countries caused other countries to postpone their ratification procedures, and leaders are contemplating a shorter version.

Council of ministers is a governing body that forms, along with the European Parliament, the legislative arm of the EU. It contains ministers of the governments of each of the member states.

"democratic deficit" refers to the perceived democratic shortcomings of the EU due to the shift of policy making to the Commission and Council and away from national parliaments. First used in the 1980s, it now mostly concerns questions on how to increase the limited powers of the Parliament and civic participation.

direct action refers to cases in which the European Court is called upon to settle a dispute between two or more parties and where the parties bring their case directly to court. This contrasts with preliminary rulings in which the European Court gives its opinion on EU law to enable national courts to make a ruling.

direct effect the doctrine developed by the ECJ where unimplemented directives in conflict with national law nonetheless carry direct legal force.

directive a collective legislative act of the EU which requires member states to achieve a particular result without dictating the means of achieving that result.

directorate general (DG) the Commission is organized into 27 distinct departments, or DGs, each of which is responsible for specific tasks or policy areas and led by a commissioner. Eventually, this number will be reduced to 18 and national governments will no longer be automatically guaranteed a commissioner.

doctrine of supremacy has no direct reference in the treaties but member states recognize that European law takes precedence over national law in order to promote a uniform or consistent EU legal order.

Economic and Monetary Union part of the Treaty of European Union (1993) and committed countries to abolish national currencies and adopt a European currency (euro). It also created the European Central Bank, which is responsible for monetary policy within the euro zone.

ECU key feature of the EMS and was a "fake" currency representing the basket of currencies of EC member states, which had to prevent movements above 2.25 percent around parity in bilateral exchange rates with other member countries.

euro launched in 1998 with 12 member states, which had met the convergence criteria. Physical coins and banknotes were introduced on January 1, 2002. Slovenia joined in January 2007, bringing total Eurozone membership to over 316 million people and 13 member states.

European Central Bank responsible for monetary policy covering the 13 member countries of the Eurozone. It also prints and mints all notes and coins. It was established in 1998 and its headquarters are located in Frankfurt.

European Coal and Steel Community founded in 1951 (Treaty of Paris), by France, West Germany, Italy, Belgium, Luxembourg, and the Netherlands to pool the steel and coal resources of its member states. It was also strongly supported by the United States.

European Commission formally the **Commission of the European Communities,** is the executive body of the EU. It is located in Brussels and has a staff of 20,000.

European Council refers to the European summit meeting of the heads of state and the president of the EU. It is held at least twice a year and is chaired by the country which holds the council presidency.

European Court of Justice ensures that the law is observed in the interpretation and application of the treaties and of the decisions laid down by community institutions. It rules on applications for annulment or actions for failure to act brought by a member state or an institution, actions against member states for failure to fulfill obligations, and answers queries through preliminary reference.

European Economic Community was established with the signing of the Treaty of Rome in 1957. The "Economic" was removed in 1967 when the EEC was merged with Euratom and the European Coal and Steel Community. It was subsequently called European Community until 1993, when it became the European Union.

European Monetary System (EMS) established in 1979 when most nations of the EC linked their currencies to prevent large fluctuations relative to one another. It is the precursor to EMU because it led to a loss of monetary autonomy and increased willingness to phase out national currencies.

European Parliament directly elected by EU citizens once every five years. Together with the Council of Ministers, it composes the legislative branch of the institutions of the union. It meets in two locations: Strasbourg and Brussels. It has restricted legislative power because it cannot initiate legislation, but it can amend or veto it in many policy areas.

intergovernmental conference (ICG) the formal procedure for negotiating amendments to the founding treaties. Under the treaties, an IGC is called by the European Council, and is composed of heads of state, with the Commission, and to a lesser degree the Parliament.

Lisbon treaty was ratified by European leaders in 2007 after the failure of the constitutional treaty in 2005. It introduces a long list of innovations such as a full-time president of the European Council and an EU foreign minister (known as the high representative), reduction in the number of commissioners from 27 to 18. It also includes a Charter of Fundamental Rights, which will guarantee social and employment rights. The EU will gain "legal personality" so it can sign international treaties in its own right. QMV will be extended into 50 areas of policy making.

"mutual recognition" important breakthrough in the creation of the single market. According to this principle, promulgated first by the ECJ in 1979, a product or a service is allowed access to the markets of other member states if it has been approved or legalized by authorities in the country of origin. Barriers to free movement of goods and services will be illegal unless justified by a set of specifically provided rules in the EC Treaty. It alleviated the need to establish uniform standards for each and every product or service.

pillars the EU consists of three pillars: European Community; common foreign and security policy; and police and judicial cooperation. The pillar structure came into being after the ratification of the Treaty of European Union. Governments desired to add powers to the Community in the areas of foreign policy, security and defense policy, asylum and immigration policy, criminal cooperation, and judicial cooperation. But many leaders felt that these matters directly intersected with national sovereignty and preferred to keep them away from the Commission and European Parliament.

Police and Judicial Cooperation in Criminal Matters third area of policy making in the EU and concerns cooperation in the fight against crime. This pillar was originally named Justice and Home Affairs but since 1997 asylum, migration, and judicial cooperation in civil matters have been transferred to the Community pillar.

preliminary reference is specific to EU law because the European Court of Justice (ECJ) is not the only judicial body empowered to apply EU law. National courts retain jurisdiction to review the implementation of EU law and they also guarantee that rights conferred to EU citizens through regulations or directives are upheld. National courts turn to the ECJ to seek clarification of a judicial issue concerning the interpretation of community law to ascertain whether their national legislation complies with that law.

president of the European Commission the highest-ranking unelected official within the EU bureaucracy, appointed by heads of state; both leads the Commission and is the public face of the EU.

qualified majority voting a voting procedure employed in the Council of Ministers for all decisions coming from the community pillar. Each member state has a fixed number of votes, which is roughly determined by its population, but progressively weighted in favor of smaller countries.

regulation a legislative act of the EU that does not require any implementing measures.

Single European Act entered into force on July 1987 and introduced the first wave of institutional reforms to prepare the institutions for completing the single market. It introduced qualified majority voting to areas related to the single market and granted more decision-making powers to the European Parliament.

single European market agreed upon in 1986, it involved a huge program of removing barriers to the free movement of all the four factors of production (goods, services, capital, and labor). The ultimate aim was to increase the international competitiveness of European economies.

spill-over the idea that intense cooperation in economics will eventually spill over into more sensitive high political arenas and thus lay the foundation for political integration.

subsidiarity the principle that the EU should only act where separate national legislation would be insufficient. It was proposed during the negotiations for the TEU.

treaties of the EU the basic constitutional texts of the EU that set out the objectives of the EU and establish various institutions that are intended to achieve those aims. There have been four additional treaties since the ratification of the Treaty of Rome in 1957.

Treaty of Amsterdam entered into force in 1999 and made substantial changes to the Treaty on European Union (1993) by increasing the powers for the European Parliament, adding a social dimension to the EU, and introducing a community area of freedom, security, and justice, and began the reform of the institutions in the run-up to enlargement.

Treaty of European Union entered into force in November 1993 and changed the name of the European Community to European Union. It also introduced a new structure to the EU by dividing policy areas into three areas or pillars. It added two new policy areas that remained under the auspices of member governments: foreign and defense policies as well as internal security.

Treaty of Nice entered into force in February 2003 and readied the EU for further enlargement by putting a ceiling on the number of MEPs and the European Commission.

Treaty of Rome established the European Economic Community and was signed in March 1957. Six countries joined: France, Italy, Germany, and Benelux. It had two major components, the European Economic Community and Euratom.

STUDY QUESTIONS

1. What lessons does European integration hold for other regions in the world?

2. Why is/was the Franco-German partnership a key feature of European institution building?

3. What were the main objectives of the single European market and the Single European Act?

4. How would you describe the balance of power between the various components of the EU: Commission, Council, Parliament, and Court?

5. What has greatly contributed to the increased influence of the European Court of Justice?

6. How are the policy responsibilities between the Commission and Council determined?

7. What led to the increase of power of the European Parliament, and how has it influenced the policy process and regional integration?

8. What are some of the contributing factors that account for the stunted development of a European identity and Euro-level public participation?

9. How do we begin to understand why European countries agreed to abolish their currencies and adopt a brand new untested currency, namely the euro?

10. How would you compare the development of interests, identities, and institutions in the EU to that of any of the country studies examined in this volume?

11. How would you assess the impact of "globalization" in the formation of the EU and in the launching of various ambitious programs and objectives?

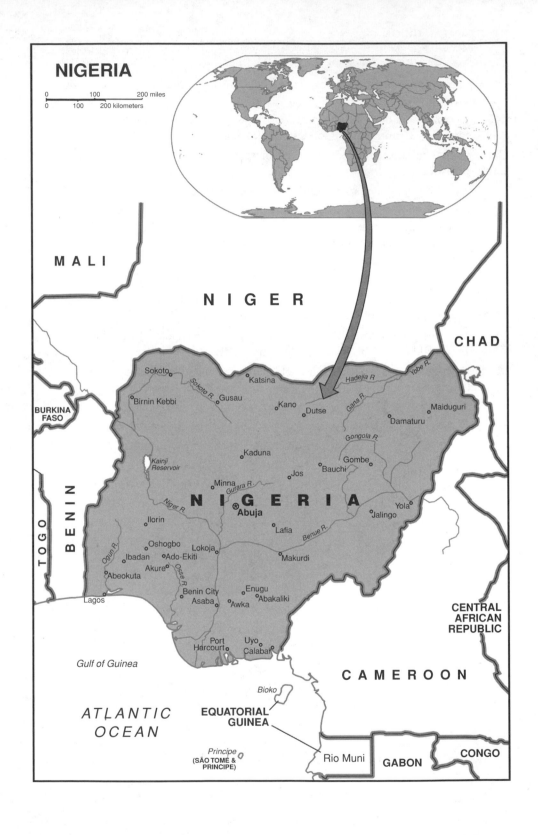

CHAPTER FOURTEEN

Nigeria

Okechukwu Iheduru

Introduction

Three mutually reinforcing sets of factors have played a central role in shaping Nigeria's political development from the precolonial through the colonial to the postcolonial era. These are the material interests and competing identities of its roughly 150 million peoples and 250 ethnic groups mediated by the type of institutions (that is, those long-term, authoritative rules and procedures that structure how power flows) created by the people and those who have exercised political authority over this territory. These material interests, identities, and institutions have in turn been shaped by the international environment in which Nigerians in each of these periods in their history interacted among themselves and with the outside world. What makes Nigerian politics interesting also is the constant proliferation of these material interests and identities – often arising from both domestic and global pressures – and the myriad ways in which they have either been accommodated or rejected by the given political order, as well as the extent to which these dynamic interactions have enhanced or undermined the existing order.

The combination of these four variables provides a robust framework for analyzing the general family of events that have shaped the political life of this fascinating country. The first set of these events falls within the historical and social origins of the entity that make up Nigeria today. These include events that took place in the colonial period (1914–1960), in the period from independence to the fall of the First Republic and the Biafran war (1960–1970), and during the rise of "military federalism" and the petroleum economy, or the "curse of black gold" (1970–1979). The second set of events comprises developments that occurred during the Second Republic (1979–1983) and the era of military dictatorships and a stillborn Third Republic (1983–1998) that followed the collapse of the Second Republic. The final set of events centers around the return to democracy since 1999. The interests, identities, and institutions developed within these social and historical contexts and mediated by global developments have given rise to a certain kind of formal and informal political culture that has come to define independent Nigeria. The chapter ends by exploring what became of these material interests, identities, and institutions during the unprecedented, unbroken eight years of electoral democracy that began in 1999, and how they have been affected by global developments.

Social and Historical Origins

CONQUEST AND COLONIALISM: THE SOURCES OF IDENTITY AND UNITY IN NIGERIA

In 2006, the National Population Commission estimated Nigeria's population at about 140 million people, but with a 3.2 percent annual growth rate, the country's population was roughly 150 million in 2007. One in five Africans is Nigerian, and they speak more than 250 mutually unintelligible languages. Three of these linguistic-ethnic groups, namely the **Hausa-Fulani** in the north, the **Yoruba** in the southwest, and the **Igbo** in the southeast have dominated much of the country's political and economic life. Following the British abolition in 1807 of the transatlantic slave trade (of which the areas that form modern Nigeria supplied a substantial proportion of the estimated 15 million Africans sold into slavery), Nigerians' ancestors were brought under British colonial rule between 1861 and 1902. Colonialism was instituted through a combination of wars of conquest, treaties of "protection" between the British and besieged rulers and communities, and Christian missionary activities that sowed discord among the people. There were also conquest and control by British trading companies, namely the **Royal Niger Company**, which was granted a charter by the British Crown to administer the areas along the River Niger as its colony from 1886 until 1900. No matter how each community was brought under British rule, the process was driven by – and operated for – a mixture of commercial interests and booty-hunters, as well as local participants and imperial interests in London, a history of state–society relations that was to shape political life in postcolonial Nigeria.

At the turn of the nineteenth century, two separate colonies, the Colony of Lagos and **Protectorate** of Southern Nigeria (administered from Lagos) and the **Protectorate** of Northern Nigeria (administered from Kaduna) were firmly established. In 1914, the British, concerned primarily about the cost of administering a largely poor territory, brought the two colonies under one entity ruled by one governor (based in Lagos) in what is now known as the "**amalgamation**" of Northern and Southern Nigeria. These disparate ethnic groups and cultures were given the name "Nigeria" by an English woman, Flora Shaw, who later married the British officer, **Sir Frederick Lugard**, who supervised this amalgamation. While most parts of the south had only been under colonial rule for barely a decade before this forced merger (thus lacking any sense of common political identity), much of the north had been ruled as a single colonial political entity – and developed a high degree of political identity beyond the century-old **emirate political system** – over the course of more than forty years. Even then, the two colonies, now called provinces, each under a lieutenant governor, continued life as two separate entities until 1947, thus ensuring that their historical, cultural, linguistic, and religious differences mediated by colonial institutions and local and foreign interests would play a pivotal (mostly negative) role in what would later become contemporary Nigeria. Not surprisingly, some Nigerians in frustration have continued to blame the "**mistake of 1914**" enforced by Lugard for much of the country's checkered political history.

One of those "mistakes" introduced in 1903 was the "**indirect rule**" **system** whereby the British ruled conquered territories through existing "traditional" or "natural" political institutions and sought to disrupt the extant local institutions as little as possible. Northern Nigeria was suited to this system of rule because of the centralized political system on which the emirates in the precolonial era were based. The people (now British colonial subjects) hardly noticed any change, while the emirs and their palace officials and tributary chiefs continued with their daily functions except that they henceforth had to take instructions from the district officer ("the Crown on the ground") and his handful of police and military officers and court officials. While this policy was successful in the north, quite a number of emirs refused to cooperate with Lugard's proclamation subjecting them under his rule, and they were immediately deposed and exiled from their territories. Indirect rule was fairly successful in western Nigeria, where a variety of centralized monarchical political systems also predated colonial rule.

The east and southeast of Nigeria (the homeland of the Igbo and other minority ethnic groups) were more challenging because precolonial society in these areas was characterized by ritualized decentralized segmented political systems often described by anthropologists as "stateless" or "acephalous" societies. These are the societies masterfully described in Chinua Achebe's classic novels, *Things Fall Apart* and *Arrow of God*, where there were no kings or chiefs with political authority and the all-male village assembly was the highest form of political organization. Consequently, the British imposed "**warrant chiefs**" in these areas to conform with the indirect-rule policies largely informed by their experience in mostly Islamic northern Nigeria.

COLONIAL LEGACIES: EMERGING INTERESTS, IDENTITIES, AND INSTITUTIONS

Colonial rule generated tremendous anger and frustration as the whole system of indirect rule turned many of the new rulers into tyrants acting on behalf of the colonial government and the emerging colonial economy. The colonial economy was export oriented and required immediate integration of peasants and the precolonial subsistence economy into the modern capitalist system through the system of taxation and commodification of land. This was accompanied by the development of modern systems of transportation and communication, especially railways and roads, to convey agricultural and mineral produce to the newly developed seaports at the coast for shipment to European factories. Inevitably, this gave rise to budding urban centers, largely segregated according to race in the south, but also along ethnic groups in the north, where recent migrants from the south (many of whom had recently converted to Christianity and received some form of Western education) were granted settlement spaces outside the old city walls, called **Sabon Gari**, or "stranger quarters."

Not only did urbanization create new interests and institutions, it also created cleavages between the rural areas controlled by the "natural rulers" and the newly mobilized urban dwellers, just as it brought Africans in constant friction with entrenched European, Lebanese, and Indian commercial interests. The latter two had accompanied European colonialism to Africa as service providers and/or indentured servants but never returned to their homelands, and were placed a notch above Africans in the colonial racial pecking order. Although their populations have gradually diminished over the years, more than 100 years later they have never fully integrated into Nigerian society.

Perhaps the most lasting legacy of British colonialism in Nigeria has been the introduction of an anomalous federal system of government in 1954 comprising the government at the center based in Lagos and three regional governments – East, North, and West. Not only was the Northern Region geographically larger than the two other regions combined, each region was also dominated economically and politically by one of the three largest ethnic groups – the Igbo in the East, the Hausa-Fulani in the North, and the Yoruba in the West. Each region was also identified with the three export products that became the mainstay of the Nigerian economy at the time: coal in the East, cocoa in the West, and peanuts (groundnuts) in the North. Most accounts of ethnicity have, for good reasons, tended to focus on the competitions and cooperation among the trio of Hausa-Fulani, Yoruba, and Igbo. The heart of ethnicization of Nigerian politics, however, lies with the numerous minority groups in each region who since 1954 have continued to agitate against their "marginalization" and consequently for further state creation as a panacea for their perceived right of self-determination. We shall return to this issue later in this chapter, but suffice to say that ethnicity or "tribalism" is a quintessential example of the interplay of interests, identities, and institutions in the shaping of politics in contemporary Nigeria. Finally, the state bequeathed to Nigerians in 1960 was – and has remained – highly nondemocratic and prone to using force, rather than dialogue, in its interactions with citizens and other social forces.

NATIONALISM AND THE ANTICOLONIAL MOVEMENT

British colonialism in Nigeria lasted anywhere from 60 to 100 years, depending on the date of each community's conquest and/or incorporation into the British Empire. However, agitation against colonial rule began in one form or another almost as soon as incorporation took place. The earlier forms of resistance, often referred to as "protonationalism," ranged from scattered peasant revolts to agitations by newly educated Nigerians for inclusion in the colonial governing structures or to be treated like "civilized" men like the Europeans. Some African merchants also complained about colonial laws and policies that discriminated against "natives" or that outlawed competition with European merchants. The colonial government and other European interests, however, undermined these putative nationalist risings through the time-tested divide-and-rule tactics that pitted one "tribal" interest against the others, further setting the stage for the political saliency of ethnic identities in the country's political development.

The relatively peaceful era of colonialism in Nigeria was jolted out of its slumber in the mid-1940s by the rise of militant anticolonial nationalism. The rise of urban centers attracted large numbers of migrants who, while retaining their ethnic identities, had begun to develop a common identity, especially against the racially discriminatory Europeans. This putative "national" identity was further sharpened by the founding of newspapers by indigenous Nigerians, especially the American-educated **Dr. Benjamin Nnamdi Azikiwe**, whose chain of newspapers became the mouthpiece of the movement. Dissatisfied with the "gentleman" politics of the extant elite and urban-based political parties in Lagos, Dr. Azikiwe later founded Nigeria's first truly national political party, the National Council of Nigeria and the Cameroons (NCNC) in 1944, whose call for independence made it popular with both the urban and rural dwellers.

The rise of labor unions in these urban centers added more fodder to the anticolonial movement, particularly after the three-month civil service strike in 1945 that almost crippled the colonial government. As secondary (and some university) educational opportunities widened and reached the urban and rural areas, Nigerian student unions and fledgling professional associations, both at home and overseas, provided additional pressure on the colonial government to quit. The return of hundreds of thousands of ex-servicemen, many of whom had fought more gallantly than their European comrades in Europe, Africa, and Asia during World War II, finally put an end to the myth of white supremacy and the white man's entitlement to rule the native. Internationally, the 1945 Pan-African Congress in Manchester, England (attended by many Nigerian politicians and students), which called Africans to go back to their respective countries and demand "independence now," as well as the independence of India and Pakistan from Britain in 1947, further whetted the appetite of the agitators and made them more impatient with British rule.

Britain, now severely weakened by the war, responded by massively investing the huge reserves accumulated by colonial Nigeria during the war in public infrastructure, social welfare, and education. A new constitution, which created the three regions, was introduced in 1947, but was denounced by the nationalists almost immediately. It was replaced by another one in 1951, which for the first time created a federal structure of government in Nigeria, ostensibly to allow each region to develop politically and economically at its own pace. This arrangement would later not only exacerbate the differential impact of Westernization in the north and the south, but also laid the foundation for the creation of new geographic identities, which have since become overlain with preexisting ones. The nationalists nonetheless pushed ahead with their demand for an end to British rule, making often fatal compromises along the way so long as the end was achieved, especially after Dr. Kwame Nkrumah's Ghana upstaged Nigeria in 1957 to become sub-Saharan Africa's first country to become independent.

As part of its colonial disengagement plans, the British granted self-government to Eastern and Western Nigerian regions in 1957, with the Northern Region following in 1959. On October 1, 1960, Nigeria became an independent country, with a central government that was structurally and administratively weaker than the three regional governments, saddled with the task of building a new nation in an increasingly complex and diverse society. In fact, Nigeria's most powerful and experienced indigenous politicians and administrators either from personal preference or as a result of political power games, opted to stay behind in the regions (Chief **Obafemi Awolowo** in the West and Sir **Ahmadu Bello** in the North as premiers, respectively), while the central government machinery was led by less competent subordinates and officials. The only possible exception was Dr. Azikiwe, arguably the foremost nationalist and the founder of the NCNC, who gave up the premier's position in the East to one of his subordinates in order to take up the ceremonial post of governor-general and representative of the British Crown in Nigeria. When Nigeria became a republic in 1963, Dr. Azikiwe became president of the Federal Republic of Nigeria, but his functions remained unchanged, an institutional arrangement that later became a source of friction between him and the prime minister, Sir Abubakar Tafawa Balewa – a northerner and the actual power holder – a few years later.

From Independence to the Fall of the First Republic

FEDERALISM AND THE QUEST FOR UNITY IN DIVERSITY

Nigeria entered postcolonial life with an explicitly federal constitution accepted by the political class as the only guarantee for "unity in diversity." Although **federalism** resolved many of the political questions arising from the country's competing ethno-religious and economic interests and identities, it created many more and exacerbated existing ones. By allowing considerable devolution of power to the three regions (increased to four in 1962), the three major ethnic groups were not only able to manage their differences but actually engaged in tremendous healthy competition that led to some of the best development efforts Nigeria has ever accomplished. The availability of more lucrative opportunities in the regions also restrained the ambitions of many local politicians and led to a rapid growth in the number of professional and technocratic cadres of managers and administrators, more than in any other African country in the first few years of independence. Since then, each major constitutional revision (1963, 1979, 1989, and 1999) has maintained the sanctity of this power-sharing arrangement. The premium that Nigerians put on federalism can be seen in the angry reactions to the unitary system of government introduced by **Major General Johnson T. U. Aguiyi-Ironsi** after the first coup d'état in 1966, for which he was eventually overthrown and killed, as well as the national uproar that accompanied a 1990 abortive coup whose ringleaders had hinted at abolishing the federal arrangement.

Paradoxically, the logic of federalism has also exacerbated the perpetual quest for more devolution of powers, especially the creation of more states. Every new region or state created, ostensibly to assuage the agitation of minorities for self-determination, immediately spawned new "minorities," sparking a new cycle of devolution that has seen the number of regions/states grow from three in 1960 to 36 in 1995. Although that number remained unchanged during the first eight years of the Fourth Republic (founded in 1999), there were no fewer than 25 active movements for state creation with varying degrees of cohesion and rationality in their agitations from 1999 to 2007. State creation is a volatile issue with serious consequences for the equally hotly contested issues of population and **resource control**. Hence, with the exception of the creation of Midwest Region out of the old Western Region in 1962, subsequent state creation has been done only by the military (12 in 1967; 19 in 1975; 35 in 1987; and 36 in 1995). Unlike many federal systems, the 1979, 1989, and 1999 constitutions in Nigeria went a step further by enshrining a three-tier federal structure, with local government councils (now 774 in all) having constitutionally guaranteed political and fiscal authority with minimal control by state governments, although the other two tiers have yet to learn to respect this constitutional guarantee.

Behind these demands for state creation (and consequently for local councils) lie the politics of "**fiscal federalism**" by which all the federating units theoretically contribute to, and derive allocations from, federally collected revenue equitably. In the First Republic, revenue distribution was based on the formula of "derivation," allocating 51 percent of the revenue back to where it was collected. This revenue-sharing formula made the regions more powerful and more attractive than the government at the center, even as it tended to widen the gap between the relatively better endowed Eastern and Western regions (relying on palm oil and coal and cocoa, respectively) and their poorer northern neighbors, whose revenue came mainly from peanuts. While various military regimes since 1966 retained the federal principle, the 29 years of military dictatorship actually resulted in more centralization of both state power and revenue – producing the oxymoronic phrase "military federalism" – which remained unchanged under the Fourth Republic.

That military rule was dominated by northern military officers seen by some southern activists as bent on perpetuating northern domination of Nigerian politics financed by wealth increasingly derived from the south (mostly in areas occupied by ethnic minorities) did not help matters, either. Hence, there have been occasional agitations for "regional" or "zonal" armies and police forces to counterbalance northern domination. Since 1979, military and civilian regimes have implemented the principle of "**federal character**," Nigeria's version of affirmative action, seeking to guarantee a proportionate share of federal positions, including admissions into educational institutions and military academies, civil service, and so on, to all states (increasingly based on ethnic group identification). In reality, this policy was introduced to ensure against southern domination of public life, given the wide gap that continues to exist between the north and the south, even though the latter controlled political power for much of the country's history. These gaps are rooted in the differential impact of economic development, the political choices made by the northern political elite prior to independence to limit Westernization in the region, as well corruption and ineptitude of subsequent rulers.

ETHNICITY, PATRONAGE POLITICS, AND PARTY POLITICS

The federal imperative arises from the fact that Nigeria's 250 ethnic groups, with their distinct (and mostly mutually unintelligible) languages and cultural characteristics, are geographically separated. Almost any one with a passing knowledge of Nigeria would be familiar with the "tripod" – Hausa-Fulani, Igbo, and Yoruba – who are unquestionably the most numerous and most influential in the country's politics. There are, however, several politically and economically powerful smaller ones that further complicate the interethnic political competition for access to, or control over, economic and political power, as well as the general resentment toward the influence of the tripod over national political life. Indeed, it is this competition and resentment of the trio that has led to more geographic separation of these ethnic groups through the creation of more states, as we discussed earlier.

Until 1947, the colonial government and the colonial economy had unwittingly encouraged the migration of mostly southern Nigerians into other parts of the country through the expansion of roads, railways, the colonial civil service, and the rise of urban centers and the general colonial economy. Migrants into these new urban centers formed numerous cultural and "hometown" associations that helped them maintain ties to their "traditional" ethnic group's homeland, and also provided an anchor and source of help to newly arrived co-ethnics. While most southerners residing in the North were segregated into the *Sabon Gari*, northern migrants in southern cities and rural areas generally concentrated in the *Hausa Quarters*, or colonies. While the North had developed a longer sense of common identity due to precolonial institutions and longer experience of colonialism, the political saliency of ethnicity was minimal up to this time. Despite this separate existence, some sense of "one Nigeria" was actually developing, as evidenced by the election of a Hausa mayor for Enugu in the East; Azikiwe's political successes in the West; the large and influential Yoruba community in Kaduna; and the prominent role of some northerners such as Said Zungur in the Igbo-dominated Zikist Movement (youth arm of the NCNC). The trend toward a politically homogeneous country and common citizenship was halted with the introduction of the Richards Constitution in 1948 (named after Sir Arthur Richards, Lord Milverton, the colonial governor). This constitution split the country into three regions: the Northern Region, dominated by the Hausa-Fulani, the Western Region, dominated by the Yoruba, and the Eastern Region, dominated by the Igbo, even as the country continued to operate a unitary system of government.

The Richards Constitution also introduced a legislative council for the "natives" in Lagos in which representation was to be based on political parties. The previous all-white legislative council was gradually opened up to a few "civilized natives" and gave rise to Nigeria's first political party, the Nigerian Democratic Party, founded by Herbert Macaulay, who often competes for the title of "father of Nigerian nationalism" with Dr. Azikiwe. The imperatives of nationwide party representation in the new council quickly led to the transformation of some of the larger hitherto cultural associations into mass political parties. With the exception of Azikiwe's NCNC, formed in 1944 with a multiethnic membership and hence more "nationalistic," the other parties that emerged were largely ethnic-based mass movements led by very charismatic ethnic identity brokers hitherto preoccupied with ethnic mobilization for new opportunities or economic development of their homelands. The Action Group (AG), which would later dominate politics in the West, emerged from the Yoruba cultural association, *Egbe Omo Oduduwa*, while the Northern People's Congress (NPC) – whose regional and exclusionist outlook could not be mistaken – simply mutated from *Jamiyaa Mutanem Arewa*, the cultural association dominated by the Hausa-Fulani, especially the princes of the emirates conquered by Captain Lugard in 1886. Minority groups similarly formed their own political parties, such as the radical Northern Elements Progressive Union (NEPU) representing the indigenous minority groups in the North; the Middle Belt Congress in the central Benue-Plateau region; and the Independent Party and Mid-West Union representing minority groups in the East and West, respectively.

This more divisive form of ethnic identity mobilization spilled over into economic and social life as Nigerians sought and competed for opportunities in education, employment (in the civil service and the putative private sector), and even residential patterns. The Yoruba were initially most favored to compete in the emerging economic and political order, given their longer experience with Westernization (especially education), dating back to 1861, when the Crown Colony of Lagos was formally incorporated. Within a few decades, the Igbo, who were formally conquered in 1902, quickly caught up with the Yoruba, igniting often a more vicious interethnic competition, stereotypes, and mutual suspicion that persists to this day between the two groups. The North, which had agreed with Lugard to bar the entry of Christian missionaries into the region ostensibly to minimize the corrupting influence of the West, continued to lag behind other regions, further triggering fear and resentment about "southern domination" that has continued to define much of north–south relations for most of the country's history. Ethnic considerations also influenced recruitment into the armed and security forces as well as the bureaucracy, as the country pursued an "Africanization" policy to fast-track Nigerians into positions of authority vacated by the departing colonialists.

The introduction of a federal constitution and granting of executive and legislative powers to regions dominated by the three major ethnic groups in 1954 further cemented this geographical separation and ethnic identity of Nigerians. Ethnicity finally crept into the anticolonial movement, splitting northern and southern leaders. The North, fearing complete domination by the South in an independent Nigeria, wanted a slower process of decolonization, while the West and the East wanted "independence now" as recommended by the 1945 Pan-African Congress in Manchester. A "premature" motion for independence by southern politicians in the colonial legislature led to the infamous Kano Riots of 1954 in which hundreds of southerners (mostly Igbo) were killed and "stranger" properties were burned and looted. The North–South divide was further witnessed in 1957 when both the Eastern and Western regions were granted self-government status, while the Northern

Region declined the offer until 1959, just a few months before the country gained independence in 1960.

At independence, therefore, Nigeria was a deeply divided country that truly needed "unity in diversity" if the entity described by the leader of the Action Group as "a mere geographical expression" were to survive at all. While other African countries may have entered postcolonial life with a semblance of national unity that later fizzled out, the Nigerian political elite faced serious ethnic cleavages that belied contemporary – often quite generous – prognoses about the prospects for economic development and political stability of the new country. The Northern Region was bigger than the Eastern and Western regions combined, its main political party, the NPC, made little effort to expand its reach into other regions – not surprising given its exclusivist self-definition. In order to govern, the NPC needed the support of the dominant party in either the West or the East. Instead of uniting to defeat the NPC (which would probably have ended the federation), the NCNC and the AG focused primarily on exploiting ethnic minority resentment in each other's region to enable them to acquire enough political power to share power with the NPC, whose solid political power base was hardly dented by its much weaker ethnic minority-based political parties.

In 1960, the NCNC (with predominant Igbo leadership but also a multi-ethnic following) allied with the NPC, shutting out the Yoruba from the new government and further exacerbating the Igbo–Yoruba rivalry and mutual suspicion. Alhaji A. T. Balewa of the NPC became federal prime minister, while NCNC's Dr. Azikiwe settled for the ceremonial office of governor-general (representing the British monarch, very odd for the acclaimed "father of Nigerian nationalism"), which was later changed to "president" when Nigeria became a republic in 1963. The exclusion of the Action Group (hence, the Yoruba ethnic group) from the new national government resulted in a revolt in the Action Group, especially among the minorities. This was happily exploited by the NPC-NCNC alliance, who quickly declared a state of emergency in the Western Region that removed Awolowo and the AG from power. Chief Awolowo was later jailed for sedition and treason. Emergency rule opened up a window of opportunity for the creation of the Midwest Region in 1962 by the federal government to further weaken Yoruba/AG influence. Similar ethnic minority agitations in the other two regions governed by the NPC and NCNC were, however, muzzled or neutralized, sometimes very brutally.

By 1964, the "marriage of convenience" between the Igbo-led NCNC and the NPC had collapsed, with the latter engineering a split in the AG and forming a new governing alliance with an AG splinter group called Nigerian National Democratic Party (NNDP). Meanwhile a disputed national census conducted in 1963 that put the Northern Region at more than half of the country's population had raised the ethnic political temperature to boiling point, while massive rigging of the 1965 federal elections, especially in the Western Region, resulted in lingering violence in the region. An aloof NPC/NNDP federal government ignored calls to declare emergency rule in the West and stem the tide of a violent orgy gripping the country, even as it focused its interest in hosting a Commonwealth Heads of Government summit that year. The elite compromises premised primarily on capturing political power also left wide gaps in political authority that encouraged massive corruption and misuse of public funds by politicians. Corruption was so prominent in government that the name of the federal finance minister at the time, Chief Festus Okotie-Eboh, became synonymous with financial corruption in Nigeria, which was also common at the regional levels.

MILITARY INTERVENTION AND THE BIAFRAN WAR OF SECESSION

Nigeria's First Republic was ended by a long-rumored military coup d'état on January 15, 1966, similar to the ignominious end of the corrupt civilian regime in Achebe's fictional novel, *A Man of the People*, published in December 1965. The coup, led by five army majors, all but one of whom was Igbo, resulted in the death of the federal prime minister (a northerner), the Northern Region premier, the federal finance minister, and a number of senior army officers of northern and western origin. No Igbo or eastern senior politician was killed or arrested, while the president, Dr. Azikiwe (an Igbo) had left the country for a medical check-up overseas shortly before the coup. The indiscipline among those who had carried out the coup, especially those detailed to carry out the operation in the Eastern Region and in the West, brought about its quick collapse. The Igbo general officer commanding (GOC) Nigerian Army, Major General Aguiyi-Ironsi, who had been listed for elimination, was able to mobilize troops and negotiated an end to the coup with the leader of the group, Major Chukwuma Kaduna Nzeogwu, after three days.

Instead of reconstituting the shattered civilian government, General Ironsi and his advisers went ahead and established a military government led by a Supreme Military Council supported by a Federal Executive Council (of military and civilian appointees), and military governors for each of the four regions. Another similarity with *A Man of the People* was the wild celebration and dancing in the streets all over the country by Nigerians relieved that Major Nzeogwu and his coconspirators (who became instant national heroes, though less so in the North) had ended the menace of the corrupt and insensitive politicians who had seemed invincible only the day before. The celebration quickly turned into a nightmare as the military stayed in power for 29 years (interrupted briefly by the Second Republic, from 1979 to 1983), turning Nigeria into a coup-prone, politically unstable country.

Contrary to the assertion that the first coup was an "Igbo coup" intended to allegedly foist Igbo domination on the rest of the country, the putschists claimed to have been motivated purely by patriotism to end corruption, restore integrity to government, and maintain national stability – and recent accounts by one of the surviving perpetrators and by their military contemporaries have lent credence to this claim. In 2007 the private secretary to Chief Awolowo (jailed leader of the Action Group) made a startling revelation that the coup plotters intended to release Awolowo from prison and make him head of state, whether or not he liked it, as he was more amenable to their inchoate socialist rhetoric. Had this occurred, that Igbo officers would overthrow the government and invite a Yoruba politician to head the new government would have been incomprehensible to (and probably caused more social strife among) both the Yoruba and the Igbo, who supposedly hated each other. In the poisoned atmosphere of the early 1960s, the plotters' motive – whether rational or not – was, however, overshadowed by the deep divisions among the political class at the time. The mutual suspicion generated by the coup was compounded by the ethnic composition of the coup-plot victims and by the fact that General Ironsi, the head of the SMC, was himself Igbo. Ironsi's government did not help matters either when it enacted **Decree no. 34 of 1966**, which unified the federal bureaucracy and police forces and provided further ammunition to those alleging an Igbo conspiracy.

The unification decree, more than the coup itself, undermined the most important elite pact, federalism, which had managed to keep the country together, even as it had militated against genuine nation building and had become the source of most of the schizophrenia and growing pains of the First Republic. Consequently, on July 29, 1966, General Ironsi and several Igbo army officers were killed in a counter-coup – again, long-rumored – led by officers of northern origin, who installed Lt. Col. Yakubu Gowon (General Ironsi's deputy, who had several times denied rumors of the coup to his superior) as the head of the SMC and commander in chief of the Armed Forces of Nigeria. After initially flirting with the threat by the Northern Region to finally secede from the federation, Gowon quickly retraced his steps (at the urging of the British) and declared his commitment to "one Nigeria."

The counter-coup was followed by a **pogrom** that left more than 10,000 eastern civilians (mostly Igbos) living mostly in northern Nigeria and scores of Igbo army officers dead at the hands of their colleagues, who had mixed with or led hordes of cheering northerners as they went on a house-to-house hunt for their innocent victims. Despite assurances by the federal government about the safety of all Nigerians in all parts of the country (which encouraged many easterners to return to their places of residence in other parts of the country), another more deadly pogrom occurred three months later. This put the total number of what would probably be classified today as genocide against Igbo civilians that year at over 100,000, plus over 200 Igbo army officers, numerous reports of rape of Igbo women, and looting and destruction of their property. The Eastern Region military government subsequently asked all easterners living in other parts of Nigeria to return to the East since the federal and other regional governments could no longer guarantee their safety. The number of other Nigerians that left the Eastern Region paled in significance and effect compared to the misery and political tension and passion generated by the mass exodus of Igbos to the East that followed the pogroms.

Tensions also flared as the Igbo military governor of Eastern Nigeria, Lt. Col. Chukwuemeka Odumegwu Ojukwu, refused to accept the legitimacy of Lt. Col. Gowon and the government that replaced General Ironsi, arguing that Gowon was not the most senior officer in rank to replace the slain head of state. Negotiations by military and civilian leaders of all the regions and mediation efforts by foreigners failed to produce an acceptable elite pact to reunify the country. The most famous of such efforts was the agreement brokered by the Ghanaian government known as the "Aburi Accords" (after the town where the meetings took place). However, it collapsed even before the details of its provision for an even weaker central government (a sort of confederacy) could be worked out. The federal government subsequently embargoed the Eastern Region for its "intransigence," while the Eastern Region confiscated all federal properties in the region, and refused to turn over revenue due the center.

On May 27, 1967, the federal government, determined to finally end Igbo domination of politics in the East and to preempt a rumored secession by the region, divided the country into 12 states, three of which emerged from the old Eastern Region. The Eastern regional government responded on May 30, 1967, by declaring the former Eastern Region "**the Sovereign Independent Republic of Biafra.**" The following week, General Gowon ordered federal forces to initiate "police action" in the breakaway region. This quickly ballooned into a 30-month civil war, pitting ill-equipped, but determined Biafrans against better-trained, well-equipped, and internationally supported (by the United Kingdom and Russia) federal forces. Only four mostly inconsequential countries, Côte d'Ivoire, Haiti, Tanzania, and Trinidad and Tobago, recognized the Biafran state. The war, which ended on January 12, 1970, with the Biafran surrender, is generally acclaimed to be one of the most devastating civil wars of the twentieth century, and one that caused more than two million Biafran deaths – mostly children – from starvation because the Nigerian government refused to lift its embargo on relief materials and supplies getting to rebel-held territories.

The Rise of "Military Federalism" and the Oil Boom Era

MILITARY RULE, PREBENDALISM, AND THE "CURSE OF BLACK GOLD" (1970–1979)

The new military regime sacked the legislature and abolished the 1963 constitution and began ruling by decrees. The political instability and the ensuing civil war quickly led to a militarization of the economy, in the sense that much of the national effort was devoted to prosecuting the war. Following the Biafran surrender in 1970, the government declared an official policy of "no victor no vanquished" and embarked on a policy of "reconciliation, reconstruction, and rehabilitation" – the three Rs, as they came to be called. To their credit, the military government's three Rs largely succeeded, with the East (now broken up into three states) quickly recovering, while the government adopted a number of measures to encourage civic education and absorption of some members of Igbos and other easterners who had been dislocated by the civil war into the civil service and the private sector. The government also embarked on rapid demobilization of the army (which had grown from a mere 8,000 in 1966 to about 600,000 in 1970) and their removal from much of Igboland, which they had occupied following the collapse of the rebellion.

Given that all policies emanated from the SMC in Lagos and state governors were appointees and lower-ranking officers of the regime, it was inevitable – given the nature of military organization – that centralization tendencies would trump the centripetal forces of federalism. Hence, the irony of military rule in Nigeria was that the Gowon regime in fact implemented Decree no. 34 of 1966, for which General Ironsi had been deposed and assassinated and over 100,000 Igbos slaughtered in the infamous pogroms that followed. One new policy that undermined the competitive development policies of the erstwhile regions was the government takeover of schools, including universities, and the standardization of curricula, thus permanently imposing the power of the central government over a concurrent legislative matter. The three regional universities at Nsukka (East), Ife (West), and Zaria (North) became federal universities, along with the federal university already in Lagos. By 1979, Nigeria had 13 federal universities, with federal agencies coordinating admissions and general administration and accreditation. Another centralizing trend was the growth in the central government's share of federal revenue, which increased to 58 percent; this reversed the power balance of the First Republic, when regional governments had had more resources and were thus more attractive than the center. Civil service rules became centralized, while regional and emirate police forces were abolished. Consequently, large numbers of bureaucrats in the regional/state governments joined the federal civil service, even as the service massively recruited personnel to match its activities, which had grown tremendously. The local government system was "centralized" in that a national framework (later codified in the 1979 and subsequent constitutions) mandated a uniform structure, irrespective of the culture or stage of development. Finally, the military regime enacted the **Land Use Decree of 1978**, which brought all land tenure laws and norms under one uniform legal structure in which land use rights were vested in the state governor. While the goal was to ensure that access to land did not impede national development, the decree created much discontent in that it failed to truly reflect extant land tenure cultures in many parts of the country. Some observers have described this trend toward centralization while also maintaining power-sharing structures and institutions as "military federalism."

The mainstay of this "military federalism" – a misnomer – was the sudden infusion of oil revenue – otherwise called the "oil boom" – which had become the main source of national revenue (about 90 percent) by 1979. Although petroleum was first discovered in Oloibiri in the Niger Delta in 1958, it was not a prominent feature of the economy during the First Republic. Moreover, the civil war (1967–1970) stopped all exports. The war's end coincided with a number of developments in the international arena, namely the 1973 Yom Kippur war between Israel and its Arab neighbors and the Iranian Revolution of 1978, which drove the price of oil to as high as $39 per barrel. Consequently, the revenue accruing to the Nigerian government grew so dramatically that the head of state, General Gowon, actually claimed that Nigeria's biggest problem was what to do with its money. The resulting oil boom, from what seemed like an endless supply of revenue (amounting to about 85 percent of export earnings even by 2007), triggered a spending spree that saw Nigerians importing all manner of goods from all over the world, in addition to several capital projects back home. The most memorable reminder of that era was the infamous "cement armada," whereby more than 400 merchant ships laden with cement were waiting to anchor along Nigeria's coast at any given time from 1975 to 1977 due to unprecedented port congestion. The oil boom, with its massive infusion of wealth in the cities, also accelerated massive population movement from rural to urban areas, increasing the country's rate of urbanization from 20 percent in 1970 to 39 percent of the population by the end of the 1980s.

With the oil boom also came massive corruption and leakage of political authority. The military regime that had prosecuted the war and did a laudable job of reintegrating the country lost its focus and reneged on its promise to hand over power to civilians in 1976. The national census it conducted in 1973 was a total flop and had to be rejected. Graft and stealing of public funds became commonplace among the top military officers in government as well as in the federal bureaucracy, which had become bloated (from 71,693 employees in 1960 to 630,000, not counting 250,000 in military service, by 1974), clumsier, and inept either because of or despite the reliance of the regime on the counsel of the so-called "super-permanent" secretaries.

When General Muritala Mohammed came to power in a palace coup in 1975, he dismissed or retired an estimated 11,000 administrators, while embarking on vigorous anticorruption measures that many still remember with nostalgia even today. Yet, such upheaval that eliminated experienced administrators drastically undermined the capacity of the bureaucracy and partly accounts for the continued capacity challenges of the civil service.

Nonetheless, the military went ahead in 1977 to host the biggest cultural extravaganza of the period, called the Second World Festival of Black Culture (FESTAC), which brought very little in return to either Nigeria or the thousands of the African diaspora that trooped to the country for the event. The oil bonanza, which should have accelerated sustainable economic development under more effective planning, management, and efficient allocation of resources, became a "resource curse" in that it became the major source of the problems the country now faced. Moreover, it also exacerbated those already generated by the competing interests, identities, and institutions created over the years and mediated by forces operating outside the country's borders as our discussion later on of militancy and piracy in the Niger Delta will show.

Despite these maladies, the military governments scored some successes, especially rebuilding a broken country and healing the wounds of the war. With lots of petro-dollars at its disposal, the military regime threw its weight around as the "big brother" in Africa and even challenged great powers and superpowers on African issues (such as the independence of Angola in 1975, the apartheid regime in South Africa, and the white minority regime in then Rhodesia). Several African countries benefited from Nigeria's concessional oil supplies; anticolonial liberation movements received financial and diplomatic support; and the military regimes often bankrolled several regional integration initiatives, such as the Economic Community of West African States (ECOWAS), founded in 1975. Through these activist foreign policy measures, the military was able to rekindle a high degree of self-confidence and patriotism (and possibly arrogance) in most Nigerians of that generation.

Yet, the national planners during this period failed not only to invest in productive activities but also to anticipate the impending collapse of the world price of oil as they prepared to exit the political scene in 1979. Even in the field of education, where they achieved tremendous successes, lack of resources and planning, infrastructure, and instructors at all levels nearly crippled the educational system so that the governments had little choice but to massively import personnel from anywhere in the world, further creating loopholes in the already weakened governing and administrative machinery of the state.

MIXED ECONOMY AND STATE-MEDIATED CAPITAL ACCUMULATION

Emboldened nationalism and patriotism also manifested themselves in the domestic economy as Nigeria's post–civil war rulers sought to minimize the vestiges of neocolonialism and the country's dependency on the very multinational corporations (MNCs) and other businesses that were part of the colonial economy. The Second National Development Plan (1972–1975) was based on the import-substitution industrialization model; this sought to create a mixed economy whereby the private sector would exist side-by-side with government control over the "commanding heights of the economy."

The indigenous private sector was considered either too weak to engage the MNCs, or too profit driven to lead the nationalist quest for rapid economic development.

By the late 1970s, several capital projects such the Ajaokuta Steel Mill and four other steel rolling mills were planned or constructed. Government created, single-handedly or in joint ventures with MNCs, scores of state-owned enterprises (SOEs) in banking, insurance, roads, air and maritime transport (including massive shipping and port development), manufacturing (including auto assembly plants and textiles), and construction sectors. Massive sums were invested in creating about 15 River Basin Development authorities as the foundation for the takeoff of mechanized agriculture, just as investments in the national electricity grid, telephone and telegraph, and communications increased. Symbols and trappings of nationhood such as Nigeria Airways, Nigerian National Shipping Lines, the Nigerian National Petroleum Corporation (NNPC), fertilizer and newsprint, and even manufactured food distribution outlets constituted part of the "commanding heights" of the economy, now under complete government control or through joint ventures.

The government also tried to foster the rise of an indigenous entrepreneurial class emasculated during and after colonial rule by the activities of MNCs and Lebanese, Syrian, and Indian businesses. In 1972, the government introduced the **Nigerian Indigenization Policy**, reserving low-skill sectors of the economy for local businesses, while medium- and high-skill sector businesses had to be joint ventures either with the government or with local business. Foreign-owned banks, insurance companies, and manufacturing and retail companies in all sectors were compelled to sell their shares to Nigerians, while the government in some cases provided investment loans to enable indigenes to purchase such shares. Further refinements were made in this policy in 1974 to accommodate the avalanche of complaints that inevitably accompanied this state-mediated wealth accumulation, including cases of corruption and Nigerians fronting for the foreign businesses the government was determined to indigenize.

Perhaps the most enduring consequence of the indigenization policy was the politicization of Nigerian capitalism, in that one section of the country, the Yoruba, benefited the most from corporate divestiture and government loan programs. The Hausa-Fulani had political power and controlled the military, but not economic power, having yet to recover from the differential impact of economic development that had continued to exacerbate the historical north–south divide. The worst hit were the Igbos, many of whom were still recovering from the aftermath of the civil war; they were especially devastated by the federal military government's postwar policy of paying only £20 to all depositors, irrespective of the amount they had in the bank in Biafra. Even then, few Igbos actually received this paltry sum to start a new life, only to be confronted two years later with one of the biggest and most lopsided wealth transfers in the country's history.

By the time the military retreated to their barracks temporarily in 1979, the southwest of Nigeria, the Yoruba heartland, was so firmly in control of the Nigerian economy that one northern sociologist contended that about 80 percent of the amount of any contract awarded anywhere in Nigeria would be circulating between Ibadan and Lagos within two weeks of closing on the contract. While some aspects of the mixed-economy policy did expand the level of industrialization in the country, the strategy actually crowded out the indigenous private sector and largely became a conduit for capital accumulation by the political elite. The resultant state–society relations have been described as **prebendalism**, defined as a form of corruption whereby state offices are regarded as patronage given by an official or a ruler to individual clients in return for their loyalty and used to generate material benefits for the officeholders and their constituents and kin groups. Overall, this has created a sense of entitlement in many people in Nigeria. Elected officials, government workers, and members of the ethnic and religious groups to which they belong all feel they have a right to a share of government revenues. As control over state resources (instead of entrepreneurship) became the quickest means to accumulate personal wealth, competition for state power (especially in the military) became a matter of life or death requiring the use of any means, including violence, to attain power. Competing religious and ethnic identities were also caught in the elite struggle for economic and political power as competitors used them to gain power, or blamed such identities for their losses. Access to, and consolidation of, power also depended on patron–client networks that provided political support to the political class while providing economic rent and other benefits to their supporters at lower levels.

THE SECOND REPUBLIC (1979–1983)

The military, led by general **Olusegun Obasanjo**, relinquished power and returned to the barracks in 1979. A new American-style presidential constitution was drawn up ostensibly to avoid the "mistakes of the past." The Westminster parliamentary system of government and its winner-take-all nature was said to be unsuitable to a divided society like Nigeria, where no political party was capable of winning a majority and where ruling coalitions were largely unstable. The 1979 constitution enshrined complete separation of powers among the three arms of government: a strong executive (headed by a popularly elected president and limited to only two terms); a dual chamber legislature (Senate and House of Representatives, both popularly elected); and the judiciary appointed by state or federal chief executives and ratified by the legislature.

In striving to create "genuine and truly national political parties," as opposed to the regional and culturally based parties in the First Republic, the new constitution stipulated that support for candidates for president must reflect the "federal character" of Nigeria, that is, candidates must win 25 percent of the votes cast in each of at least two-thirds of the now 19 states of the federation. Elections became a national function implemented by a Federal Election Commission (FEDECO) which also was given the authority to register only those political parties that meet the "federal character" test, that is, two-thirds of the states must be represented in the party leadership. Governments at the state level had elected governors as head of the executive branch and single chamber legislatures (House of Assembly) and a judiciary appointed by the governor with legislative approval. Local government councils were recognized in the constitution as "the third tier" of governmental power, with guaranteed revenue but still subject to supervision by the state governments.

Political parties were again made legal in 1978. Nigeria's political class responded like hungry lions and founded about 150 political parties, but in the end, the military regime registered only five of them. Yet, the ghost of the First Republic hung over the transition program and re-created old problems in new guises. The National Party of Nigeria (NPN) was led by Alhaji Shehu Shagari and scions of the NPC, while the Nigerian People's Party (NPP) was led by Azikiwe and his former NCNC stalwarts. The Unity Party of Nigeria (UPN) simply reconstructed Awolowo's Action Group and the Great Nigeria People's Party (GNPP) was a breakaway faction from NPP. The People's Redemption Party (PRP) brought together the same radicals in the banned Northern Elements Political Union led by the highly revered and indomitable Mallam Aminu Kano, who spent his entire political career fighting for the poor indigenous communities against the NPC elite. The Nigerian Advance Party (NAP) was a late addition led by the alliance of labor and pseudo-socialist activists, perhaps to play the old game of countering the influence of Chief Awolowo in the West.

In the presidential elections of 1979, the NPN's Shagari emerged the president by barely winning at least 25 percent of the votes in 12 and two-thirds of the states. Despite the controversy over the meaning of "two-thirds of 19 states" (eventually resolved by the Supreme Court) and allegations that it was favored by the departing military regime, the NPN was the only true "national" party among these five, winning five states in the north and three in the southeast, and thereby complicating the ethno-religious formations that reemerged in the Second Republic. The UPN dominated five states (all in the Yoruba southwest and the old Midwest Region); NPP carried two Igbo states and one in the central-middle belt; Aminu Kano's PRP won Kano (his home state) while a PRP governor won in an NPN-dominated legislature in neighboring Kaduna state; GNPP won two, while NAP failed to win any states. At the national level, the NPN – which failed to win a majority in the

National Assembly – formed a governing alliance with the NPP which, as in the First Republic, broke down very quickly.

Despite early warnings about the country's dwindling revenue from oil, the civilian leadership of the Second Republic behaved as if they had learned nothing from the country's tragic past and continued the profligate spending and lack of proper planning of the departing military regime. From its peak in 1979, crude oil output fell from 2.1 million barrels per day (bpd) to 0.9 million bpd, while Nigeria's oil export revenue dropped from $1.33 billion to $700 million. The Shagari administration was forced to borrow about $2.8 billion from the IMF to cover the country's foreign debt, followed by half-hearted **austerity measures** to curtail public spending. Even these measures were unraveled by the 1983 general elections, in which the NPN-led government did everything it could to win the election, especially in NPP and UPN strongholds in the east and west, respectively. There were accusations of massive vote-rigging and election violence, even as corruption and brazen flaunting of ill-gotten wealth became the hallmark of the regime.

President Shagari was generally perceived as inept and incapable of controlling the excesses of his subordinates. The old demons of ethnic and sectarian violence reappeared, while more sinister forms of patron–client networks characterized daily political life, making it extremely difficult for the government to address the urgent issues that faced the country, especially the economic austerity measures introduced by Shagari. In the end, the confluence of identities, interests, and institutions mediated by the external environment once again shaped the course of events and seriously dashed the hopes and expectations of Nigerians to build a sustainable democratic society.

THE RETURN OF MILITARY DICTATORSHIPS AND "TRANSITION WITHOUT END" (1983–1998)

President Shagari's 1983 election victory was short lived because the government was deposed in a coup led by General Muhammadu Buhari, a Northern Fulani infantry officer, on December 31, 1983, launching the country into another round of military dictatorships that ended 16 years later, in 1999. General Buhari and his deputy, General Tunde Idiagbon (also a Muslim from north-central Nigeria), rode on the crest of nationalist resentments against Nigeria's acceptance of the structural adjustment program (SAP) imposed on Nigeria by the IMF and promptly broke off negotiations with the organization. Like previous military regimes, he sacked the civilian government and legislatures and incarcerated many politicians (including the Igbo vice-president, Alex Ekwueme) accused of corruption and ruining the economy. Remarkably, President Shagari was not similarly imprisoned or held accountable for any of the transgressions of his government, a move that cast serious doubts about the new regime's ethnic and religious impartiality.

In 1985, General Ibrahim Babangida, Buhari's defense chief, deposed him in a palace coup and took on the title of president. Babangida moved quickly to allow Nigerians to "democratically" decide whether or not to accept further loans – and therefore more SAP – from the IMF. More importantly, Babangida promised a quick return to civilian rule, an issue on which General Buhari had been noncommittal. A national "great debate" soon ensued over SAP and in the end Babangida declared that Nigerians had decided to implement SAP without recourse to IMF loans. This set Nigeria on an ill-conceived economic reform program characterized by massive devaluation of the local currency (which impoverished millions of Nigerians overnight), public sector lay-offs, and privatization of state-owned enterprises.

Inevitably, the regime faced resistance to these measures from organized labor, students, market women, and civil society groups, but Babangida was able to buy off opposition (especially from civil society organizations) with state largesse and outright bribery in the shape of huge sums in synthetic twine bags that Nigerians call "Ghana must go" bags. Media outlets that were critical of government were silenced or banned, while some journalists were jailed or forced underground and into exile. The most notorious example of media harassment during this period was the case of Dele Giwa of the highly regarded *Newswatch* weekly magazine who was killed by a letter bomb allegedly sent by agents of the regime. General Babangida also established a number of high-sounding propaganda outfits such as the Directorate for Social Mobilization or Mass Mobilization for Self-Reliance, Economic Recovery and Social Justice (MAMSER), whose mission was to cultivate a mass political culture supportive of democracy. The Center for Democratic Studies (CDS) in Abuja, also run by several academics formerly critical of the regime, served similar functions. Babangida elevated the role of the first lady to the status of royalty, and her many questionable pet projects were paid for by the public treasury. Through his wife's "better life for rural women" project, for instance, Babangida was able to co-opt large numbers of lower- and middle-class women as support networks for the regime. The institution of public corruption and abuse of office known in Nigeria as "settlement," or co-optation of critics or opposition through financial inducement, was introduced by General Babangida, only to be turned into a national pastime by subsequent regimes.

In 1992, the regime created and funded two political parties to which all politicians were compelled to belong. One of them, the Social Democratic Party (SDP), was supposedly "a little to the Left" while the other, the National Republican Convention (NRC), was "a little to the Right." The forced two-party system was an ill-conceived contraption devised by "the evil genius" to use nonexistent ideological or class identities to defuse ethnic and sectarian political mobilization that the professional politicians had allegedly failed to eschew. The NRC selected Chief Moshood K. Abiola, a Yoruba multi-billionnaire business mogul and friend of various military officers and regimes as its presidential candidate, while SDP selected another Muslim, Alhaji Ibrahim Tofa from Kano State in the north, as its flag-bearer.

Babangida's two-party system seemed to have succeeded because the June 12, 1993, election (**June 12** hereafter) fought by the two parties sanctioned by the Banangida regime was judged to be the fairest and freest in the history of Nigeria. The 1993 elections demonstrated the capacity of the Nigerian voter to rise above ethnic and religious identities in the sense that the two presidential candidates were both Muslims, and Chief Abiola won across ethnic, religious, gender, and class lines in all zones and also beat his opponent in his own ward in Kano. Press reports even claimed that a majority of junior officers had voted for the Yoruba politician in the election. However, after several days of delay in announcing the results and heightened apprehension across the country, the military government annulled the result, popularly believed to have been won by Abiola. Indeed, initial results released by the National Electoral Commission showed Abiola winning in 11 of 14 states, while the results later published by the Campaign for Democracy, a human rights group, increased his win to 19 of 30 states. General Babangida claimed to have based the annulment on a dubious high court injunction against certification of the polls granted to a faceless organization called Association for a Better Nigeria (ABN). ABN was founded by the maverick Igbo politician Chief Arthur Nzeribe, who was popularly believed to be acting at the behest of the military and other civilians (including some Yorubas) who were not comfortable with an Abiola presidency.

Following the annulment, Babangida "stepped aside" in August 1993 and appointed an Interim National Government led by Chief Ernest Shonekan, a Yoruba businessman, although power actually lay with **General Sani Abacha**, the chief of army staff. Shonekan was not only shunned by his Yoruba coethnics, he also had virtually no support across the country, let alone around the world. It was therefore relatively easy for General Abacha to push him out in November 1993, and thus began the story of the most brutal and brazenly corrupt military dictatorship Nigerians had experienced. A year later, on the anniversary of the annulled 1993 election, Chief Abiola declared himself president, having exhausted his patience waiting for Abacha's duplicitous promise to grant Abiola his mandate to be fulfilled; it was on the basis of that promise that Abiola had allegedly supported Shonekan's removal from office. On June 23, 1994, Abacha arrested Abiola, charged him with three counts of treason, and remanded him in prison, where he died in 1998.

With the presumed winner of the 1993 elections out of the way, General Abacha, who had been central to the two preceding military regimes, took Babangida's political trickery and Machiavellian tactics to unprecedented levels. The regime was, however, buffeted by a more vocal civil society, now mobilized to pressure the government to restore the June 12 mandate to Abiola. In July 1994, the National Union of Petroleum and Gas Workers (NUPENG) and the Petroleum and Natural Gas Senior Staff Association (PENGASSAN) embarked on strike action that paralyzed the country. Abacha promptly arrested Frank Kokori, secretary of NUPENG, and forced most members of the two associations back to work. University faculty, staff, and students became more vocal and many campuses were shut down for months, with armored personnel carriers guarding every entrance point in the most riot-prone campuses. The Nigerian Labor Congress and its 17 affiliates (including local government employee unions and the Nigerian Association of Resident Doctors) all had running battles with the military during this period.

General Abacha had the biggest headache from human rights and prodemocracy groups, such as the Civil Liberties Organization (CLO), the National Democratic Coalition (NADECO), the Campaign for Democracy (CD), and the Constitutional Rights Project. Their international connections and affiliations with global civil society groups rankled the regime, but their effectiveness was limited because of their ethnic and middle- and upper-class composition and authoritarian leadership which led to frequent fragmentation, and which the regime exploited to the fullest.

The singular most important action that sealed Abacha's reign in infamy was his execution of writer and environmental activist Ken Saro-Wiwa and eight other Ogoni activists in November 1995 for allegedly ordering the murder of four Ogoni chiefs in 1994. Saro-Wiwa was the founder of the **Movement for the Survival of Ogoni People** (**MOSOP**), which campaigned against the environmental degradation caused by oil drilling by Shell Petroleum Development Corporation (SPDC) and from which the 500,000 Ogoni people had derived few economic benefits. As MOSOP began to disrupt oil production, Saro-Wiwa was arrested several times, but managed to link up with global environmental and social justice activist networks eager to help popularize the problems of the Niger Delta and their connections to the global economy. In 1994, four Ogoni chiefs were murdered by young MOSOP militants and Abacha – who had now militarized Ogoniland – placed Saro-Wiwa and 14 others under house arrest and charged them with murder and incitement to commit murder. Saro-Wiwa and eight other Ogoni activists were convicted by a kangaroo military court in October 1995, and despite last minute pleas for clemency by world leaders, including South Africa's Nelson Mandela, Abacha had them hanged in November of that year. Not only would Abacha not recover from the international opprobrium this action earned him, the killing of the Ogoni Nine in turn galvanized other Niger Delta communities to rise up against the government and oil companies, and at times against one another, making this the most intractable ethnic mobilization problem Nigeria has ever faced since independence.

Moreover, by the time he died in 1998, Abacha had joined the league of Africa's kleptocratic dictators and had stolen more than $6 billion from the Nigerian treasury, which he stashed away in banks in Switzerland, France, the United Kingdom, and the United States. His family's business empire reached every sector of the Nigerian economy from petroleum to banks and construction companies and choice government real estate. It took the subsequent civilian government almost eight years to repatriate less than half of Abacha's loot, even as his family engaged the government in a long-drawn legal battle over his estate.

Ironically, the most enduring legacy of the Abacha dictatorship is the strong endorsement given to the concept of "zoning" of political offices at all levels of government by his carefully selected Constitutional Conference in 1995. Table 14.1 shows the six geographic zones which were designed as another strategy to strengthen Nigeria's federalism and weaken ethnic and sectarian conflicts. The seemingly intractable nature of Nigeria's pluralism and the added loads of ethnic mistrust injected into the polity by the June 12 saga – and speculations of secession by the Yoruba ethnic group – informed the need to assure every major group of a turn at the presidency and other top posts. States had become too weak compared to the center, and some would not be financially viable without allocations from the center. Zoning was therefore seen as an alternative to the call by some for a return to the federal structure of the First Republic, where stronger regions lessened the political significance of capturing power at the center. As we will see later in this chapter, zoning, which is not officially recognized in the constitution, has become an important basis for political identities and resource allocation in the Fourth Republic.

Despite the outward appearance of a tough infantry officer without whom Nigeria would supposedly fall apart, General Abacha was deeply paranoid and rarely attended public functions, let alone traveled out of the country. He retired or reassigned "problem" military officers frequently and unleashed his security apparatus (including killer squads) – a first in the history of Nigeria – on perceived and real opponents of the regime. Yet, alleged coup plots in 1995 and 1997 that resulted in death sentences for a large number of officers and civilians (including General Oladapo Diya, Abacha's Yoruba deputy in 1997) could not be carried out due to disagreements within the now mortally fractured and seriously deprofessionalized military.

Nonetheless, Abacha remained enigmatically vague about his vaunted transition plans until 1997, when he allowed the creation of seven political parties that contested local and state elections. Critics referred to them as "the seven dwarfs" because they not only agreed to Abacha's demand that they refrain from criticizing the regime but also "adopted" Abacha as their "consensus

TABLE 14.1. Nigeria's Six Geographic Zones

Geographic zone	States in the zone
North-Central	Benue Kogi Nasarawa Niger Plateau Federal Capital Territory–Abuja
North-East	Adamawa Bauchi Borno Gombe Taraba Yobe
North-West	Jigawa Kaduna Kano Katsina Kebbi Sokoto Zamfara
South-East	Abia Anambra Ebonyi Enugu Imo
South-South	Akwa-Ibom Bayelsa Cross-River Delta Edo Rivers
South-West	Ekiti Ogun Ondo Osun Oyo Lagos

candidate" for the upcoming presidential election in 1998. Like Babangida, Abacha also funded the creation of several civil society organizations (most notably Youths Energized for Abacha – YEA), and co-opted several academics and religious and traditional rulers who were "settled"; they became vocal supporters of the regime's self-succession transition plans, which they tried to sell to the international community as the only antidote to the alleged imminent collapse of the Nigerian state. Abacha's sudden death in June 1998 abruptly ended "the game of the seven dwarfs" and the closest Nigeria had come to a military dictator giving up his khaki military uniform for the *agbada*, the flowing, colorful, and ridiculously expensive gowns that have now become the trademark of most Nigerian politicians

The Return to Democracy and the Fourth Republic

INSTITUTIONS AND ELITE COALITION POLITICS

By 1998, the military itself had become weary of ruling the country (for 29 years), as it was being blamed by all and sundry for every political, economic, and social problem in the country. The military itself, as an institution, had become a mere shadow of its former self, wracked by all forms of factionalism, loss of professionalism, esprit de corps, and sense of mission, and hijacked by rapacious politicians in military uniform. For much of this period, enlisted soldiers and officers of lower ranks saw little direct benefit from military rule, and preferred a return to rule by civilian politicians, who dared not offend the military too much for fear of coups. Feverish deliberations about what to do with Chief Abiola, the presumed winner of the 1993 election, were still going on when Abiola suddenly died in his prison guesthouse in the presence of visiting American diplomats. Under such circumstances, Abacha's successor, General Abdusalami Abubakar, had little choice but to quickly cobble together a transition program, which eventually returned the country to elected civilian government on May 29, 1999. Marginal changes were made to the 1979 constitution, but the presidential system of government and the principles of federalism with Nigerian peculiarities were retained in the 1999 constitution.

The transition process started with local council elections. Three of the nine major political parties that received the most votes in the December 1998 elections into the country's 774 local councils were subsequently allowed to contest the presidential and general elections in 1999. These were the People's Democratic Party (PDP) which won 389 local councils; All People's Party (APP) 182; and Alliance for Democracy (AD) 100 – other parties won the remaining 103 local council seats. Unofficially, the presidency was zoned to the Yoruba southwest, ostensibly to assuage the injustice of the June 12 debacle and Abiola's subsequent death, and to blunt mooted secessionist moves by the Yoruba. Retired general Obasanjo – who relinquished power to civilians in 1979 and who had just been released from prison following Abacha's demise – was "invited" by the PDP to be their candidate, while Chief Olu Falae, also a Yoruba, Yale University–trained economist and former finance minister and former secretary to the federal government under Babangida, became the joint flag-bearer of the AD and APP. Obasanjo won the presidential election with 62.8 percent of the votes, while Falae received a mere 37.2 percent. Obasanjo's PDP also won a majority of the parliamentary seats in both the Senate and the federal House of Representatives.

Like all previous elections, the 1999 elections were characterized by reports and allegations of vote-rigging and other electoral irregularities, most of them stemming from the limited time the Abubakar regime had to organize the polls. Indeed, Falae's unexpectedly poor showing was attributed to the strong backing given to Obasanjo by retired and departing military officers, who allegedly could not trust civilians to protect their interests. In comparison to the 2007 general elections held after eight years of democratic government, which we will discuss later, Abubakar's transition program was executed with remarkable success. Another interesting feature of the transition process was the virtual eclipse of prodemocracy and human rights movements in the post-military elite pacts and power-sharing arrangements that followed. Some have speculated that the unofficial zoning of the presidency to the southwest by the departing military and the emergence of two prominent Yoruba presidential candidates in 1999 simply pulled the rug out from under an otherwise ethnic Yoruba-dominated prodemocracy movement. One prodemocracy activist, however, explained that they did not believe that the military was serious about the transition, given their past experience. Hence they continued to fight while "charlatans, crooks and 419ers" jumped in and took up positions in the new government and have since made it almost impossible for anyone to dislodge them from power.

President Obasanjo's international connections, reputation (including as vice-president of Transparency International and founder of Africa Leadership Forum), and rhetoric captured the imagination and hopes of Nigerians and the world. Indeed, no Nigerian government had ever come to power with such domestic and international legitimacy as the Obasanjo administration in 1999. The president even whetted the appetite of Nigerians for an end to political corruption and militarization of Nigerian politics by dismissing, a day after his inauguration, 90 senior military officers who had political ambitions or were tainted by their involvement in previous military regimes. He also quickly embarked on a program of reprofessionalization of the armed forces, especially to institutionalize civilian control of the military.

Indeed, most Nigerians genuinely expected President Obasanjo to borrow a leaf from South Africa's Nelson Mandela and serve only one term, during which he was expected to stabilize the polity and use his postmilitary national and international goodwill to extricate Nigeria from its Abacha-era pariah status and reintegrate the country into the world community. Ironically, Obasanjo, who had become a born-again Christian in jail, seemed to have learned from his nemesis, Abacha, by keeping mum, saying only that God would determine whether or not he would be a candidate for the 2003

TABLE 14.2. Nigeria: Federal Election Results of 2003

Type of vote	Peoples Democratic Party	All Nigeria People's Party	Alliance for Democracy	Others
Presidential election	61.9%	32.2%	no candidate	5.9%
House of Rep. (seats)	54.5% (213)	27.4% (95)	9.3% (31)	8.8% (7)
Senate (seats)	53.7% (73)	27.9% (28)	9.7% (6)	8.7% (0)

Source: The Independent National Election Commission, 2003.

election. By 2002, most PDP governors had fallen out with the president and were urging his vice-president, Alhaji Abubakar Atiku (who was instrumental to the PDP adopting Obasanjo in 1998), to run against Obasanjo in the party primaries, which Atiku declined. In the end, Obasanjo did run, beating his closest opponent, General Muhammadu Buhari of the All Nigeria People's Party (formerly APP) and a tough-talking northern military dictator in the 1980s, still with an unblemished reputation for unflinching patriotism and zero tolerance for corruption. In addition to the landslide electoral victory shown in Table 14.2, the PDP, now in charge of the state machinery including the electoral commission, also won 28 out of 36 governorships, and began to refer to itself as "Africa's biggest political party." Whereas Obasanjo had been shunned by his southwest Yoruba people (including a humiliating loss in his village ward) in 1999, the PDP in 2003 captured five governorship positions from the AD in the Yoruba southwest. The disunity among the 30 registered political parties (26 of which fielded presidential candidates) may have split the opposition vote, while General Buhari was unable to erase his record of brutal dictatorship and human rights abuses when he was military ruler and his support for the introduction of sharia law by 12 states in northern Nigeria following the end of military rule. Additionally, the Yoruba-dominated AD was so fractured that it either was unable to agree on a presidential candidate or played the ethnic card by unofficially adopting Obasanjo as its candidate for the presidential vote. Nonetheless, the 2003 election must rank as among the most rigged in the history of Nigeria. Indeed, General Buhari spent vast sums of money and 23 months seeking to overturn the elections in the courts, which eventually sustained most of the rigging claims but ruled that the widespread rigging by the PDP was not sufficient to have a different electoral outcome. The appeal court even agreed (later reversed by the Supreme Court) that in Ogun State (Obasanjo's home state), the number of votes reported for the PDP governorship candidate who purportedly won the election was far greater than the total number of votes actually cast in the general elections.

THE POLITICS OF "RESOURCE CONTROL"

One of the most divisive issues in the Fourth Republic has been – and will continue to be – increased agitation for more local control over resources generated in each group's homeland. Return to civilian rule created new opportunities to challenge the 1992 revenue allocation formula decreed by the military as follows: federal government 48.5 percent; states 24 percent; local governments 20 percent; Special Fund 7.5 percent (made up of Federal Capital Territory 1 percent, Ecological Fund 2 percent, Economic Stabilization 1.5 percent, and Natural Resources 3 percent).

Obasanjo's proposal to increase the Special Fund's allocation to 11.7 percent resulted in the infamous "Resource Control" suit in the Supreme Court by oil-producing coastal states seeking clarification about which tier of government was entitled to offshore oil revenues, as well as the right of central government to exempt certain expenses from the federally collected revenue. In April 2002, the Supreme Court declared the Special Fund unconstitutional and ordered the following revenue allocations: federal government 56 percent; states 24 percent; and local governments 20 percent. After a series of disputes among the three levels of government, the president by executive order in March 2003 (and against the recommendation of the Revenue Mobilization, Allocation and Fiscal Commission – RMAFC) allocated 52.68 percent to the federal government, 26.72 percent to states, and 20.6 percent to local governments. By creating the perception that lopsided revenue allocation was to blame for underdevelopment, lack of public infrastructure, and massive poverty and unemployment, oil-producing state governors fueled much of the "youth restiveness" in the Niger Delta, and this set them on a collision course with President Obasanjo, who in 2007 controversially indicted some of these "resource control agitators" for corruption.

POPULATION COUNT, ETHNIC MOBILIZATION, AND INSURGENCY MOVEMENTS

The national population census has been highly politicized in Nigeria, beginning with the introduction of limited representative government in 1948. Since then every head count has either been rejected outright (1958 and 1973) or been a source of controversy (1963, 1992, and 2006) for the simple reason that population is also a basis for federal revenue allocation and political representation and state creation, hence, an important marker of identity. Besides, almost every head count in the country since the 1930s has given the north a majority which most southerners reject, arguing that Nigeria is the only country where the farther away one moves from the coast the larger the population, instead of the universal experience of population concentration in coastal areas. In 2006, the federal government therefore decided to expunge religious and ethnic identities from the head count, ostensibly to blunt the saliency of factors in national politics.

The provisional population totals by geographic zones give the three zones in the old Northern Region a combined 52.6 percent of Nigeria's population. One controversial surprise from the 2006 census data was that Kano State had 9.3 million people, surpassing Lagos – one of Africa's most notorious mega-cities – at 9.01 million. Indeed, the government of Lagos State was so dissatisfied with the results that it actually published its own population estimate giving the state about 12 million people. The southeast (Igbo) states – now clearly a national minority – also noted that because most Igbos actually lived outside the five states in the zone, the exclusion of ethnic and religious information from the census was intended to deliberately undercount them.

Related to demographic politics is ethnic mobilization, which not only continued during the 29 years of military dictatorship, but actually multiplied, especially in the Niger Delta, in the Fourth Republic. Throughout Obasanjo's tenure there was bloody anarchy in the Niger Delta, which produces most of Nigeria's 2.5 million barrels per day of oil and increasing volumes of gas. At least 1,000 people a year were killed in battles on land and sea between the 50-odd militia groups, including the Movement for the Emancipation of the Niger Delta (MEND) and the Niger Delta Peoples' Volunteer Force (NDPVF), who fight the authorities as well as each other for opportunities to steal oil. More than 400 Nigerians and foreigners (most, but not all of them, connected to the oil industry) have been kidnapped for ransom since 1999, with about 250 abducted since the start of 2006. In October 2007, the Central Bank of Nigeria estimated that over 600,000 barrels of oil per day – as much as 20 percent of Nigeria's oil exports – were stolen or disrupted by the insurgency from 1999 to 2006, while the federal Ministry of Finance estimated that the country lost about $58.3 billion from 1999 to 2007, with $14.4 billion in tax and royalty lost between February and December 2006. While some of the militants genuinely want the federal government to cede control of the oil industry to Niger Delta states, where the crude is pumped, most of them are criminal gangs and thugs trained and equipped by rival corrupt politicians (including extremely corrupt oil-state governors) who use them for their political purposes, including vote rigging, intimidation of opponents, and extortion of money from oil companies and the various levels of government.

In the first of a series of actions taken by the federal government to forestall any threats to its oil revenue, the government sent in the army to level the village of Odi in Bayelsa State in 1999 in what human rights groups consider an act of genocide. The government response to the crisis since then has centered on a Joint Task Force (JTF) of all security agencies, which has essentially been reactive, often leading to complete destruction of fishing villages accused of harboring the militants, even as the JTF itself has continued to lose scores of personnel, material, and equipment. Yet, the prospects for more deadly violence remain high as Nigeria's "restive youth" population climbed to about

70 million and the bandwagon effect of vigilante groups like the Egbesu Boys, MEND, and the NDPVF, of the Niger Delta has spread to all parts of the country. More troubling is the fact that more than 75 percent of the youth remain unemployed, making them easy prey and fodder for state political elite and ethnic identity entrepreneurs and brokers bent on using the youth to achieve their selfish political ends.

Ethnic mobilization – as well as fragmentation often blamed on Obasanjo – have similarly occurred among the much bigger ethnic groups, namely Afenifere (Yoruba) and Yoruba Council of Elders, the Arewa Consultative Forum (Hausa-Fulani or the so-called Old Core North), and Ohanaeze (Igbo), while the Ijaw National Council competes for space in the Niger Delta with various splinter or micronationalist groups that seem to spring up by the day. Often these elitist groups are upstaged by their more militant competitors, namely O'dua Peoples' Congress (OPC) in the southwest, the Movement for the Actualization of the Sovereignty State of Biafra (MASSOB) in the southeast, the MEND, NDPVF, and ethnic vigilante groups like the Egbesu Boys and Bakassi Boys. By 2005, some of these violent groups had either been co-opted or subdued by arrest and indefinite imprisonment of their leaders. Yet, several human rights groups report that more that 15,000 people had died in more than 10 instances of intercommunal violence during the Fourth Republic. These have occurred in Zaki Biam in the middle belt between the Tiv and Jukun, as well as among supposedly homogenous societies such as the perennial Ife-Modakeke wars in Oyo State; and the Umuleri-Aguleri communal clashes in Anambra State.

FEDERALISM, FEDERAL CHARACTER, AND THE POLITICS OF ZONING

The zoning policy introduced under General Abacha as a further refinement of the "federal character" principle became a crucial basis for interest aggregation, allocation of the spoils of office, and identity brokerage for the political class. In the preceding section, we noted how the departing northern military and the political cabal that ruled the country from 1983 to 1998 zoned the presidency in the upcoming Fourth Republic in 1999 to the Yoruba. The president chose a vice-president from the north-east zone, while the senate president (third in the line of succession) went to the Igbo. The position of Supreme Court chief justice was zoned to the north-central zone, while chief of the armed forces and deputy senate president were from the central Benue-Plateau zone. In a classical balancing act, all the military service chiefs were chosen from ethnic minority groups that did not occupy top positions in the government. Similarly, legislative leadership and committee assignments, ministerial appointments, as well as capital projects ("federal presence") were allocated along zonal lines. Ideally, the presidency would eventually rotate to the other zones, namely the south-south and the south-east, before returning to the north again. The 2007 elections, however, seem to have confirmed speculations in 1999 that General Obasanjo at the time may have struck a deal to return the presidency to the North after eight years. In 2007, Obasanjo handed over power to Alhaji Umaru Yar'Adua, the governor of Katsina state in the north-west zone who in turn chose a vice-president from the Ijaw ethnic group in the south-south zone.

The zoning logic applied to the allocation of all political party positions (not just the ruling party), as well as top-level career civil service, armed forces, and diplomatic corps positions, especially those understood to be end-of-career, political appointments. Zoning, rotation, "state character," and even "local government character" have become the mantra, and often the source of serious protracted political contestations and violence whenever politicians attempted to ignore this arrangement. Critics point to the deficiencies and obvious perversions of this system when individuals are appointed or selected as representatives of their zones, states, or local councils, and not because of their competence or integrity. Yet, the institution seems to have served the country well in terms of political stability in the sense that it gives hope to the political class from all zones (especially the minorities) that they might one day have their turn at ruling the country, a scenario that is highly unlikely under any other "democratic" power-sharing arrangement.

ECONOMIC REFORMS AND THE POLITICS OF DEVELOPMENT AND DEINDUSTRIALIZATION

From 1999 to 2007, Obasanjo and his officials embarked on many laudable economic reform programs – from consolidating the nation's banking and insurance sectors to privatization of state assets, and elimination of archaic laws that crowded out the private sector and favored treasury-busting, corrupt, and inefficient state monopolies. There were also reforms of corporate governance laws (including enforceable codes of good conduct) which have encouraged inflow of foreign direct investment and equity funds into the banking, insurance, and manufacturing sectors, not just into the petroleum sector as in the past. The level of transparency arising from the new corporate governance culture can be gauged from the ready acceptance of Nigerian firms (mostly banks) seeking offshore listing in the West African subregion, the United Kingdom, and the United States; the positive ratings they have garnered from global rating agencies; and the numerous corporate governance awards received by Nigerian businesses and their executives.

The reforms were anchored on the government's National Economic Empowerment and Development (NEEDS) program setting measurable benchmarks for federal and state governments. Government adopted the "Publish What You Earn" (PWYE) program whereby oil revenue and its disbursement to the three tiers of government are published on a monthly basis, bringing some degree of sanity into what used to be the fountainhead of corruption in Nigeria. Similarly, in 2005, the government introduced open bidding for oil exploration blocks, increasing government revenue from "signature bonuses" from less than $600 million in 1999 to $1.5 billion in 2006, a far more open system than the nightly, one-man discretionary allocation that prevailed under Abacha. The National Economic Summit Group and the National Extractive Industries Transparency Initiative, statutory bodies appointed from the public and private sector, now monitor the status of these reforms. The government finally achieved an exchange rates convergence after 20 years of ill-conceived devaluation of the naira (the Nigerian currency); and external reserves stood at about $48 billion in October 2007, compared to about $5.4 billion in 1999, thanks to much higher oil prices and improved non-oil revenue collection, but also largely due to more prudent financial management and levels of transparency never seen in the country's treasury for decades. The highlight of the reforms was the reduction of the country's foreign debt, down from a high of $36 billion in 1999 to $3 billion in 2007, earning the country a debt relief of $18 billion from the London and Paris club of creditors.

These reforms were, however, marred by the haphazardness and inconsistency of the vital ingredient for success – good governance – made worse by corruption, rent-seeking, and more brazen forms of prebendalism and assault on the rule of law. For instance, amid controversy over the rationality of paying off such huge debt in the midst of cruel poverty, the government borrowed an additional $5 billion on the eve of leaving office and left a domestic debt of over $18 billion. The most glaring example of performance legitimacy failure is the power sector, where the president in 2000 promised Nigerians "regular, uninterrupted power supply" by the end of 2001. Frustrated with persistent interruption of power supplies by the National Electric Power Authority (NEPA), Nigerians refer to NEPA as "Never Expect Power Always." Practically every business concern must provide its own power supply while NEPA became a backup, resulting in industrial capacity utilization of about 34 percent.

Pursuant to his pledge, Obasanjo set up a technical board of experts, threw over $10 billion into the pledge, and appointed four successive ministers for the sector, while NEPA was broken up into 18 separate companies, privatized and renamed Power Holding Company of Nigeria (PHCN). By May 2007, the government's ineptitude and corruption had plunged the country further into unremitting darkness, with few areas "enjoying" more than three hours of electricity in any given day, as power generation declined from 3,600 megawatts hours (MwH) in 1999 to a mere 1,000 MwH in early 2007. Several investors in Nigeria reportedly began migrating to neighboring countries to escape the destructive effects of the power sector crisis and other antibusiness policies. The change in name from NEPA to PHCN was more noticeable in the continued deterioration of the power sector; hence, Nigerians now refer to the new entity as "Problem Has Changed Name."

The Obasanjo era was also characterized by perennial shortages of petrol and black market for petrol, as none of the country's three refineries ever worked in eight years despite huge funds thrown at the problem, and the world's seventh largest oil exporter continued to import refined petroleum for domestic use. Some of the men surrounding Obasanjo were alleged to be part of a "mafia" that made billions from importing oil, and therefore had every reason to thwart any effort to refine petroleum locally. Agriculture and food production similarly suffered under Obasanjo. Despite huge subsidies to farmers, especially fertilizer (about $722 million from 2002 to 2007), Nigeria remains a net food importer as more and more people left the farms to swell the population of urban areas. Attempts to make the country become self-sufficient in fertilizer production followed the general pattern of failed state-led industrialization as two plants established in 1973 and 1987 had long ceased production and were privatized by the government.

Another qualified success is the privatization of scores of state-owned enterprises – from steel mills to airlines, banks, and other financial institutions – that has since 2000 begun to unshackle Nigeria's notoriously state-dependent organized private sector (OPS). In the telecommunications sector, for example, the overall installed capacity number of telephone subscribers ballooned from 866,782 connected lines in 2001 after the entry of mobile network operators to nearly 61 million lines and 45.5 million subscribers at the end of August 2007. This explosion in telephone service has led to the creation of over 100,000 jobs, making Nigeria one of the world's fastest growing and most lucrative telephone markets in the world. However, with privatization came the very opposite of what the people were promised – massive public sector layoffs and more money taken from the poor majority and concentrated in even fewer hands than even the military could have contemplated. The most dramatic evidence of deindustrialization occurred in the textile industry, which declined from 175 functioning mills (with 300,000 direct and 700,000 indirect jobs) in 1980 to 26 mills employing just 26,000 workers in 2007.

CORRUPTION: FIGHTING THE CANKER WORM IN THE SOCIAL FABRIC

Corruption became more widespread in Nigeria under Obasanjo (ironically the world vice-president of Transparency International until 1999), with the country ranking 152nd out of 158 countries in Transparency International's *Corruption Perception Index* in 2005, an improvement from being the second most corrupt in 1999. According to a 2006 estimate by the International Monetary Fund, as much as $384.6 billion (revised upward in 2007 to $600 billion by Nigeria's Central Bank) in ill-gotten gains are sitting in foreign bank accounts while about 70 percent of the population live on less than a

TABLE 14.3. What Does $384.6 Billion Buy?

BBC.com estimates	Saharareporters.com estimates
• 225 space shuttles • 795,115 Rolls Royce Phantoms • 400 million PC computers • 32 million primary school classrooms • 3,800 kilograms of rice for each of the 150 million Nigerians	• 30,899 kilometers of railway lines • 1,536 Boeing 747 aircrafts manufactured in February 2006 • 64 nuclear power plants • 38 universities with endowments the size of Harvard University • 4,800 hospitals the standard of Mayo Clinic in Minnesota • 3.8 million farm/agricultural tractors • 38 zillion liters of clean water (probably distilled) • 2.4 million Harvard graduates, etc.

Source: http://www.bbc.co.uk and http://www.saharareporters.com.

dollar a day. Table 14.3 shows the opportunity costs to Nigeria of this colossal amount.

Yet, Obasanjo's was the first administration to seriously embark on an anticorruption war by establishing institutions with the legal authority to go after the big fish and sacred cows of Nigeria's corruption industry. The **Economic and Financial Crimes Commission (EFCC)** was set up in 2002 as the lead agency in the anticorruption war. Other organs include the Independent Corrupt Practices Bureau (ICPB), the Code of Conduct Bureau, the Transparency in Budget Office, the NESG, the Publish What You Earn program mentioned earlier, and of course the introduction of open bidding for oil blocks in 2005. Civil society organizations (in partnership with anticorruption global NGOs) have also begun to develop the capacity to monitor and report graft in government. The most hated Nigerian in the Fourth Republic is probably Mallam Nuhu Ribadu, the chairman of the EFCC, who has come to personify the anticorruption effort. Under his watch, the EFCC has convicted over 150 persons involved in economic and financial crimes since 2003. Some of the most prominent cases include the trial and conviction of Emmanuel Nwude and others in the biggest bank fraud in the world and the theft by a former inspector general of police, Tafa Balogun, of about $135 million meant for his very poorly paid and shamefully ill-equipped police force.

Similarly, the National Food and Drug Administration and Control (NAFDAC) has brought some sanity into the infamous fake drug industry in Nigeria by destroying over $135 million worth of fake drugs linked to criminal syndicates in India, Lebanon, and the entire West African subregion. Finally, the consolidation exercise carried out by the Central Bank of Nigeria not only pruned down the number of banks from as high as 98 to 25, but also ended the fraudulent banking culture and feasting on the foreign exchange market and government deposits that went on for decades in the name of banking.

Ironically, Obasanjo's regime was deeply implicated in serious and blatant cases of public corruption, beginning with the first speaker of the House of Representatives, who was found guilty of certificate forgery in 1999 and left office. There were numerous allegations of and indictments for bribery and corruption leveled against many legislators and 26 of the country's immensely powerful 36 state governors, only five of whom had been charged to court as of October 2007. Three successive senate presidents were removed from office for corruption and embezzlement of public funds and abuse of office, while the EFCC described the country's 774 local councils as "stealing factories." Overall, the EFCC claimed to have recovered $5 billion of stolen assets in three years.

Most Nigerians believe the EFCC granted immunity to many "big men" and godfathers of the ruling PDP, and was reluctant to probe President Obasanjo's alleged self-enrichment, particularly the latter's willingness to accept billions of naira from individuals as well as corporate entities in the name of fund-raising for his presidential library in 2005. The top donors to the library fund were beneficiaries of his transfers of huge public assets to private hands, especially through the notorious Transnational Corporation (Transcorp), a mega corporation put together in 2005 by the private sector at the behest of the president, who also bought about N200 million Transcorp shares. In the same vein, while the president's friends had rescued his Temperance Farms from a court-ordered bankruptcy that would have derailed his election in 1999, his personal assistants claimed in 2005 that the same farm had been earning profits of $300,000 per year since he assumed office. The EFCC allowed itself to be used by Obasanjo to smear Vice-President Atiku with a view to preventing him from running for president in 2007. The agency also engineered the rash of impeachments of governors who, although clearly corrupt, were known to have lost favor with the presidency. Four of those impeachments were later voided by the Supreme Court – and the impeached governors reinstated – because the affected state legislatures, under tremendous pressure from the EFCC, failed to follow constitutionally mandated procedures.

POVERTY, UNEMPLOYMENT, AND GENERAL INSECURITY

Although Nigeria is rich in both human and material resources, it has paradoxically experienced the worst forms of poverty since the return to civilian rule in 1999. According to the World Bank, the percentage of the population subsisting on a dollar or less a day grew from a mere 36 percent in 1980 to about 75 percent in 2006. President Obasanjo repeatedly rejected the above statistic, arguing that although a lot of Nigerians did not earn the equivalent of a dollar a day, they nevertheless ate three square meals per day from what they were able to produce on their farms. Unemployment in the rural areas could be as high as 60 percent. The United Nations Human Development Index report of 2006 ranked Nigeria 158th out of the 177 countries surveyed. Another survey of 103 developing countries in 2005 on a Human Poverty Index (HPI) ranked the country 75th with a 38.8 percent score.

The economic impact of perennial power failure in Nigeria, especially the imperative of installing private power generating plants in homes and businesses, has led to escalating manufacturing costs, resulting in massive loss of jobs in various sectors of the economy. The government's own commitment to "downsizing" the public sector to the tune of over 100,000 jobs, as well as its failure to create the millions of jobs it had promised would flow from these reforms, further compounded the unemployment situation. Finally, better exposure or integration into the world economy through market reforms has been accompanied by social disintegration. Open borders have resulted in better access to small arms by insurgent groups, militants, political thugs, and armed robbers, and with deadly weapons comes greater insecurity; knowledge of new markets has been accompanied with unimproved exchange rates. Nigeria has consequently reaped a harvest of rampant insecurity as youths roam the streets without jobs or hope for the future. There is hardly any part of the country today that is safe from the menace of armed robbers who have been on the rampage, wasting lives and property and paralyzing economic activities with little, if any, challenge from the police. Kidnapping for ransom has grown beyond the notorious insurgency in the Niger Delta to now include almost daily abduction of aged parents and children of prominent politicians and wealthy civilians in many parts of the country.

FROM THE "THIRD-TERM" PLOT DEBACLE TO A STRENGTHENED PRESIDENCY

Obasanjo's efforts to institutionalize needed reforms for political and economic development were matched or surpassed by actions or policies that undermined the regime's legitimacy and public trust in institutions of government. The most baffling and contentious example was his ill-fated plot to change the constitution to allow him to run for a third term as president. The "**third-term**" **plot** was disguised in a bill that included 103 other legally unassailable amendments aimed at smoothing the rough edges of the 1999 constitution imposed by the military and which the president and the ruling PDP wanted to ram through the legislature. The plot was eventually stopped by both chambers of the National Assembly in one of those rare moments when the legislature truly asserted its independence as a coequal arm of government. The collapse of the third-term plot plunged Nigeria into a crisis that may have mortally undermined the presidency and other institutions of government more than any other maladies discussed in this chapter.

A humiliated Obasanjo turned against a number of state agencies officially intended to curb the crimes of corruption and electoral malfeasance (for example, the EFCC, the Independent Corrupt Practices Bureau, and the Code of Conduct Bureau) on anyone who may have disagreed with him, especially on his desire to extend his tenure. Meanwhile, several notoriously corrupt prominent politicians and godfathers around the president were spared, even after some of these agencies had submitted damning indictments against them. The biggest fallout from this failed plot was an open fight between Obasanjo and his vice-president, Abubakar Atiku, that publicly ridiculed Nigeria's image and scandalized the citizenry. Atiku had openly opposed the third-term agenda from the very moment the idea was mooted in 2003. As we noted earlier, in 2003 Atiku had managed to convince the PDP (especially state governors) to allow Obasanjo to run for a second term with the understanding that he would "naturally" be the party's presidential flag-bearer in the 2007 presidential elections. Obasanjo, however, vowed not to allow Atiku to run for president, accusing him of disloyalty, corruption, and misuse of public funds belonging to the Petroleum Development Trust Fund (PTDF), of which Atiku was in charge as vice-president – a charge which the vice-president flatly denied. Instead, in December 2006, Obasanjo engineered a seriously flawed PDP primary that anointed Umaru Yar'Adua, a quiet former chemistry lecturer and incumbent governor of the northern sharia state of Katsina, as his successor.

Based on the findings of a federal administrative panel (composed of his ministers) and an investigative report by the EFFC, Obasanjo purportedly "dismissed" the vice-president and subsequently reported him to the National Assembly, where he expected Atiku to be impeached and removed from office. The administrative panel, composed of Obasanjo's trusted ministers, based its indictment of the vice-president on the EFCC report, itself supposedly triggered by a request for assistance from the Federal Bureau of Investigation (FBI) of the United States in connection with a money-laundering investigation against William Jefferson, a Louisiana congressman and acquaintance of the Nigerian vice-president. Within hours of the administrative panel's submission of its report, the Federal Executive Council (FEC) met hurriedly to ratify the report and quickly gazetted the controversial indictment.

When Atiku announced his presidential ambition and picked up the ticket of a new political party, the Action Congress (AC), he was barred from standing by the Independent Electoral Commission (INEC), which cited his indictment for corruption. Critics – including the vice-president – countered that the EFCC report and the administrative panel indictment were a ruse to satisfy Section 137 of the 1999 Constitution, which bars those indicted by a tribunal or an administrative panel from running for office in Nigeria. In the end, Atiku successfully challenged the ban up to the Supreme Court, which ruled just three days prior to the April 21, 2007, election that INEC did not have the power to disqualify candidates for office and therefore ordered the reinstatement of Atiku's candidacy.

In a twist of fate, the PTDF affair, which the president had expected to result in the impeachment and removal of the vice-president by the legislators, resulted in a parliamentary committee hearing and report that, instead, indicted both President Obasanjo and the vice-president. While Atiku was found culpable of unlawfully approving $20 million on October 14, 2003, for deposit in a bank (which allegedly benefited his business associates) without the authority of the president, Obasanjo was found guilty of giving approval and retroactive ratification for the funding of projects not within the mandate of the PTDF. About three weeks before the end of his tenure, the National Assembly voted to quash Obasanjo's indictment while sustaining the guilty verdict on Atiku, leaving the embattled vice-president open to possible future prosecution.

The 2007 Elections and Nigerian Politics in the Twenty-First Century

INTERESTS, INSTITUTIONS, AND THE 2007 FLAWED ELECTIONS

We have seen in the preceding sections that Nigeria has had more than five general elections since its independence on October 1, 1960, two of them conducted by military regimes preparatory to their disengagement from formal politics. The only exception was the 1983 general election that saw the then incumbent, Alhaji Shehu Shagari, succeeding himself. However, the events that led to his overthrow by the military three months after the election testified to the credibility or otherwise of that exercise. The 2007 presidential election was therefore more than just another election. Indeed, as a pivotal election it was billed to permanently redefine Nigerian politics and to give a mighty fillip to the democratic project in Africa in the twenty-first century. There were 55 registered political parties, but only 25 fielded candidates for president. A total of 61,567,036 Nigerians were registered by INEC for the vote, compared to the 60,823,022 registered in 2003. At least 120,000 polling stations were designated, while local and international election observers numbered more than 100,000 and covered almost every part of the country. With a population of about 150 million people, fewer than 40 percent supposedly decided who will run the affairs of the nation in the next four years.

Unfortunately, this unprecedented transfer of power from one elected president to another was not executed cleanly at all. While a new president was sworn in on May 29, 2007, the process was marred by unprecedented and embarrassing widespread fraud and violence. The 2007 polls, like all previous

elections, unleashed the worst aspects of a system increasingly run by political godfathers – state governors, political contractors, Western powers, and
local and foreign multinational corporations – who forge deals and alliances
to support candidates. Depending on whose figures one chooses, anywhere
from 100 to 300 people were killed or died in political clashes or related events
between November 2006 and April 2007, a figure that grew following bouts
of predicted postelection violence.

The Alliance for Credible Elections and the Transition Monitoring Group
called the elections a "charade," while international observer groups (such as
the International Republican Institute, the National Democratic Institute,
ECOWAS Election Observer Mission, the European Union, and the Commonwealth Observer Group) concluded that elections "failed to meet acceptable minimum standards." Specifically, there was colossal rigging, falsification
of results, rampant cases of ballot-bag snatching at gunpoint, underage voting, shortage of voting materials, and general intimidation of the electorate
and opposition party agents during the elections.

Compounding the problem was INEC, whose credibility took a precipitous
nosedive following its disastrous voter registration exercise in 2006. This saw
the number of voters miraculously leap from 50 million to 61 million, while
hundreds of thousands of people were clearly unable to register because of
the chaos emanating from the Electronic Data Capture machines used in
the exercise. INEC's partisan pronouncements and actions (for which it was
severally chastised by the high courts) and its sheer ineptitude in conducting
the state and federal elections equally took Nigeria to new lows in electoral
politics. In the notoriously rancorous Anambra State in the southeast, the
commission was forced to adjust the votes of the declared winner from 1.9
million to one million after discovering that the total number of registered
voters was 1.7 million. In Rivers State, where the 2006 census gave the adult
population as two million, or about 45 percent of the total 5.1 million population, INEC curiously stated that the winner of the governorship election
polled 1.9 million votes. The implication that each one of the adult population registered and voted for the PDP when there were 49 other political parties further made the commission's claims seriously suspect. By the
time Yar'Adua was inaugurated, there were election petitions in all states for
almost every seat, including about five seeking to invalidate the presidential
election.

Despite these monumental failures, the significance of the 2007 election
and the civilian-to-civilian transition cannot be underestimated. Since independence, Nigeria has not had this kind of election in which 26 out of
36 state governors were virtually in transition and the president himself agreed
(although reluctantly) to leave office at the expiration of his term and handed
over power to another person. As the Fourth Republic marches into its ninth
year, it does so with a completely different gamut of executives at the center

and a completely new team in the various states and at the national level to run the affairs of the country.

Second, despite all its imperfections, the events of 2007 were the first civilian-to-civilian transition in the country featuring 25 presidential candidates, even though about 55 political parties were registered. Besides, the symbolic power structure in Nigeria in which the northerners are regarded as the power brokers makes this maiden transition being brokered by a president from the south politically significant. Moreover, it is the first time voter registration and general elections were conducted electronically. There were also signs of change that ought not to be dismissed in this season of disappointment. Several diaspora Nigerians either ran for elective office or mobilized to compel candidates to address issues, while the New Democrat Party (whose presidential and vice-presidential candidates hold United States citizenship) actually won landmark legal victories, including the constitutional rights of Nigerians with dual citizenships to run for office. Indeed, during the election campaigns, major cities in North America and Europe became favored stumping grounds for many Nigerian politicians, even as state agencies such as the EFCC and INEC frequently traveled overseas to explain their programs to an increasingly vocal and visible Nigerian diaspora. Like their Ghanaian counterparts, who won the right to vote in future Ghanaian elections, the Nigerian diaspora have been mobilizing – and actually instituted an ongoing legal action – to compel INEC to make necessary arrangements for Nigeria's reported 10 million diaspora (whom the Central Bank of Nigeria reports send home over $4 billion annually) to vote in future elections.

Perhaps, most importantly, Nigerians successfully eliminated the likelihood of an incumbent fighting to retain the presidency by killing President Obasanjo's third-term plot. That "emperor" Obasanjo stepped down voluntarily after eight years in power says something for the strength of Nigeria's fledgling parliament, which derailed the third-term plot. While most parliaments in Africa are yet to evolve beyond their rubber stamp destiny, Nigeria's parliament, especially between 2005 and 2007, demonstrated remarkable political will to restore the integrity of the legislature. By late October 2007, the House of Representatives was still embroiled in a two-month-old battle to remove the first female speaker, an Obasanjo protégé, indicted for embezzling about $5 million barely three months after her inauguration, despite pressure from the ruling PDP.

THE JUDICIARY: COMPROMISED AND RESILIENT

The judiciary in the Fourth Republic also had a similarly mixed bag of experiences, even as it still reeled from the fallout from aiding and abetting the masterminds of the annulment of the June 12, 1993, elections. During Obasanjo's first four years, the judiciary had a somewhat timid relationship with the executive. A number of judges were removed from office by the National Judicial Council for various offenses that demonstrated the extent of bribery and corruption in the judiciary. Two judges sitting on the Anambra South Senatorial Election Tribunal were dismissed for accepting N15 million and N12 million bribes, respectively. Similarly, the chairman and three other members of the Akwa Ibom State Governorship Election Tribunal were dismissed for taking bribes and compromising their personal integrity and betraying their oath of office. The credibility of the judiciary was also weakened by decisions by several electoral tribunals (often ratified by higher courts) in cases of outright vote rigging and other electoral malpractices against the ruling PDP candidates following the 2003 elections. Some PDP candidates whose seats were declared vacant by the courts were allowed to continue to serve out their terms in the National Assembly.

The Supreme Court also alienated many minority groups by siding with the federal government in its legal action to quash the quest by minorities to exercise more control over mineral resources in their areas. More damaging to the judiciary was the impunity with which the government, especially the Nigeria Police Force, either ignored or selectively implemented judicial decisions against it and/or the PDP. We have already noted the way the judiciary handled the petitions following the 2003 elections, especially the appellate court's 2005 ruling in the gubernatorial elections in Ogun State, a decision that was later reversed by the Supreme Court. The federal government also ignored high court rulings ordering it to defreeze the revenue allocations to Lagos State ordered by Obasanjo in response to the decision of this and other states to create new local government councils without the consent of the National Assembly. Moreover, several state high court judges became cheap accomplices in the abuse of the impeachment process that led to the removal of three governors from office between 2005 and 2007. Four of these illegal impeachments were later reversed by the Supreme Court. State and federal high courts have also become notorious for issuing "black market" injunctions preventing authorities (especially the EFCC) from arresting and prosecuting corrupt politicians or confiscating their ill-gotten wealth.

It was only in the last two years of Obasanjo's administration (2005–2007) that the judiciary began to assert its authority, thereby regaining some of the credibility which it had lost, along with every other discredited institution of government in Nigeria, over the past three decades. As noted already, the courts overturned the impeachments of three governors who were removed allegedly at the behest the president. Perhaps the most audacious assertion of boldness, courage, and judicial independence occurred in the context of the face-off between Obasanjo and his vice-president. Three days prior to the presidential election in 2004, the Supreme Court ruled clearly that the INEC did not have the power to disqualify candidates for election and should therefore not have excluded Atiku's name from the list of presidential candidates for the election. That landmark decision was the 14th legal victory scored by Atiku over the government in his bid to quash the purported indictments against him and the dogged determination of INEC and the president to exclude him from the ballot. While it would be worthy of celebration to win once or twice in Nigeria's courts, which are still wedded to archaic rules, to win a dozen or more cases before different judges in different courts confirms that the judiciary could be trusted as the last line of defense for people's rights and Nigeria's journey toward consolidated democracy.

Unlike the previous Nigerian experience, where archaic court rules and a corrupt judiciary and electoral commissions made it extremely difficult to overturn even clear cases of electoral irregularities, the courts have acted expeditiously to resolve election petitions following the 2007 elections. The opening salvo of this renewed judicial activism was the voiding by the Supreme Court of the 2007 gubernatorial election in Anambra State in which Obasanjo's former valet Andy Ubah was foisted on the state and the reinstatement of former governor Peter Obi of the All Peoples Grand Alliance (APGA). Mr. Obi's mandate had earlier been stolen by a PDP governor in 2003. He spent three years in the courts seeking his mandate, which he obtained in 2006, only to be impeached barely six months later by a PDP-dominated state assembly instigated by President Obasanjo and his godfather allies in the state. By late October 2007, the courts had overturned the elections of five PDP governors, two senators, and over a dozen House of Representatives and State Assembly (mostly PDP) seats, even as dozens more cases worked their way through the courts.

This emboldened activism, however, masks serious problems facing Nigeria's judiciary, especially the continued erosion of talent as more experienced jurists refuse appointments to the bench. Some governments retaliate against the judiciary by starving it of funds, while the massive public corruption and brazen stealing of public funds that have come to define Nigeria's identity has not escaped the courts as we have already noted. Courts are generally understaffed and have over two-year backlogs of cases, while judges still record proceedings by hand. In fact, many attorneys complain that they are unable to pursue appeals simply because the judges either failed to record the court proceedings accurately or bluntly refused to do so unless material inducements are provided. It is rare to find computers in most courts, especially at the magistrate's courts level, the real courts of first instance in Nigeria. Ill-educated and massively corrupt police officers continue to be the prosecutors with infinite drag on any semblance of efficiency that still exists in the courts. Access to lawyers and justice thus still remains a pipedream to most Nigerians, while the authoritarianism of some judges and the penchant for bribes from litigants and their attorneys suggests that any claim to judicial independence and fairness must be taken in context.

WHAT FUTURE FOR AN EPILEPTIC GIANT?

Given the history of Nigeria and its corrupt leadership no one would be faulted for expressing little hope that this enigmatic but fascinating country would ever evolve those institutions, interests, identities, and global connections capable of enabling its political class to replace bribes, vote rigging, and intimidation of rivals with genuine electoral franchise and consolidated democracy. As the elections closed in April 2007, Nigeria resounded with prophecies of clashes and chaos, including civil war or military intruding yet again into politics. Nigeria, as an "epileptic" giant, has had similar political seizures in the past as discussed earlier in this chapter. Remarkably, this national tendency to predict disaster and head for the precipice in the past always ended with remarkable swerves to avoid it at the last second. As noted by Richard Dowden, director of the Royal African Society in London, the trouble in the twenty-first century is that this tendency to head for disaster and then pull back is a terrifying nightmare for Nigeria's neighbors on the road they hope will lead to prosperity and stability. The extent of this nightmare was captured in what one minister told Professor Dowden during one of his visits to Ghana on the eve of Nigeria's 2007 elections: "Please beg those Nigerians for all our sakes to stay cool and calm. We don't want a disaster that will damage us, too." As the post-Obasanjo era reaches its half-year mark, Nigeria the "crippled" giant appears to have veered off the precipice once again, even though none of its ailments has been cured.

While history may judge the first eight years of the Fourth Republic and Obasanjo harshly for the way he pursued personal power and his half-hearted anticorruption crusade, the administration must be given credit for the apparent permanent exclusion of serving military officers from government. As we noted earlier, the process began with the dismissal in 1999 of about 90 senior military officers tainted by their involvement in politics under military rule who might have the potential to nurse political ambitions. Many Nigerians today believe that civilian control of the military is so entrenched that they do not envisage gunmen holding the population for ransom again while pillaging the state treasury. Obasanjo may have looked the other way as many of his party men robbed the country blind, but he was quite decisive about the military and what their role should be in his government. The ease with which he frequently changed or eased out insubordinate or potentially troublesome service chiefs and generals (including the 13 generals he retired three weeks before his leaving office on May 29, 2007) could not even be contemplated under military rule. His successor, Yar'Adua, similarly retired and reassigned scores of senior military officers two months after taking office as a matter of routine.

Nonetheless, it is a sad commentary that Obasanjo and his men and women, who were expected to use the tremendous goodwill and support of Nigerians to steer the country away from its chaotic past, would now go down in history as a mixed bag, if not outright failure. Their failure was not necessarily because there was anything wrong with them or that they failed to build institutions; it may be because there is everything wrong with Nigeria – her structure and her terms of existence, the institutions, identities, and interests – as this chapter has shown. Yet, the failure to do anything concrete to create sustainable institutions in a good eight years is the most disastrous failure of the Obasanjo administration. One may even be tempted to come to the inescapable conclusion that the country's founding fathers and mothers by their actions, choices, or omissions inadvertently created a country where mediocrity is celebrated or where people limit themselves to personal gain, as would booty-hunters. In that respect, the Fourth Republic has been both remarkably similar to, and an extension of, its predecessors to the extent that the post–military rule political class have taken the unfortunate history of postcolonial Nigeria – one of perpetual struggle by the people against bad leadership – to new heights.

Breaking this jinx in order to free the people from the tyranny of a few self-righteous individuals, however, depends on the outcome of a number of related aspects of democratic struggles that have always underlain Nigerian politics. These are the struggle between dictatorial temptations of one or a few individuals and irrepressible popular demand for democracy; the rule of law versus arbitrariness; an entrenched culture of impunity versus due process; and the booty-hunter mentality and selfish interests of a few individuals versus the national interest. Nothing short of a complete break from the chaotic history highlighted in this chapter can fix Nigeria's problems while tapping into its immense potential. Despite serious concerns about the legitimacy of his government, the Yar'Adua administration has taken several reassuring steps to give Nigerians hope for a stable democratic future. His professed zero tolerance for corruption, emphasis on the rule of law, his calm demeanor, and portrayal of himself as a "servant-leader" have won the new president plaudits from most Nigerians, including those contesting his victory at the election petition tribunal.

Yar'Adua's *Seven Plus Two Point Agenda to Transform Nigeria* – namely power and energy, food security and agriculture, wealth creation and employment, mass transportation, land reform, security, qualitative and functional education – and an ambitious but credible economic development masterplan for the Niger Delta as well as empowerment of disadvantaged groups sound all the right notes and have the potential to consolidate the needed (but erratically executed) reforms initiated by his predecessor. He has since formed a government of national unity and inaugurated an electoral reform commission, streamlined revenue allocation, and reiterated his government's respect for the federal principle. Yet, the ghosts of those

TABLE 14.4. Key Phases in Nigeria's Political Development

Time period	Regime	Global context	Interests/identities/institutions	Developmental path
Until 19th century	empires, kingdoms, emirates and hundreds of village-level councils; company rule	trans-Atlantic slave trade	African chiefs and kings; Islamic revolutionaries and state-makers; emergent trading city-states; European merchants and booty-hunters; missionaries; returnee slaves	unequal exchange; imperialism and mercantilism; trade in human, natural, and agricultural resources
1860–1914	Crown Colony of Lagos; Protectorate of Northern Nigeria; Oil Rivers Protectorate; Protectorate of Southern Nigeria; amalgamation	renewed European mercantilism, industrialization, rise of new states; World War I	indirect rule with emirs, obas, and warrant chiefs; European trading firms; competition among various communities	promotion of cash-crop economy; monetization of the economy
1914–1945	colonialism (authoritarian)	European imperialism; World War II	native authority (indirect rule); newly educated class; nascent urban commercial interests; missionary and European merchants; nascent political parties; national identity began to clash with ethnic/tribal cultures and identities	amalgamation of Northern and Southern Nigeria; infrastructural development to promote cash-crop economy; disarticulation of indigenous economies
1945–1960	colonialism; local/regional autonomy/self-government	Cold War and trend toward decolonization	militant nationalist movement; nascent trade unions; mass-based cultural organizations and political parties; print media; loca and Asian, Levant and European merchants; marginalized women	infrastructural development; mining; cash-crop economy; poll tax and self-financing colonial administration
1960–1966	First Republic: Northern People's Congress dominance and alliance with either Igbo or Yoruba parties	Cold War and nonaligned movement	weak central government and powerful regions; religious and ethnic diversity; parliament and judiciary; Hausa-Fulani, Igbo and Yoruba dominance and minority rights agitations; peasant and working-class interests	state-dominated import-substitution industrialization; planned development

(continued)

TABLE 14.4 (continued)

Time period	Regime	Global context	Interests/identities/institutions	Developmental path
1966–1979	military rule (authoritarian) and civil war	Cold War; non-aligned movement; oil and rise of OPEC	cessation and Biafran civil war; state-creation; "military federalism"; labor unions, students; multinational oil companies	state-dominated import-substitution industrialization; indigenization/economic nationalism
1979–1983	Second Republic; National Party of Nigeria dominance and alliance with Igbo-led Nigerian People's Party	Cold War; nonaligned movement; collapse of oil price and reduced impact of OPEC	military disengagement; federalism and "federal character" principle; 19 states, parliaments; courts; organized labor and students; state-dependent foreign and local capital; prebendalism and corruption	state-dominated import-substitution industrialization; indigenization; first phase of structural economic adjustment
1983–1999	military (authoritarian); still-born Third Republic	late Cold War; end of Cold War, globalization	return of the military; minority rights agitation and 36-state structure; revenue allocation; religious and ethnic conflicts; organized labor and mobilized prodemocracy civil society; ethnic militias and youth insurgency in the Niger Delta; corruption	neoliberal economic reforms and structural adjustment; quest for export-led growth
1999–present	Fourth Republic; People's Democratic Party dominance	post–Cold War globalization	federalism, zoning and revenue allocation, and "resource control" politics; political parties, organized labor, civil society; religious and ethnic mobilization and increased youth and militia insurgency; oil multinationals	neoliberal economic reforms and structural adjustment; export-led growth and privatization

very interests, institutions, and competing identities that stopped Obasanjo from fulfilling his promises to Nigerians in eight years still lurk nearby and will certainly stop Yar'Adua (or the next president, should he be removed from office by the Presidential Election Petition Tribunal) unless these ghosts are finally neutralized. The country's future will also depend on whether or not most Nigerians will finally go out to fight for their freedom – like South Africans and other aggrieved peoples elsewhere did – but this will equally be a function of the mutual interactions among those interests, institutions, and identities mediated by global forces.

BIBLIOGRAPHY

Achebe, Chinua. *The Trouble with Nigeria*. London and Exeter, NH: Heinemann Educational Books, 1983.

Ajayi, Gboyega I. *The Military and the Nigerian State, 1966–1993: A Study of the Strategies of Political Power Control*. Trenton, NJ: Africa World Press, 2007.

Ake, Claude. *Political Economy of Nigeria*. London and New York: Longman, 1985.

Beckett, Paul, and Crawford Young, eds. *Dilemmas of Democracy in Nigeria*. Rochester, NY: University of Rochester Press, 1997.

Bratton, Michael, and Peter Lewis. "The Durability of Political Goods? Evidence from Nigeria's New Democracy." *Commonwealth and Comparative Politics* 45, no. 1 (March 2007): 1–33.

Coleman, James S. *Nigeria: Background to Nationalism*. Berkeley: University of California Press, 1958.

Diamond, Larry. *Class, Ethnicity and Democracy in Nigeria: The Failure of the First Republic*. Basingstoke, UK: Macmillan, 1988.

Diamond, Larry, Anthony Kirk-Greene, and Oyeleye Oyediran, eds. *Transition without End: Nigerian Politics and Civil Society under Babangida*. Boulder, CO: Lynne Rienner Publishers, 1997.

Elaigwu, J. Isawa. *The Politics of Federalism in Nigeria*. London: Adonis & Abbey, 2007.

Falola, Toyin, and Julius Ihonvbere, eds. *The Rise and Fall of Nigeria's Second Republic, 1979–84*. London: Zed Books, 1985.

Forrest, Tom G. *Politics and Economic Development in Nigeria*. Boulder, CO: Westview Press, 1995.

Herskovits, Jean. "Nigeria's Rigged Democracy." *Foreign Affairs* 86, no. 4 (July/August 2007): 115–130.

Ihonvbere, Julius O. *Nigeria: The Politics of Adjustment and Democracy*. New Brunswick, NJ: Transaction Publishers, 1994.

Ilesanmi, Simeon O. *Religious Pluralism and Nigerian State*. Athens, OH: Ohio University Press, 1997.

Joseph, Richard A. *Democracy and Prebendal Politics in Nigeria: The Rise and Fall of the Second Republic*. New York: Cambridge University Press, 1987.

Kuka, Matthew H. *Religion, Politics and Power in Northern Nigeria*. Ibadan: Spectrum Press, 1994.

Maier, Karl. *This House Has Fallen: Midnight in Nigeria*. New York: Public Affairs Press, 2000.

Nnoli, Okwudiba. *Ethnicity and Development in Nigeria*. Aldershot, UK, and Brookfield, VT: Avebury, 1995.

Odetola, Theophus. *Military Politics in Nigeria: Economic Development and Political Stability*. New Brunswick, NJ: Transaction Books, 1978.

Okonjo, Isaac M. *British Administration in Nigeria 1900–1950: A Nigerian View*. New York: NOK Publishers, 1974.

Okonta, Ike, and Oronto Douglas. *Where Vultures Feast: Shell, Human Rights, and Oil*. London: Verso, 2003.

Okpaku, Joseph, ed. *Nigeria: Dilemma of Nationhood: An African Analysis of the Biafran Conflict*. New York, Third Press, 1972.

Osaghae, Eghosa. *Crippled Giant: Nigeria since Independence*. Bloomington, IN: University Press, 1998.

Rotberg, Robert, ed. *Crafting the New Nigeria: Confronting the Challenges*. Boulder, CO: Lynne Rienner Publishers, 2004.

Schwarz, Frederick O. *Nigeria: The Tribes, the Nation, or the Race: The Politics of Independence*. Cambridge, MA: MIT Press, 1965.

Sklar, Richard. *Nigerian Political Parties: Power in an Emergent African Nation*. Princeton, NJ: Princeton University Press, 1963.

Soyinka, Wole. *The Open Sore of a Continent: A Personal Narrative of the Nigerian Crisis*. New York: Oxford University Press, 1996.

Suberu, Rotimi T. *Federalism and Ethnic Conflict in Nigeria*. Washington, DC: United States Institute of Peace Press, 2001.

Suberu, Rotimi T. "Nigeria's Muddled Elections." *Journal of Democracy* 18, no. 4 (October 2007): 95–110.

IMPORTANT TERMS

Sanni Abacha Nigeria's brutal dictator from 1993 to 1998, reputed for corruption and stashing up to $6 billion in foreign accounts, who died before actualizing plans to transform himself into a civilian president.

Major General Johnson T. U. Aguiyi-Ironsi a major-general and general officer commanding Nigerian Armed Forces during the first military coup in 1966; became Nigeria's first military ruler and was killed in the July 29, 1966, anti-Igbo counter coup.

"amalgamation" the merging of previously separate administrative units into one for ease of administration: for example, the amalgamation of the protectorates of Northern and Southern Nigeria into one British Colony of Nigeria in 1914 by Sir Frederick Lugard.

austerity measures structural adjustment program (SAP) to curtail public spending, especially on social services and subsidies.

Obafemi Awolowo (1906–1987) often called the father of opposition politics in Nigeria; leader and founder of the Action Group; premier of the then Western

Region, later imprisoned for sedition, and presidential candidate of the Unity Party of Nigeria (UPN) in the Second Republic.

Benjamin Nnamdi Azikiwe (1904–1986) often called the father of the Nigerian nationalist movement; leader and founder of the National Council of Nigerian Citizens (NCNC); premier of the then Eastern Region, president of the First Republic of Nigeria, and presidential candidate of the Nigerian People's Party (NPP) in the Second Republic.

Ahmadu Bello (Sadauna of Sokoto) leader and founder of the Northern People's Congress and premier of the then Northern Region killed in the 1966 coup.

Sovereign Independent Republic of Biafra the ill-fated breakaway Eastern Region dominated by the Igbo ethnic group; collapsed on January 12, 1970, after civil war in which more than two million Igbos died.

Decree no. 34 of 1966 introduced by General Ironsi's regime to unify the federal bureaucracy and police forces; allegedly undermined national consensus on federalism.

Economic and Financial Crimes Commission (EFCC) Nigeria's anticorruption watchdog, which convicted over 150 persons and confiscated over $5 billion of ill-gotten wealth from 2002 to 2007, but was also used by President Olesugun Obasanjo against his political enemies.

emirate political system the Islamic political system in the emirates defeated by the British in 1886 which became the model of British colonial administration (indirect rule) in Nigeria – successful in the north, fairly successful in the west, but a colossal failure in the east.

federal character Nigeria's version of affirmative action, seeking to guarantee a proportionate share of federal positions for all states, especially to protect "educationally backward areas."

federalism a power-sharing arrangement between the central government and the federating units; Nigeria is unusual in that the constitution includes local councils as a coequal third tier of power.

fiscal federalism an arrangement by which all the federating units theoretically contribute to, and derive equitable allocations from, federally collected revenue.

Hausa-Fulani the ethno-linguistic group that has historically dominated the politics and economy of northern Nigeria; also dominant in Nigeria's politics and the armed forces since independence in contention with the Igbo and Yoruba, Nigeria's two other major ethnic groups.

indirect rule system a system of rule by which the British ruled conquered territories through existing "traditional" or "natural" political institutions and sought to disrupt the extant local institutions as little as possible.

Igbo the ethno-linguistic group that has historically dominated the politics and economy of eastern Nigeria; the nucleus of the ill-fated breakaway Republic of Biafra; and often in contention with the Hausa-Fulani and Yoruba, Nigeria's two other major ethnic groups; the language spoken by the Igbo.

June 12 refers to the June 12, 1993, presidential election won by Yoruba business mogul Moshood K. Abiola but which was annulled by the military.

Land Use Decree of 1978 brought all land tenure laws and norms under one uniform legal structure in which land use rights are vested in the state governor.

Sir Frederick Lugard British colonial officer (initially a captain) who conquered and ruled northern Nigeria from 1900 to 1914, the year he effected the amalgamation of the two protectorates of Northern and Southern Nigeria. Lugard (referred to as Nigeria's first "evil genius") then became governor of colonial Nigeria, a policy still regarded by Nigerians today as "the mistake of 1914."

"mistake of 1914" the British policy that merged or "amalgamated" the two protectorates of Northern and Southern Nigeria in 1914 under the governorship of Sir Frederick Lugard.

Movement for the Survival of Ogoni People (MOSOP) founded by writer Ken Saro-Wiwa, who was hanged in 1995 (with eight others) for campaigning against the environmental degradation caused by oil drilling by Shell in Ogoniland.

Nigerian Indigenization Policy sought to restrict ownership and management of 40–60 percent of the national (especially "the commanding heights") economy to Nigerian nationals.

Olusegun Obasanjo military ruler from 1976 to 1979, when he handed power back to a civilian regime; ruled again from 1999 to 2007 as elected civilian president.

pogrom massacre of over 100,000 innocent civilians and more than 200 army officers of Igbo origin in various parts of (especially northern) Nigeria, following the January 15, 1966, and July 29, 1966, military coups against the Igbo; sometimes referred to as genocide.

prebendalism a form of corruption whereby state offices are appropriated by officeholders who use them to generate material benefits for themselves and their constituents and kin groups.

protectorate a colonial territory acquired through the signing (often under duress) of a "treaty of protection" between a European power and an African ruler or community.

resource control a continuation of the politics of revenue allocation whereby oil-producing states seek more local control of the revenue derived from the resource instead of the current lopsided control by the federal government.

Royal Niger Company British trading company granted royal charter to administer areas along the River Niger, 1886–1900.

Sabon Gari "stranger quarters" or residential enclaves for non-Muslim migrants from southern Nigeria found in many cities in northern Nigeria.

third-term plot a plot by President Obasanjo to amend the constitution so as to allow him to seek a third term as civilian president but which was defeated by Parliament in response to domestic and external pressure.

warrant chiefs local rulers whose authority was modeled on the emirate system in northern Nigeria and imposed by the British on southeastern Nigeria, especially among the Igbo, who did not have widespread tradition of kingship.

Yoruba the ethno-linguistic group that has historically dominated the politics and economy of western Nigeria; also dominant in Nigeria's economy since independence; and often in contention with the Igbo and Hausa-Fulani, Nigeria's two other major ethnic groups; language spoken by the Yoruba.

STUDY QUESTIONS

1. Compare and contrast civilian and military governments in Nigeria in terms of how they have dealt with the problems of corruption, minority interest groups, and overall economic development. What accounts for their differences and/or similarities?

2. Compare and contrast the institutional arrangements to share power among the various tiers of government in India, Nigeria, and the United States. Which country has done a better job at protecting the interests of minorities?

3. What are the costs and benefits associated with the federal and presidential systems of government adopted by Nigeria since 1979? Is "zoning" of political offices an improvement over earlier problems associated with the dilemma of implementing the "federal character" principle and running an efficient and effective government?

4. What are the immediate causes of the Biafran war (1966–1970)? In what ways does that war differ from the ongoing insurgency in the Niger Delta?

5. What do Nigerians mean by "the mistake of 1914"? To what extent have those "mistakes" shaped the politics of ethnicity and "resource control" since independence in Nigeria?

6. What lessons can we take from the 2007 general and presidential elections in Nigeria in terms of democracy promotion and consolidation of democratic regimes?

7. In what ways did the legacies of British colonial rule shape the institutions, material interests, and identities that have structured the nature of interactions among Nigerians and post-colonial politics? How have these institutions, material interests, and identities been affected by global economic, social and political processes?

8. If you were a Nigerian voter and a member of civil society groups, what would you do regarding the government of President Umaru Yar'Adua, which succeeded the Obasanjo administration in May 2007, given the verdict by local and international election observers that the poll "failed to meet acceptable minimal standards of fairness"?

STOP AND COMPARE

EARLY DEVELOPERS, MIDDLE DEVELOPERS, LATE DEVELOPERS, AND EXPERIMENTAL DEVELOPERS

Taken together, the chapters you have just read underscore the importance of domestic political responses to international political challenges. In fact, a different title for the book might well have been "Liberal Democracy and Its Challengers." As we have seen, Britain and France developed first, each with its own institutional variation on the liberal democratic theme. This development, as positively as we may now evaluate it from our own perspective, made these two states powerful and ultimately threatening to Europe and the rest of the world.

Still, because of British and French successes, other countries sought to emulate the experience of the initial developers. In terms of our five-step framework: (1) While middle developers Germany and Japan reacted to British and French development, devising variations on the initial British and French innovations, they were never actually able to replicate them for the simple reason that they were trying to catch up from behind. (2) As middle developers, middle-class interests were weaker, nationalist identity more pronounced, and bureaucratic state-institutions stronger and democracy weaker. (3) These different circumstances of development ultimately weakened liberalism in Germany and Japan, which paved the way for the Nazi and fascist responses. It makes sense therefore to speak of a fascist path to the modern world. (4) The Nazis and the Japanese launched World War II, which ultimately led to occupation by the core liberal powers and a recasting of domestic identities, interests, and institutions. (5) In contemporary democratic Germany and Japan interests, identities, and institutions grapple with the economic and political legacies of their distinctive authoritarian path to the modern world.

The late developers in this book are the (post) communist giants Russia and China. In terms of our five-step framework: (1) Both tried to industrialize their societies in a global order dominated by liberal democratic and fascist capitalist states. (2) As late developers, middle-class interests were even weaker, nationalist identity more pronounced, bureaucratic state-institutions even stronger, and democracy even weaker. (3) These different circumstances of development cut off both the liberal democratic and fascist paths and paved the way for communism – the twentieth century's third main contender for a path to the modern world. (4) After an initial flirtation with global dominance, both the Soviet Union and China settled into an effort to legitimate their specific response to liberalism with superior economic performance under communist economic institutions. (5) Both failed. After desperately trying to repair a basically unworkable communist economic and political model in the decades after Stalin's death, the Russian response was to give up communism and introduce democracy and markets in the hope of rejoining the democratic capitalist world system. Neither democracy nor markets were terribly successful in Russia after communism. Under President Putin's strong hand and buoyed by high energy prices, Russia reverted to a relatively stable form of authoritarian-led market development. China, on the other hand, shed its communist economy but not its communist party. Under the influence of the other successful semi-authoritarian capitalist states in East Asia, the Chinese response was to introduce markets into their society, while attempting to maintain communist party dominance. Whether either country is able to succeed in its newfound flirtation with a complete or partial reintegration with the international liberal order remains to be seen.

EXPERIMENTAL DEVELOPERS: MEXICO, INDIA, IRAN, SOUTH AFRICA, THE EUROPEAN UNION, AND NIGERIA

Our final group of countries embodies a distinctive global historical heritage and shares common links. Most often, this commonality is colonial. Mexico, India, Iran, South Africa, and Nigeria experienced the impact of European colonial power. All now confront the cultural, institutional, and economic pressures of the global economy. Despite these similarities, each of these countries has distinctive, if modal, kinds of political problems that are of great interest to comparativists.

South Africa and India respectively conduct democratic politics in countries with very high levels of ethnic and racial diversity. Both have developed an innovative set of institutional arrangements for adjudicating conflicting ethnic and racial interests and identities within the parameters of what we normally think of as democratic institutions. Their experiments with multicultural democracy may even provide lessons, both positive and negative, for more industrialized, Western societies. Furthermore, both confront the problem of sustaining democracy in environments of economic scarcity.

Nigeria also has attempted to structure democratic politics in a highly diverse society. Before independence the British colonial authorities encouraged and even strengthened ethnic fragmentation as a tool of colonial rule. After independence, the demands of so many competing ethnic groups in an environment of economic scarcity put tremendous strain on the country's institutions and has not made for stable democratic politics. Nigeria is also in many ways cursed with having so much oil. The rich countries of the world are interested in this country primarily for its oil and Nigeria's elites have frequently misused and even stolen the country's wealth rather than cobble together a set of economic policies that would enable high energy prices to foster sustained economic growth.

Iran experienced decades of steady Westernization under a dictator, the Shah. After an Islamic revolution in 1980, it sought to reshape its society and live under the rules of political Islam. It thus stands as a fascinating case of the religious reaction to global cultural, economic competition, and political pressure. The recent on-again, off-again turn to more moderate leadership in Iran illustrates vividly just how powerful are the homogenizing forces of global liberalism. It remains unclear whether these latest developments signal a gradual return to the modernizing path taken before the Islamic revolution or whether it is a sign that the Islamic revolution is now institutionally stable and has indeed carved out a viable alternative to the liberal democratic and global capitalist order that it consciously rejected.

Finally, Mexico has taken precisely the opposite route from Iran, choosing economically to integrate itself as closely with the United States as it can. Integration into the global trading system, however, has created both new political elites that are supportive of this move and new social movements that oppose it. Until the year 2000 Mexico was steadily (if corruptly) ruled by one party (the PRI). The election of Vincente Fox in 2000, however, turned a new and important page in Mexican history. Whether the new political elites and social movements that have emerged as a result of rapid economic change will contribute to the consolidation of liberal democracy remains an open question.

Perhaps the most challenging experiment of all has been the European Union (EU). In some ways, this case does not really fit into this book at all. The European Union is not a country and of course it has never been colonized. Instead, the EU is an experiment that challenges one of the key assumptions of comparative politics – that the world is divided into relatively independent states. The entire purpose of the EU has been to secure peace and prosperity for the multiple peoples of Europe by pooling the one resource that is normally guarded by national elites: sovereignty. Rather than figuring out ways to prevent the powerful currents of international markets and the rise of new powers from undermining national authority, the members of the European Union have embraced economic and political integration on a regional level. The intention is to build and preserve something that is distinctly European and banish war from the European landmass forever. The question remains, however, what the final destination of integration will be. What began as a trade organization has developed into something much more serious and complex with its own set of interests, identities, and institutions. Europeans disagree about whether the purpose of the EU is to promote trade or to create a new overarching European identity. They disagree about how much sovereignty should be ceded to Brussels and where the member states should pursue their own interests and strengthen their own identities. Finally, they also disagree about the limits on enlargement and where Europe's "borders" lie. Which countries should be admitted and which excluded? How these disagreements are resolved will determine whether the EU becomes a model for other regions of the world or remains an entity particular to the European experience.

In sum: six cases, six experiments. Mexico's grand experiment is independence: Is it possible for a country to be autonomous when its northern neighbor happens to be the most powerful nation in the world? Iran's grand experiment is Islam: Is it possible for a country to be economically and politically powerful when it has had an Islamic revolution that creates an Islamic state? India's grand experiment is nonrevolutionary democracy: Is it possible for a large postcolonial country to be a democracy when it has had a major independence movement but not a social revolution? South Africa's grand experiment is interracial democracy. Is it possible for ethno-constitutional democracy and markets to survive in a country that made a relatively peaceful transition from colonialism and apartheid? Nigeria's experiment combines the challenges of all of these: the diversity and nonrevolutionary colonial heritage of India, the difficulties of democracy amid tribal fragmentation of South Africa, and the dependence on oil revenues of Mexico and Iran – all in an environment of dire scarcity. What is the long-run fate of democratic rule with such unfavorable initial conditions? Our final experiment, the European Union, is not a country but a new form of political organization that raises the crucial question of whether states and societies are willing to give up their sovereignty in pursuit of peace and prosperity. Will the European experience be exportable to other regions of the world?

More generally: 12 cases, 12 experiments. The closer we look the more we discover that there have been 12 developmental paths to the modern world. States made their own development choices and evolved local institutional variations of globally dominant political economies. In the words of our framework: (1) the constant of global context influences (2) the types of domestic interests, identities, and institutions which produce (3) the variables of developmental paths to the modern world, which, in turn, generate (4) international-relations feedback effects on the global context and (5) comparative-politics feedback effects on domestic interests, identities, and institutions.

Index